Praise for
Zen and the Art of Making a Living

"The subtitle of this book is *A Practical Guide to Creative Career Design* and it is that and more. The best book, by far, that I have come across on how to identify what your strengths are, how to visualize your ideal job and how to go about bringing it into existence. Hundreds of inspiring quotes and dozens of thoughtful checklists. If you go through this book with care, it will assuredly be life changing in addition to thought provoking."

—Srikumar S. Rao, adjunct professor,
Columbia School of Business, former
contributing editor to *Forbes, Financial
World,* and *Success* magazines

"Once again Laurence Boldt gives us the tools we need to live our passion, follow our true work, and make our living in harmony with our true spiritual path."

—Michael Toms, cofounder of
New Dimensions Radio, coauthor of
*True Work: Doing What You Love
and Loving What You Do*

"*Zen and the Art of Making a Living* has been, for many years, a treasured and often referred to addition to my very selective library. It is that rare combination of the inspirational and the practical."

—Dick Richards, author of
Artful Work and *Is Your Genius at Work?*

"The parachute books are useful, and there are hundreds about finding purpose, meaning, work you love, etc. The best is Boldt's 600-page workbook [*Zen and the Art of Making a Living*]. Lots of philosophy and quotations mixed with a practical guide for creative career design. The sections are easy to move in and out of depending on your needs. Comprehensive, useful, and maybe even life changing."

—Mark S. Albion, Ph.D., author of
*True to Yourself: Leading a Values-
Based Business*

"*Zen and the Art of Making a Living* is one hell of a book. I [feel] that [it] really challenges *What Color Is Your Parachute?* for leadership in the career field. Nice Job!"

—Daniel Lauber, author of
Non-Profit & Education Job Finder

Comments from Readers

"I had a problem that my family and friends kept trying to convince me was no problem at all. I was earning a high six-figure income on Wall Street and getting no personal satisfaction from it at all. I dreaded going to work each day . . . I felt as though [*Zen and the Art of Making a Living*] had been written expressly for me . . . To make a long story short, I resigned from my company ten months ago and am now spending each day doing what I love—and what my teachers all the way back to elementary school told me I had a special aptitude for—writing. One final note. I'm making more money now than I ever did on Wall Street. (Oh, the irony.) Many thanks to Laurence Boldt for his sage advice."
— Alexander Green, Orlando, Florida

"How can I possibly express the life-transforming realizations *Zen and the Art of Making a Living* has helped me to see? I truly feel blessed to have found it. It's given me a whole new perspective on work and couldn't have come along at a better time in my life. I've been longing to make a career change for many years, and your book has inspired me to go for it."
— Dave Powell, Newman, Georgia

"I'm only a quarter of the way through *Zen and the Art of Making a Living* and I already realize that it is one of the most important books that I've ever read. If you're planning a career switch, seek this book out. If you're not planning a career change, read it anyway."
— Marc Leonetti, Cherry Hill, New Jersey

"I found [*Zen and the Art of Making a Living*] fascinating, stimulating, meaningful, and helpful. You truly helped me to resolve to take the first steps on a new path (my quest) for which my heart and my mind have been yearning for years. It has served, not only as an invaluable resource for information and ideas, but also as a source of wisdom and a jumping-off place for discovery."
— Jeffrey R. Kastin, La Jolla, California

"I found [Laurence Boldt's] writing both very inspiring and pith, and the writing exercises were completely remarkable . . . I would begin an exercise by thinking 'I don't know if this is going to uncover anything!' and as soon as I would begin to write, important insights would bubble up. Through this book, I gained what Buddhists called 'vipashana,' which means 'awareness.' I was motivated by awareness of a 'bigger picture' of my life's work, and when I told myself the truth, I could see that this work had deep integrity and meaning and purpose. This book should be a prerequisite . . . for anyone who has a dream that seems too hard to reach."
— Anne Kerry Ford, Ojai, California

"Laurence's books are an inspiration. They work. They give you the courage and the confidence to pursue and achieve your dreams. Brilliant!"
— Jonathan Perks, Lincolnshire, England

"I would like to thank Laurence Boldt for writing the amazing book, *Zen and the Art of Making a Living*. This book has had a profound influence on the way I look at work and understanding how it is an integral part of one's life."
— Ajit Pyati, Los Angeles, California

PENGUIN BOOKS

ZEN AND THE ART OF MAKING A LIVING

For more than two decades, career coach and author Laurence Boldt has been helping people clarify and achieve their career goals. A recognized leader in the career development field, he is a sought-after public speaker and a longtime student of Eastern philosophy. Boldt has appeared on hundreds of radio and television programs around the country and has been featured in numerous newspaper and magazine articles. In addition to career classic *Zen and the Art of Making a Living,* his other books include *How to Find the Work You Love* (2004), *Zen Soup* (1997), and *The Tao of Abundance* (1999).

Zen

and the Art of Making a Living

A Practical Guide to Creative Career Design

LAURENCE G. BOLDT

PENGUIN BOOKS

PENGUIN BOOKS
Published by the Penguin Group
Penguin Group (USA) Inc., 375 Hudson Street, New York, New York 10014, U.S.A.
Penguin Group (Canada), 90 Eglinton Avenue East, Suite 700, Toronto,
Ontario, Canada M4P 2Y3 (a division of Pearson Penguin Canada Inc.)
Penguin Books Ltd, 80 Strand, London WC2R 0RL, England
Penguin Ireland, 25 St Stephen's Green, Dublin 2, Ireland (a division of Penguin Books Ltd)
Penguin Group (Australia), 250 Camberwell Road, Camberwell,
Victoria 3124, Australia (a division of Pearson Australia Group Pty Ltd)
Penguin Books India Pvt Ltd, 11 Community Centre, Panchsheel Park, New Delhi – 110 017, India
Penguin Group (NZ), 67 Apollo Drive, Rosedale, North Shore 0632,
New Zealand (a division of Pearson New Zealand Ltd)
Penguin Books (South Africa) (Pty) Ltd, 24 Sturdee Avenue, Rosebank, Johannesburg 2196, South Africa

Penguin Books Ltd, Registered Offices: 80 Strand, London WC2R 0RL, England

First published in the United States of America as *Zen and the Art of Making a Living
in the Post-Modern World* by Lightning Press 1991
Revised edition published in Arkana, an imprint of Penguin Books USA Inc. 1993
Second revised edition published 1999
This third revised edition published in Penguin Books 2009

5 7 9 10 8 6

Illustrations used with permission of Suzuki, Daisetz T., *Zen and Japanese Culture*, Bolligen Series LXIV. Copyright © 1959 by Princeton University Press. Illustrations from *Zen Painting and Calligraphy* by Jan Fontein and Money L. Hickman. Copyright © 1970 by Museum of Fine Arts, Boston, Massachusetts. Used by permission. Illustrations from *The Art of Zen* by Stephen Addiss used with permission of Stephen Addiss. Copyright © 1989 by Harry N. Abrams. Lu K'uan Yu (Charles Luk), *Taoist Yoga*, © Lu K'uan Yu, 1973 (York Beach, ME: Samuel Weiser, Inc., 1973), p. 150. Used by permission. Lu K'uan Yu (Charles Luk), *The Secrets of Chinese Meditation* © Charles Luk, 1964 (York Beach, ME: Samuel Weiser, Inc. 1964), p.16. Used by permission. Illustrations from *Pelican History of Art. Art and Architecture of India*, by Benjamin Rowland. © 1953 by Yale University Press. Used by permission. #28—Yantra of Krsna, courtesy of John Stevens; #32—The six chakra, courtesy of John Stevens; #145a—"Katsujinken," "The sword that gives life" by Gempo, courtesy of John Stevens; #203b—"Namu amida butsu" by Ryokan, courtesy of the Kimura Collection; and #207—"Dai birushanabutsu," "Mahavairocana Buddha" by Juin, courtesy of the Kinami Collection from *Sacred Calligraphy of the East* by John Stevens, © 1981. By arrangement with Shambhala Publications Inc., Boston. Excerpts from *Foundations of Tibetan Mysticism* by Lama Anagarka Govinda, copyright © 1969, 1991, Samuel Weiser, Inc., York Beach, ME. Used by permission. Excerpts from *The Tao of Power* by R. L. Wing. Copyright © 1986 by Immedia. Used by permission of Doubleday, a division of Bantam, Doubleday, & Dell Publishing Group, Inc. Excerpts from *Winning the Marketing War: A Field Manual for Business Leaders* by Gerald A. Michaelson. Published by Madison Books/Abt Books. Copyright © 1987 by Abt Books. Reprinted by permission of the publishers. Excerpts from *The California Nonprofit Corporation Handbook* by Anthony Mancuso. Published by Nolo Press. Copyright © 1991 by Anthony Mancuso. Reprinted by permission of publishers.

LIBRARY OF CONGRESS CATALOGING IN PUBLICATION DATA
Boldt, Laurence G.
Zen and the art of making a living : a practical guide to creative career design / Laurence G. Boldt.—Rev. ed.
p. cm.
Includes bibliographical references and index.
ISBN 978-0-14-311459-8
1. Zen Buddhism.   2. Religious life—Zen Buddhism.   I. Title.
BQ9286.B65 2009
650.14—dc22   2009019516

Printed in the United States of America

When one happens on a book of this kind, he is well advised to throw it away.
                                        Shū-an

C O N T E N T S

Acknowledgments

To John Panama

I t is no exaggeration to say that this book would not have been possible without the help of many. To all who have contributed, my heartfelt thanks. I am especially grateful for the input of my clients and of seminar participants. The program was originally developed as a response to your interests and desires. Your input has been critical at every stage. Additionally, your kind words have been a tremendous encouragement along the way. Many thanks.

Further thanks are due to several dedicated volunteers for their excellent work. Kim Grant is a capable editor whose enthusiasm for the book has been a large part of making it happen. Beyond her typesetting and layout assistance, Susan Shapiro's continuing commitment and support have been indispensable to all iterations of this book. Sonny King's persistent and tenacious proofreading has saved me from incomprehensibility too many times to count. I would also like to thank my wife Tina for her help on this revised edition.

I also want to thank several people for making possible the Penguin edition of this book. Thanks to my agent, Peter Beren, and to Michael Jacobs for seeing the potential of the book. Thanks also to my editor at Penguin, David Stanford, for his careful handling of the book and his easy manner and good humor throughout.

While I am most grateful to these and others for their efforts, responsibility for the book and all of its shortcomings and errors remains mine. A project of this size is bound to have errors and need revision to stay up to date. I encourage you to contact me with any corrections, updates, or information you think might be of interest to readers of future editions of this book. Feedback of all kinds is most welcome. Please be advised that, though I read all communications, time constraints may keep me from responding. Thank you for your understanding and cooperation.

Preface to the Revised Edition

To love what you do and feel that it matters—how could anything be more fun?
Katherine Graham

More than twenty years ago, I began this work with the conviction that people of all ages and professional levels were ready to embrace the challenge of creating work they truly love. Through good economic times and bad, I've seen this conviction borne out in the lives of countless dedicated individuals who have found their own ways to put their passions to work. The success of this book and, even more, the many letters and comments I've received from readers who've found it helpful in mapping their own journeys to fulfilling work have been truly gratifying. This revised edition has given me an opportunity to sharpen and clarify my thoughts on a number of topics. Considerable revisions have been made throughout. The entire text has been updated, and a lot of new material has been added. For those familiar with this book, the bibliography and most of the Web resources that appeared in its previous incarnations have been greatly expanded and put online (empoweryou.com), where they can more easily be kept current.

This book is really about two things: the "what" and the "how" of creating a fulfilling experience of work. Most of the new material in this revised edition addresses issues related to the "how." For example, I've incorporated a variety of new tactics for career development and marketing made possible by the advent of new technologies. Nevertheless, most of the essential principles remain unchanged, with respect to both the "what" and the strategic elements of the "how." Since this is a large book, it may prove useful at the outset to briefly sketch some of these principles. (The "prologue" and four "acts" mentioned below refer to the book's five major units; see "How to Use This Book.")

What to Do: Embracing Your Trajectory

First you must find your trajectory, and then comes the social coordination.

Joseph Campbell

When it comes to the fundamentals of vocational guidance (determining what to do), nothing significant has changed since this book was first written. Indeed, nothing essential has changed in the more than two thousand years since Aristotle wrote, "Where your talent and the needs of the world cross, there lies your vocation." Were he alive today and whispering in your ear, Aristotle could give no more relevant or timely advice. Over seven hundred years ago, the Sufi poet Rumi wrote, "Everyone has been made for some particular work and the desire for that work has been placed in every heart." This too is every bit as relevant today as it was the day it was first written. In a sense, either of these formulations (Rumi's or Aristotle's) provides everything you need to identify your vocation or life's work.

If we were to recast Rumi's maxim as a question, we might come up with something like, What was I born to do? or, What does my heart tell me to do? If we were to reframe Aristotle's dictum, we might get, Where (or what) is the nexus between my talents and the needs of the world? or, Where can I find a mix of passion and purpose, of joy and meaning? Now, I've found that most people have a difficult time answering any of these questions straightaway. On the other hand, if you ask folks a targeted series of more manageable questions, you find that many move definitely (though at first almost imperceptibly) toward an answer to the larger questions.

Act I of this book addresses this process, approaching the big questions in bite-sized pieces. I call it the "quest" for life's work for the simple reason that questions provide the compass points with which to chart the path to purpose and passion. To ask the questions relevant to fulfilling work is to seek the answers that will transform your work life. The quest for your life trajectory, direction, or purpose moves through the field of visions and the forest of values. In the field of visions, you articulate your worldview, clarify your perceptions, and see where your imagination wants to take you. In the forest of values, you sort out the meanings of life. Competing interests pull you this way and that; yet you find the deepest, most enduring well of motivation and the sustaining values of your life in what moves your heart and soul the most. The quest for passion goes by way of talents and goals. Your talents are your innate strengths—the things you're *naturally* good at. Expressing your talents has joy, energy, and creative engagement in it. Goals arise from your desire to grow, to achieve, to complete. In moving toward, fighting for, and completing goals, energy is renewed and released, and as Blake said, "Energy is Bliss!" If you listen to them, your visions and values, talents and lifelong objectives will tell you what you want to do with your life.

When it comes to vocational choice, I don't rely on personality tests, for the simple reason that the personality is not the soul. The soul, or deep Self, is the source of one's true passion and purpose, while the personality (from Latin *persona*, "mask") is inexorably linked to familial and societal conditioning. The questions suggested by Rumi's and Aristotle's vocational formulations are addressed to the soul. Typically, answers to these kinds of questions are not lying around on the surface but are the fruit of a deep inner work. Joseph Campbell called this work "finding your own trajectory"; Carl Jung, "individuation." The outlines of this inner work are discussed in the Prologue of this book. I call it the "art" of life's work because the beginning of all creative transformations (whether of form or experience) lies within—in consciousness. More often than not, the recognition of vocation results from a journey of self-discovery. This journey may be undertaken deliberately, or it may be forced on us by circumstances. Either way, it moves us toward that deeper Self, where clarity is found. Some advanced souls seek their own trajectories from an early age. Many more get caught up for a time in socially defined images of themselves and don't seek their own trajectories until their mid-thirties or well beyond. (If you are in either of these groups, consider yourself fortunate.)

Most of us have been taught to approach work as though the requirements of our souls are superfluous or peripheral to the real business of living. The body demands food and sex; the ego, attention. The emotions want security; the mind, knowledge. In the market society we live in, money is in one way or another tied to the fulfillment of all of these aims. Most of our lives, we are chasing food, sex, attention, knowledge, security, and—most of all—money. Without the real engagement of our souls, all this can seem quite empty as the years go by. For the soul too has its demands. It has a way of letting us know when we neglect or abandon its imperatives—authenticity and responsibility, joy and compassion. At some point, many come to realize that listening to their hearts and souls isn't a luxury but an essential part of their psychological and spiritual health. With respect to work, they understand that it makes a difference whether they work to go on earning or earn to go on doing what they love.

While they want more from their experience of work, many aren't sure if it's really possible to get it. Most of us start with an unexamined but deeply ingrained belief framed in a dichotomy between soul and money. Why worry about what my soul wants? I need money, and I can't possibly make money doing what my soul wants. Why should I get in touch with my purpose and passion? I will never be able to make a living with those. This reminds me of the fairy tale where people hear rumors of a great and wonderful city over yonder but are told that if they venture over the mountain, some terrible monster will get them. That's enough to keep most at home. Of course, some do venture over the mountain and discover that the "monster" isn't nearly as fearsome as it's cracked up to be. In much the same way, some discover that they can make a nice living—thank you very much—doing what they love. Now, to extend the metaphor, you still have to climb the first mountain (identify your passion), you still have to traverse the peaks and valleys twixt it and the city (develop competency), and you still have to gain the support of others along the way (find a way to market yourself doing what you love). I'm not suggesting that it's easy to climb the mountain of self-awareness, develop the knowledge and skill you need for the journey, or gain the support you need to succeed. What I am saying is that the path is knowable and has been traversed by many before you.

Identifying what moves you, your passion and purpose, is the place to start. After all, if you don't know what you are aiming for, your chances of hitting it aren't very good. Many who can't or won't admit what they want to do hide behind the "impossible" meme. Since the desires of the soul must subordinate themselves to the demands of money—why even bother identifying those desires? This is a rationalization—not an argument. It's clearly possible for people to make a living doing what they love to do, since many are doing it every day. The real question is: Can *you* do it? Once we admit what we want in our hearts, we immediately confront another challenge. At one of my workshops, the group listened intently to a young woman who stood speaking before them. With obvious joy and elation, she was telling the group what her true passion was. She described the profound sense of freedom she felt in proclaiming before others what she really wanted to do with her life. She was describing how she had come to this realization and what it meant to her, when, suddenly, she stopped abruptly and said, "I feel scared." She turned from the group toward me and asked, "Is that normal?" I assured her that she was expressing something I'd heard many times before (and since). When we reveal our heart's desire with respect to work, we feel an emotional vulnerability not unlike what we feel in our first confessions of love for a would-be partner. In contrast to the responses of a would-be lover, we have much more—though far from complete—control over our career destinies. Still, it's worth pointing out that there is a marked emotional difference between claiming what we would really love to do and discussing the merits of a good job or sensible career. Yet it is only after making that claim that we have a chance of creating a life where what we do matches what we are at the deepest levels.

How to Do It:
Making the Social Coordination

Make your work to be in keeping with your purpose.
Leonardo da Vinci

For purpose and passion, we must rely, not on society, but on ourselves. On the other hand, if we are to transform our inner motivations into viable work, we must coordinate our efforts with the existing social order. We must be capable of doing the work we desire and capable of getting others to help us. That's what the second half of this book is about. It's concerned with "how to do" your "what to do" in the world we live in today.

Choose a Career Vehicle: The first coordinating step is choosing a career role. More than anything, society defines us by the career roles we play. I call Act II the "game" of life's work because, while others will define us by our roles, we are better off seeing our careers as vehicles for fulfilling our self-defined "what to do's" (purpose and passion). The word *career* comes from the Latin *carrus*, meaning "a wheeled vehicle." The point of any vehicle isn't so much the thing itself, but where you can go with it and how it feels when you're in it. A beautiful car without a battery isn't going anywhere. An expensive but cramped sports coupe may look great but leave you with a sore back or stiff neck. To the extent that a career role allows you to fulfill your purpose, it can get you where you want to go. To the extent that a career role allows you to be and express yourself—to do what you are naturally good at—you will enjoy the ride. A career role is a vehicle through which to pursue your purpose and express your passion, and it gives others a way of relating to you so they can help you achieve your goals. Act II is designed to help you choose a career that works for you, before you engage in the often expensive and time-intensive process of retraining.

Develop a Marketing Strategy: Since we live in a market society, we all have to market ourselves in one way or another. This is the subject of Act III. Marketing just means getting people to help you do what you want to do—be it someone to hire you or people to buy your products or services or to fund your nonprofit organization. Of course, the higher the quality of your work, the more inclined people will be to help you. But in a market society, there is more to it than that. You have to *communicate* what you do in ways that connect with your (paying) audience—employers, clients, customers, financial backers, etc. How you market yourself will depend on your purpose and passion and the career role you choose. I call Act III the "battle" for life's work because however you choose to market yourself, it will take courage and strength to resist the temptation to settle for less than your best, to keep fighting for your "what to do" in the face of resistance. Act III explores a variety of marketing options including conducting an aggressive job search, starting your own business or freelance operation, and starting a nonprofit corporation.

Plan on Growth: Depending on your current circumstances and future goals, additional knowledge and skill may be required to qualify for, and/or to succeed in, your new career. I call Act IV the "school" of life's work because learning and growing are necessary not only to gain mastery of the work you want to do but also to live a rich and full life. More often than not, what separates us from what we want to do is what we don't know. This section addresses developing a strategy for transitioning into your new career and includes information on how to maximize and expedite your efforts to acquire new knowledge and skills, how to maintain a positive self-image, and how to gain the support of your family and friends as you make the transition. It also considers how to maintain the positive energy you need to make the transition—by loving what you're doing until you are doing what you love.

Preface to the
First Edition

As you've probably guessed by now, this is not your typical career-planning guide. Many of those books seem to have been written for automatons. This is a career guide for human beings. It's really a book about love in action, about joy, about beauty, about caring. It's for people who want to express their talents in meaningful ways that serve others. Its purpose is not to cram you into some category or stuff you into a gray flannel box. Its aim is to assist you in expressing the best within you in the world of work. In other words, it's designed to help you do your thing. If you don't know what your thing is, it will even help you find it. That's the good news, and, for those who apply themselves, there is no question that the program at the heart of this book works.

Now here comes the bad news. Well, sort of . . . It takes a lot of work. Yes, that's right, w-o-r-k. It takes "inner work" like soul-searching, intuition, thought, and decision making, and it takes "outer work" like research, learning, outreach, and follow-through. The information and the step-by-step planning process outlined in this book will help, but in the end, you are the one making all the decisions. If you don't like decision making, you'd probably be better off reading one of those "put you into a gray flannel box" career guides. They have all kinds of neat little tests that tell you what you should be. I don't know what you should be, and to tell you the truth, neither does any other career coach—no matter how impressive their tests. Fortunately, you do know.

You may not think so, but you really do know what you are here to do. Many of you are carrying around a great secret that you have yet to let yourself in on. One purpose of this book is to get the part of you that knows to start talking to the part of you that thinks it doesn't know. Of course, it's really up to you; you are the active ingredient. Your sincerity, intensity, and desire are what will make this process work for you. If you're the kind of person who enjoys self-discovery and adventure, you'll find most of the work in this process challenging and fun. In fact, once you get into it, you will start getting really turned on by the discoveries you make about yourself and the strategies and plans you develop to realize your visions of life at its best.

That's the action of this book—designing creative strategies for realizing your life's work. In addition to its unique vocational guidance program, you'll find many of the same subjects that are discussed in more traditional career books. You'll find information on how to write a resume, how to assess your skills, how to take a job interview—all the basics. In addition, you'll find a wealth of information not generally found in career-planning guides, information on starting your own business, working as a freelance, founding a nonprofit corporation, managing multiple careers, and much, much more.

Most importantly, all of this information will be presented within the context of viewing work as your creative expression of love in action. Right along, you'll be reminded of the opportunities and rewards as well as the challenges and pitfalls that face those who have the courage to be themselves in their work lives. Traditionally, career success has been defined by externals like salary, benefits, recognition, status in the community, and long-term security. From the standpoint of *Zen and the Art of Making a Living*, these parameters are inadequate. Money is a wonderful compensation *for* work, but is a terrible reason *to* work, especially if it means suppressing the desires of your heart and soul in the bargain. External rewards may dazzle others, but only your heart can tell you whether you have found fool's gold or the real McCoy. Being true to yourself, sharing your unique gifts in a way that matters to you, is what counts in the end.

Some of you may be judging yourselves for not already knowing what your life's work is. You may feel like kicking yourself for spending year after year working at something that wasn't really you. Look, there is nobody here but you and me, and just between the two of us, I'm not perfect either. So take a load off. Relax. Kick off your shoes, loosen your belt. On this journey, it doesn't matter where you have been. This journey is about where you are going, and consciously engaging the process of getting there . . . one step at a time.

For my part, I promise not to bore you on purpose. I want you to come along for the entire ride, and I know that for that to happen, you have to be having fun along the way. True, some parts of this book may not be as thrilling as jumping out of an airplane. I'm not going to tell you that researching a potential new career is more fun than a night on the town; but it can be more fun than peeling onions, and we all know that if we want onions in the soup, somebody's got to peel them. It's the same with organizing a targeted job search, or writing a business plan or a grant proposal, or doing some of the other work suggested in this book. There are times when somebody's got to do it, and that somebody usually ought to be you. These things may not be intrinsically thrilling, but on the other hand, if you have the right attitude, you *can* have fun doing them. Most of all, you'll feel good about yourself for having done what's good for you.

Why This Book Was Written

I first got into the career field because I recognized how central work is to the happiness of the individual and the character of any society. Work offers the individual the opportunity to share acts of love and beauty, to see himself reflected in the image of his work. By the work that a society chooses to do or *not* to do, it defines its values and shapes its future. Since work is what we do with most of our waking lives, we must, if we count life valuable, consider what we are working for.

I also realized that today, for all too many, work is drudgery, the thing to do to pay the bills, or a mad chase for material wealth and social status. I saw how bored, alienated, underchallenged, or overstressed so many are in their work, and how their unhappiness at work affects their families, friends, and communities. It seemed to me that the popular conception of work as principally a matter of economics and social status was at the heart of the matter. Many individual tragedies of alienation, emptiness, and despair, as well as community, national, and global problems, seemed to be aggravated, if not in fact caused, by this conception of work.

For many who came to me seeking career guidance, a "better job" (as defined by pay and benefits alone) was not enough. There was a real desire for a broader conception of work—one that would reflect the spiritual as well as the material life of human beings. My search for such a vision of work led me finally to the notion of work as art, the unique creative expression of the individual. (I cannot begin to acknowledge all the influences in shaping this view, though the work of Joseph Campbell, Ananda K. Coomaraswamy, and Alan W. Watts must be mentioned.) The essence of a vision of work as art is inspiration and excellence. Work, inspired in conception and spirited in performance, is art. This vision of work will be discussed in detail in the section called "Prologue: The Art of Life's Work." As time goes by, I've become convinced that this vision contains the seed of a profound cultural transformation. More immediately, I've seen many discover in their own lives that, when they stop thinking about work primarily as a tool for making money and put doing what they love first, money has a way of taking care of itself. Far beyond this, they have the satisfaction of being more fully alive and engaged every single day of their lives.

Even as the conventional notion of work was failing many, so too the conventional career-planning methodologies that had arisen out of this conception were, for many, inadequate. Many people who were looking for more fulfilling work were completely turned off by the conventional career-planning process. It isn't hard to understand why. Vocational guidance programs were originally designed to help employers better fit employees into positions within their organizational structures. They were never intended as a means of helping individuals realize their creative potential or achieve their own best work.

Over the years, career planning and vocational guidance evolved, but this notion of "finding the fit" was carried over as an integral part of conventional career-planning theory. Programs cut from this cloth tended to reduce human beings to collections of personality traits, aptitudes, or skills that could be matched with preexisting job slots. They focused on developing ever more elaborate tests and measures to find the perfect fit. Yet no matter how logical and systematic these programs might have seemed, they often failed to reach people where they lived. Like painting by numbers or dating by computer, something seemed to be missing from these programs—the LIFE of spontaneous engagement. The "best fit" model, after all, tends to view people as static, interchangeable parts in a grand machine, not as living, growing, and conscious beings.

On the other hand, there were inspirational books that failed to offer any practical help for dealing with the details of making things happen in the real world. People would read these books and get inspired for a time, but take no action. It all seemed so overwhelming. They didn't know where to begin. I saw the need for a program that would speak to people's hearts and souls, yet be practical enough to help them take definite action.

Over a number of years, I worked to develop such a program. That program formed the core of this book. Its purpose is to enhance human creativity in work, and in so doing, to assist people to experience the full joy of living. It has three key ingredients: a spiritual perspective on life in general and work in particular, an emphasis on service and on freedom of choice, and a wide range of options with which to construct a viable life's work.

An Integrated Approach to Work

Why is this one book and not two? What is all this stuff about Zen and mythic archetypes doing in a career book loaded with practical material about finding a job and all the rest? This *is* the Zen of it—the spirit in the everyday. Zen is the integration of the spiritual and material—the shattering of any artificial separation we might impose between the two. In the words of Kakuzo Okakura, "A special contribution of Zen to Eastern thought was its recognition of the mundane as of equal importance with the spiritual."[1] It seems to me that in our alienated, fractured modern life, this is a contribution *we* desperately need—an awareness of the sacred in the ordinary. Therefore, in its approach to work, this book acknowledges a vital role for spirit and soul.

For better or worse, as Carl Jung often pointed out, we cannot escape the psyche and the power that the imagination has in shaping our lives. The purpose of including the material on myth and archetypes is to provide tools with which to consciously and constructively engage this power in your life. Tapping into the deep well of psychic energy embedded in the archetypes will motivate and vitalize your efforts throughout the process of creating the work you love.

A Service Orientation

It is a fundamental premise of this book that to attempt to make a career choice without examining our values, or considering the impact that our "doing" has upon society, is to make an immature choice. It is immature because it lacks the confidence to face up to our responsibility to ourselves and to humanity. To ignore or discount your own values when making a career choice is to sell yourself short. "They" are never going to make the world a better place. It's up to you and me, and we *can* do it—if we have the love, the courage, and the patience.

We must have the love to go for what we know is right, even if it means paying a price. We who love life must work with life for life, while celebrating the mystery that is life. In short, we must be actively engaged in making the world the best it can be, while loving it exactly as it is. We must have the courage to believe that our dreams of a better world will one day be made manifest and that what we do as individuals makes a difference. We must have the courage to reject the idea of settling for work that is destructive of, or even indifferent to, human happiness. We must have the patience to view the movement toward life's work as an unfolding lifelong process—not something we can do in a week, a month, or a year, but something that takes a deep commitment and the patience to see it through.

Freedom of Choice

Those who take up their work as a creative pursuit, those who are ready to work from "the inside out," need a wider range of alternatives than the traditional nine-to-five job format alone. This book contains a complete section on mounting the kind of targeted job search that will put you in control of the hiring process. Beyond this, you'll find sections on starting your own business and on working as a freelance or independent contractor. There is even preliminary information on starting a nonprofit organization. There are sections on networking and negotiating, on writing grants and obtaining publicity, as well as information on volunteering and internships. You'll find tools for evaluating whether or not you ought to go back to school, and information on obtaining financial aid, should you decide to do so. There's a section on choosing the right strategy for making the transition between what you are doing now and what you ultimately decide you want to do. I've included a wide range of information and tools to give you more options to work with when you set about designing your new career. Be creative in the way you think about career and take advantage of the wide range of options available to you.

This book provides a set of tools for finding and doing the work you love within the existing economic, educational, and social structures. For the most part, these structures do not encourage one to be oneself or to serve one's fellow man in a spirit of love and beauty. At a later point, a new vocational technology will be required, but this can only gain wide currency when society's narrow focus on economics expands to include spiritual and humanitarian values, when education has become more a matter of developing the individual than of filling his head, when the organization of work is less centralized, and when the individual members of the society participate more fully in its decision making at all levels— in short, when we are more spiritually evolved. At times, this book points at how things might one day be, but it is written to be used with things as they are now. It's about creating the work you love in the world we find ourselves in today.

About the Title

This work is an attempt to apply the spirit of Zen to the human activity of living and working in the postmodern world. I am not a Buddhist or any "ist," but as D. T. Suzuki says, "Zen professes itself to be the spirit of Buddhism, but in fact, it is the spirit of all religions and philosophies." It is in this transcendent sense that I use the word *Zen*. I am not talking about a particular religion or dogma, or even a historical or cultural point of view, but of awareness and spirit applied to everyday life and work.

> To remain caught up in ideas and words about Zen is, as the old masters say, to "stink of Zen."
> *Alan Watts*

The "Zen lessons" in this book can be applied as easily by Christians, Jews, Hindus, Muslims, agnostics, and atheists as by Buddhists. I trust that the monastic purists will not take offense at my use of "Zen words" but will see the moon I'm pointing at. Still, I will use a minimum of Zen terminology. This is intended to be a popular book, not a book for scholastics or monastics. Where I can find a Western word or metaphor that fits the feel, I will prefer it.

Even as Bodhidharma brought Zen from India to China, so have the likes of D. T. Suzuki, Reginald Blyth, Alan Watts, and more recently a flood of Zen monastics brought Zen to the West.

Bodhidharma planted the Zen seed in a (Chinese) cultural milieu vastly different from that of his native India. In China, Zen (Ch'an) teachings evolved to integrate and express Taoist and Confucian elements. After Eisai brought the Ch'an teachings to Japan, Zen adapted to the native Samurai and Shinto traditions. Similar adaptations occurred in Zen's encounter with Korean, Vietnamese, and Thai cultures. As D. T. Suzuki puts it, Zen "is extremely flexible in adapting to almost any philosophy or moral doctrine."[2] Though Chinese, Japanese, and Korean Zen each has its own flavor and character, Zen remains Zen. At its heart, Zen is not the various Zen religions, sects, or schools, but what all of these are pointing at.

Now that Zen has reached the West, we can expect further adaptation of its expression as it encounters a radically different culture. Beyond adapting to culture, Zen today finds humanity facing crises unknown to the Ch'an patriarchs. Today, human survival itself is in jeopardy from nuclear destruction, climate change, overpopulation, and rampant environmental degradation. These threats too are, no doubt, bringing a further adaptation of Zen.

Even as the Zen experience is expressed differently in various cultures, so each individual expresses the Zen experience in his or her own way. For me, Zen says simply and emphatically: *We are one. This is it.* If we have realized this, then to act otherwise is lunacy. Sane or loony, we are all here together, and, like it or not, this is it.

*A Note about Language and Grammar

Like the content of this book, the use of language and grammar is at times unconventional. The occasional use of slang or nontraditional punctuation is intended to enhance a conversational tone. Further, since the content varies greatly throughout the book, the style varies accordingly. As for gender-specific pronouns, I use both he and she, not in clumsy combination, but by shuffling back and forth between the two.

How to Use This Book

Change and growth take place when a person has risked himself and dares to become involved with experimenting with his own life.

Herbert Otto

This is a big book, one that may seem a little daunting at first. The purpose of this section is to give you an overview of what's in it—so that you can begin to think about how to get the most out of it. I've found that people use this book in several different ways. You may gain benefit from any of these ways, or some combination. They are listed below according to the amount of effort required—starting with the most and moving to the least. (The highlight on page xxxi will help you find your way around the book.)

Five Ways to Use This Book

1. **A Lifework Planning Book.** Beginning in Act I, there are interactive exercises at the end of most chapters. You certainly don't have to work through all of these. However, I do encourage you to engage the exercises in the areas of interest to you. If you are looking to identify your passion, a fulfilling life's work, answering the questions in the exercises in Act I will prove helpful. If you are weighing a variety of career options or want to better understand if a particular career is right for you, see the exercises in Act II. If you are considering how to market yourself in a new or existing career, or thinking of starting your own business or nonprofit foundation, see those in Act III. If you are considering retraining for a new career or simply looking for ways to continue growing in your field, see those in Act IV.

2. **A General Interest Book on "The Way" or Art of Life's Work.** A second way to use this book is simply to read it and engage the ideas presented in it. Based on the comments of thousands of readers, I know that many have found this a rewarding, even life-transforming experience. The philosophy of work and the methodology of vocational guidance and career development that I have developed are based on a critique and a proposed remedy. Briefly, the critique is this: conventionally, we've tried to separate work from our souls and from love for, and responsibilities to, our fellow human beings and the natural world. This separation has proved detrimental to the individual, to society, and to the natural world. With respect to the remedy, I have endeavored to present a practical philosophy of work that reintegrates these elements into career decision making and development. At times, it may seem that the discussion drifts away from the subject of work, but this is only because of the extremely narrow way it is conventionally defined. In applying this approach, I invite you to view your life's work as an Art, a Quest, a Game, a Battle, and a School. To get an overview of these elements and how they fit together, see the diagram on page xxix.

3. **A "How-to" Career Guide.** A third way to use the book is as a "how-to" book of specific information. If, for example, you would like specific information on how to research a particular career that interests you, how you might go about setting yourself up as a freelance, how to conduct an effective job search, or how to gain publicity for yourself, your business, or your nonprofit foundation—you can simply look up this information in the appropriate sections.

Zen and the Art of Making a Living:
A Practical Philosophy of Work

Prologue: The Art of Life's Work. Your life's work is an Art in the sense of expressing your essential self in the world of time and space. The inspiration and the discipline of the artist provide a metaphor for a new vision of work. Lessons from mythology can help us to approach a creative psychology of work (see chapter 1, page 38).

Act I: The Quest for Life's Work. Your life's work is a Quest, in the sense that through it, you discover yourself. Like the heroes of old, those who follow the path of life's work make of their lives a quest for the shining apparition of their own best selves (see "The Quest for Your Best," page 126).

Act II: The Game of Life's Work. Your life's work is a Game, in the sense that to fulfill it, you must play roles—such as a career role. Working from a strong sense of purpose allows you to approach the game with a sense of play. You are invited to choose a "career game" you can get into—then play on purpose (see "Playing the Game: Winners, Losers, and Choosers," page 250).

Act III: The Battle for Life's Work. Your life's work is a Battle, in the sense that the effort to execute it takes place within socioeconomic and temporal-spatial limitations. No matter how good our intentions, how loving our motives, without aggressive action and a knowledge of the marketplace, we may abandon our grand intentions to the realm of mere dreams (see "Winning in the Marketplace," page 326).

Act IV: The School of Life's Work. Your life's work is a School, in the sense that it is a constant learning process. Learning is essential, both in creating the changes you intend and in responding well to the changes happening all around you (see "Learning to Change: The Old Boy and the Student-Sage," page 482).

4. **A Book of Inspirational Quotations.** A fourth way to use this book is as a compendium of inspiring quotes. Many people find they enjoy browsing through the book from time to time, finding inspiration and stimulation from a wealth of carefully selected quotations.

5. **A Career Resource Reference.** Previous editions of this book have included extensive Web and book resources. While a few have been retained, most of these resources have been moved to the Web site (empoweryou.com) in order to keep them relevant and up to date between editions of the book.

Lifework Planning

Since the other ways of using this book are pretty straightforward, the remaining discussion will focus on using this as a lifework-planning book. The process of lifework planning can be defined, in a general sense, as envisioning the world you want to live in and then determining what your part is in creating it. It takes being part dreamer, part builder. If we are not dreamers, our aspirations will be too low, and we will leave nothing of lasting value to those who follow. Yet, if we are not builders, if our dreams are not given the shape, form, and substance of living reality, they are nothing more than phantoms, the mirages we chase to escape a world we are unwilling to confront and love. The true idealist is no dewy-eyed dreamer, but a committed foot soldier in the cause of his or her vision.

To get the most out of this book, you'll probably want to take on the questions it raises. One way or another, you'll need to answer many of these questions on the road to your life's work. You may answer them by tackling the exercises in this book, or you may grapple with them some other way, perhaps without even realizing that you are. The important thing is not the form but the quest, the journey, and your commitment to it.

No book can tell you how to find your way; it can at best catalyze and awaken the way within you. You can paint by numbers, but you'll never produce a masterpiece that way. A masterpiece requires the soul and inspiration of an artist. To paint the masterpiece of your life, you need more than forms and systems. You need a commitment to your best self. Born in your heart, tempered by your head, shaped with your hands, and walked with your own two feet, your life's work is your unique expression of yourself—your special gift for mankind.

What follows is an attempt to point at some of the significant landmarks along the way to your life's work. It is not the only way. It is not even a way, per se. It is simply a description of some of the

Zen and the Art of Making a Living
Lifework Planning Program in a Nutshell

Act I: The Quest for Life's Work. In this unit, you will consider your place in the world and identify your core values. You'll go on to identify your work purpose, your key talents, and the specific objectives you would like to accomplish in the course of your work life. This unit includes a special section on breaking through the fear barriers to unleashing your full potential. See page 143 for a more complete overview of the exercises in Act I.

Act II: The Game of Life's Work. You begin by mentally projecting yourself into the career roles that will best enable you to express your passion or mission in life. Next, you are guided through the sometimes difficult process of conducting research on the careers you have envisioned. Finally, you have a chance to make a thorough and critical evaluation of the careers you have selected, to help you determine what's really right for you. See page 270 for a more complete overview of the exercises in Act II.

Act III: The Battle for Life's Work. In this unit, you will develop your personal marketing strategy. Whether you decide to build your own organization or work for an existing one, this unit is packed with the kind of practical information you need to move ahead. With the information and resources in this unit, you will be able to assemble what you need to capture your market share or make the job interviewer sit up in his chair. See page 343 for a more complete overview of the process work in Act III.

Act IV: The School of Life's Work. In this unit, you will develop a strategy for making the transition from what you are doing now, into your new career. You'll find sections devoted to increasing your ability, credibility, and marketability. You'll learn how to improve your self-image, enlist the support of friends and loved ones, and how "to love what you're doing till you're doing what you love." See page 506 for a more complete overview of the process work in Act IV.

The beginning is the most important part of the work.

Plato

important scenery along the way. You must find your own way, the road to your Self and its expression in the world. This process should be approached with a spirit of introspection, adventure, and fun. You must rely upon yourself over any form, system, or structure. Having said all this, see the plan in a nutshell on the previous page.

Working Through the Time, Space, and Stuff

The biggest difficulty in any work is getting started. Therefore, determine to begin as soon as possible. Make a conscious decision that you're going to work through the questions in the exercises until you have arrived at answers that satisfy you. Consistent attention to the questions presented in this book will yield exciting, even life-transforming, results. The following are some tips that will help you to get the most of your lifework planning efforts.

The Time: Schedule your lifework-planning sessions. Determine in advance when and how long each session will be. An hour to an hour and a half once a week works best for most people. Try to work at the same time each week if at all possible—for example, eight o'clock on Wednesday evenings. This will enlist the aid of your subconscious mind in working on the process in the interim. When you know that at eight o'clock on Wednesdays you'll be focusing on and writing about your life's work, your subconscious mind will be working with these ideas throughout the week. You may find that you wake up in the morning with ideas or that in the middle of a shower or a conversation or while driving home from work—ideas suddenly appear. When you work on a regular basis, you can incorporate these gifts from your creative subconscious into your scheduled planning sessions.

It's also helpful to review your work on a regular basis. Try to do this in a leisurely and relaxed fashion. You might take a portion of a Sunday afternoon and look over everything you've written. Let it rumble around in your mind. Listen to what your answers are telling you. Whether these review sessions serve to confirm your current thinking or stimulate you to revise it, they can prove invaluable.

The Space: If at all possible, establish a regular place where you can work without interruption. If you don't have an office or study in your home, try to set up a special table or desk in a designated area. Keep distractions to an absolute minimum. You'll want to do a good deal of concentrated thinking and reflecting, and a quiet workspace helps. Be sure that your family or the people you live with understand that you require their cooperation in giving you the space you need to do your lifework planning. Let them know you're not to be interrupted during this time. Arrange to have someone watching the children, and hold the telephone calls. Additionally, a designated work area will help you keep all of your work in one place. This becomes especially important as you get into the research phase of the process.

The Stuff: At times, you may feel stuck, but if you persevere, you will move through the blocks. Being aware of and accepting of your emotional responses throughout this process will help you to stay on course. You may experience feeling regretful, depressed, or angry from time to time. A Chinese proverb says even a hurricane doesn't last a day. So don't worry, the emotional storms will pass. The parts of our subconscious minds that are hooked into negativity and limitation may begin to create certain problems or symptoms. These may include feeling sleepy or fatigued, anxious or restless. Assuming you are otherwise healthy, these symptoms are simply a part of moving through the emotional terrain involved in getting to clarity and commitment. It is worth recognizing that creating a life's work is a process. Much of that process involves coming to new levels of inner strength and confidence. After all, if you were there now, you would already be doing work you loved and valued. Accept the growing pains.

Our demons are our own limitations, which shut us off from the realization of the ubiquity of the spirit . . . each of these demons is conquered in a vision quest.

Joseph Campbell

While it's true that our socioeconomic system doesn't support people finding and expressing their unique gifts, more often than not it is we who block ourselves from realizing our full potentials. Our own conscious or subconscious beliefs can keep us from either identifying fulfilling life's work or taking the necessary action to make it a reality. If we're going to transcend old limiting beliefs and hang-ups, we're going to have to deal with things we've avoided in the past. For example, some people have difficulty answering probing questions that require introspection and self-examination. Others have difficulty doing the necessary research and goal-setting work. Persist through the difficulties, whatever they may be, and you will open doors to a deeper, richer experience of yourself and your work.

The Art of Life's Work

*Wherein we consider the spirit at work
and meet our hero*

Where the spirit does not work with the hand, there is no art.

Leonardo da Vinci

In "Prologue: The Art of Life's Work," we set the stage for the four-act play that follows. The theme of this unit is to consider how we can express our full creative potential and aliveness through work. In the introduction, we begin our discussion of the "Art of Life's Work" by contrasting the prevailing myth of the "little king" with the philosophy of work as art. Chapter 1 explores approaching work as creative self-expression and contrasts this with the more traditional problem-solving approach to work. Chapter 2 draws on lessons from Zen and the creative arts in an attempt to discover how each of us can make our work poetry in motion—love in action. Chapter 3 considers how we can enhance our experience of work through a conscious and creative encounter with universal, mythic, or archetypal energies. Chapter 4 speaks to awakening the heroic consciousness in our lives and work, and explores the potential for greatness and heroic action within us all.

The Grail Quest or the Bourgeois Nest?

If you follow your bliss, you put yourself on a kind of track, which has been there all the while waiting for you, and the life that you ought to be living is the one you are living.

                                        Joseph Campbell

Work is one of the great topics of humankind. We can know no people—their culture, history, art, or religion—without understanding their approach to work. In seeking to understand a historically distant culture, the anthropologist is interested in not only the work these people did and how they did it but also *why* they did it. It is not enough for the anthropologist to know a people's artifacts and technologies; she must to be able to surmise something of their worldview, the myths they lived by, if she would understand them. In the same way, we cannot understand ourselves without understanding the myths we live and work by. This introduction will briefly explore a central myth that has shaped our attitudes toward work in the Modern Age. It will also suggest an alternative vision of work for the Postmodern Era.

Myths shape our attitudes and aspirations in ways we scarcely recognize, grabbing hold of our imaginations and channeling our energies into prescribed patterns of behavior. Today, our dominant myth about work is the myth of "a world of little kings." This myth provides a social ideal, a measure for judging the relative worth of various activities and members of society. Today, it is a view of life that many find personally empty and socially ruinous. They, perhaps like you, are questing for another way.

Modern Times: Man in the Machine Age

It all began, not with the water wheel or the steam engine, the railroad or mass production—the modern world was born with the ticking of a clock. We don't really know when the first clock appeared in Europe. We do know that by 1335, the people of Milan could hear their all-mechanical town clock strike out the hours. Later in the same century, domestic versions of the clock became available throughout Europe. By the sixteenth century, we had personal time in the form of the watch. These early "time machines" were harbingers of a profound shift in worldview—one that would touch virtually every aspect of human life—the dawn of the machine age.

> *The hours of folly are measured by the clock; but of wisdom, no clock can measure.*
> *William Blake*

We have been gearing up ever since. Time has become more precise and more "valuable" as the years have rolled by. Today time *is* money, as every child in day care knows. We save, borrow, and spend time until our bodily gears are exhausted. If we could travel back in time, we would, no doubt, have a difficult time explaining to a thirteenth century peasant that today we "have no time," that we feel under time "pressure," that time is "getting away from us," that we are in a "time crunch."

Gears, clocks, and hourly wages just weren't known in the Middle Ages. Man lived by the calendar, the sacred holidays and festivals marking the passage of cyclical time, recounting an endless drama of life, death, and regeneration. While calendarial time is based on nature's seasons and the earth's place in the universe, clock time is an abstraction of the mind.[1] The shift from calendar to clock took natural man into an abstract, linear world, sectioned off into minute particles. Life was no longer to be organized around the rhythms of nature, but around a machine.

Today, the clock has become an almost trite symbol of the Industrial Revolution, where the gears of industry turned on the labor of the punch-clock worker. In compensation for his labors, the worker became "geared" toward the pursuit of the "good life." Why, it was only a matter of time before the marvels of science would allow the common man to enjoy the good life once known only to the aristocracy.

The Little King's Paradise: A Promise Unfulfilled

About the time the Industrial Revolution was really getting into gear, political revolutions were everywhere replacing kings with parliaments, presidents, and promises. The key promise was that the common man would one day soon be king. He would possess for his own the kingly prerogatives of power, leisure, and security—power over his station in life, the liberty of leisure, and the security of property.

Mass education would destroy class distinction and give every man the power over his station. Scientific technology and free market capitalism would supply him with the labor-saving devices that would ensure his leisure. Government would guarantee his security through old-age benefits and either state assignment of housing or governmental support and incentives for home ownership.

Every man would be king, enjoying the goods of life made possible through machines and mass production. There would soon arise whole nations of little kings, each at home in his castle; if not a palace, then perhaps a country estate; if not a country estate, then a home in the suburbs, a condo, an apartment, a mobile home—any kingdom, no matter how small. This is what we worked for. *We labored for a kingdom and the promise of the leisure to enjoy it.*

Too many people spend money they haven't earned, to buy things they don't want, to impress people they don't like.

Will Rogers

We aspired to the kingly life of leisure, a life of ease, a life to do with whatever we pleased, to be as irresponsible as we imagined the aristocracy to be. Labor unions advocated less work for more benefits—never challenging the nature or objectives of the work, only demanding more leisure and security *away* from work. Golf and

Of Cabbage and Kings:
Power, Leisure, and Security

Power Through Technology and Trade: The Corporate Society.
We put our faith in the power of technology and the "free market" to solve
all of our problems. As the production of weapons of mass destruction
demonstrates, technology is simply power and not necessarily a good unto
itself. The danger is not with technology per se, but in either elevating it
to a religion—science as savior—or allowing it to be used solely as a tool
for profit. The doctrine of the inherent benevolence of the "free market" is
taken as gospel. Despite the fact that modern markets and the corporations that dominate them are creations of the state, we pretend a godlike
invisible hand moves across the land bringing justice through the law of
supply and demand. Markets and technologies can be used for good or ill,
and are finally no better than the motives behind them.

Individualism Through Leisure: The Consumer Society. The advance of so-called "Western individualism" has strangely failed to include
individual expression through work. It has not meant better craftsmanship or fuller individual participation in the purpose and goals of work. It
has rather come to mean pleasure in "leisure," or rather consumption. We
claim to be an individualistic society, yet we reside in cracker-box houses
and scurry about in cookie-cutter cars. We live in suburbs that look so
much alike it requires a road map to tell them apart. We toil away at dull
or meaningless jobs, and suppress our individuality and creative zest in
hopes of acquiring the status symbols that Madison Avenue tells us we need
in order to be *individuals*. Today, people in the third world want in on the
act. Irreplaceable resources dwindle, but still we try to consume our way
to heaven. Perhaps if we were happier we wouldn't *need* so much stuff.

Security Through Secularism: The Bureaucratic State Society.
Secularism has developed into reliance upon the state, the government.
Big Brother will take care of us in old age, solve all of our social ills, and
create the Great Society. The sum of our duty to our fellow man, to nature, and to the environment is to be a good "citizen" and vote for the best
candidates. We have relied on political solutions rather than individual
spiritual development and social cooperation. Bureaucracies abound, but
they have not reduced anxiety, nor produced lasting security.

tennis, the games of the aristocrats, became the staples (with the stables) of the country club set, where the new upper middle class could play the part of landed gentry on a subscription basis. The more ambitious were not content with little kingdoms and playing weekend gentry. They would be empire builders. They would rule whole industries and employ thousands, have their own armies, and crush all opposition. While these industrial giants set out to conquer ever-larger domains, the less ambitious or advantaged had to content themselves with whatever leisure and security they could manage.

No doubt kingly life (at least that of the better kings) was more than power, leisure, and security, but these were what we coveted. Duty, responsibility, wisdom, honor, courage, magnanimity—these kingly virtues might be admired in passing, but they were not envied like the others. Like a younger sibling, jealous of the privileges of an older brother, we viewed the king from afar and ogled the privileges we would one day have for ourselves. *We would be kings and take for ourselves as much power, leisure, and security as we thought we deserved and could get away with.*

The promise of a future kingdom kept the wageworker toiling away. If he wasn't enjoying what he was doing, well, the age of leisure was just around the corner. It is amusing today to read predictions made as late as the mid-1970s about the life of leisure that was just around the corner for the common man. Today, children of the two-career family, who seldom see either parent, scoff at the notion that they will grow up to a life of leisure. Still, we rush to get our share of the goods of life, before our time runs out. We cling to the hope that, if not by the miracles of science, then perhaps by the miracle of the credit card, we can live the life of kings. (Increasingly, leisure has become associated, not with rest, refinement, or a contemplative life—but with consumption. *Leisure,* which we get from the Latin *licere*, "to be permitted," has come to mean permission to consume as much as we want, without consideration for others or the environment.)[2]

By now many realize that the promise was empty indeed. We were promised that we would be little kings, and yet it seems we have so little control over the direction of our lives. The little king is a prisoner of his own "freedom"—from responsibility and conscience. He is free to fit in—not free to live his own life. His inner life is barren and hollow; his humanity, atrophied; his creativity, flat. Not surprisingly, some of the most telling criticism of modern society has come from some of our most insightful psychiatrists, people who see firsthand the psychological anguish of "the little king." Erich Fromm described modern life as producing men "who feel free and independent, not subject to any authority or principle

Come out of the circle of time, and into the circle of love.

Rumi

of conscience—yet willing to be commanded, to do what is expected of them, to fit into the social machine without friction; who can be guided without force, led without leaders, prompted without aim—except the one to make good, to be on the move, to function, to go ahead."[3] To be obsessed with control, yet unable to direct his own life, to consume without satisfaction, to seek security in isolating conformity—such is the lot of the little king—such, his "freedom."

Victor Frankl, author of *Man's Search for Meaning,* put it like this: "For too long we have been dreaming a dream from which we are now waking up; the dream that if we improve the socioeconomic situation of people, everything will be okay, people will become happy. The truth is that as the struggle for survival has subsided, the question has emerged: Survival for what?"[4] While the struggle for survival remains paramount for much of humanity, those of us who have the luxury of asking this question have a responsibility not only to ourselves but also to those who don't.

It is preoccupation with possessions, more than anything else, that prevents us from living freely and nobly.
                                        Bertrand Russell

The dream from which we are now awakening is what I've called the "Myth of the Little King." Now, some would say that today we have no myth to live by, and, in the archaic sense of the term, this is so. (Chapter 3 will discuss myth in this context.) Yet, as much as nature, the mind of man—his imagination—abhors a vacuum. If we have no genuine myth to show us the way of life, then a pseudo-myth arises to fill the void. Today, we live by the pseudo-myth of the little king.

Of course, most of us don't actually live like kings; yet most are still caught up in the myth. We wish it were so. So high school kids rent limousines on prom night; we dream of the "lifestyles of the rich and famous" and hope to win the lottery. To wish for something is to believe in it (the *lief* in *belief* originally meant "wish"). If you believe in the myth, not intellectually, but deeply—subconsciously, you accept it as the standard by which you judge yourself and others.

The little-king myth is today at once a practical anachronism and a popular worldview that holds great currency in the imaginative life of the global culture. While most of us in the West still believe in the myth (and we are busy exporting it to the far reaches of the globe), many are coming to see it for the empty fiction that it is. Working for security, status, and consumer items is simply not enough for many today. We have a sense that work ought to nurture and uplift us spiritually and psychologically. The little king myth and the values it promotes are increasingly seen as inadequate. Two major factors are peeling away the scales from our eyes.

1. The growing recognition of the importance of nonmaterial, psychological, and spiritual factors to happiness and fulfillment in life generally and at work in particular.

2. The achievement of the global village and the recognition of the critical state of issues related to the environment, the global economy, and world peace. Increasingly, we recognize that we are all in this together.

These are really flip sides of the same coin. We cannot address the needs of the community, the nation, or the world apart from consideration of the psychological and spiritual needs of the individual, or vice versa. The great fallacy of the little-king myth is its suggestion that the individual ego is a thing apart—apart from nature, from the spirit of life, from his fellows, and even from his own psyche. To conceive of ourselves as separate is to create an artificial boundary between "me" (the ego) and "them" (everything and everyone else). Our separate kingdoms become our prisons. We can't lock "them" out without locking ourselves in. Individual alienation and social and environmental conflict must result from this separative consciousness.

This time, like all times, is a very good one, if we but know what to do with it.

Emerson

For the Bold: Breaking with the Mold

The myth of the little king and the values that it inculcates—avarice, consumerism, and security in conformity—give us a prescription for how we are supposed to live our lives. To want something different is to enter the dark forest of uncharted experience. As Joseph Campbell put it, "You don't have to go very far off the interpreted path to find yourself in very difficult situations. The courage to face the trials and to bring a whole new body of possibilities into the field of interpreted experience for other people to experience—

that is the hero's deed."[5] The hero, in living her own life, in being true to herself—radiates a light by which others may see their own way.

> *What each must seek in his life never was on land or sea. It is something out of his own unique potentiality for experience, something that never has been and never could have been experienced by anyone else.*
>
> Joseph Campbell

This is no easy task, but one demanding the greatest integrity, courage, and skill. As Colin Wilson has written, "modern civilisation, with its mechanised rigidity, is producing more outsiders than ever before—people who are too intelligent to do some repetitive job, but not intelligent enough to make their own terms with society."[6] Those Wilson calls "outsiders" see through the absurdity of devoting year after year to work they neither love nor respect. Those "intelligent enough" to make their own terms with society are what I will later refer to as "artists of life." The outsider views himself as a product of a culture he rejects—the artist views himself as a culture-builder. As would-be artists, we must begin with the right attitudes or, as the Buddhists say, "right views"—taking a mature approach beyond mere protest and complaint—accepting the responsibility to *create* the life we would live. Everything in the remainder of this book is there for this purpose: to encourage and assist you in engaging this creative process. Clearly, if we are to accomplish this, we will require a new image of what work is and what work is for.

Life shrinks or expands in proportion to one's courage.

Anaïs Nin

A Question of Balance

On our way to developing a new image of work, we can take a lesson from Jungian psychology. According to Jung, the individual psyche (of both men and women) has feminine and masculine aspects or values. Roughly speaking, the feminine values are concerned with *being*; the masculine, with *doing*. In the Jungian conception, the masculine aspect of self is concerned with *controlling* the external world. Technology is the preeminent means of achieving control. In a society where masculine values dominate, technology is highly valued and advanced. The feminine aspect of self is concerned with enlarging the individual's *experience* of the world as it is—that is, with being. In a society where masculine values dominate, people have little experience with being; they lose touch with what Joseph Campbell called "the rapture of being alive."

The key to psychological maturity, Jung would tell us, is balance.[7] The balanced individual is free, in the words of Joseph Campbell, "to pass back and forth across the world division, from the perspective of the apparitions of *time* [the world of doing] to that of the causal deep [the world of being] and back—not contaminating the principles of the one with those of the other, yet permitting the mind to know the one by virtue of the other."[8] Modern man is a prisoner of time—so involved in his doings that he has lost touch with his being. As individuals and as a society, we have lost our balance. We might ask with Anne Morrow Lindbergh, "Why have we been seduced into abandoning this timeless inner strength of woman [the feminine values] for the temporal outer strength of man [the masculine values]?"[9]

> *Only those who will risk going too far can possibly find out how far one can go.*
>
> T. S. Eliot

The effects of this cultural bias are not merely academic. They are everyday life, where good has become synonymous with expensive; practical, with commercial; science, with technology. The good doctor or lawyer is the one who costs the most money. Practical decisions are ones that make the largest short-term profit, regardless of long-term costs. Science is no longer the pursuit of knowledge, but the pursuit of commercially viable technological "solutions." The problem is we accept all of this as though it were the only way. The starving artist is cliché, but we seldom hear of the starving engineer.

Today, even art has become commercialized. It has too often become a tool for profit and, therefore, a means for better controlling the environment, rather than the revelation of deep inner experience. The same can be said of much of religion, which is often little more than a social club. Religion serves as a means of abating the loneliness and isolation of an existence lived without an experience of spirit. It has, to a large degree, lost its fire, its bliss. Philosophy has been left to the technical specialists, and wisdom, especially in high places, runs in short supply.

Certainly our common-man-as-king myth, with its exclusive emphasis on controlling the environment, produces a half-formed individual, alienated from the life-vivifying powers of nature and spirit—cut off from his own conscience. Without the balance of the feminine values, the sanctioned drives for power, leisure, and security are more apt to produce little tyrants than philosopher-

The feminine values are the fountain of bliss.

kings. The feminine values are the wellspring of life, the fountain of bliss, the ocean of life eternal. Without the regeneration of these living waters, life becomes the barren *Waste Land* of T. S. Eliot. We become slaves to time and technology. The more enslaved and stuck in time we feel, the more desperately we try to control our time and our lives. Yet the more we attempt to gain control through our mechanical creations (both mental machinations and material gadgetry), the more controlled by them we feel. Today the mechanical gear has been replaced by the electronic chip, and the pace of time has become a frantic clip.

We miss the bliss, the touch of the eternal. We are stuck in time, stuck in trying to control, stuck with a sense of missing something. We miss the bliss, and so content ourselves with seeking stimulation or sedation. Imitation bliss comes and goes, and too soon time again comes marching in. Bliss is rest, but we are restless.

> *Know the masculine,*
> *Keep to the feminine.*
> *Lao Tzu*

To date, the women's movement has provided little challenge to our overly masculine value structure. It has been more concerned with finding a place for women within the existing structure than with challenging the assumptions upon which it is based. (If the common man can be king, why not the common woman?) In its wake, we have not become a more feminine (that is, a more spiritual/artistic) society. The introduction of women en masse into the workplace means women, as well as men, feel the pressure to conform to the existing masculine-dominated value structure.

The Whole 'n' Parting

In his effort to control his world, modern man rejected all he could not understand through reason or experiment. He accepted that "such knowledge as is not empirical is meaningless."[10] He denied the great Mystery of Life and put his faith in ratio-nality. A ratio is a portion, a part. The analytical mind divides life into parts; but in endless fragmentation, we miss the experience of the whole. Life is simultaneously the ratio (the part) and the whole—at once the same and different. A stream remains a stream, though each moment different water is running though it. Starting from the ratio, life is an endless series of problems to be solved. Starting from the whole, life is a mystery to be revealed.

The rational point of view tells us that life is a problem to be solved. Problems can be solved through analysis, but new problems always take their place. This is the endless tail chase of Q and A—the Hydra that sprouts new heads every time you cut one off. The poet, the sage, the scriptures, the mythologies of the world suggest that life is not a problem to be solved, but a mystery to be revealed. But alas, toward these we turned a deaf ear.

We rejected the Mystery of the whole and came to rely on the fraction. This gave us a one-at-a-time (abstract, linear) sense of reality—a world of separate things. We fixated on a kind of spotlight consciousness. Our way of dealing with a world of separate parts was to attempt to exercise ever-greater control over those portions of it that came under our individual and collective spotlights. We became so proud of what we were doing under our various spotlights that we failed to notice what we were doing to the global stage we were playing on. We were so busy trying to straighten out a world we perceived as a jumbled mess of separate things that we failed to notice the mess we were making of things. It was, we thought, up to us to impose law and order on this chaos. We would put our faith in political laws to control the wills of others and scientific laws to regulate nature. In the modern era, first politics, then technology, and finally money became the principal religions of the little king. Religions concerned with controlling the parts are frightened of the prospect of opening to the whole. The emphasis on fragmentary knowledge and the felt need for control arise together—head and tail of the same dragon.

Nothing divides one so much as thought.
Reginald Blyth

Today, most see the "problem of life" as a matter of addition. Our whole effort is to gain and hold, acquire and defend. The cry of the little king is, "More, more, more!" The answer to our social problems is ever greater economic growth (a good unto itself) and more and better technological solutions. On the personal level, the answer is more stuff of one kind or another: money, knowledge, fame, recognition, etc. Perhaps, we dream, if we get enough parts, they will add up to a whole. But alas, all the king's horses and all the king's men can't put poor ol' Humpty Dumpty back together again. While the Western tradition is obsessed with addition, the Eastern tradition tells us that there is also value in subtraction—in letting go of our attachments to the parts long enough to open to the whole. It says that to the extent that we become conscious of this whole, we put ourselves in touch with a higher order of

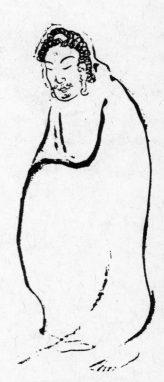

O, Heart, remember thee That Man is none, Save One.

Coventry Patmore

intelligence and a greater source of energy than we can ever find in the parts. The mind plays in the realm of parts, but the whole comes through the heart.

Society tells us that the only thing that matters is matter— the only things that count are the things that can be counted. We start counting with toys, then grades, then friends, then bank accounts, then years to retirement. What is there to life that can't be counted? That can't be measured? That can't be dissected or analyzed? What is this, that wiggles away when you try to reduce it or that vanishes the moment you try to grab it? No matter how we try to comprehend it, life remains an indefinable mystery.

Science can record similarities or differences in nature, but it can't touch the Mystery. Below, Isaac Newton states the difficulty of trying to understand any whole from a series of parts.

> The orbit of any one planet depends on the combined motion of all the planets, not to mention the action of all these on each other. But to consider simultaneously all these causes of motion and to define these motions by exact laws allowing of convenient calculation exceeds, unless I am mistaken, the force of the entire human intellect.[11]

The difficulty he describes is not a matter of a backward seventeenth-century technology, but a fundamental limitation of analysis for ever comprehending the whole. There are mysteries that simply defy analysis. If we limit our knowledge to that which can be quantified, we miss not only the wonder of the Mystery but also the possibility of its revelation.

It has been said that Mystery is revealed through purification. Zen tells us that we must purify even the idea of purification; we must enter into the Mystery direct. All can approach the Mystery in nature. The Taoists and Western transcendental poets contemplated the Mystery this way—in landscape and rain, in birdsong and nightfall. Looking in nature, we catch glimpses of an order— patterns within a leaf, rings on a tree, cycles of seasons, migrations of birds. These glimpses hint at an incomprehensible, transcendent Mystery. The more of the Mystery we glimpse, the more we are struck by its incomprehensibility, and the more deeply we are moved to purify our sense of separation, our fixation on ourselves as little parts.

The Art of Life's Work:
The Mystery of Being in Action

The image of work presented in this book can be called "The Art of Life's Work." Life's work is not machine work, obsessed with control—negating the Mystery of Life. It is an integrated expression of Being and Doing—what Zen calls the "infinite way of doing finite things." It is a celebration of the Mystery of Life in the everyday activities of life. We needn't be desperate prisoners of the time machine, struggling to lord it over our separate little kingdoms. We can live in cognizance of the Eternal, and in harmony with nature and one another. We can dedicate ourselves to loving and serving humanity in the realization that we are all a part of the great Mystery of Life. We can go beyond doing things we neither love nor respect just so we can go on earning. We can find our soul's passion and earn so we can go on doing it. Do from the depth of your *being*—this is what is meant by "follow your bliss." Act in time from the ecstasy of the timeless.

A life's work comes out of the Living Mystery. It moves into the limited world of time and forms; this is the work, hence, life's work. Life and work are not things apart. Work is more than gaining privileges and possessions; it is ongoing, ecstatic, *living* experience. When we really love what we are doing, we no longer feel as though we must be king. We can just be ALIVE at work. *When we live in the bliss, there is no difficulty that is insurmountable. If we miss the bliss, there is no compensation that is adequate.*

> We are kept out of the Garden by our own fear and desire in relation to what we think to be the goods of our life.
>
> Joseph Campbell

The highest order of duty to self is to follow your bliss. To thine own self be true. The highest order of duty to society is to make your greatest contribution to its well-being. These duties meet in life's work. They may appear (especially in the short term) to be in conflict, but in the long run of a life span, they can be seen to be threads interwoven so tightly as to be almost indistinguishable. It cannot be said where one begins and the other ends.

Freud said the basic requirements of human existence are love and work.[12] A genuine life's work breaks down any barriers we might impose to separate the two. Love is not a category, a compartment of life separate from work. It is pervasive. When we are in love, we feel boundless life. We touch the timeless. Work

Artists in each of the arts seek after and care for nothing but love.

Marsilio Ficino

is simply the forms into which we pour this living substance of love. In life's work, we honor both the timeless love that fills our hearts and the time-bound world of form we live in. Freud was right: Love (and through it, the timeless pulse of life) and work (and through it, the world of time and forms) are the basic stuff of human life. Work without love is dry and empty. Love without work is incomplete. Our task is to tap into the eternal ocean of bliss and somehow express that energy in the world of forms and time. This is the art of creative living. While engaged in life's work, we can be said to be practicing artists—motivated, not by external rewards, but by the intrinsic joys of self-expression and service to humanity.

A Postmodern Vision: Everyone an Artist

Art is the proper task of life.
Friedrich Nietzsche

At first, some may find it hard to accept that Nietzsche's statement above applies to them. Throughout this book, I will insist that every man or woman is a potential artist and, when living authentically, one indeed. If that doesn't resonate, it may be because you are thinking about art in a different way than is intended here. Art is not limited to what we today call "fine" art. Ananda K. Coomaraswamy wrote, "However broad or narrow, noble or ignoble, the subject of the art, however elegant or crude the language, art is always recognizable as art. *All that we demand of an artist is that he should offer us living water:* for this water has a miraculous quality, and even though it be offered in a thimble it will fill a bowl"[13] [emphasis added].

An experience I had many years ago shaped my own views of work as art. I had arrived in Europe for the first time, there to study the art and architecture of the Old World. After traveling all night, I arrived early in the morning and went straight to a downtown hotel to check in. There was no one at the desk, but I heard the most incredible singing ringing through the building. A voice of such spirit, beauty, and joy as I had never heard. It was "not the tongue, but our very life singing." Following the voice, I went upstairs. There, in the third-floor hallway, was the origin of the voice—a young woman on her hands and knees, pushing a bristle brush with both hands. In this woman, I had encountered a genuine artist of life. Her art echoed in me long after the noise of so many museum images had faded.

The Whole Business of Man Is The Arts, & All Things Common.

William Blake

This little story illustrates a couple of important points: that we not mistake art for artifact, or again, that we not mistake the art with the craft. As Coomaraswamy wrote, "The thing is a work *of* art, made *by* art, but it is not art itself; the art remains in the artist."[14] If we can enter into what Coomaraswamy is saying here (and he is by no means alone in this view; see pages 48 and 75), we can understand that not only *can* we all be artists, but artists are what we naturally are. The art is in the man or woman—in their consciousness. The Zen saying, "How wondrous this, how mysterious! I carry fuel, I draw water,"[15] gives this perfectly. Again emphasizing consciousness over craft, Blake said, "Jesus & his Apostles & Disciples were all Artists."[16] If you cannot find art in your consciousness, you will never find it at all.

The most awkward means are adequate to the communication of authentic experience, and the finest words no compensation for lack of it. It is for this reason that we are moved by the true Primitives and that the most accomplished art craftsmanship leaves us cold.

Ananda K. Coomaraswamy

The artist's craft may be a "fine" or "applied" art. I am not suggesting that all of us can or should be "fine" artists, but that we err if we assume "that there is one kind of man that can imagine, and another that cannot; or to speak more honestly, another kind whom we cannot afford to imagine without doing hurt to business."[17] Of course, there are greater and lesser artists, whatever the craft. The test of greatness is in the depth of the artist's vision, and only secondarily in the skill of her technique. As Coomaraswamy would say, it is the artist's vision (love) from which the "living waters" spring. "It is not by an intellectual or categorical activity that we can judge the intensity of an artist's vision. We cannot judge except by our response and whether or not we *can* respond will depend on our own state of grace" [emphasis added].[18]

The First Work of the Artist Is Herself

The artist must be a developed individual—an authentic hero—and never a mere product of society. The hero, as Dorothea Dooling so aptly put it, "may be you or me, but only at the highest reaches of our most impossible possibility."[19] Her role is to release the active powers of nature, soul, and spirit into the lives of humanity. The intensity of her vision is reflected in her capacity to fuse these three into a radiant, harmonious whole. Nature provides the medium and energy of the work—the dancer's body, the painter's colors, the sculptor's stone, the composer's instruments, the poet's paper and ink or computer chip—as well as the body's transformation of these. The musician trains her ear; the painter, his eye and hand; the dancer, her body. The soul provides the symbols, the mythic forms, the archetypal energies through which a universally human art is made intelligible. The spirit arrests the mind—projecting the experiencer out of himself into the realm of the infinite, the transcendent Mystery.

> *The purpose of the whole (work) is to remove those who are living in this life from a state of wretchedness and lead them to the state of blessedness.*
> *Dante*

Before she can express them in art, the artist must deeply encounter these energies in life. Modern life is so configured as to negate the powers of nature, soul, and spirit—to encourage you to put all of your eggs (faith and aspirations) into society's basket. Society tries to make you think that it is your only source of nourishment and protection, power and refreshment. And who is this society? None other than our little king—the adolescent ego. Traditional cultures understood that society is always essentially adolescent and sought to honor, celebrate, and make conscious the greater powers of nature, soul, and spirit through communally shared myths, rituals, and initiations, and in the higher religions, through individual spiritual transformation. Here we must distinguish between society and culture. A society can be interested in a man or woman only as a political or economic entity; a culture is interested in more. Culture means literally "to cultivate" or "to care for."[20] Cultures care for their peoples as natural, spiritual beings and not simply as workers or consumers. Cultures cultivate an awareness of the deep energies of life and of the particular gifts of the individual, and so naturally produce art. Modern society (the little king with his machines) has usurped the role of the greater powers in seeking to make itself the Alpha and Omega of human experience.

The trick of society is to make you think it is the whole banana of life. For your physical food, you are to depend, not on the bounty of Mother Nature, but on supermarket chains, chemical conglomerates, and giant agribusiness firms. Western man has become increasingly alienated from his body and nature. You are to depend on society for its evaluation of your sanity—measured, not in terms of the

Industry without art is brutality.

*Ananda K.
Coomaraswamy*

ancient wisdom or sacred psychologies, but in terms of "normality"—the sharing of the society-dominant worldview. Western man has become alienated from his conscience and the universally human. You are to depend upon social religion to tell you what God is or upon social science to tell you that God isn't. Western man stands alienated from his divinity and from Ultimate Reality. (By Western man I mean, not simply those who live in the West, but all who embrace its vision of life.) All of this puts extreme pressure on the social dimension to fulfill all of our needs, and puts pressure on us to conform; for unlike in other cultures, we have no other concept of power, no other source of protection.

> *For, in order to turn the individual into a function of the State, his dependence on anything beside the State must be taken from him.*
>
> *Carl Jung*

Again, our task is to vitalize the life of society with the living energies of nature, spirit, and psyche. This is always the work of the artist—opening, as Blake said, "the immortal Eyes of man" to the reality beyond and beneath his mental abstractions. Having come to recognize and trust the energies that support it, we may come at last to develop a relationship of trust with society, not in unexamined innocence, but in the full acceptance of our responsibilities to it. We can only trust society when we are no longer exclusively dependent upon it—when we can live as natural human beings in touch with the deeply spiritual within. The first work of the artist, then, is not the transformation of matter into artifacts, but the transformation of his own consciousness, or put another way, transforming his relationships to nature, spirit, psyche, and society.

The key to these transformations lies in developing relationships of trust with each of these aspects. Trust is not arrived at through an effort of will or conscious intention; it comes in the simple recognition that we are not separate from, but one with, nature, spirit, the universally human, and our unique historical and cultural context. All of these are forces greater than our little personality kingdoms. All may be trusted on their own terms, but these terms must be understood and not confused. Trusting these powers begins with acknowledging (or acting-in-the-knowledge-of) them. Act in the knowledge of nature—its spontaneous growth and its inherent polarity. Act in the knowledge of spirit and its transcendent Mystery. Act in the knowledge of the psyche and its archetypal energies. Act in the knowledge of society and serve it

When Nations grow Old,
The Arts grow Cold
And Commerce settles on every Tree.

William Blake

The Little-King Model

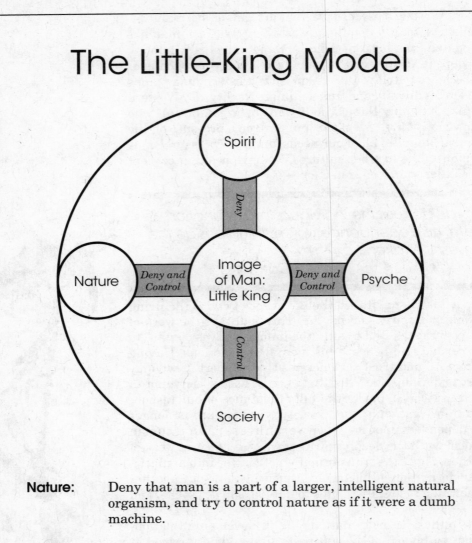

Nature: Deny that man is a part of a larger, intelligent natural organism, and try to control nature as if it were a dumb machine.

Spirit: Spirit is dismissed by science as superstition or confined by religion to limited images (spirit denied as immanent).

Psyche: Deny soul and its intelligence, the universally human archetypes, and then invent a psychology of adjustment to society.

Society: Society dominates as the axis of control—man's whole life is defined in terms of society.

The Way of the Artist

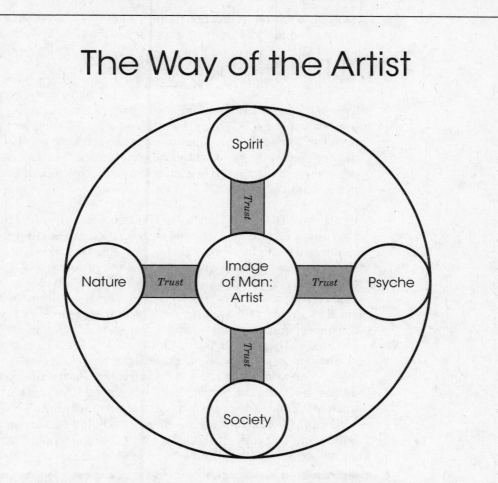

Nature: Transform relationship to nature: trust nature's spontaneous growth from the inside out and its polarity, black and white, birth and death.

Spirit: Transform relationship to spirit from king, judge, or dead God image to the living spirit—immanent in all things, yet transcendent to them.

Psyche: Transform relationship to psyche by opening to its intuitions and taking instruction from the myths and ancient wisdom teachings.

Society: Transform relationship to society by viewing it in terms of the responsibility to one's fellow man and in openness to higher powers.

as a *culture builder,* and not simply as a *cultural product.* Together, these energies will guide you on your journey to life's work.

Transforming Our Relationship to Nature

Transforming our relationship to nature begins with understanding how we approach it. Today, most of us have little direct experience of nature (or so we think), and so we are left with our ideas about nature. Below I sketch three big ones: nature is inferior to the conscious mind, nature is a machine to be controlled, and nature is not good enough.

Eradicate Inferior (or Sinful) Nature: Nature is not inferior to the conscious mind, but is the source of its life. The conscious mind requires a brain to think, which it gets courtesy of Mother Nature. Yet somehow (perhaps from our old-time religion?) we got the notion that nature has it all wrong, and it is the job of man, with his superior conscious mind, to set things straight. This is the wild and woolly view of nature so prevalent in the nineteenth and twentieth centuries, and carrying over into our own. *Modern* came to be associated with man-made, and all things natural came to be seen as dirty, messy, or heathen. Traditional peoples living "in nature" were inferior races; women, who are more closely associated with nature, became "the inferior sex"; natural bodily functions became unclean. The modern notion was to put nature out of sight and out of mind—to attack it. Of course, we couldn't go around blindly bulldozing and cementing nature "out there" without losing touch with nature "in here." And lose touch we did.

> *Technology is destructive only in the hands of people who do not realize that they are one and the same process as the universe.*
>
> Alan Watts

Control the Machine, Nature: Where we could not eradicate nature, we attempted to control it as if it were a machine—a kind of giant clockwork. As much as possible, we attempted to make natural functions into social, mechanical ones. We start with childbirth, where life is not given by the mother as the embodiment of Mother Nature, but by a socially licensed doctor and his marvelous machines. We are fed, not mother's milk, but a product of a mechanized factory. We try to act as though we are the boss of nature—that through our marvelous science, we can piecemeal manipulate it—without bothering to respect, much less to understand it. Often our attempts at control only make a bigger mess of things. Nature *can* be improved upon, as in a Japanese tea garden or a beautiful city park. Yet this is best accomplished when we work with nature and by our own nature—so that the city park is as natural a human action as a beaver's dam or an eagle's nest.

Nature is not a dead machine but a living miracle. Your conscious mind is not required to digest your food or beat your heart. Nor can it direct the movements of the stars, the orbiting of planets, the migration of birds, the sprouting of seeds. If one stops to contemplate this, she recognizes that this great natural intelligence lives within. Right now you are sitting in the midst of a miracle. Acknowledge it. Honor it. Nature is neither a wild creature to be tamed, nor a machine that can be adroitly controlled by pushing all the right levers. Nothing you can do from conscious intention can in any way rival the mystery of the life happening spontaneously within you—right now.

A man is related to all nature.

Emerson

> *Thus, those who say they would have right without its correlate, wrong; or good government without its correlate, misrule, do not apprehend the great principles of the universe, nor the nature of all creation.*
>
> *Chuang Tzu*

Avoid the Polarity of Nature: Nature is not the one-sided affair that we seem to wish it were. Having attempted to eradicate and control nature, to discount its blessings, we are all the more shocked by its destructive power. For most of us, nature is not the birth of a child, the bounty of food, a gentle summer day, or the extraordinary internal processes that maintain our health and existence—nature is a hurricane, an earthquake, a flood, or an illness. Traditional peoples living in nature, as a part of nature, are naturally attuned to its ways. They know the lesson of nature is polarity: life/death, day/night, gain/loss—that the way of nature is the way of sacrifice. Creation *is* suffering. The image is there in childbirth—for you to enter life, your mother must suffer. It is there every time you take a meal—some being (plant or animal) has died to give you life.

Traditional peoples love the animal while stalking, killing, and carving it. We buy our meat prepackaged in cellophane—we don't want to be reminded of death or sacrifice. We want good without bad, happiness without suffering, beginnings without ends, life without death. We try to sugarcoat or avoid the pains of life. The sick, the old, and the dying are shunned. They remind us of our own mortality. Whether we like it or not, nature's way is our way. We must come into accord with it, not as an intellectual understanding, but deeply felt in the depths of our being—opening our hearts to the sorrows as well as the joys of life. Nature's way is only shocking for someone who lives in an artificial world of his own imagining, where everything is at right angles, and nothing is crooked.

Nature in Art: Coomaraswamy defined art as "the involuntary dramatization of subjective experience."[21] *Involuntary* here means "spontaneous"; even as love cannot be coerced or willed, neither can creativity be forced. The art of creative living is not the execution of some intentional program for life, but a natural, evolving expression. Chapter 1 will explore how we might learn to trust nature, growing spontaneously, as it does, from the inside out. Following your natural impulses will lead you to your innate strengths and gifts. These, in turn, will give frame and energy to your life's work.

Transforming Our Relationship to Spirit

At least since the Council of Constantinople in 869, the spirit has been denied as essential in Western man. Both our traditional religion and modern science dismiss the spirit as irrelevant to daily life. Religion does admit of the soul and the Holy Spirit (which comes to us from without, but is not innate to us), yet the *emphasis* is on the ethical—good vs. bad, right vs. wrong. As Joseph Campbell said, contemporary "religious life is ethical; it is not mystical."[22]

For modern science, *mystical* is a kind of dirty word. The spirit is a childish superstition from a bygone era. The word *science* originally meant simply "knowledge," and as the quote below by Plotinus indicates, philosophers have long recognized that there are different kinds (orders) of knowledge. (Plotinus is hardly alone in this, following Pythagoras, Socrates, Plato, and many other great Eastern and Western philosophers.) Modern science is only interested in knowledge perceivable through the senses, either directly or through augmenting instrumentation. An empirical methodology is well suited to investigations of physical phenomena. The problem comes when we try to equate all knowledge with that subject to this particular methodology. But this is what we in the West have done over the last few centuries.

This cultural bias rejects knowledge of the realm of ideas as well as the realm of spirit. Because ideas cannot be sensibly perceived

*Know Ye not . . .
that the spirit of God
dwelleth within you?*

I Corinthians 3:16

doesn't mean they do not exist. (Mathematics are proved by logic, not by measurement.) Likewise, the spiritual is no less real because it cannot be measured by the senses or proved by logic. (Immanuel Kant dealt definitively with this.)[23] So much of the modern disdain for the spiritual or mystical results from a confused understanding of the word *science*. We retain its original meaning, "knowledge," (i.e., that which is intelligible); yet we graft onto it a new meaning that limits all knowledge to the empirical.

Knowledge has three degrees—opinion, science, illumination. The means or instrument of the first is sense; of the second, dialectic; of the third, intuition.
                                                    Plotinus

Spiritual knowledge is recognized through intuition. It is a methodology as appropriate to spiritual understanding as empiricism is to the understanding of physical phenomena. The current fashion of denying spiritual knowledge and its methodology runs contrary to the great mystical and philosophical teachings of the world. The term *Philosophia Perennis* or Perennial Philosophy was apparently first used by Gottfried Leibniz and developed in modern times by Ananda K. Coomaraswamy and Aldous Huxley. The Perennial Philosophy is what Huxley called "the Highest Common Good" in all traditions—cutting across religious traditions, historical epochs, ethnic inflections—Hindu, Taoist, Buddhist, Greek, Jewish, Christian, Islamic. It belongs to no religion, but is the essence of them all. Huxley renders the crux of the Perennial Philosophy thus:

The Man who never in his Mind and Thoughts travel'd to Heaven Is No Artist.

William Blake

> *First: the phenomenal world of matter and of individual consciousness . . . is the manifestation of a Divine Ground within which all partial realities have their being, and apart from which they would be nonexistent.*

> *Second: human beings are capable not merely of knowing about the Divine Ground by inference; they can also realize its existence by a direct intuition . . . [uniting] the knower with that which is known.*

> *Third: man possesses a double nature, a phenomenal ego and an eternal Self, which is the inner man, the spirit, the spark of divinity within the soul. It is possible for a man, if he desires, to identify himself with the spirit and therefore the Divine Ground, which is of the same or like nature with the spirit.*[24]

Even if you haven't fully identified with this spirit and, thereby, had direct experience, you can intuit that the spirit within you is one with the Divine Ground out of which all things have arisen and into which they will again return. This cannot be proved by evidence of the senses nor understood by logic or deduction, and is therefore called Mystery. There is no genuine art that does not in some way acknowledge (act-in-the-knowledge-of) this Mystery. That the Perennial Philosophy is currently out of fashion or that it "makes no sense" (again, it is transcendent or trans-sense-able) in no way reflects on its efficacy or veracity. For in these matters, as Joseph Campbell said, the majority is always wrong. "The majority's function in relation to spirit is to try to listen and open up to someone who's had an experience beyond that of food, shelter, progeny, and wealth."[25] These "someones" are the genuine artists, mystics, sages. The consistency of their revelations across time and culture lead the open-minded individual to recognize in the Perennial Philosophy inherent truth about the Reality of who we are.[26]

If we are to learn to trust spirit, we in the West must venture beyond our primitive images of God as king, judge, or dead man. The Roman Catholic tradition epitomizes the king model. Early Roman Catholic churches were called "basilicas," or "royal houses." The pope wears a crown and carries a staff; you kneel to kiss his ring. I once saw the pope entering St. Peter's at the Vatican. There he was with all of his attendants—being carried slowly down the aisle on a palanquin—the Swiss Guards standing sharply at attention. When at last he sat upon the throne, the entire congregation broke into applause. This is a king. The pope is standing in for King God. The accent in this model is on authority and decrees issued from on high.

> *The religious idea of God cannot do full duty for the metaphysical infinity.*
>
> *Alan Watts*

From the Jewish tradition, we get the judge model. Read the Book of Judges: this is how the Hebrews organized society. Even when they took a king in Saul, this was recognized as adopting something foreign—the judge was the homegrown model. In this model, you get a heavy emphasis on judging by the letter of the law. The accent is on collective righteousness enforced, not by the king, but by the group—everyone is checking up on you to make sure you are doing it right. This is picked up again in the Protestant religions. The Protestant church typically resembles,

Thou shalt know God without image and without means.

Meister Eckhart

not a throne room, but a courtroom. You have the minister in the black robe, who comes out to the pulpit like a kind of prosecuting attorney and throws the book at you—with the rest of the congregation playing the role of jury. (Of course, I am speaking here of the common sense of these religions. There are many examples of Catholic, Jewish, and Protestant mystics who have articulated profound revelations of spiritual truth.)

You have, no doubt, also heard that God is dead. You probably have an image of an old guy with a gray beard who just up and died one day. The old codger got so tired of being the boss and the judge that he just croaked. We might not want to admit it, but these are our images of God—way back in our subconscious minds. They shape the way we approach the world. If you imagine God as the big king, then you want to be the little king—the boss of your little world. If you think God is the judge, then you think, I'll be a good little judge and go around making sure *they* are doing things right. If you think God is dead, you feel yourself to be an orphan, forsaken and adrift in a sea of meaninglessness—a kind of Sartrean existentialist.

Most likely you have a combination of all three God images. (God is there in the back of your mind bossing and judging you, but dead when you need Him.) I've called the controlling pseudo-myth the little-king model, yet we can see elements of the Judge and the dead God within it. From the king, we get our ambition; from the judge, our hyperconformity; and from the dead God, our insatiable consumerism and focus on banal entertainment. A genuine experience of spirit requires that we move beyond these primitive images of God. For this reason, I will speak of spirit in terms of Zen—though I could have just as easily used Western mystics; for in matters of spirit, there are no contradictions.

Spirit in Art: Chapter 2 will explore the Zen spirit at work. I will say nothing here of the role of spirit in art except to quote two great artists and two great philosophers:

> *Where the spirit does not work with the hand there is no art.*
>
> *Leonardo da Vinci*

> *The greatest productions of art, whether painting, music, sculpture or poetry, have invariably this quality—something approaching the work of God.*
>
> *D. T. Suzuki*

One comes to be of just such stuff as that on which the mind is set.

Upanishads

Can it really be said that before the day of our pretentious science, humanity was composed solely of imbeciles and the superstitious?

R. Schwaller de Lubicz

The human mind cannot go beyond the gift of God, the Holy Ghost. To suppose that art can go beyond the finest specimens of art that are now in the world is not knowing what art is; it is being blind to the gifts of the spirit.

> *William Blake*

All that is true, by whomsoever it has been said has its origin in the Spirit.

> *Thomas Aquinas*

Transforming Our Relationship to Psyche

We know ourselves as human beings through the psyche, the human imagination. Traditionally, the Chinese said that in the human (soul), Heaven (spirit) and Earth (nature) unite. Through the human, nature makes love to (becomes fully conscious of) spirit. The human psyche (literally, soul) is universal in its nature and individual in its expression. To say that there is a universal human soul or imagination may be out of fashion, yet how else can we account for the amazing correspondences in the art and mythologies of the world? How else can we account for human compassion, the readiness of one human being to *suffer with* another? For, as Arthur Schopenhauer suggested, when we act in compassion at the risk of our own lives, it is because we recognize the other to be, in fact, our very own self.[27] Careful examination will bear up what we intuitively know. After fifty years of studying diverse cultures, the great American anthropologist Franz Boas concluded that "in the main the mental characteristics of man are the same all over the world."[28]

The psyche is the realm where the universal human imagination meets the individual conscience. A man or woman in touch with conscience (literally, "together with" [con] "knowledge" [science] or "the inner Knower") and the potent energies of the soul is an authentic human being and not easily controlled by the pressure to conform to social norms.[29] She knows where she is in the universe, in the stages of life, and in relation to the archetypal energies. Mythology speaks to the Knower within us all. It tells us what it is to be human and how to live in accord with the energies of life. Carl Jung wrote that man is "a being operated and manoevred by archetypal forces instead of his 'free will,' that is, his arbitrary egoism and his limited consciousness. He should learn that he is not the master in his own house and that he should carefully study the other side of his psychical world [the shadow], which seems to be the true ruler of his fate."[30]

Jung's statement echoes the lessons of the world's great mythologies: there are archetypal forces inherent in man, which he must recognize and come into accord with before he can be thought of as a mature individual. The role of mythology and genuine psychology is to guide the individual in this "inner work." Today, our notion of psychology rejects the soul and its inner work, reducing "psychology" to a means of effecting, with the aid of academically trained specialists, chemical "equilibrium," social "adjustment," or behavior "modification." The genuine psychology of the "inner work" is not the domain of the specialist, but of every living human being.

We must get beyond the simpleminded notion that psychology is something "invented" in the nineteenth century by Dr. Freud (or William James or Alexander Bain). Psychology, as the word itself indicates, is properly the study of the soul. Thousands of years of wisdom precede the good Viennese doctor. To toss this treasure overboard in favor of a narrow "scientific" psychology is a crime no less heinous than the burning of the library of Alexandria. (Jung, for example, recognized that one could not properly call himself a student of psychology and dismiss the wisdom of ancient China, India, Egypt, or Tibet, much less Greece and the folktales of Europe—and fortunately for us, he didn't.)

> *Mythology is the womb of man's initiation to life and death.*
>
> *Joseph Campbell*

In many fields today, overspecialization is a positively dangerous trend. Buckminster Fuller wrote, "The more specialized society becomes, the less attention does it pay to the discoveries of the mind, which are intuitively beamed to the brain, there to be received only if the switches are on. Specialization tends to shut off the wide-band tuning searches and thus to preclude further discovery of all-powerful generalized principles."[31] More than this, overspecialization tends to separate us from the pearls of wisdom already pulled from the depths of the human psyche.

In our overly specialized culture, we've lost the value of the universalist, the generalist. The universalist is a humanist in the best sense of the word. His subject is man, not in relation to any particular historical or cultural context, not in narrow specialization, but man whole, as he is. Especially in our time of great transition and upheaval, it is vital that we integrate the lessons of those who have made it their task to study what is constant in the human

I am in you and you in me, mutual in love divine.

William Blake

experience. In the last century, we had many great universalists, among them Carl Jung in psychology, Joseph Campbell in mythology, Ananda K. Coomaraswamy in art, Aldous Huxley and Frithjof Schuon in religion, Buckminster Fuller in the study of the structure of the universe. All had their difficulties with academic narrow-mindedness, and yet all have left legacies well worth mining.

In the encounter with the universally human (the human soul), you recognize your own soul and its promptings toward your unique life's work. Ironically, the most original work often occurs in exploration of the most unoriginal themes—the universal human themes. Only by embracing these themes is there the possibility of genuine art. One's true work is never merely "my work," but humanity's work. It's not really self-expression, unless by "self" we mean it with a capital *S*, and that Self is the Self within all mankind.

Psyche in Art: Chapter 3 will explore the role of the psyche in work. It will consider how we can come to trust our psyche by developing a constructive relationship with conscience, by learning to face our own shadow, or dark side, and by accessing mythic archetypes, the creative energies of the soul. Joseph Campbell said, "The artist is the one who communicates myth for today. But he has to be an artist who understands mythology and humanity."[32] Tapping into the power of myth will provide understanding, meaning, and motivation on your journey toward life's work.

Transforming Our Relationship to Society

Society *is* a source of power and a protection for the individual. It teaches and protects us through our many years of dependence. As human beings, we are born into a long period of dependency and incompleteness. The moment the umbilical cord is cut, we are helpless. We are biologically incomplete and dependent upon others for our survival. This physiological fact has a profound effect on our psychology. We develop a psychology of approval-seeking as a reaction to our biological helplessness. This *is* an effective strategy. First, in seeking the approval of our parents, we win their affection and support: they take care of us. Second, seeking approval becomes the motivating force to learn and thereby to complete ourselves as full members of adult society. We learn to walk, talk, and all the rest we need to function as members of our society.

Even as approval motivates, disapproval has tremendous power to limit or correct our behavior. Because we associate winning approval with survival, signs of disapproval are experienced as threats to our survival and become effective tools for social conditioning. While efficacious in our youth, remaining locked in the psychology of approval-seeking is a positive drag on our development as mature adults. Traditional cultures helped individuals through this transition or transformation of consciousness with rites of initiation. In the modern world, we are left to work this out for ourselves.

Society and Art: Chapter 4 will consider how we can develop a relationship of trust with society—not as conformists that take its model hook, line, and sinker, but in the recognition of our responsibilities to our fellow human beings. In the seventeenth and eighteenth centuries, a revolution in thinking turned the existing social order on its head. It was the realization of "the rights of man." The next great revolution in thinking has already begun. It is the realization of "the responsibilities of man." While continuing to protect and enlarge human rights, we must, if we are going to make a world worth living in, be equally concerned with human responsibilities. This includes the responsibility to make a meaningful contribution through our work. After all, most of us spend more of our waking adult lives working than doing anything else.

Taken together, what we choose to do as individuals becomes what we as a society choose to do. As responsible individuals, we cannot make our career choices as if oblivious to this fact. Even if we wanted to, we could not bury our heads in the sand. Reminders of our responsibility are all around us. It is fair to say that, up to now, we have collectively made some rather poor choices. Currently, as a global society, we are choosing to pollute and abuse our environment to the point of risking our own life support system; we are choosing to live in a world of vast inequities in the distribution of wealth and resources; we are choosing to live under the constant threat from weapons of mass destruction. Of course, we are also collectively choosing to do many good and noble things. Still, the enormity of our collective challenges requires each of us to consider our responsibilities to the world we live in when making our individual career choices. But then this has always been the wise course for a well-lived life. Indeed, it was the vocational advice that Aristotle gave some 2,400 years ago: "Where your talents and the needs of the world cross, there lies your vocation."

Man must cease attributing his problems to his environment, and learn again to exercise his will—his personal responsibility.

Albert Einstein

*If all men lead
mechanical,
unpoetical lives,
this is the real nihilism,
the real undoing
of the world.*

Reginald Blyth

> *We begin from the recognition that all beings cherish happiness and do not want suffering. It then becomes both morally wrong and pragmatically unwise to pursue only one's own happiness oblivious to the feelings and aspirations of all others who surround us as members of the same human family. The wiser course is to think of others when pursuing our own happiness.*
>
> *The Fourteenth Dalai Lama*

Today, we stand at a crossroads in human history. We have the opportunity to create a new image of ourselves at work, one that will surely trigger a revolution as profound, as dramatic, as the Industrial Revolution. Even as the Industrial Revolution could not occur until there was a massive shift in society's view of work and wealth, so must an equally profound change in thinking regarding work and wealth occur before the next quantum leap in man's social evolution can flourish. We can no more conceptualize the impact of such a change than a pre-industrial miller in the hills of England or New Hampshire could have conceptualized the impact of the Industrial Revolution he was helping to foster. We are charting new ground. We must.

Humanity: A Multidimensional Phenomenon

The "work-as-art" or "human-as-artist" paradigm briefly sketched above provides a tool for choosing and evaluating your work. (It will be explored in much greater depth in "Prologue: The Art of Life's Work.") The remainder of this discussion touches on some of the social and cultural ramifications of this perspective on work. Of course, a work-as-art paradigm implies a different set of values around which to organize society. It recognizes people as multidimensional beings. It is concerned with the expansion of (individual) consciousness and the integration of that consciousness into the life of society. It does not, as is the prevailing fashion, see human problems and solutions as residing exclusively, or even primarily, in politics or economics. It does not put its faith in the free market, in democracy, in social-welfare programs, in economic growth, in the redistribution of wealth, etc. Neither is it inherently opposed to any of these. It does not suggest that if "everything were equal" or "the playing field level," everyone would be happy, nor does it trust the market to supply the individual with meaning, joy, or direction. The market is only interested in the individual as a supplier of capital, a unit of production, or a consumer of goods. It doesn't recognize, much less address, the human soul. On the other hand, owning the means of production—without having some sense of what to do with them—will hardly "save the masses."

The work-as-art paradigm doesn't view the unhappy worker making six figures as fundamentally better off than the unhappy worker who makes far less. If he is doing work he neither loves nor respects, he is wasting the time of his life in either case. Today, we have been conditioned to believe that human life is measured in money. In fact, we are no different from human beings who lived two thousand, five thousand, or ten thousand years ago. Like them, our lives are measured in time. What you do with the time of life is your life—whether you earn $500,000 or $50,000 a year. It is true that the higher one's income, the more choices one has about how one's time is spent away from work. But if he is vexed in his soul, if he is an alienated and unhappy creature, the high earner will not necessarily use that time in a way that enriches his life.

> I think the person who takes a job in order to live—that is to say, (just) for the money—has turned himself into a slave.
>
> Joseph Campbell

We live in a market society and so must necessarily address its demands. But its demands are not the only demands, nor—beyond a certain level—are they the most important. If we discount the call of our innate talents, if we reject our soul's passion and purpose, if we silence the stirring of the spirit, simply to meet the market's demands, then we have alienated ourselves from ourselves in a profound way. We risk becoming inauthentic shadows of who we truly are. We are not one-dimensional but multidimensional beings. If we limit ourselves to a one-dimensional consciousness, we feel constrained, boxed in, and vaguely empty. We are anxious and ill at ease, like the man whose pants are too tight—he can "neither stand nor lie nor sit."[33] Or we are like the Sisyphus of mythic fame, endlessly, and often frenetically, pushing our loads up the hill, only to watch them roll back down again—and, then, do it all over again. In either case, we sense or know that something must

A craft can only have meaning when it serves a spiritual way.

Titus Burkhardt

Thoroughly to know oneself, is above all art, for it is the highest art.

Theologia Germanica

change. This "something" is not merely adding to or rearranging of the furniture within the box, but an expansion of consciousness into areas we have heretofore ignored or neglected.

The artist of life moves from the inside out. Having identified his own gifts and purpose, his passion and desire, he confronts the market on his terms, ready to adapt and adjust to it—but not ready to surrender his core. There are signs that many today are ready for this expansion in consciousness—ready to grow and expand, as all nature does, from the inside out. As E. F. Schumacher wrote, "Some people are no longer angry when told that *restoration must come from within:* the belief that everything is 'politics' and that radical rearrangements of the 'system' will suffice to save civilisation is no longer held with the same fanaticism [that it once was.]"[34] In this there is great promise. If we desire a fundamental transformation of society, the place to begin is not with society but within ourselves. By engaging this inner work, we begin the journey to becoming artists of life in whatever work we may end up doing.

"Art-quality" for All

Some may object that the image of the human as artist is elitist—that the common man or woman cannot attain to art, either in consciousness or in the execution of their craft. It could be argued in reply that many so-called primitive cultures did, in fact, achieve a "society of artists." Yet this is not a wholly adequate response, for they did so while operating within fixed traditional systems, having limited vocational choice and a shared mythic and symbolic vocabulary—neither of which apply to our situation today. Our task, then, is a new and more difficult one. There is no model we can imitate or "get back to." Yet today we recognize that the underlying truths that the great art of the world sought to represent are universal and not limited to any particular ethnic inflection. They belong, finally, to all humanity.

The way of the artist is a universally human way, not dependent upon a shared religion, myth, geography, or even technology. It works as well in Bali as in New York City, in China as in the Middle East. Ultimately, quality is for everyone—in terms of both aspirations and end results. We all benefit from quality workmanship, from the products of men and women who know themselves as total beings and not simply as "job-holders." Were all to aspire to be artists, all would benefit from more beautiful meals, clothing, parks, homes, schools, etc. We would benefit further from living with people—not alienated from but happy in—their work. Those capable of the greatest art would not waste their talents in a vain struggle to be king of the hill, but would release the gifts they hold deep within their souls.

The little-king view of life is no less elitist in theory, yet far more destructive in its effect. Everyone cannot be king, and while this image dominates our imaginations, we view life in terms of separation and competition, and therefore, conflict. On the other hand, the way of the artist is inclusive—respecting and celebrating the wonders of nature, the dignity of humanity, and the radiance of the Transcendent Mystery. No genuine artist views himself as superior in essence to others.

Still, aren't we just substituting one ideal or image for another, and doesn't the truth stand behind any image? Of course, words or any symbolic images are always only maps of the territory of truth, never reality itself. No map, no matter how excellent, is ever to be confused with the territory that it indicates. Yet, since few know the territory directly, most are left dealing with maps—and, to be sure, there are better and worse maps. At the dawn of the third millennium CE, the little-king map has us totally lost and utterly confused. The map laid out here may help us find our way again. The way of the artist offers us an image of humanity in harmony with nature, the deep rhythms of the human soul, and the Transcendent Mystery. In the end, it may produce, if not an enlightened society, at least a happier and more humane one.

The Art of Everyday Living

You can experience your everyday life as art by bringing to it the qualities of the artist—inspiration and absorption, creativity and resourcefulness, play and delight. But first, unwind. No one can live as an artist who feels anxious, knotted up in fear. Fortunately, there are only two great fears—the fear that life is going to end and the fear that it isn't. It is easy to see that the fear of death arises from attachment to the temporal—from holding on to what must be let go of. But why should we fear living?

We fear living because we don't believe we are adequate to life. Tangled in the mumbo jumbo of conditioned beliefs, we get so hung up on limitation that we fail to recognize our basic adequacy as human beings. Denying limitation or obsessing on it keeps us knotted up in fear. Artists play with limitation. They neither deny it, nor are they overwhelmed by it. There are only so many words in any language, but that doesn't keep the poet from writing. There is only a certain range of color the eye can see, but this doesn't keep the painter from painting. There are a limited number of notes that we can hear, but that doesn't keep the composer from composing. The artist accepts the limitations of form, not with fear and dread, but as the starting point of creation.

You can be the artist of your life by recognizing that, for all of your limitations, you are basically adequate to life. For all of its difficulties, life is basically adequate for you. Accept that, while it may not fit some imaginary conception of perfection, the world is basically adequate, and you are basically adequate to the world. Be here now with what is, and play with the stuff of your life. If you have twelve crayons in your box, use your creativity and resourcefulness to make the best picture you can with these. Don't spend your time worrying that someone else has forty-eight or sixty-four crayons. As you are, you are basically adequate to life.

Your basic adequacy is not won or done. It is not because you own a home or because you have a good job, not because you have a big bank balance or because you have a certain relationship, not because you are American or politically correct. Your basic adequacy is in your breath, in your beating heart—in your life. You are adequate to life because you *are* life. You have all you need—a heart, a body, an imaginative mind, a basic connection with all of life. You have an earth to walk on. It has gravity to hold you. It has water and fire, plants and trees, mountains and valleys. It's an adequate earth. The sky is adequate. It has sun and moon. It has stars—not too many, not too few. As you begin to attune to the adequacy of life all around and within you, you will see ever more opportunities for creative play. Even as the artist accepts the tools of her craft and creates with these, accept all the stuff of your life and creatively play with it.

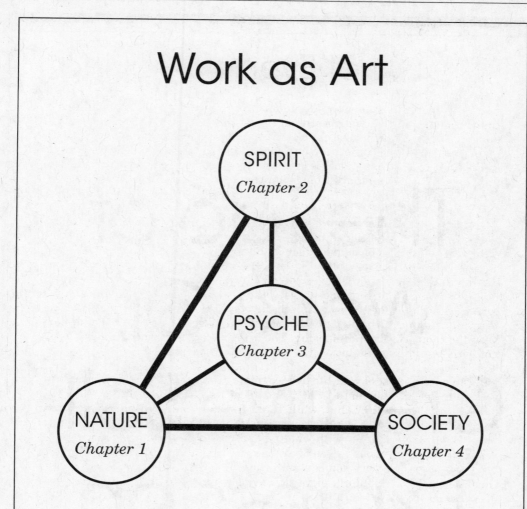

Work as Art

This is a book about work. Work can be most simply and broadly defined as human action—our doing. In the West, we have separated our doing from our Being. This separation, or alienation, has profound consequences on the quality of our lives. It is for precisely this reason that we have, as Ananda K. Coomaraswamy said, "for the first time in history created an industry without art."[35] Everything in the remainder of "Prologue: The Art of Life's Work"—the lessons it draws from Taoism, from Zen, from art and myth, and from the great humanitarian activists—will be with a view toward discovering how we might unite our doing with our Being.

CHAPTER 1

The Tao of Work; Or, Creative Self-Expression

*Let everything be allowed to do what it naturally does,
so that its nature will be satisfied.*
                        Chuang Tzu

How can we make of work a genuine art—an expression of
our deepest selves? We can begin by asking, What are we
working for; is the purpose of work to solve problems or to
creatively express ourselves? The way each of us answers
this question shapes our lives as individuals and our world.
It affects our psychology as well as our activities—the way
we feel about the world and the things we do in it. We can't
really get too far into this without at least briefly considering
worldview, the way we approach the world. After examining
some of the underlying assumptions behind conventional
attitudes toward work, this chapter explores how the approach to career design presented in this book differs from
more traditional career-planning models.

Follow that will and that way which experience confirms to be your own.

Carl Jung

The Western view of life, inherited from Middle Eastern mythology, tends to see man as a stranger in a strange land. Thrust out of the Garden into a hostile world, he is condemned to toil and sweat, to eke out his existence in a perpetual struggle against nature and his fellow man. The ancient "man as stranger" element of the religious worldview remained implicit in the "scientific" worldview developed over the last few centuries. Briefly stated, the common sense of the scientific worldview goes something like this: Quite by accident, man has arisen out of a dead and dumb universe. He has every reason to fear that he may fall back into it. Consequently, he makes it his business to distinguish himself from nature at every turn. This is his dirty little secret: He is a sort of bastard child of stars and slime, of animal violence and lust. Since he is embarrassed by his connection with the natural world, he distinguishes himself from it by trying to make it submit.

Nature is a mess he will put right. He will straighten it out, figure it out, reason this insane chaos into a predictable set of rules that he can deal with. His one great tool in this noble endeavor is his rational mind and the technologies he can construct with it. It will save him from the ravages of wild and cruel nature. Though it cannot beat his heart, digest his food, or maintain other vital functions, that part of his brain responsible for conscious attention he considers the summum bonum of the human species. It's as if one portion of his brain (that responsible for conscious attention) refuses to admit that it is connected to the rest of his brain, let alone the rest of his body or the rest of the natural world. It alone is "intelligent."

The worldview of traditional Taoists (and of many traditional cultures) begins with a different set of assumptions.[1] Man was not thrust into a strange world; he came out of it as naturally as water comes out of a bubbling brook. He is not against nature; he cannot be separated from it—he is in nature, and nature in him. Nature is not dead and dumb; all of nature is alive and intelligent. It is not hostile and chaotic, but friendly and ordered. Man's purpose is not to conquer and lord over nature, but to come into accord with it. The Taoist understands that there is in nature a profound intelligence that the rational mind can never comprehend. This intelligence is wild, spontaneous, and free. On the other hand, because it depends on symbolic language of one sort or another, the rational mind remains encased in a world of abstraction. It is forever using symbols to map the world. Some maps guide; some mislead. But we should never confuse a map with the world it represents or delude ourselves into believing that what can't be mapped doesn't exist.

While Taoism trusts nature, including what it calls "Self Nature," our Western approach puts its faith in symbolic abstractions of the world. As we saw in the introduction, this orientation gives an analytical, problem-solving approach to life, one that denies the Mystery of life, the inexplicable fount of creative living. A society at odds with nature will be at odds with the creative. For where are the mysterious creative powers more evident than in nature—from the miracle of the seed to the genesis of the galaxies?

Creativity is a function of the nature within us; call it intuition, native intelligence, or the subconscious mind. The rational conscious mind can intend, but it cannot, of itself, create. A conscious mind can intend a child, but it cannot create one. A conscious mind can intend a work of art, but cannot, of itself, create it. If we are to live a creative life, we must learn to trust nature within and without. Taoist master Chuang Tzu told the following story: Once a one-legged dragon named Hui asked a centipede, "How do you manage all those legs? I can hardly manage one!" "As a matter of fact," replied the centipede, "I do not manage them." The centipede that doesn't trust nature can hardly walk; the human being who doesn't trust nature can hardly live his own life. Creativity bubbles up from within when we open to trust what the Taoist calls our "original nature."

If we view the world as hostile, we seek security in our minds, in abstractions. We erect "thought barricades" between our world and ourselves. From behind our barricades, we try to fix a world we cannot *feel*. We don't trust nature—in the environment, in others, or in ourselves; we don't trust our innate creativity. From a one-with-nature, intuitive approach, we open to life and its infinite creative possibilities. We trust ourselves to be ourselves and trust that that which arises from within us will be supported by the world from which it (and we) have sprung. We can easily see how the differences in these worldviews affect our attitudes toward work. In the simplest terms, work can be defined as human activity. So we are back to the question we started with, namely: Is work, is human activity, principally for problem solving or self-expression?

The approach of traditional career models is to help people defend against problems. The implicit assumption is a notion of work as a means of defending against the problems of poverty, ridicule, boredom, and the like. A problem-solving approach to work puts us in a defensive posture, from which we hope for escape—ultimately, from work itself. (Defending, after all, is a rather tiresome business.) Since work is something we are forced to do to solve our problems, the implication is that no problems equals no work. So, many dream of winning the lottery and "solving all their problems" and not "having to" work.

This book is designed to assist you in creating your life's work. From this perspective, work is viewed, not as a means of achieving

Art always has something of the Unconscious about it.

D. T. Suzuki

The Tao is near and people seek it far away.

Menicus

freedom from problems, but as a vehicle for expressing the *freedom to create*. Creating your life's work is not solving the occupation problem. It is the art of creative living. You are not a problem but a creative, living being. Work is not a problem but a natural, on-going, creative process. Vocational guidance is not helping people come up with workable solutions to the career problem, but helping them to tap into their innate passion and creativity. When you find your passion, you find it in a field of native intelligence that will show you the way—if you trust it. On the other hand, if you miss your passion, you've left something of yourself behind, even if you succeed financially.

Your life's work does not exist "out there" in a world apart. You can't order up the perfect career or set of careers the way you might order a book from Amazon.com. Being too concerned with what is "out there" before you know what you want "in here" puts you in a position of powerlessness. On the other hand, when you identify what you really want and begin to move confidently and deliberately in that direction, you seize the initiative. In this way, you move from strength and remain in creative control.

If it's truly creative, the direction of your life's work is "from the inside out." In later chapters, you will find tools to help you tap into your inner passion and innate gifts, tools to help you better understand what's "out there," and tools to help coordinate your inner passion with the outer realities. Traditional career models tend to view your creativity, energy, and zest for life as rough edges that must be shaved off so you can better fit what's "out there." Exactly what doesn't fit (the rough edges of the old model) is what will drive the process of creating a life's work—your creativity, energy, and zest for life.

We have been told that we must face the facts of life; but we must also, if we are really going to live, face the spirit and the emotional power in life. To describe Michelangelo's *David* as a marble statue of a Hebrew king in his youth gives you the facts, but none of the spirit or emotional power of the work. To say that *Don Quixote* is a story about the wanderings of a madman misses the power, spirit, and heart of its message. It is no less ridiculous to reduce your life to a set of facts. You are not your place of birth, your height, weight, or degrees, your resume, or credit history. You are a being of spirit, emotional power, and intelligence.

Traditional career models are only interested in the facts of your work life, your education, skills, training, and experience. The approach taken in this book considers the facts, but also the all-important creative intangibles. From the perspective of the art of life's work, the facts of your life are the media with which you will create. Color is not painting. Notes are not music. Words are not poetry. For color to become painting; notes, music; or words, poetry, there must be knowledge of technique, emotional power, and the radiance of spirit. Likewise, the facts or raw materials of your work life only become really interesting when imbued with emotional power and spiritual energy and transformed through the application of intelligence. This is not to negate the importance of your career facts. They provide the necessary color with which to paint your masterpiece. But remember, as the French painter Jean-Baptiste Chardin said, "One uses color, but *paints* with feeling" [emphasis added].

An exclusive emphasis on facts limits creativity. While a hardheaded, nothing-but-the-facts approach is often touted as an objective or scientific approach to reality, modern physics understands the limitations and fallacy of this view. As physicist Werner Heisenberg put it, "The mere act of observing something changes the nature of the thing observed."[2] This statement of what scientists call the "observer effect" means, in essence, that there is no objective reality we can discern with our senses. In our relationship to reality, a hard head is of less use than an open mind. The truly creative, whether in science or art, would agree with Albert Einstein's assertion that "imagination is more important than knowledge" or that "the only really valuable thing is intuition." Intuitions, and not facts—imaginations, and not data banks—are the beginnings of creations. Don't get so caught up with your career facts that you neglect the role that intuition and imagination can play in transforming your experience of work.

> It is the natural instinct of a child to work from within outwards; "First I think, and then I draw my think." What wasted efforts we make to teach the child to stop thinking, and only to observe!
> Ananda K. Coomaraswamy

The problem-solving approach to life generates feelings of insecurity and anxiety. On the other hand, as Rollo May put it, "What the artist or creative scientist feels is not anxiety or fear; it is joy. The artist, at the moment of creating, does not experience gratification or satisfaction [as one might at solving a problem] but . . . joy." May defines joy as "the emotion that goes with heightened consciousness, the mood that accompanies the experience of actualizing one's own potentialities."[3] This gets to the crux of it—creating the joyous life or struggling from fear and powerlessness.

Since our problem-solving efforts are always tail-chasing and do not resolve, we ultimately tire of them and seek relief in escape.

Facts, to become poetic, must be fused with being.

Gerald Sykes

To be properly expressed a thing must proceed from within, moved by its form.

Meister Eckhart

From a problem-solving approach, escape is what passes for joy. It is not the bliss of "heightened consciousness," but the limited pleasure of diminished awareness. Many social critics have pointed out the escapism of modern life and its many manifestations. There are the individual manifestations seen in narcissism, alcohol and drug abuse, compulsive consumption, and addiction to television and entertainments. There are the collective manifestations of environmental destruction, war, national debt, and the like. As long as we seek to defend against problems, we try to escape from them. As long as we view work as a means of solving problems, we "live for the weekends."

Escapism generates still more problems that, in turn, we seek to defend against and ultimately to escape from. This is the vicious cycle of modern life. Of course, the tendency to escape from life is hardly a modern invention. (The Buddha gave his Four Noble Truths over two thousand years ago as a strategy for living beyond escape.) Yet our modern worldview has produced unparalleled (and dangerous) levels of escapism.

Learning to approach life creatively is the challenge before us as individuals and as the human race. Our innate creativity holds a powerful key to the transformation of reality. Lewis Mumford wrote, "Every transformation of man . . . has rested on a new image of the cosmos and the nature of man." Indeed, these images are how we mark history into eras: the Classical Era, the Middle Ages, the Renaissance, the Modern Age, etc. Our hostile-world, problem-solving approach evolved over time into an image of the world, indeed of the universe, as a giant machine. The conception of the universe as a machine marks the Modern Age.

Ironically, science, the pride of the Modern Age, has been at the forefront in exposing the limitations of the machine model. Quantum mechanics and ecology, for example, have demonstrated that an image of a universe of separate, isolated parts is not a terribly useful way of conceiving of reality. While increasingly outdated, even from a scientific point of view, the legacy of the machine model affects the way we think about a range of subjects, including work. We find its legacy in our everyday speech, where work is "the old grind" or "the treadmill" (a machine designed to go nowhere). We must "gear up" for work so we can "crank it out." One's relationship to work is a matter of "fitting in" or of "meshing with." Economies are job-making "engines." (Incidentally, our word *job* originates from the Middle English *jobbe,* meaning "mouthful," and clearly comes from the notion of work as a solution to the feeding problem.)[4] From this perspective, work is a very serious affair, a boring routine or a frantic chase to we know not where. Since this is what people think work is, it's no wonder they want to escape from it.

From an organic worldview, we get an image of work as living, growing, evolving, creative action. Work comes out of life the way grass grows, the way apple trees "apple." Because human beings are active creatures, they naturally work, not like machines, but as integral parts of nature. Because all life is creative, humans naturally create. Similarly, human creativity naturally transcends the reproductive function we share with plants and other animals. Human beings can ask: "Why to create?" "What to create?" "How to create?" That human beings ask these questions is no less natural than pear trees "pearing" or monkeys "monkeying around." We are naturally creative, questioning creatures and must be unnaturally molded into mindless machine workers. Where spontaneity is the enemy of the machine society, it is the essence of natural action and, therefore, of work.

Throughout human history, work has been the individual's primary means of self-expression.[5] In the modern world, we're taught to see self-expression in our consumption and possession, not in our work. (Suppress yourself at work, so you can express yourself when you are done.) Finding your creative self-expression in what you are naturally good at gives a life of integrity, service, enjoyment, and excellence (see page 51). Your natural self-expression moves out of your authentic self. And if you are true to yourself, as Shakespeare said, you can't be false to anyone else. It is naturally your highest and best service, since the best thing you can do for others is to be yourself—and, thus, give the gifts that are innately yours. Self-expression is naturally engaging and joyous, and naturally prompts one to work with excellence. When you are doing something you love, you naturally want to make it the best you can—the way you want to give a friend a lovely present. Your self-expression is your gift to the world. Discovering your life's work is not a mechanical process of assembling facts; it's a matter of trusting yourself. Realizing it is a matter of trusting yourself *and* gaining specific knowledge, taking definite action, and persevering.

To know oneself, one should assert oneself.

Albert Camus

Going with the Flow and Creating What You Want

The great challenges of life are to BE and to EXPRESS. These are the lessons of "Zen" and of "the Art of . . ." Lose your spontaneity, your ability to sense and move with the flow of your deepest being, and you become stiff, numb, out of sync with life. Lack the ability to create structure, and you risk remaining socially marginal and/or psychologically alienated—unable to express yourself in a full and enlivening way. In either case, you risk an inauthentic life. Spontaneity and structure—these two have a creative tension, recalling the notion of the authentic life as a razor's edge.

The Tao's principle is spontaneity.

Lao Tzu

In some circles, there is a long-standing argument about whether 'tis nobler to "go with the flow" or to "create what you want." There is really no conflict between the two. In fact, "creating what you want" is a natural extension of "going with the flow." This is so if by "going with the flow" you mean "following your bliss," moving with the flow—the energy—of your deepest desires. Your deepest desires are at one with the universe, a natural expression of it. Your deepest desires (not commercially manufactured ones) are as organic as any towering tree, roaring stream, or flowering bush. To resist their flow is to block your own natural growth and, collectively, our natural evolution. Desire, deep desire, is the sap of the tree of life.

Going with the flow is, then, the first step to creating what you want. Yet in itself, it is incomplete. To get into a truly positive, creative relationship with life, we must confront structure. Structure is necessary to every creative work. The composition of a musical score requires the creation of a structure; the writing of a book requires the creation of a structure; the scripting of a comedy act requires the creation of a structure. So too starting a business, a nonprofit foundation, or even creating the job you want—all require that you create a structure. The simple truth is this: Structure cannot be avoided. If you don't create your own structure, you have to deal with someone else's.

I must Create a System or be enslav'd by another Man's.   *William Blake*

Executing a targeted job search, the kind discussed in Act III, demands a more structured job-hunting effort than merely answering want ads or posting scores of resumes. Starting your own business, setting yourself up as a freelance, or founding a nonprofit foundation requires the creation of still more structure, as well as the creation of additional structures for their maintenance and growth. The more involved you are in creating the structures of your life, the greater the sense of freedom and self-expression you will experience in your work. This is true so long as the original impulse, the creative vision that generates these structures, comes out of your own being, out of your desire, and not from some abstract idea of what you "should do," and so long as you continue to remain responsive to additional creative intuitions. In other words, so long as you continue to grow and evolve.

The most effective structures naturally present themselves when we move out of creative openness—out of spontaneity—going with the flow of our hearts. In this way, structure is intuitively perceived in principle before it is realized in practice, and it is continuously evolving. When creating structure, we don't want to get locked into some dead end, but to remain open to spontaneous evolution. As artist Julia Jones puts it, "This is the way I approach the creation of art: I always have a plan [structure], but I allow things to happen." In this way, structure serves our creative vision; we are not blindly serving structure.

Perhaps because we so often feel ourselves to be prisoners of structures we had no hand in creating—structures that, however inspired in their origin, have hardened into lifeless, grinding machines—many of us resist structure altogether. In this, we miss the possibility of realizing our own fullest creative potential. We *can* create structure without getting stuck in it. Yet to do this, we must continue to "go with the flow," never imagining that we have achieved the ultimate structure, or indeed that one even exists. Structures are vehicles through which to express creative desires and must not be taken as ends in themselves.

"Going with the flow" requires that you be here now, that you not allow yourself to drift automatically into a lackadaisical conformity to structure. It also requires respecting your humanity and holding it inviolate. Work doesn't have to be a dehumanizing experience and should not be accepted as such. One of the main tenets of Mahatma Gandhi's theory and practice of nonviolence is noncooperation with anything that diminishes human dignity. Of course, noncooperation means not engaging in anything that is blatantly oppressive or abusive to others. It also means avoiding that which is oppressive to one's own soul—to one's innate sense of humanity.

For example, when people are treated as machinelike workers and not taken seriously as human beings, tremendous emotional suffering results. Resentment and self-loathing are sure to build in those who remain in these situations. If we are to become a humane society, we must recognize that this emotional suffering is every bit as real as physical suffering—and put an end to it. This pain is mother to an army of social and psychological ills, which we desperately try to solve piecemeal, only to find new manifestations. Humane work has to take into account the fact that people are emotional and spiritual, as well as intellectual and physical, beings.

So often today, white-collar workers are hired for their brains alone; blue-collar and service workers, for their bodies only, as though these could be detached from the beings who possess them. As a consequence, there is so much emotional pain around work in our culture. This pain spills over into virtually every aspect of life. Families, relationships, and communities are deeply affected by it. We can't really blame anyone for this, or at least it does us no good to do so. Freedom can't be demanded from others—it must be created for ourselves. In his essay "Self-Reliance," Emerson writes,

Is not the core of
nature in the
heart of man?

Goethe

The Natural Art of Human Living

The great German author Thomas Mann wrote, "Art is the spirit in matter, the natural instinct toward humanization, that is, toward the spiritualization of life."[6] Mann's conception of art as *the natural instinct toward humanization, or spiritualization,* provides a bridge uniting the fine and the practical arts, the spiritual life with the art of creative living. The *impulse to humanize,* the movement "toward the spiritualization of life" is the origin of art, the progenitor of all that is noble in the creative arts, in science, in humanitarian service, indeed, in all fields of endeavor.

This conception unites the work of Gandhi with the Japanese tea ceremony, the mission work of Albert Schweitzer with Mozart's *Magic Flute,* Navaho sand painting with the great cathedrals of Europe, the work of Mother Teresa with that of Goethe, the poetry of the troubadours with the scriptures of India, the work of Albert Einstein with that of the anonymous but devoted local elementary school teacher. All of these are art because they spring from what Mann calls the "*natural instinct toward humanization.*" Setting aside for the moment the issue of the relative merit of these or of any other works of art, we can recognize this natural impulse as their common origin.

Following your natural instinct toward humanization is the road to your art, your life's work. This is another way of saying, "Follow your bliss." While we tend to think of art as something for a privileged few, Mann's conception recognizes art as the natural expression of our humanity. As such, art is not exceptional, but ordinary. In many traditional cultures, it was expected that all people were, or ought to be, artists. In regaining our naturalness, we regain our humanity and our art.

There *are* significant differences in the relative value of the arts and in the quality of their execution. Nevertheless, there is something to be gained in the recognition of the one impulse that gives rise to all the arts. *Major or minor, epic or commonplace, the arts are the works of the spirit.* They are acts of love that unite and "spiritualize" our lives. On the other hand, as Leonardo da Vinci said, "Where the spirit does not work with the hand, there is no art,"[7] no matter the virtuosity of the technique employed. All true art ought be celebrated for the sake of the impulse to humanity that gives it birth. This impulse is itself the art; it is what makes life worth living and, more than that, a thing of wonder, glory, and splendor.

In their contemplation, the genuine arts call out our humanity. If we study the arts with a view toward recognizing the underlying patterns, the ever-recurring Universal archetypes they evoke, we cannot help but recognize that the ground from which they emanate is the universal ground of Being in which man, the earth, the universe, and all things reside. The Ever-Becoming of this Being—the grand play of creation in which we are privileged to participate—is itself the Great Art to which all of the lesser arts point. As the sunlight reflects and recalls the Sun, so the radiance of the arts reflects and recalls the Great Art of Infinite Being, Ever-Becoming. Naturally.

"But now we are a mob. Man does not stand in awe of man, nor is his genius admonished to stay at home, to put itself in communication with the *internal* ocean, but it goes abroad to beg a cup of water of the urns of other men" [emphasis added].[8]

We must first become self-reliant; while we are still begging, pointing the finger serves no purpose. We can only learn to relax more deeply into the now-eternal moment of our being and learn to create, like artists, structures that have definite use and meaning in our lives. We can learn to be truly self-reliant, trusting in our innate humanity and in our ability to create, maintain, and dissolve structures as appropriate.

Gandhi also emphasized the importance of self-reliance. Self-reliance is critical to creating structures we can live with, and to remaining free of confining structures imposed by others (or even those of our own making). Self-reliance is a matter of spiritual and emotional maturity. It doesn't mean everyone out for him- or herself. Many of the most important things to be done in this world require that we work together. The critical points are that those working in a structure have some part in creating it—that it be useful and meaningful in their lives—and that structure never become "just the way it is." Structures, even at their best, are never "the way it is," but only limited vehicles for the expression of use and meaning. When they outlive either their use or their meaning, structures ought to be dissolved. The sad truth is that today, far too many have little, if any, input on the structures they work with; their work is experienced as neither useful nor meaningful, but "just the way it is."

When we lack self-reliance, when we depend upon someone else's structure for direction and support, we never know when it is going to shrink, collapse, or simply replace the part that we play in it. The corporation, the federal, state, or local government, can suddenly and unilaterally decide that what you are doing, and may have been doing for many years, is no longer necessary. This is often experienced as painful and disheartening. Perhaps it is all the more painful because we, at least obliquely, realize that all along, our work was not principally a means of self-expression, but of problem-solving, and damn it anyway, now we are right back to the problem—and know nothing more of our self-expression in the bargain.

The freedom to create, then, means that we can, to whatever degree, BE in touch with the essential core of Self and Life, and that we can EXPRESS through structures that we have some part in creating. We can say that the maximum experience of freedom in work requires the ability to freely and deliberately create structure, the ability to maintain structure through adaptation, the ability to freely let go of structure, and the ability to know when each is appropriate.

But then if I do not strive, who will?

Chuang Tzu

For one who has conquered the mind,
The mind is the best of friends,
But for one who has failed to do so,
His very mind will be the greatest enemy.
                    Bhagavad-Gita

Many Westerners think of Eastern religion as seeking to induce a mindless, negative, trancelike state called *Nirvana*. As the quote above clearly indicates, the enlightened person is not a tranced-out dope. His mind is his friend. He uses it creatively to express. He can think—clearly. And he can simply Be. He can rest and he can move to express. His thinking is not the mental chatter born of unconscious preoccupation or anxious self-consciousness many call thinking. It is deliberate—holding and developing the thought of some creative vision or idea, for the accomplishment of some human purpose.

One way or another, we all have to find what best fosters the flowering of our humanity in this contemporary life, and dedicate ourselves to that.
                    Joseph Campbell

Don't listen to friends when the Friend inside you says "Do this."

Gandhi

To express is to take an idea, not of what one is, but of what one can make or manifest, and make or manifest it. In this sense, creative expression always has an impersonal quality to it. For example, we have a sense of the world's great art as belonging to humanity and not to the individuals who created it. Unique self-expression turns out to resonate with all of humanity, while conformist work seems strangely alienated and isolating. The deeper we go within ourselves, the closer we are to everyone. In regard to work, the question "What do you want to be?" throws us off track. Better questions are: What do you want to do or make? What do you want to express? What do you want to create? The thing to be is yourself; the thing to do is what moves you.

Many today are seeking a holistic approach to life and work, one that integrates the spiritual and material. Too often these seem separated by a wide chasm bounded by steep cliffs. Our lives take on a schizophrenic quality—spiritual here, practical there. We require a bridge or bridges—effective ways of uniting the spiritual and material, the sacred and the ordinary. My goal in writing this book is to provide some principles of creative design and some materials with which you can build *your* bridge. To bridge the sacred and the ordinary, we must tap the spirit and emotional power of creative living, and gain knowledge of how things are and how they work. In this way, we can create the life of our inborn nature.

I.S.E.E. My Life's Work

While I cannot tell you what your life's work is, I can suggest a few terms to serve as a frame of reference while you are making your search. In your life's work, you will find a mix of integrity, service, enjoyment, and excellence.

Integrity: Your life's work is something you deeply care about. In line with your values and ideals, it's something you can be proud to work for. Of course, it is important that your work not conflict with your values and ideals. More than this, a life's work is born out of your visions, values, and ideals. It's giving life to your values, anchoring them in the everyday world of action. **Key Words:** purposeful, meaningful, responsible, honest, truthful. **Essential Question: Who Am I?**

Service: Your life's work is your way of making this world a better place. It's something you can make an important contribution to. We all want to give, to know that what we do is benefiting others. Your life's work is an opportunity to put your love in action. It's your way of taking a stand to help your fellow man. **Key Words:** helping, caring, loving, giving, contributing. **Essential Question: How can I make this world a better place?**

Enjoyment: Your life's work is something you love to do, something your talents can find full expression through. If we enjoy our work, we are sure to bring our creativity and enthusiasm to it. If we do not, we are sure to get burnt out, frustrated, resentful, or indifferent. No matter how noble the ideal or seemingly valuable your service, you must find joy in your work if you are to be truly successful. Work without joy is a chore or a bore. Channel your creative powers into meaningful contributions. **Key Words:** talents, creating, feedback, joy, gratitude. **Essential Question: What do I love to do?**

Excellence: Your life's work is something you can give your all to. Something you can dedicate yourself to. The dancer has his body pain, the writer struggles and racks his brain, the craftsman sweats every detail, the musician has his endless scales. Always quality has its price. It takes extra effort to make it nice. **Key Words:** dedication, persistence, determination, quality. **Essential Question: What can I dedicate to enough to persist to excellence?**

CHAPTER 2

Zen at Work; Or, Poetry in Motion

The truth of Zen, just a little bit of it, is what turns one's hum drum life, a life of monotonous, uninspiring commonplaceness, into one of art, full of genuine inner creativity.

D. T. Suzuki

This book is called *Zen and the Art of Making a Living,* and you may well ask, What is Zen? A Sufi was once asked, "What is a Sufi?" He replied, "A Sufi is a Sufi." What is Zen? Zen is Zen.[1] Big help, you may say. Ask a Zen master, and he might choke you, or hit you with a stick, or laugh, or insult you, or spit in your face.

If you're still asking, What is Zen?, look at the question—it's all words. Words are symbols. Symbols are not what they stand for. Water is not these five letters *w-a-t-e-r*. Only an idiot would confuse the fluid reality with the letter symbols. You can't drink letters on a hot day. The reality behind all symbols has been called the *Mystery*, the *Unnameable*, the *Unexplainable*, the *Tao*, *God*, many names. Whatever you name it, you can't name it; whatever symbol you invent, it cannot hold the reality it represents. Since it can't be named, Zen is as good a name as any. But Zen is not about knowing about this reality. Zen is drinking it in everyday life.

I was first introduced to Zen through my interest in poetry. Poetry is our best (though entirely inadequate) attempt to reveal the Great Mystery in mere words. Zen poets seem to have an uncanny knack for providing awakening glimpses of the Mystery in the ordinary. Their poems are slices of ordinary life, lived with extraordinary vigor, insight, grace, and humor. The attentive reader can't help but feel refreshed and amused, ready to meet the situations of his own life with new energy and detachment.

> Zen makes use, to a great extent, of poetical expressions; Zen is wedded to poetry.
> D. T. Suzuki

Of course, Zen poems are not alone in this. East or West, inspired poetry has been called scripture, or sacred verse. Writing about the Old Testament prophets, David Ben-Gurion notes that "it is a strange but significant fact that all the prophets were poets, so much so that any prose passages in the prophetic writings must be suspected of being later additions."[2] In *Mahayana Buddhism*, author Paul Williams instructs that "the Mahayana *sutras* were not the words of the Buddha but rather the works of poets."[3] We will not belabor the point beyond restating Aldous Huxley's general assertion that "the original scriptures of *most* religions are poetical and unsystematic" [emphasis added].[4]

Poetry is not to be thought of as mere words upon a printed page. A poem is an interactive relationship of word and consciousness. It is the act of hearing that makes the poem come alive. Indeed, *sruti*, the Sanskrit word for "scriptures," literally means "hearing."[5] Until they are heard, scriptures are not scriptures— poems are not poems. Rightly heard, poetry can be a gateway to Mystery.

Likewise, poetry can serve as a metaphor for a vision of work as art. From the Western vantage point, the notion of equating poetry with work may seem peculiar. We are used to thinking of work as a necessary drudgery or a moral responsibility, as a means to economic gain or ego gratification, but hardly as poetry. Work is what you have to do when you grow up, or it's a way of paying the bills, relieving boredom, achieving status, exercising power, or getting rich. This is life and work as "prose"—driven by the fears and ambitions of the mind, haunted by the necessities of the body—functional, but soulless.

"Poetic" work comes from the heart. Where "prosaic" work struggles to satisfy the material demands of the body and the ego demands of the mind, poetic work delights in the spirit of living.

Spirit-led and -fed, there isn't a trace of otherworldliness, moral superiority, or retreat about it. Not a matter of engaging in superior occupations, poetic work intensifies and exalts human experience in whatever it finds itself engaged. While it goes without saying that it does not become involved in that which would violate its source (the heart), poetic work differs from the prosaic, not so much in content as in its approach.

Perhaps the best way to give a sense of the difference between these two approaches is to look at two phrases: "have to" and "want to." "Have to's" have a bit of grudge to them, a holding back, an inner struggle. "Want to's" move ahead directly. I *have to* work. I *have to* pay the bills. I *have to* impress people. I *have to* get rich. I *have to* beat the competition. I *have to* save the world. I *want to* work. I *want to* buy things. I *want to* be myself. I *want to* make money. I *want to* win. I *want to* share love. Feel the difference?

The things you have done because you truly wanted to—you experienced. The things you have done because you thought you had to—you missed. Zen says, This is it! Don't miss it with a lot of "have to" concepts. Dig on life! Zen embraces life; necessities, it calls *desires*. Since it lives, it "wants to" live. Since it works, it "wants to" work. Zen is not fighting with itself.

*Everywhere I go I find
a poet has been
there before me.*

Sigmund Freud

---

*Desires that are just are termed Truth.
Without desires, Truth cannot be understood.
                Hung Tzu-ch'eng*

How can we bring to work the spirit of Zen—of poetry in motion? We can start by listening to the "want to's" of our hearts, of our original nature. Poetry, after all, is all in the hearing. As a poem depends upon the "hearer" to make it Poetry, a life depends on a "liver" to make it Alive. Inspired poetic works can be analyzed, but that is so much nonsense if they are not heard. Lives can be planned, controlled, and organized, but that is so much nonsense if they are not lived. Zen says, LIVE! Be what you are!

Dare to Be the Poet of Your Life's Song

A poet is one who hears and one who *makes*. In fact, our word *poet* comes from the Greek *poietes*—"one who makes."[6] To make is to bring into form. The poet brings into form what she hears in the depth of her heart—the echo of her life's destiny. Oh, maybe she can only make out a couple of notes. They roam around in the back of her mind and won't let go. Maybe she hears only a refrain

Look with thine ears.

Shakespeare

or a simple tune. Perhaps she hears a glorious symphony in full orchestration. Whatever music she hears, she plays it with intense energy. She makes the song of her heart sing through her life.

A poem is the realization of love.
René Char

Again, poetic work is not limited to stanzas on a printed page. Mother Teresa is a poet, and Einstein. St. Francis is a poet, and Martin Luther King. Michelangelo is a poet, and so is Mozart. All who hear a voice calling them to a mighty purpose and labor to give it expression are poets. Still, all poems are not epics. There are farmer poets and cleaning poets, healing poets and sewing poets, cooking poets and building poets. Some hear better than others, and some are better at making, but all can be the poets of their own lives by joining the hearing and making—the inspiration and the action.

We can carry the metaphor of work as poetry (hearing and making) a step further by introducing two terms, one from the Western tradition, one from the Eastern. The Western term is *vocation;* the Eastern, *Dō.* The word *vocation* means "calling." Your vocation is the work you are called to perform. *Dō* is a Japanese word that has been translated "way" or "art of," as in the art of flower arrangement or the art of archery. *Dō* is a mindful attitude and manner of performance. It has been called "the infinite way of doing finite things."

In the Supreme Presence of Mind
there is total absence of "mine."

Your life's work is a matter of the *use* that you are called to make of your life (vocation) and the *way* (*Dō*) in which you execute it. The *use* is the function served; the *way,* the manner in which it is served. The use of a meal is to eat. The way that the food is selected, prepared, served, and eaten will spell the difference between enjoyment and a lot of gas. The right vocation and the right way of executing it—this is life's work.

Vocation: Hearing the Call

Again, *vocation* means "calling." To hear the call, you have to be listening. It's hard to listen when you have a lot of preconceived notions about what you should do, or fears of inadequacy, or prejudices about how one kind of work is better or more worthy than another, or vested interests (like having trained and worked so long at something that isn't really you). If you want to find your true calling, you have to forget all of that and follow your Bliss.

Dive deeply into being, beyond identity and form. Encompass all around you. Penetrate into absorption—absorb into bliss—sail on bliss—into complete quietness. Enter into emptiness—where "self" is no more. Silence the noise of fear and craving, the static of social obligation. Have no fear; in silence the image or form of your life's natural expression will become clear. It is in your heart; it has been there all along. As the great poet Rumi has written, "Everyone has been made for some particular work, and the desire for that work has been put in every heart."[7]

Can you hear it? Can you silence the confusion of the mind and its conflicts and listen for your Bliss—the voice of your heart? Listen now for the voice out of The Silence. Listen for what moves or draws you the most. Listen for what you can dedicate yourself to. Listen to what you love. If many things attract your attention, you're still on the surface. Go deeper. A relative few will speak powerfully to you. When you hear this call, what will it say? Make this—bring this into being. A poet is one who hears and one who makes.

If you ask him: "What is silence?" he will answer, "It is the Great Mystery! The holy silence is His voice!" If you ask: "What are the fruits of silence?" he will say: "They are self-control, true courage or endurance, patience, dignity, and reverence. Silence is the cornerstone of character."

Ohiyesa (Charles Eastman)

We All Have It: The Desire to Be Useful

Have you ever noticed what energetic creatures we humans are? Most of us appear happier when we are busy than when we are not. We seem to feel the need to do something. Many of the other animals seem to have this as well. But we humans have this other thing—this notion of being useful. We don't want to do just anything. We want to do something meaningful, something useful.

Everyone has been made for some particular work, and the desire for that work has been put in every heart.

Rumi

The words of truth are always paradoxical.

Lao Tzu

> *The vocation, whether it be that of the farmer or the architect, is a function; the exercise of this function as regards the man himself is the most indispensable means of spiritual development, and as regards his relation to society the measure of his worth.*
>
> Ananda K. Coomaraswamy

Now, some may protest that none of us are terribly useful, but that doesn't keep us from trying. The Chinese sage Lao Tzu (or the poets writing in his name) wrote that those who know do not speak, and those who speak do not know.[8] One wonders why he bothers to break his own silence to tell us this. Perhaps there is something in our nature that is bound and determined to be useful—even if it knows better.

The modern Indian philosopher and teacher J. Krishnamurti would often say, "Do not accept it [what he was saying] because the speaker is telling you. The speaker is not important." Still he went on speaking right to the end. Even after there were dozens of books, tapes, and films, he kept talking on into his nineties. If the speaker was altogether unimportant, and everyone knew what he had to say, why keep saying it? Maybe next time someone would hear! Maybe he just loved to talk. Or maybe he just couldn't help making himself useful.

Your calling is your natural way of being useful, the way it was natural for Lao Tzu to be useful in speaking to remind us that those who speak do not know. Apparently, he just couldn't keep himself from sharing—naturally. Just as naturally, you have a calling, a unique way of being useful. Struggling and straining to find your calling is a good way to miss it. It's natural, after all.

> *Consciously or unconsciously, every one of us does render some service or other. If we cultivate the habit of doing this service deliberately, our desire for service will steadily grow stronger, and will make, not only for our own happiness, but that of the world at large.*
>
> Mahatma Gandhi

You have heard that life is a dance. And if you have seen cells dividing, or the sun on the water, or birds before they mate, you can see that it *is* a dance. If you think too much when you're dancing, you trip over your feet. In the same way, if you miss the rhythm of your life (with too much self-conscious "have to" thinking), you'll stumble through it a bit awkward and out of place. The graceful dancer listens for the music and trusts her feet to respond.

Follow Your Native Compassion and Bliss

In listening for the song of your life's work, the notes to follow are your native compassion and bliss, or *karuna* and *ananda*.[9] We can call *compassion* the desire to act for the benefit of others—to eliminate their suffering or increase their happiness. *Bliss* we can call the energy of transcendent consciousness, Life Ecstatic.

Like all the great sages, the Buddha tells us that it is the craving desire to act for self-interest that binds us to suffering. Jesus said, to save yourself, lose yourself—lose these self-interested cravings. Yet how can we eliminate desire? Desire is the very stuff of life— to kill it would be to destroy life itself. We cannot destroy desire, but we can begin to recognize that beyond the transient desires of ego lie deeper desires for love and service to all mankind. We can "lose ourselves" in our desire to give of our love and talent. This, we have been told by all the great teachers, is the road to happiness.

To love is to transform; to be a poet.
Norman O. Brown

Why, then, is this road so little traveled? Most of us are too busy running down approval alley. Our years of dependency, from infancy through adolescence, condition us to try to *please* others in order to get from them what we need (or think we need) to survive. The conditioned drive to please to get approval is a learned mental process, based on the memory of past experience and the hope or threat of future consequences. It moves us out of the now-present-moment of spontaneous giving into concern for gaining approval or avoiding disapproval in the future. Where pleasing is a calculated mental process, compassion comes straight from the heart. Out of a here-and-now feeling of identity arises a spontaneous urge to act for the benefit of others.

Many of us find the please-for-approval habit a hard one to break. Doing so means accepting full responsibility for our own lives—breaking our chains of emotional dependence, letting go of our unending approval demands. Only then can we hear the com-

The art of life,
of a poet's life,
is, not having
anything to do,
to do something.

Henry David Thoreau

passion note echoing from within. Only then can we move in the direction it wants to take us. As we accept responsibility for our own lives, our desire to serve others increases. It seems we have more energy to give. Energy once tied up in the infantile desire to please can now find release in the compassion of universal love.

Zen finds in *trshna*, selfish ego-centered love, the seed of *karuna*, universal compassion. Melting ice changes in form, not in essence. All the while, the ice of selfish love contains the water of universal compassion. Rearranging the letters in the word *please*, we get the word *ASLEEP*. The "please" mode is simply sleeping compassion. Awakening genuine compassion leads you to the best use of your life—"a purpose recognized by yourself as a mighty one."[10]

The Buddha has further told us that our fundamental nature is Ecstatic Bliss. Yet, paradoxically, we miss the Bliss in our desperate attempts to find happiness. When we stake our happiness on other people, places, things, or circumstances, we are sure to come up wanting. This brings to life the sense of a rollercoaster ride of elation and depression, an endless cycle of ups and downs. Of course, gains and losses, advances and reversals are inevitable in life, but they *cause* us neither to be happy nor to be unhappy. In our attachment to and investment in these turns of events, we miss the ecstatic pulse of life, its radiant Bliss. Bliss is not pleasure without pain. Genuine Bliss holds infinite sorrow as space holds the earth, without effort or weariness. Even as we miss Compassion in trying to please, so we miss Bliss in trying to find happiness.

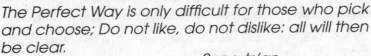

The Perfect Way is only difficult for those who pick and choose; Do not like, do not dislike: all will then be clear.

Seng-ts'an

The Buddha enjoins us to hold to the middle—recognize that pleasure and pain (like and dislike) are but two sides of the same coin. Sometimes it comes up heads; sometimes, tails. Aware of pleasure and pain, but neither attached to the one nor repulsed by the other, the Buddha resides in the center of Bliss.

Zen masters laugh at our vain attempts to find happiness in outer circumstances. In this, we are like a man standing in a clear stream while dying of thirst, or as the Polynesian saying goes, we are "standing on a whale, fishing for minnows." Bliss, the sages tell us, is not a thing to be acquired, conquered, or possessed by outer means; rather, it is an ongoing experience to relax into. Ever abiding and without cause—Bliss simply Is. To recognize this, to

To the mind that is still, the whole universe surrenders.

Lieh Tzu

know it in the gut, is to awaken the sleeper. The Zen masters call this the recognition of one's own "original [blissful] nature."

Now, getting back to work, whatever gets you really turned on, enough to work for with dedication, sacrifice, and excellence, has the quality of this blissful, original nature in it and is moving you toward your life's work. If you find great joy in your work *and* you are ready to sacrifice for it, you are on the right track. You are following your bliss—beyond the pairs of opposites.

> *To be willing to suffer in order to create is one thing; to realize that one's creation necessitates one's suffering, that suffering is one of the greatest of God's gifts, is almost to reach a mystical solution to the problem of evil.*
>
> *J. W. Sullivan*

The compassion and bliss notes are usually drowned out by all the "have to" static over the security, approval (status), and power needs that occupy so much of society's time and interest. Money is usually mixed up with all three. Joseph Campbell said, "Social pressure is the enemy!"[11] Society gives us preconceived, abstract notions of how our lives are supposed to be and puts on tremendous pressure to see that we conform.

Then, of course, there is our own weakness and rigidity. We fear change. We try to create a predictable life that is as unthreatening as possible. Yet it's not knowing what's coming around the corner that makes life interesting. Look at nature; it's full of surprises. It curves, zigzags, wiggles, and bends. Its forms grow, expand, decay, and die. Change is everywhere, ongoing. Yet for all its changes, nature has an order, an intelligence.

So it is with compassion and bliss. Follow them; they know where to take you. Don't interfere with growth; yield to it. There is an intelligence in this. Often it can only be understood in retrospect. Though we may not have understood at the time, something was guiding us all the while. When we yield to our compassionate, blissful nature, its intelligence takes the lead. We are moved by something at once intrinsically a part of ourselves, and yet infinitely larger.

Allow your natural compassion and bliss to ripen, and you are sure to find your vocation sooner or later. It may not come out like you thought, but that's part of the adventure of life—and the fun! Pay attention to where compassion and bliss take you, and watch the thing unfold. Even if you miss the *heart* promptings of compassion and bliss, you can still *mentally* recognize your desire to be useful. (Watch how children naturally want to help.) Since we can't help trying to be useful, we may as well decide to be useful at things that foster harmony, increase beauty, and generally make life more palatable. Certainly we can decide not to be useful at things that are destructive, dull, or drab.

If the notion of following your compassion and bliss to your vocation seems a little vague or nebulous, don't worry. Later, we will confront vocation in much more concrete terms. For now, simply recognize your desire to be useful, and see where it wants to take you.

Dō: Making the Art of Zen

Zen is as much at home with the practical business of everyday living as it is with transcendent realization. It delights in "the infinite way of doing finite things." Unlike some spiritual traditions, Zen does not reject or abhor the "world." It takes a middle path that embraces the phenomenal world while seeing through its illusions. Its fundamental insight is that all dualistic distinctions—life/death, creator/created, self/other, *nirvana/samsara*—are illusionary. Everything is mutually arising, mutually dependent, and constantly changing. You cannot conceive of anything apart from its relation to something else. And both the "anythings" and their relations are constantly changing. Therefore, it is said, Nothing exists. At the same time, things appear to have form and substance. Recognize this appearance, the stage in which the cosmic drama unfolds, as none other than the no-thing-ness. Play in the field of forms without becoming deceived into believing that any form, including the one I call "myself," has any permanence or an independent existence.

The one named myself is at odds with the world, simply because its endless desires are frustrated by the world. It seems to always be pushing against the world and feeling the world push against it. It is tense, on guard, playing defense. In this posture, it is difficult to create or to play. When I relinquish myself, I drop the tension and regain my original (creative, playful) nature. (Better said: Self relinquished, breath returns, play appears.) Now the "Buddha nature" in, and of, every-thing (form) becomes perceptible. As my Zen teacher used to say over and again, "I become the Buddha, whole universe become the Buddha" (sic). In this awakening, everything changes, though nothing is different.

D. T. Suzuki wrote, "Enlightenment . . . is an act of intuition born of the will."[12] We cannot realize enlightenment *by* or *through* will. Awakening comes through intuition, direct experience. Yet this experience will almost certainly elude us if we haven't devel-

Take thy Bliss O Man!

William Blake

oped a strong will. Why? Because we already have so many bad habits that obscure our "original nature." These habits (*samskara*) keep us in darkness. More than anything, these are habits of the mind. You become angry and say or do this or that. You become fearful and do this or that. You become bored and do this or that. You become despondent, or greedy, or whatever and do this or that. Most of the time, we focus on the "this or that." We justify or condemn our behavior. But we seldom ask, Why did I become angry, fearful, bored, or despondent? I didn't choose to have these feelings; they were suddenly just there—automatically. Habitually. Spiritual ignorance is not lack of (intellectual) knowledge, but lack of awareness. In the face of habit, awareness takes will. Awareness in action is the essence of *Dō*.

Since most of us spend more of our waking lives working than doing anything else, work provides an excellent opportunity to strengthen will and develop awareness. If we conceive of ourselves as being on a spiritual path (however we define it), the what and the how of the work we do makes a difference. If I am working forty-plus hours a week, my spiritual path will always be peripheral if I don't take it to work with me. It is wonderful if you can sit still in mediation for twenty minutes or an hour every day. Still, if at work you are "meditating" on anxiety, resentment, boredom, or hostility for hours each day, this too will have consequences. The idea behind vocation is doing what you are naturally suited to do. A turtle is a good swimmer but a slow walker. A cheetah is a great runner but it can't fly. An eagle is a lousy runner but a good swimmer and a great flier. In the same way, each of us is naturally suited in our inclinations and innate abilities to some kind of work. In my career coaching work, I see many eagles trying to run and a lot of turtles that never get near the water. It is always a great delight to see how different individuals move naturally toward this or that arena, once they begin to tune in to their natural inclinations and abilities. For most people, an appropriate vocation facilitates full engagement in their work. Full engagement in the now activities of work takes the focus off the ego. This helps one stay centered in love, which, in turn, increases one's ability.

Whatever your vocation, your way of being useful, how you go about it is as much "your work" as what you do. If *use* is purpose, *Dō*, or *way,* is purposefulness. Zen influence on Japanese culture gave rise to many *Dō's,* or ways. Anyone who has ever experienced a Japanese tea ceremony has some idea what purposeful action is. Here, in the simple act of serving and taking tea, life is artistry. Human dignity, strength, and grace are honored in purposeful, present action. On the other hand, even a grand intention (purpose) undertaken with a shaky consciousness produces a dubious result. Every work reflects

You wish to see; Listen. Hearing is a step toward Vision.

St. Bernard

its creator, his spiritual strengths and flaws, his skill, patience, and resolve. The role of the *Dō* is to develop the artist's awareness.

> *There are various Ways. There is the Way of salvation by the law of Buddha, the Way of Confucius governing the Way of learning, the Way of healing as a doctor, as a poet teaching the Way of Waka, tea, archery, and many arts and skills. Each man practices as he feels inclined.*
>
> Miyamoto Musashi

The dictionary defines art as "the disposition or modification of things by human skill, to answer the purpose intended." Our word *art* comes from the Greek *artunein*—"to arrange."[13] We arrange by sight. Where *vocation* is a matter of hearing what to do, *making* is a matter of seeing how to do it. We *see* how to arrange things to answer the purpose intended. Seeing may come in a flash, whole and complete, or it may come around the corner, bit by bit. The artist encounters human society, physical nature, and the particular medium, tools, or objects of his work, and transforms these according to the image in his consciousness. Whether our making involves the production of some service, the production and distribution of beneficial products, the investigation into some knowledge, the transmission of some wisdom, or whatever else—art has lessons for all of us. While the discussion below will be framed in terms of the formal arts, everything that will be said applies to all work undertaken as art.

In giving form to her vision, the creative artist measures her efforts against the inner vision she holds. The final product is always inadequate. Yet, as Michelangelo said, it's in striving for perfection that the artist touches the divine. This striving for perfection, for the fullest realization of the thing imagined, elevates ordinary life to the level of sublime, transcendent experience. Striving for perfection is the passion of art—the ready sacrifice of the artist to realize some inner vision in the outer world of form. Her dedication requires no external motivation but is driven from within.

> *The way of the mystic and the way of the artist are related, except that the mystic doesn't have the craft.*
>
> Jean Erdman

While it is this striving for perfection that gives art its passion, imagination gives it its play. Both in the sense of enjoyment and in the sense of the dramatic, art is play. The revelations of imagination, the *satori* of every genuine artistic inspiration, are sublime delight. Art is magical or, in Zen terms, *marvelous*, when vision, content, design, and technique form an inseparable unity. Today we rely heavily upon technique, but as D. T. Suzuki put it, "Technical knowledge is not enough. One must transcend techniques so that the art becomes the artless art." "Artless art" has the quality of revelation. One feels that in beholding it, he has received a precious gift; a conscious spirit has moved over this form, in turn evoking the spirit of the beholder. This sense of the gift is equally present in the practical and the contemplative arts—as much in entering a well-made home or sitting down to a well-prepared meal as in enjoying a fine piece of music or poetry. It is the essence of the experience of any work as art. The all-embracing humanity of Zen tells us that there is no sphere of human life exempt from the display of this gift-giving spirit.

Although profoundly "inconsequential," the Zen experience has consequences in the sense that it may be applied in any direction, to any conceivable human activity, and that wherever it is so applied it lends an unmistakable quality to the work.
Alan Watts

It is easier and more useful to talk about what art does than what it is. Art communicates awareness—consciousness. All art reflects some *theory* (in the original sense of the word, i.e., "a way of seeing").[14] This is true whether or not the theory is ever articulated or even understood by the artist. A way of seeing, or *theory,* of art is expressed through a work's *content* and *design* language. Of course, the language of art is not limited to words. Movement, sound, light, shape, color—all design elements are a kind of artistic language. Additionally, every art has a *technique,* a way of "modifying things by human skill." The discussion below considers the theory, content, design, and technique of art. We can draw on these elements in shaping any life's work.

Vision or Theory of Art: As we have seen, in its origin the word *art* means "to arrange." The true artist is a master arranger or master of arrangements. He may "arrange" in any field of action— in any of the making or doing arts. An art theory is simply a vision

There is no patriotic art and no patriotic science.

Goethe

of how to make beautiful arrangements. Philosophers, artists, and critics from around the world have offered many excellent theories or ways of seeing art. The discussion below draws on a simple, yet profound, theory articulated by James Joyce in *Portrait of the Artist as a Young Man.*[15] To begin with, Joyce distinguishes between "proper" and "improper" art in terms of their effects on their "audience." Proper art produces what Joyce calls "aesthetic arrest" (more on this below). He says that improper art comes in two general categories: the "pornographic" and the "didactic." Pornographic art arouses a *desire to possess* the object represented. Pornographic art is seen in the advertising barrage to which we are daily subjected. "Make the thing look sexy, alluring, sensually enticing, so they will want to possess it." Didactic art excites a sense of *fear and loathing* in relation to the object represented (not unlike the "pleasure" many seem to get from watching horror films). Didactic art is often used as a vehicle for propaganda, social criticism, or protest. "Political," "confessional," or "movement" art is typically didactic. On the other hand, genuine art is timeless and universal, appealing to the essential humanity in us all. It is not exclusively addressed to any particular ethnicity, race, or gender. Georgia O'Keeffe put it emphatically, "There is no man's art or woman's art; there is just Art."

Be still and cool in thy own mind and spirit.
George Fox

The productions of all arts are kinds of poetry and their craftsmen are all poets.

Plato

This capital *A* Art that Georgia O'Keeffe is referring to above is what Joyce calls "proper art." In Joyce's view, proper art has a *static* quality, while improper art has a *kinetic,* or moving, quality. Improper art excites the mind to move toward or away from its object. Proper art brings the mind to rest. Joyce explains that while the pleasures of improper art are desire and loathing, the pleasure of proper art is "aesthetic arrest," stopping or arresting the motions of the mind. In contemplation of the work of art, "the mind is arrested and raised above desire and loathing."[16] This is exactly the goal of meditation—to arrest the mind—transcending attachment (desire) and repulsion (loathing). Thus, genuine art, both in its contemplation and in its practice, is meditation—mind-arresting. And this is Zen. The word *Zen* itself is Japanese for the Indian *dhyana,* usually translated "meditation."[17] The static quality of "aesthetic arrest" corresponds with the Zen concept of "No-Mind."[18] So we can say that in proper art, the motions of the mind are arrested in the rest of No-Mind.

In Zen the important thing is to stop the course of the mind.

Traditional Zen Saying

The motive of proper art is neither "for" nor "against," but to bring out what Joyce calls "the radiance." The *radiance* of a work of art shows in its ability to arrest the mind. We want to linger and absorb the beauty of the work. Blissful serenity, intense stillness, this is radiance. While Joyce's theory of art was intended for the contemplation of the fine arts, we can see in it keys to *Dō*, or working in the way of art, in any field of human endeavor. As the Buddhist art critic, Sōetsu Yanagi put it, "Beauty is that which has been liberated—or freed—from duality."[19] All action is beautiful (art) when it arises out of the cosmic crack between this and that. Similarly, as the Buddha said, "the *contemplation* of beauty eliminates selfish desire"—liberating us, if only temporarily, from duality.

We have, then, come round again to the essential point: *The pleasure in art, both in its practice and in its contemplation, is meditation—arresting or liberating the mind from duality*. We lose ourselves in art. As Arthur Schopenhauer noted, the contemplation of art switches off the sense of self and other. As we merge our consciousness with the work of art, we lose the sense of ourselves as a thing apart.[20] In this "loss of self," we feel the ecstatic Bliss of our original nature. Rodin was getting at something similar when he said, "Art is contemplation. It is the *joy* of the intelligence" [emphasis mine]. Likewise, in the practice of art, the sense of self is lost in ecstatic absorption. While here on earth, attending to the most practical of affairs, the artist, as Blake would say, "travels in his mind to Heaven." He loses himself (identification with ego) and gains eternity. This is Zen at work, the essence of work as art—liberation from the little self, returning to the Bliss of our original nature.

The heart has its reasons that the mind knows nothing of.

Blaise Pascal

If you realize what the real problem is—losing yourself—you realize that this itself is the ultimate trial.
Joseph Campbell

Dō is active contemplation or meditation—moving or doing in aesthetic arrest. Or we could say it is moving without moving—moving without the motions of the mind. Lao Tzu wrote, "The secret of the magic of life is in using action to attain non-action."[21] It is making your work (action) your meditation (nonaction). For St. Augustine, "our whole business in this life is to restore the health of the eye of the heart whereby God (the Infinite) may be seen."[22] Our business (career) need not keep us from "our business in this life." Indeed, working in the way of the artist does not impede, but enhances and expresses spiritual life. Work engaged in this way purifies "the personal system so that it moves over into the universal."[23] In the making of the art, we are remaking ourselves, gaining confidence in what Zen calls our "original nature."

Having now some inkling of how we might approach work as *Dō* or "the art of . . . ," it's worth asking: How we can recognize a work of art, be it our own life's work or the art of another? The four essentials below are useful guideposts that apply equally to the "fine" and "everyday" arts.

1. **The work of art is inspired.** It is conceived of the spirit, born of the Buddha nature, whispered by the muse—however you want to say it—the work of art in some way echoes the transcendent Mystery. It suggests something more than itself. What Joseph Campbell said of myth—that it is a "metaphor transparent to transcendence"—applies to the work of art. Both in the making arts and in the doing arts, the radiance of spirit shines through. We recognize a Beauty that transcends the beautiful and the ugly. This is the **integrity** of the work of art—that it arises from the essential self of the artist. *The secret of art lies in the artist himself* (Kuo Jo-hsu).[24]

2. **The work of art is useful.** The artist feels a sense of responsibility to humanity, and therefore, he makes that which can be put to good use. The use intended may be for the practical life of the body, the refreshment of the mind, or the awakening of the soul. In every case, the artist has in mind the use of the work. It arises out of compassion for humanity. "The secret of art," as the sculptor Antoine Bourdelle put it, "is love."[25] This is the quality of **service** in the work of art—that the artist makes the work, not simply for himself, but for all mankind. *The general end of art is the good of man* (Aristotle).[26]

3. **The work of art is natural.** The artist is naturally suited to his work. Be he a carpenter, an orator, a doctor, or a poet, his work is what he naturally does, that is, loves. This is what gives work the quality of play. While working at what is naturally his to do, the artist enters into the work so completely, he loses himself in it. This is the **enjoyment** of the work of art—the natural, spontaneous self-abandonment of the artist in what he loves. *It is certain that the secret of all art . . . lies in self-oblivion* (Ricciotto Canudo).[27]

4. The work of art is beautiful. Beauty is not an end in itself, but the by-product of making or doing things well. The beautiful results from the aspiration to perfection, yet it accepts, even celebrates, natural human imperfections. Beauty is not found in mechanical correctness, but in human aspiration—in making and doing with love. If in-spiration is the call of Heaven, a-spiration is the desire to realize Heaven on Earth. The artist knows that, as Michelangelo said, "trifles make perfection and perfection is no trifle." This is what gives the work of art the quality of **excellence**—the artist's striving for perfection. *O Excellence! how narrow are thy paths, how arduous thy ways! Happy the man who can climb thy paths and tread thy ways!* (Gottfried von Strassburg).[28]

*   The "Vision Questing" and "Clarifying Values" sections of "Act I: The Quest for Life's Work" are designed to help you explore and develop a *theory* for the art of your life. The idea is to see where your work fits in the context of the wider world and your inner core.

Content: The content of "proper art" may be virtually anything approached in a sacred way. Some art historians categorize the content of works of art in terms of the "superordinary sacred" and the "ordinary sacred." The sacred art of India or medieval Europe reflects the sacred in the superordinary aspect. The subject is theistic—God in splendor, majesty, and miraculous exploits. Zen art more typically represents the sacred in the ordinary aspect: the rock gardens, the calligraphy, the tea ceremony, the martial arts. Ordinary things like rocks and trees, ordinary activities like writing, taking tea, and fighting are approached with a presence and a sense of wonder that can only be called sacred.

> *What is particularly intriguing, in fact, is that whereas many peoples tend to locate this experience (of the sacred) in certain unusual, if not "supernatural" moments and circumstances . . . the Oriental focus is upon mystery in the most obvious, ordinary, mundane—the most natural—situations of life.*
>
> Conrad Hyers

In the West, this sacred-in-the-ordinary aspect can be seen in works such as Cézanne's still lifes or his paintings of Mont Sainte-Victoire, in van Gogh's *Boots with Laces* or *Starry Night,* or even in T. S. Eliot's *The Cocktail Party.* Of course, the two (superordinary and ordinary) are not mutually exclusive. Blake, Rembrandt, Mozart,

The work will teach you how to do it.

Estonian Proverb

Love is love's reward.

John Dryden

and many others have revealed the sacred in both superordinary and ordinary content. Extending this metaphor beyond the so-called "fine" arts, we could say that one could choose to practice his or her spiritual life in the superordinary way, as a monk or renunciate, or in an ordinary way by working as an artist in whatever field he or she is naturally drawn to.

✳ The "Pointing to Purpose," "Targeting Talents," and "Marking Mission Objectives" sections of "Act I: The Quest for Life's Work" are designed to help you discover the *content* of your life's work.

Design: We have seen that "proper art" is a kind of meditation and that its content may be any work approached in a sacred manner. What about its design? Our word *design* originates in the Latin *designare,* "to mark out."[29] By her design, the artist marks out the time and space boundaries through which she will reveal the infinite. In approaching your work as art, your first design marking is your choice of career. Every career has its own unique boundaries, limitations, and patterns, and as Joseph Campbell put it, "When you choose a vocation, you have actually chosen a model, and it will fit you in a little while."[30] Make sure it's a fit you want to live with. (Act I of this book addresses some of the "sizing" questions you may want to explore before you pick a model.)

William Blake said, "Eternity is in love with the productions of time."[31] Design is in time, both in the sense that a poem, a painting, a song, or a life's work lives in the finite world of form, and in the sense that every design reflects the historical and cultural context in which it is produced. The Infinite in Bach echoes through Baroque musical forms—e.g., fugues, masses, and concertos. The Infinite in Shakespeare speaks through the design forms of Elizabethan sonnets, comedies, histories, and tragedies. The Infinite in Michelangelo shines forth through the forms of High Renaissance sculpture, painting, and architecture. The Japanese poet Matsuo Basho revealed the Infinite in the seventeen-syllable haiku form. One feels that these great souls would have somehow expressed the Infinite, no matter the time, place, or form of their work.

The design forms these artists selected reflect the historical and cultural contexts in which they lived, as well as their own unique style. Similarly, your life's work will be shaped by the time you live in, yet it will be your own unique expression. The design of your work, the career you choose, ought to be a natural vehicle for your unique talents and temperament, so that you will be able to say with Henri Matisse, "I am unable to distinguish between the feeling I have for life and my way of expressing it." This is the essence of vocation.

＊ You will have the opportunity to shape the *design* (i.e., select your career role) of your life's work in "Act II: The Game of Life's Work."

Technique: Driven to excel in his craft, the true artist becomes a master of technique. The artist is so engaged "that he naturally possesses a sustained interest strong enough to impel and guide him through a lifetime of searching for an adequate . . . vocabulary, with which to objectify his subjective impulses."[32] Strive to be the best you can be at what you do, to expand your vocabulary in the language of your art. The essence of technique is discipline. Even as Zen embraces the necessities of physical survival, so it embraces the necessities of the *Dō* (the discipline of the work). Without regret, second thought, or self-pity, it plunges in. What must be done to perfect oneself or one's craft *is* done, without pausing to consider, Do I like to do it? As D. T. Suzuki put it, "Zen wants to act, and the most effective act is, once the mind is made up, to go on without looking backward."[33] In this way, the artist becomes first master of himself, and then of his art. Look at a painting by Zen master. In a few deliberate brushstrokes, a world of images is born. Rigorous discipline ultimately produces spontaneous ease.

All labor that uplifts humanity has dignity and importance and should be undertaken with painstaking excellence.
Martin Luther King, Jr.

＊ You will have the opportunity to consider how you can improve your capacity to excel in your career field by improving your *technique* in "Act IV: The School of Life's Work."

The Poetic Work Is Hearing and Making

Hearing	Making
Inspiration	Action
Idea	Form
Reception	Creation
Vocation	*Dō*
Use	Way
Imagination	Discipline
Inflow	Outflow
Subjective	Objective

The Life of Beauty

Modern life has altogether too much ugliness. This is doubly so since most of it is so unnecessary. The ugliness of poverty may be excused, but the ugliness of the mediocre, the bland, and the lifeless is an appalling waste. Beauty sensitizes the soul—evoking the finer, subtler feelings and inspiring noble thoughts. Ugliness depresses and diminishes life—sapping the creative spirit of the individual and weakening the character of society.

> *We have come to think of art and work as incompatible, or at least independent categories, and have for the first time in history created an industry without art.   Ananda K. Coomaraswamy*

A first-rate soup is more creative than a second-rate painting.

Abraham Maslow

There is unnecessary ugliness, not only in the things we make, but in the way we make them. Mass production ensures that quantity dominates quality and profit rules beauty. White collar or blue, the worker is taken to be a machine. Engaged, not as a whole person, but as a tool of production, he becomes alienated from his work and himself. No wonder the worker is more interested in sports or gossip than in his or her work. No wonder, in the words of popular bumper stickers, he "would rather be golfing" or she "would rather be shopping." Work devoid of meaning and spirit, work without the discipline and satisfaction of a job well done, is work without joy. So work has gotten a bad name, and we live for the weekends. Art curator and philosopher Ananda K. Coomaraswamy put it like this: "It is taken for granted that while at work we are doing what we like least, and at play what we should wish to be doing all the time."[34]

Zen and art can teach us how to work beautifully. From Zen, we can learn to embrace work, to accept responsibility for ourselves and our world, without seeking to escape. We can go deeper in our experience of Reality—finding what *lives* between the pairs of opposites. From art we can draw on the lessons of the spirit at work (the inspiration of the artist) and the lessons of dedication to and sacrifice for the vision one sees. Zen says: No sense waiting for Heaven. This very life on earth is the Buddha Realm. Therefore, let it be a beautiful life. The Buddha nature is within all things; therefore, treat them with love and kindness, care and compassion.

Conceiving of ourselves as artists in whatever work we do gives us a metaphor for a life of integrity, service, enjoyment, and excellence. We can draw strength from the lives of the great artists and cultivate an appreciation of their works. Really, there is no significant transformation of our increasingly global culture without changing our ideas about what work is and what work is for. Conceiving of ourselves as artists and injecting the spirit of beauty into our work from beginning to end can play an important role in this transformation. Cultivating an appreciation of art and the artistic life fosters a desire to serve humanity in a spirit of beauty—no matter one's calling.

Learning to appreciate the art of others is as much a part of building a beautiful world as developing the artist within ourselves. Real art appreciation will produce not only more and better contemplative or "fine" artists but also better carpenters, nurses, scientists, teachers, humanitarians, and entrepreneurs, and most importantly, better (more awake) human beings. Art is for the sake of the living everywhere. Its lessons, traditions, and revelations belong to us all.

Many today would have us believe that art is for the cultured few—the museum hounds and the wine-and-cheese set. The implication is that art is too good to be contaminated with the vulgar business of living. While art is safely locked away from the soiling hands of the common man, the greatest vulgarity of all is perpetuated. Art is reduced to an investment commodity to be hoarded or exchanged like so many trade beads.

Beauty is truth, truth beauty,—that is all Ye know on earth, and all ye need to know.

John Keats

To have great poets, there must be great audiences.

Walt Whitman

It is clear that even without cultivating a deep appreciation or understanding, art speaks to us all. One doesn't have to understand a cathedral to appreciate its beauty, or comprehend a musical composition to be moved by it. You certainly don't have to be a poet, playwright, director, or scholar to appreciate a Shakespearean play. Something within us recognizes art. Perhaps it is because we ourselves are artists at heart. Even as we all share in a spiritual life, whether we are "enlightened" or not, so we are all artists—whether masters, journeymen, apprentices, or hacks. Cultivating awareness of the art we are called to perform and awareness of the manner in which we perform it can only improve us as craftsmen and as human beings.

To say that everyone can be an artist is in no way meant to denigrate the arts—to cheapen or to lessen the standards of excellence in any of the arts. It is not that we all take dance classes and are suddenly "dancers" or that we take creative writing classes

For man is by nature an artist.

Tagore

and are now "poets." It is rather that in whatever our craft, we lift ourselves to the highest standards of excellence in that field. This doesn't mean that we cannot as amateurs enjoy dancing or writing or singing; indeed, these brighten our lives. (What we practice as amateurs may enrich our vocations or even turn out to be our vocations.) It is simply to recognize the difference between being an amateur and being an artist in any field. Of course, all arts or artists are not equal. It is absurd to compare a well-cooked meal with Mozart's *Requiem*, or the local home architect with Michelangelo; but it is even more absurd to eat tasteless meals or live in cracker-box houses because their makers aren't Mozarts or Michelangelos. If we are called to be cooks or architects, brain surgeons, or whatever-it-might-be, we can aspire to be the best we can be at our professions. Beautiful clothing, lovely meals, well-designed homes, parks, and cities uplift the spirit of man. They reveal a vision of beauty, of the mystery of life, and in this, they are art.

In Japan, the place where "the art" is practiced is called the *"Dō-Jo,"* or "house of enlightenment." There is a popular saying: "The *Dō-Jo* is everywhere." Wherever work is done in a present, conscious way, there is the house of enlightenment. Transformation is the action of both spiritual liberation and art. Zen sees, in the stuff of suffering, the tools for liberation. For the artist, the physical world provides the raw materials for revealing a higher consciousness of Beauty.

The only lasting beauty is the beauty of the heart.
Rumi

It is, of course, in the imagination that all art begins. In the words of Jacob Bronowski, "The characteristic gift that makes us human is . . . the gift of imagination. The power that man has over nature and himself lies in his command of imaginary experience."[35] The art of life is facing that awful power and leading it in the way of Beauty, until it learns to find its way—naturally. Dostoyevsky said, "Beauty will save the world." Beauty rightly understood and widely practiced *will* save the world. It is not too far-fetched to imagine a civilization of artists working in love and joy to reveal a world of Beauty. Though it may take a thousand years, we can begin at once.

To believe that what has not occurred in history will not occur at all, is to argue disbelief in the dignity of man.

Mahatma Gandhi

Modern Artists on Spirit

Everything passes, and what remains of former times, what remains of life, is the spiritual. In everything we do, the claim of the Absolute is unchanging.
            Paul Klee

Whoever does not detach himself from the ego never attains the Absolute and never deciphers life.
            Constantin Brâncuşi

If the universal is the essential, then it is the basis of all life and art. Recognizing and uniting with the universal therefore gives us the greatest aesthetic satisfaction, the greatest emotion of beauty. The more this union with the universal is felt, the more individual subjectivity declines.
            Piet Mondrian

Construction on a purely spiritual basis is a slow business . . . The artist must train not only his eye but also his soul.
            Wassily Kandinsky

Something sacred, that's it. We ought to be able to say that such and such a painting is as it is, with its capacity for power, because it is "touched by God."
            Pablo Picasso

Firmament and planets both disappeared, but the mighty breath which gives life to all things and in which all is bound up remained.

            Vincent van Gogh,
            describing Starry Night

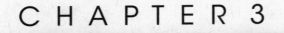

CHAPTER 3

Myth at Work; Or, Crafting the Story of Your Life

The role of the artist I now understood as that of revealing through the world-surfaces the implicit forms of the soul, and the great agent to assist the artist was the myth.
Joseph Campbell

T he word *myth* means story. But a genuine myth is not just any story. It is a story of an encounter with universal human energies and experience. It is, as Joseph Campbell said in his final and most refined definition, "a metaphor transparent to transcendence."[1] If we approach myth as fact, it is clearly ridiculous. We don't really think that a god named Zeus had a splitting headache from which (with the help of an ax) Athena sprang, or that a guy named Ulysses went around in a boat encountering Sirens and Cyclopes. It is not as fact but as metaphor that the mythic stories speak to us. To approach myth as fact is to miss the point. Similarly, to view your life as "nothing but the facts" is to miss an opportunity for a marvelous adventure, a conscious encounter with the universal energies and dilemmas of the human experience. In this encounter, we take the hero's journey, we experience life as art, we put "soul" into our work.

Think of a work of art, a great literary work, for example. A great work of art *is* a great work of art because it reveals the universal in the particular—so that across time, place, and culture, we experience the works of Homer or Virgil, Dante or Shakespeare, speaking directly to us. To view your life as a mythic story, to approach it as a work of art, is to recognize the play of the universal in the particulars of your life. This chapter will identify some of these "universal energies" and how you might consciously, constructively, and artistically engage them on the way to creating your life's work.

The myths hold keys to a timeless psychology of creativity. Clearly, if we are to be artists of life, it is useful for us to have some understanding of the psychology of the creative process. But what does myth have to do with psychology? To begin with, in its life-instructing function—in what it can tell us about how to live—myth *is* psychology, in the literal meaning of the word *psycho* (soul) and *logos* (description). As the word itself implies, the work of any genuine psychology is to chart the landscape of the soul. This landscape comes to life in vivid detail in the world's great mythology.

Where the Zen poetry of work is in the now, immediate experience of *being*, the psychology or mythology of work considers the process of *becoming*. It describes the soul's journey, the pilgrim's progress, if you will, and the inner territory one encounters on this journey of becoming. Through the ages and across cultures, there have been many psychologies (soul descriptions). They were traditionally expressed in the intuitive language of myth and symbol, a language we have largely forgotten. As a result, much of the wisdom of these ancient psychologies remains a mystery to us. Recently, Jungian psychology (the only widely popular modern psychology that, in fact, *is* one, i.e., the only one concerned with describing the landscape of the soul) has begun to provide a framework through which we can begin to approach some of these soul mysteries. The discussion below will briefly consider three basic elements of this framework—myth, archetype, and symbol—and then go on to consider four universal or archetypal energies that we can play with in creating life's work.

Myth and Archetype: For Joseph Campbell, "myth is the secret opening through which the inexhaustible energies of the cosmos pour into human cultural manifestation."[2] These "inexhaustible energies" of the cosmos are what Carl Jung referred to as *archetypes*. Archetypes, as Jung defined them, are the primordial energies that underlie human consciousness. How these energies got there is not entirely clear. Yet whether they are a sort of a human

The one thing in the world, of value, is the active soul.

Emerson

microcosm of the great macrocosmic energies of the universe, an intrinsic part of human biology, or dispositions acquired through common human experience is not the central point for Jung. The point is that they *exist* as a fundamental part of human experience, and that we are better off for learning to recognize and come to terms with them.

The archetypes provide the cosmic or psychic raw material of myth. Across cultures and time, we see this same basic psychic stuff, or raw material, worked and reworked in great variety. The mythic stories, their heroes, friends, and foes, their deeds and adventures, are particular representations of these archetypal energies. No matter how the stories of world mythology differ in detail, one can always recognize common themes. These common themes arise from the universality of the archetypes.

Symbol: If the archetypes are the raw material of myth, then symbols are its vocabulary. Symbols are the language of the imagination—the active ingredients of mythology and psychology. As Carl Jung said, "The psychological mechanism that transforms energy is the symbol."[3] He elsewhere tells us what this "transformation" is all about: "The symbols act as transformers, their function is to convert libido from a 'lower' into a 'higher' form."[4]

> *The degradation of the sense of symbol in modern society is one of its many signs of spiritual decay.*
> Thomas Merton

Symbols transform the energy of the individual and collective psyche. The power of symbol lies in its capacity to transcend the limits of reason—to penetrate the conscious mind and communicate directly with the subconscious. While this power is enormous, it is not always well used. Allowing, as Jung suggests, that the *true function* of symbol is to convert "lower" libido energies into a "higher" form, we mustn't get the idea that the power of symbol (or sign) can't be used for more malevolent aims. The mass hysteria of the Nazis, for example, relied upon a peculiar brand of mythic interpretation and the very deliberate, effective, and perverse use of symbol and ritual.

The secret of art is love.

Antoine Bourdelle

The power of symbol should hardly surprise us. We need not be students of mythology or history to understand its effect. Advertisers use symbols every day to try to transform our energy so we will buy their products. The logical connections between cowboys and cigarettes, half-naked women and beer, babies and tires may be dubious, but the power of these images is not in dispute.

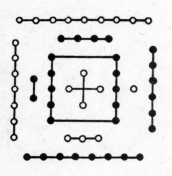

Whoever controls the media—the images—controls the culture.

Allen Ginsberg

Today, the power of symbol is wielded with greatest effect, not by its traditional keepers in religion and art, but by Madison Avenue and political image-makers, Hollywood and commercial television, MTV and the recording "industry." We are everywhere surrounded by what James Joyce called "pornographic art," the use of symbols as tools of manipulation (see chapter 2).

While dictators and advertisers certainly know and use the power of symbols as psychological tools of transformation, the scientific view of life and "scientific psychology" in particular tend to downplay their power in the inner life of the individual. This has important consequences. As Jung says, "Modern man does not understand how much his 'rationalism' (which has destroyed his capacity to respond to numinous symbols and ideas) has put him at the mercy of the psychic underworld. He has freed himself from 'superstition' (or so he believes), but in the process, he has lost his spiritual values to a positively dangerous degree."[5] One of Jung's principal arguments is that the psychic energy field we call the "subconscious" is an inescapable part of the structure of the human being. We can no more step outside of this field than we can exist without the water that comprises most of our bodies. We delude ourselves if we think we can deny or rationalize it away. Symbols are important because they both activate and reveal this psychic field.

Through the centuries, religion and art used the power of symbol *as an end in itself* for the transformation of consciousness, to uplift and awaken. Today their influence is minimal. Instead, politicians use this power *as a means* to gain and maintain control; commercialists use it to sell products. If we are to take control of our own destinies, we must reclaim this power for ourselves as individuals. We must consciously develop our own relationships to myth, archetype, and symbol.

Symbolism is no mere idle fancy or corrupt degeneration: it is inherent in the very texture of human life.

Alfred North Whitehead

That's what this chapter is all about—encouraging you: first, to experience your life as myth, as a story of the individual encounter with the universal; second, and as a part of the first, to learn to recognize the universal or archetypal energies; third, to develop your own creative relationship to these energies. In this way, the "inexhaustible energies" of the cosmos can pour into your life and, in so doing, transform you and the world around you.

This chapter will present four archetypes that I trust you will recognize and hope you will engage on your journey to life's work. These are the Hero, the Magician, the Warrior, and the Scholar (or Student-Sage). Developing your own symbolic relationship with these archetypal energies can transform your experience of work (and life). These four archetypes can help us to begin to approach a psychology of work—work as a means of soul development—as well as providing deep insight into the creative process. These archetypes show up all over the place in mythic stories and adventures. Are they the only ones? Of course not. I've chosen these particular archetypes because I've found them to be especially useful in creating life's work. While they do in some way parallel the four wisdoms of Zen Buddhism (The Great Perfect Mirror Wisdom, The Marvelous Observing Wisdom, The Perfecting-of-Action Wisdom, and The Universal Nature Wisdom),[6] they do not belong to any tradition, but arise, as it were, from life itself. Names for these universal energies vary and are less important than the energies themselves.

Around the world, teachings relating to the four directions or four wisdoms abound. The four directions of the Native American medicine wheel, the four rivers of the Garden of Eden, the four gardens of the Islamic Paradise, the four sons of Horus in Egyptian mythology, and the four Holy Living Creatures of Ezekiel's vision (eagle, lion, man, bull), often portrayed as the four authors of the gospels in Christian sacred art, are just a few examples. Of course, this list is hardly complete. My aim is not to catalogue representations of the fourfold energies, but to show how we can engage these universal energies in the specific and ongoing process of creating and maintaining a life's work. Still, I would be remiss if I did not point out that the presentation that follows only hints at the profound wisdom of the sacred four as revealed in wisdom teachings from around the world.

Before exploring each of the archetypes in greater detail, it's worth emphasizing that archetypal energies are simply that—energies. Like the four elements to which they, in some essential way, correspond, these energies may take positive or negative expression. We can experience water as refreshing spring or raging flood; fire, as light and heat or as hellish holocaust. Air can kiss with a cool, gentle breeze or ravage with a mighty cyclone; earth can give the bounty of food, or quake with terror and spit molten rock. The value of working deliberately with the archetypes is to move into a conscious and constructive experience of the vital energies they represent. Whether we are aware of it or not, we are all dealing with archetypal energies. In Jungian terms, negative manifestations of archetypal energies result from their denial or suppression, and are

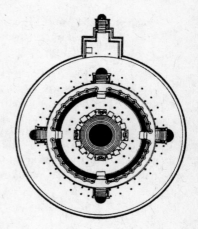

The Universal is always the same, the specifics are always different.

Robert Aitken

Symbols of the Archetypes

Perhaps the best or easiest way to understand the action or function of the archetypes we are referring to is to consider the symbols with which they are often associated.

The Hero

The Seeker of the Grail—The Decider of Roads: Two of the strongest symbols of the Hero are the cup, or Grail, and the road, or path of adventure. The Grail represents the Quest, the Hero as Seeker. It signifies the fullest potential of life, the yearning for one's true life. The road represents choice, the crossroads of decision, the Hero as Decider. What will you give your life for? Whom does the Grail serve? The key for the Hero is consecration to a higher-than-self purpose. The test is the choice between creative problems and neurotic problems. Decide to seek and decide to honor what you find.

The Magician

The Showman—The Shaman: Two of the strongest symbols of the Magician are the mask and the wand. The mask represents the play in illusion, the Showman Magician donning costume and role. The wand represents the mastery of the forces of nature, the Shaman or Master Magician consciously invoking the cosmic powers of Light. The key for the Magician is developing detachment and clear perception. The test is: Are you psyched up or psyched out for the game of life? Imagine how to make your work play.

The Warrior

The Horseman—The Swordsman: Prime symbols of the Warrior are the horse and the sword. Riding the horse signifies the mastery of the animal nature, or aggressive energy. The Warrior can mount the magic horse of creative aggression and ride like the wind. The Warrior's sword, spear, lance, or arrow is that which penetrates. Penetration is achieved through concentration. The Warrior has developed the power of single-minded concentration. The key for the Warrior is endurance. The test is: Will you persist or give up? Will yourself to fight for what you love.

The Scholar (Student-Sage)

The Child—The Old Wise Ones: Two of the strongest symbols for this aspect are the child and the old wise ones or grandparents. The Nativity is a kind of veneration of the child. All hope, all potential for growth and learning are there in the child. All the suffering of humanity, and the compassion we feel for all humanity, are there in the child. (One who can't feel compassion for children can't feel at all.) The veneration of the old wise ones signifies respect for the wisdom tradition. Myths and stories represent the wisdom and knowledge of the old, the continuity of human experience. The key for the Scholar is the heart of intuition. The test is: Are you a steward or owner of knowledge? Keep growing and giving all your days.

called *shadow* aspects (more on this below). The four archetypical energies considered in this chapter are sketched below.

Hero—The Creative Power of Decision: Decision making is an essential part of human life; no matter what you do, you will always make decisions. The power to decide what to focus on, in other words the power to decide what is important and the power to decide what you want to create, are essential to the creative life. The decisions we make about our work lives are especially important, since most of us will spend more of our waking lives working than doing anything else. Your choices will affect not only yourself and those closest to you but also, in some way, the whole world. The Hero energy is about claiming the decision-making power, being conscious of the decisions you make, and accepting responsibility for them.

Magician—The Creative Power of Imagination: Imagination is an essential part of human life; no matter what you do, your imagination is doing something. If imagination is not set to the task of building a creative life, it busies itself weaving a web of fear and doubt, blame and excuse. How well you use your imagination can mean the difference between succeeding and failing in your work. The power to deliberately and effectively move your imagination and the power to receive and interpret the spontaneous promptings of your imagination are essential to the creative life. The Magician energy is about embracing imaginative power, being conscious of what your imagination is doing in shaping and responding to the events of your life, and accepting responsibility for how you use this power.

Warrior—The Creative Power of Aggressive Action: Aggressive energy is an essential part of human life; no matter what you do, you will always have aggressive energy. You can use it for good or for ill, or deny it altogether and turn it against yourself. Nevertheless, aggressive energy will always be a part of your life. The power to summon aggressive energy (willpower) and the power to direct this energy toward the accomplishment of constructive purposes are essential to the creative life. It will take the disciplined and concentrated use of aggressive energy to accomplish your life's work. Wimping out, getting bitter or hostile, will limit your creative capacity. The Warrior energy is about fully embracing the aggressive power, being conscious of how you are channeling your aggressive energy, and accepting responsibility for how you use this power.

Scholar—The Creative Power of Learning and Teaching: Learning and teaching are essential to human life; no matter what

Myths are clues to the spiritual potentialities of the human life.

Joseph Campbell

you do, you will always be learning and teaching something. You can learn about sports or celebrity gossip, about what time various television shows come on, or you can learn about that which, in some way, makes your world a better place. You can, by your example, teach about greed and indifference, derision and confusion, or you can, by example, teach how we can all live together in harmonious and beautiful ways. To succeed in the new economy, you will need to become a lifelong learner. You will also likely want to exemplify (teach by example) what you consider to be constructive and uplifting. The Scholar energy is about claiming the learning/teaching power, being fully conscious of what you are learning and teaching, and fully accepting responsibility for how you use this power.

> *Look within. Within is the fountain of good, and it will ever bubble up, if thou wilt ever dig.*
> *Marcus Aurelius*

We can think of the Self as the artist of life, wielding the awesome creative powers of decision making, imagination, will (aggressive action), and learning and teaching—building a life of beauty on these four pillars. The key is consciousness. As Jung put it, "In the history of the collective, as in the history of the individual, everything depends on the development of consciousness."[7] *Becoming fully conscious of these inner powers and creatively engaging them in your own life can transform your experience in a variety of ways.*

The Hero (The Quest for Life's Work)

Imagine, for example, that in approaching the Quest for life's work, you view and experience yourself as a hero or heroine tracking a great treasure which, having won, you will bring back for all to see and enjoy.[8] This is a qualitatively different experience from "looking for a good job" or "finding a niche." You are a Parzival or Psyche. However you frame it, or name it, you are a hero—moving into the field of the Quest—following your bliss. You are not a confused, pathetic groper who doesn't know what to do with your life; you are a Hero on a Quest for your own best Self. You have decided to continue seeking until you find what is really meaningful for you.

The Seeker of the Grail

You can tell when people are putting their whole selves into their work and you can tell when they are just going through the motions.

More often than not, those who put their entire selves into their work are the ones who put their entire selves into the Quest to find it—and who keep questing the whole of their lives. Embracing the Quest puts you on a continuingly unfolding path of self-discovery. People often remain in untenable work situations (or any untenable situation) because they put a negative frame around the process of looking for a better way. It's not that these folks are lazy. It's that they feel threatened by the process of questioning themselves and their assumptions about work on a deeper level. They are uncomfortable asking questions that they don't have ready answers for.

The Hero is comfortable with not knowing, yet unwilling to tolerate confusion. His comfort with not knowing gets him going on the Quest; his unwillingness to tolerate confusion keeps him going until he has answers that ring true for *him*. Behind every significant invention, creative work of art, or advance in scientific understanding, there was someone who was willing to experience the tension between not knowing and not accepting confusion. This creative discontent is beautifully expressed by Albert Einstein: "The years of searching in the dark for a truth that one feels but cannot express, the intense desire and the alternations of confidence and misgiving, until one breaks through to clarity and understanding, are only known to him who has himself experienced them." This is hero stuff—seeking and searching for a better way, bravely moving through the dark unknowing.

Think of how embarrassed most people are with not knowing what they are going to do next. While the Hero is comfortable with "I don't know yet; I am still seeking, probing, searching," the average Joe thinks he must have all the answers right away. He feels anxiety at the prospect of not knowing, and so clings to something pat—in other words, to something he has been told and has accepted without examination. He has no aim. He doesn't know what to do with his life. He's been told that an MBA or a law degree, a computer science degree or sales training, or whatever else, will do the trick. After that, it's just play the game and rise to the top. Typically, he'll get so caught up in this game, so busy trying to succeed or just keep up, that he dare not ask if he's doing what he wants to do. Then, as he approaches forty, it hits him. This *is* his life.

Some grasp at pat answers; others accept confusion and muddling as the natural order of things. They've resigned themselves to not knowing and have given up even the idea of the Quest. Their "not knowing" isn't a matter of having yet to find an answer. Indeed, they shape no question. Confusion hangs over them, an amorphous, ubiquitous cloud of doubt and despair. Those who cling to pat answers tend toward anxiety and defensiveness; the more

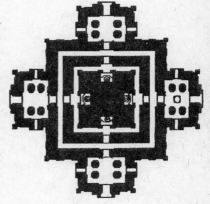

Be patient toward all that is unresolved in your heart and try to love the questions themselves.

Rainer Maria Rilke

The hero's will is not that of his ancestors nor of his society, but his own. This will to be oneself is heroism.

Ortega y Gasset

resigned, toward depression. True Heroes have the strength to ask the really big questions, questions like Who am I? and What in the world am I doing here?—and the strength to stay with them until they find satisfying answers.

The Hero as seeker decides what to focus on. He makes value choices. The Hero exercises judgment, selecting what is worthy of his time, attention, and energy—what is worthy of his life. George Bernard Shaw said of the creative process, "You imagine what you desire; you will what you imagine; and at last you create what you will." Desire begins the creative process, setting imagination and will (aggressive action) to work. The Hero's seeking informs desire—before he wants, he asks what to want. He recognizes that we tend to desire what we focus our attention on, and that what we focus on is often more someone else's doing than our own. Parents, teachers, television programmers, movie producers, newspaper editors, etc., select what we focus on, and in so doing, shape our desires. The Hero decides for himself what to focus his attention on (what is important), and, in so doing, he determines what the story of his life will be about.

Man's activity consists in either a making or doing. Both of these aspects of the active life depend for their correction upon the contemplative life (that is, the Hero).

Ananda K. Coomaraswamy

Many of us first contact this seeking aspect of the Hero in our youth. Sometime in our late high school or early college years, a lot of us begin to examine where the values and ideologies that inform our society match and conflict with the directions we'd like to take in our own lives. We are young and idealistic and not yet heavily invested in the status quo. Exposure to history, anthropology, sociology, art, mythology, literature, and philosophy, etc., teaches us that ours is not the only way to organize this thing called human society. We begin to see more clearly the nature of our particular culture from the reference point of others. If we are fortunate enough to travel abroad, all of this is brought home even more dramatically.

The realization of choice and the potential for change hit us like a bolt of lightning—the way we do it in this society is *not* the only way. There are many ways. There is nothing sacrosanct about the choices we have made—as individuals or collectively. We understand that many options are available to us now, and that, in some way, they always will be in the future. We are exposed to so many ideas, values, choices. We may even come to realize that "social reality" exists only because people agree to it, and only for as long as they agree to it. Likewise, we may realize that our individual "reality" is plastic, molded by the questions we choose to answer with our lives.

About the time we're really getting into all this, we're faced with the fact that our college days will soon be history. Now it's time to go out into the "real world." "Real" here, of course, means sanctioned, socially approved, conventional, having no more or less reality than any other social order—past, present, or possible. The "real" world of today's Western society may ignore values you identified with in your youthful questing, while emphasizing values that you've come to reject for yourself. But now, all of a sudden: *Nobody's asking what you think, buster.*

It's time to get a job. Time to forget all that stuff about choices. Don't think about visions or values. Don't concern yourself with whys. Just be responsible [*sic*] and concentrate on how you can get the "best" job. Suppress your awareness of yourself as an observer and creator of social reality and plunge into playing the game as it is already defined, with your eyes closed. We have seen other ways. We are aware of choice, and yet if we are to be "responsible" citizens, we must try to forget. Be a good kid, now, and get yourself heavily involved in the game of winning social approval—anything else and you risk ostracism. That's enough to keep most of us in line for a long time. We still think about these things—now and then. We may talk about it some weekend, late at night, over a few beers or glasses of wine. As we grow older, we may bore our children with repeated tellings of stories about the good old days of our freedom (of choice). What was questing, searching, evaluating now gets stuffed, shelved, and compartmentalized. But make no mistake; it is not dead. It is only sleeping.

Once we've seen the light of choice, we must put on blinders in order to go back to sleep. The trouble is, we put these blinders on by choice, and in awareness of the choice. We will go along, though we know the emperor has no clothes. This makes it difficult to fall into a really deep sleep. It's more of a waking trance. We may struggle to keep our eyes closed, but from time to time, the light gets in anyway. Its perception reminds us of how alienated we feel, mostly from ourselves. Whatever happened to all those choices, all those possibilities? What happened to the life you intended? Now everything seems set in stone, and we are quickly turning into stone. Of course, whether you've gotten off the trail or are just taking it up for the first time, it's never too late to take up the Quest.

Awaken the Hero. Don't be afraid to seek, to ask deep questions, or to stay with them until you have answers that really work for you. In Norse mythology, the first man was named *Ask*. It's our ability to ask questions that sets us apart from other sentient

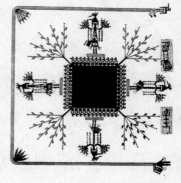

I was so full of sleep at the time that I left the true way.

Dante

*Questions are the
creative acts
of intelligence.*

Frank Kingdon-Ward

beings. Humans ask. Whether or not we are conscious of it, our lives are the answers to the questions we ask. Most only ask the questions prescribed by their societies. The Hero asks his or her own questions. In "Act I: The Quest for Life's Work," you will be encouraged to identify the questions you were asking that put you in your current work situation, and invited to engage new questions that will bring you a more fulfilling experience of work.

The Decider or Chooser of Roads

As well as the quester or questioner, the Hero is the inner King or Queen, the chooser, the decider, the one who gives directions, who sets the life course. This is the aspect of the Hero as conscience. In Sanskrit, it's called *buddhi*, the higher intelligence that perceives, discerns, and decides. *Buddhi* is sometimes translated "discriminative will" because it takes effort to see things as they are and decide to change. When you are sleepy in the morning, it takes effort to wake up and get out of bed. In the same way, when we're unconsciously following some life pattern, it takes effort to wake up and assert a new direction. The Hero ventures into the dark forest of the unknown, and when he comes to see the light, he is determined to live by the light he sees. Because his vision, or clarity, is hard-won, he is not easily dissuaded from his insights. Homer describes the Hero when he says, "What he greatly thought he nobly dared." To "greatly think" and consciously decide what your life will be about—this is Hero work.

Life is either a daring adventure or it is nothing.
Helen Keller

The Hero is the chooser at the crossroads of life. She admits that she and we always have a choice and that she and we are always responsible for what is chosen. The first choice of the Hero is the choice to be one, to live a life of consciousness and responsibility. *To choose a life direction is the Hero's greatest choice.* The Hero's life course is never merely an automatic or conditioned response to events. It is a choice. She chooses to be conscious of the choices she makes and accepts full responsibility for the same. She knows that the greater her awareness, the better the choices she will make. She makes awareness a friend that she is willing to listen to, even when this friend tells her it's time to make major changes in her life.

While our culture celebrates the executive function (Warrior), we hardly recognize, let alone honor, the Hero as the one who decides what is worthy of being done. The Hero takes time to look and see before moving forward. Most rush ahead, too busy to think about where they are going or why. Together we crash about like a giant headless horseman, hardly aware of where we are going or the effect we are having on the world around us. The Hero is the one who sets the direction for the Warrior. The warrior energy of the insecure nowhere man is ripe for the plucking. Since he has no purpose of his own, he is only all too ready to give his will, his ambition, his drive, over to someone else's aims. He can be, and often is, manipulated for all kinds of foolishness. In this, we can wonder with Shakespeare at "what men do daily not knowing what they do." We are often told that it takes courage to be a Warrior, but it takes even more courage to be a Hero. The Hero has the courage to be an individual, to follow a path he chooses for himself.

The Hero's motivation is love. He is moved by something bigger than his self-interest. Inspired and nourished by a larger-than-self purpose, his life is so radically transformed that without anything changing—everything is different. The suffering he experiences is no longer merely personal suffering, but human suffering. The work that he does is no longer personal work, but humanity's work. The energies that he employs are no longer mere personality traits, but aspects of great mythological archetypes.

> *When we quit thinking primarily about ourselves and our own self-preservation, we undergo a truly heroic transformation of consciousness.*
> *Joseph Campbell*

The Hero sets the agenda for the other creative powers, commanding them to transform his or her visions into reality. When the Hero is in charge, the Magician, the Warrior, and the Scholar serve the life directions that the Hero sets forth. When the Hero post is occupied by the insecure nowhere man, these other energies are left to fend for themselves. They are then as likely to create mischief as they are to bring us benefit. Because in relation to the other archetypes the Hero is first among equals, this archetype will be discussed at length in the next chapter.

Shadow Play: The shadow hero is the nowhere man, without self-awareness or real direction. The nowhere man is insecure and indecisive. He doesn't know who he is, what he wants, or where he is going. The nowhere man thinks: It's a beautiful day, someone paid me a compliment, the deal closed, or it's payday. Life is good. But the next day, it's cold and raining, he feels his aches and pains a little more acutely, his boss is upset, he lost money in the stock

All truth is an achievement. If you would have truth at its value, go win it.

T. T. Munger

market or finds out he has unexpected expenses. He thinks: Life sucks. His days go on like this, a virtual roller coaster of elation and depression. That is why he's called the nowhere man. As he has no deep well of meaning, no enduring Bliss, his happiness is subject to the winds of fortune, which blow him this way, then that.

The Magician (The Game of Life's Work)

Once the Hero has determined a direction or outcome he would like to pursue, he hands the project over to the Magician. The inner Hero says, Imagine this! and the inner Magician goes to work making a mental mock-up of the result. The Magician is the ruler of the I-Magi-Nation. The true Magi, or Magicians, are those who have mastered the creative powers of the imagination. Of course, the inner Magician, or imagination, is just as active when it's under the muddled command of the nowhere man. Depending on who is in charge, the magician is a powerful, creative ally, a pesky nuisance, or a positively dangerous foe.

The true Magician makes her magic in accord with the Hero's directions and as a reflection of the poetic view of life. At work, she plays out the ritual game of career, puts on costume and mask, and wields the secret knowledge of her craft. She knows there is magic in making, in creating. In antiquity, gods and goddesses and/or magical rites were associated with all the crafts: weaving, metallurgy, healing, writing, dance, theater, farming, cooking, architecture, music, oratory, history, etc. In ancient Hawaii, the spirit masters were called *kahunas*. One *kahuna* might be a sorcerer (shaman); another, a healer; a third, an expert canoe maker. Yet, as all worked in the realm of the spirit, all made magic. Today, we can treat the work we do with a similar sense of reverence and respect. We make our own "magic arts" by working in a sacred manner.

Artist! You are a magician: Art is the great miracle.
Péladan

Cosmic Theater: The Great Magic Show

Theater and stagecraft have a kind of magic in their capacity to pull us into a world of illusion. East Indian cosmology views the world, indeed the entire material creation, as a kind of giant cosmic theater—the *lila,* or play, of creation in the realm of *maya,* or illusion.[9] Shakespeare gives us a similar notion in his "All the world's a stage, and all the men and women merely players." Our word *illusion* originates from the Latin *illudere*, literally "to play on."[10] Illusion is what we play on and in. Think of a Hollywood set version of a town from the Old West. The illusion of a town is created by a series of storefront facades. It's not a "real" town, yet the storefronts are made of "real" stuff—boards, nails, and paint. Likewise, Hindu cosmology tells us that the appearance of the world around us is an illusion, a stage set, but that this set is made of real stuff. The Buddha said that it is with our minds (imaginations) that we shape the world into its many appearances. Individually and collectively, we can consciously wield the awesome power of imagination to create the results we seek or we can allow our unconscious minds to squander this power in self-defeating or destructive ways.

> *We are what we think. All that we are arises with our thoughts. With our thoughts we make the world.*
> *Buddha*

The Showman and His Box of Magic Props

The Magician is always dealing with image and perception. The showman Magician (illusionist) knows how the illusion is created. If you do a sleight-of-hand trick for me and I say, "Wow, that's magic!"—you don't think that you really made the ball or quarter disappear. You know how the trick is done. For one not to be fooled by illusion, he must first be disillusioned; that is, he must see how the trick is done. This is when, as Alan Watts said, the life of Zen begins.[11] If you need to be somebody special or always on top, if it matters too much to you what people think or you're ashamed of this or that, then you're ready to be tricked. Before you can be a real Magician, you must first become disillusioned with all of that (see "Playing the Game: Winners, Losers, and Choosers," page 250). When we understand that we are not these egos or *persona* masks that we pretend to be, we are freer to play with the illusion stuff of ego and personality—freer to play the Magician. Seeing through the illusion keeps you from being intimidated or overly impressed by the images (magic) that others project. Refuse to believe that anyone is fundamentally better or worse than you, and you liberate psychic energy that can be channeled into creating the outcomes you envision.

Where we encounter ceremony, rituals, secrets, the psychic—be it the psych up or the psych out—this is the realm of the Magician. We may think of this type of magic as a relic from bygone days when

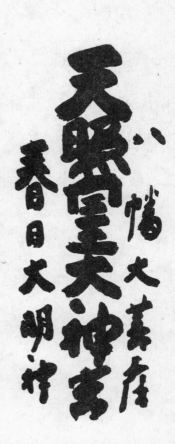

> *Men are so simple and yield so readily to the desires of the moment that he who will trick will always find another who will suffer himself to be tricked.*
>
> *Machiavelli*

superstitious people lived in fear of ghosts and demons. Still, we can recognize magical elements in a host of rituals that populate modern life. For example, why do judges still wear black robes? What practical purpose do these serve? Perhaps the donning of the ceremonial costume is meant to impress upon the minds of the participants that this is no mere mortal, but one possessed with the supernatural power to preside over the fates of others. Why do high school and college students still don the medieval cap and gown at their graduations? Why do we wear white at weddings, or black at funerals? We have some sense of these events as magic rituals that require the proper costumes.

The Magician uses tools such as symbol, suggestion, visualization, ritual, costume, language, and space to make his art. For better or worse, this kind of magic is all around us, though we often fail to appreciate the effect it has on us. Just a few of the many elements of magic that play out in our everyday lives are considered below.

The Magic of Symbol: Symbols have the power to elicit positive or negative reactions at a subtle unconscious level. Corporations spend millions on the design and marketing of their corporate logos because they recognize the psychological power of symbols. Chrysler and the five-pointed star, Safeway and the *Tai Chi* symbol, Swiss financial giant UBS and the three inverted keys—none of these symbols were chosen by accident. All have deep unconscious resonances. The Great Seal of the United States of America (printed on every dollar bill) is a kind of super-symbol loaded with occult symbols. The swastika, ancient symbol of life, has come to be so closely associated with the Nazis that today many cannot look at it without feeling fear, horror, or anger. National flags are such powerful symbols that people are ready to die for them. The Upanishads (*Chhāndogya*) declare that OM is the greatest symbol—the one we should follow. More than we may realize, we are following symbols of one kind or another.

The Magic of Suggestion: Advertisers use the magic of suggestion in the endless barrage of commercial messages to which we are all subjected. Politicians know that by endlessly repeating slogans or attack lines they can influence many voters. The news media use a kind of suggestive power in what they select as worthy of coverage. Peer pressure has suggestive power, as does association. It's a truism that people tend to become like those with whom they associate. Parents who tell their children they are stupid and will never amount to anything, and people who tell themselves they will succeed, are using the power of suggestion. Whether or not we are aware of it, the magic of suggestion is shaping our experience of the world.

The Magic of Visualization: In recent years, a growing number of books and scientific articles have documented the extraordinary power that visualization has to affect physical results. If visualization can actually increase the weight Olympic weight lifters can lift or can reduce the size of cancerous tumors, it can certainly be a powerful tool in creating the results you want in your life.[12] Today, visualization exercises have been integrated into programs designed for business, education, health, wellness, sports, and more (see page 538). But the truth is, we are visualizing all the time. The mental pictures we repeatedly focus on shape our lives, whether or not we are even aware of them. For better or worse, what we repeatedly see in our mind's eye has a way of manifesting in our lives.

The Magic of Ritual: Ritual is so much a part of our daily lives that we scarcely notice it. The handshake ritual is said to have developed as a means of demonstrating that people held no weapons; the wine-tasting ritual, as a means of discovering whether or not the vino was poisoned. We still carry important papers about in animal skins and wear hides on our feet and around our waists. Surely, there is some old animal magic in this. From the minutiae of etiquette to elaborate ceremonies, the diplomatic relations between nations are highly ritualized. In business, the typical job interview is a kind of ritual, with each party acting from an unwritten script. Prior to their performances, many athletes, actors, and others engage in personal rituals that may be merely superstitious or that may provide psychological anchors to certain attitudes or states of mind they want to invoke prior to their performance. At their best, rituals elevate consciousness or diffuse potentially discordant situations.

The Magic of Costume: For the last couple hundred years, men have worn the suit and tie uniform. In the last fifty years, many business and professional women have worn some variation of the traditional man's suit. Prior to the French Revolution, men's dress (to say nothing of women's) was more varied and, at least among the well-to-do, much more colorful, ornate, and elegant. The stoic military-like costume of the suit and tie grew out of the infatuation with Roman law, custom, and culture that attended the French Revolution. Putting on the suit and tie is a ritual that affects body carriage, speech, and ways of relating. When a group of men in this attire change into more comfortable clothing, different manners of speech, movement, and interaction are immediately apparent. To appreciate the power of costume magic, imagine people the world over forsaking the suit for more comfortable and colorful clothing.

大毘盧舍那佛

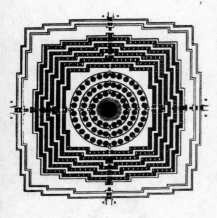

You can't depend on your judgment when your imagination is out of focus.

Mark Twain

This alone would change the world. Whatever career role you play, be aware of the effect your costume has on you and others and how you respond to the costumes worn by others.

The Magic of Language: Most professions have their own secret language. Why do doctors still write prescriptions in Latin? Why are legal terms loaded with French and Latin? Why do so many fields have their own jargon? Some special terms may be necessary to distinguish fine points of meaning; many are simply code words designed to keep the initiated unintelligible to the masses. Diplomas or professional certifications usually indicate initiation into some "secret society" marked by its own special language. Beyond specialized jargon, any spoken or written language can be used to communicate and illuminate or to deceive and befuddle. Similarly, the ability to create a narrative for your life, your company or organization, or your nation, is a kind of magic that can be used to deceive or illuminate.

The Magic of Space: Territorial boundaries—the corner office, the physical and people barriers that separate the "big boss" from the rest—these involve the magic of space. The boundaries of the in-group are marked by gates patrolled by security guards. Limousine rides, private jets, and yachts all reflect a kind of magic in one's ability to use and control space. A little over a hundred years ago, flying over mountains or across oceans would certainly have been considered magic. Any physical space that impresses people to the point where they forget themselves is a magical use of space. Bankers, for example, use this magic when they give their buildings the appearance of imposing temples. The ancient Chinese art of *Feng Shui* has long been practiced to create harmonious environments through the skillful use of (and arrangements within) space. *Feng Shui* masters know that good or bad "magic" can result from the use of space.

These are just a few of the elements of everyday "magic." Whatever you do to psych yourself up is a part of your magic. Incorporate into your own daily "ritual" those things that help you to feel and project confidence. At the same time, be aware that some use elements of the magic show to try to psych you out. If you can be intimidated or seduced, you can be psyched out. When you are impressed by others, you lose your center and move into their field of control. They take the power. This is why the Zen *bushido* master says, "Don't show weakness," or the Jedi Warrior Obi-Wan Kenobi says, "Hide your feelings, Luke."[13] In playing the game of career, don't let them see you sweat—or too impressed.

The Genius, The Shaman, and the Creative Womb of Emptiness

The Chinese sage Lao Tzu tells us that the usefulness of things is in their emptiness. The useful part of a wheel is the hub; the useful part of a pot is the empty space within.[14] Consider the mystery of the seed; throw it in the seemingly empty earth and watch life spring forth from the emptiness. There is mystery, magic, and creative power in the emptiness. Think of the creative artist. She knows that for all her searching, concentrating, and disciplined effort, the really exciting breakthroughs will come as inspirations from the emptiness.

The goal, the Hero's direction, is a seed, a potential; throw it on the emptiness of the imagination. Let imagination show you the way. Learn to trust in its magic subconscious power. Walk in expectancy, looking for signs of its revelations along the way. If we only move into what we already know how to do, if we are not willing to let imagination show us the way, we limit our creative potential. The creative life unfolds like a growing plant when we listen to and trust in what our imaginations are telling us.

From What-is all the world of things was born
But What-is sprang in turn from What-is-not.
Lao Tzu

We all know that nature abhors a vacuum. The same is true of our imaginations. The Magician makes this principle work for him. Drawing a magic circle, he creates an empty space in which to work his magic. You can think of your goals as providing the boundaries of a magic circle. Within the empty space of this circle, your imagination or inner magician works to create the outcomes you desire. On the other hand, if we don't give our imaginations constructive things to do, they tend to fill up with junk and recycle images of negativity and doubt. It's up to the Hero to supply the inner Magician with challenging creative demands that will keep it constructively engaged and out of mischief. Because our imaginations abhor a vacuum, they are our best friends or our worst enemies. The true Magician makes her imagination her friend; she both listens to it and protects it.

The two-headed Janus was the Roman god of doors and gates.[15] Like Janus, the Magician is a two-headed gatekeeper. She looks within and without, guarding the gate between the conscious and subconscious mind. In traditional cultures, a shaman was one who could intentionally pass through the gate into the realm of the

The faculty of imagination is both the rudder and the bridle of the senses.

Leonardo da Vinci

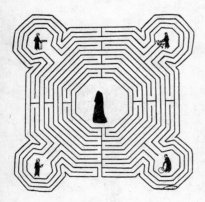

*All poetic inspiration
is but dream
interpretation.*

Hans Sachs

subconscious and come safely back out again with new information or insight that he had discovered there. A shaman is one who can "contact and utilize an ordinarily hidden reality in order to acquire knowledge, power, and to help other persons."[16] While perhaps not to the same degree or in the same way as the shaman, we can all develop the capacity to contact an "ordinarily hidden reality" and draw from it what will be useful to our daily lives. I'm not talking about performing any kind of strange rites, but simply developing the capacity to see that there may be more or less to things than immediately meets the eye. We can learn to, as Plotinus said, "close our eyes and invoke a new manner of seeing."[17]

For example, some make use of "dream therapy." Through this practice, one learns to read the signs and symbols of the hidden world of dreams with the aim of discovering what his or her subconscious, or even the collective unconscious, might be "saying" at a particular time. Dreams can be a rich source of creative inspirations. They can supply us with uncommon wisdom and insight. To gain real value from our dreams, we must develop the capacity not only to clearly recall them but also to interpret their messages and meanings. The Bible emphasizes the significance of the interpretative function in its stories of how Daniel and Joseph interpreted the dreams of King Nebuchadnezzar and "Pharaoh." In each case, the ruler recalled a dream in precise and graphic detail; yet until he found someone with the insight to interpret it, the information transmitted through the dream remained useless to him. So it is—not just with dreams, but with all information that arises spontaneously from the emptiness of the subconscious mind. Potential inspirations and insights from the unconscious must be recognized and interpreted by the conscious mind before they can be actualized. This brings us back to the image of Janus, looking within the subconscious mind and looking without, interpreting with the conscious mind. In my career coaching work, I've observed that people too often ignore or discount inspirations and intuitions they've had about the direction of their lives. Often finding your life's work is simply a matter of picking up or dusting off inspirations you have discarded or put on the shelf. In the world's great myths, we often see the archetypal Hero receiving aid from the archetypal Magician. Even as the great kings and queens of old relied on magi, oracles, and wizards to give them knowledge from the hidden reality, let the inspirations and intuitions of your deep subconscious help you find your way.

The great Magicians of myth and legend did not think their magic extraordinary. Rather, they saw themselves as evoking natural laws. Similarly, there is value for us in seeing the magic in everyday life, in honoring the creative imagination as an intrinsic part of our human makeup. We don't have to *become* creative, but only learn to recognize and utilize our innate creativity. We have our personal, idiosyncratic ways of blocking this innate ability, but when we allow it to work its magic, we find ourselves at one with people of all times and cultures who have touched this realm of enchantment.

Shadow Play: A Magician can be a Magus, a dark sorcerer, a bumbler, or a charlatan, depending on the depth of his knowledge and the purity of his motive. Those who don't have a spiritual Quest or a larger-than-self purpose are left using their imaginations for other purposes. While few deliberately use their "magic" in a destructive way, many end up recycling negative psychic raw material from their family upbringing or societal conditioning in unconscious imaginings. In dark tormented minds, the shadow Magician has dreamed up many a heinous crime. More often than this, it whips up garden-variety neurosis. Robbing joy, stealing ease, and sapping strength at every turn, the shadow Magician has a lot to learn.

The Warrior (The Battle for Life's Work)

The Hero makes the decision; the Magician develops a plan; the Warrior's job is to carry it out. King Arthur makes a decision, gains magical help from Merlin, and sends his knights out to do his bidding. Without his warrior knights, the King's decisions are meaningless. As King Lear so poignantly learned in Shakespeare's tragedy, a ruler without warriors to execute his aims is useless indeed. The Warrior says, "What you have imagined, do. What you have dreamed, live." The Warrior gets you off your rear and gets things done on the physical plane.

As a Warrior, you have a sense of yourself as a champion of your vision, the larger-than-self purpose to which your inner Hero has committed. This becomes your banner, and with it held high, you ride out to slay the dragons of doubt and fear, to defeat the view of life that holds nothing dear. The Warrior starts down this road, inspired and full of optimism—and runs smack into obstacles, blocks, and opposition. These test his character and resolve. They tempt him to forsake his duty (to himself and others) and abandon the vision of his Quest. As he battles external foes or resistance, his own inner fears and doubts kick in. Some obstacles threaten, intimidate, or coerce; others seduce, entice, and charm him from his duty. In any case, they prey upon his weakness and tempt him to relent, to give in to the belief that life doesn't make a difference and that choice is not. The Warrior battles the whole of his life,

within and without, against the notion that life doesn't make a difference.

> *Has fear ever held a man back from anything he really wanted, or a woman either?*
> *George Bernard Shaw*

The Warrior perseveres in the face of difficulties and doubts. Study the myths of the world, and you will see this theme repeated again and again. As soon as the Hero gets the call, the obstacles arise, and there's something difficult to do. There are dragons to slay, raging seas to cross, or wicked stepmothers to outwit. In other words, there is hard and/or scary stuff to do. The minute you answer the Hero's call, the Warrior's tests begin. How you handle these tests will determine whether you will live as a free man, a free woman—or cower in bondage to circumstance.

Riding the Windhorse of Creative Aggression

Now, all our hero wants to do is to realize some larger-than-self purpose; all our poet wants to do is express her vision of beauty in the world. Most would agree these are nice things to do. The problem is, if he's too much of a nice guy, or she too much of a nice gal, these goals will never be realized. For all their grand intentions, sooner or later, this guy and gal are going to run into obstacles, hurdles that must be jumped over, hoops that must be jumped through. He may think, Do I really want to do this? She may ask herself, Is this really *that* important? Now, either the Warrior energy steps up to save the day or the would-be goals are frittered away. Good intentions are not enough; commitment and perseverance are needed.

> *Let me not pray to be sheltered from dangers*
> *but to be fearless in facing them.*
> *Let me not beg for the stilling of my pain*
> *but for the heart to conquer it.*
> *Tagore*

The Warrior's strength comes from his or her discipline. Warriors embrace discipline, not as something imposed from without, but as the foundation upon which their freedom is built. Where most crave comfort, Warriors seek opportunities to challenge and strengthen themselves. Warriors succeed because they have to—because they put themselves in situations that demand their all. The "nice guy" (wimp) hopes that if he kisses enough rear, somebody will do it for him; the Warrior relies on himself. True Warriors have the integrity that comes from commitment to a larger-than-self purpose and the dignity that comes from self-reliance. Their obvious self-confidence is not mere bravado, but comes from having been tested and proven under fire. One of the great themes of world literature and drama is the transformation of the youth (or, if older, the wimp, rogue, or thug) into the Warrior. A heroic, larger-than-self purpose gives the Warrior a reason to excel, to transcend limiting notions of herself. It is for others that she becomes a stronger, more self-reliant individual and acquires the dignity that all people crave. She no longer doubts her basic goodness as a human being. She rides the *windhorse* of dignity, self-respect, and power.

> *Anyone who proposes to do good must not expect people to roll stones out of his way, but must accept his lot calmly, even if they roll a few more upon it.*
> *Albert Schweitzer*

We can think of Warrior energy as penetrating and protecting, piercing barriers and defending what is precious. The Warrior protects life and pierces the boundaries of limitation and stagnation. Both require creative aggression. The Warrior is master of aggressive energy. People with a lot of aggressive energy (strong wills) determine the sociocultural landscape: Those who work for good serve the heart with this power; those who work for ill, whether consciously or not, use this power to serve baser instincts. One way or another, aggression is a part of the human experience. For some, *aggression* is a bad word. They associate it with violence, cruelty, tyranny, and oppression. Yet aggression—the assertion of will—is required for every creative as well as every destructive act. Concentration is the assertion of a single idea, image, or train of thought to the exclusion of all else. That exclusion is aggressive. Great artists through history have been known for aggressive concentration on their work. One had better not interrupt Beethoven while he is composing, or Michelangelo while he is carving.

> *Life is a fight. You must remain concentrated and not reveal your defects; through continuous training and self-control, gradually you discard them.*
> *Taisen Deshimaru*

Zen masters have been known to be extremely aggressive in their teaching techniques—hitting, kicking, spitting, throwing things—shocking the student out of his slumber. Jesus was aggressive while confronting the money changers in the temple. Elsewhere he called men vipers, hypocrites, and serpents—aggressive terms, to be sure. Mahatma Gandhi's use of fasting was an aggressive act. He held his own body hostage and threatened to destroy it unless the changes he wanted were adopted. Mother Teresa was aggressive in fighting for those in her care and in the demands she made upon the sisters in her order. If her followers couldn't accept the very strict discipline she imposed—and cheerfully—they were dropped. Martin Luther King's March on Washington was an aggressive act. The point of these examples is simply to demonstrate that Warrior aggression is necessary for positive, creative action, and that aggression is not necessarily violent.

The Sword of Present Concentration

From Japanese *bushido*, or "way of the warrior," we can learn three keys for making aggressive energy serve our creative visions: *be present, be focused*, and *be strong*.

Be Present: The Warrior is totally alive because he is ready to die. He accepts his life and his death. Most people accept neither. They live in terror of death and muddle through life half-asleep, scarcely aware of the dangers and opportunities that lie all around them. Native American warriors cried on their way to battle, "Today is a good day to die!" Muhammad said, "Die before you die."[18] Japanese *bushido* teaches the warrior to be internally dead, meaning *still*. Being dead within, the samurai is completely free to respond—immediately and in all directions—without. The aliveness of the Warrior, his alert presence, arises from his inner deadness. In Japanese *bushido*, this consciousness is called the *shin*, or "spirit" aspect.

Be Focused: The warrior must also be a master of technique (*wasa*). Mastery of technique is achieved through concentration. One way of conceiving of the Japanese *Dō's*, e.g., *Aikido, Judo, Kendo* (sword), *Kyudo* (archery), *Chado* (Tea), is as a means of concentrating on a single act. When you arrive at the day when you can wield a sword, arrange flowers, or serve tea with total presence, you discover that your whole life (consciousness) has been transformed in the process of getting there. The person who does things in a sloppy fashion never develops concentration and so never becomes an authentic Warrior. True technique is neither

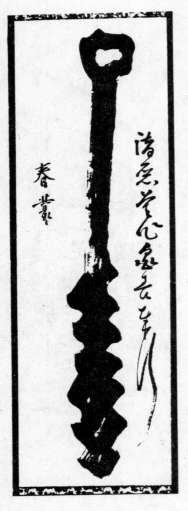

Those who reach greatness on earth reach it through concentration.

Upanishads

sloppy nor mechanical. It must become instinctive, spontaneous. The samurai who has to think about what he is doing in combat will soon be dead. The calligrapher who thinks too much about his strokes never achieves grace. Technique must become total, uniting body and mind.

Be Strong: The third element is physical strength. The Warrior must have a strong body, because he will ask it to do uncomfortable stuff. If your body is weak, it becomes the boss. When your body is strong, it obeys the commands of mind and spirit. It is said: Good technique defeats bodily strength. Good *shin*, or consciousness, defeats good technique. This is why the old *Dō-Jo* master in his eighties will whip the strong young student every time. The old master has the patience to look for weakness—in Japanese, *suki*, or opportunity. When he sees it, he strikes. The student, too eager or self-conscious, leaves himself open. Develop the physical strength to endure, but rely on your presence and concentration to see you through.

Courage is not the absence of fear, but rather the judgment that something else is more important than fear.

Ambrose Redmoon

From the European tradition of the medieval knights, we can learn something about the Warrior's relation to the Poet (spirit). Beginning in the twelfth century, certain knights began to practice what has come to be called "the art of courtly love." Recently, several scholars have provided convincing evidence that the etiquette of courtly love was, in fact, a ritualized spiritual practice and not, as many imagine, a code for conducting illicit affairs.[19] In this ritualized courting, both the knight and the lady were playing prescribed, symbolic roles. The Lady (standing for the knight's True Self) says, in effect, "Kill me some dragons." The knight goes out and slays the dragons or defeats the opponents. He comes back all full of himself and thinks, "Ah, what a fine thing I have done." And the Lady says, "Is that all? That's not much. The heroes of old who really loved their Ladies did truly great and heroic deeds. Go out and do something really great, and then I'll consider if you're really serious." His love for his Lady inspired the knight to ever greater deeds. Moreover, the frustrations of his (unconsummated) love provided the impetus for his spiritual transformation. Through the art of courtly love, the knight learned strength, humility, and detachment. Even as the knight's Lady taunted her suitor to ever

There is nothing stronger in the world than gentleness.

Han Suyin

greater heroism, so we can be inspired by the literature of spirit (mythic and poetic)—spurred and egged on to the Avalon of our Quest. True Warriors endure for Love. (For more on the warrior, see "Winning in the Marketplace" in Act III.)

Shadow Play: The shadow warrior might be a mercenary, selling his aggressive energy to the highest bidder, an accommodating lackey, ingratiating himself with the powers-that-be, or a self-effacing wimp. The bully enforcer, the sycophantic brown-noser, and the timid milquetoast—each in his own way has sold out. All have hardened their hearts. Where the true Warrior has courage (from Old French *corage,* or "heart"), the shadow warrior has only meanness, be it cruelty, guile, or wretchedness. The disciplined Warrior learns to use aggressive energy to serve the inner Hero— that is, a consciously chosen larger-than-self purpose. The shadow Warrior seeks power or comfort for its own sake.

The Scholar (The School of Life's Work)

What is meant here by *Scholar* is not necessarily a bookish fellow with a gray beard. The archetypal Scholar might appear in various cultures as the grandfathers or the grandmothers, the keepers of the knowledge and the wisdom of the people. I once saw a film about an African family in an arid climate. The grandfather knew the old ways of his people, which had been passed on for thousands of years. His son had a few years of elementary school and began to lose the old ways. The old man's grandson, in turn, went off to the university and knew virtually nothing of the traditional teachings. One day, the grandson arrived at the village with a strange and noisy machine. He was very excited—telling everyone that with this contraption he could find water. There he was bumbling about with this noisy machine, looking quite ridiculous and having little luck besides, when the old grandfather happened onto the scene. "What are you doing?" asked the old man. "Looking for water," came the reply. The old man laughed. He walked out into the desert, and where he saw certain plants, he began to dig. Sure enough, he found water. Now, if finding water is important, the old man, who never had a day of schooling in his life, is a better scholar than the university-trained grandson.[20]

This story gives a sense of what I mean by the archetypal Scholar. The Scholars are the knowledge and wisdom keepers of a people, a culture, and of humanity as a whole. *Scholar* is not really a satisfactory word to describe this archetype. I've coined the term *Student-Sage,* which gets closer to the meaning, but is a

Your motive in working should be to set others, by your example, on the path of duty.

Bhagavad-Gita

bit clumsy to use. I will use the terms Scholar and Student-Sage interchangeably throughout this discussion.

The Hero sets the direction, determining what to create; the Magician develops the plan; the Warrior executes it; the Scholar is the course-corrector. The Scholar's wisdom, patience, and willingness to learn keep you on track. The inner Scholar has a keen awareness of process, and it is from this awareness that wisdom flows. Think of planting strawberry seeds with an impatient young child. He may not know that the seed must germinate and begin to establish roots beneath the ground before it will become visible on the surface. He may not understand that the plant must be watered and weeded, not just once or now and then, but consistently for some time. All the child can think about is seeing and eating the strawberries. This analogy applies to growth in many areas of our lives. The goal must be worked into the underground of the subconscious mind and nurtured and protected by the action of the Warrior. Because the Scholar understands the process of growth, she gives us the patience we need to succeed. She tempers the Warrior's aggression and tendency to frustration. She recognizes when the Magician and Warrior need to adjust their attitudes, plans, or tactics. The inner Scholar prompts us to learn what is necessary to continue growing and advancing toward our goals. She looks at the situations of her life as opportunities to learn and as opportunities to exemplify what she believes in. Recognizing the Student-Sage in your life comes in the realization that you are learning and teaching twenty-four hours a day.

In one sense, we never stop learning—collecting and storing new data. But real learning is more than this. It's making new connections with our world and seeing new relationships between and among things. We are meant to grow naturally, expanding like trees into ever-widening circles of knowledge, wisdom, and ability. This is how young children learn—freely, spontaneously, wholeheartedly. When we lose this passion for learning, something in us dies. Even as learning is more than storing facts, teaching isn't limited to formal instruction in a classroom. We all teach by example. In the way we live our lives, we are teaching others what is important and valuable to us. Of course, what we say we believe in and what we actually exemplify are not always the same. Whether we choose to exemplify the selfish, the mediocre, or the indifferent or to take a creative approach to life, we are constantly teaching. The Student-Sage recognizes that even as she is teaching others, others are teaching her. As a wise friend of mine often says, "Some people are teaching you where it's at; some are teaching you where it's not at."

The Scholar includes both what Blake called "The Wisdom of Innocence" and "The Wisdom of Experience." In myth, this archetype

Without love the acquisition of knowledge only increases confusion and leads to self-destruction.

J. Krishnamurti

Is not indeed every man a student, and do not all things exist for the student's behoof?

Emerson

presents itself in images such as the Divine Child, or Innocent, and as the Old Wise Man, the Crone, or the Wise Old Grandmother. (The dual nature of this archetype is expressed in mythic figures such as Pluto, who is represented here as a bearded old wise man and there as a playful youth.) The special relationship of children and grandparents represents the twin aspects of this learning-teaching archetype we call the Student-Sage. The child represents the learning or growth potential within us; the grandparent, the tested wisdom of experience. In traditional cultures, elders pass on knowledge through hands-on apprenticeship and through storytelling.

The Student: Child Apprentice, Beginner's Mind

Apprenticeship is the way of learning with love. Think of times when you learned something one-on-one: your mother taught you how to cook, or your father taught you how to play baseball or to do some kind of handiwork, or perhaps a friend taught you how to play a game or do a new dance step. Remember the sweetness of this? Learning in the physical presence of the one who teaches you to do a thing—this is a tender and beautiful experience. You always feel like a child when you are learning from someone who loves you. Now imagine if someone taught you to do your work in this way, not hovering over you constantly, but from time to time being there, physically present, showing you. The important thing is that learning come with love, in a spirit of goodwill and rapport.

If you go to work for a corporation and they put you through an "orientation" program and then assign someone to watch over you, you don't experience this sense of the apprenticeship. You're probably a bit suspicious of the watcher's motives. You may think of this watcher (and perhaps with good reason), not as a friendly and supportive *mentor,* but as a sort of *monitor,* sent to keep an eye on you. The difference between a monitor and a mentor is the human element, caring for the person as a person and not simply as a "colleague," "worker," or employee. Bureaucracies, corporate or otherwise, tend to encourage people to act as monitors, not mentors. While it happens here and there, real mentorship is sorely lacking in the modern workplace. Beyond encouraging people to act like machines, bureaucratic systems tend to reduce knowledge to bits of information with all the humanity blanched out. In our reliance on automated instruction via digital technologies, we are losing something profound. People taught only by machines will become machinelike. People taught by loving humans will become loving humans.

In addition to the loss of mentoring and apprenticeship and the move toward automated instruction, our society is enamored with the cram-to-learn method of instruction. The test of learning is what we can consistently apply, not what we can regurgitate on a given day. Of course, the cram-for-the-test approach to learning is hardly new. A thousand years ago, critics complained that it was destroying the moral fabric of Chinese society. Once passing exams in Confucian (and other) classics became required for placement in virtually every position of responsibility or social standing, it wasn't long before students became more concerned with passing tests than with learning for its own sake. Education became perverted from a means of learning to a vehicle for social advancement.[21] We have fallen into the same pattern today.

Running parallel to this, we've devalued knowledge that doesn't have commercial application and wisdom that can't be measured by objective tests. Art, music, and the humanities are superfluous subjects. They are nice elective interests, but not terribly important. The real subjects are math, science, engineering, finance, economics, and business. There was a time (long ago) when one wouldn't dream of calling himself educated unless he was well versed in philosophy. Today, philosophy is left to a small cadre of professionals engaged in intramural debates. Once an educated person was expected not only to understand philosophy but also to demonstrate wisdom in his or her own life. The Student-Sage is interested in teaching that which humanizes and inspires the love of wisdom (philosophy). Beyond this, she wants the teaching of all the practical arts and activities of daily life to come in a spirit of love and humanity. This was the time-honored way in which crafts from weaving to stone masonry, from candle making to cloth spinning, were taught for centuries. When love accompanies instruction, something more than knowledge is shared. However amorphous, some substance of the human soul transfers from one person to another. If we are to be good Student-Sages, then this is our way through life: receiving this "human substance," along with knowledge, as students and giving it, along with knowledge, as teachers or sages.

The Sage: Grandmother and Grandfather Story

In addition to, and often as a part of, apprenticeship, traditional cultures transmitted wisdom-knowledge through storytelling, song, dance, theater, visual art, etc.—but principally, storytelling. Dance, art, and theater, etc., originally grew out of the desire to convey the story of a particular people, their deities, origins, folkways, and so on. The Sage knows and values stories: the story of her life, the story of her people, the story of humanity, perhaps even the story of life itself. She has a sense of being a trustee, a steward, and a

达磨元来觀自在

Education is not filling a bucket but lighting a fire.

William Butler Yeats

record keeper, part of an unbroken chain extending backward and forward, honoring those who have gone before and feeling profound responsibility for those yet to come.

The world is our school for spiritual discovery.
Paul Brunton

History is a nightmare from which I am trying to awake.

James Joyce

Today we are story-starved, hungry for stories that will feed our souls. Oh, we have plenty of stories. We consume more stories than any people in human history. Television sitcoms, crime and hospital dramas, formula movies full of violence or escapist fantasies, and romance and mystery novels are cranked out by their respective "industries" like so many widgets on an assembly line. But it's a hollow diet. Most of these stories lack spiritual nutrition—direction, insight, inspiration, or awakening. It isn't just pop culture—the stories of many of our "serious" writers are equally devoid of soul food. As with junk foods, we can consume these stories in great quantities and remain malnourished. The Student-Sage respects the art of storytelling. She knows that stories, from children's nursery rhymes to great novels and everything in between, make a profound difference in the lives of individuals and in the character of a society. Whether we want to admit it or not, stories, *all stories*, teach values in a uniquely powerful way—by giving them life in our imaginations.

Myth, drama, ritual, dance, and art, in addition to whatever else they may be, are vehicles for conveying profound knowledge about the human experience. They can teach us about the wide range of creative strategies humanity has developed over many thousands of years for living rich and meaningful lives. More fundamentally, they can teach us about the human experience we all share across time and culture. In his classic *Wen Fu (The Art of Writing)*, the Chinese poet Lu Chi instructs, "There are no new ideas, only those which rhyme with certain classics."[22] In the West, we have that line from Proverbs: "There is nothing new under the sun." The new that doesn't rhyme with the best of the old cannot be said to be wise. We might even say with Aquinas that truth has but one author. "All that is true, by whomsoever it has been said, has its origin in the Spirit."[23] The Student-Sage recognizes and honors the timeless wisdom that binds us all together.

This chapter began with a discussion of a mythic approach to life—viewing your life as a story of an encounter with the universal in everyday life. The Sage aspect of the Student-Sage has a sense of where you are in the story of your life. Her insights give continuity and meaning to the events of your life. Her long-term perspective and detachment encourage the Student to learn what will enrich and better her own life and all humanity. In this we have the completing of a cycle begun by the Hero as seeker. The Hero is shaking things up, questing, seeking, moving into the unknown, until direction is found. The Sage aspect of the Student-Sage examines whether or not one is, in fact, realizing what she (as Hero) set out to do. She considers the lessons learned and yet to be learned on the journey through life. (For more on the Student-Sage, see "Learning to Change: The Old Boy and the Student-Sage" in Act IV.)

Shadow Play: The shadow Scholar views knowledge as his personal possession. He might be an opportunist who, without conscience or compassion, sells his knowledge to the highest bidder. He reasons that the labors of his studies have earned him an expertise that he now "owns" as a kind of personal commodity to trade as he wills. He has no sense of a debt owed to generations past for the knowledge he possesses, nor does he feel responsibility to generations to come. He lacks a sense of story in his life—and the wisdom and the patience that this engenders. He has a difficult time being at rest or at peace. He fears the course correction he might receive from the inner Sage if he were ever quiet long enough to hear it. He fears getting old.

Working with the Archetypes

Carl Jung emphasized that for the individual to gain real value in working with the archetypes emotional involvement is critical. Archetypes are not dead images from the past. "They are living pieces of life itself—images that are integrally connected to the individual by the bridge of the emotions." He stresses that it is "by being charged with emotion [that] the image gains numinosity (or psychic energy)."[24] Active engagement with the archetypes intensifies our experience of life—moving us out of the mundane, drab, half-asleep life, into the wide-awake intensity of life lived to the fullest. Nothing is as intense as play. Constructively engaging the archetypes in a spirit of play energizes and intensifies life to a surprising degree.

It is a myth, not a mandate, a fable not a logic, and symbol rather than a reason by which men are moved.

Irwin Edman

Joseph Campbell said of myth, "Once this subject catches you, there is such a *feeling* . . . of information of a deep, rich, *life-vivifying* sort that you don't want to give it up"[25] [emphasis added]. In even the most cursory study of mythology, you encounter a language of symbols that gives meaning and understanding to your everyday experience. Myths can help guide you through the labyrinth of the unconscious and inspire and guide you in the realization of your Quest. Familiarizing yourself with the recurring themes and symbols of mythology can help you construct a personally meaningful set of symbols. In the modern world, many once-potent symbols have been drained of their psychic power through neglect or through the inoculation that occurs when these are appropriated by commercial advertisers. Reading myths or books with mythic themes, or seeing plays or films that draw on mythic images, can reawaken awareness of our own individual relationships to the archetypical challenges dramatized in these stories.

I think that what we're seeking is an experience of being alive, so that our life experiences on the purely physical plane will have resonances within our own innermost being and reality, so that we actually feel the rapture of being alive.

Joseph Campbell

Life is not watching television. It is not passively reacting to a world programmed and controlled by ambivalent or even hostile forces beyond our reach. We needn't feel alienated from the joy or overwhelmed by the pain of the world. We can creatively engage the whole of life, and the myths and archetypes can help in this. They teach us to embrace the world-as-it-is as the setting on which the stories of our lives play out. They tell us that we can use our imaginations to shape, and imaginatively respond to, events. They remind us that all the victories and obstacles, all the angels and devils of our inner and outer lives, are but dramatic elements in the stories of our lives—stories we are simultaneously writing and acting in.

Around the Wheel

The Poet doesn't tell his story or history. He tells The Story. The Story is the encounter of the individual with the universal. Whether consciously intended or not, great literature has a mythic or poetic dimension. We understand that it is not a story about an individual,

All wrong-doing arises because of mind. If mind is transformed can wrong-doing remain?

Buddha

that is, a history; it is a story of an encounter of the individual with the universal, that is, a poetry. If the spiritual or poetic life is the capstone of human experience, then the four wisdoms are the foundation on which this capstone rests. Similarly, if the poetic center is the source of all great inspiration, then these four aspects are the vehicles through which the inspiration becomes manifest.

Around the world, all who teach the sacred four indicate that we must pass through all four directions—that we must develop ourselves in all four aspects if we are to be complete and balanced human beings. Ask yourself: How do I relate to the Hero archetype? What kind of Hero am I? How do I relate to the Magician archetype? What kind of Magician am I? How do I relate to the Warrior archetype? What kind of Warrior am I? How do I relate to the Student-Sage archetype? What kind of Student-Sage am I? Our relationships with these powerful archetypes will determine not only what we are able to accomplish but also the quality, the richness, of our lives.

Even if we can't yet hear the voice of the heart, the direct intuition of the Poet, we can, in the meantime, be developing as Heroes, Magicians, Warriors, and Scholars. We can, as Heroes, learn to respect the dictates of our conscience and develop our discriminative will, the capacity to discern and decide without vacillation. We can, as Magicians, creatively direct imaginative power and develop the ability to see the soul (or inner meaning) of things. We can, as Warriors, develop the alertness, concentration, strength, and endurance we will need when the time comes to answer the call. We can, as Student-Sages, grow in learning and teaching that which is life-affirming and life-preserving. By consciously making all we make—we make ourselves ready to hear the voice of the heart.

Light on the Shadows

It is clear to many that, if we are even to survive on this planet, human society is in critical need of change. But how to change? Jung points out that our typical idea of change is to blame others or the "system." He goes on, "It would be much more to the point for us to make a serious attempt to recognize our own shadow and its nefarious doings. If we could see our shadow (the dark side of our nature), we should be immune to any moral and mental infection and insinuation."[26] In other words, learning to recognize our own shadow inoculates us from the destructive elements of the collective unconscious and mass culture. This is an individual process, indeed an individuating process: it takes the courage to face one's dark side.

*"What is the path?"
the Zen Master
Nan-sen was asked.
"Everyday life is the
path," he answered.*

> *He then learns that in going down into the secrets of his own mind he has descended into the secrets of all minds.*   Emerson

As I become more aware of these archetypal energies, I must be willing to admit that I am affected by decisions, which I have made, and for which I am responsible, but of which I am now hardly aware. I must be willing to recognize that much of my imagined freedom is little more than slavish obedience to habits and chasing irrational phantoms born of repressed memory, collective and individual. I must be willing to recognize where I am using the creative powers of my imagination, not as an artist creating a life of beauty, but as a kind of black magician—conjuring demons and monsters in thoughts of fear and guilt, jealousy and revenge. I must be willing to recognize within myself the dark warrior whose undisciplined and unfocused aggression wreaks havoc and destruction, turning green fields to barren wastelands. I must be willing to face that I may be using the knowledge of my craft, or any knowledge for that matter, for destructive or indifferent aims.

Only if I am willing to conceive of myself as a slave to conditioned habits and unexamined choices will the possibility of acting as a true Hero, a conscious quester and chooser, become a viable option. Only as I am willing to conceive of myself as having an imagination populated, perhaps even dominated, by dark psychic forces, does the possibility of being a true Magician arise. Only if I am willing to conceive of myself as a destructive warrior, abusing the aggressive energy of life or bottling it up in self-destructive and world-polluting stagnation, can I possibly become a true Warrior—a brave and gentle knight. Only if I am willing to conceive of myself as playing the whore with the knowledge I possess, selling it for destructive or indifferent aims, can I become a true Scholar. Ask yourself:

- Right now, are my choices conscious or automatic? Do I accept responsibility for my life, for my choices, or do I seek to escape?

- Right now, in this instant, is my imagination creating beauty, blandness, or misery?

- Right now, in this moment, is my aggressive energy serving a higher purpose, or is it stagnating or openly destructive?

- Right now, in this instant, is my knowledge serving the greater good, or is it going unused or serving destructive aims?

In earlier times, working with these energies was something that was done in community. Today we are left to work these things out on our own. Part of the inner Magician's work is to consciously invoke these energies into our lives. Toward this end, you might create your own dramas, rituals, and creative relationships to symbol. If you enjoy writing, you might write your autobiography—your life journey or story—from the standpoint of your relationships with these energies. This can be an illuminating process and is only one example of the many ways you can begin to creatively engage these energies.

The final chapter of this Prologue will look more closely at the Hero. The remainder of this book is organized around the themes of the Quest, the Game, the Battle, and the School of Life's Work. The four archetypes (Hero, Magician, Warrior, Scholar) correspond to these four Acts. Of course, these energies do not fit into neat little compartments or categories; they show up all over the place. The point of suggesting correspondences is simply to show which energies predominate at each point. The subject of this book is life's work, and we can easily see that these are energies that we will, in one way or another, work with for the rest of our lives.

It doesn't happen all at once . . . You become. It takes a long time.

Margery Williams

CHAPTER 4

The World Calls for the Postmodern (Blissful) Hero

Have we not come to such an impasse in the modern world that we must love our enemies—or else?
The chain reaction of evil—hate begetting hate, wars producing more wars—must be broken, or else we shall be plunged into the dark abyss of annihilation.
Martin Luther King, Jr.

I f ever there was a time that called for heroic action, it is the one we live in today. Never before in history has humanity possessed the awesome capacities for self-destruction that we now hold. From the immediate destructive power of nuclear holocaust to the slow death of environmental decay, we live in dangerous times. We cannot simply go on with business as usual. Perilous times call for heroic action. It is time that we suspend our preoccupation with economic life to the exclusion of all other values and put love into action in every sphere of life.

Today, heroic action is not a matter of conquering new lands, slaying dragons, or crossing uncharted seas. The heroic life awaits all who are ready to take up the challenge of making this world the best it can be. Even as the hero of old had to confront the unknown, today we must confront the known. We must confront the world we find ourselves in while keeping before us the image of the world that could be. We must face our conditions and "breathe into them the breath recuperative of sane and heroic life" (Walt Whitman).

After the final no there comes a yes and on that yes the future of the world depends.
Wallace Stevens

Perhaps inspired by Shakespeare's *Hamlet*, Albert Camus said that the fundamental choice is suicide or life.[1] The intellectually honest person must face up to the choice: To be or to not be. Among the living, there are but two kinds of people: those who have said YES to life and those who have ducked the question. Those who have honestly decided that life is not worth living are no longer with us. That which says YES to life can be called the heroic view of life. That which ducks the question is something else again. We can call it the "maybe view of life." The heroic YES must be total, unequivocal—the affirmation of a love that embraces human life exactly as it is. On the other hand, "maybe" muddles in avoidance born of fear. It endeavors to build an abstract ideational world that emphasizes either the "good" or the "bad," but as we shall see, neither Pollyanna positivism nor cynical resignation is intellectually honest.

I believe in life after birth!

Maxie Dunham

The Heroic View of Life: Love for Existence

The intellectually honest person must face the fact that his very existence is dependent upon the destruction of other living beings. Whether it is plants or animals that I consume to sustain my life, I'm a killer. I can try to rationalize, prepackage, or otherwise avoid it, but I live on destruction. This alone is enough to make a person feel guilt and repulsion. After all, how can I justify my existence when it depends upon the destruction of others? I cannot. I can only accept that it's the way of life, that death, decay, and destruction are as much a part of life as birth, growth, and regeneration. Life is full of pairs of opposites. Night and day, winter and summer, birth and death, on and on. ***Heroic love transcends the opposites in its embrace of them.***

In life's work, bliss and sacrifice are two sides of the same coin, complementary opposites. It takes disciplined effort to produce beauty in art, music, or even the presentation of an evening meal. What is most pleasing to our senses often comes, not from sensual pursuit, but from meticulous effort. George Bernard Shaw said, "This is the true joy in life, the being used for a purpose recognized by yourself as a mighty one."[2] The joy is the bliss; the being used, the sacrifice. Shaw is saying that if we want to know the greatest joy in life, we ought to dedicate ourselves to a purpose that we conceive of as a mighty-heroic-valuable-meaningful one and give our very all to it.

Today, it's out of fashion to speak in terms of "sacrifice" or of "being used." We are told we must assert ourselves and "look out for number one." Yet when we look at the origin of the word *sacrifice,* we find a verb that means "to make sacred." Sacrificing your life, then, is making it sacred; or rather, it is acting in the recognition that all life—including yours—already is sacred. It's simply embracing reality. "Being used" in the sense that Shaw refers to it in the quote above means being fully engaged in life while you have it. After all, when we die, our lives will have been used up in one way or another. The question is: For what? Will it be for purposes we recognize as mighty ones, or will it simply be because we have muddled through to the end? Will we meet our ends knowing that we put our all into life, or will we be left with regrets and might-have-beens?

> *I want to be thoroughly used up when I die, for the harder I work the more I live. I rejoice in life for its own sake.*
>
> George Bernard Shaw

Back to Bliss: Unzipping the Ego

Today, we seek quick happiness, not lasting bliss. Though we've been told of agony and ecstasy—of losing oneself to save oneself—we run from the pain of the world. In our effort to block out the pain, we miss the bliss. How then do we get back to bliss? The better question might be: How did we lose it? Every child knows the joy of living. His bliss is innocent. He has not yet felt the weight his culture will soon hoist upon him. The weight of social manners and customs, of conflicting roles and obligations, of proving himself acceptable, makes him capable of functioning in his society. But in the process, he is robbed of his innocence—and his bliss.

You can and you must expect suffering.

Mother Teresa

He is wrapped in mental cellophane and shipped off to become a useful member of society. What is the wrapping about? Mental cellophane is protection from the direct experience of life. It's an ideational insulation from pain. It's endless categories and types; it's prejudices, "should-be's," and hypes. It's using our brains to cover our hearts. The mind's ability to concentrate, think, and create suffers from the strain of keeping the world at bay. We go through our lives with armored hearts and distracted brains and wonder what happened to our creativity and sense of play.

We're so engaged in doing things to achieve purposes of outer value that we forget the inner value, the rapture that is associated with being alive, is what it is all about.

Joseph Campbell

The older we get, the more difficult it is to keep out the pain of the world, so we add layer after layer of mental cellophane. By middle age, a lot of us can hardly breathe. Wrapped up in cellophane, we are awkward and stiff, slowly suffocating talking heads, devoid of direct experience.

Reclaim the bliss! Split the seam of your cellophane wrap! Step out of thought and convention. Leave your mind behind. Feel the breeze, dance naked in the moonlight, move freely, spontaneously, blissfully. It feels good out here. Don't worry, you will be able to handle pain when it comes. You are strong now.

How do we split the seam once and for all? How can we live naked and unwrapped? By learning to live with pain. Not in spite of it, not in hope of its end, not crushed by it, but with it. As a tree must anchor its roots deep in the earth in order to stretch forth to the skies, so must we who would reach the greatest heights of human experience be ready to meet the pain of this world head-on. Like the Buddha, the innocent child in her bliss will one day discover that this world is full of pain and, if she is to live fully, she must live with it.

Heroic love is not something that can be hyped, pep-talked, or adroitly argued into someone. It must be felt by each alone. It is not a matter of majority vote or popular consensus. *Each must conquer for him- or herself the desire to run away from life.* There's no escaping from life, really. You are here. There is no denying it. Maybe you don't know why or how, but you are here. You may as well decide to love it as you find it. Life, after all, is for living.

Is not life a thousand times too short for us to bore ourselves?

Friedrich Nietzsche

Either you think that life should not exist, that it's all a big mistake—or you affirm its basic goodness. You say YES to life, with all of its pain and joy, horror and majesty, sorrow and bliss. It is good that life exists. It's as simple as that. **Oh, yes, do all you can to make the world a better place, but remember— that comes out of acceptance, not out of rejection.** Love in its truest form is without condition. It accepts life exactly as it is. Yet paradoxically, love is also the strongest force of change.

Zen wants us to be the Mother of All Things, to embrace everything exactly as it is—to see all that is as "thy will" being done on earth. Total acceptance. Zen also asks us to be the Father of Creative Movement—to change, to transform, to evolve. So, in this understanding, we can say with Lao Tzu, "Know the masculine, but keep to the feminine"—act for change from the embrace of things as they are. This is the only action or creative movement. All else is reaction.

Humanity: One of a Kind

All people share in a state and relationship we call the human condition. In this we are one, we are of a kind. You are human, I am human, they are human—we are all human. Since we're all of a kind, we might as well act that way. Really, aren't we all doing everything we do to gain happiness or avoid suffering? Of course, many of our efforts are misguided in that they do not bring the results we seek. Still, we are all, in our own ways, trying to be happy.

> Today . . . we know that all living beings who strive to maintain life and who long to be spared pain— all living beings on earth are our neighbors.
> Albert Schweitzer

Through the ages, philosophers and sages have offered various formulas for happiness. Perhaps the simplest is: Be kind—treat all people with kindness. We can say that to see *kind* is to be kind—for who would want to injure oneself or those of one's kind? Beyond gender, race, religion, nationality, social or economic status, education, talent, or political persuasion, we share our humanity. Differences, of course, exist, and it is well to recognize and honor these, but never at the expense of forgetting our essential "kindness" as humans—not, at least, if we would be happy. Acting with kindness doesn't have to fit any preconceived notion of proper action. In this recognition, you can trust—remember your "kindness" and act.

We cannot be more sensitive to pleasure without being more sensitive to pain.

Alan Watts

The Maybe View of Life: Self-Contempt

The maybe view of life is based, not on love, but on shame. Where love breeds confidence and self-respect, shame brings doubt and self-contempt. Where love comes out of an identification of kind, shame sets up a need for separation. The need to be separate comes out of the belief that humanity is a low level of life. You must separate yourself from that lot. What makes you different is what makes you good. Your difference might be that you are an American, or Christian, or Jewish, or rich, or intellectual, or conservative, or liberal, or whatever.

It is only when we realize that life is taking us nowhere that it begins to have meaning.

P. D. Ouspensky

No work of love will flourish out of guilt, fear, or hollowness of heart, just as no valid plans for the future can be made by those who have no capacity for living now.   *Alan Watts*

Although few would dare to say it so bluntly, the internal rationalization goes something like this: "The normal run of folks comprise a sort of contemptuous mob. I would be in that mob were it not for my smartness, holiness, coolness, 'wealthiness,' 'causiness' (whatever it is that separates me from the masses)." Only when we fail to love ourselves as we are do we feel the need to separate ourselves from the rest of humanity. If we don't meet the world with love, we meet it with demands. We make demands upon life, demands upon ourselves, and demands upon others. We will love when our demands are met and not a minute before. If life were more to my liking, I would love it; if I were more to my liking, I would love me; if others were more to my liking, I would love them. In the meantime, I will hold back, and I will hold on to what I think distinguishes me from the rest of the rabble.

The miracle is not that we do this work, but that we are happy to do it.
                                    Mother Teresa

When one tries to stake his identity on some distinctive possession, he is on insecure ground. It matters not whether the possession is an accumulation of wealth or knowledge, a title, a career, a social status, a marriage partner, or a cause—it is sure to bring him anxiety. The owner becomes anxious about losing his possession because he equates this with losing his distinctive identity. Once more, he is confronted with an image of himself indistinguishable from the mob he so deplores.

"Doing good" can become a distinctive possession that separates you from the "masses." That is why the motive of the hero must be love, first, foremost, and always, love. Love for existence—your own and that of others. If you secretly hate yourself, but you're "trying to do good," your hatred will color the water. You can only give to others what you experience yourself.

The hero must first be a lover. Then she may attempt to heal others: their minds with high ideals, their emotions with loving feelings, their bodies with nourishment and touch. But these things are secondary. It is the existence that she loves, and it is the love that makes the difference. Mother Teresa's work with the poor and the dying was certainly a heroic work. She emphasized to those in her order the importance of doing their work with a spirit of joy and a feeling of love. She said, "If you can't do it with love and cheerfulness, don't do it at all, go home."[3] She understood that you can't heal the particular need while holding bitterness in your heart. Heroic love embraces all that we typically reject in the world, in ourselves, and in others.

> *There is nothing with which every man is so afraid as getting to know how enormously much he is capable of doing and becoming.*
> Søren Kierkegaard

The test of our spiritual development is not the zeal with which we profess our beliefs, but our willingness to love others and ourselves exactly as we are. Keeping this in mind helps us understand how so many wars have been fought in the name of religion, or how seemingly good intentions or high ideals often bring destructive results. The fault is not with the religion or the ideal, but with the practitioner's contempt for humanity and the resulting need to cling to some separating identity. In the Crusades, the Christians marched into battle crying, "God is mighty!" The Muslims cried, "God is all!" But because each side claimed "God" for their own purposes, neither side could comprehend their own slogans. In the name of the proletariat, self-proclaimed Marxists sacrificed millions of ordinary people. Cynics point to these kinds of atrocities to dismiss any kind of spiritual life or to discount any sense of responsibility to our fellow beings. Surely hypocrisy exists, but that in no way diminishes spiritual reality, nor does it relieve us of our responsibility to one another. It is contempt for humanity that must be overcome, not our impulse to spiritual awakening, or our desire

One cannot always be a hero, but one can always be a (hu)man.

Goethe

to love and serve one another. If we are to survive and flourish as a species, we must remake, not only our society, but ourselves as individuals. Ironically, we cannot succeed in remaking ourselves until we accept ourselves as we are. Only in love will we find the courage to be what we truly are. Only with love do we say yes to life. Yes to life with all of its beauty and terror. Yes to life with all of its brilliance and depravity. Yes to life with all of its sorrow and bliss.

Love Makes a World of Difference

Love until it hurts. Real love is always painful and hurts; then it is real and pure.

Mother Teresa

> *My life is an indivisible whole, and all my activities run into one another; and they have their rise in my insatiable love of mankind.*
>
> *Mahatma Gandhi*

It's easy to imagine that making the world a better place is simply a matter of throwing money at its problems. Of course, money helps make things happen, but it is secondary to love and character. As Albert Einstein put it, "I am absolutely convinced that no wealth in the world can help humanity forward, even in the hands of the most devoted worker in this cause. The example of great and pure individuals is the only thing that can lead us to noble thoughts and deeds. Money only appeals to selfishness, and irresistibly invites abuse. Can anyone imagine Moses, Jesus, or Gandhi armed with . . . money bags . . . ?"[4]

The fear of pain and death makes most of us but shadows of what we might be. Yet even suffering, mixed with love, with purpose, with joy, becomes heroic—an exaltation of the human spirit. And what of death? Listen to the speech Dr. Martin Luther King made days before he was shot. You can tell, somehow, he knew it was coming. Still, he went ahead undaunted, unbowed. Like a thousand heroes before him, he held on to a vision of man mightier than fear. Heroic action cuts the bounds of fear and triumphantly asserts that there is a spirit in us that is noble and mighty. This loving spirit exists within all life, including yours. *The heroic life lives in dormancy in all and in active expression in the great men and women.*

The heroic life is a beautiful life. You cannot hear Martin Luther King's "I Have a Dream" speech and miss hearing the beauty. You cannot see Mother Teresa and miss seeing the beauty. You cannot study Gandhi's life and miss sensing the beauty. You just can't. I think everyone sees it. But what does it take to transfer that beauty into an active force in our own lives?

Identification. We must be able to identify with the hero as being fundamentally like ourselves. Otherwise, heroic action is dismissed as the peculiar behavior of some peculiarly great individual. This behavior is worthy of admiration, to be sure, but not capable of imitation by the ordinary man and woman. Heroes, whether living or dead legends, are seen as fundamentally different from the rest of us. Of course, we are not all equally gifted or talented, but we are all capable of heroic action.

How then do we create identification with heroic models?

1. **By realizing that the greats of history were human beings, cut from the same cloth as we.** They put their pants on one leg at a time. They had to deal with the same emotions and inner doubts, the same outside pressures and concerns.

2. **By seeing that they are all around us.** Every day, many thousands of so-called ordinary people are involved in heroic service. Most of this service goes unrecognized and unnoticed by the wider public because it does not fit with the conventional view of what is valuable and important.

> *Everybody can be great. Because anybody can serve. You don't have to have a college degree to serve. You don't have to make your subject and verb agree to serve. You don't have to know about Plato and Aristotle . . . (or) Einstein's Theory of Relativity . . . (or) the Second Theory of Thermodynamics in physics to serve. You only need a heart full of grace. A soul generated by love.*
> *Martin Luther King, Jr.*

The point of telling the hero's story is that our identification with the hero allows us, at least for a time, to move beyond the fear and defensive hesitation that hold us back from full participation in life. We experience what the Greeks call *catharsis*.[5] Catharsis doesn't mean rant and rave and scream and yell, and then there is catharsis. The cathartic experience is the release experienced in the cessation of the emotions that ordinarily dominate life, namely fear and guilt. Catharsis happens when we identify with the character and move along his emotional track until he and we are free of guilt and fear.

That's why the stories from ages old have been told—so that you might feel, if only for an instant, what it is to be so bold. So ALIVE.

The Way is not far from man; if we take the Way as something superhuman, beyond man, this is not the real Way.

Confucius

In that, you find life. You find bliss. You find courage. You can feel it. Where did it come from? It was there all along, beneath the clouds of shame and fear. Cathartic identification has temporarily blown the clouds away. Now you feel the pure brilliance of your being. Courage isn't something you've put on. Fear is something you've taken off. You feel the power and grace of your naked Self.

We all have the capacity to inspire and uplift one another. When you see someone heroically facing a tragedy of some kind, or heroically working to express their vision of love in action—it's an inspiration. That person could be black, white, yellow, red, rich, or poor, Protestant, Catholic, Muslim, or Jew; it doesn't matter. *It's the spirit that you identify with*. It lifts your spirit to see someone exalting theirs. Each of us can approach our daily lives in a way that exalts the human spirit. We can be living examples of human dignity, love, and brotherhood. We can create a society based on love for one another and respect for the mystery of life.

I have not the shadow of a doubt that any man or woman can achieve what I have, if he or she would make the same effort and cultivate the same hope and faith.

Mahatma Gandhi

You have seen the earth from space. Maybe it was only a photograph, but you have seen it. Having seen ourselves from somewhere else, we can no longer be so much in the dark about where we are. We are on earth, together with the great oceans and landmasses, together with seven billion of our fellow humans, we are on earth. For the first time, that image is a part of our psyche; and for the first time, we have a global culture. We can decry this culture and its banality. We can try to stop the push toward universality by emphasizing ethnic or cultural differences, but inevitably we are moving to one world. Our efforts are better spent in attempting to elevate this culture than in reverting to separation.

How can we elevate this culture we live in? How can we make it more human, more sane? What kind of values do we want represented in the images that bounce around the world in an instant? What will we televise? What will we glorify? What will we compute? Will it be about love or loot? We are deciding.

I cry: Love! Love! happy happy Love!
free as the mountain wind!
William Blake

Living on the Edge

Look at Bodhidharma's fierce scowl. Strong as an ox, he won't take any bull. He's a radical, a rebel, a revolutionary. He knows that it's society's job to tame the individual, and the individual's job to get free.

Society's propaganda will tell you that you are inadequate, that it's your fate to live in fear and beg for the approval of others, that things are just the way they are, and there's nothing you can do about it. You must resign yourself to a gray existence; you must go along to get along.

But there is Bodhidharma, fiery eyes, teeth showing, intent and determined, a free spirit who will not buy the propaganda of mediocrity. He challenges you to be free enough of society to actually help transform it for the better.

That's what this book is about. It's about being personally free and socially active. It is not for wimps. It takes the courage to say no to every attempt to fit you into a category and make you a carbon copy of your next-door neighbor. It takes the courage to say no to every attempt to turn you into a beggar, pleading for the approval of others. It takes the courage to say no to the needless suffering of your fellow man. No to becoming hypnotized and tranquilized. No to becoming greedy and indifferent. No to becoming clay in somebody else's hand.

Things were no different in Bodhidharma's day. Society has always been the free man's greatest enemy. And the free man has always been society's greatest friend. How did society treat Jesus or Socrates, Galileo or Martin Luther King? Yet look what they have left humankind.

Bodhidharma, if we could get him to talk, would tell us that it's our wanting to be somebody special that turns us into slaves of approval. He is a nobody who works for everybody, who kowtows to none, condemns none, loves all in his rascal way. I'm not your leader, he might say. Don't follow me. Be your own leader.

This book says: What is in you, let it out. What you really want to do, do it. Don't yield to doubt. Love is the greatest religion, the greatest philosophy, the guiding light of the free man. Love is what it's all about.

The Quest for Life's Work

Wherein our hero asks:
What in the world am I doing here?

Not I—not anyone else, can travel that road for you,
You must travel it for yourself.

Walt Whitman

A lifelong adventure awaits those who are ready to take up the quest for their life's work. The first step on this journey is to determine the direction you want your life to take. In "Act I: The Quest for Life's Work," you will be invited to examine several key landmarks to help you get your bearings. These include: your vision for the kind of world you want to live in, your values, your purpose in life, your talents, and specific objectives you would like to accomplish while on this earth. With these landmarks and your commitment, you will be able to determine, at least in a general sense, what your life's work is.

The Quest
for Your Best

*"Each entered the forest at a point he,
himself, had chosen, where it was darkest
and there was no path."*

T he lines above come from a medieval story that has come to be known as *The Quest of the Holy Grail*.[1] It is a story rich in psychological meaning and spiritual significance. Having seen an apparition of the Grail through a veil, the knights of King Arthur's court determined to go on a quest to find it. And they thought, "We should go out together to find the Grail." But then they realized that this would be "a disgrace." No, each must go alone into the forest and enter at the point he himself would choose, "where it was darkest and there was no path."

Entering the forest alone at the darkest spot, this is taking the road less traveled. To walk this pathless path is to take the hero's journey. This book is for those who, like the mythic heroes of old, are ready to make of their lives a quest for the shining apparition of their own best self—ready to take the hero's journey. The word *hero* is etymologically related to *heresy* and *heretic*. All three are derived from the Greek *hairétikos,* meaning "able to choose."[2] A hero is a chooser. A hero chooses the questions of his or her life, and thereby his or her quest.

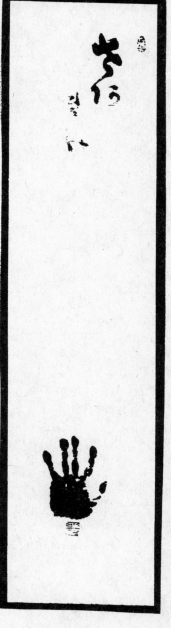

If a man does not keep pace with his companions perhaps it is because he hears a different drummer. Let him step to the music he hears, however measured or far away.

Henry David Thoreau

For all of us, *the question is the quest-I-on.* In other words, the questions we ask or fail to ask shape the journeys of our lives. While most blindly go where the conventional questions of their society take them, heroes consciously choose and earnestly pursue the questions that shape their lives. As Joseph Campbell puts it, "The usual person is more than content, he is even proud, to remain within the indicated bounds, and popular belief gives him every reason to fear so much as the first step into the unexplored."[3] Will you live your life spontaneously from the heart and its pathless call, or conventionally from prescribed role? Will you take the path less traveled or the well-trodden road? This is the dilemma that Zen and the Grail Myth put to us, each in its own inimitable way.

Despite obvious differences, there are many underlying parallels between the Western Grail tradition and the Eastern Zen insights. Both say loud and clear: Trust your original nature. Be yourself—be done with fear. Both say: Beware the conventional and its deadening influence. Both instruct us to walk the pathless path, and remind us that only in trusting our original, spontaneous nature are we authentic—or even safe.

In both approaches, the Question is imperative. In the Zen (Rinzai) tradition, questions are central to *kensho*—seeing into one's own real nature. The Zen student meditates upon a *koan,* or "impossible question," as a means of awakening what Søren Kierkegaard calls "the supreme paradox": "The supreme paradox of all thought is the attempt to discover something that thought cannot think." In repeated attempts to "answer" the *koan,* the Zen student finds himself stumbling in the dark, tripping over his own mind until—finally—it stands still, and he sees by the light of his

If you observe well your own heart will answer.

R. Schwaller de Lubicz

original nature. Likewise, the Question is central to the Grail stories. As Grail scholar John Matthews writes, "Many, if not all, of the Grail mysteries are about self-discovery, hence, the emphasis on questions. The Quest is a journey inward as well as through the lands of the Grail."[4]

Man is not the creature of circumstances.
Circumstances are the creatures of men.
Benjamin Disraeli

Wisdom asks the right questions. Many of the world's myths, legends, and even children's fairy stories revolve around questions: How was the world created? When and how did humans first appear? What should one ask for when given three wishes? Likewise, many of the world's sacred writings revolve around questions. In the stories of the Zen masters and in much of the Buddhist writings, in Sufi stories and in much of the Upanishads, we find a question/answer format. The whole of the Bhagavad-Gita is in this style. Jesus questions his disciples and answers theirs. The Book of Job is an extended "What if?" question. Plato's *Dialogues* are full of questions, and philosophy generally is concerned with questions. Where wisdom is after the right questions, Enlightenment is getting back behind the questioner, the hungry, restless mind. Zen calls this "seeing into your own self-nature," into the loving, blissful consciousness that is before question, attention, or mind, and out of which these seem to arise. As the Sixth Cha'n (Chinese Zen) patriarch Hui Neng puts it, "From the first not a thing is." Where nothing is, there is nothing to get or to ask.

What is this place where thought is useless?
Knowledge and emotion cannot fathom it!
Yun-men Wen-yan

Questions are also central to creative work. In his wonderful book *The Craft of Novel Writing*, author Colin Wilson writes, "Go to the heart of most novels and you will find a question mark. This applies also, of course, to stories, which are simply novels on a smaller scale."[5] Literature is not alone. In every creative medium, we find creative work formed, fired, and glazed by questions. For example, Leonardo da Vinci said that while creating his *Last Supper* he was asking how he could make "the movements of the figures represent the passions of their souls."[6] Scientific discoveries are likewise fueled by questions: How does this work? How can this be? How does this affect that?

We follow questions on inner and outer journeys. Different questions lead us to different destinations. Colin Wilson begins his assessment of the relative merits of several centuries of novels by examining the expanse of their worldviews. He places novels that reflect what he calls a "Communal [Conventional] Life World" at the bottom of his list. In the middle, he puts those with an "Individual Life World." At the top, he puts those that approach the universal human condition in a category he calls "Purely Objective Vision."[7] These three worldviews correspond to the stages of psychological development on the path to enlightenment—moving out of the *conformity* of convention into the *individuation* of self, and then transcending the individual self in *universalization*—what in the East is referred to as *mukta,* or "liberation." The Self that is not self. The hero, literary or actual, must individuate from the mass of automatic conformity—become him- or herself—and then begin to discover the relationship of this self to all of life.

We have to remember that what we observe is not nature in itself but nature exposed to our method of questioning.

Werner Heisenberg

Wilson suggests that "the novel is a form of thought experiment ... The aim of all these thought experiments is the exploration of human freedom."[8] Similarly, the Grail Legend is a thought experiment that guides us through the psychological terrain of the hero's journey into the freedom of the authentic self (more on this below). The Zen *koan* too is a thought experiment aimed at spiritual freedom—beyond the limits of thought itself. We can make our own lives creative thought experiments that probe the boundaries of human freedom. Ask more expansive questions than convention dictates, and you widen your consciousness. Stay with these questions, and you deepen it. In exploring the range of human freedom, we can benefit from those who have gone before. We can learn from those who have, through spiritual and/or artistic "thought experiments," probed the boundaries of human limitation and gone beyond. George Bernard Shaw said, "You use a glass mirror to see your face; you use works of art to see your soul."[9] Scriptures and mythology likewise have this soul-reflective quality. Midas asks for gold; Solomon, for wisdom; Arjuna, for understanding. What are you asking for?

The only journey is the one within.

Rainer Maria Rilke

Ask and it shall be given unto you.
Seek and ye shall find.
                            Luke 11:9

Colin Wilson observes, "You can't write a really effective play—or a novel—about someone who doesn't know what he wants."[10] So it is with the story of your life; it doesn't get really interesting until you know what you're after. The first step to knowing what you want is to choose the questions you want to explore. Then determine to work them out, like a skilled novelist exploring a theme. Wilson distinguishes between high-flying and low-flying novel writers based on the questions they set out to explore—the bigger the questions, the greater the degree of difficulty. A competitive gymnast may execute a simple exercise perfectly and receive lower marks than another who attempts a far more difficult task but does it imperfectly. Similarly, a novelist can write a nice little story about achieving "Communal Life World" objectives, or she can attempt to take on bigger questions. Obviously, the more difficult the questions, the bigger the challenges, and the greater the possibility of failure. As with novelists and their stories, so with all of us and our lives. We can take our questions from the "Communal Life World" (What do they want me to do?) or from the "Individual Life World" (What do I want to do?), or we can ask, "What does humanity, or the universal Self, want me to do?" We can be high-fliers or low-flyers. Heroes are high-fliers. Sometimes they crash and sometimes they succeed brilliantly—but they are always after the big questions.

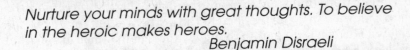

Nurture your minds with great thoughts. To believe in the heroic makes heroes.
                            Benjamin Disraeli

The mind runs on questions. Questions ignite the mind the way spark plugs ignite an automobile engine. All imaginative journeys are prompted by questions, be they the mundane questions of moving the body about (Is it time to get up? What shall I wear? What shall I have for breakfast? What is my schedule for today?) or the psychological need questions (Will she make me happy? Will he be faithful? Will my children fail or succeed? What will people think?) or the deeper attitudinal questions (How can I defend myself? How can I be approved of by others? How can I stay positive? How can I get ahead of people or back at them?). Most of this inner questioning is so automatic that we hardly notice it.

Human beings can alter their lives by altering their attitudes of mind.

William James

We call it "subconscious" and either dismiss it altogether or try to psychoanalyze it into "normality," whatever that is.

Your conscious or subconscious imaginative life, then, is just a matter of questions, or rather of chasing after answers to questions. Most everything you've thought or imagined came from some question you asked or from following the process or results of someone else's questioning. When you find your mind drifting in fantasy, some question sent it on that journey. When you imagine a better world, some question sent you on that journey. Becoming mindful is becoming aware of the questions you are asking. Moving toward your life's work is coming to ask the questions appropriate to it, and persisting with them.

Your Book of Questions

What questions dominate your life? These more than anything will determine its direction and shape. They form a kind of skeletal structure upon which your life is built. No matter what materials you use to cover the skeletal structure of a geodesic dome, you can't, by the covering alone, change it into the form of a forty-story skyscraper, the Statue of Liberty, or a canoe. So it is in our lives; we can put a fresh coat of paint on things, new siding or roofing, but this will not change their fundamental shape. New questions deeply asked will shape a new life. Further, in the process of tearing down one structure and building another, we may happen upon the mystery behind all structures and see the true nature of the raw materials used to build them.

You can't make a silk purse out of a sow's ear, and you can't follow the bliss of your life's work by asking conventional questions. As Emerson said, "Whoso would be a man [or woman] must be a nonconformist."[11] Think of the questions that shape most people's experience of work: How can I make good money? How can I win approval? How can I get to the top? Then consider questions like: Who am I? What in the world am I doing here? What is my passion? How can I make a real difference in the lives of others? Clearly these two sets of questions lead to fundamentally different lives.

How can I be useful, of what service can I be? There is something inside me, what can it be?

Vincent van Gogh

Live the questions now.
Rainer Maria Rilke

The latter set of questions held with sincerity and tenacity are as much *koans* as the well-known "What is the sound of one hand clapping?" If you think that the question "Who am I?" is any less a *koan* or any less difficult to answer, then you haven't ever really asked it, not deeply, as a *koan* is to be examined. To take these questions as *koans* is to awaken to an experience that those who pass by these questions, because they are simple or obvious on the one hand or obtuse or unanswerable on the other, will never know. What will be the *koans* of your life and work? Whether you choose your own questions or take those handed to you by society, your questions will shape your journey through life.

> *Underlying great doubt there is great satori, where there is thorough questioning there will be thoroughgoing experience of awakening.*
> *Zen Saying Quoted by Hakuin*

And his own thoughts, along that rugged way, Pursued, like raging hounds, their father and their prey.

Shelley

The road to individuation, the way to live as-king of your own life, is the way of asking your own questions. Zen historian Heinrich Dumoulin notes that, while today the Zen master usually chooses the student's *koan*, "in former times, the disciple chose the *koan* himself."[12] Choose your life questions, your *koans*. Embrace them with the totality of your being. Hold on tight to the questions but don't force the answers. Let them come to you. It helps if you can quiet the mind. It needn't be *zazen* or any kind of formal meditation but—in whatever way works for you—stop the mental chatter and just be still. The voice you hear in stillness is the One worth listening to.

Zen master Hakuin gave three essentials to the Zen practice of the *koan*: the great root of faith, the great ball of doubt, and tenacity of purpose.[13] The faith is in one's original nature, in the ultimate reality of the Buddha (literally, "Awakened") experience. The great ball of doubt means applying "concentrated doubt" to the *koans*. Pushing deeper, moving past the cynical and trite, going beneath the phony and affected—abandoning the quick fix that hides—exposing yourself. Tenacity of purpose is the intensity of commitment, the firm resolve that ultimately "shatters" doubt. These (faith, doubt, and tenacity of purpose) are just the same qualities of all the great mythic heroes. Certainly they are the qualities of Parzival, the hero of the Grail myth.

They are also essential qualities for those who would seek the call of their life's work. The great root of faith shows in your confidence in your vision for a better world and in your own part in it. The great ball of doubt represents the inner fears, doubts, vagaries, and the outer obstacles and adversities en route. The tenacity of purpose is the dogged determination to see it through. Take a *koan* for your life's work: What am I doing here? Where is my bliss? What is my passion? Where do I find meaning? Whatever your question, however you frame it, enter into it with emotional intensity and full imaginative engagement.

Lacking this imaginative questing, life becomes a dry, barren wasteland. To reclaim our vitality, we "must become as little children." We must allow our imaginations the freedom to explore in humility and openness. We must have what Zen calls a "beginner's mind." All the great explorers have this childlike humility and openness. Isaac Newton wrote, "I do not know what I may appear to the world; but to myself I seem to have been only like a boy playing on the seashore, and diverting myself in now and then finding a smoother pebble or a prettier shell than the ordinary, whilst the great ocean of truth lay all undiscovered before me." Einstein said, "The more I learn, the more I realize I don't know." In every field, the "big" people have little pretension. They are always open to a new question.

Now let's return to the Grail myth. Who is the hero of the Grail myth? Called variously Parzival, Perceval, Gallahad, or Bors in different versions of the story, he is the one adequate to "Grail Quest." His adequacy is not a matter of big muscles or intellectual refinement, but of a simple, childlike heart. Parzival (from here on, I am drawing on Wolfram von Eschenbach's version of the Grail story[14]) often seems something of a fool. The line between the hero and the fool is always thin indeed.

The greatest obstacle to being heroic is the doubt whether one may not be going to prove one's self a fool; the truest heroism is, to resist the doubt; and the profoundest wisdom, to know when it ought to be resisted, and when to be obeyed.
Nathaniel Hawthorne

Within our impure mind the pure one is to be found.

Hui Neng

Parzival is raised by his mother. His father was a knight who came to his end in the way knights often do. Mother would that the same not happen to her fair-haired boy. She isolates him from knightly stories and things, but of course this fails, for no one can be kept from his destiny. One day, three knights show up in bright and shining armor, and the boy is enchanted. Mother then hopes to have him ridiculed out of his quest, for as she observes, people are usually ready to "turn away from mockery."

She wants him to give up this foolish business of grand and heroic intentions. (Many young men do give up their dreams to please Mother, or "Mother" projected onto their wives.) So she gives him a pitiful old nag of a horse and a ridiculous costume, one that Wolfram tells us makes him look exactly like a fool.[15] The lesson is clear:

everyone who takes up the Quest must be prepared to face ridicule. One who accepts the prescribed role seems sure of himself. He knows what to do even if he is just doing what he is told. The one who breaks out of the conventional mold must figure out for himself what he is about. It is not only his desire for "something different" but also his searching after he-knows-not-what that makes him seem a fool.

This is precisely where one requires what Zen calls "the root of faith." It has been said that the meanest form of atheism is to not believe in oneself. This kind of atheist, if he takes up the quest at all, is soon ridiculed out of it. The following quote from Dag Hammarskjöld gives the sense of the kind of faith required for a heroic quest.

> He broke fresh ground—because, and only because, he had the courage to go ahead without asking whether others were following or even understood. He had no need for the divided responsibility in which others seek to be safe from ridicule, because he had been granted a faith which required no confirmation—a contact with reality, light and intense like the touch of a loved hand: a union in self-surrender without self-destruction, where his heart was lucid and his mind was loving.[16]

The crux of Parzival's story and his quest for the Grail is suggested in his first encounter in the Grail castle. After various adventures, Parzival sort of stumbles into the Grail castle. This is the wisdom of innocence. The purity of the simple fellow gets him into the Grail castle—the field of psychic transformation. In the castle lives a king who is sorely wounded. The king's illness has brought devastation to the kingdom—it has become the Wasteland.

> *The theme of the Grail is the bringing of life into what is known as "the wasteland." The wasteland is the preliminary theme to which the Grail is the answer . . . It's the world of people living inauthentic lives—doing what they are supposed to do.*
>
> *Joseph Campbell*

Parzival can redeem king and kingdom by asking a simple question. The wounded king is brought before him, and Parzival wants to ask, "What ails thee, brother?" But he has been told good knights don't ask a lot of questions. He is faced with the choice between acting spontaneously from his heart or conventionally from his role as a knight. He fails the test; innocence is not enough, for he has already been socially indoctrinated. It has caused him to doubt the promptings of his heart, and as Wolfram says in the very first line of his Parzival, "If vacillation dwell with the heart the soul will rue it."[17]

He chose to act conventionally, the way he thought he was supposed to. He muffed his opportunity for the Grail because he was trying so hard to be a good boy. He goes to bed that night, and when he gets up in the morning, the castle is empty. As he leaves the castle, he hears a voice shouting, "You silly goose. Why didn't you open your gob and ask the lord the Question?"[18] Though a little dense, he soon comes to realize that he has missed a great opportunity. He is sorely bummed out. As Wolfram says, "It was a cause of great remorse to the warrior that he had been so slow to ask the Question as he sat beside the sorrowing king."[19] Now for five long years he tries desperately to find his way back to the castle. In his travels, he is booed and jeered. Everyone knows he has failed, and everywhere before him is the desolation of the Wasteland.

He is gaining the wisdom of experience, of commitment, loyalty, and dedication. He must face the great ball of doubt. His journey now weaves through a maze-like set of experiences through which he, at long last, comes to understand and redeem his past. Like the ball of string the Greek hero Theseus unwound to find his way out of the labyrinth after his encounter with the Minotaur, Parzival's commitment to his quest, his question, provides him with a way through the wasteland and back to the Grail castle. Of course, he eventually triumphs and, in fact, becomes the Grail King. Through his tenacity of purpose, his loyalty to the Quest, he is told he has changed God's law. "A greater marvel never occurred . . . you have wrung the concession from God."[20] Just so, all who take up the great Quest-I-ons of life and hold tenaciously to them will enter into a marvelous life, the life of their destiny.

For Parzival, the basic issue is compassion. In other words, "What ails thee, brother?" In the Buddhist Bodhisattva tradition, this compassion is called "joyful participation in the sorrows of others"—the consecration of action in service to humanity. Without compassion, without the heart of spontaneous action, all one has is conventionality in one form or another. Of course, we can be conventionally spiritual, intellectual, yuppie, hippie, "revolutionary," or whatever. It's still the wasteland. You can recognize it right away. It lacks spontaneity, freshness, energy—life. Zen.

The way out is through the heart. The heart is the heart of things, the center of life. If the heart is not the center of your life, you are not really living; you are inauthentic—this is what the Grail myth is telling us. You're stuck in the wasteland of the conventional. Again, as Wolfram says, "If vacillation dwell with the heart the soul will rue it." The victory of the Grail Quest is the assertion of the spontaneous impulse of the heart over the auto-

Life's most urgent question is, what are you doing for others?

Martin Luther King, Jr.

mated, conventional monotony of uninspired, unimaginative life. It begins with choosing to make the questions of your own heart more important than those thrust upon you by social convention.

In another and older version of the Grail story, the one told by Chrétien de Troyes, the critical Question on which the story turns is: "Whom does the Grail serve?"[21] While the phrasing of the Question is different, the issue remains essentially the same. Is life for the endless desires, fears, and hostilities of the ego or for something larger than this? Not only the Grail story but also many of the great souls from various ages and places have told us reality and authentic living transcend the barren life of ego entrapment in societal convention.

In the World of Reality there is no self, / There is no other-than-self.   *Seng-ts'an*

What is reality? Selflessness.
               Sufi saying

I believe that unarmed truth and unconditional love will have the final word in reality.
            Martin Luther King, Jr.

The spontaneous, loving heart is the reality of human life. The mechanical, fortressed, inauthentic life of the ego is a transitory, dreamlike phase we seem to pass through on an apparent journey from innocence to experience and beyond. The desire to be what you are, to know the reality of love beyond self and other, begins to awaken the sleeper from his slumber.

A joyful heart is the inevitable result of a heart burning with love.
            Mother Teresa

You may have experienced that before you awaken from a dream, you sometimes incorporate events of the "real world" (the sound of an alarm clock or a dog barking) into your dream. Though you are still dreaming, the sound of the "real world" is moving into your awareness. If it's loud enough or if it persists long enough, it will soon wake you up. In the same way, the "desire to serve" is the sound of the real world intruding on an inauthentic life of a dream world. While we think, "I have a desire to serve," we are still dreaming, but hearing a sound from the real world. When we awaken, we know that we do not possess love as a thing apart, but

A person starts to live when he can live outside of himself.

Albert Einstein

that we *are* that love; we do not have a desire to serve—we *are* service and cannot be otherwise.

Focusing on your desire to serve is asking to be roused into your real life. As Mahatma Gandhi put it, "Consciously or unconsciously, every one of us does render some service or other. If we cultivate the habit of doing this service deliberately, our desire for service will steadily grow stronger, and make, not only for our own happiness, but that of the world at large."[22] We can think, I have this mind, and I'll put it in the service of humanity. I have emotions, and I want to put those in service to humanity. I have these talents and abilities; I want to put them to service for humanity. And out of this will come the particular manifestations of our work—the entrée is the desire to serve. Hear the call from the real world waking you to the way of happiness. Scattered through these pages in various quotations are many voices, calling us to heed the desire to serve. Below are just a few:

> *I don't know what your destiny will be, but one thing I know: the only ones among you who will be really happy are those who have sought and found how to serve.*
> Albert Schweitzer

> *Get beyond love and grief; exist for the good of man.*
> Yamamoto Tsunemoto

> *The sole meaning of life is to serve humanity.*
> Tolstoy

When will our consciences grow so tender that we will act to prevent human misery rather than avenge it?

Eleanor Roosevelt

Of course, it only makes sense that, as all of these (and so many more wise ones) have said, your mission in life is to serve humanity. You can't get to your life's work by asking: What's going to make me hot, rich, or let me get off easy? These questions won't give you your life's work, because they are not asking for it. If you want the seed thought that's going to give you your life's work, this is it: How is humanity to be served by this existence? or, expressed another way: What is my real life? The specific forms of your life's work arise out of this deep desire to serve humanity—to know your real life. Compassion moves us to serve, to ask, "What ails thee, brother?" Wisdom wants us to ask, Whom does the Grail serve?—in other words, What is my real life? or Who am I? Following these questions is living the Quest.

Right now, in this moment, you contain everything you need. Zen says, let go of the conception of yourself as a lack walking around waiting for fulfillment. The seed is within. It is not something that needs to be added or invented. All you can do is create the right circumstances for its germination. The questions that you will find in the pages that follow are not there so that you can come up with brilliant answers (though you may), but rather that through the process of questioning (questing) you might put a new light on the seed or add just a tad more water and suddenly—germination.

What Gets You Going and Keeps You Going on the Quest?

What gets the hero going on the quest? What sustains her in her seeking? The beautiful and the sublime. Art and life, through the Beautiful and the Sublime, call us to the Quest and nourish us along the way. To the sensitive heart, Beauty, the radiance of the veiled Grail, calls one out of the world of convention. Stop and think of it. What are the world's great scriptures, poetry, mythology, music, paintings, etc.? Beauty! Beauty is, as Plato said, "the splendor of truth"—not truth itself—only its reflection. Beauty is the transcendent made transparent in the world of form and time. The perception of beauty in nature and art stimulates the sensitive beholder to seek its source. It starts the hero on the Grail Quest, and if he achieves it, then he too will make things of Beauty, which will call the next generation of heroes to the questing life.

> *The most beautiful thing we can experience is the mysterious. It is the source of all true art and all science. He to whom this emotion is a stranger, who can no longer pause to wonder and stand rapt in awe, is as good as dead: his eyes are closed.*
> *Albert Einstein*

There is another way, the way of the terrible or, as it is sometimes called, "the sublime." Edmund Burke describes the sublime thus: "Whatever is fitted in any sort to excite the ideas of pain and danger, that is to say, whatever is in any sort terrible, or is conversant about terrible objects, or operates in a manner analogous to terror, is a source of the sublime."[23] Confrontation with death and death at its most terrible, war, can open one up to a new experience of life.

War is an extreme example, but we confront the sublime at every turn. We face the sublime in encountering the sheer horror of life—destruction, suffering, pain, war, and tragedy of every kind. Religious experience and ritual attempt in some way to come to terms with the sublime. In the Christian communion, we drink the blood of Christ; in Tibetan Buddhism, instruments of sacred music are crafted from human skulls and thighbones; in the Hindu religion, the goddess Kali stands with a garland of skulls, drinking the blood of her victims. In primitive or traditional cultures, ritual

Compared to what we ought to be, we are half awake.

William James

animal and even human sacrifice and painful initiatory rites are an attempt to reconcile the human psyche with the sublime.

Much of the art and literature of the modern era deals especially with the sublime. The awakening of Pierre, one of the main characters in Tolstoy's *War and Peace*, involves his encounter with the sublime. Like Parzival, he too is troubled by questions. Pierre is a thoughtful fellow earnestly seeking meaning. He travels up on this philosophy, and down on that disillusionment, until finally the shock, the overwhelming horror of war gives him release from his quest for meaning. "What had worried him in the old days, what he had always been seeking to solve, the question of the object of life, did not exist for him now. That seeking for an object in life was over for him now; and it was not fortuitously or temporarily that it was over . . . And it was just the absence of an object that gave him that complete and joyful sense of freedom that at this time made his happiness."[24] He had, as Zen would say, awakened his mind without fixing it anywhere.

> Man is unhappy because he doesn't know he's happy . . . If anyone finds out he'll become happy at once.
>
> Dostoyevsky, The Possessed

This release gave him a kind of, from the conventional perspective, madness. "Pierre's madness showed itself in his not waiting, as in the old days, for those personal grounds, which he called good qualities in people, in order to love them; but as love was brimming over in his heart he loved men without cause."[25]

Of course, this experience sounds good, like something many of us would like to know for ourselves. The difficulty is, we must cross the wasteland to get there—the barren, empty, dry, and desolate places of our inner lives—the great ball of doubt. We cannot pretend to have put an end to the questions until they are, in fact and forever, silenced by the quest itself. We can only be where we are now, while keeping in view the reality of our destiny (and awakening). The heroic spirit carries on in the quest for real life and work, in spite of inner doubts and outer obstacles.

Driven on by creative discontent, refusing to settle for less, he stays the course, she keeps on keeping on. This is the theme of Goethe's masterpiece, *Faust*. If Faust becomes satisfied, Mephistopheles gets him. The "devil" and his hellish wasteland gets the man or woman who becomes self-satisfied. With reference to work, Peter Drucker has put it like this: "No matter what job it is, it ain't final. The first few years are trials. The probability that the first choice you

> You ask me for a motto. Here it is: SERVICE.
>
> Albert Schweitzer

*All the fish needs
Is to get lost
in the water.
All man needs
is to get lost
In Tao.*

Chuang Tzu

make is right for you is roughly one in a million. If you decide your first choice is the right one, chances are you are just plain lazy."[26]

Keep away from people who try to belittle your ambitions. Small people always do that, but the really great make you feel that you, too, can become great.　　　　　　　　　　　　*Mark Twain*

And what becomes of those who hear the call and refuse? Joseph Campbell writes, "Refusal of the summons converts the adventure into its negative . . . the subject loses the power of significant affirmative action and becomes a victim to be saved. His flowering world becomes a wasteland of dry stones and his life feels meaningless . . . All he can do is create new problems for himself [and others] and await the gradual approach of his disintegration."[27] All I can do is encourage you to respond to the call you hear—invite you to consecrate yourself to your best for the sake of all humankind.

The *Koan* of Creativity

In his early essays, Zen writer D. T. Suzuki discussed the process through which the Zen student moves in contemplation of the *koan* to the *satori* of enlightenment. He said that the process was marked by stages of *accumulation, saturation*, and *explosion*.[28] These three exactly parallel the creative process known to creative artists and scientists. Let's briefly consider these three stages: first with reference to the *koan,* and then in terms of creative work.

In the *accumulation* stage, one learns to sit still and draw scattering energy back into oneself. One's concentration improves and with it, one's confidence, but the restless mind is still untamed. The *koan* answers at this stage come from memory or intellect, being cute or straining to get it right. They are disappointing failures. One's initial confidence is followed by doubt, as one moves into the *saturation* stage. Though it seems he has gotten nowhere, the student is now awake enough to recognize his sleep. But brief waking moments only serve to illustrate the depth of a slumber so deep that he begins to doubt if he will ever wake up. Nevertheless, he presses on in his meditation, reminding himself of what Hakuin said about great doubt—complete saturation—eventually bringing great *satori*.

Achieving total saturation may take more or less time—time is not as important as intensity. Imagine that you are trying to melt copper, which has a melting temperature of around two thousand degrees Fahrenheit. You could keep it at four hundred degrees for a very long time without getting anywhere. To get the transformation, you have to reach the critical point of intensity—in this case, two thousand degrees. It doesn't matter whether it takes a day or a week, one year or twenty; you have to reach the critical point of intensity before you have the melt, the transformation. So it is with the *koan*: extreme intensity of faith and doubt brings the *explosion*—the awakening melt. Now let's consider the role of *accumulation, saturation*, and *explosion* in the creative process.

Accumulation: This is the initial phase of the creative process. We might call it "great beginnings." This is the stage when the idea first occurs and generates the initial action. For this stage to come to its fullest development, one must do everything she can to accumulate that which supports the initial revelation. She might accumulate knowledge or materials, the support of other people, or her own energy through the scheduling of time. Her love for the vision she has seen sets her in motion, collecting the technical, material, intellectual, and human resources she requires to manifest it. She moves with confidence, trusting that, as George Herbert said, "Love makes one fit for any work."[29]

Saturation: This is the second phase of the creative process. We might call this stage "great absorption" or "magnificent obsession." It's the one that separates the men from the boys, the women from the girls. At this point, we find out that there is a world of difference between being *interested by* something and being *interested in* something. You might be *interested by* an attractive person walking down the street, but to create a relationship with someone, you have to be consistently *interested in* that person—warts and all. The original creative idea might have seemed interesting to you, but are you ready to stay with it—to keep creating interest in it, even when you're not sure of what you're doing? This is the test of saturation.

In the first stage, the creative idea comes to you; in the last stage, it takes on its own life; in the middle, the saturation stage, it takes your life. It temporarily embodies in you. Because of your love for this vision, you freely give yourself over to it. Think of a creative idea as a living entity that exists on another plane of existence. This entity wants to live on the physical plane. The problem is, it doesn't have a physical body; so it will borrow yours while you make one for it. The entity will tell you how to construct its new body and will work through you to do it. Time and again, creative artists report on this process.

Often labor pains are associated with the body-building process. This is why the lives of creative artists sometimes take on a tragic quality. Until they have set the idea free, they hang suspended,

The excellency of every art is its intensity, capable of making all disagreeables evaporate.

John Keats

as it were, between two worlds (the idea realm of the creative vision and the physical world of manifestation). Saturation in the creative vision may cause them to neglect other areas of their lives. The artist lives for the work even more than for himself. One biographer of Mozart has written of the great composer, "Artistically he succeeded, though he died penniless. Throughout [he was]... a creative artist with a goal that had to be achieved. No matter what, he adhered to his vision."[30] This is creative saturation—that no matter what, you adhere to your vision.

Intensity is the essence of saturation. Sometimes the work comes out all at once. Mozart was said to have written many of his compositions as if taking dictation. On the other hand, many reworkings are often necessary to realize the original vision. Beethoven reworked the theme of the *adagio* movement of his Fifth Symphony at least a dozen times; James Joyce spent nineteen years on *Finnegans Wake;* Cézanne, at least eight years on his great *The Large Bathers*.[31] Often the artist is forced by the demands of the vision to grow—to develop in ways that make him better able to express the creative image. After many years of work, part one of Goethe's *Faust* was published in 1808. Twenty-four years later, part two was published. Goethe was still at work on his masterpiece in the last months of his life. One can say without question that the man who wrote part one was not the same man who wrote part two. He grew with the work. He remained intensely saturated in it throughout.[32]

Explosion: This is the final stage of the creative process. We might call it "happy endings." In this stage, the work becomes a thing in itself, whole and complete. A tremendous explosive relief often accompanies the completion of a creative work. The thing has its own life now and is done with you (though something of you is in it). There may be a sense of loss. If we hold too tightly to that which now has its own life, if after the high voltage of saturation we find our energy dropping to a more mundane level, if we no longer feel useful, or if we are struck at how far the creation seems to stand from the original vision, we may feel a sense of loss or letdown.

On the other hand, we might experience great joy on completion. One may feel as though a great burden has been lifted from his shoulders. He may feel free to pursue other creative endeavors that were not possible while he was saturated in the previous creative work. Even as a pregnant woman cannot conceive, we are not free to begin great new projects while in the midst of building the body for a great idea. The joy of the completion is in the total release of saturated energy. As we can see, each stage of the creative process has its own joy. There is the enthusiastic joy of the new idea, the concentrated joy of absorption or saturation, and the explosive joy of completion.

What is Art? It is the response of man's creative soul to the call of the Real.

Tagore

What's Ahead in Act I

There are a number of ways to slice a cake. There are, likewise, a number of ways to find your life's work. No matter how you slice it, cake is cake. No matter how you find it, your life's work is your life's work. In the reminder of "Act I: The Quest for Life's Work," you will encounter several methods to assist you in tapping into your life's work. Each approach stands on its own as a means of discovery. Yet combining all of these methods will help you to see your work with a clarity and breadth not possible through any single method. Each method can be thought of as tapping into a different level of awareness. Some of these approaches may resonate with you more than others do. Whatever method you use, the key ingredient in finding your life's work is your desire. With enough desire and commitment, any of these methods or others will work for you. Lacking sufficient desire, all methods are inadequate.

It is the first of all problems for a man (or woman) to find out what kind of work he (or she) is to do in this universe.

Thomas Carlyle

"Scene I: Vision Questing" invites you to consider your worldview (the way you see the world) and the effect that it has in shaping the world. Further, it asks you to consider what world, national, or community problems you might like to work toward solving. Finally, it asks you to use your imagination in seeing the world as it could be and to recognize and honor the inspirations that have already come to you.

"Scene II: Clarifying Values" asks you to answer questions like: What values are most important to me? What is my basic philosophy of life? What are the most important lessons I have learned in life? What seemed most important to me as a child? What do I most want to accomplish before I die?

"Scene III: Pointing to Purpose" invites you to answer questions like: What am I doing here? What is my part in this grand play of life? How can I make a difference? What do I want to do?

"Scene IV: Targeting Talents" asks you to answer questions like: What do I love to do? What am I naturally good at? What are my natural strengths and abilities? Further, it asks you to consider how you can best put your talents to work in service to your vision, values, and purpose.

"Scene V: Marking Mission Objectives" invites you to answer questions like: What specific outcomes do I want to effect? What can I realistically achieve in the span of my life? What *must* I do?

Detour #1: The Denial Trap

Man is a social animal. This statement is a truism, one we all accept and pass by without contemplating the meaning. If man is a social animal, then his existence and action cannot but affect his fellows. Man, fully conscious of himself as a social being (regardless of whatever else he may be), recognizes that he affects and creates social reality in his individual choices and actions. If he is a social animal, he cannot do otherwise. Therefore, to say that he has a responsibility to the social order he is creating and perpetuating is almost too clumsy an expression, for that responsibility is no different from the responsibility to himself. It is simply a matter of being what he is.

The denial of the social aspect of man is a denial of self. It is a denial of one's own nature. This denial takes two forms: "Don't Care" and "Don't Know." "Don't care about others" equals "Don't care about self." "Don't know what I can contribute to others" means "I don't know myself." It is in hiding behind "Don't Care" and "Don't Know" that we perpetuate folly. For to act without self-knowledge (self-awareness) is to make action itself a denial of self. By self-knowledge here, I do not mean some mystical apparition, but simply the realization that man *is* a social animal.

One can now begin to understand how we have come to make such a mess of our world. We have been acting without basic self-awareness. We have been acting as if we were not social. Precisely because this denial has been so strong, we are now beginning to break free of it. Our denial has produced weapons of destruction and environmental consequences that put in jeopardy the entire human species. The individual's denial of social nature has come at last to put the individual at risk. We are being forced to face the fact that we are all in this together, that indeed man is a social animal.

Don't Care: "Social responsibility" is not an afterthought of an "enlightened person"; it is a fundamental part of being true to what one is. The pursuit of so-called "self-interest" apart from the realization of the social nature of self is immature because it is unaware. The mature individual cares, not out of largesse, but because he cares about himself.

Don't Know: "Don't know what to do" is the last hiding place from awareness (see page 237). Suffice to say here: Do something that needs to be done. Don't do things that are better left undone. Support those who are doing things that need to be done. Find what needs to be done that goes undone and do it.

Crafting the Story of Your Life

Throughout this book, you'll be asked to think of your life as a story. When most novelists sit down to write, they don't know everything that is going to happen in their story. They start with an idea, a compelling central question that they work out through the plot and characters. We invite you to approach the story of your life in this way—to start with the life questions you want most to explore, and shape these into a rough outline. Don't worry about the details or about how you will accomplish your objectives. We will get to that later. Start by letting your imagination follow the track of the questions or issues that grab you.

Of course, you are the main character of your life's story as well as the author. In a good novel, the main character grows and develops; so too in a good life. A good novel has an interesting plot; so does a good life. An author must be able to step back and see her story from a distance—to objectively consider whether or not it achieves her purpose. Ask yourself, "If I could look at it objectively, would I want to read the story of my life? Does it grab and hold my attention? Does it have the elements of a good story: challenges to overcome, growth, direction, confidence, a larger-than-self purpose?" If the answer is no, then perhaps the main character needs development; the plot needs to be clarified, expanded, sharpened; or excitement needs to be generated by increasing the tension between what could be and what is. If you can honestly answer yes, then—where is the next chapter going?

Your Story's Elements

You can conceive of the action of lifework planning in terms of the elements that go into crafting a story.

Act I—The Quest for Life's Work: **Fixing the Central Questions.** Finding voice. Outlining the plot.

Act II—The Game of Life's Work: **Developing the Characters and Their Roles**. Particularly the main character.

Act III—The Battle for Life's Work: **Clarifying the Conflicts.** Tension between what could be and what is.

Act IV—The School of Life's Work: **Identifying Character Growth.** How is the main character (you) to become a better, more capable person?

The Quest for Life's Work Affirmations

1. I am now willing to see the vision of my life's work.

2. Whatever fears or blocks may have kept me from seeing my work in the past are now dissolved by my desire to know and be my very best.

3. I am open to receiving the vision of my life's work easily and with joy. I now receive it.

4. I am willing to accept this vision and promise to be responsible to and for it.

5. Having seen the vision of my life's work, I trust that it will continue to reveal itself more fully to me as time goes by.

6. I am confident of my ability to manifest the vision I see.

7. I boldly take each and every step necessary to make this vision manifest.

8. My strongest talents and abilities are now made clear to me. I accept and embrace them with gratitude.

9. I am happy that I am a unique individual, endowed with unique talents and abilities. I never spend my precious time and energy comparing my talents with those of others.

10. I like me, and I like being who I am. I am glad I have the talents that I have, and I use them wisely in service to others.

11. Each and every day, it becomes clearer to me how I can best apply my talents to my life's work.

12. The more I focus on my desire to achieve the vision of my life's work, the more my talents become clear to me and the more effectively I use them.

Vision Questing

If we want to make something really superb of this planet, there is nothing whatever that can stop us.
                    Shepherd Mead

I dentifying your visions of and for the world starts you on the quest for your best. You project your vision beyond myopic concerns that often block the perception of a life's work. As you deeply consider what you would like to see for mankind and the world, your own part in that process will begin to come into view. In this section, you will have the opportunity to consider your worldview (the way you see the world), the clarity of your perception, and the depth of your imagination. You will be challenged to love the world as it is, while holding an image of the world that could be.

Though anatomically modern humans—people who look like you and me—have been on this planet for at least 160,000 years, it is only in the last few generations that human beings have had a chance to see where they are. We've seen the pictures of our world taken from space, and we now know we are drifting on a circular life raft in a vast sea of emptiness. It is one thing to be told that our planet revolves around the sun or that our solar system is in the outer third of the Milky Way. It is quite another to recognize this beautiful blue-white ball as our home. For eons, humans have been generating and focusing on symbols that reinforce tribal, religious, racial, ideological, and national divisions. All these distinctions vanish in the new image of our common home. It is the one symbol that unites every human being, indeed, every creature on this planet. This dramatic new vision of where we are and of who we are in relation to one another will necessarily bring profound change to the reality of life on this planet, provided, of course, that we can integrate it in time. Today, a vision of life that recognizes our place within the universe and the interdependence of all life on earth is bumping up against the "man against nature" view that has dominated Western thinking for at least the last three hundred years and, by now, has been exported to every corner of the globe.

The discussion that follows will consider: vision as *worldview,* that is, as a way of seeing; vision as *a process of perception*; and vision as *an imaginative, or creative, process.* Your vision for the future is expressed in the way you see the world today. This applies to both your worldview and your ability to accurately perceive what is going on in it. Vision as an imaginative process means simply this: everything that has ever been created began as an idea—we create what we imagine.

Vision in Three Aspects

1. Worldview: Vision as a Way of Seeing
2. Perception: The Vision to See What Is Going On
3. Imagination: The Vision to See What Could Be

Worldview: Vision as a Way of Seeing

Without vision the people perish.
Proverbs 29:18

The way you look at the world—the Germans call it *weltanschauung,* or "worldview." A worldview is a "general perspective from which one sees and interprets the world."[1] Put another way, your worldview is your metaphysical window to the world. *Metaphysical* simply means "beyond (*meta*) the physical (*physic*)." A metaphysic is a view that cannot be justified by empirical evidence; it can neither be proved nor disproved by fact or argument. It's an overarching way of seeing that colors all our so-called objective observations and logical interpretations. For a very long time, the principal metaphysical debate in the West was over whether or not God exists. It seems to me that today the fundamental metaphysical debate is over whether life is to be viewed as sacred or as a commodity.

A commodity worldview equates value and meaning with economics. Any activity, thing, or event that can be converted into economic gain is valuable; any that cannot be, isn't. Similarly, economics is the meaningful criterion for establishing relative value between and within categories of things, events, activities, or people. From a commodity worldview, maximizing economic gain is the raison d'être of the individual, the community, and the state. Life serves economics. In the name of economic growth, life (its organisms, activities, events, and processes) must be subjected to ever-greater domination and control. Only by exploiting human and natural resources to the utmost can their full potential for economic gain be realized.

An entirely new system of thought is needed, a system based on attention to people, and not primarily attention to goods.

E. F. Schumacher

A sacred worldview values life for its own sake. It gives birth to feelings of responsibility, compassion, and love. Implicit within it is an *internal* constraint against the exploitation of other individuals, groups, or species. While from the standpoint of the commodity worldview the relevant activity is the conversion of life into economics (i.e., "monetizable commodities"), from a sacred worldview the relevant activity is the appreciation of life. Both of these activities represent a transformation. To convert a life (human, bovine, cereal, arboreal) or activity of life (labor, learning, leisure, sex) into a commodity is to fundamentally transform that life or life activity. Likewise, a life or activity of life is transformed by the appreciation of it. The transformation born of appreciation is called "art." The transformation born of commodification is called "commerce." While commerce is a necessary and legitimate social activity, embracing a worldview that demands ever-increasing

The universe is made of one kind of whatever-it-is, which cannot be defined.

Thaddeus Golas

commodification is neither necessary nor wise. History and cultural anthropology teach us that commerce can be contained (in both senses of the word) within a sacred worldview. Whether or not the relatively recent phenomenon of rampant commodification can long endure is an open question.

Our word *sacred* comes from the Latin *sacer* "from the root seen also in *sanus*, sane."[2] A sacred worldview is a sane view of life. You needn't be religious to hold a sacred worldview. There are those who claim no God or religion, yet have a sense of the sacredness of life. On the other hand, there are those who profess belief in God, yet seem to view life as a commodity. Whether Christian or Jew, Muslim or Hindu, Buddhist or humanist, pantheist or shamanist, atheist or agnostic, those who hold life sacred may have much more in common than is generally supposed. While there are endless differences in the interpretation and emphasis made by those who hold a sacred, or sane, view of life, a few essentials are commonly accepted. These include *wholeness*, *harmony*, and *radiance*. These terms are from James Joyce's theory of art (see chapter 2). Notice the parallels with the Eastern *sat, cit, ananda* — being, consciousness, and bliss — or the Christian Father, Son, and Holy Spirit.

The Wholeness of Life: *Beyond the understanding of human intellect, there is an intelligent life order.* This life order may be called divine or natural intelligence, cosmic or scientific law, or a host of other names, but anyhow, it exists. More than a sum of its parts, this life order is an integrated whole. In fact, quantum mechanics has revealed that the perception of a world of separate, discrete things reflects the limitations of our senses and language and not the underlying (subatomic) reality. Physicist Fritjof Capra put it like this: "The constituents of matter and the basic phenomena involving them are all interconnected; they cannot be understood as isolated entities but only as integral parts of a unified whole."[3]

The Harmony of Life: *Everything is in relationship to everything else.* The universe is better understood as a living organism than as a machine. Events in one part of the organism affect the whole of the organism. Since every change affects the entire system, we ought to seek harmony in the system rather than the advantage of any individual, group, or species over others. As Martin Luther King, Jr., wrote, "It really boils down to this: that all life is interrelated. We are all caught in an inescapable network of mutuality, tied into a single garment of destiny. Whatever affects one directly, affects all indirectly."

The Radiance of Life: *Life's very existence is an awe-inspiring mystery.* Encounters with the energy that is life bring feelings of awe, wonder, and joy, all of which evoke respect. In the words of Albert Schweitzer, "We can no longer say that there is a senseless existence with which we can do as we please. We recognize that all existence is a mystery like our own existence."[4] Beyond any purpose we can imagine, life itself is valuable and ought to be celebrated, preserved, and protected. Save the whales or rain forests, whether profitable or not; avoid war; uphold human dignity, because life is valuable.

Everything in Nature contains all the powers of Nature. Everything is made of hidden stuff.
                                        Emerson

Many do not know that we are here in this world to live in harmony.

Dhammapada

Again, these terms of the sacred do not belong to any particular religion or even to religion per se. The following from Albert Einstein has all the elements of a sacred view of life: "[The scientist's] religious feeling takes the form of a rapturous amazement [radiance] at the harmony [harmony] of natural law, which reveals an intelligence of such superiority [wholeness] that, compared with it, all systematic thinking and acting of human beings is utterly insignificant."[5]

For the purposes of this discussion, I will assume you hold a sacred view of life. While the facts and logic that support a sacred view are, to those who hold it, overwhelmingly persuasive; for those who don't, they're not. It would be fruitless to try to convince those who are not already so inclined. For those who want convincing, *Small Is Beautiful: Economics as if People Mattered*, by E. F. Schumacher, and *The Tao of Physics*, by Fritjof Capra, state the case well, not to mention the Bible, the Talmud, the Upanishads, the Tao Te Ching, the Bhagavad-Gita, the Koran, the Dhammapada, etc.

Out of a sacred worldview, ethics flow naturally. From a commodity view, efforts at moral or ethical restraints must rely on reward and punishment. Holding to a sacred view, we can let ethics take care of themselves. Losing a sacred view, ethics are always artificial, inadequate, and bound to create resistance and opposition.

Commodity ethics: *Everything is for sale, and the one with the gold rules . . .*

Sacred ethics: *Do unto others as you would have them do unto you . . . Love your neighbor as yourself. What goes around comes around, etc.*

Again, sacred or not, a worldview is a metaphysic, and metaphysics are, indeed, *meta* (beyond) the physical. While a metaphysic can never be proved or disproved by facts, a metaphysic does select out the facts that support it and ignore those that do not. For example, happiness is not a matter of fact but of attitude. If one is unhappy, he finds the facts to substantiate his unhappiness; if happy, the facts to support his happiness. Happiness, while independent of facts as a cause, can itself become a fact. We all can recognize the fact of a happy man or woman. Occasionally, such a recognition of fact can trigger a spontaneous change of attitude. This is the effect that an example can have on us. The happy man has not proved the efficacy of his view by logic; rather, he has demonstrated it by example.

If we're going to change the quality of life in any appreciable way, we must begin, not with facts, but with attitudes. Significant social change always begins with a change of attitude. Albert Einstein called this change of attitude "a new level of thinking." He said, "The world we have made as a result of a level of thinking we have done thus far creates problems we cannot solve at the same level at which we created them."[6] Acting from the attitude of a sacred view of life creates a new set of facts, as well as a different perception of the existing facts. It represents a "new level of thinking."

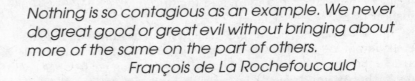

Nothing is so contagious as an example. We never do great good or great evil without bringing about more of the same on the part of others.
François de La Rochefoucauld

It is less important that we change the minds of others than that we have the courage to put our sacred vision into practice. Those who are caught up in the commodity worldview will likely remain unconvinced, at least in the near term. They may try to involve you in "proving" the viability of your vision, or discount it as unrealistic or even simpleminded. Remember, from a commodity worldview, economic profit is what is real and valuable. All other values are secondary, even superfluous: "It's nice to do good, but what REALLY matters is the bottom line." The commodity worldview is not fundamentally interested in what is right or necessary, beautiful or wise, but in what will sell. Its important facts are dollar signs and profit potentials, and often only short-term ones at that. Other facts may not register through the filter of the commodity metaphysic.

Apart from business, economics has become the sole, or at least dominant, criterion by which projects in science, art, and education are judged. In considering whether a project is "worthy of support,"

Continue to soil your bed and you will one night suffocate in your own waste.

*Chief Seattle
1844*

its purpose or quality is less important than its bottom-line potential. The term *viable*, which originally meant "able to live," has come to mean "economically profitable." This redefinition has meant the extinction of thousands of species of plants and animals, not to mention the elimination of many human pursuits that are seen as superfluous to profit. All this, it is argued, is a necessary part of the high standard of living we enjoy. But, as E. F. Schumacher has noted, "high standards of living do not necessarily mean high standards of life."[7]

The more I study physics, the more I am drawn to metaphysics.

Albert Einstein

Those with a commodity worldview may have difficulty seeing, let alone supporting, what you are trying to do. (Unless, of course, you frame it in commodity terms, for example, "green profits.") "Good works" are agreeable from the commodity standpoint, so long as their advocacy does not challenge the legitimacy of the commodity view itself. For example, it is worthwhile to educate and train the inner-city poor *because* we need skilled workers to "stay competitive." This is an acceptable commodity argument. On the other hand, assertions that every human life is sacred and, therefore, deserves a decent (even a beautiful) existence may not be heard by those with a commodity perspective.

Make a profit coming and going; this is progress, from the commodity perspective. We needn't worry if the commodity worldview has been the ruin of the environment, because we are told it is now ready to turn "saving" the environment into a commodity. The business magazines trumpet the big profits waiting to be made on the environment. Water polluted and loaded down with chemicals from industrial waste and agricultural runoff? Don't ask fundamental questions about the ethics of the commodity worldview; delight in the fact that bottled water is now the fastest growing part of the "beverage industry." The commodity worldview that gave us preserved, processed, and "enriched" foods will now give us the original "all natural" foods as high-priced specialty items.

The commodity worldview holds that the creation of life itself is a commodity to be owned and sold for profit. We've had patented "grain food commodities" for many years. (Meanwhile, the genetic diversity of the planet's food grains has shrunk dramatically.) In recent decades, patents for other food crops, as well as for fish and livestock, have proliferated. Even water, upon which all of life ultimately depends, is increasingly being exploited as a commodity.

I exist as I am, that is enough.

Walt Whitman

While all of the above are taken as signs of progress from the commodity view, they are clearly dangerous from any sane perspective interested in the long-term quality of life on this planet.

The purpose of this discussion is not to condemn or complain, but simply to demonstrate that so much of the insanity of this world makes perfect sense (is understandable) from the commodity metaphysic. If we are going to change the world in any fundamental way, we must collectively change the way we see the world, and ourselves in it. This, of course, can only happen one individual at a time. The writer who gives up his art for a life in advertising or the executive who takes less pay and more hours to work for a nonprofit foundation engaged in a service he believes in—each is deciding in his own way the future of the world. The victories and defeats are one at a time—not a matter of "them," but of you and me. Gandhi put it eloquently: "I believe that if one man gains spiritually, the whole world gains with him, and if one man falls, the whole world falls to that extent."[8]

Of course, the sacred view of life is still the minority view in the developed world. From the standpoint of the commodity metaphysic, it is a dangerous heresy. If you put your sacred worldview into practice, you may be ridiculed or scorned, not because your view is unsubstantiated by the facts, but because it is not yet the prevailing one. (All minority views are considered stupid until they gain acceptance.) You may be told to "grow up" or to "get with it." Certainly we can all grow more mature. Yet it is lunacy to imagine that rejecting the sacredness of life is a necessary element of the maturation process. If it is, we will shortly mature our species out of existence. "Get with it" may mean: "Get into step. March your way into consumer heaven. Never mind the larger social perspective or the deeper spiritual one—just get what you can while you can."

> *Every great movement must experience three stages: ridicule, discussion, adoption.*
> *John Stuart Mill*

If you are out of step because you are taking the time to reflect upon your direction or because you are already acting out of a sacred view, be undaunted in the face of the pressure to conform. You cannot prove the validity of a sacred view of life, but you can over time create and leave behind something that others can recognize. See life as sacred, and work to make it so. From the context of a sacred view of life, we create from perceiving a need or directly from inspiration. Later, we will consider creating from inspiration. For now, let's consider how we create from perception.

Whoso would be a man must be a nonconformist.

Emerson

Perception: The Vision to See What Is Going On

The second aspect of vision is *perception.* Even as we create the world by our attitudes toward it, so do we create the world by our perceptions of it. It is one of the great marvels of consciousness that whatever situation we clearly perceive, we improve. To see is to see a better way; to perceive any problem clearly is to begin to create its solution. All we need is the wisdom and patience to keep looking, and the love to hold what we see up to the light of under-standing. Only when we doubt our capacity to create (love) do we begin to block and distort our perceptions of the world. Only then do we fear to look at it square-on. From the love and confidence of clear perception, the world must become a better place.

> *Nothing has such power to broaden the mind as the ability to investigate systematically and truly all that comes under thy observation in life.*
> *Marcus Aurelius*

Participate joyfully in the sorrows of the world. We cannot cure the world of sorrows, but we can choose to live in joy

Joseph Campbell

Again, whatever we give our loving attention to, naturally improves. We all know, for example, that plants respond to loving kindness and attention. *The Secret Life of Plants,* by Peter Tompkins and Christopher Bird gives incredible testimony to the power of loving attention to affect plant growth and well-being.[9] What is true for plants is certainly true for the "higher" forms of life. We all have had practical experience with this; areas of our lives that we avoid and neglect become problem areas. Once we begin to give these areas loving attention, they start to improve.

We usually move from avoidance and confusion to attention and clarity only when we perceive that it is necessary. It was Plato who gave us that wonderful maxim: Necessity is the mother of invention. Necessity is simply the perception that something must be given more attention (i.e., improved) and that the perceiver is the one to do something about it. Once we deem it necessary, we begin to look over what we had previously overlooked, until we see a better way. Necessity often forces us out of the prejudices and conceptual limitations that have heretofore blocked our perception. Necessity has an intensity, an urgency, to it. Without this intensity, there is no drive to keep looking for a better way.

For example, well over 50 percent of all employed Americans consistently report that they are dissatisfied in their work.[10] Most, however, never allow their dissatisfaction to reach the point where action becomes a necessity. They never know the kind of necessity

*The soul
never thinks
without a picture.*

Aristotle

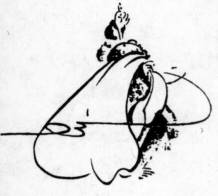

that would compel them to thoroughly examine themselves and their environments until they perceive a truer vision of their life's work.

Of course, necessity, like beauty, is in the eye of the beholder. No matter how deplorable a situation may seem to an outsider, the individual involved finds no reason to look for a better way until, for him, it becomes a necessity. When discontent reaches the point of necessity, we demand of ourselves and our world that a better way be shown. Until then, we put up with less. Because we fear and hate the problems that seem to trap us, we find no way out. It is often necessary that we find more confidence and love before things can start to improve.

*I clearly see how the Eternal Light
Shines in your mind,
So that upon its mere sight, love is enkindled.*
Dante

This applies to the bigger picture of planetary and community problems as well as to our individual concerns. We are stuck in these problems until we have the confidence and strength to look at them with love. The gift of the innovator is his ability to keep his attention on what most of us avoid. He makes it a necessity to find a better way. She keeps looking until she does. We can say that it was a necessity for Jonas Salk to discover the cure for polio, for Maria Montessori to design a better way of educating children, or for Gandhi to devise an effective means of nonviolent social change. Creative discontent was driving them all.

Where is creative discontent taking you? What is the better way you see for the world as a whole, or in some particular arena? Perhaps it's the cure for some contagious disease or a means of more efficient energy use. Perhaps it's a way of improving communication within families. Maybe it's a necessity for you to create a better way of dealing with drug addiction or a better way of coordinating nonprofit resources and activities. Maybe it's a necessity to create a better way of utilizing the knowledge, skill, and energy of the elderly. Perhaps it's a necessity for you to bring about an advance in whatever field you work in or want to work in. What are your necessary discoveries? If you don't know yet, keep looking. Sharpen your observation skills.

Don't listen to what they say. Go see.
Chinese Proverb

Leonardo da Vinci kept extensive notebooks. Hundreds of detailed drawings of everything from the flight of cannonballs to the structure of plants, from human anatomy to fish eggs, honed his observation skills. What he learned from these detailed observations was of great benefit to him in his later inventions and artistic creations.[11] In the same way, keeping track of your observations can stimulate creative insights.

Buckminster Fuller kept detailed diaries in what he called his "Chronofile." Fuller viewed himself as a guinea pig and the world as his laboratory. Careful observation of both led him to an important discovery. In his words: "Chronofile observation showed that the larger the number for whom I worked, the more positively effective I became. Thus it became obvious that if I worked always and only for humanity, I would be optimally effective." It was on the basis of these observations that he determined to commit all of his "productivity potentials to dealing with our whole planet Earth."[12] His discovery of optimal effectiveness in world service was probably his single most important discovery, since all later discoveries depended upon his fixing his attention on global problems.

> *A man of science doesn't discover in order to know, he wants to know in order to discover.*
> *Alfred North Whitehead*

Careful observation helps to keep the mind in shape. In the words of Leonardo da Vinci, "Iron rusts from disuse; water loses its purity from stagnation, and in cold weather becomes frozen; even so does inaction sap the vigors of the mind."[13] All the great minds seem to be saying, "Don't be afraid of problems. Take a creative look at them." Creative solutions arise spontaneously upon the clear perception of particular personal, community, or planetary problems. Whatever level you are working on, get clear on exactly what the problems are. Penetrate to the essence. According to Einstein, "The formulation of a problem is far more essential than its solution." When we see problems clearly, solutions present themselves.

For ignorance is in reality the Buddha nature.

Cheng-Tao-Ko

Seeing with the Eyes of Patience: Unmasking the Ignorance Blinder

Often our ignorance blocks us from creative solutions. We cannot see a solution until we have sufficient data. We must have the patience to persist until we see a problem clearly enough for a so-

For the contemplative is the path of knowledge: for the active is the path of selfless action.

Bhagavad-Gita

lution to occur. Many times the solutions are right in front of our noses, but we don't see them. For example, Buckminster Fuller was able to demonstrate that we have all the energy we need on the planet to exist in a high standard of living, without having to destroy nonreplenishable resources.

There is nothing so difficult but that it may be found out by seeking.

Terence

Most of us accept the conventional assumptions of lack because we are ignorant of the facts and lack the patience to investigate. But Buckminster Fuller "demonstrated beyond any argument that humanity can carry on handsomely and adequately when advantaged only by its daily energy income from the Sun-gravity system." As with energy supply, so too, food: "We can take ample care of all human food needs."[14]

Time and again, we accept limitations simply because we don't know any better. We must exert the confidence and maintain the patience to investigate until we see a better way. Two hundred years ago, Alexander Hamilton described this kind of confident patience when he said, "Men give me credit for some genius. All the genius I have lies in this; when I have a subject in hand, I study it profoundly. Day and night it is before me. My mind becomes pervaded by it. Then the effort I have made is what people are pleased to call the fruit of genius. It is the fruit of labor and thought."

It is our duty as men and women to proceed as though the limits of our abilities do not exist.

Pierre Teilhard de Chardin

Remember, people were once told that bleeding was the best cure for disease and that slavery was an economic necessity. We have been told we must sell out to get along and that many of the world's problems are insurmountable. Always we can yield to the blinder of ignorance or make resolute our determination to look until we see a better way. It has been wisely said that there is nothing that will not reveal its secrets to you if you love it enough. All things improve with loving attention.

Seeing with the Eyes of Strength:
Unmasking the Fear Blinder

It is not ignorance alone that keeps us from perceiving our personal, community, and planetary problems or from acting to abate them. For example, we daily see scenes of war, injustice, indignity, and violence flashed before us on our television screens. Yet many of us have insulated and isolated ourselves from the suffering of the world. The need seems so great, the hunger so vast, as to be almost overwhelming. In fear of being overwhelmed, we dull our senses.

It *is* a hungry world we live in. This world is hungry, not just in material terms, not just because over 20 percent of its population faces chronic malnourishment or starvation. It's hungry in so many ways—hungry for knowledge, hungry for wisdom, hungry for caring, hungry for justice, hungry for beauty, hungry for peace, hungry for joy, hungry for love—your love. Rather than to fear the enormity of the world's problems, we can act with courage, responding to the particular hungers we are called to feed. Mother Teresa put it like this: "What we do is nothing but a drop in the ocean, but if we didn't do it, the ocean would be one drop less." Mahatma Gandhi said, "Whatever you do may seem insignificant, but it is very important that you do it."

All the world is full of suffering, it is also full of overcoming it.

Helen Keller

The hunger of the world cries out for the food of your loving attention. Listen and discover what kind of food you have; then distribute it where it is most needed and wanted. Do you have spiritual food or the food of laughter? Do you have wisdom food or affection food? Do you have beauty food or confidence food? Whatever food you have, share it. We can all feed each other our best food, and in so doing, nourish all life. Remember, there are so many ways to serve. It needn't look any particular way. It is up to you to see clearly—to find your way.

Of course, to see suffering is to feel suffering. Many fear that they won't be able to handle the suffering of the world and its people. Many of us have dedicated our lives to feeling good, to avoiding suffering at all costs. We want day without night, beauty without ugliness, comedy without tragedy. Sooner or later, we must find a love big enough and strong enough to love life exactly as it is.

Alas! the fearful Unbelief is unbelief in yourself.

Thomas Carlyle

Man was made for Joy and Woe;
And when this we rightly know,
Thro' the World we safely go,
Joy and woe are woven fine,
A clothing for the soul divine.
                    William Blake

If it hurts to see the suffering of the world, it also hurts to avoid it. Avoidance has its pain, no matter how we try to deaden it. Each year, Americans spend more on psychiatric drugs than the entire GNP of two-thirds of the world's nations. According to the National Institutes for Health, one in twelve Americans abuse alcohol. An estimated thirty-two million Americans suffer from insomnia. Americans spend over ninety billion dollars annually on illicit drugs. More than sixty million Americans (one in five) are obese. These are problems that cut across ethnic, educational, and class boundaries.

Clearly, we cannot run from the pain of the world. Rather, we can learn to look with eyes of strength into the darkest abyss and not flinch. We can gain confidence in the knowledge that only that which we avoid as individuals and as a species will, in the long run, hurt us. What we refuse to be aware of does not go away. If anything, it only becomes more pronounced. Below are a few facts that we must not be afraid to be aware of. Information about the state of the world is readily available, you simply have to get on your favorite search engine and start looking in areas of interest to you.

No one must shut his eyes and regard as nonexistent the sufferings of which he spares himself the sight. Let no one regard as light the burden of his responsibility.

Albert Schweitzer

- There are around seven billion people living on the planet today. If everyone consumed at the level of those in high-income developed countries, the planet could support fewer than two billion people.

- Americans make up 5 percent of the world's population and consume one-quarter of the world's energy.

- In 2008, for the first time in human history, more than half the people on the planet lived in urban centers. By 2030, urban dwellers are projected to comprise 60 to 65 percent of the world's population. Most of the urban population growth will be in developing nations.

- More than a billion people lack clean water and more than twice that many lack proper sanitation. Worldwide, more deaths result from the lack of clean water and sanitation than from any other source.

- Each year, more than eleven million children on our planet die from preventable diseases.

- Five percent of the U.S. population owns as much wealth as the remaining 95 percent. The income gap between rich and poor is greater in America than in any other major industrialized nation.

- According to the USDA, thirty-six million Americans (including 18 percent of all children) live in households considered to be "food insecure."

> *Can I see another's woe*
> *And not be in sorrow too?*
> *Can I see another's grief*
> *And not seek forkind relief?*
> *William Blake*

Seeing with the Eyes of Beauty: Unmasking the Hatred Blinder

It is easy to hate and often difficult to love. With clear perception, we see the weakness of man, his greed, folly, and capacity for cruelty. It seems that everywhere we look, we see man's inhumanity to man. We are tempted to hate—to be angry and bitter at "them," for making such a mess of the world. Or we hate the people we have known whom we perceive as hurting or blocking us as individuals. It seems we have a thousand reasons to hate.

Yet to do so is to violate the basic necessity of our being—love. Without love, we cannot be what we are. We may think we have every right to hate, or that we hate for the right reasons, but all the while, hatred is shaping us in the image of the thing we detest. In our efforts to rid the world of evil, we can ourselves become caught up in the evil of hatred. Once tricked into returning hate for hate, we become locked in a vicious circle. Hatred disables our creative capacities and sucks all the beauty out of life. This brings us no advantage, but only increases the chance that we will suffer more injury—so then, more hate. On and on it can go . . . Surely we can accomplish no great good or have lasting happiness with hatred in our hearts.

There is some soul of goodness in things evil,
Would men observingly distill it out.

Shakespeare

When we see people acting in ways that seem to injure others or ourselves, we feel an impulse to hate them as people. Of course, with a bit of detachment, we see that the problem is simply ignorance and fear. To hate people for their ignorance or fear is to become a part of the problem. The solution can only come with the understanding of wisdom and the strength of love. The Buddha said, *Never has hatred ended by hatred. Only by love does hatred cease.*[15]

From a sacred point of view, life is not merely random combinations of inert matter; life is conscious, and consciousness is life. The more conscious we are, the more alive we are; the less conscious, the less alive. "Aliveness" gives us the energy to experience and handle the situations of life. *The more we are willing to be aware of, the more energy we have to create with.* Love is the energy of accepting awareness (life). Fear is the energy of resisting (or avoiding) awareness. When we resist awareness of some thing or event, we suppress our consciousness *and* our energy. We tie up, in denial and defensive reactions, energy that we need in order to enjoy and handle the situations of life. The greater our avoidance and denial, the less energy we have to create with and the more we will tend to feel like victims—pushed around by life.

I hold myself to be incapable of hating any being on earth. By a long course of prayerful discipline, I have ceased for over forty years to hate anybody. I know this is a big claim. Nevertheless, I make it in all humility.

Mahatma Gandhi

Bless relaxes,
damn braces.

William Blake

We all seek safety. We could say that everything we do is an attempt to *make safe*. This is true no matter how dangerous the action appears. It applies to the heroic risk-takers attempting to make their group or the whole of humanity safer (e.g., Gandhi, Martin Luther King, Jr.) or to make safe the integrity of their own souls (e.g., Socrates, Sir Thomas More). It also applies to the miser, addict, and criminal attempting to make safe their bodies or egos. While the hero acts out of love and furthers life, the others act from ignorance and fear and diminish it. All are attempting to make safe; the difference is that, while love creates a better way, hatred born of fear can only destroy.

Our wisdom (or folly) is reflected in what we believe will gain us the safety we seek. The miser, addict, and criminal are all trying to be safe (right) while feeling desperately unsafe (wrong). They are attempting to make safe within a context of avoidance. *While in avoidance, the greater the effort to make safe, the greater the actual danger we place ourselves in.* Love is the only safe way. This is so since only in love do we enjoy full consciousness—the full aliveness to enjoy and handle life.

If I keep a green bough in my heart, the singing bird will come.

Chinese Proverb

Of course, the examples above are extreme, but the principle applies to all of us: ***while we hate, we block our capacity to create.*** While in the spell of hatred, the world seems dark and gloomy, bleak and hopeless. Love restores the eyes of beauty, the eyes of the artist. Only with the eyes of beauty can we see the way to a better world. To have a sense of the right without being self-righteous, to have the strength to see the evil of the world and yet to give back love and understanding—is to retain the ability to create a better life for yourself and others.

There is a comfort in the strength of love;
'Twill make a thing endurable, which else
Would overset the brain, or break the heart.
William Wordsworth

Imagination: The Vision to See What Could Be

The third aspect of vision is *imagination*. Even as we can open our physical eyes to the problems and opportunities of the world as it is, so we can open our mind's eye to the possibilities of as yet unseen realities. To fully open our perceptive capacities, we must learn to trust that we can look at whatever we see, through the eyes of love. Whether personal, community, or planetary, problems can be faced head-on. To fully open our imaginative capacities, we must learn to trust that in some way we will make what we see in our mind's eye manifest in the world of form. Intuitions and inspirations are to be embraced, even when we have no idea how we will realize them.

Though it is crude to do so, we can say that the vision of perception is the vision of the scientist, and the vision of imagination is the vision of the artist. Of course, these classifications are meant to describe differences in methodologies, not to classify individuals. (Many of the true geniuses in art and science have been both acutely perceptive and highly imaginative.) Both types of vision are creative. *Perception* involves seeing clearly what exists in the outer world; *imagination* means "the act or power of forming mental images of what is not actually present."[16] In the former, we give our attention to some situation until we see a better way; in the latter, the creative image seems to come from nowhere. It comes all at once as a bug in the ear, the whispering of the muse.

> *When your thinking rises above concern for your own welfare, wisdom which is independent of thought appears.*
>
> *Yamamoto Tsunemoto*

Hagakure (*Hidden Leaves*), a seventeenth century Japanese samurai text, describes the distinction between the two kinds of vision in practical terms: "Some men are prone to having sudden inspirations. Some... arrive at the answer after slow consideration."[17] Usually, we are best at one type of vision or the other. Of course, we all use both, and we all can learn to use each better. However we arrive at our creative visions, it is important that we claim them and commit ourselves to making them happen. As each of us acts on our visions for the world, we better ourselves, almost without trying. Confucius said, "He who wishes to secure the good of others has already secured his own."[18]

Since it is an intuitive, right-brain process, the vision of imagination doesn't lend itself to systematic, left-brain analysis. Let's just say that if necessity is the mother of invention, then playfulness is the father. Playfulness is the dew-fresh, childlike spirit of wonder. A roving, wandering, wondering, what-if kind of a rascal. Unconventional, lightning-flash, sailing through the cracks, images come, free and unattached.

The right-brain process hinted at here is not logical and measured. It is intuitive and spontaneous. If it sounds a little silly, it is important to recognize that it works. Michael Faraday imagined living the life of an atom. He went on to discover the electromagnetic theory. Albert Einstein imagined himself flying through space at light speed. Such play as this was significant in the development of the general theory of relativity. It is said that in the beginning, the telescope was just a toy for Galileo.

Without this playing with fantasy no creative work has ever yet come to birth. The debt we owe to the play of the imagination is incalculable.

C. G. Jung

Go on a vision quest. Consecrate yourself to a higher purpose, then let go—when inspirations come, make them manifest in a form that can be enjoyed by others. Remember that the process of imaginative vision has more to do with receptivity than concentrated effort. Struggling and straining don't help; they actually impede the process. Start by relaxing, playing, keeping an open mind. After all, ideas are all around us. Like radio waves, they fill the air. We have simply to open to receive them.

You enhance your receptivity as you relax into stillness and play. Meditation eliminates the mental clutter and clatter that block inspirations. Play gives your mind the freedom to wander where it will. Alfred Binet said, "I find that images appear only if we give our minds uncontrolled freedom." Just let yourself be in a state of reverie. Inspirations come to a mind that is relaxed and alert. The Zen saying is, "Awaken the mind without fixing it anywhere."

When open, our minds have tremendous power to receive ideas. Yet much of the time we jam our creative imaginations with the static of negativity and limiting beliefs. We are so sure of how things are that we lose all perspective on how things could be. We have lost the wonder of the childlike mind. We tend to think alike. This conformity of thought maintains society's

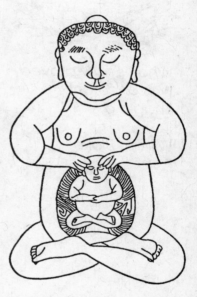

Awaken the mind without fixing it anywhere.

Diamond Sutra

What is now proved was once only imagin'd.

William Blake

traditions on the one hand and perpetuates its misconceptions on the other.

An original concept . . . prefers the mind imbued with the love of Nature, untainted with hidden plans for Her exploitation.
R. G. H. Sui, Tao of Science

Artistic revelation for the artist and artistic perception for the beholder of art come as "Aha!" The artist is as surprised (or more) at his discovery as anyone. From the reference of his conscious mind, it is coming from somewhere else. Call it "the muse," "the mind that is no mind," or "Dionysian ecstasy," a power greater than himself is working itself through him. Intense love has shattered the conscious control barrier, revealing something of the greater-than-self mind and its awful majesty. Less mystically, we can say that love relaxes the stranglehold of the conscious over the subconscious and allows the artist to tap a far deeper and richer well of inspiration.

Where *do* creative visions come from? When it comes to ideas, there is nothing new under the sun. In a sense, all ideas already exist. Newton's discovery of the law of gravity illustrates the point; if the law of gravity is operative, then it was always so, even before the fateful day that the apple came his way (or so they say). He didn't invent or make up gravity; he simply discovered an already-existing idea. Before man began to use fire to warm himself and cook his food, the capacity of fire to do these things existed. In a sense, these uses were latent within the idea of fire. The property and action of the law of displacement was operative long before Archimedes took his famous bath.

I invent nothing; I rediscover.
Rodin

All creative ideas are discovered. The new world called "America" existed before Columbus or Leif Ericson (or whoever else had dibs on it) bumped their boats on its shores. They did not create America from nothing. They simply made it known to people (including themselves) who were previously ignorant of its existence. So it is with all discoveries. Every discovery, whether through observation or direct inspiration, opens a new world to the discoverer. Further, if the discoverer can somehow communicate her discovery, it becomes a boon she bestows on her society.

To help us understand how all ideas exist now, imagine a universe of ideas, a vast, timeless realm that contains all ideas. Now imagine within this broad universe a smaller subset of all known ideas. These are the ideas that have been discovered. Their time has come. Voltaire said, "There is one thing stronger than all the armies in the world, and that is an idea whose time has come."[19] How it is that an idea's time comes, we cannot say. But when it does, it transforms the world.

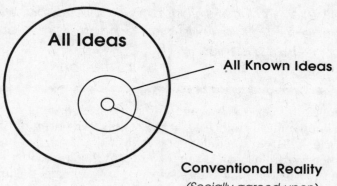

All Ideas

All Known Ideas

Conventional Reality
(Socially agreed-upon)

There is often a significant lag between the discovery of an idea and its manifestation. Leonardo da Vinci envisioned the modern submarine and helicopter four hundred years before their actual manifestation. In 1690, Denis Papin, inventor of the pressure cooker, first proposed the idea of a piston-driven automobile. Another two hundred years passed before a piston-driven auto was built. This lag principle applies to social and spiritual ideas as well as to physical inventions. Some have suggested the notion of a critical mass or a "hundredth monkey theory" to explain the lag. These theories suggest that when a certain portion (by no means a majority) of the population adopt a new idea, it becomes a part of the conventional, socially agreed-upon reality.[20]

Enlighten the people generally, and tyranny and oppressions of body and mind will vanish like evil spirits at the dawn of day.

Thomas Jefferson

If all ideas already exist, what is the role of the genius? Geniuses are those whose receptivity or keen observation allows them to discover previously unexplored or long-forgotten sectors of the universe of ideas. A genius explores sectors that lie beyond the reach of ordinary awareness and brings the ideas she finds there "down to earth" by expressing them in a way that the rest of us can comprehend. Much like Jack in "Jack and the Beanstalk," she climbs the ladder of consciousness and returns with the gold-laying goose of newly discovered or rediscovered ideas, often with the giant of entrenched mediocrity hot on her trail.

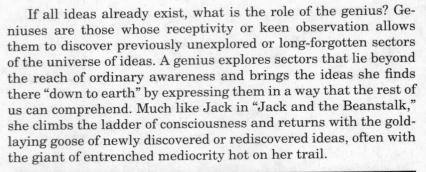

To believe your own thought, to believe that what is true for you in your private heart is true for all men—that is genius.

Emerson

The genius serves as a conduit for ideas, expanding the subset of all known ideas to include a greater portion of the universe of all ideas. Einstein's genius lies, not in the difficulty of his ideas (his theory of relativity is taught to many high school students), but in their potential to enlarge our understanding of the universe we live in. You too have the potential for genius, the potential to expand your known universe.

We are familiar with the great scientific and technological discoveries. Those of Copernicus, Newton, Edison, and Einstein are just a few examples. Equally important is the process through which each one of us comes to discover for ourselves the answers to the age-old questions: Who am I? and What am I doing here? Thoreau said, "Man's capacities have never been measured, nor are we to judge of what he can do by any precedent, so little has been tried."[21] Imagine what wonderful new worlds of ideas are yet to be discovered. They exist now and await discovery, even as the lightbulb waited for Edison; relativity, for Einstein; *The Magic Flute,* for Mozart. Like all ideas, your creative visions already exist, whether or not you have discovered them. You may be the next Einstein; yet even if you are not, the way in which you live your life is of great importance to yourself, your loved ones, and in some significant way, to the world as a whole. At this point, you may be asking yourself, But how do I go about discovering the important visions of my life?

When an inspiration hits you, *pay attention*. This is how you develop confidence in your imagination—one step at a time, by acting on your inspirations. As you continue in this, you may gain

Image creates desire. You will want what you imagine.

J. G. Gallimore

the confidence to tap into ever higher realms of thought and take responsibility for ever greater visions. Often we ignore our inspirations and then wonder why our lives seem to lack the marvelous or magical quality we felt as children. Children trust their imaginations and are not afraid of seeming ridiculous. We really needn't fear; we all *are* a little ridiculous.

A genuine vision is a pregnant idea, teeming with life and possibilities. Visionary ideas give birth to other ideas, as well as to the actions that materialize them. Even with ideas that come directly from inspiration, we often have to keep looking for ways to apply them, or for other ideas that support them. When asked how he got his ideas, Einstein replied that he only had one. According to Einstein, the rest of his work was merely the development of a single visionary idea. Imagine that.

Francis Bacon said, "A man would do well to carry a pencil in his pocket, and write down the thoughts of the moment. Those that come unsought for are commonly the most valuable, and should be secured, because they seldom return." That's still good advice. Keep a notebook or journal with you and near your bed. Catch the ideas as they come in. Your dreams can be an important source of creative visions. Your mind is a maker of models. Seeing the image of your vision builds the first model. Getting it down on paper builds the second, and so on. Don't expect complete perfection on the first attempt to make this vision manifest. Just begin your sketch, no matter how blind or foolish you may feel. Remember: A journey of a thousand miles begins with the first step, no matter how awkward or tenuous that step may be.

Everything around you—this book, the room you are in, the clothes you are wearing, the political and economic systems you live in—began as an idea in someone's head. Come to think of it, every created thing began as an idea in some fertile mind. In the words of

Your imagination is your preview of life's coming attractions.

Albert Einstein

Robert Collier, "The source and center of all man's creative power . . . is his power of making images, or the power of imagination."

You have probably had inspirations that you have discounted. Perhaps you have a vision of a better way in art, science, education, child care, health care, nutrition, farming, social philosophy, or politics. Whatever your vision, recognize it and work to give it expression. *Recollecting your creative inspirations will reconnect you with a potent energy source in your life.* Tune in again, and watch the very thought of the vision charge you with positive feelings and set you in motion.

The visionary artist sees and gives expression to the deeper inner reality that we all experience. Through his art, we are able to experience more deeply our humanity, the mysteries of existence, and the godlike beauty of the human spirit. The poet gives voice to what we all know, but cannot express. The artist shapes, forms, and colors the sublime radiance of life. Let them speak:

> *I am the poet of the body and I am the poet of the Soul.*
> *The pleasures of Heaven are with me and the pains of Hell*
> *   are with me.*
> *The first I graft and increase upon myself, the latter I*
> *   translate into a new tongue.*
> Walt Whitman

> *In every block of marble I see a statue as plain as though it stood before me, shaped and perfect in attitude and action. I have only to hew away the rough walls that imprison the lovely apparition to reveal it to the other eyes as mine see it.*
> Michelangelo

You must be the change you wish to see in the world.

Mahatma Gandhi

But I am no artist, you may protest. Yet is your life any less a canvas because you do not paint? Is your voice any less potent because you do not give it pen? Is your soul barren of song because you compose no notes? No, a thousand times! Life well lived is the greatest art of all. The art of your life is not a matter of talent. It is a matter of MOUNTING THE COURAGE TO LIVE.

It's mounting the courage to SEE what you really are, to be dazzled by the Radiance that is You. Mounting the courage to imagine what this world could be. Mounting the courage to die a thousand deaths to LIVE one life to the fullest. Translate the pains of hell into a new song. Lovely apparitions of possibilities as yet undreamed await those whose hands are strong and steady enough to hew away the rough walls and make their creative vision a manifest reality.

No one knows what he can do until he tries.
Publilius Syrus

Making visible the glorious inner life in the everyday world of form is the creative process. Neurosis is but expression denied. We can't hide and express at the same time any more than we can move forward and backward at once. We hide because we do not accept ourselves as we are. We will not admit the pains of hell, fearing we have not the courage to translate them into a new song. We hide in shame outside the Gates of Eden, invisible to ourselves, blind to others.

Fear not: Your hands are worthy to chisel out the divine image. Live in openness to the possibilities. The muse will visit without call, but she only abides with those who make works of her inspirations. None but your very self can tell you that you are worthy to be her scribe, her errand boy, or her handmaiden. Seek her out. Serve well the images she inspires. O noble son, O noble daughter, you are worthy of her divine touch. Consecrate yourself to the sacred vision you see.

Fear not: You can bear the pains of hell and translate them into a new song. As all heroes before you, you must conquer the pains of hell. Open eyes will shed tears, for this world is full of sorrow. The flames of hell reflected in wet pools of tender eyes blaze brilliant the light of love. The sorrow of the world humbles and purifies all idle vanities. Look upon the world, stripped bare, not in a blank stare, but gently with eyes that care. Mother Teresa, who had reason to know, has said, "Sorrow shared becomes joy." What sorrows in this world do we not share, you and I, my brother, my sister?

A man's value to the community primarily
depends on how far his feelings, thoughts,
and actions are directed towards promoting
the good of his fellows.
Albert Einstein

Creating from Vision

All that is is a result of what we have thought.
                    Suttapitaka

Man is what he believes.

                    Anton Chekhov

Imagination rules the world.
                    Napoleon I

The idea that is not dangerous is unworthy of being
called an idea at all.
                    Elbert Hubbard

The only real valuable thing is intuition.
                    Albert Einstein

A man's dreams are an index to his greatness.
                    Zadok Rabinowitz

Look within. Within is the fountain of good, and it
will ever bubble up, if thou wilt ever dig.
                    Marcus Aurelius

There will be a decrease in the desire for individual
advancement, and an increase in the desire for the
advancement of the race as a whole.
                    Eugene E. Thomas

What in the World Could Be?

In the space below, write your vision of the world you would like to live in. Do not concern yourself with how realistic your vision is, how it would be implemented, or what your part in creating it might be. Simply write your vision as though you could wave a magic wand and have it manifest in one fell swoop. This is your opportunity to create your utopia.

Write your vision of the world you would like to live in.

_____
_____
_____
_____
_____
_____
_____
_____
_____

Now write your vision of the nation you would like to live in.

_____
_____
_____
_____
_____
_____
_____
_____
_____
_____
_____

You see things and say, "why?" but I dream things that never were and say, "why not?"
George Bernard Shaw

Now write your vision of the community you would like to live in.

_____

_____

_____

_____

_____

_____

_____

_____

_____

_____

_____

After reviewing what you have written above, ask yourself, "What insights do my answers give me about the direction I would like my life to take?"

_____

_____

_____

_____

_____

_____

_____

_____

_____

_____

_____

_____

_____

_____

Attitudes are more important than facts.
Carl Menninger

Your World Needs Your Love

This process provides you with the opportunity to assess the needs of your world, nation, and community. One of the key components to a satisfying and fulfilling life's work is the sense that you are making a contribution to the world you live in. This exercise is a problem-solving approach to your world, which will help you determine what you can do to make it better.

In your estimation, what are the most critical needs on the planet that are going unmet, or what are the greatest sources of pain and suffering in the world?

_____

_____

_____

_____

In your nation?

_____

_____

_____

_____

In your community?

_____

_____

_____

_____

What situation or need in your community, nation, or world most moves you to want to take action? *"More than anything, I really want to do something about."*

_____

_____

_____

_____

_____

_____

 No one is useless in this world who lightens the burdens of another.

Charles Dickens

What situation in the world, in your nation, or in your community do you notice yourself complaining about the most? *"Somebody really ought to do something about . . . "*

_____

_____

_____

_____

_____

How could you ultimately be most effective in working on these problems? *"If I were to take responsibility to do something about this, I would."*

_____

_____

_____

_____

_____

What elements of human suffering speak to your heart?

_____

_____

_____

_____

_____

After reviewing what you have written above, ask yourself, "What insights do my answers give me about the direction I would like my life to take?"

_____

_____

_____

_____

_____

_____

_____

In nothing do men approach so nearly to the gods as in doing good to men.
Marcus Cicero

Through the Eyes of a Child

The premise behind these questions is that somewhere in the back of your mind, you have always known what you are here to do. Recalling your childhood may help you unlock this inner sense of knowing, which children are more readily aware of because they have not yet accepted the limiting beliefs or the sense of defeat that often hinders adults.

As a child, what did you most want to give to the world?

_____

_____

_____

_____

_____

_____

As a child, what situation in the world most hurt, disturbed, or upset you?

_____

_____

_____

_____

_____

_____

_____

What did you want to do about it?

_____

_____

_____

_____

_____

_____

_____

  *In youthful idealism man perceives the truth.
In youthful idealism he possesses riches that
should not be bartered for anything on earth.*
Albert Schweitzer

When you were a child, what did you most love to do?

_____

_____

_____

_____

_____

_____

If you could wave a magic wand, and the world would instantly be the way you want it to be, how would it be different?

_____

_____

_____

_____

_____

_____

_____

What insights do the answers to these questions give you?

_____

_____

_____

_____

_____

_____

_____

_____

 The greater part of all the mischief in the world arises from the fact that men do not sufficiently understand their own aims.

Goethe

Through the Eyes of the Wisdom of Age

Imagine that you have been told you have five years left to live. In terms of your work life, what is it that you most want to accomplish in your remaining years?

_____
_____
_____
_____
_____
_____
_____
_____
_____
_____
_____

Imagine yourself on your deathbed, filled with regret, with a painful sense of having missed your life's calling. What is it that you most regret not accomplishing?

_____
_____
_____
_____
_____
_____
_____
_____
_____
_____
_____

In the long run you hit only what you aim at.
Therefore, though you should fail immediately,
you had better aim at something high.
Henry David Thoreau

Now again, imagine yourself on your deathbed. This time, imagine that you feel at peace with the world and ready to pass on. You are surrounded by your friends and family. You feel as though you have completed or accomplished what you came here to do in this life. What do you consider to have been your most important accomplishments?

_____

_____

_____

_____

_____

_____

_____

_____

_____

_____

_____

More than anything, what do you want the message of your life to have been when all is said and done? How could you best exemplify this?

_____

_____

_____

_____

_____

_____

_____

_____

_____

_____

_____

_____

Web and Book Resources

Find out more about global issues and challenges
@ Empoweryou.com.

Clarifying Values

Why not spend some time determining what is right for us, and then go after that?

William Ross

Thomas Jefferson gave us a worthy maxim for sorting out the importances of life. He said, "In matters of principle, stand like a rock. In matters of taste, swim with the current."[1] What principles do you want to stand for? What values are central to your life? The choices you make will determine your future and, with the choices of others, the future of life on our planet. The objective of this section is to assist you in identifying and clarifying your values.

"Know thyself," the ancient wise men said. Today, knowing yourself is no less important than it was twenty-five centuries ago when Thales, the reputed father of Greek philosophy, first articulated this maxim. Yet modern life runs at such a pace that we seldom take the time to examine our lives. We become strangers to ourselves—so caught up in seeking the approval of others or in oiling the great machinery of society that we take little time to pause and reflect upon the deeper meaning of our existence.

For the secret of man's being is not only to live but to have something to live for.

Dostoyevsky

Our educational system is of little help. We aren't trained to be critical thinkers, to perceive the fundamental principles or values behind a given political, economic, social, or interpersonal agenda. The mass media tell us their version of current events, with little debate about the fundamental value choices involved in major policy decisions. It is up to each of us to discern the cornerstone principles upon which our society stands and determine for ourselves their merit or fallacy. It's up to each of us to determine the kind of future society we will create, by deciding on the kind of values we will emphasize today.

For good or for ill, ideas and the values they reflect have tremendous power to shape our world. The great debate of ideas must not be left to a few academics in ivory towers or "experts" on talk shows. It must become an integral part of everyday life if we are to create a sane and healthy society. We owe it to ourselves and our society to consciously examine and make explicit our values.

The individual who takes the time and makes the effort to discover for him- or herself what is valuable and what is peripheral in life has internal guideposts to live by. Of course, in practice, making value choices is not as easy as it sounds. At times, values conflict. One esteemed value or principle seems to run against another. Much of the great literature of the world—from Abraham and Isaac to Arjuna and Krishna, from the plays of Sophocles to the death of Socrates, from Hamlet to Huck Finn—turns on how individuals resolve their moral dilemmas.

Only those with strongly held principles face the great tests of character that come with moral dilemmas. Today, we too often take the convenience-store approach to values: whatever one we need, we'll just run in and get it. We take whatever value seems expedient in the moment to justify our actions. We then elevate moral neglect into high duty by invoking the doctrine that all value assertions are

Know Thyself.

Thales

relative. In our efforts to rid ourselves of the responsibilities (and anguish) of moral dilemmas, we have thrown out our best chances to develop character. However trying moral dilemmas may be, they are healthier for the individual and the society than eliminating all value conflict by eliminating all conviction.

The Ch'an masters who carried Zen to Japan brought with them Confucian ethics. They advocated the adoption of Confucian values as a means of promoting the welfare of the society and providing a cultural environment favorable to Zen realization.[2] In discussing the role of fundamental values in guiding individual behavior, Confucius said, "If a man will *carefully cultivate* these in his conduct, he may still err a little, but he won't be far from the standard of truth."[3] We seldom err when we make explicit our core convictions and endeavor to align our behavior with them.

Below, you will be invited to consider three categories of values in human life: universal (or archetypal) values, cultural (or ethnic) values, and individual (or personal) values.

Universal Values

Freedom consists not in refusing to recognize anything above us, but in respecting something which is above us; for by respecting it, we raise ourselves to it, and, by our very acknowledgement, prove that we bear within ourselves what is higher, and are worthy to be on a level with it.

Goethe

Who am I? What is there of me that is not simply the forces of socialization and heredity? What is the essential? Who am I, stripped of the particular social and cultural milieu into which I was born? Is there anything of me that cannot be explained away by genes or social means?

Universal values reveal and inform the essence of the human condition. Through the universal values, we link our individual experience with the rest of humanity and the cosmos. In the universal values, the barriers of time and place, language and culture, crumble before the eternal dance of life. Universal values are experienced, not comprehended. Can you comprehend a sunrise? Fathom a flower? Translate a smile?

That the Upanishads, the Bible, or the plays of Sophocles can speak with relevance to our lives today tells us that there are, at

Be still, and know that I am God.

Psalms 46:10

the core, certain timeless constants to the human condition. That we feel wonder at the Sphinx, awe at the cathedrals of Notre Dame or Chartres, or serenity at the Taj Mahal tells us that these values cannot be contained by words. That we can be moved by Beethoven, soothed by Mozart, can identify with Hamlet or Faust speaks tomes on the mystery of universal values and the laugh they have on time, place, and death.

Universal values are not the exclusive domain of the poet, artist, mystic, or monk. No fair-minded reader of Carl Jung, Joseph Campbell, or Erich Neumann can dispute the presence of universal values in the myths and legends by which all peoples have sought meaning and direction. Today, we are so occupied in material and economic pursuits that universal values receive little attention. Still, when we deny them in our waking lives, they haunt us in our dreams, as Jung has shown. Universal values move us out of our separate roles and identities, into the vast expanse of timeless reality.

Universal Values can be experienced as: life, joy, brotherhood, love, peace, unity, sacrifice, service, God, eternity, bliss, etc.

Cultural Values

> *Society is a necessary condition of life in this world and a necessary medium of personal self-realization through community; that is why we hold it to be a part of the order of creation.*
> *Will Herberg*

Cultural values are the generally agreed-upon social values of the day. They serve to establish and maintain social order. They are peculiar to time and place and can be extremely volatile. Cultural values are concerned with ethics, with right and wrong, with good and bad, with manners and customs. We see cultural values reflected in the ideas and behaviors a society rewards as well as those it punishes. Cultural values are a mixed bag for the individual. Especially in a highly complex society like the late twentieth century Western culture, there is likely to be much with which the individual resonates and much with which he does not.

Man has speculated for centuries on the best ways to organize human society—from Plato's *Republic* to More's *Utopia*, from Bacon's *New Atlantis* to Wells's *Anticipations*. The society in which we live is itself a speculation. It is man's attempt, with his limited knowledge and psychological and spiritual development, to construct the best world he can imagine.

The world is his who can see through its pretension. What deafness, what stone-blind custom, what overgrown error you behold, is there only by sufferance—your sufferance. See it to be a lie, and you have already dealt it its mortal blow.

Emerson

Of course, there is nothing wrong with speculating, but it is dangerous to forget that we are. When speculation becomes "truth," opinion "fact," and prejudice a "holy cause," demagoguery is not far behind. When we mistake cultural values for universal ones and proclaim them as doctrine, we risk intolerance, chauvinism, oppression, and every form of brutality and stupidity. While cultural values may be (as Claude Levi-Strauss and others have suggested) functional, they are, nevertheless, essentially arbitrary. There is no contradiction here. A shovel serves the function of turning over earth, but so can a grader, a bulldozer, a plow, a shoehorn, a coin, or a bare hand. The fact that a cultural value or custom serves a given function does not necessarily imply that it is the only, or even the best, way of doing so. In certain primitive cultures, human sacrifice no doubt served a function, but in other cultures, that same function was served by animal sacrifice, and in still others without any loss of life.

That we in this culture have chosen the automobile as the dominant mode of transportation has ramifications on virtually every aspect of social life. Suburbs, supermarkets, freeways, shopping malls, parking lots, and drive-through restaurants all owe their existence to the auto. Yet if one were asked to specify exactly what caused, and continues to cause, reliance on the automobile, one would be hard put to come up with a definitive, rational explanation.

The engineer has his explanation; the sociologist, hers; the management professor, his; the historian, hers; the cultural anthropologist, his; the economist, hers. Each considers important those factors peculiar to his or her specialization. Some pontificate, but all speculate. Rational attempts to comprehend causes for the peculiarities in various social orders are always approximations.

While attempts to trace the origins and development of cultural patterns rely upon speculation, they can, nevertheless, help us bet-

Economics and politics are the governing powers of life today, and that's why everything is screwy.

Joseph Campbell

The good man is the friend of all living things.

Mahatma Gandhi

ter understand ourselves and our world. Speculation will always be incomplete. In this sense, history *is* bunk. Still, speculating on the history of ideas, the origins and propagation of cultural values, is more than entertainment. With careful execution, it becomes a source of insight into our psyche, time, and society. It provides an opportunity to step out of our cultural skins and observe our common prejudice, taboo, and superstition, as well as our cultural strengths.

In a sense, every culture is a person. As with people, when cultures meet, there is the potential for conflict and for creative interaction. We are too familiar with cultural conflicts and the destruction these have wrought. Yet, it is well to remember that the meetings of cultures have also triggered tremendous creative explosions. Zen was born in a meeting of Chinese and Indian cultures. The Renaissance sprang from a meeting of the ancient Greek and medieval European cultures. A number of scholars have recognized a Buddhist influence in Neoplatonic thought. Jazz is African meets European music. Some have said that the great medieval romance poetry evolved out of a meeting of the Islamic (Sufi) and European cultures.[4] American Transcendentalists studied the Indian Vedas and Upanishads. Many of the German philosophers of the nineteenth century (e.g., Schopenhauer and Nietzsche) were influenced by the philosophies of China and India.

Modern writers including Hermann Hesse, E. M. Forster, Somerset Maugham, Aldous Huxley, Alan Watts, Carl Jung, Joseph Campbell, and the Beat poets, to name only a few, were heavily influenced by the East. Van Gogh shows Japanese influence. Gandhi drew heavily from Tolstoy, and Martin Luther King, Jr., in turn, from Gandhi. Modern dance began by cross-pollinating ballet with aboriginal dance. These are only a few illustrations; much of what we find exciting and interesting has come from a meeting of cultures.

If you see in any given situation only what everybody else can see, you can be said to be so much a representative of your culture that you are a victim of it.

S. I. Hayakawa

If all one knows is one's own culture, one has only met one person. Those who know no culture but their own tend to be narcissistic, simply because they've never known anyone else to have a relationship with. Much of what we understand as unique personality is simply the mask (*persona*) of culture. Psychology since Freud has placed great importance on childhood experience and particularly the role that parents play in shaping personality. Of course, parents do not fall from the skies and are themselves the products of culture.

The study of other cultures helps you to see yourself as both a *spectator* and a *participant* in your personal life drama. It gives you a frame of reference. Of course, moving to Japan to live in a high-rise, commute by subway, and work for a large corporation is not necessarily meeting another culture. (One tea ceremony will teach you more about Japanese culture than weeks in Tokyo nightclubs.) Oswald Spengler suggested that the key to understanding any culture is to study its "culture forming" (poetic, mythic, religious) tradition.[5] A century before, William Blake put it like this: "It is not Arts that follow & attend upon Empire, / but Empire that attends upon & follows the Arts."

We see our silly cultural ethnocentricity in books, and indeed entire academic departments, that purport to be "world history," when they are in fact European or, at best, Western history. We are told that the history of Western art is "THE HISTORY OF ART," that Western philosophy is "PHILOSOPHY." We teach world literature without *The Mahabharata* or *The Ramayana*. Of late, there has been a trend to incorporate snippets from other cultures into "world courses," but these are, for the most part, merely token. Of course, we are not alone in this. The Chinese thought Westerners barbarians and made no attempt to learn from them until it was too late. When Gandhi was asked what he thought of Western civilization, he reportedly said that he thought it would be a good idea.

Cultural Values are seen reflected in language, ethics, status systems, aesthetics, education, government, law, economics, philosophy, social conventions (of every kind), social institutions (of every kind), etc.

Individual Values

Individual values are our private meanings. These result from individual temperament and experience. Individual meanings can be a source of individual strength (as in a marriage vow or the consecration of a knight) or weakness (as in idiosyncratic fears). Personal role models, parents, teachers, and childhood chums shape individual values. Biology and physical environment also play a role.

Scatter Joy.

Emerson

Two men respond to war wounds in different ways. One remains cheerful, buoyant, and productive; the other becomes bitter, morose, and difficult. No doubt the injury means something different to each. The proverbial straw that breaks the camel's back does so because of the weight of individual meaning given to it.

Moral courage and character go hand in hand . . . a man of real character is consistently courageous, being imbued with a basic integrity and a firm sense of principle.

Martha Boaz

The concept of a life script has been suggested to account for the individual differences in attributing meaning to experience. We tend to project early personal relationships onto the present and replay the issues of these relationships over and over again. We distort perception and impute personal meanings resurrected from images of the past. A client's decision not to buy one's product is taken as a personal rejection, unconsciously recalling a negative and critical father who withheld the support one craved. A friend's pain or bad mood becomes a personal affront, unconsciously recalling a cold and emotionally distant mother.

An earlier experience of pain can lead us to hold associated stimuli with disdain. Embarrassment or ridicule at school can, by association, lead one to reject learning *in toto*. Others may have difficulty understanding how strongly these private meanings affect us.

Any object, event, or idea can take on individual meaning. What others find the odd piece is, to the sentimental owner, a cherished treasure. Personal "power spots," a special piece of ribbon, a baseball player's favorite number, these have personal meaning. Even objects that hold cultural significance may represent, to the individual, values and feelings beyond those culturally assigned to them. For example, a marriage ring may represent more than a social contract of fidelity. For one person, it may symbolize inspiration, joy, and the strength to do one's best. For another, it might represent bondage to an unhappy existence. The difference in meaning is individual.

Individual Values are reflected in individual goals, humor, vows, relationships, commitments, personal objects (of every kind), personal preferences (of every kind), etc.

In addition to determining which universal, cultural, and individual values are most meaningful for you, consider the relative priority of each of the categories of values. For me, the universal values top the list. Each of the categories of meaning has its place, but it is through the universal values that we experience a sense of oneness with the entire human race and, indeed, the cosmos. Encountering universal values gives an experience so rich and profound as to make the others seem shallow by comparison.

Today, in the midst of writing this, I took a stroll past the county courthouse. There, a photographer, quite intently engaged in his craft, asked me for the time. Nothing peculiar in this, except that he was standing beneath an enormous clock on the side of the building. I thought of how often we are like this photographer, so focused on a narrow part of the landscape that we miss the wider view. Our personal and cultural biases limit and distort our perception of the universal wonder that is life.

Even as the hands of a clock are powered from the center, which remains ever still, so the universal values remain ever at the center of human life, no matter where the hands of time are pointing—past, present, or future.

Of course, all three categories of meaning overlap. An artist may use his *personal* experience to express *universals* in a *culturally* relevant motif. On a universal level, the image of Jesus on the cross may symbolize transcending the lower self through sacrifice to a higher purpose, dying to the old self to be born to the new, or the regeneration of life from death. Culturally, the image may represent the impact of the Christian church on European history and the Western psyche, the Roman Catholic Church as an institution, or a popular motif in Western art. Personally, it may represent the abhorrence one feels toward aspects of the Christian legacy he rejects, or it might represent a personal relationship with a living God. Of course, at each value level, there are myriad possibilities. Since, as Goethe said, "everything transitory is but a reference,"[6] any *thing* can stand for anything (idea). The important thing is to decide what you stand for.

That civilization perishes in which the individual thwarts the revelation of the universal.

Tagore

Values

Cowardice asks the question, Is it safe? Expediency asks the question, Is it politic? Vanity asks the question, Is it popular? But conscience asks the question, Is it right? And there comes a time when one must take a position that is neither safe, nor politic, nor popular, but he must take it because his conscience tells him it is right.
        Martin Luther

Thus to be independent of public opinion is the first formal condition of achieving anything great.
        G. W. F. Hegel

Think nothing profitable to you which compels you to break a promise, to lose your self-respect, to hate any person, to suspect, to curse, to act the hypocrite, to desire anything that needs walls and curtains about it.
        Marcus Aurelius

We are prone to judge success by the index of our salaries or the size of our automobiles rather than by the quality of our service and relationship to mankind.
        Martin Luther King, Jr.

We cannot live only for ourselves. A thousand fibers connect us with our fellow-men; and along those fibers, as sympathetic threads, our actions run as causes, and they come back to us as effects.
        Herman Melville

Your Philosophy of Life

If you could share one bit of wisdom with the whole world, what would it be?

_____
_____
_____
_____

Is there anything you would be willing to put it all on the line for? If so, what?

_____
_____
_____
_____

What has been the most important lesson you have learned in your life? Why was it the most important?

_____
_____
_____
_____

Briefly, what is the basic philosophy of your life?

_____
_____
_____
_____
_____
_____
_____

 Few men ever drop dead from overwork, but many quietly curl up and die because of undersatisfaction.
  Sidney J. Harris

Personal Bill of Rights and Responsibilities

Take the opportunity to declare your "Personal Bill of Rights and Responsibilities." In creating this list, you will clarify your personal standards of behavior: what you expect of yourself, what you view as your responsibility to others, and what you will and will not tolerate—of yourself or of others.

1. _____
   _____

2. _____
   _____

3. _____
   _____

4. _____
   _____

5. _____
   _____

6. _____
   _____

7. _____
   _____

8. _____
   _____

9. _____
   _____

10. _____
    _____

 It is the chiefest point of happiness that a man is willing to be what he is.
Desiderius Erasmus

Instant Recall

Reviewing highlights from your past may reveal clues to your life's work. Additionally, the following questions may help you get a feeling for what it would be like to actually be engaged in your life's work. When giving your answers to the questions below, do not limit yourself to previous work experience. Draw upon your entire life experience.

Recall times when you have been most creative. These are times when you created something (an event, a thing, a product, a system).

_____

_____

_____

Recall times when you have been most committed. These are times when you were deeply involved, emotionally committed, and determined to persist in spite of all obstacles. _____

_____

_____

Recall times when you were most decisive. These are times when you knew exactly what to do. You knew you were right, and you acted deliberately and confidently, perhaps even in spite of the doubt and objections of others. _____

_____

_____

Recall a time when everyone said you couldn't do it, but you knew you could, and you did it anyway. What was it? How did it feel?_____

_____

_____

Recall times when you have been so absorbed in what you were doing that you hardly noticed the time. What were you doing? _____

_____

_____

You will find as you look back upon your life that the moments when you have really lived are the moments when you have done things in a spirit of love.
Henry Drummond

What do you consider to be the greatest accomplishment of your life? Why?

_____
_____
_____
_____
_____
_____

What is the most exciting thing you have done in your life? Why?

_____
_____
_____
_____
_____
_____

When have you taken the strongest stand in your life? What were you standing for?

_____
_____
_____
_____
_____
_____

Review your answers to the questions above with a view toward what they might suggest to you about your life's work. Look for patterns, redundancies, events that you repeatedly recalled. What insights do your answers suggest? Write these in the space below. _____

_____
_____
_____
_____
_____

Work to become, not to acquire.
Elbert Hubbard

Know Thy Values

After you have read the preceding discussion, answer the questions below. (Refer to the examples given in the discussion if you are unclear as to the nature of each kind of value.)

What universal values speak most powerfully to you? Why?_____

_____

_____

_____

_____

_____

_____

_____

What cultural values speak most powerfully to you? Why?_____

_____

_____

_____

_____

_____

_____

_____

What individual values speak most powerfully to you? Why?_____

_____

_____

_____

_____

_____

_____

_____

The more a man lays stress on false posses-sions, and the less sensitivity he has for what is essential, the less satisfying is his life.
                                                    Carl Jung

Below is a list of values. Put a check in front of those that are most important to you. Check no more than ten.

___ Truth	___ Honesty	___ Service
___ Peace	___ Leisure	___ Compassion
___ Love	___ Nonviolence	___ Strength
___ Loyalty	___ God	___ Patience
___ Integrity	___ Creativity	___ Drive
___ Innovation	___ Fame	___ Ambition
___ Health	___ Wealth	___ Achievement
___ Beauty	___ Justice	___ Unity
___ Abundance	___ Courtesy	
___ Gentleness	___ Nonattachment	*Other*
___ Resourcefulness	___ Discipline	1. _____
___ Calmness	___ Sense of belonging	2. _____
___ Community	___ Courage	3. _____
___ Family	___ Independence	4. _____
___ Freedom	___ Simplicity	5. _____
___ Humility	___ Friendship	6. _____

Which values do you most want to characterize your life?

_____

_____

_____

_____

_____

_____

Overall, which values are most important to you in your life?

_____

_____

_____

_____

_____

_____

_____

Prioritize your top values and list them below.

1._____

2._____

3._____

4._____

5._____

Then, define each of these values in terms of its significance and meaning to you.

Value #1:_____

_____

_____

_____

_____

Value #2:_____

_____

_____

_____

_____

Value #3:_____

_____

_____

_____

_____

Value #4:_____

_____

_____

_____

_____

Value #5:_____

_____

_____

_____

_____

Your Mission Statement

Review all of your answers to the "Vision Questing" and "Clarifying Values" sections; then write out your life's mission in the space below. Your Mission Statement answers the question, "What am I here to do on this earth?"

_____

_____

_____

_____

_____

_____

_____

_____

_____

_____

_____

_____

_____

_____

_____

_____

_____

_____

_____

_____

_____

_____

Now review what you have written, and write a condensed Mission Statement. State the mission of your life in no more than two sentences.

_____

_____

_____

_____

_____

Pointing to Purpose

All the world's a stage,
And all the men and women merely players.
Shakespeare

All the world's a stage, and all of us are players. We have our time upon the stage of life and then depart. While on the stage, we play our parts, however poorly or well. Each character in this grand play of life has lines to deliver and action to make while he "struts and frets" upon the stage. What is the message you want your life to proclaim? Is it about beauty or cooperation, wisdom or inspiration, peace or enlightenment? What is it that you want your life to say when it is all said and done? Answering these kinds of questions is what this section is all about.

It's motive alone that gives character to the actions of men.

Jean de la Bruyère

You can think of your purpose as the essential message of your life. In a well-staged play, every word, movement, lighting effect, costume, and prop—or its absence—delivers a message. In the grand play of life, every actor has something to say. Ask yourself, Why has this character made his entrance? What is the purpose of the action of her life? What is the message you want an audience of seven billion to get from the action of your life? What is your part in *this* Globe Theater?

In an essay entitled "The Basis of Artistic Creation in Literature," playwright Maxwell Anderson articulated several key elements he found essential in all great plays. In his words, "A play can't be written without them—or at least it can't be a success."[1] Below, I explore a few of these elements and consider how they apply to playing your part on the grand stage of life. (Unless otherwise indicated, quotes below are from *The Bases of Artistic Creation* by Maxwell Anderson.)

1. The outer is symbolic of the inner. "The story of a play must be the story of what happens within . . . the heart of a man or woman. It cannot deal primarily with external events. The external events are only symbolic of what goes on within." The spiritual or inner life cannot be separated from work—or from anything else, for that matter. All action is self-reflecting; what you do reflects what you are within. To be authentic, the play, or action of your life, must flow from your heart and soul.

2. The quality of the inner life is tested in the outer world. "The story of a play must be a conflict—and specifically, a conflict between the forces of good and evil within a single individual." This inner conflict gives life its drama and creative tension. The good of your best self is engaged in an ongoing conflict with the "evil" of settling for less. The authentic actor in the play of life views external obstacles and inner deficiencies as challenges to be overcome—not reasons to quit. This does not mean there won't be setbacks along the way. It means we are willing to live, and therefore to test, the highest truths we know.

3. The protagonist must grow. "The protagonist of a play cannot be a perfect person. If he were, he could not improve, and he must come out at the end of the play a more admirable human being than he went in." Surely all of us hope to come out of this play of life more admirable people for having lived it. Embracing a larger-than-self purpose gives us something to live up to now and a reason to keep growing into the future.

4. The soul is the scorecard. "Excellence on the stage is always moral excellence. A struggle on the part of the hero to better his material circumstances is of no interest unless his character is somehow tried in the fire, unless he comes out of the trial a better man." There is nothing wrong with money or trinkets, but the wise person values his soul before all else. By its light, she sees her place in the world; by its reckoning, he keeps score. Every ego separates; but no soul is an island. Ordinary life takes on a heroic dimension when we commit ourselves to a "soul purpose." A hero is, in the words of Joseph Campbell, "someone who has given his or her life to something bigger than oneself."[2] This is what makes his character interesting. This is why we root for him. Heroic action can come from any of us. In Campbell's words, "When we stop thinking primarily about ourselves and our own self-preservation we undergo a truly heroic transformation of consciousness."[3] When we embrace a larger-than-self purpose we move beyond the surface desires of the ego and honor the deeper prompting of our souls.

To Find Your Part: Don't Exaggerate, Deny, or Minimize Your Importance

Many fall into patterns that limit their capacities to recognize their parts in the play of life. There are those who *exaggerate* their importance in the overall scheme of things. There are those who *deny* that they have any effect on the world. Still others admit their effect, but *minimize* their abilities. Any of these extremes impedes the process of discovering your purpose, or part, in the play of life.

> *The importance and unimportance of the self cannot be exaggerated.*
>
> *Reginald Blyth*

It's easy to *exaggerate* our importance in the overall scheme of things. Many are blocked from tapping into their purpose in life by their insistence that it come with a personalized name tag. They expect the sky to open and a deep bass voice from on high to say, "Well, my son (or daughter), this is your purpose..." Choirs of angels, lightning, and thunder are optional, but the bass voice is a must.

Don't overpersonalize; great purposes are not individual. They have historical continuity. They were begun before you and will

*Wherefore by their
fruits ye shall know
them.*

Matthew 7:20

continue long after you. Rome was not built in a day; neither was science, art, or culture. We stand on the shoulders of those who have come before and owe our best to those who will follow. No great purpose relies upon any single individual. It is always a group effort. This may be a little difficult for our egos to accept, but it will make finding our purpose less difficult.

Many *deny* that there is any purpose or message to what they do. For example, some screenwriters, playwrights, and authors claim that there is no purpose to their work—beyond, of course, making money. It's just a movie, a play, a book. It has no "message." Of course, this is silly. It may not be didactic, but everything we do communicates something. Every action conveys a message in the way that every musical note conveys a sound. There are no soundless notes any more than there are "messageless" actions or characters. Think of a Zen garden. We hear "everything counts" in the careful placement of each and every object. Think of a run-down urban, or a bland suburban, landscape—it too conveys a message. Whether motivated by love or fear, cynicism or greed, resignation or exaltation, actions send ripples that extend beyond the immediate field in which they play out. Each person carries the resonance generated by all of his or her own actions. As long as we are alive, we are making ripples through our actions; we are resonating at our own unique frequencies.

I will act as if what I do makes a difference.
William James

There is no getting around purpose. If you work, you have a work purpose, whether or not you have articulated (or even thought about) it. If you work for an organization, your work purpose is linked to the organization's purpose. Figuring out your current work purpose is simply a matter of determining your organization's purpose and where you fit within it. If you work in the private sector, you can determine the purpose of your organization by identifying how it makes its money. Even if you work in a corporate headquarters and never have any immediate experience with what your company sells, what it sells is what you are working for. In our world, money is an essential part of work. Corporation or nonprofit, entrepreneur or employee, all must generate income to sustain their efforts. Yet money is supposed to be a medium of exchange—not an end in itself. One might hope that something of real value is involved in the exchange for money.

Again, there is no getting around purpose. If we don't believe we can claim a purpose for our work, we may try to work it out in a different way. We might say, "I don't think much of my organization's purpose but . . . I need the money" or "I like the lifestyle it provides my family and myself" or "I derive meaning from my relationships with colleagues, coworkers, or clients." There is nothing wrong with working just for money for a time; but sooner or later, your soul will likely want more from you. While many will say they do what they do because they "need the money," those a notch or two up the economic scale will often say they do it because of "the lifestyle it provides my family." I've had many more affluent clients tell me that for years they had tried to view their purpose for work, not in its content, but in its ability to provide a great lifestyle for their families. (Ironically, in addition to feeling alienated from their work, virtually every one of these folks was working and/or traveling so much that they had little quality time with their families.) Others will say that, though they can't get excited about the purpose of their work, they derive satisfaction from their relationships with colleagues, coworkers, or clients. Of course, it should be apparent that one could have a self-defined purpose and also have money, meaningful work relationships, and a lifestyle one enjoys.

Much of the work that gets done in our society depends upon people viewing themselves and their labor, brains, and energy as commodities for hire. They should feel lucky if they are employed— never mind at what. Their biggest aspiration should be to make enough money so they can buy more stuff and/or buy the labor of others to do the stuff they don't want to do. They shouldn't expect meaning or worry about the purpose of their work. Work is for the pocketbook—not the soul. If not in so many words, we've all heard this message. Some have it drilled in so hard they can't imagine any deeper purpose than hoping to someday be able to comfortably retire. What about the forty to fifty years most will work before retirement? Is it just so we can go earning and spending and saving for the end?

Of course, if we haven't identified or claimed what we want to do—the purpose we want to accomplish through our work—there are always plenty who are more than happy to engage us in their purposes. More often than not, these revolve around money. Don't know what you want to do? That's fine—you can help me get richer. Give me your labor, your brains, your education; I know what to do with them. If life is cheap, its only value is what someone will pay for it. All I can do is try to get the best deal I can on my package of skills, education, and experience. On the other hand, if life has intrinsic value, then it matters what I do with it. It's not pretentious to believe that what you do makes a difference or to imagine a purpose to your life. What we claim for ourselves we affirm for

*Your work is to
discover your work
and then with all
your heart to give
yourself to it.*

Buddha

all. What we deny to ourselves we reject for others. If life has intrinsic value, then so does yours. If life makes a difference, then it makes a difference what you do with your life. *The life spent in doing what you love is a different life indeed from putting yourself out for hire to the highest bidder.*

Remember that you are an actor in a play and the Playwright chooses the manner of it . . . your business is to act the character that is given you and act it well; the choice of the cast is Another's.
                                                    Epictetus

While some *exaggerate* their importance and others *deny* having any effect, still others *minimize* the importance of their contribution. They don't deny that it makes a difference what each of us does with our lives. Indeed, these folks tend to admire those who embrace a larger purpose. They simply claim that they themselves cannot do much. No doubt they underestimate their abilities, as we will discuss below. Still, if you think you are in this camp, remember the advice that great actors give to their protégés: Better to have a small part in a great play than a large part in a bad play. The ages-old drama of love, brotherhood, and human advancement is a great play. A small role in this epic, played with sincerity, dignity, and strength, adds immeasurably to the play. Everyone can't be a star, and yet where would the stars be without the supporting cast? In the end, it's not the size of your role, but how well you play it.

It is better to do your own duty, however imperfectly, than to assume the duties of another person, however successfully. Prefer to die doing your own duties: the duties of another will bring you into great spiritual danger.   *Bhagavad-Gita*

Most of us tend to underestimate the contributions we can make. We hold ourselves hostage to our pasts. We erect boundaries around our creative imaginations, lest they venture too far beyond what we have already achieved. Blast the boundaries. Go beyond the tried and true, dare something new. When you raise your expectations of yourself, you create a space to grow into. At first, it may seem like an empty space, but over time you will fill it with new responsibilities and skills. You want to be realistic—but if you are to err, you are better off overestimating what you can do and coming up short than you are in underestimating yourself and settling for less than your best.

It's not enough to say, "I'm earning enough to live and support my family. I do my work well. I'm a good father. I'm a good churchgoer." That's all very well BUT YOU MUST DO SOMETHING MORE.
Albert Schweitzer

Stretch beyond self-imposed limits. Expand your vision of what you can contribute. Create into the gap between what you imagine yourself capable of doing and what you are actually doing now. Remember, when the distance between your current performance and your ultimate vision is too small, you will feel bored, harried, or confined. When the gap is too big, you may feel overwhelmed. When the distance is right, you will feel alive, challenged, and creatively stimulated.

What's in a Purpose?

Your work purpose is what you are working for, both in the sense of motivation and direction. What motivates you with respect to your work life? If you want a work that you love, it goes without saying that love will be the principal sustaining motivation for that work. The discovery of the work you love is not so much a product of analysis as it is a matter of allowing yourself to be led by love. Your love for the content of a work (a subject matter, an activity, an art form) can lead you to a work you love. Your love and compassion for others can lead you to the recognition of a work that allows you to serve them in a personally meaningful way. (Albert Schweitzer said that his career in music came out of the first kind of love while his career in medicine and humanitarian service came out of the second.) A work that is motivated by love has meaning and joy already built into it. A work that has a self-defined direction already has creative tension, opportunities for growth, and challenge built in. The direction you want to move in is determined by your vision for the future and that, in turn, is shaped by your values. (This is why you were asked to address these in the previous two sections before identifying your purpose.) In beginning to define your work purpose, it can be helpful to ask: What moves me the most? Whom do I want to serve? and How many do I want to reach?

What Moves You the Most?

Perhaps there is some situation in your community, nation, or world that moves you so strongly, so irresistibly, that you have to act. It is so out of alignment with your vision of the world you want to live in that you feel compelled to do something about it. Perhaps you want to see to the material comfort of humanity. You feel moved to see that everyone has adequate food, shelter, and clothing. Perhaps you are moved by the neglect or abuse of children, and you want to make a difference in this area. Perhaps it's ignorance or illiteracy that moves you to act. Perhaps you are moved to protect animals or the environment. You might work against poverty, injustice, indignity, ill health, or mental deprivation. Martin Luther King, Jr., and Mahatma Gandhi were moved by the injustice with which man treated his fellow man.

Just as we can be moved to try to alleviate suffering, so we can be moved to bring joy, beauty, knowledge, or truth to our world. Do you want to share your love and passion for some subject matter, art form, interest, or activity with others? Maybe you are moved to write beautiful music or to share your vision for the world through art or dance. You might be moved to explore some mystery or make some discovery. Einstein was touched by a desire to know where we stand in the universe. Mozart was moved by music that still inspires today. Luther Burbank was moved to discover how plants and man could better care for one another.

When people are serving life is no longer meaning-less.

John Gardner

Whether you are working to end suffering or to spread joy, you are part of building the world you want to live in. In any case, you must be powerfully moved, personally inspired. You will need that inspiration later on, when you begin to confront the challenges of manifesting your vision. Respond to a need or build from an inspiration, but go with what moves you the most. Trust the voice of your heart—it will lead you to your life's work.

What thou lovest well remains, the rest is dross
What thou lov'st well shall not be reft from thee
What thou lov'st well is thy true heritage.
        Ezra Pound

Whom Do You Want to Serve?

Is there any particular group or sector of the population that you feel particularly drawn to serve? Perhaps you grew up in a rural area, and you have decided that you want to provide health-care services for folks in your community. You know these people. You know their needs, wants, and aspirations. Perhaps you feel particularly drawn to working with children or the elderly. Maybe you are a member of a particular ethnic or racial group, and you want to help people in your group. Perhaps you feel a particular tug on your heartstrings when you encounter a certain group or kind of people. Follow that tug.

How Many Do You Want to Reach and How Deeply?

When contemplating your life's work, consider the scope of the impact you want to make. Is the change or benefit you want to make at the level of the individual, family, community, nation, or planet? How many lives do you want to reach and at what level of depth? The quality or depth of the impact that you make upon others can be as important as the breadth of your impact. For example, an elementary school teacher may profoundly impact the twenty-five students that she teaches each day for a year. Her students will grow up to be better people and to give more to the world because of her effort and love.

You may have heard it said that effectiveness is a matter of doing the right things, and efficiency is doing things right. *Your work purpose reflects what you think are the right things to do*. It is the why-you-do that precedes the how-to-do. If you have a strong enough why, you will figure out the how. When we continue to act on and into purpose, the results have a way of taking care of themselves, even as when we care for a tree, the fruit takes care of itself. Thoreau said, "Be not simply good—be good for something." Discover what you are good for! Look within your heart and out upon the world. Look at how much the world needs your love and at how much you want to give it. Then determine to live your life on purpose, to play your part as it was meant to be played.

And whosoever of you will be the chiefest, shall be the servant of all.

Mark 10:44

What: The Way You Want to Serve

Your Mission Statement (see page 198) was a general statement about why you are here on this earth. In the exercises that follow, you will step that down a bit and begin to construct a "Work-Purpose Statement." The first step to developing your work-purpose statement is to identify what you would like to do by identifying the fields in which you would most like to make a contribution. Below are examples of "I want to" statements that express work purposes. You may be able to use one of these as a skeleton of your work-purpose statement and amend or adjust it to suit your purpose. You may want to start entirely from scratch, using the statements that follow as guides in constructing your own work-purpose statement. However you arrive at it, your work-purpose statement should be your own, reflecting what you most want to express or accomplish.

You may realize that you have more than one work purpose. In that case, pick the one that represents the area you want to focus on most over the next seven to ten years. If you still end up with several areas of focus, rank them and pick one major area of focus. The alphabetical list below is not intended to be complete or exhaustive. It represents just a few of the more common areas in which people with whom we have worked have expressed interest.

Agriculture: I want to produce or advance the production of the foodstuffs that will provide people sustenance and nourishment in a manner that is environmentally sound.

Animal Care: I want to see to it that the animals are protected and treated with care, compassion, and dignity.

Architecture: I want to design structures that are at once functional and uplifting to the spirit.

Art: I want to portray, through artistic media, universal truths that uplift and inspire.

Business: I want to provide valuable products and services including: _____

Clothing: I want to design, manufacture, or distribute quality clothing that is aesthetically pleasing, comfortable, and healthful.

Communication: I want to provide communication technologies and/or services that will help people to achieve their goals.

Culinary Arts: I want to design, prepare, and/or produce delicious, nutritious foods. I want to provide an atmosphere that will make eating a fulfilling, even spiritual experience.

Defense: I want to provide for national security and defense. I want to see to it that people are safe, protected, and free to pursue happiness in their own way.

Economic Development: I want to assist people in developing a higher standard of living. I want to do so in a manner that respects values of human dignity and ecological balance. I want to ensure that economic growth is based on the production of useful goods and services.

Education: I want to train and develop people's minds, character, knowledge, and skills. I want to help people to broaden their horizons and deepen their understanding.

Energy: I want to design, develop, or promote safe, efficient, nonpolluting, and replenishable energy systems. I want to increase the efficiency of existing energy systems until new ones are in place.

Engineering: I want to design, construct, or manage roadworks, waterworks, building, machinery, etc., which will serve to improve people's quality of life.

Entertainment: I want to provide laughter, drama, song, or dance to lighten and enlighten people's lives.

Environment: I want to clean up and protect the environment and to do all I can to see that it is kept as safe and as pure as possible.

Family: I want to provide services that will strengthen and support family units and family happiness.

Government: I want to work with government institutions to ensure that government remains responsive to the people and provides them with the best possible services.

Health: I want to share with people the skill, knowledge, love, and energy necessary to care for their health and physical well-being.

History: I want to help people to better understand their past, to see how things have come to be as they are, and to understand the great historical processes of change and their consequences.

Industry: I want to manufacture materials that will make people's lives more fulfilling, free, and productive.

Information Services: I want to provide people, in an easy-to-use and readily available form, the information they need to make informed and effective decisions.

Interior Design: I want to create the kinds of interior spaces that elevate people's spirits and bring out the very best in them.

Journalism: I want to inform people about current events and issues. I want to help them to be aware of the people and events that shape their lives.

Justice: I want to protect people's rights and ensure that they are treated fairly and with human dignity.

Landscaping: I want to create exterior environments that provide people with upliftment and joy.

Law: I want to write, interpret, or practice legal remedies for human problems, conflicts, or grievances.

Life Sciences: I want to help people better understand and utilize the biological and organic processes of life to further their well-being and minimize the dangers to their health.

Management: I want to manage organizations that serve people's needs and aspirations.

Music: I want to share beauty, joy, understanding, and harmony through the vehicle of music.

Organization: I want to help people to be more effective by organizing personnel, material, ideas, and financial resources that will facilitate the achievement of their goals.

Peace: I want to promote world peace. I want to further international cooperation, understanding, and harmony. I want to exemplify and promote universal love and brotherhood.

Performing Arts: I want to take an active role in portraying the wonder, poignancy, beauty, and drama of the human experience before live audiences.

Philosophy: I want to challenge people to think of the deep and fundamental issues of life. I want to encourage them to examine their beliefs and the effect that holding these ideas has upon themselves and others. I want to share with them the wisdom of the ages.

Physical Education: I want to teach people how to utilize their bodies to maximize efficiency, promote health and longevity, and reduce physical stress and tension.

Physical Science: I want to help people understand the physical world in which they live and how it can be made to serve them even better.

Politics: I want to help people to gain a voice in the decisions that affect their lives.

Psychology: I want to help people better understand their minds and emotions, their motivations, drives, and desires. I want to help them unlock the power of their minds and emotions to achieve their highest potential.

Recreation: I want to help people relax, play, and rejuvenate. I want to facilitate the relaxation of their bodies, minds, and spirits.

Religion: I want to minister to people's spiritual needs. I want to help them to discover who they are, what it is to be, and how to be free.

Sports: I want to help people discover the joys of effort, persistence, cooperation, teamwork, and physical development that sports provide.

Technology: I want to design, manufacture, or promote technological advances that will help people to achieve a happier, richer, more productive lifestyle.

Trade: I want to promote goodwill and cultural interaction by helping people to trade their products and services with others.

Transportation: I want to help people to get from place to place in a clean, economical, and safe manner and in a way that makes the most efficient and least destructive use of natural resources.

In the space below, construct your own statement indicating how you want to serve in the areas you most want to make a contribution. If you have more than one work purpose, indicate the one that you most want. **Example:** *I want to assist people in developing higher self-esteem.*

Statement of the Way I Want to Serve:

_____

_____

_____

Whom: The People You Want to Serve

Your next step is to identify the people you want to serve. These people are your constituency, the people for whom you are responsible in your work. The purpose of work is to serve, to contribute. We are all serving someone. Review the list below and identify the primary beneficiaries of your work.

Age

Prenatal
Infants
Preschoolers
Children
Adolescents
Young Adults
Middle Age
Elderly
All ages

Income

Destitute
Economically deprived
Lower middle
Middle
Upper middle
Wealthy
Extremely wealthy
All incomes

Special cases

Prisoners
Homeless
Pregnant
Physically disabled
Mentally disabled
Victims of specific diseases
People of other countries
Disaster victims
Armed forces
Orphans
Illiterate
Animals
Delinquents
Hungry
Sick
Veterans
Immigrants
Dying
Other

Ethnicity

White
African-American
Hispanic
Asian-American
Native American
Other
All races

Sex

Males
Females
Both sexes

Now construct a statement that explains who you want to serve. **Example:** *I want to serve adolescents from economically deprived areas who need help in improving their academic ability.*

Statement of Whom I Want to Serve:

_____

_____

_____

_____

_____

_____

How Many: The Scope of the Impact You Want to Make

The final step in writing your work-purpose statement is to determine the scope of the impact or the size of the playing field on which you choose to operate.

For example, do you work best alone, in small groups, or within large organizations?

Consider the following choices:

_____*Individuals*   _____*Countywide*

_____*Small groups*   _____*Statewide*

_____*Neighborhood*   _____*National region*

_____*Community*   _____*Multinational*

_____*Citywide*   _____*Worldwide (Global)*

Write the scope or the scale of service that you primarily want to operate on. **Example:** *I want to begin working on a community level and eventually expand to a statewide program.*

Statement of the Scale I Want to Work At:

_____

_____

_____

_____

_____

_____

_____

_____

_____

_____

_____

_____

_____

 One person with a belief is a social power equal to ninety-nine who have only interests.
John Stuart Mill

Your Work-Purpose Statement

Review your answers to the three preceding exercises, and restate them in the spaces provided below.

What: The way I want to contribute is . . .

_____

_____

_____

_____

_____

Whom: The people I want to serve are . . .

_____

_____

_____

_____

_____

How Many: The scale I want to work at is . . .

_____

_____

_____

_____

Now write a work-purpose statement that includes whom you want to serve, the way you want to serve them, and the scope of the impact you want to make.

My Work-Purpose Statement

_____

_____

_____

_____

_____

_____

_____

_____

Living on Purpose

The way to be happy is to make others so.
Robert Ingersoll

Live your life as though every act were to become a universal law.

Henry David Thoreau

Live as you will have wished to have lived when you are dying.

Christian Fürchtegott Gellert

Nothing comes from nothing.
Shakespeare

Here is the test to find whether your mission on earth is finished: If you're alive, it isn't.
Richard Bach

A man has to live with himself, and he should see to it that he always has good company.
Charles Hughes

The most sublime act is to set another before you.
William Blake

Targeting Talents

Every man has his own vocation,
talent is the call.

> *Emerson*

Your talents provide a window that opens into the discovery of your life's work. The purpose of this section is to help you identify your talents and start thinking about how you can put them to work building the kind of world you want to live in. What are your gifts to the world? What is it that you have to share with the rest of us that will make our lives richer, more fulfilling, and more enjoyable? Many of us think of talents in relation to writing, music, or dance—as artistic, dramatic, or entertainment skills. But talents are more than these; they include a wide range of natural abilities. I invite you to follow your talents and follow your bliss.

Talent Is More Than Skill

Every man's leading propensity ought to be call'd his leading Virtue & his good Angel.

William Blake

Don't confuse talents with skills. Talent is natural; skill, learned. Skills are acquired abilities, learned through study, imitation, training, and practice. We can think of talents as our genetic endowment. While skills are important (skills will be discussed at length in Act II), talents provide an open door into the discovery of your life's work. Your talents are not simply what you do well. You can have an undeveloped or undiscovered talent or be reasonably proficient in areas where you have no special talent. Your talents are found in the things you truly love to do.

While your talents are unique to you, your skills are often as much the result of someone else's doing as your own. Your mother decides you will learn to play the piano; your father starts you in the family business; grandma reminds you, "There are three generations of lawyers in this family," and so on. Much of what we have become skilled at is simply what was in front of us—hodgepodge collections of familial, geographic, social, and economic influences that, to borrow from Shakespeare, "signify nothing." The often random and haphazard way that skills are acquired makes them unreliable indicators for life's work.

Beyond this, it is a mistake to draw conclusions about potential ability solely from past experience. No one would look at a healthy infant and say he will never walk or talk, simply because he hasn't done so before. While it is important to value what you have already learned to do, it is equally important to recognize that you are still in the process of growing. You may have undiscovered talents. With a relatively small degree of talent and considerable training and technical skill, you may achieve competency, perhaps even a high degree of commercial success, but if you pursue what you have real talent in, you will experience the joy of being fully alive in your work.

Often we have so much invested in training and developing our skills in a given field that we are unwilling to admit we have little real talent for that field. When we do admit it, we feel a sense of relief, for now we can go on to discover our genuine talents and pursue them with a passion. Developing talent is the road to your creative best. Don't let a poor investment (of your time and energy) continue to rob you of what could be the greatest joy in your life. If you've made a poor investment, cut your losses, and begin at once to exploit your talents to the ultimate.

Your talents can hardly wait to express. They are itching to get out and about. To go through life without releasing your strongest talents leads to feelings of frustration, resentment, even depression. You feel bottled up, envious, and discouraged. You may even question why you exist at all. It's as if you were damming a great river of energy. The release of talent is one of the great joys in life. The moment of expression is timeless, effortless, fluid, and vivifying. You feel a deep harmony—self, humanity, and the physical world are one. You feel right with the world.

Focusing on Purpose Releases Talent

More talent has been squandered by the low expectations that result from lack of purpose than from any other cause. Purpose marshals talent. You can spend your time analyzing your talents, comparing yours with those of others, wishing you had more, or feeling superior for those you do possess, but you will never tap into the deepest well of your own innate abilities until you set yourself to some great purpose.

When you are inspired by some great purpose, some extraordinary project, all your thoughts break their bounds: Your mind transcends limitations, your consciousness expands in every direction and you find yourself in a new, great and wonderful world. Dormant forces, faculties and talents become alive, and you discover yourself to be a greater person by far than you ever dreamed yourself to be.

Patañjali

If people knew how hard I worked to get my mastery, it wouldn't seem so wonderful after all.

Michelangelo

If you are dedicated to your purpose, you will find a way to express your talents through it. We are not drawn to areas where we have no talent or latent ability. On the contrary, we are drawn to a particular field because we know we have an important contribution to make to it. Talent is said to be raw when it is undeveloped. Talent is incomplete, however developed, when it is not aligned with your vision, values, and purpose. When it is integrated with these, there is no telling how far you can go.

You may currently be a "two" on a one-to-ten scale of competency in the area that best reflects your vision, purpose, and talents and a "nine and a half" in another area. Work at what you love the most, even if you're only a "two." Trust that your love for what you are doing will see you through. That's not easy, but better to grow into what you love than to pretend you're satisfied with a developmental dead end.

Talents Are a Sacred Trust

From the commodity view of life (see "Scene I: Vision Questing"), talents are possessions, tools for personal gratification. From a sacred view of life, talents are gifts that we hold in trust. After Michelangelo completed his first *Pietà*, he heard rumors that another artist was getting credit for having done this work. One night, he stole into the cathedral and carved his name on the back of the *Pietà*. Later he called this act an abomination and a desecration. This *Pietà* was the only work he ever signed. Michelangelo recognized that the sacred gift of talent cannot be possessed.[1] One has a responsibility to share his talents without trying to own them.

It is your work in life that is the ultimate seduction.

Pablo Picasso

> *When one is engaged in a favorite pursuit or a subject absorbingly interesting, the normal conception of labor or time and artificial social distinctions disappear from the mind. In fact, life itself is absorbed in the engagement, or it may be said that one's life is tuned in harmony with eternal life.*
>
> *G. Koizumi (Judo Master)*

Jesus told the parable of the talents.[2] In the story, the faithful stewards have risked and invested their talents and doubled their worth. They are given greater responsibility. The unfaithful steward buried his talent out of fear of taking a risk. His little responsibility was taken away. The story applies to discovering and utilizing your natural abilities. Risk investing yourself fully into the talents you now recognize, and you may discover others that you never knew you had. You won't discover or express your talents while playing defense, while seeking the safe and sure, the tried and secure. You have to risk, take chances, fully invest yourself if you want to discover and express your talents. We needn't get bogged down in either false modesty or arrogant pride. Talents are natural gifts, developed through the discipline and concentration that come from caring.

Talents Are What You Enjoy

What great joy it is to work and to see how we can effect change in the world, how we can build, shape, and make it better. We love feedback. Consider a child playing in the water. He seems fascinated by the effect he is having. He splashes in the water—it strikes him in the face—he laughs. What fun is feedback! How wonderful it is to build something of value, to give your love and understanding and see the effect you are having. Joy and play expand as you put your talents to work. Your talents are the way you can make the biggest splash and have the biggest laugh. As a practical matter, when you are looking for your talents, look for:

1. What you enjoy doing
2. What you enjoy thinking about
3. What you enjoy learning about
4. What you enjoy as a process

What You Enjoy Doing

What do you have the most fun doing? This is the first tip-off to your talents. Talent is the kind of thing you can lose yourself in while you are doing it. Yet, because it is so much a part of you, its pursuit brings you to an ever deeper experience of yourself. We enjoy doing what we are naturally good at.

A musician must make his music, an artist must paint, a poet must write if he is to ultimately be at peace with himself.

Abraham Maslow

What do you most enjoy doing? Writing or hiking, discussing politics or playing with children, making things with your hands or dancing? Do you enjoy gardening or reading, painting or public speaking? If you especially enjoy doing some activity, and you want to discover if you have real talent in this area, ask yourself if you also enjoy thinking about it, learning about it, and if you enjoy it as a process. These additional questions may help you to discover talent in areas where, up till now, you have had little experience.

What You Enjoy Thinking About

Do you find yourself pondering the nature of the universe or thinking about the varieties of social organization and their effects? Do you spend a good deal of time ruminating about the psychological or physical makeup of man? Do you spend time thinking about mythological stories or international relations? Do you compose

We know what we are, not what we may become.

Shakespeare

songs or music in your head? What do you enjoy thinking and talking about? Your idea of a fascinating conversation would be a discussion about . . . ?

What You Enjoy Learning About

One of the best tip-offs to talent comes in observing what you most enjoy learning about. Since talent seeks expression, you naturally enjoy learning that which makes possible the fuller expression of your talents. You will learn quickly and develop rapidly in areas where you have real talent. You can even enjoy learning about the more mundane aspects because they move you toward the full release of talent. The joy that you experience in stretching out the envelope of your abilities inspires you to ever greater heights. The strength you gain in honing your talent translates into every aspect of your life. You are not only a happier person for pursuing your talent, but a stronger and more resilient one as well.

What You Enjoy As a Process

There is a difference between what you might enjoy as a simple event and what you enjoy as a process. Process is a better tip-off to talent. Let's suppose you enjoy writing letters. This "doing of writing" is a tip-off, but it is an entirely different process from writing books or even articles. These involve problems of organization, style, research, logic, concentration, and persistence, which generally do not apply in writing personal letters. Greater self-confidence is also required, simply because one is taking on a much larger task. You might enjoy "doing singing" in the car or the shower or with a group of friends; but this is altogether different from enjoying the process of rigorous voice training, the scales, the breathing exercises, and the endless hours of practice required of the professional.

Having talent in an area does not mean that you are necessarily going to be thrilled or in wild ecstasy over every part of the process. It doesn't mean you won't have difficulties and frustrations. It doesn't mean that there won't be things to do that you would (in the short-term) rather not do. Still, you must in some measure enjoy the process of growing into the fullness of your ability.

The musician, the architect, the teacher, the philosopher, the dancer, the poet, the government leader, those who protect the earth and the animals, those who protect the children and the poor, those true scientists who seek to know, those who make things grow—it takes all kinds. Identify your talents, and begin to think about how you can put them to work building the kind of world you want to live in.

Releasing Talent

We never know how high we are
Till we are called to rise.
And then, if we are true to plan
Our statures touch the skies.

Emily Dickinson

Man's capacities have never been measured, nor are we
to judge of what he can do by any precedent, so little
has been tried.

Henry David Thoreau

Do what you can with what you have, where you are.
Theodore Roosevelt

[One] who is naturally and constitutionally adapted
to and trained in some one or another kind of making,
even though he earns his living by this making, is
really doing what he likes most, and if he is forced
by circumstances to do some other kind of work, even
though more highly paid, is actually unhappy.

Ananda K. Coomaraswamy

If you do what you like, you never really work. Your
work is your play.

Hans Selye

Although men are accused of not knowing their own
weakness, perhaps few know their strength.
Jonathan Swift

A.C.T. to Release Your Talents

Don't worry if you can't get at your talents right off. There are things you can do to create favorable conditions for their recognition and ultimate expression. For starters, cultivate the soil in which your talents can germinate by practicing *attitude* and *creativity* in all you do. Recognize that the expression of talent is simply the greatest pleasure in work. You can develop your capacity for this pleasure. With attitude and creativity, you can act your way to the full release of talent.

Attitude: Cultivating a constructive attitude gives you the energy you will need for the full release of talent. The essence of a Zen attitude can be put like this: No self-pity! Suffering in the material world is inevitable; therefore, do not be shocked or upset by it. Bring to your work a spirit of gratitude. Be glad to be alive and happy to have the opportunity to work, to give in any capacity. In cultivating this attitude, you become more active in your inner life—quickening your imagination. Zen tells us to practice attitude while doing any work, however menial, monotonous, or mundane it may seem. Do not resent work— embrace it. *When you have finished your rice, wash your bowl.*

Creativity: The practice of creativity gives you the confidence you will need to express your talent. The first level of enjoyment in work is attitude. Next comes creativity. Creativity requires still greater inner aliveness, a more active imagination, and so, is more pleasurable. From the standpoint of Zen, we can say that creativity shows in applying *upaya*—"skillful means," or resourcefulness— to your work. To be resourceful, you must first accept things as they are, then go on to make a masterful arrangement of them. For example, because one is poor, he needn't live in an ugly way. The creative, resourceful one will make of his clothing and home beautiful arrangements that show his love and humanity. Creative resourcefulness is bold and confident, unafraid of obstacles or difficulties, using them as catalysts to spark ever greater creative achievement.

Talent: Talent is the final expression of joy in work. Attitude says: Don't resent. Creativity says: Invent, arrange, play. Talent is silent—bliss. While practicing your talent, your art, you are not. You have forgotten yourself. To forget oneself is the greatest of all pleasures—the ultimate joy. For it means destroying time—the greatest of all barriers. One who has not developed attitude is frustrated: time and self-remembrance weigh heavy on him. Attitude frees; creativity, still more; but in the expression of talent, one becomes the slayer of time. He enters into the time-less. When you are fully expressing your strongest talents, your joy is complete. "Do I then strive after *happiness?* I strive after my work!" (Nietzsche).[3]

Tapping into What You Enjoy

What do you enjoy most about your current work? (Even if you dislike most of it, there may be one feature that you enjoy.)

_____
_____
_____
_____

What do you most enjoy doing when you're not working? (Hobbies, recreational interests, etc.)

_____
_____
_____
_____

What do you most enjoy learning about?

_____
_____
_____
_____

What do you most enjoy making? (What do you enjoy as a beginning-to-end process?)

_____
_____
_____
_____

If you were financially independent and money was not a factor, what kind of work would you do?

_____
_____
_____
_____

 It sometimes seems that intense desire creates not only its own opportunities, but its own talents.
Eric Hoffer

Taking the Talent Quiz

Rank each of the following talents on a scale of one to ten, with ten representing an extraordinary level of talent; five, an average level of talent; one, an extremely small amount of talent.

Rating

1. An ability to organize   ____
2. An ability to motivate   ____
3. An ability to mediate   ____
4. An ability to instruct   ____
5. An ability to manage   ____
6. An ability to execute   ____
7. An ability to lead   ____
8. An ability to inspire   ____
9. An ability to counsel   ____
10. An ability to make things work (mechanical ability)   ____
11. An ability to build things   ____
12. An ability to design things   ____
13. An ability to heal   ____
14. An ability to put people at ease (diplomacy)   ____
15. An ability to contemplate (philosophize)   ____
16. An ability to arrange things beautifully   ____
17. An ability to make beautiful things   ____
18. An ability to perform (entertain)   ____
19. An ability to communicate through speech   ____
20. An ability to tell stories that instruct   ____
21. An ability to be playful   ____
22. An ability to persist   ____
23. An ability to perceive the essential   ____
24. An ability to juggle many responsibilities or activities at once   ____
25. An ability for efficiency   ____
26. An ability to be loyal   ____
27. An ability to be appropriate   ____
28. An ability to be self-disciplined   ____
29. An ability to be tolerant   ____
30. An ability to concentrate   ____
31. An ability to love   ____
32. An ability to be happy   ____
33. An ability to be balanced   ____
34. An ability to be generous   ____

35. An ability to be compassionate   _____
36. An ability to be dignified   _____
37. An ability to be tender   _____
38. An ability to be strong   _____
39. An ability to be impeccable   _____
40. An ability to be popular   _____
41. An ability to be enthusiastic   _____
42. An ability to express through the written word (writing)   _____
43. An ability to express through movement (dance)   _____
44. An ability to express through the visual arts   _____
45. An ability to express through music   _____
46. An ability to analyze   _____
47. An ability to be persuasive   _____
48. An ability to synthesize ideas   _____
49. An ability for logical or abstract thought   _____
50. An ability for imagination and vision   _____
51. An ability for athletics   _____
52. An ability for tactics   _____
53. An ability to strategize   _____
54. An ability to interpret or translate languages   _____
55. An ability to make things grow (plants)   _____
56. An ability to negotiate   _____
57. An ability to protect or defend   _____
58. An ability to invent things   _____
59. An ability to evaluate or judge   _____
60. An ability to explore or discover   _____
61. An ability to experiment   _____
62. An ability to nurture   _____
63. An ability to invest   _____
64. An ability to cooperate   _____
65. An ability to inspect   _____
66. An ability to investigate   _____
67. An ability to plan   _____
68. An ability to discern   _____
69. An ability to perceive opportunities   _____
70. An ability to clarify   _____
71. An ability to harmonize   _____
72. An ability to establish rapport   _____
73. An ability to be decisive   _____
74. An ability to initiate or begin   _____
75. An ability to complete or conclude   _____

Identifying Your Top Talents

Now, having ranked yourself on each of the talents indicated in the "Talent Quiz," go back and review your answers. From the talents that received the highest scores, construct a list of your top ten talents. For those who have many highly rated talents, it may take a good deal of thought to narrow it down to ten. Continue until you are satisfied that you have identified your top ten talents.

1._____   6._____
2._____   7._____
3._____   8._____
4._____   9._____
5._____   10._____

Talent Feedback: Now give your list to at least five people who know you in different ways (e.g., your spouse, a friend, coworker, boss, or mentor). Ask them to examine your list and give you feedback on how well you have evaluated your talents. Tell them their honest opinion will be greatly appreciated. Ask them to indicate to you if perhaps you've overrated yourself in a certain area, or if there are any obvious omissions, or areas where you have a strong ability that you may have overlooked. Write what you learn in the space below.

_____
_____
_____
_____
_____
_____
_____
_____
_____
_____
_____
_____
_____

Many individuals have, like uncut diamonds,
shining qualities beneath a rough exterior.
Juvenal

Your Top Five Talents

After receiving feedback from others and doing your own careful analysis, write your top five natural strengths or talents below.

My Top Five Talents

1. _____

2. _____

3. _____

4. _____

5. _____

Now restate your work-purpose statement below:

_____

_____

_____

_____

_____

_____

_____

_____

_____

Integrating Your Talents and Purpose: How will you employ your talents in the furtherance of your life's work? Review your work-purpose statement and think of how you can put each of your top five talents to work in the pursuit of your life's work.

Talent #1: _____

I can use my ability to: _____

to further my work purpose by: _____

_____

_____

_____

_____

_____

On another sheet of paper, do the same for each of the rest of your top five talents.

Your Personal Strengths

When it comes to your career, you are more than a sum of your education, skills, and work experience. You have already considered your visions, values, purpose, talents, and goals. Beyond this, what are the personal qualities that make you a unique individual?

_____

_____

_____

What do you consider your strongest character traits?

_____

_____

_____

Below is a list of traits or personal qualities. Selecting from these (or others you may want to add), choose the five traits (no more) that **best** describe you.

Adventurous	Courageous	Happy	Kind	Responsible
Amiable	Creative	Hard-charging	Levelheaded	Self-motivated
Artistic	Curious	Hardworking	Loving	Self-assured
Assertive	Dedicated	Honest	Loyal	Spiritual
Athletic	Dramatic	Humorous	Persuasive	Tactful
Aware	Empathetic	Imaginative	Philosophical	Thoughtful
Calm	Energetic	Independent	Playful	Tolerant
Commanding	Entertaining	Intellectual	Positive	Trustworthy
Committed	Enthusiastic	Intelligent	Practical	Wise
Compassionate	Excitable	Intuitive	Rational	
Confident	Gentle	Joyous	Reliable	

My five strongest character traits or personal qualities

1._____

2._____

3._____

4._____

5._____

More than anything, what sets you apart as a unique individual?

_____

_____

_____

_____

Marking Mission Objectives

If you only care enough for a result, you will almost certainly attain it.

William James

The next step is to identify some of your *mission objectives*. A mission objective is a statement of a specific outcome you want to effect in your lifetime, in other words, a lifelong work goal. Unlike a work purpose, a mission objective is limited in time; that is, it is either done or it isn't. To build an orphanage, to create a foundation, to publish a book, to produce a film—these are all possible mission objectives. They are either done or not. The purpose of this section is to give you an opportunity to mark out your mission objectives.

Establishing long-term goals, or mission objectives, gives you a point of focus. In a sea of constant change and turmoil, you have an anchor for your attention and a direction for your life. The Japanese have a saying: "The focused mind can pierce through stone." When you lack focus, your energy is scattered and dispersed. Focus pulls your energy together and magnifies its impact. A laser can cut through a sheet of solid steel with the amount of energy required to illuminate an ordinary lightbulb. The quantity of energy is the same, yet focus intensifies its power.

Imagine shooting an arrow into the air. The arrow soars for a time and then falls limply to the ground. Now imagine taking aim upon a definite target. Your sight clearly fixed on the bull's-eye, you let go the arrow. You hear the satisfying thud as the arrow slams into the target. Without a target, you have nothing to aim at; and without aim, you have virtually no chance of hitting the target. Focus, then, requires a target and concentrated aim. Long-term goals serve as your targets, and repeated concentration on these targets helps you hit the mark.

> *If you do not look at things on a large scale it will be difficult for you to master strategy.*
> *Miyamoto Musashi*

It's clear that a great many personal, social, environmental, and global problems have resulted from shortsighted thinking. Adopting a long-term perspective helps us improve the quality of the decisions we make. For example, if we thought more about those who will follow, we would no doubt take better care of our environment. As nations, we would balance our national budgets and not throw our children and grandchildren into debt. As companies, we would think less in terms of short-term profits and more in terms of bringing long-term benefits. Our educational institutions would concentrate on developing individuals who can think for themselves and on arming them with the tools they need to succeed in the twenty-first century, rather than pushing endless standardized tests on them. In short, if we are to take seriously our responsibility to future generations, we must make choices with the long view in mind.

In the same way that taking into account our responsibility to those who follow influences our choice of work, it influences the quality of our performance—our commitment to excellence. Do we write books, produce films, or compose music that will be enjoyed by those of as yet unborn generations, or do we go for the quick

If you have love you will do all things well.

Thomas Merton

buck? Do we build beautiful, quality buildings that will stand for centuries, or do we slap together bland boxes and cubes? Do we raise the next generation on healthy, nourishing food, or do we feed them microwaved, processed fare? Do we create organizations that build harmony and understanding, protect the environment, and promote world peace, or do we leave it to someone else? The good things you really want to do and accomplish—*do* them.

But don't you have to be realistic? Don't you have to compromise? Never compromise your deepest desires. Never give up on your desire to be your best, or on doing your best to make it manifest. Don't sell out your ideals—easy to say, I know, but hard to live up to. It can sometimes seem like a battle. Something within us is urging us on to our best; yet something seems to pull us down to settling for less. All I can say is: *Stand strong*. Do the best you can. If you fall (and we all do), get back up, and focus on that which seems to pull the good out from you. Give your attention to that which, when you focus on it, makes you feel strength, dignity, self-respect, and a sense of being destined to achieve your best life—whatever that means to you.

Ideas must work through the brains and the arms of good and brave men, or they are no better than dreams.

Emerson

Of course, you may have to compromise in the way your objectives take shape. It is often necessary to start small. As you gain confidence, knowledge, and experience, you move closer to the objectives you have set for yourself. Perhaps even in the end your accomplishments will fall short of your original vision. Perhaps others who follow will complete what you begin. Still, holding the vision, the ideal, out in front of you will encourage you to give more than you might ever have dreamed possible. We can rise only as high as our aspirations; we can only achieve what we intend. Set your sights high.

We all want to give our best. Giving is as natural as breathing and, if we are *really* to live, just as necessary. When expression of the desire to give is somehow blocked, trouble starts. Energy that would naturally go into making constructive contributions gets diverted into less healthy pursuits. The most common ways in which these diversions manifest are confessing unimportance and pulling for the pity of others (passive hostility) or feigning exaggerated importance and demanding their admiration (aggressive hostil-

*For what profit
a man, if he gain
the whole world and
lose his own soul?
Or what shall a man
give in exchange
for his soul?*

Mark 8:36,37

ity). Variations on these two themes are virtually endless. History is replete with examples. *As a practical matter, we have simply to remember that a blocked expression of the desire to contribute produces anger, frustration, and resentment.* Whether we turn the anger inward in the form of self-sabotage or outward in the form of verbal or physical violence, it eats up our lives. Held over time, this anger can destroy relationships, weaken health, and sap creativity.

*Resolve to be thyself, and know that he
Who finds himself, loses his misery.*
> Coventry Patmore

Many a good relationship has been destroyed when one or both parties in that relationship have failed to achieve a clear sense of direction, or purpose, in their lives. The aimless party feels badly about him- or herself and so begins to find fault with the other and make excessive demands on that person. They demand attention, wanting the other to constantly reassure them that they are lovable and okay. This becomes a horribly destructive and draining game.

Another, equally destructive game is to play off many different "lovers." The object of this game is to fill with admirers the void left by your failure to adequately express yourself. Its object is, again, to reassure you that you are okay. You may create great anxiety for yourself and your loved ones by living far beyond your means. Again, this is an attempt to impress upon yourself and others that you have made it, that you are okay. The point is that you are not here to *be* someone else or just to be *with* someone else. You're here to be yourself, to make your unique contribution to the world. In the end, giving your best is the best you can do for your relationships and yourself.

For years, it has been known that stress is a contributing factor to many types of illness. Recently, researchers at Columbia University have made the link between illness and an individual's sense of control in his or her life. For example, people who work in jobs where they have little control (e.g., cooks and assembly line workers, etc.) are more likely to suffer heart attacks than those who have greater control. Apparently, as you increase control in your life, you reduce negative stress. Overeating, drug abuse, smoking, and alcoholism are frequently the result of the stress associated with not having taken responsibility to create a meaningful life's work, a work that gives you a sense of direction and control. Committing yourself to giving your best fosters good health by reducing negative stress.

It is hard to feel creative in a job that you are doing just to get by. Creativity is a way of life, not a matter of chance or a mysterious force to be summoned out of the ethers. If what you are doing most of the day requires no creative skill, chances are your creativity is on the way downhill. You're not going to walk in the door and suddenly be creative at home if all day you've been vegetating at your work. Your creative powers grow and develop through use. The more you are challenged, the more you grow. The point is: don't settle for less; follow your desire, and work to make it manifest.

Our plans miscarry because they have no aim. When a man does not know what harbor he is making for, no wind is the right wind.
                                        Seneca

There is no getting away from difficulties in this life. You're either going to have the creative challenges that come with realizing this vision of yours, or the neurotic problems that arise from the suppression of desire. Creative challenges test you and spur you to your best. Neurotic problems are simply the murky water of suppressed desire. Let's face it, your deepest desires aren't going away. Talk to people in nursing homes. See if many don't still have the idea of the thing they always wanted to do, but didn't. They are haunted by regret. Their desires didn't go away just because they didn't act on them. Your desire isn't going away either. Honor it, and do your best to give it expression. Keep coming back to it; feed it more and more attention. Let your desire become so strong that no fear from within or obstacle from without can stop your commitment to give your best.

In the exercise that follows, you will be encouraged to list your mission objectives, things you would most like to accomplish in your life. Don't expect that your list is necessarily going to be complete, or even accurate. Don't worry; you're not setting anything in stone. There may be omissions. Your list may not reflect the full range of all you want to accomplish. Once you get your feet wet, you may discover a host of additional possibilities that you haven't even considered. There may be inaccuracies. Once you begin, you may discover that you no longer want to accomplish things that were your original objectives. Again, you are not setting anything in stone. You are beginning to mark out the territory of your life's work with specific targets that you can use as reference points along the way.

Sooner murder an infant in its cradle than nurse unacted desires.

William Blake

Transforming Visions into Goals

Let's be honest. For a lot of us, writing goals just isn't as much fun as dreaming about visions. A vision is, in a sense, complete within itself, while a goal represents a great deal of effort for only a fraction of the vision. In your imagination, you can experience the totality of the vision now, with practically no effort, while working toward goals demands effort and the capacity to overcome resistance. Resistance results from the physical limitations of the natural world—time, space, energy, and matter. Resistance is overcome by concentrating and focusing energy. Writing definite goals is a powerful step to concentrating your energy.

Written Goals Are Best: A goal is a measurable written statement of a definite next step toward the realization of a vision you want to see manifest. If it's not written down, it's not really a goal. It's a wish, a dream, a vision, a hope, but not a goal. Writing your goals down forces you to clarify and refine them. Several studies have shown that a written goal is more likely to be achieved than one that is merely thought or talked about. For example, in 1954 a survey was made of individuals graduating from Yale University. It was found that only 3 percent had definite written financial goals; 10 percent had a clear idea, but had not written it down; 87 percent had no idea of their goals. Twenty years later, these Yale graduates were again interviewed. The 3 percent who had written goals had made more money than all the rest combined. Leaders in business, industry, and finance have long known the power of written goals in achieving success. Today, more and more individuals are writing personally meaningful goals in all areas of their lives, including career.

Goals Can Promote Well-being: There are indications that identifying goals reduces stress and improve one's sense of psychological well-being. In his book *A Strategy for Daily Living*, Dr. Ari Kiev writes, "In my practice as a psychiatrist, I have found that helping people to develop personal goals has proved to be *the most effective way* to help them cope with problems" [emphasis added]. Many psychological problems are the result of an abundance of unchanneled or unfocused psychic energy. When we lack direction or creative challenge, life seems alternatively dull and boring or overwhelming and confusing. Establishing clear goals puts you in charge of your life. You're not at the whim of changing circumstances or opinions of others. You know exactly what you want. You look forward to the coming years because you know that you will progress and how you will progress.

Goals Increase Motivation: Once a goal is clearly fixed in your mind and written down on paper, you can begin to measure progress toward that goal. Psychologists studying motivation in the workplace have identified clear and consistent feedback as the most effective means of improving motivation and increasing performance. Feedback is only meaningful to the extent that it is the measurement of progress toward clear, definite goals. I encourage you to take the time to identify long-range career goals—your mission objectives.

Your Mission: Give Birth to the Great Idea of Your Life

Everyone has a great idea for his or her life. For many it remains unfertil-ized, unrecognized. Some abort the idea before it ever has a chance to grow. Some abandon it in its infancy. Still others chain the idea to themselves and make it twisted and distorted. And some set it free. Discover the great idea of your life, and set it free. But don't kid yourself. It will take every ounce of you. No weak, halfhearted effort will raise this child. Only a mother's love will get the job done.

In raising an idea, as in raising a child, there are joys and sorrows, frustra-tions and victories, agony and ecstasy. A child can get you up at three o'clock in the morning; so can an idea. A child can keep you up all night because it's sick and in need of care; so can an idea. Child or idea, you thrill when it says its first word or takes its first step, when it has its first day at school, when it first falls in love, and when, finally, it is free of you and yet full of you. The work of the creative person is to make her idea independent of her, just as the work of a parent is to make her child independent.

He who wants to do good knocks at the gate; he who loves finds the gate open.

Tagore

Many times people are afraid to embrace their idea, their vision, because deep down they know that they will become responsible for it, and it will hold them, like a child holds a mother, until it is free of them. Just as a mother becomes a servant of the child, so the creator becomes the servant of her creation. Like any parent, she is both happy and sad the day she sets it free. It's a labor of love. What we mean by "giving your best" is taking on the great idea of your life and carrying it, nurturing it, loving it until it can stand on its own two feet, and you are free. Take an idea that will grab hold of you and not let you go until it has squeezed the very best from you.

That idea is your life's mission. Your mission is your special gift to mankind. It is the most appropriate vehicle through which to express your unique talents, interests, and abilities. A life's mission is not simply an occupa-tion. Rather, it's a steady application of effort to the lifelong challenge of remaining true to your best. It's the love of your life in action.

Mission Objectives

In the space below, write your important mission objectives. A mission objective is a statement of a specific work-related goal that you want to accomplish in your lifetime. While a work purpose is open-ended, a mission objective is limited in time. It is either done or it isn't. To publish a book, create a foundation, produce a film, open a store, or create an online resource center—these are all possible mission objectives.

Mission Objective #1:

_____

_____

_____

_____

Mission Objective #2:

_____

_____

_____

_____

Mission Objective #3:

_____

_____

_____

_____

Mission Objective #4:

_____

_____

_____

_____

Mission Objective #5:

_____

_____

_____

_____

What If You Still Don't Know?

Most ignorance is vincible ignorance: We don't know because we don't want to know.
        Aldous Huxley

What if, after doing the exercises in Act I and contemplating on your own, you still don't know what your life's work is? In my work with clients, I always assume that they do know, and I tell them so. I simply don't believe their "not knowing." I ask them to consider *why they might not want to know.* I suggest to them that they might not want to be aware of knowing because of the responsibility for action that knowledge brings. If I profess not to know what my work is, then I can't be blamed for not having achieved it. If I do know, then how can I justify not taking action, either to myself or to others? How can I justify not making a sincere effort to develop myself so that I will be better able to work in this area? Again, knowledge brings responsibility.

So far, I've asked you to examine your vision for the kind of world you want to live in, to clarify your values, articulate your purpose, identify your talents, and list major accomplishments you would like to make in the course (or remainder) of your work life. My best advice is that you attempt to do or redo the exercises at the end of each scene in Act I. If, after having done that, you still don't know what your life's work is, you may want to:

1. Continue to put your attention on the kind of world you want to live in, on what the world needs, and on what you have to give (see "Act I: Action Steps" on page 245).

2. Understand why you might not want to know. Below are a few of the more popular "reasons" why people "do not know" what they want to do.

"Reasons" Why You Might Not Want to Know What Your Life's Work Is

1. Fear of failure
2. Fear of rejection
3. Fear of reality
4. Fear of losing identity (face)
5. Fear of pain (and sacrifice)
6. Fear of commitment
7. Fear of making the "wrong choice"
8. Fear of not being in control
9. Fear that it will never work

Fear of Failure

Fear of failure often results from a false definition of what failure is, and by extension, of what success is. If failure is defined only in terms of ends, outcomes, and completions, then the possibility of failure is a real one. Likewise, if failure is measured by the standards and judgments of others, it is a very real possibility. If, on the other hand, you measure your success in terms of doing your best to realize your highest potential and make your maximum contribution, failure is only a failure of effort, the failure to fully apply yourself. To overcome fear of failure: (1) value your process as well as your results; (2) don't make comparisons, except with yourself; and (3) don't be lazy. Make your best effort. *Since we as individuals are completely in control of any effort that we*

make, we are better advised to make our best efforts than to involve ourselves in fear and worry, which, after all, can only hamper our performance.

Fear of Rejection

Our society is extremely approval oriented. There's tremendous pressure to conform to narrowly defined images of success. People, by and large, understand static positions and finished products far better than dynamic creative processes. *A great inventor is a silly tinkerer until his invention is perfected and accepted.* The process of pursuing your life's work may not bring immediately obvious results. It may appear to others as though you are "doing nothing" while you're going through the process of self-examination, research, learning, training, or developing products or services.

> *Our doubts are traitors and make us lose the good we oft might win by fearing to attempt.*
>
> Shakespeare

While this kind of work is absolutely vital to attaining your life's work, it is not currently highly valued in society. This is especially true if it means loss of income or social status in the process. While a temporary loss of income and status may be a necessary and constructive step toward the achievement of your life's work, it is often viewed by others whose opinion one values as a step backward. They may think that you are slipping or "losing it" and may pressure you to "give up this foolishness" and return to a more "secure" position. If we are overly dependent upon the approval of others, its withdrawal may seem like the end of the world. Happily, the end of one world is often the beginning of a new, far richer and more fulfilling one.

Additionally, you may risk social rejection for taking controversial stands or for attempting to do things that haven't been done before. If you are particularly sensitive to the fear of rejection, you may view the pursuit of your life's work as threatening the approval of friends and loved ones as well as more general social approval. *Recognize that while approval comes and goes, we ultimately have to live with what we think of ourselves: remaining true to your conscience is the safest possible course.*

Fear of Reality

This fear arises in those who have consistently denied reality and have constructed fantasy worlds. In their fantasy worlds, they're always good, accomplished, beautiful. They are, in a word—perfect. In the real world, none of us is perfect. People who tend to be perfectionists dread the thought of being evaluated on their performance. After all, performance always has a measure of imperfection in it. We can maintain our perfect dream of ourselves in our heads and never have to confront our limitations. In my mind, I can imagine a perfect book. But the one you are reading, as I am well aware, is imperfect. Its imperfection reflects not only the limitations of the material world, but those of its author. Still, I offer it to you, imperfect as it is, in hope that it may be of value to you. Your offerings will likewise be imperfect, but they can nevertheless be valuable.

> *I believe that anyone can conquer fear by doing the things he fears to do.*
>
> Eleanor Roosevelt

While the fears of failure and rejection are largely concerned with how others perceive us, the fear of reality is concerned with how we perceive ourselves. Are we willing to leave our mental ivory towers and face our imperfection, our smallness in the grand scheme of things, our frailness and humanity? In the imaginary fantasy world, I am not only perfect, I am omnipotent. In the real world, I am neither. It's hard to venture forth and risk much when you live inside a protective bubble designed to preserve your cherished illusions. In pursuing your life's work, you will burst the bubble of your fantasy world. ***Your caring and desire to give will push you to risk facing the reality of your shortcomings as well as the limitations of this world.***

Fear of Losing Identity

Individuals who do not have a strong sense of their own identity attach a great deal of significance to titles and positions. A focus on title or position is static and, as such, perceived as secure (at least as long as one maintains the title or position). The pursuit of a life's work, on the other hand, is dynamic. Its success is measured, not in terms of positions or titles achieved, but in terms of the degree to which one realizes a self-defined purpose. The pursuit of a life's work may require the abandonment of a certain title or position that, even though unfulfilling, gives one some sense of security. ***When you know you are more than the positions or titles you hold, you are free to do your best without being afraid of the tests.***

Fear of Pain (and Sacrifice)

The fear of pain could also be called the reluctance to make the necessary sacrifices. If, when you meet resistance or encounter obstacles, you habitually retreat into your protective bubble, you probably suffer from this fear. For some, contemplation of their life's work requires a quantity and depth of thought to which they are unaccustomed. They have resistance to thinking about or concentrating on this subject because it forces them to confront their values and beliefs, to answer the age-old questions: Who am I? and What am I doing here? Many people find these questions painful.

This is particularly true since they recognize that once they have been successful in discovering their life's work, they may be setting up a course with even greater challenges. A cartoon appearing some years ago in a popular magazine depicted two well-dressed men seated in armchairs by a blazing fire with one saying to the other, "I used to ask myself, 'What can I do to help my fellow man?' but I couldn't think of anything that wouldn't have put me to considerable inconvenience." ***You must be willing to put yourself to "considerable inconvenience."***

Fear of Commitment

Today, while commitment is widely touted, it is rarely practiced. People are particularly sensitive about making commitments. This is true in areas beyond work, for example, in marriage and relationships. Our popular concept of freedom is freedom from commitment or obligation. Given this, it is not surprising that we tend to avoid voluntarily committing ourselves. The fault in this kind of thinking lies in our ideas of what freedom is and how best to achieve it. If we view freedom as a hedonistic lack of restraint, we are unlikely to equate it with the discipline necessary to achieve a life's work. Discipline must be embraced as the road to freedom. ***We pursue our life's work, not to diminish our freedom, but rather to expand it; we expand our freedom by leading lives that are fully integrated, by doing our best to practice what we preach, by putting our ideals to work.***

Fear always springs from ignorance.

Emerson

Fear of Making the "Wrong Choice"

Decision making requires not only that we accept definite limitations, but that we, in fact, impose them on ourselves. There is a certain aspect of human nature that resists limits of any kind. Yet, if we are to fully embrace life as a creative adventure, we must learn to put limits on our activities (not our potentials). Every truly creative person does so. Classical art, poetry, music, and drama all operate within the definite limits of form. These limits do not impede creativity, but rather challenge the composer to make his message fit the formal structure. Limits force him to make every line, every note, every scene count.

> *Nothing is terrible except fear itself.*
> *Francis Bacon*

When making decisions, you must leave behind the billowy clouds of vision and confront the practical limitations of space, time, energy, and matter. In other words, you have to make your visions work for you in the world in which you live. In this world, you can't do all things at once; you can't be all things to all people. You have to choose what you are about as an individual and establish the priorities of your life. Recognize that when you decide to focus on a particular vision, you may have to let go of one or several others, at least for a time. You have to make a choice.

The important thing is that you make the best choice possible for you at this time. If it is not your ultimate choice, don't be concerned. You will have plenty of opportunities to refine and reconsider your course, once you have begun it. The important thing is to begin. The worst choice is no choice. The best choice is choosing what you love the best. ***Choosing your priorities and values makes the strongest possible statement about who you are in this life.***

Fear of Not Being in Control

The fear of losing control is the fear that you will get in over your head. There will be too much to learn, too much information to process, too much to do. The remedy to this fear is simply the recognition that creating your life's work is a step-by-step process that you control from beginning to end. Establish the parameters of your area of expertise. Continued focus and study in this area will bring added knowledge and, with it, increased confidence.

What we cannot control is the fact that we have a limited time on this earth, and therefore we must choose how we will use it. ***Make the most of the time you have. Be deliberate. Take it step by step. Control what you can; forget the rest.***

Fear That It Will Never Work

People who have this fear have decided that "it" simply won't work for them. They believe their lives cannot really be the way they want them to be. They feel beaten down—defeated by life. They suffer from chronic low self-esteem. They've lost belief in themselves and, with it, the power to dream. If you fall into this group, identify when it was that you decided it was over, that it couldn't work—the point where you stopped believing in yourself. What were the events that precipitated this decision?

> *There are costs and risks to a program of action, but they are far less than the long range risks and costs of comfortable inaction.*
>
> *John F. Kennedy*

Objectively analyze the situation and the reasons for your failure to achieve the results you wanted. Perhaps you didn't have adequate information. Perhaps you didn't make enough effort. Perhaps you listened to those who said you would fail. Whatever the reasons, objectively identify them. A great high jumper may miss a height that is well within his reach. But he *does not* conclude that he is a failure as an athlete. He says, "My approach was too slow. My hip was too low . . ." He identifies specifics that he can correct. ***Understand specific reasons for past failures, and you free yourself to try again.***

Fear can be a factor at any step of the process of moving toward your life's work. I've placed this discussion here because if you don't get past your initial fears, you're not even in the ballpark. If you overcome them in the early stages of the process, you can apply what you've learned about mastering fear to any issues that come up later.

Putting Fear on the Run

If you are having difficulty identifying your life's work, review the nine fears above. Indicate the top three that slow you down and what you plan to do to overcome them. Keep acting into fear until it is no more.

Fear 1: _____

What I will do to overcome this: _____
_____
_____
_____
_____
_____
_____

Act into Fear and Watch It Disappear

Fear 2: _____

What I will do to overcome this: _____
_____
_____
_____
_____
_____

Act into Fear and Watch It Disappear

Fear 3: _____

What I will do to overcome this: _____
_____
_____
_____
_____
_____

Act into Fear and Watch It Disappear

Act I: Action Steps

If you still don't know what your life's work is, do and learn until you do.

1. Volunteer your time working for causes you believe in.

2. Study global, national, and/or community problems, firsthand if possible.

3. Study philosophy, religion, mythology, sociology, history, anthropology, science, art, etc., with a view toward developing personally meaningful values.

4. Read the biographies of great individuals with a view toward learning effective strategies and raising your expectations.

5. Study success principles generally, and develop or strengthen a positive mental and emotional attitude toward life.

6. Develop skills that will stand you in good stead, regardless of your later career choices. For example:

   a. Speaking
   b. Writing
   c. Negotiating
   d. Managing
   e. Teaching
   f. Mentoring
   g. Performing well under pressure
   h. Planning
   i. Critical thinking
   j. Creative thinking
   k. Public relations

7. Learn techniques such as speed-reading, superlearning, and meditation, which will help you to keep up with all you will need to learn, and yet remain relatively unburdened by it.

Act I Review

My Mission Statement: *(page 198)*

My Work-Purpose Statement: *(page 213)*

My Top Five Talents: *(page 227)*

1.
2.
3.
4.
5.

Integrating My Talents and Purpose:

(page 227)

Talent #1:
I can use my ability to:
to further my work purpose by:

Talent #2:
I can use my ability to:
to further my work purpose by:

Talent #3:
I can use my ability to:
to further my work purpose by:

Talent #4:
I can use my ability to:
to further my work purpose by:

Talent #5:
I can use my ability to:
to further my work purpose by:

My Mission Objectives:

(page 236)

The Game of Life's Work

Wherein our hero makes a career choice

Is the system going to flatten you out and deny you your humanity, or are you going to be able to make use of the system to the attainment of human purposes?
Joseph Campbell

Assuming you've completed the exercises in Act I, you should have a general sense of what your life's work is. Now, in "Act II: The Game of Life's Work," it's time to begin identifying and investigating career roles that will enable you to pursue this work. In shaping your vision of the work life you want to create, your intuition, desire, and imagination have been the key drivers. Now, as you begin developing a career strategy for realizing that vision, you'll want to bring research, critical-thinking, and decision-making skills into the mix. Because it is a decision that will affect your daily life for years to come, you know that making a career choice is a task that deserves thorough research and careful consideration. Ironically, knowledge of the importance of a decision can sometimes prevent us from making it. Viewing career choice as the identification of a suitable vehicle for pursuing your purpose and expressing your passion rather than as the selection of a personal identity can go a long way in reducing the angst around it. Before investigating potential career options and making a choice, let's step back and consider the game of career and its place in the larger game of society.

Playing the Game:
Winners, Losers, and Choosers

The play's the thing.
Shakespeare

The correspondence between the archetypical Magician and the Game of Life's Work was discussed in chapter 3. The Magician's domain is the realm of imagination, of theater. The magic of the theater comes to life on an empty stage. A few painted scenes, a few simple props, a few scraps of material fashioned into costumes, some well-placed lights—and an entire world is born. Throw in some actors to animate this world and you become lost in the magic of theater. Under its spell, the once-empty stage seems transformed into a tropical island or a medieval kingdom, a Roman courtyard or a modern courtroom. Yet, when the show is over and the lights come back up, you realize that the world you inhabited had gained its sense of reality from the belief you placed in it. It was just a stage full of props and pretenders. Whatever life this make-believe world seemed to possess ultimately came from you.

In the discussion that follows, we're going to attempt to discover the magic behind society's theater, or game. We're going to unlock some of the secrets of its stagecraft. Be forewarned that this may be somewhat disillusioning. For what had once seemed inevitable and enduring will look far more ephemeral with the house lights turned up. You will still be able to enjoy the play—in fact, all the more. Yet its effects will never charm or frighten you to the same degree, once you know how the magic is made. After considering society's game, we'll turn to the game of career and how to play it.

Society's game can play tricks on our imaginations. Like Dorothy and her companions, we are seduced by the apparent majesty of a Great Wizard of Oz. We venture far out of our way to seek his blessing, only to find ourselves quaking before the awful images he projects. However, once we see how these images are constructed, we no longer fear or fetch for them. No longer do we imagine that the Great Oz can do for us what we can only do for ourselves. Now we are free to unleash the full creative power of our hearts and minds, right where we are, in our own backyards. Yet first we must gather the courage to peek behind the veil—to see how this silly little man projects the fearful image of the Magnificent Oz. To our shock or delight, we will discover that we are that funny little man. We, alone and together, have projected the Great Oz of social convention out of our own imaginations.

The theater of the mind, the magic realm of imagination, is perhaps most easily approached through the study of dreams. In the twentieth century, the once strange and remote world of dreams first came under scientific scrutiny. Researchers recognized a phenomenon referred to as "lucid dreaming." It was noted that for lucid dreamers, dreams do not simply "happen" as they do for most. Lucid dreamers are actually able to consciously create and direct the course of their dreams. Researchers also discovered that the capacity for lucid dreaming could be developed through a deliberate training.[1] The critical stage in this development comes when the individual recognizes in the midst of a dream that he or she has the power to control the dream images. He becomes, as it were, awake while dreaming. She awakens to the choice that she has in creating, directing, and editing the images that play upon the nocturnal theater of the mind. In much the same way, when we turn up the house lights, when we awaken within the dream of unconscious living, we become aware of the magic that makes up society's game. Just as the lucid dreamer remains conscious within the dream, so we can remain aware in the midst of the collective dream called "society's game."

Society has a game going. Like it or not, you were recruited into this game. Every game needs ends, goals, outcomes, prizes. In other words, it needs a way of separating winners from losers.

Nothing can bring you peace but yourself.

Emerson

Winners are those who get the prizes and titles. Losers are those who don't. Society's game is based on a conventional *winning model*, confirmed through *title acquisition*. Conforming to the conventional winning model and acquiring sanctioned titles makes you a "winner." Deviating from the winning model and/or failing to acquire sanctioned titles makes you a "loser."

Of course, no one invites you to choose the winning model by which you will be judged and by which, most likely, you will come to judge yourself. Society does, however, entice you with rewards and chasten you with ridicule into accepting the winning model as the only game in town. Though individuals are not invited to choose the model, the model's continuance depends on most people choosing to play for its prizes. This is the irony of the game—the key to its drama. *We choose to forget that we have a choice, that we have chosen the game that runs our lives.*

> The beater and the beaten: Mere players of a game ephemeral as a dream.
>
> Muso Soseki

Society's game is like a giant lotto. Everyone buys a ticket and plays along in the hope of being one of the lucky few who strike it rich. Everyone starts out trying to win; yet, in order for the model to maintain its allure, most people can't win. Who would strive to win a prize everyone has? Societies arrange their games to give the appearance that things have to be a certain way—the way they are. The discussion that follows will consider the ways this plays out in our society: through *envy for rank and property titles* and *the shame of social ridicule.*

Rank Titles: A Position of Deference

Near the end of the Cold War, the Romanian dictator called out the army to quash a popular uprising. Instead, the army sided with the people, and the dictator was executed. In an instant, the most powerful man in the nation became a helpless outcast unable to save his own skin. This story illustrates a fundamental maxim of society's game: *A person's power and position within society depend upon the deference that others choose to give to their title.* The all-powerful king or dictator is virtually powerless after the revolution.

We seek titles with the expectation that once we possess them, others will have to give us deference. It's the title that gets the deference, not the person holding the title. It's not Joan Smith who gets deference, but Dr. Joan Smith, MD; not Bill Jones, but Bill Jones, CEO of Widgets International. Richard Nixon's deference level plummeted the day he resigned the title President.

Titles win us deference, and though we attempt to hold them for perpetuity, they are subject to the slings and arrows of outrageous fortune. CFO Robert L. Doe can one day find himself without the corner office or the morning limo ride that go with the title. Dr. Joan Smith can (heaven forbid!) lose her license to practice. General Douglas MacArthur can find himself without an army to command. Even Popes have lost their titles. Most people find the deference that accompanies titles gratifying to their egos and their pocketbooks. They will fight, scratch, and kiss the proverbial rear to keep a T.I.T.L.E. they hold dear.

Still, despite our best efforts, titles remain insecure. The higher the rank, the bigger the fall, and the better the gunslingers ready for a showdown. The hot star in business, sports, entertainment, or politics quickly becomes yesterday's news when he or she "fails to produce." What, then, can we hold on to? Better than rank titles are property titles. Through convention, we have come to give more permanence to property titles than rank titles.

Property Titles: A Position of Power

Rank is rarely held for life and can't be passed on. Where it appears to be, as in the case of the chairman of the firm passing the title on to an heir, the authority to do so is based on ownership, not on rank. Hostile takeovers demonstrate the priority of property titles over rank titles. The founder and chairman can find himself without a company if others are able to acquire a controlling interest in the stock property of the company.

Realizing the insecurity of rank, rank-holders try to convert rank advantage into property titles. The chart-topping *Rock Star* buys a Beverly Hills mansion. The *Queen of Daytime Talk* buys a grand estate in Santa Barbara; the *Corporate CEO,* a palatial villa on the Florida coast. In Latin America, the corrupt *Chief of Police* builds the multimillion-dollar home on a hill overlooking the city. The significance of these properties goes beyond their capacity to provide beautiful surroundings. They are a statement. "I have made it." "I have won what cannot be taken away." "I'm above it all."

Property, then, is the big prize, *the ultimate form of legitimacy in our society.* And, of course, real estate is but one of the many kinds of property we value. With enough property titles, you can control many rank titles in many spheres of influence, without possessing any rank title yourself. Although, with very few exceptions, you must continue

Once the game is over, the king and the pawn go back into the same box.

Italian Proverb

to prove that you are worthy of rank, you seldom have to prove that you are worthy of property. Another name for "serious property holdings" is financial independence. For most, it is only a dream.

Most people don't own much property. (In America, the bottom 95 percent own less wealth than the top 5 percent.) They depend on rank for deference and status. That's why companies have twelve vice presidents and garbage collectors are called "sanitary engineers." People work for rank titles today (even if the title is First Assistant to the Senior Assistant of the Executive Assistant to the Chief of Miscellaneous Services) and the dream of big-time property tomorrow.

The powers that be, meaning those who hold the most property and the "best" titles, have the most to lose by people not taking all this seriously. It behooves them to perpetuate the notion that all rankings are real, important, and just. Even more, the "property rules" rule must remain unquestioned. In our society, this is the mother of all rules, the one upon which the entire game depends. One should accept that property titles are earned or deserved, and that it is more or less the inalienable right of their owners to keep them forever—through their offspring. It's a tough break for losers, but that's the way it is. Besides, with enough pluck and luck, they too could become winners. Of course, acquiring and maintaining property is not without its set of problems. As William James said, "Lives based on having are less free than lives based on either doing or being."[2] "Winners" often end up psychologically chained to their possessions, property, or rank.

He who possesses most must be most afraid of loss.
Leonardo da Vinci

Because of the role property plays as the ultimate prize in the social game, there is great ceremony around the legitimacy of its possession. Once upon a time, the king's role as the realm's ultimate property holder was confirmed in elaborate ceremonies blessed by wizards or priests. Today, major property holders buy and collect works of art to confer spiritual legitimacy to their status. They support the status quo by endowing, often in their own names, important rank-conferring institutions, such as the prestigious universities. Ceremony helps to preserve social stability and the existing (rank/property) title system.

The aim is to make the status quo seem a kind of divine, or at least natural, order. I live in California, where it was okay for the Spaniards to take land from the Indians, and the Mexicans from the Spaniards, and the Americans from the Mexicans. Yet it's not okay for you to take it from the guy who owns it now. Why? Well,

The trouble with the rat race is that even if you win you're still a rat.

Lily Tomlin

the most obvious answer is the law and the force behind it. If you did, the police would come arrest you. But, ultimately, any law relies on the consent, or at least the acquiescence, of the governed. When most people decide to break a given law, it becomes unenforceable. The highway patrol doesn't strictly enforce the posted speed limit because most people drive at least a few miles faster. There's no way they can catch them all. It's the same with any law, written or unwritten. Most enforcement is self-enforcement. A society that needs zillions of police is on shaky ground.

Life must be lived as play.

Plato

Social Ridicule: Shame on You

How, then, do you get people to take the game seriously? With juicy, alluring prizes, to be sure; but remember, only a few people can win the really big prizes or they won't mean much. The primary means of getting people to take the game seriously is social ridicule. Social ridicule is based upon shame, the shame of being a loser. To the degree that you can be shamed, you will be manipulated by ridicule. *Every society uses ridicule as a means of social control.* Look at societies from a standpoint of what they ridicule, and you can understand their winning models and why they have developed the way they have.

Ridicule says, "Get back in line, you loser, you." And it's very effective. *Remember, most of us are losers.* We are losers for two reasons. First, we do not fit the winning model (serious property), and second, we choose to accept the model as a guide to our worth. Losers can be shamed by ridicule. Losers accept themselves as losers and feel defeated. Still, they do not want to be EXPOSED as losers. Being ridiculed is being exposed. Once you decide that you can't win, the next step is to play defense against the ridicule of being exposed as a loser.

Humour is the only test of gravity, and gravity of humour. For a subject which will not bear raillery is suspicious; and a jest which will not bear a serious examination is certainly false wit.

(Quoted by Aristotle)

So we go along and act extra nice, hoping no one will expose us. Our motto becomes: Don't rock the boat. We put down others (who obviously are bigger losers than we are). Poor people, "stupid" people, people with physical or mental disabilities are frequent targets, as are those of other races, ethnicities, and sexual orientations. We make up reasons for losing—extenuating circumstances. We had a deprived childhood, or our parents didn't love us; we were jilted by a lover or treated unfairly by a boss. We have chronic aches and pains.

We try extra hard to look like winners, living beyond our means. Or we try to deaden the pain of losing by becoming addicted to things that take us mentally or emotionally away. Drugs, alcohol, television, affairs—any convincing escape will do. We get into attacking the model or calling the "winners" cheaters, scoundrels, or worse. If you don't think you can get good titles, you may go for bad titles. Something distinguishing. If you don't think you can be the world's greatest X, and you're still into having titles, then you possibly could be the world's worst something. When all else fails, some try to destroy the game through individual acts of violence or collective acts of terrorism. Remember, all of this presupposes that we choose to accept the game's winning model, and define ourselves as losers.

What if we observe the game and come to the conclusion that we are not particularly delighted about the prizes being offered? What if we think that the whole lotto concept of a few winners and many losers is fallacious? What if we come to see the particular game we are playing in today's global society as downright destructive? When you observe people playing a destructive game, you have a number of options: You can try to oppose them. You can start another game and try to get them interested in playing. You can remind them of the infinite game possibilities and the fact that they are always the choosers, and that in this sense, there are no winners and losers. Let's explore these options.

Opposing the Game: AKA, Fighting the System

Fighting the game's property-ranking system tends to actually maintain it, with minor adjustments. Losers may trade places with winners, but the game remains essentially the same. *It is for this reason that violent political revolutions seldom change much.* Typically, some segment of an oppressed people takes up arms and tries to overthrow the powers that be. Somewhere along the way, they are so transformed by the brutality of the struggle that they become the new oppressors when they ultimately seize control. (There is an old Hebrew saying: *Don't hate your enemy, or you become like him.*) Of course, their interest was not in changing the game but in changing the status of in- and out-groups. I call these struggles "pie fights," fighting over who gets what piece of the pie. Occasionally, pie fighters do manage to recut the pie without taking the old leadership's slice for themselves—but this is very rare. Few political revolutions of any kind ever succeed; most collapse when their leaders are bought off, threatened, jailed, or otherwise silenced. Successful or not, pie fights usually get very messy.

Changing the Rules of the Game: New Models, New Ridicule

Fighting the ranking system is about political revolution. Changing the rules of the game is about social revolution. Changing the rules of the game means changing ideas about what it means to be a winner and a loser. This has happened more rarely, and the effects have been more profound. A genuine social revolution changes the winning model and, thus, what is rewarded and ridiculed.

For example, hoarding is a rewarded activity in our society. The "biggest people" are those with the largest hoards. The "littlest people" are the homeless, with but tiny hoards. They are ridiculed for their paltry possessions, not their lack of industry. A lazy man with many possessions is not a bum; he leads a "charmed life." In some traditional societies, the "biggest people" are those who give away the most. The "littlest people" are the possessive ones, ridiculed for their hoarding. In both cases, conformity with the winning model is rewarded and deviation from it is ridiculed. In both cases, the model and the ridicule are means of social control, but the resulting societies and the values they emphasize are fundamentally different.

If Men were Wise, the Most arbitrary Princes could not hurt them. If they are not wise, the Freest Government is compelled to be a Tyranny.
William Blake

Many believe that, in today's global society, a winning model defined in terms of hoarded property is unsustainable. They fear that it could lead to the termination of all play on earth. Increased population and the fact that more and more people in the developing world are playing the game every year put tremendous pressure on the earth's life-support system. Some who view the current game as placing human survival in jeopardy are trying to change the rules of the game by setting up model communities based on alternative values. Others attempt to communicate their points of view through various media in hopes of convincing a sizable sector of the population to agree to a new social game. They propose new models and new types of social ridicule. The environmental movement is one of the more visible examples. It holds up the model of sustainable living, and ridicules overconsumption and environmental degradation.

Ironically, efforts at social change are most effective when those so engaged are not attached to winning, in other words—when they are willing to allow others the freedom to change or not. When we need others to change, we often evoke resistance from them. People who might otherwise be ready to change will recoil against the effort to push them into it.

Choosers Playing Games: Not Taking Any Game Seriously

Are there any other possibilities besides striving to win, defending against losing, fighting the system, or attempting to change the rules of the game? When you choose to remain lucid in the midst of the collective dream, the possibilities become virtually endless. See society's game for what it is and you can release its psychological hold on you. Turn up the houselights and recognize how the game sucks you in emotionally. From this place, you can seek rank for the power it gives to achieve results. You just stop believing that your rank makes you better or worse than anyone else. Similarly, you can seek property for enjoyment, security, or service. You just stop believing that possessing or not possessing property makes you better or worse than anyone else.

Because it is a collective dream, society's game doesn't end just because you awaken within it. What changes is your psychological investment in its winning model and ranking system. You no longer use these as a guide to your own worth or that of others. In other words, while in the midst of society's game, you choose to play your own. Remember you are the chooser, and play. *Playing doesn't mean indifference*. You can play with commitment and intensity. You can play heroically and passionately. You can play with determination and perseverance. In fact, you can't play halfheartedly. You can go through the motions, but that ain't playing. It really is true that it's not about winning or losing, but how you play the game.

> *Love and do as you please.*
> St. Augustine

You can play the game, or it can play you. Playing the game is fun; getting played—not so much. Playing begins not with action, but with contemplation. Our word *contemplation* comes from the Latin *contemplari*, "to see things as they really are." See the game for what it is and you are free to play. Recognize that the trick of the game is to seduce you into feeling superior and/or to manipulate or intimidate you into feeling inferior. When you honor all people for their humanity and don't see anyone as essentially better, worse, or different from yourself, you can no longer be tricked. You no longer need submit to projections of inferiority or crave an enviable position from which to lord it over others. You can concentrate on expressing your creative best without being unduly concerned about social approval. Hold your own and the dignity of all human beings inviolate, and you are free to play.

Put another way, the trick of the game is to capture your imagination. Society's game links rank and title with images that become symbolically associated with winning and losing. These images enter your subconscious mind, where they become invested with emotional energy until they grow to larger-than-life-sized in your imagination. Image and emotion work together to draw you into the life prescribed by society. The creative power of your imagination becomes involved in building a defensive ego fortress, complete with watchtowers that scan the surrounding territory for possible threats (social ridicule) or possible new areas of conquest. Unfortunately, while your imagination is so engaged, it's not available for creating the life you want to live.

> *Zen is the game of insight, the game of discovering who you are beneath the social masks.*
> *Reginald Blyth*

Seeing through the game allows you to reclaim your imaginative power. You are free to use your imagination to create a life born out of the impulses of your own creative center. Instead of living in the hope of future reward or the fear of future shame, you put your faith in your creative intuitions and rely on your innate talents and abilities to take you to the life you want to live. You see your happiness in expressing what you are, not in gaining approval or avoiding its loss. Emotional reactions (like envy and shame) keep you from playing, precisely because they keep you from contemplating—seeing things as they really are. They stir up and muddy the water. When the water is still, you can see all the way to the bottom of things. Zen tells us that if we want to be free to play, we must be done with the agitation of envy and shame. Otherwise, we can be triggered, through prizes and ridicule, into performing like trained monkeys—without ever knowing how or why.

Zen encourages us to recognize the transitory nature of gain and loss and remain awake to choice. It reminds us that we are not pushed around by society as much as we are by our own emotions. After all, through the ages, there have been many political and economic systems. Though some are better than others, none

Human affairs are like a chess game: Only those who do not take it seriously can be called good players.

Hung Tzu-ch'eng

have yet, nor ever will, give us genuine freedom. Ultimately, we are not enslaved or freed by a social system, but by ourselves. As the Hindu classic the Bhagavad-Gita puts it, "All living creatures are led astray as soon as they are born, by the delusion that this relative world is permanent. This delusion arises from their own desire and hatred." (We might equate *desire* with envy, and *hatred*, really self-hatred, with shame.)

In Hindu cosmology, *maya* is an illusory experience of the world made all too real by the emotional investment we make in a fictional character called "me." When I go searching for this "me," I find nothing more than mental images, memories. The sense that this "me" or ego identity is winning or losing, succeeding or faltering, improving or backsliding is an emotional response to the mental process of comparing pictures (memories). You cannot compare yourself to anything or anyone without summoning memories—even if the memories are only fractions of a second old. To the extent that you put your attention on memory, you miss the life now happening within and around you. Now of course, you need a "me" and its memories to function in society. But to attach to these as an ultimate identity misses the point. Looking for yourself in your memories is a sure way to miss you. It's *maya*'s cosmic game of hide-and-seek. Seeking the "I" that is not "me-mories" is the game called enlightenment.

Our (or any) society's game is but a little game within this cosmic game of *maya*. Careers (social roles and duties), in turn, are games played within the games of *maya* and society. This goes on and on like a Chinese box, one game inside of another and another and another. Zen would say that since we find ourselves in all these games, we might as well accept that we have chosen to play. At any level where you deny choice, you have seriousness, unfunness, stuckness. If I forget that I made "me" up out of a bag of memories, I feel burdened by the effort of dragging it around. If I forget that it's my desire for approval that makes me conform, I feel resentment or sorrow over the life I haven't dared to live. If I forget that I put myself in a career and/or job I don't love or respect, I feel trapped in a rut. At any level where you deny choice, you get caught in a game. It's playing you; you're not playing it. If you are into forgetting, then you think life is FOR-GETTING something to hold on to. It's the holding on that leaves you feeling pushed around. Be awake to choice—let go—and the spirit of play will return.

Suppressing choice while unconsciously chasing titles sucks the life out of life. Some people marry because they want the title "married person." Most would agree that's a very different experience from choosing (and choosing again and again) to be with someone you love. It's the same with any title. The greater the psychological identification we make with our titles, the more stuck we become on the idea that we aren't good enough without them. Ultimately, it's only the attachment to winning that can make us feel like losers. *Trust that you are good enough, and you don't have to spend your life proving that you are.*

> Never for a moment do we lay aside our mistrust of the ideals established by society, and of the convictions which are kept by it in circulation. We always know that society is full of folly and will deceive us in the matter of humanity. It is an unreliable horse, and blind into the bargain. Woe to the driver if he falls asleep.
>
> *Albert Schweitzer*

The reward of all action is to be found in enlightenment.

Bhagavad-Gita

Remember, titles are societal abstractions, but life is living. Titles were won in the past in the hope of exercising the benefits they grant in the future. Life is here and now. Titles focus on differentiation. Life is a unified field. While titles can be extended, they cannot grow. Life grows. Life is FOR-GIVING Life. Life gives naturally, endlessly, the way a plant gives its bounty of food; and yet in the seed, nothing is lost. If you realize that it's a game AND CHOOSE TO BE AWAKE, you can be *in* the world and not *of* it, with or without titles or ridicule. You can play "winning" or "changing the social game" without getting serious, without losing your playfulness. The truth is, we always have a choice. Choose to recognize the choices you've made, and you open yourself to new ones. You get back in the game. Look again at all your choices, but this time—hold off on the shame.

It may occur to you that a lot of people aren't going to get free of envy and shame or get hip to choice anytime soon. They will be pretty serious and probably not much into *playing* with you. In the meantime, you may want to work on changing the rules of the game, or on taking care of people who get lost in the shuffle. You may decide to acquire a particular title so that you can use the accompanying power and deference toward these ends or others. Remember, it doesn't have to be a certain way. It can be any way you want to play.

From awareness, there are many ways to play. Here are a few:

Game 1: You can play "Win the Game," without taking it seriously.

Game 2: You can play "Retreating from the World," without taking yourself too seriously.

Game 3: You can play "Taking Care of Others," without getting maudlin, uptight, burned-out, or serious.

Game 4: You can play "Making Social Change," without getting maudlin, uptight, burned-out, or serious.

Game 5: You can play "Professional Waker-Upper," the true poet, artist, mystic, without taking yourself too seriously.

Wanted: Life Beyond Rewards

Can you work long-term, without the bait of future reward? Of course—if you are playing. You make play of work when you're fully present with what you're doing—when you enjoy it for its own sake. In this moment, as I write this, I've been working on this book off and on for the better part of three years. I don't have an agent, an advance, or a publisher, and I am having great fun. If I thought I *had to* write this book to get approval or the reward of money or fame (or had to finish it because I started it), it would quickly get serious. I am playing writing a book because I want to say something—many things actually. The world has gotten on quite nicely without my having said them and will get along just fine without ever hearing them.

> *The hook is your desire to be approved of by others. The bait is any kind of reward. The minute you go for the bait, the game is playing you. You are no longer playing the game. You get serious.*

Still, when I have said what I want to say, I will play the game of promoting this book. Because I am playing, writing this book is teaching me many things. I trust that playing promoting it will teach me even more. I tell you this, not because it is any big deal, but only to convey that I *know* that you can be highly motivated and committed to your work without the hope of future reward or recognition. The doing *is* the reward; the reward, the doing. (Note for revised edition: I wrote this nearly twenty years ago. The book went on to become a bestseller.)

Can you take rewards without getting hooked? Yes, but only if you don't take them too seriously. Society tries to arrange things so as to convince you that you *need* its rewards. Take learning. From Baghdad to Granada, the Saracens operated great centers of learning for hundreds of years. Everyone could come and play the learning game with the wise and knowledgeable there assembled.

The superior man loves his soul, the inferior man loves his property.

Confucius

After auditioning potential teachers, students selected (and paid) the ones they believed could help them learn. These scholars did not, however, grant degrees or titles. They feared that granting titles would subvert the very purpose of education. They reasoned that if they began to grant degrees, students would become more concerned with winning titles than with learning for its own sake. They also thought giving a title suggested some kind of finish, or completion, as though someone were now certifiably learned and needn't bother keeping an open mind.[3]

> *The life of Zen begins, therefore, in a disillusion with the pursuit of goals which do not really exist—the good without the bad, the gratification of a self which is no more than an idea, and the morrow which never comes.*
>
> *Alan Watts*

In modern society, we measure by degree. Degree titles become commodities that can be traded in the marketplace for rank titles. The acquisition of knowledge, to say nothing of the development of wisdom and creative intelligence, is secondary to the acquisition of a degree title. Never mind if the man is speaking gibberish, he is, after all, "Grade-A Learned" and has the papers to prove it. Checking up on credentials is less taxing than paying attention in the moment to find out if the person has anything worthwhile to say. Whatever their relationship to knowledge or wisdom, degrees, like all titles, are taken very seriously in our society. Parents fret over their children's entrance into the proper certifying institutions. You want to tell me what you are learning? Oh, that's nice, dear. What I really want to know is HOW ARE YOUR GRADES? It's in striving for grades, in the grades, to make the grade, that most of us first get hooked into working for the promise of reward rather than the enjoyment of what we are actually doing. Because we are psychologically removed from NOW, we chase a future that never quite gets HERE.

Striving for rewards can become a habit as addictive as any narcotic. Like a narcotic, breaking this addiction may require a period of withdrawal and recovery. Often referred to as "burning out" or "taking time out," a period of withdrawal can allow you to begin paying attention to long-neglected emotional needs and spiritual aspirations. Recovery begins by taking one day at a time—finding your own center and integrating its impulses with the world of work and society. If you don't need or can't afford a period of withdrawal, begin paying more attention as you go. At work, bring yourself into what you are doing NOW. Cultivate an attitude of enjoying work for its own sake. You'll have more fun now, and this attitude will serve you for the rest of your life. If you're a student, get the degree, but don't forget that the purpose of education is learning. You'll have more fun now, and the love of learning you cultivate will serve you for the rest of your life.

Playing the Career Game

The dominant game in Western society at the beginning of the third millennium CE was briefly considered above. Now let's consider the game of career. Every career field is a mini-society, complete with its own winning model, its own game rules and conventions. A given career game may parallel the game of the larger society or emphasize a different set of values. In choosing among career roles, investigate the game in each field, and determine how disposed you are to play it—disposed from the standpoint of skills, yes, but perhaps more importantly, disposed from the standpoint of intention. If you find that you will be railing against the absurdities of a particular career game or that a lot of your energy is likely to be consumed in protesting the game rules, you should probably choose another field.

The key to selecting an appropriate career game is to understand what you are working for—your purpose. A clear sense of purpose helps you coordinate your inner promptings (visions, values, and talents) with the social demands of work. Once in a given career, staying focused on purpose will help you to play the career game without taking it seriously. Lack of purpose (or lack of attention to purpose) is responsible for the two big problems in work. The first is obsession—getting so lost in the game that you forget what you are doing. The second is disaffection—unwillingness to fully engage the game. When we work on purpose, we can play the career game without becoming consumed by it, on the one hand, or refusing to fully engage, on the other.

But do your thing and I shall know you.

Emerson

Work on Purpose

Some of us become so consumed by the game that we lose sight of our purpose. We become obsessed with having the right lifestyle accessories, compulsive about the way we are perceived. We lose our balance and perspective and fall into the traps of one-upmanship, jealousy, and competition. We become so intent on what we are trying to be that we forget what we have set out to do. It's easy to get lost in the striving. Without a clearly defined purpose of our own, we have no way of measuring success, except in terms of society's game.

Many a businessman feels himself the prisoner of the commodities he sells; he has a feeling of fraudulency about his product and a secret contempt for it. Most important of all, he hates himself, because he sees his life passing him by without making any sense beyond the momentary intoxication of success.

Erich Fromm

Understanding that career is a game doesn't mean we are to take it as something trivial or unimportant. It *is* important, but only in reference to our purpose, that is, only in terms of doing what we have set out to do. For example, the purpose of medicine is health and healing. Anything doctors do to further health and healing is important. Everything else is not. The fact that they went through many years of training, or spent long and arduous hours of internship, or that they are up to date with the latest technologies is only important to the degree that these now aid the doctor in "doing" health and healing. A doctor may become so distracted by technologies, drugs, prestige, income, etc., that he "forgets" the purpose of medicine—health and healing. There is nothing sinister in this: technologies are fascinating; drugs are quickly and easily prescribed; prestige boosts the ego; and money is power in our society. Yet it serves to illustrate a fundamental career axiom: *In the game of careers, peripherals move in to fill the void left by lack of purpose.*

In today's world, it's impossible to eliminate all peripherals. Many are social demands with which we simply must comply. Still, we can keep the peripherals under control by keeping our purpose in mind. The happiness of the individual worker and the beauty and humanity of a society diminish to the degree that peripherals replace purpose in work. Much of our personal alienation and global waste is simply a matter of peripherals dominating. Even benign peripherals can become malignant when they get out of hand. Career, then, can be a dangerous game if we attempt to play it without a clear, constructive purpose. Playing it effectively requires an ability to distinguish between purposeful and peripheral matters, and to act on the purposeful ones.

When you no longer identify your Self with your career and instead focus on your work purpose, you expand the range of career options available to you. At the same time, you sharpen your criteria for deciding between careers. Moreover, a clearly defined purpose gives you more latitude in playing whatever career game (or games) you ultimately choose. It gives you a touchstone that helps you to recognize and maximize opportunities and recognize

To be contented is noble, but to be lethargic does not enable one to benefit men or to utilize things.

Hung Tzu-ch'eng

and overcome limitations within the field. Without a clear purpose, you likely feel at effect of the game, pushed around by forces you can't control. Your anxiety increases as you come to believe that you *must* continue to play a game you can't control. At the same time, your sense of insecurity increases because you don't know what you would do if you ever got off this not-so-merry-go-round. Putting purpose first gets you focused on the why of work before you get lost in the how. It gives you something to hold on to when circumstances, economies, or careers change. You have a constant reference point in a sea of change. A clear sense of purpose helps you understand and direct the events of your life.

Accepting the Game

While some of us become consumed by the game, others of us resent it with a passion! We are rebels without a cause (purpose). We rail against the unfairness, the futility, or the silliness of the game. We're out to show the world how ridiculous all these games are, and so we play the game of pointing out how ridiculous all the games are. We see so clearly the blindness of those who get lost in the game, but we may not see the problems we cause by our refusal to play. Francis Bacon said, "For good thoughts . . . towards men, are little better than dreams, except they be put into action; and that cannot be, without power and place."[4] We who refuse the game leave power and place to others and complain about the way they are handling things.

Working on purpose allows you to approach the game with a spirit of play. You concentrate on your purpose and choose a career game appropriate to its expression. You don't get overwhelmed by fighting the system or trying to escape from it. You choose a game you can work with and stay focused on purpose. You don't spend your emotional energy in minor (or major) skirmishes over trifles. You don't isolate yourself on the sidelines. You choose a humane game and play.

Make Sure Your Choice Is Your Own

When we play the career game without a personally meaningful purpose, we allow others to assess our failure or success. In our culture, others will generally define your success by the money (property) and status (rank) rewards you have acquired. Many believe that these (wealth and status) comprise the sum and substance of career. They have no larger purpose than to seek security or to acquire the rank and property they believe will make them a "success."

What drives the ladder-climber on the fast track to wealth and success? It may seem that he or she is chasing after money or power. If we look a little closer, we find that more often than not what they are really after is approval. If he can buy more approved-of things, he will be more esteemed by others. If she can gain a more valued rank, she will be more valued by others. Though they may define or rationalize it in a variety of ways, many ended up in the careers they're in because they were looking for approval. Rank and money are simply the means of attaining the approval they crave. When we say that we have to have a certain standard of living, many of us in the middle class and above are talking about a standard of living necessary to gain the approval we think we need. Our entire economy is fueled by our desire for approval. We earn for approval and we spend for approval.

We seek our parents' approval. We seek the approval of siblings and peers. Men seek the approval of women—their wives or lovers. Women seek the approval of men—their husbands or boyfriends. And it's not just our friends and families; we crave approval from people we don't even know. Success in work is often measured in terms of the approval we receive from family, friends, and society in general. Even while we chase after the approval of others, we are smart enough to know (at least subconsciously) that the minute we stop playing this game, we will be confronted with a more difficult problem, a problem called: What do I want? What do I believe in? What do I stand for? What am I all about?

It's not just that we fear the disapproval of others. We doubt our own ability to find answers. The courage to risk the disapproval of others, while at the same time moving through the doubt that accompanies self-examination, is rare. When we begin to deeply examine our values, we often feel most insecure. It is then that we most look for approval. Finding none, many abandon the quest. This is the time for courage and perseverance—the time to seek out the support of those who believe in your quest to realize your best.

---

to be nobody-but-yourself—in a world which is doing its best, night and day, to make you everybody else—means to fight the hardest battle which any human being can fight; and never stop fighting.
e. e. cummings

Abraham Maslow articulated a hierarchy of values with security at the base, followed by belonging, ego-fulfillment, and finally, self-actualization. The most striking difference between the self-actualized individual and others is the degree to which he creates his life out of his own values. Self-actualized people are not dependent upon the approval of others when making major life decisions. They

A happy life is one which is in accordance with its own nature.

Seneca

I'm not at all contemptuous of comforts, but they have their place, and it is not first.

E. F. Schumacher

rely on their intuitions, values, and principles. Again, make sure your choice is your own. You are the one who is going to have to live with it.

There are two general categories of information necessary to making good career choices. The first has to do with what people in this career role typically do. This includes the kinds of things you might find in a job description: the skills, knowledge, experience, and training required to actually do the work. The second category includes the social dynamics or unwritten rules by which a particular career game is typically played. This takes into account all aspects of the career that are not directly tied to work performance. Later, you'll have an opportunity to assess the job description elements: the component skills, knowledge, experience, and training necessary to perform this career role (see "Scene II: Reality Testing"). For now, let's consider how the game is played in various career fields.

Choose a Game You Can Get Into

Traditional career-planning models tend to ignore the game-playing aspect, as though a career or a job were limited to the elements of a job description. Job descriptions reflect what's really happening on the job about as much as formal organizational charts reflect the power dynamics within large organizations. Job descriptions and organizational charts are more theory than reality. In many career fields, you will be judged on your ability to play the game at least as much as on your work performance.

If you don't think so, try showing up to work at the office in your bathrobe. Try speaking in slang or obscenities at a formal business meeting. You probably won't find the ability to tie a tie or make up your face on your job description, but don't do these things, and you will soon discover how important they are to certain career games. They may not directly affect your ability to do the actual work (many people working at home do quite nicely in their bathrobes), but they do affect the way you play the game.

A man I'll call "Robert" was an untenured professor at a prestigious private college. He was an excellent teacher who consistently received high marks for his classroom performance in university staff evaluations. His students also rated him highly. There was only one problem. Robert didn't go to informal faculty social gatherings. These meetings were not part of his job per se. He attended formal departmental meetings and the like, but couldn't get into the game of socializing with the school faculty in his free time. Robert didn't make tenure, and is no longer working at this school. Understand the rules of the game before you decide to play.

Business lunches, cocktail parties, weekends entertaining for the boss, the clients, the staff—these may be a part of the career game in your field. If you wouldn't pick these people solely for the interesting and pleasant companionship they provide, then your "entertaining" is work. There are so many aspects to the career game. Let's say that you consistently outproduce a coworker who gets the promotion, the raise, the added responsibility. You know you are doing more; still, this person is getting more. Before you decide that life is unfair, stop to consider that he or she may be playing the game better than you and that in your career or job, game playing matters more than you thought. Remember, when you choose a career game, you are choosing to abide by rules you have not made and will probably have little impact on changing. Choose a game that works for you.

> *There is nothing so easy but that it becomes difficult when you do it reluctantly.*
>
> *Terence*

Intention is the starting place for learning. (More on this in Act IV.) If you really "can't get into" the game in your field, you probably won't have an intention strong enough to learn to play it well. If your intention is strong, you can get into a game, even if you've never played it before and even if it runs a little counter to your personality. If your intention is lacking, trying to force yourself is not a good idea.

Enjoy the Game You Are Playing

The best way to enjoy the career game is to remember that it is one. We play best when we don't take the game too seriously. We take the game too seriously when we make the roles we are playing more important than our reasons for playing them. We get caught up in defending our positions instead of accomplishing our missions. Concentrate on your purpose, and you needn't exaggerate the importance of your role. You can relax and enjoy the game. You know it's theater, so you concentrate on acting on purpose. As a conscious player on the stage of life, play your career role; don't let it play you.

A career role is a vehicle through which to express and fulfill your life's work. It is a tool to be used consciously and deliberately to express talents and realize your purpose. A career role is not an end; it is a means. It is not an achievement; it's a means of achieving. Not merely something to *be*, it's a way to *do* the work you love.

What's Ahead in Act II

Act II begins with **"Scene I, Your New Career: Getting a Picture."** The purpose of this section is to give you an opportunity to mentally project yourself into potential career roles. By "pre-experiencing" the doing and the "gaming" of a given field, you'll get a sense of how well you resonate with it. This will allow you to eliminate inappropriate career roles before you begin the time-consuming research process discussed in the next section.

In **"Scene II, Reality Testing,"** you'll have the opportunity to test your notions of potential career choices against reality. You'll thoroughly investigate these options to ensure that you fully understand what a given career entails *before* you consider making a change. Where you are now in your work life is a direct result of the decisions you have made or decided not to make. The quality of these decisions was based upon your awareness at the time. We see so much better with hindsight because of the additional awareness we have gained. The exercises in this section will help you improve your *foresight* by increasing your awareness before you make a major career decision.

In **"Scene III, Evaluation: No or Go?"** you will have an opportunity to systematically evaluate your research and determine whether or not the career role you initially selected is one you want to pursue.

Life Is a Game

Life is a game full of games. There is no getting around the games of life. The question is not whether we will play games but rather: What games will we play? and, How well will we play them? The more we accept and understand any game, the better we are able to play it. This unit is designed to improve your general understanding of the game called "career." Additionally, and perhaps more importantly, answering the questions in the process work that follows will help you better understand the career game within the specific fields you are considering. You will have a framework for determining whether or not a particular career role is the best means for expressing your life's work at this time.

Detour #2: The Approval Trap

Every child has a desire to please, to be approved of. That desire for approval becomes linked to whatever goals, values, and behaviors are most highly esteemed by his family and society. This is a fundamental component of the process social psychologists call socialization. It is a cross-cultural phenomenon that applies equally to Eskimos and Bushmen, Europeans and Americans. Of course, the sanctioned values and behaviors vary from culture to culture, but the process operates in all.

Our Western culture is extremely materialistic. Acquisition of material resources is highly valued as an end in itself. Materialism shapes our thinking in such fundamental and pervasive ways that our perception of its impact on our lives and on the decisions we make is often obscured. Often we are not aware of being caught up in materialism; we only have a desperate sense of wanting approval.

There are two basic ways that we can sell out for approval. We can actively go after what's approved of (money), and/or we can suppress our talents because we fear to risk disapproval. We sell out when we pursue a career course primarily for the sake of money. "I really want to work in this area, but there is more demand (or pay) for that." On the other hand, we can sell short our talents to make it easier to sell our wares. "My heart and talent are really into this, but it looks safer or easier to do that." In either case, we risk our conscience. When we compromise our values in order to fit in, we mute the voice of conscience. It will be easier to sell out next time. Each time we sell out, it becomes a bit more difficult to hear the voice of the conscience, until finally it is all but silent and we have become alienated from ourselves.

Materialism: Fascination with material gain distracts us from purpose. Time and again we are confronted with tests of character. These tests often put material gain at odds with purpose. In our desire to please our fellow man, we may compromise our desire to serve him. Only firm resolve and constant attention to purpose can keep us on a steady course.

Antimaterialism: Antimaterialism rejects the resources necessary to implement purpose. It is an immature fear of power that keeps us from acquiring the resources necessary to achieve our objectives and express our talent. In fact, it is a kind of materialism, for it places concern for material resources (their denial) above purpose and talent. If you require resources to fulfill your purpose or express your talent, and you deny yourself these because of an antimaterial bias, you have sold out. Get what you need to succeed.

Zen Play

Zen talks out of both sides of its mouth. Out of one side it tells you what you think is you is a fiction, a joke, a nothing. Out of the other side: Take care about what you are doing. Do it with precision, excellence, and grace.

Most of us are consistent. If we comprehend the absurdity of our personal drama, we are often lazy and inattentive to life. If, on the other hand, we are passionately involved in the activities of the world, we come to take ourselves too seriously, imagining that our egos have some reality beyond our thoughts. Zen is singularly two-faced.

When the mind is still, you feel the love. The Buddhists call it "Karuna." *Karuna* is compassion: not sentimental, not maudlin, not condescending—just love for your fellow man and awareness of his suffering. Zen all of a sudden, you are the Buddha, and everyone is the Buddha, including the pesky neighborhood cat.

Compassion says, "Serve, love, be helpful." Buddhahood says, "Who are you helping with your helping? Everyone is already the Buddha. Getting serious about helping and 'saving' people is very silly." To walk the way of Zen is to walk a tightrope of active involvement without attachment.

To act without acting, to do without doing, to work without working, this is the Zen way. This is making life a play.

There is nothing left to you at this moment but to have a good laugh.

Zen master

Honoring the One Behind the Mask

Life is a masquerade ball. We all are wearing costumes and masks. These help us mark the roles we are playing at any particular time. While we keep in mind their purpose, role masks serve us well. When we confuse ourselves with our roles or forget that we are choosing to play a game, roles become oppressive—capable of turning even young men and women into cardboard stiffs. In *The Art of Loving,* Erich Fromm describes the condition of the modern man—caught up in a game he has forgotten he chose to play. Fromm describes a "nowhere man" who has become so attached to his masks that he has forgotten how to play—and to love. Fromm calls this "nowhere man" an automaton. Read his description below, and see if perhaps you have met this man.

> Modern man is alienated from himself, from his fellow men, and from nature. He has been transformed into a commodity, experiences his life forces as investments which must bring him the maximum profit obtainable within existing market conditions. Human relations are essentially those of alienated automatons, each basing his security on staying close to the herd, and not being different in thought, feeling, or action. While everybody tries to be as close as possible to the rest, everybody remains utterly alone, pervaded by a deep sense of insecurity, anxiety and guilt which always results when human separateness cannot be overcome . . . Automatons cannot love; they exchange their "personality packages" and hope for a fair bargain.[5]

The postmodern man (or woman) is not an automaton, but an alive and loving player in the game of life. He or she is a gamesman, not in the sense of being a shrewd manipulator, but in the sense of one who is game for life and ready to play. *The automaton struggles for ends.* He wants to *have something* that is fixed in time, for example, a title, a position, rewards of every kind. *The gamesman plays an open-ended game.* The gamesman wants to *do something,* and that changes. An automaton becomes habituated to a role. A gamesman never confuses himself with his role.

Now that you are about to frame your life's work in terms of a career role, we want to remind you to stay loose. The career game that you choose to play ought to attract you and be fun for you. Even so, beware of the trap of hiding in it, of losing your spontaneity and humanity for the sake of the role. Gamesmen remember that they have put on masks and can take them off; and every now and again, even while they are wearing them, they lift them just a bit, and peek through.

The gamesman knows that she can fall into the automaton habit, not only by concretizing into her role, but by taking the roles of others too seriously. Often we forget that the policeman or doctor, the university professor or boss, the secretary or waitress is so much more than the role each plays in our lives. Gamesmen relate to people first and foremost as human beings and only secondarily as their roles. Gamesmen see, honor, and love the one behind the mask.

The Career Game

When making career choices, we are in a general sense choosing our playing field, our teammates, the rules and regulations by which we will play, the goal lines, and (yes, Mathilda) our opponents.

Playing Field: Where will you be playing this career game of yours? Indoors or out? In a skyscraper or a storefront? Is it a static field, like an office desk, or will you be moving out and about, meeting people—traveling?

Teammates: What kind of people will you be playing with, and in what type of formations do they generally play? In some fields, you have to run tight with the pack. In others, you can plan on being the lone wolf most of the time. In some fields, teammates will play like opponents. In others, they will be very supportive. In many careers, you have to be a member of the "club" in order to play, or to play effectively. Some clubs are very traditional, formal, and obvious. Others are more spontaneous, informal, and insidious.

Rules and Regs: Some of the rules and regs are designed to expedite the work function. Some are designed to protect the organization against legal, market, or political injury. Some are designed to protect the community against the excesses of the organization or its players. Some are simply social conventions that attempt to make a given work environment predictable and understandable. Some are accepted matters of taste, e.g., in writing, it is considered bad form to start every sentence in the same paragraph with the same word. (No, Mrs. Eckhart, I haven't forgotten.) Some career fields are more into rules and regs than others.

Goal Lines: Every field has its goal lines. The goal lines are the commonly agreed-upon standards of success. As we have seen above, these may have little or nothing to do with the stated work purpose. For example, at most universities, professors are more likely to be judged based on what they do or do not write than on how well they teach. Even when the "goal lines" do not match your work purpose, you will be expected to pursue them or risk disapproval, anything from slight annoyance to major hostility. Peer pressure in many career fields is enormous. Try to choose a career where the peer pressure will push you in the direction you want to go.

Opponents: An opponent can be anyone who is holding a purpose counter to your consciously stated work purpose. This, of course, could include even yourself or your teammates from time to time. The career game itself can be an opponent when your purpose differs greatly from the accepted goals in your field.

What to Look for in a Career Game

Choose the game that best allows you to fulfill your purpose. Purpose is the engine that drives your life's work. Choose a career, not because you want to be something, but because you want to do something. If you take a career as something to be, you will get distracted by the game and forget your purpose. You may find the ideal career role for the full expression of your purpose, or you may find that it will require several career roles. These you might pursue concurrently or one after the other.

Choose a game that allows you to fully express your talents. Even as your career role must allow you to fully express your purpose, so must it allow you to fully express your talents. You can think of your talents as your built-in tool kit. Let's say that your tool kit is full of wrenches and your career role calls almost exclusively for hammers. You are not fully utilizing your talents if you're only using your wrenches for hammering. Wrenches will hammer, but they do something else better and more naturally. If you can accept this somewhat silly metaphor, you can see that it is important to know what is in your tool kit and the best way to use it.

Choose a game that is compatible with your personality. You must be ready to agree with the game in your field. In other words, the game must be agreeable to you. You ought to enjoy playing it. Of course, you may not enjoy every aspect of it, but generally it should be pleasurable to you. If you detest the game, it will be hard for you to concentrate on purpose. A fair number of the requirements of the game ought to be things you enjoy doing.

Choose a game you can commit yourself to. Choose a game you can get into playing long enough and intensely enough to excel at. Choose a game you can respect and feel a sense of honor in playing, one with a tradition you can take pride in.

 By honors, medals, titles no true man is elated.
To realize that which we are, this is the honor
for which we are created.
                                    Angelus Silesius

The Game of Life's Work Affirmations

1. I now see the career, or combination of careers, that best expresses my life's work.

2. Because I choose my career with full awareness, I am able to play with intensity without getting serious.

3. I have the will, energy, and persistence to investigate the career I have chosen and find out all pertinent information.

4. I am totally honest and realistic in my appraisal of myself and my abilities.

5. I remain confident that I can flourish in the career, or combination of careers, that best supports my life's mission.

6. I trust myself. I know that if a career is right for me, even if I do not now possess the skills and knowledge that I need to excel in this career, I will acquire all that I need and more.

7. Nothing can stop me from achieving my purpose in life. Every step that I take gives me new confidence that I will succeed in making manifest my vision for myself and others.

The process that follows is a scientific approach to career decision making. It is scientific in the sense that it applies the scientific method: developing a hypothesis, testing the hypothesis, evaluating the results of the test, then determining the validity of the hypothesis. Here, you will develop a hypothesis about which career role will best allow you to take advantage of your talents and purpose. Next you will conduct research to test your hypothesis. Then you will evaluate the results and determine if the original hypothesis was indeed correct or if you need a new one. The exercise that immediately follows will save you time by helping you to make sure your working hypothesis is reasonably sound before you conduct your research.

Your New Career:
Getting a Picture

I have learned this at least by my experiment: that if one advances confidently in the direction of his dreams, and endeavors to live the life which he has imagined, he will meet with a success unexpected in common hours.
Henry David Thoreau

Actors often must take a screen test to determine if they are right for the roles they are interested in. In this section, you'll have the opportunity take a screen test to determine if the career roles you are interested in are right for you. First, you'll identify a few potential career roles that you believe would be the best vehicles for pursuing your life's work. Then you'll select one and put it through an extensive and detailed visualization process designed to help you mentally project yourself into the role to see if it fits. Just because a career passes this initial test doesn't mean that it's right for you. You'll want to investigate it much more deeply by doing the exercises in "Scene II: Reality Testing." Nevertheless, taking the screen test may help you eliminate roles that aren't right for you before you engage in this time-intensive research; or it may get you excited to learn more about a potential new career.

Selecting Your Career Roles

Write your work-purpose statement below (see page 213). Next, generate a list of ten potential career roles that you could employ in the pursuit of this work purpose.

Work-Purpose Statement

_____

_____

_____

Possible Career Roles

1._____
2._____
3._____
4._____
5._____
6._____
7._____
8._____
9._____
10._____

Now select your top three and list these below:

1._____
2._____
3._____

Now select the one you feel most attracted to. Indicate why you believe it is the best fit for your purpose, talents, and mission objectives.

_____

_____

_____

Use the career role you have selected above for the exercises that follow.

Web and Book Resources

Find out more about investigating a range of potential career options @ Empoweryou.com.

Put Your Career Choice to the Test

Refer to the career choice you identified in the previous exercise and ask yourself the following questions:

Am I making this choice freely, or do I feel compelled to prove something?

_____

_____

_____

_____

Am I really enthusiastic about this choice? Is there anything I want more than this choice?_____

_____

_____

_____

Do I want it for me, or am I trying to please someone else?

_____

_____

_____

_____

Do any of the following terms apply to the way I feel about this career choice: "I ought to," "I have to," or "I should"? _____

_____

_____

_____

Am I committed to following through with this career choice, or am I likely to give up when things get difficult?

_____

_____

_____

_____

The privilege of a lifetime is being who you are.

Joseph Campbell

Giving Yourself a Screen Test

Think of each career option as a "role" played by you, the main character. In the exercises that follow, you'll mentally project yourself into the career roles you have selected. At this point, you haven't done the research necessary to answer these questions in anything like a definite way. Nevertheless, you may find value in mentally projecting yourself into a career role and "intuiting" the answers to these questions. You can begin to get a sense of which roles might be right for you and to eliminate inappropriate roles before you go through the time-intensive "Reality Testing" and "Evaluation: No or Go?" sections that follow.

A Day in the Life

Answer the following questions as though you were currently engaged in the career you identified earlier.

What time do you wake up for work? _____

What do you wear to work? _____

Where do you go to work? (Setting? Rural, small town, suburban, or urban area? If indoors, type of building?) _____

Who is the first person you greet (if any)? _____

At what time do you begin your workday? _____

Are you working for yourself, a small firm, large firm, or a branch of the government, etc.? _____

What are the tools you work with? (Paint and brushes? Computer and telephone? Desk? Workbench?) _____

_____

Do you have a boss? What kind of rapport do you have? Do you have subordinates or employees? What do they do? How do you interact? _____

_____

How do you spend the lion's share of your day? (In meetings? Alone? With a team? On the telephone? Making presentations?) _____

_____

Do you work primarily with people inside or outside of your organization? For example, a manager works more with people on the inside; a sales representative, more with those on the outside.) _____

Where do you have lunch? With whom? _____

At what time do you complete your workday? _____

Do you take your work home? If yes, what kind of work? _____

How much money will you earn at this work over the course of one year? _____

I like the dreams of the future better than the history of the past.

Thomas Jefferson

Looking Back on Your Life's Work: Great Moments

Answer the following questions as though you had already successfully completed your life's work.

What was the most important contribution you made through this work?

_____

_____

What was the most exciting aspect of this work? _____

_____

What was your most difficult challenge, and how did you overcome it?

_____

_____

What were you most proud of? What was most rewarding? _____

_____

_____

What were the creative highlights? _____

_____

_____

What skills have you perfected in the course of this work? _____

_____

_____

What did you enjoy most about this work? _____

_____

What did you enjoy least? _____

_____

What awards, commendations, acknowledgments, testimonials, etc., that you received were the most meaningful to you? _____

 Growth is the only evidence of life.
Cardinal Newman

Mission Accomplished!

How did you fulfill your mission in life through this career?

_____
_____
_____
_____
_____

What did you do to eliminate suffering and/or expand joy for your fellow man?

_____
_____
_____
_____
_____

How did your example inspire others to be their best?

_____
_____
_____
_____
_____

What have you left behind as a legacy?

_____
_____
_____
_____
_____

Our aspirations are our possibilities.
Robert Browning

Acknowledging the Supporting Cast

Answer the following questions as though you had already successfully completed your life's work.

Whose support was most critical to achieving your success? (If you can't give specific names, perhaps positions, titles, or relationships.)

_____

_____

_____

_____

_____

_____

What role models have influenced you the most?

_____

_____

_____

_____

_____

_____

How did the response and appreciation of the people you were serving inspire you to do and achieve more?

_____

_____

_____

_____

_____

_____

Who else has helped you to succeed, and how have they done so?

_____

_____

_____

_____

_____

_____

Reality Testing

You should investigate something to see its benefit or harm, examine whether it is appropriate and suitable or not; then after that you may carry it out.
Caotang

In Scene I of Act II, you imagined yourself in one or more career roles. When you did this, the actual knowledge you had about these careers may have been somewhat superficial. Your visualization of a given career role may have been something akin to what we see portrayed in a popular Hollywood movie. You need much more accurate information. In this section, you will have the opportunity to test your imagined sense of a given career against the reality of it.

Think of the way careers are portrayed in Hollywood. The actor is playing a part—a doctor, a lawyer, a banker, whatever. The role is indicated with a very few actions, words, props, or costume elements. A professional in this field can look at these representations and see that they are often kind of silly. Yet for the general public, it's convincing. We accept (at least for entertainment purposes) that this person is indeed a lawyer, a detective, a brain surgeon, a banker, or whatever. We accept this because enough of the image is there to fit the popular conception of the career.

Unless you've had reason to have more specific knowledge, your first imaginings of your new career were most likely from the "pop culture" understanding of what this field is and what a person in this field does. These images may be accurate or filled with misconceptions. You need to find out.

The next step is to go out and collect data. As you gather information, you will get a clearer understanding of what individuals in this field do, how they spend their days, what their problems are, what issues they face, how they interact with people, and the like. You'll move out of the fantasy image into a more realistic understanding of what it would really be like to work in this role. In the process, you will collect a wealth of information that will prove useful later on, should you decide to go ahead and pursue this career. In Scene III of this unit, you will have a chance to evaluate all you have learned about this career role and to decide if it's really right for you.

The "Reality Testing" process involves a good deal of work. You may be tempted to skip over it. I strongly recommend that you do not. The investment of time and energy that you make at this point can save you a great deal of time, money, and heartache later on. For example, if you were to begin retraining for a new career without having done the necessary research, you might find that you had wasted thousands of dollars and many precious years of your life preparing for a career that was not appropriate for you. This can be easily averted by doing adequate research in advance.

You may discover in the course of your research that the career role you were initially attracted to is not appropriate and should be discarded. If that is the case, begin again with your second career choice (see page 278). You might discover that, while your first choice is the best vehicle through which to express your life's work, it will take considerably more work than you first imagined. In that case, don't get discouraged. Continue to pursue your life's work, keeping in mind your vision of your best work and your desire to manifest it.

Determining whether a career is truly inappropriate or simply a lot of work is sometimes difficult. It's a judgment you will have to make for yourself. The important thing to remember throughout this process is: do not compromise your creative visions of your best work. *There is a way, and you will find it if you persist.* It may take a good deal of thought, creativity, and effort, but there is a way. After all, you would not have the deep desire for this work without also having the ability to achieve it.

The "Reality Testing" Process in a Nutshell

Step 1: Get on the Internet.

Step 2: Conduct interviews.

Step 3: Get firsthand experience.

Step 4: Make a skills master list.

Step 5: Identify necessary credentials.

Research Questions List

The following is a list of research questions, the answers to which will begin to put the career role you are considering into focus. Read these questions now; then refer to them throughout the course of your research. *Do not attempt to write final answers to these questions until you have done the Internet / library, interview, and firsthand experience sections that follow.*

Does the career role you have imagined already exist in the real world?_____

If the answer is yes, proceed to the next question. If the answer is no, what career roles are closest to the one you have envisioned? Pick one.

_____

How well will this career fit with your mission and work-purpose statements? That is, at what level of depth and breadth will it allow you to pursue your life's work?

_____

_____

_____

_____

_____

Who do people in this field serve on a day-to-day basis?

_____

_____

How well do your talents and interests match with what is required in this field?

_____

_____

What values do people in this field generally adhere to? How well do they match with yours?

_____

_____

What do people in this career role actually do in the course of a day?

_____

_____

What skills do they rely upon most?

_____

_____

What generally are their working conditions (environment, independence, etc.)?

_____

_____

What kind of training is required to work in this field?

_____

_____

What additional credentials enhance a person's credibility in this field?

_____

_____

Is there any area of the country where people who do this are especially concentrated? If so, where? (For example: movies and popular music/Los Angeles; theater, dance, music/New York; national politics/Washington, D.C.) If this applies, are you prepared to move there?

_____

_____

Who are the leading figures, companies, organizations, and/or institutions in this field?

_____

_____

How much do people in this field generally earn?

Entry level_____   Intermediate or average_____   Top level_____

What professional, trade, union, or other organizations do people in this field generally belong to?

_____

_____

Generally, what is the social status of people who are involved in this field? How are they viewed by others in the community?

_____

_____

What are the positive aspects of how these individuals are perceived?

_____

_____

What are the negative aspects? _____

_____

What kind of lifestyle do people in this profession generally uphold? (Journalists travel and drink a lot. New York executives are traditional and formal; California executives, more casual.)

_____

_____

What is the current market demand for this career? What are its prospects for the future? (Latin teachers are no longer in high demand.)

_____

_____

What hours, generally, do people in this field work? (It's not uncommon for people in high levels of government to work seventy-hour weeks or for beginning entrepreneurs to work fifty, sixty, or more.)

_____

_____

What personal and family sacrifices do people in this field generally make? (For example, many female executives are not married.)

_____

_____

How is the game played in this field, that is, what does it take to get to the top of it?

_____

_____

Review this list carefully, and write down any additional questions that seem important to you. These additional questions may occur to you immediately, while you are engaged in the process of doing your research, or once you have completed your initial research. If the question is important to you, write it down and find out the answer!

_____

_____

_____

_____

_____

Web and Book Resources

Find an example of a completed "Research Questions List" @ Empoweryou.com.

Get on the Internet

Now that you have your research list in hand (page 287), it's time to begin filling in the blanks. Remember, the hours you spend researching a new career before you begin training for or working in that field can save years of grief down the road. Fortunately, doing this research has never been easier. There is a wealth of career information available on the Internet. Most people are aware of the opportunities the Web offers when it comes to conducting a job search (more on this in Act III). Few, though, take full advantage of the extraordinary resources available when it comes to researching career options. You owe it to yourself to find out all you can before you make a career choice or change, and the Internet is the best place to start.

In addition to sites that provide general information (including info on training and educational requirements, requisite skills, salary ranges, and employment demand) about a wide range of career choices, there are sites that offer detailed information about specific careers. Virtually every professional and trade organization is online; many offer a wealth of career information. You can read trade and professional journals and newsletters in fields you are interested in online. You can find career-specific blogs, forums, and news articles. In addition to gathering research and conducting informal inquiries from people in your field of interest, you can use the Internet to find people (both locally and outside your area) who you can contact to set up more in-depth on-site informational interviews. These are just a few of the ways you can use the Internet to assist in researching a new career. See the link at the bottom of the page for Web and book resources that can help you make an informed choice.

Don't Forget the Library

While there is a great deal of information available for free on the Internet, libraries can still play a critical role in your research efforts. In addition to books, magazines, trade journals, and reference works, libraries today offer a wealth of digital information resources. For example, many companies charge hundreds of dollars in annual subscription fees for access to their online databases. Libraries pay these fees so that you can utilize these resources for little or no cost. Similarly, most libraries today have extensive collections of digital information resources available on CD-ROM, DVD, and other electronic formats. If you're not familiar with all your library has to offer (and few are), speak with a reference librarian at your favorite public or college library. He or she can be an invaluable resource in your research efforts.

Career Library Reference Works

Your library contains a wealth of information you can use to test potential career roles. The following are some resources you may want to investigate. If your public library does not contain the source materials listed below, you will likely be able to find them at your local college or university library or career center.

The Almanac of American Employers. Plunkett, Jack W., ed. Houston, Tex.: Plunkett Research. Updated annually. Includes: company profiles, industry associations, major trends affecting job seekers, employment statistics, and aggregate employment

Web and Book Resources
Find out more about researching potential careers
@ Empoweryou.com.

of specific industries and occupations, as well as outlooks for each.

Occupational Outlook Handbook. Bureau of Labor Statistics: Jist Works, published biennially. Provides general information about what people in a particular field do, what they earn, and what the demand outlook is.

Encyclopedia of Careers and Vocational Guidance. Ferguson Publishers. This five-volume encyclopedia provides general information on career development and a comprehensive survey of various career fields.

O*NET Dictionary of Occupational Titles. Michael Farr and Laurence Shatkin. This career reference book puts the official job descriptions and other career information from the U.S. Department of Labor's Occupational Information Network (O*NET) database into an easy-to-use form.

The Reader's Guide to Periodical Literature. H. W. Wilson Company. Look in the guide under your subject area for articles about your field. This is an especially good source for obtaining general information about trends in your field of interest, the field's relationship to the broader community, information about notables in the field, and new developments and breakthroughs.

General Books in the Field

Check your library's electronic card catalogue for books in your field of interest. A good way of researching books in your potential career area is to check out one or two general surveys of the field, as well as several more specialized books that appeal to you.

Conduct Interviews

The Internet is a great place to start. It's a good orienting point from which to begin your search, but there ain't nothin' like hearing it from the horse's mouth. If you want to learn how to do something, talk to people who are doing it. I recommend that you interview at least three individuals who are well respected within the field you are considering. You may not want to stop there; the more information, the better. However, usually after three interviews you get a good idea of what the work involves and if you really want to do it.

Many people are timid about approaching someone who is experienced in a field unfamiliar to them. Don't let pride or fear keep you from learning vital information. Remember, when you're calling for an interview, you are flattering that person by soliciting his or her "expert" opinion. For the sake of motivation, you might imagine yourself as a reporter for the *Daily Planet.* You have just got to get this scoop. Now get out there!

How to Do an Informational Interview

Setting Up the Interview

If you know competent people in the field that interests you, call them and set up appointments. If you don't, ask people you do know to refer you. Take advantage of your existing networks. Perhaps a member of an organization you belong to is working in this field. Even if you don't know that person, he

 No man is more miserable than he that hath no adversity.

Jeremy Taylor

or she is likely to respond favorably when approached by a member of his or her organization. If no one in this field belongs to any of your organizations, ask other members to suggest someone. Use the name of the person who gave you the referral to gain access to the person in the field. When you can call and say John or Mary Doe (whom they know and respect) suggested that they were an outstanding person in their field whom you should talk to, chances are good they will be accommodating.

If all else fails, check your telephone directory and do some cold calling. Expect rejection and persist. When you call, explain what you are doing and ask if you could get together for a brief interview. Set a time and meeting place for the appointment. I suggest that you invite them to lunch or coffee. This is for two reasons:

1. Their time is valuable. If you interview them at their place of work, you're more apt to be taking them away from their duties and thus to meet with resistance.

2. It's good form. You're asking them to give you something (information). It's only right that you give them something (lunch). Consider it a token of your appreciation for their valuable time and vital information.

If the interviewee would prefer to meet you in his or her office, comply with this request and ask for a time that would be relatively free of interruptions.

Doing the Interview

Be prompt to your meeting. Prepare your questions in advance. (See the list of suggested questions below.) Keep the interview brief and to the point. You may want to tape record the session, provided the other party is comfortable with this. This will help ensure that you get an accurate record of the encounter and it will free you from taking notes. Thank the interviewee at the close of the interview.

If the interview is going especially well and you feel it appropriate, ask if you might be a silent observer at the interviewee's place of work. Stress your interest in the field and your appreciation for their time. Convince them that you will be an innocuous, silent watcher who will not keep them from the performance of their duties, and that you will be ready to leave at any point they feel it appropriate (see page 295).

 The real object of education is to have a man in the condition of continually asking questions.
                                                    Bishop Creighton

Interview Questions

Here are some questions you might want to ask:

1.   How did you first get involved in this work?

2.   What was your training and background coming into this field?

3.   In what ways do you find meaning and fulfillment in this profession?

4.   What do you like most about your work?

5.   What do you like least?

6.   Knowing what you know now, how would you have approached this career differently?

7.   What would you recommend as the best course of action for someone who wanted to begin in this field?

8.   What talents or skills do you feel are most important in this work?

9.   What attitudes or values do you view as most important in this work?

10. What do you see as the future of this kind of work? Where is your field heading?

11. What is a typical workday like for you?

12. What hours do you work? What were your hours like when you first started in this field?

13. How is the game played in this field? How do you get to the top?

Make your own list using these and/or other questions that are important to you.

 What you see is what you get.
Flip Wilson

After the Interview

After the interview, send the interviewee a thank-you card expressing your appreciation. If you are especially impressed with their company, you may want to send along a resume. You might even call and tell that person you were so impressed by what they shared in the interview that you would like to work for their company. Ask them to refer you to their personnel department. Remember when conducting the interview that these individuals are potential contacts for future employment. Treat them accordingly.

Interview Profiles

In the space below, briefly summarize the key points of what you learned in your interviews.

Interview #1: _____

_____

_____

_____

_____

_____

Interview #2: _____

_____

_____

_____

_____

_____

Interview #3: _____

_____

_____

_____

_____

_____

_____

Without work, all life goes rotten. But when work is soulless, life stifles and dies.
Albert Camus

Get Firsthand Experience

In conducting your research, the Internet is good, interviews are better, and firsthand experience is best. An interview is not an entirely natural situation. People are more candid in a less formal setting, and there is nothing like seeing them in action. The following are some of the ways you can gain firsthand experience in your career area.

Short-Term

Be an Observer: Above, I suggested that you ask your informational interview subjects to allow you to observe them at work. If you did not feel it was appropriate to ask for this on the day of the interview, you may want to do so after some time has passed and they've received your thank-you note. Give them a call, and ask if you could be a silent observer for a day. Getting people to agree to let you watch is sometimes difficult, but the payoff is well worth the effort. It's an excellent way to learn a great deal in a short amount of time about what it's really like to work in a given career.

Meeting Places: You can get to know individuals socially in your career area by frequenting their favorite restaurants, bars, and health clubs. For example, Spago in Los Angeles is a favorite for Hollywood actors, screenwriters, and directors. The Tune Inn in Washington, D.C., is a favorite for congressional staff people. The Four Seasons Restaurant in New York is a favorite for publishers and authors. Also in the Big Apple is Sardi's, the place to be for the Broadway set. Entertainers, lawyers, doctors, and other professionals frequently congregate in a favorite bar, restaurant, or health club.

Find out where these places are in your community, and be there. You may make contacts that will be invaluable to your career. If you have an outgoing personality (and if you don't, fake it), you can learn a lot in a very short time. One reason is that individuals in these settings are much more relaxed and, therefore, more candid.

Association Meetings: Get yourself invited as a guest to association or trade meetings. Again, you can make contacts and friends and gain a great deal of information. Because these meetings are more formal, don't expect people at them to be as candid as they are at the watering hole or in the gym.

Conventions and Trade Shows: Most fields hold annual (or more frequent) conventions or trade shows. Many are open to the public. For those that are not, you'll need a guest pass. For your research purposes, these gatherings are somewhere in between the casual coffeehouse or the bar scene and the association or the service club meeting. They have the feeling of the association meeting by day and of the club scene by night.

Long-Term

Part-Time Work: By working part time in the new career area, you can "learn by doing" in a way that will not force you to give up your current position. This is not always appropriate or applicable, but if it is in your case, you may want to pursue it. It gets you hands-on experience, which, by the way, you might be able to parlay into full-time employment.

Volunteer Work: Benefits are similar to part-time work and some internships, with added flexibility and objectivity on the upside, but no pay on the downside.

Internships: Here, the benefits are similar to those of part-time and volunteer work. You will receive training in lieu of pay or in addition to nominal payment (see page 442).

Make a Skills Master List

From your Internet, library, interview, and firsthand research, make a list of the skills required to move into your new career. A list of skills is provided on the next page.

List the skills that you would employ in doing this work.

1._____

2._____

3._____

4._____

5._____

6._____

7._____

8._____

9._____

10._____

11._____

12._____

13._____

14._____

15._____

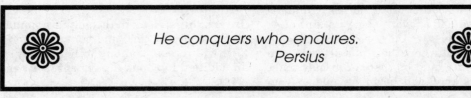

He conquers who endures.
Persius

Skill T.I.P. List

Things

1. Setting up
2. Adjusting
3. Precision working
4. Controlling/operating
5. Driving/operating
6. Manipulating
7. Tending
8. Feeding
9. Inserting
10. Throwing
11. Placing
12. Handling
13. Lifting
14. Cutting
15. Fitting
16. Pressing
17. Cleaning
18. Arranging
19. Assembling
20. Installing
21. Repairing
22. Typing
23. Operating a computer
24. Plowing
25. Drilling
26. Planting
27. Harvesting
28. Massaging

Ideas

1. Synthesizing
2. Developing concepts
3. Coordinating
4. Executing
5. Reporting
6. Analyzing
7. Examining
8. Evaluating
9. Adapting
10. Compiling
11. Gathering
12. Collating
13. Classifying
14. Computing
15. Copying
16. Transcribing
17. Entering
18. Posting
19. Comparing
20. Budgeting
21. Purchasing
22. Composing
23. Proofreading
24. Studying
25. Appraising
26. Testing
27. Visualizing
28. Writing

People

1. Mentoring
2. Advising
3. Counseling
4. Guiding
5. Negotiating
6. Debating
7. Arguing
8. Exchanging ideas
9. Selling
10. Instructing
11. Teaching
12. Training
13. Demonstrating
14. Supervising
15. Organizing
16. Managing
17. Delegating
18. Motivating
19. Entertaining
20. Performing
21. Persuading
22. Influencing
23. Speaking
24. Directing
25. Attending
26. Helping
27. Taking instructions
28. Making recommendations

You are what you do.
Anonymous

Playing-the-Game Skills List

In the space below, list all the skills necessary to playing the game in this career. Draw upon your Internet research, interviews, and firsthand experience. You may want to consult the list on the next two pages.

Playing-the-Game Skills (the auxiliary skills necessary to maintain and enhance your acceptance in this profession):

1. _____

2. _____

3. _____

4. _____

5. _____

6. _____

7. _____

8. _____

9. _____

10. _____

11. _____

12. _____

13. _____

14. _____

15. _____

16. _____

17. _____

18. _____

19. _____

20. _____

Playing-the-Game Skills: Some Examples

The following is a list of a few of the skills involved in playing the game.

Things

1. How to select a winning wardrobe
2. How to coordinate your wardrobe
3. How to select and collect things that will improve your image
4. How to buy appropriate gifts
5. How to invest your money
6. How to manage your money
7. How to have good posture
8. How to move your body in a manner that commands attention and respect
9. How to play appropriate sports
10. How to manipulate objects at table
11. How to make professional presentations of your written materials

Ideas

1. How to organize and prepare written materials
2. How to develop a powerful vocabulary
3. How to keep abreast of current topics of interest to those in your field or those who interact with the people in your field
4. How to do research on people so that you have information about them before you meet them
5. How to predict cycles and trends in your field
6. How to use metaphors to communicate your ideas
7. How to extract the essentials from large bodies of written material in a short amount of time
8. How to create systems for organizing information
9. How to ask intelligent questions in areas you know nothing about
10. How to translate technical or advanced concepts into simple language that the layman can understand
11. How to plan strategy
12. How to prove an idea through logic

13. How to explain a difficult concept in simple, successive steps

14. How to sort peripherals from essentials in any body of information

15. How to make complicated ideas seem simple

16. How to make simple ideas seem complicated

People

1. How to get noticed in a favorable way by your superiors

2. How to know where the real power is in your organization

3. How to tell the difference between a real promotion and a symbolic one

4. How to ask for a promotion or a raise

5. How to listen effectively

6. How to know what to do if you're asked to relocate

7. How to handle difficult people within your organization

8. How to sell effectively (this is important even if you're not in sales)

9. How to deal with enemies within your organization

10. How to be emotionally detached

11. How to make yourself look good at meetings

12. How to know whom to trust and how much

13. How to avoid office romances

14. How to know what the boss really means

15. How to handle criticism well

16. How to read body language

17. How to motivate your team

18. How to delegate effectively

19. How to understand the real motives of your clients or coworkers

20. How to deal effectively with authority

21. How to assume authority in an effective manner

22. How to fit in and show that you belong

23. How to develop networks

24. How to conduct an interview

25. How to build a team and get the most out of it

26. How to project a pleasing personality

27. How to make whatever you're doing sound fascinating

You May Have More Skills Than You Realize

When reflecting upon your skill development, it's worthwhile to recall that for the average adult, skill is a matter of degree. For example, Harold Figler, in his book, *The Complete Job Search Handbook* (an excellent primer on the skills necessary to the job seeker), lists what he calls the "Ten Hottest Transferable Skills." These are:

1. Budget Management
2. Supervising
3. Public Relations
4. Coping with Deadline Pressure
5. Negotiating/Arbitrating
6. Speaking
7. Writing
8. Organizing/Managing/Coordinating
9. Interviewing
10. Teaching/Instructing

Anyone who ever had an allowance as a child, or any money, for that matter, has engaged in *budget management*. Everyone who has ever babysat, looked after a younger sibling, or been a parent has engaged in *supervising*. If, on a date, you made an effort to make a favorable impression, you have engaged in *public relations* work. If you have filed an income tax form, you have dealt with *deadline pressure*. We all *negotiate* every day in our relationships. Have you ever answered a question in class? If so, you've engaged in *public speaking*. Anyone who has *written* the standard "What I Did Last Summer" paper in school has engaged in *writing*. Life in every household requires the skills of *organizing, managing,* and *coordinating;* for example, coordinating who uses the bathroom when. If you've ever asked for directions, you have conducted an *interview*. Every parent, sibling, or friend has done his or her share of *teaching* and *instructing*.

Of course, managing a multimillion-dollar budget requires a greater degree of skill than balancing a personal checkbook, and supervising a staff of hundreds requires more sophistication than babysitting the familial brood. Still, recognizing that you already possess these skills can give you the confidence to expand upon your current ability in that skill area.

Rate the Career Game

Below is a list of career game variables. Rate the career you have selected, according to the variables below. Indicate where the career you are considering stands in relation to each of these variables (one low, ten high). Next, review your assessment and ask yourself: Am I willing to agree with this game? Can I get into playing this game?

	1	2	3	4	5	6	7	8	9	10
1. Stress level										
2. Variability of tasks										
3. Flexibility of hours										
4. Physically demanding										
5. Emotionally demanding										
6. Mentally demanding										
7. Formality of dress										
8. Formality of language										
9. Formality of ethical code										
10. Opportunities for advancement										
11. Independence of work selection										

	1	2	3	4	5	6	7	8	9	10
12. Opportunities for creative thinking										
13. Degree of physical mobility										
14. Degree of social interaction within the organization										
15. Degree of social interaction outside of the organization										
16. Degree of competitiveness within the field										
17. Degree to which your personal life affects your career advancement										
18. Degree of participation of rank-and-file in management decisions										
19. Number of "off duty" hours you are expected to work or engage in work-related activities										
20. Importance of volunteer and community activities to career advancement										

Identify Necessary and Beneficial Credentials

In the space below, list the legal, de facto, and optional credentials necessary to begin work in this field.

1. Legal requirements for participation in this career (e.g., degrees, certifications, licensing required by the state or federal government, inspection standards, or updates in training).

    _____

    _____

    _____

    _____

    _____

2. Nonlegal but de facto necessary credentials (e.g., for job seekers: inside connections, physical capacities; for entrepreneurs: an office or store, association memberships, etc.).

    _____

    _____

    _____

    _____

    _____

3. Optional enhancing credentials (e.g., publishing books or articles, getting media attention, winning awards, etc.).

    _____

    _____

    _____

    _____

    _____

    _____

 As every divided kingdom falls, so every mind divided between many studies confounds and saps itself.   Leonardo da Vinci

Evaluation: No or Go?

We are free up to the point of choice. Then the choice controls the chooser.

Mary Crowley

In this section, you'll use the information gained in the "Reality Testing" section to determine whether a potential career is the right choice for you. A comprehensive ten-step evaluation process will guide you in making an intelligent and informed decision about your potential new career. More than making an informed decision, you will be in a position to make a commitment. Having thoroughly researched and evaluated your new career, you can be confident in the decision you make. If, after completing the work in this section, you determine that the career role you have selected is the right one for you, proceed to "Act III: The Battle for Life's Work." If not, go back to "Selecting Your Career Roles" on page 278 and start over again, this time working with another of the career roles you identified there.

Evaluating Your New Career in a Nutshell

In this section, you will evaluate your tentative career choice in terms of the following ten variables:

Evaluation #1:	Skills
Evaluation #2:	Purpose
Evaluation #3:	Talents
Evaluation #4:	Self-Esteem
Evaluation #5:	Personal Benefits
Evaluation #6:	Trade-offs
Evaluation #7:	Work Environment
Evaluation #8:	Retraining
Evaluation #9:	Economic Factors
Evaluation #10:	Demand and Growth

Evaluation #1: Skills
Where do I stand in relation to the skills necessary to succeed in this career?

The first step in evaluating a potential new career is to assess your skills in light of those needed for the career role you are considering. You will determine which of the necessary skills you already possess and which you have yet to acquire. Next, you will indicate the relative difficulty of each of these skills. Finally, you will determine whether the skills involved are primarily concerned with things, ideas, or people.

The end product is a "Skills Map" that will tell you at a glance how ready you are to pursue this career at this time, and what areas to concentrate on in developing greater ability. You can think of your Skills Map as the universe of skills necessary for pursuing this career.

The exercises that immediately follow require subjective self-assessment. You may feel as though you can't give exact answers. Don't be concerned about this. Simply rate each as well as you can. This exercise is but one component of the evaluation process through which you will determine whether or not you want to pursue your life's work through the career role you first imagined.

He who has a why can endure any how.
Friedrich Nietzsche

Part I
Skills: What You've Got, What You Need to Get

Enter the skills from your "Skills Master List" (on page 296) in the column provided. Rate your skill level on a scale of one to ten (one low, ten high), and check your answer on the list to the right. Finally, in the spaces to the right of the numbered list, indicate which of the skills you are already competent in and which you still need work in. All the skills you rated with scores of six or more, mark in the AC (Already Competent) column, and those less than six in the NW (Needs Work) column.

Necessary Skills	Needs Work					Already Competent					NW	AC
	1	2	3	4	5	6	7	8	9	10		
Example: *Public Speaking*			✓								✓	
1.												
2.												
3.												
4.												
5.												
6.												
7.												
8.												
9.												
10.												
11.												
12.												
13.												
14.												
15.												

Note: It is important that each skill be recorded in the same order throughout the skill assessment process.

Part II
Skills: Some Come Easy, Some Don't

The purpose of this exercise is to help you to estimate the amount of time it may take you to acquire the various skills, based upon their relative difficulty for you. Rate each of the skills from your "Skills Master List" according to the length of time required to master it. If you already possess the skill, did the acquisition of that skill take a few weeks, or did it take years to master? If you have yet to acquire the skill, do you anticipate the acquisition of that skill taking a relatively short time or significantly longer? Use the key below to assist you in selecting the appropriate space: A, B, C, D.

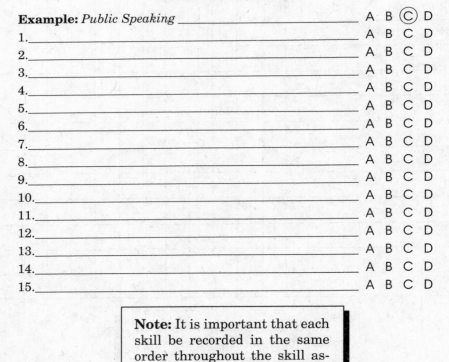

Key	
A	1–3 Months
B	3 Months–1 Year
C	1–3 Years
D	3+ Years

Necessary Skills

Example: *Public Speaking* _____ A B (C) D

1. _____ A B C D
2. _____ A B C D
3. _____ A B C D
4. _____ A B C D
5. _____ A B C D
6. _____ A B C D
7. _____ A B C D
8. _____ A B C D
9. _____ A B C D
10. _____ A B C D
11. _____ A B C D
12. _____ A B C D
13. _____ A B C D
14. _____ A B C D
15. _____ A B C D

Note: It is important that each skill be recorded in the same order throughout the skill assessment process.

Part III
Skills: Getting Some T.I.P.s as to Content

The purpose of this exercise is to help you to determine whether this career role primarily involves working with things, ideas, or people. This exercise can help you to clarify the actual content of the work and how that fits with your personality. If you are having difficulty determining whether a particular skill is primarily concerned with things, ideas, or people, refer to the "Skill T.I.P. List" on page 297.

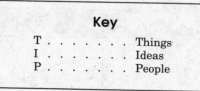

Key

T . . . . Things
I . . . . Ideas
P . . . . People

Necessary Skills

Example: *Public Speaking* _____ T I (P)

1._____ T I P
2._____ T I P
3._____ T I P
4._____ T I P
5._____ T I P
6._____ T I P
7._____ T I P
8._____ T I P
9._____ T I P
10._____ T I P
11._____ T I P
12._____ T I P
13._____ T I P
14._____ T I P
15._____ T I P

Note: It is important that each skill be recorded in the same order throughout the skill assessment process.

Charting Your Skills Map

Now refer to the three skill exercises you have just completed. Use the data from these to help you plot out your "Skills Map." Notice that your skills map has a line through the center of it. The left-hand side of the map represents the skills you are already competent in. The right-hand side of the map represents the skills you need to improve in, in order to work in your new career. The concentric circles represent the relative difficulty of each skill for you. The three pie-slice sections in both the left and right hemispheres indicate whether the skill primarily involves things, ideas, or people.

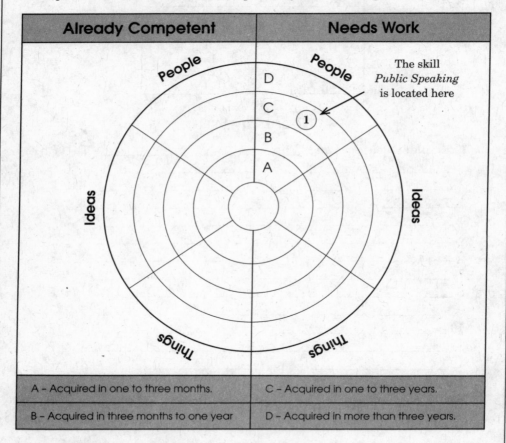

Already Competent	Needs Work

The skill *Public Speaking* is located here

A – Acquired in one to three months.	C – Acquired in one to three years.
B – Acquired in three months to one year	D – Acquired in more than three years.

Example: Public Speaking—I=NW, II=C, III=P. Let's say that you had "Public Speaking" in position number 1. This is a skill which you rated as "Needing Work," so you will enter it in the right hemisphere of your "Skills Map." It primarily involves people, so it will appear in the "People" pie slice. You estimate that it will take you one to three years to master and, therefore, corresponds to the C sphere. So skill number 1, Public Speaking, appears in the right hemisphere, in the second concentric circle of the "People" pie slice as indicated above. Chart your "Skills Map" on the next page.

My Skills Map

Career _____

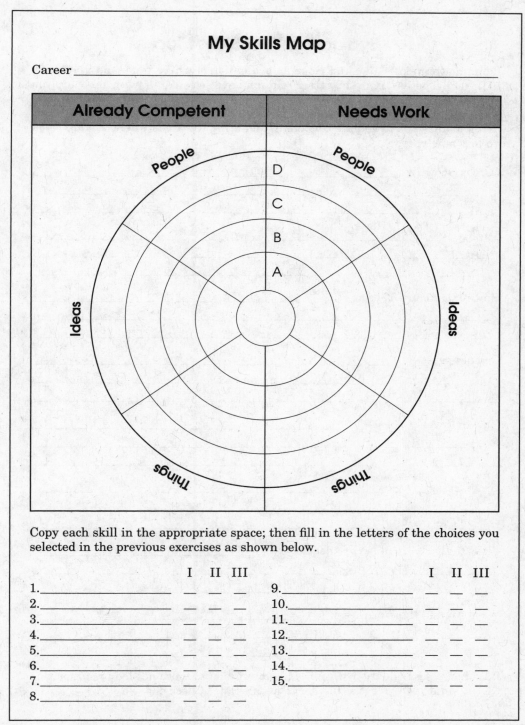

Already Competent	Needs Work

People · D · C · B · A · People

Ideas · Ideas

Things · Things

Copy each skill in the appropriate space; then fill in the letters of the choices you selected in the previous exercises as shown below.

		I	II	III			I	II	III
1.	_____	__	__	__	9.	_____	__	__	__
2.	_____	__	__	__	10.	_____	__	__	__
3.	_____	__	__	__	11.	_____	__	__	__
4.	_____	__	__	__	12.	_____	__	__	__
5.	_____	__	__	__	13.	_____	__	__	__
6.	_____	__	__	__	14.	_____	__	__	__
7.	_____	__	__	__	15.	_____	__	__	__
8.	_____	__	__	__					

Evaluating Your Skills Map

Examine your skills map and make an evaluation of where you stand in relation to the skills necessary to the career role you have selected. In what areas are you already strong? In what areas are you competent? And in what areas are you weakest? Next, indicate how you can take full advantage of the areas you excel in, develop areas where you are conpetent, and bring the areas where you are weak up to competency.

Career Objective:_____

_____

_____

Strengths:_____

_____

_____

How to Maximize These:_____

_____

_____

Competencies:_____

_____

_____

How to Develop These:_____

_____

_____

Weaknesses:_____

_____

_____

Ways to Bring Them Up to Adequacy:_____

_____

_____

Ways Around the Weakness:_____

_____

_____

Based on your evaluation of your skills in relation to those needed to pursue this career, would you give it a "no" or "go"at this time? Check one: No___ Go___

Evaluation #2: Purpose
Does this career provide an excellent opportunity to pursue my work purpose?

If you believe that this career is the optimal way of pursuing your purpose or vocation, you may determine to work at it, even if you currently lack skill or training in this field. On the other hand, even if you are well qualified for a given career, it may not be compatible with your purpose and, therefore, would not be a good choice. You initially selected this career, in part, based on your belief that it would provide an excellent opportunity to pursue your work purpose. Now that you have thoroughly researched this field, do you still believe that it will allow you to pursue your purpose?

Yes___ No____

If yes, why? _____

_____

If no, why not?_____

_____

If you chose to pursue this career, would the work you would be doing be something you could be proud of and find meaningful?

_____

_____

Does it reflect your values?

_____

_____

Does it reflect your vision of your best self?

_____

_____

Based on your evaluation of how well this career choice will enable you to pursue your purpose, would you give it a "no" or a "go" at this time? Check one: No___ Go___

 I feel the capacity to care is the thing which gives life its deepest significance and meaning.
Pablo Casals

Evaluation #3: Talents
Does this career provide the opportunity to express my talents?

In all likelihood, your new career will require a number of skills that lie outside of your talents. Nevertheless, based on your research of this field, do you feel confident that in the main this career provides ample opportunity to express your talents?

Yes___ No____

If yes, why?

_____

_____

_____

_____

_____

_____

_____

_____

If no, why not?

_____

_____

_____

_____

_____

_____

_____

Based on your evaluation of how well this career choice will enable you to express your talents, would you give it a "no" or a "go" at this time? Check one: No___ Go___

 Obstacles will look large or small to you according to whether you are large or small.
Orison Swett Marden

Evaluation #4: Self-Esteem
Do I believe I can do and ultimately excel at this work?

Considering your skills and motivation may not be enough to make an adequate evaluation of the likelihood of success in this field. You also need to know how your self-esteem compares with that of people already in the field. Some individuals are qualified for a given field (for example, starting their own business) and are even ready to make the necessary sacrifices, but they don't believe that they can do it. They lack the self-esteem necessary to make their dreams become reality.

In evaluating your self-esteem, consider how self-esteem works together with skills and experience. If you currently possess relatively few of the requisite skills, but you are willing to take the necessary steps to acquire them, and your self-esteem is such that you believe that you will ultimately be successful, you might make a "go" decision, even though your skills are relatively few. However, if your skills and self-esteem are both relatively low, you might choose an intermediate career, while building your skills and confidence.

Do you believe you can do this?_____

Generally, how does your self-esteem compare with that of people already in this field?

_____

If there is a significant gap, is it a gap you can close easily within the time you have allowed?

_____

Do you believe you can grow, learn, and change for the better? Write down examples of how you have grown as a person. List some of the new things you have learned.

_____

Are you willing to test your belief in yourself by trying new things? _____

Are your self-esteem reserves ample enough for you to risk a little by possibly failing, or are they so small that you feel you can't risk it?

_____

All in all, given your self-esteem reserves at this time, would you give this career move a "no" or a "go" at this time? Check one: No___ Go___

 A strong passion . . . will insure success, for the desire of the end will point out the means.
William Hazlitt

Evaluation #5: Personal Benefits
What will I gain personally from pursuing this career?

Okay, so you've taken a good look at what your new career endeavor is going to cost you. Now it's time to examine the benefits you can expect to enjoy. Among these are the increased contributions you can make, and improvements in your finances, in your family life, and in your psychological and physical health.

What impact are you likely to make with your new career? How will the world be better because of your efforts? _____

_____

What psychological benefits are you likely to derive? (For example, increased self-confidence and self-esteem, more energy and a greater sense of well-being, knowing that you are making the world a better place.)

_____

_____

How will this career change or improve your family life? (For example, your increased self-esteem improves your relationships with your mate and children. Your example of giving your best inspires your children to pursue theirs. Your courage to pursue your work puts your family in contact with interesting people and places. Your increased status in the community reflects well on your family. Your increased earnings make for a better lifestyle.)

_____

_____

What benefits to your health are you likely to derive from your pursuit of this career?

_____

_____

What material benefits will you derive from pursuing your new career? (For example, increases in income, and the kinds of improvements that may make possible.) _____

_____

All in all, based on the benefits you will receive as a result of this career move, would you give the move a "no" or a "go" at this time? Check one: No___ Go___

 Isn't the fulfillment of our duty towards our neighbor an expression of deepest desire?
Dag Hammarskjöld

Evaluation #6: Trade-offs
What will it cost me in the short and long term?

One way or another, everything has a price. This process provides you with the opportunity to think in advance about the likely sacrifices you'll need to make in terms of time, money, and your personal life in order to succeed in your new career.

Time

From your research, how many years or months of training do people in this field have? Will you need this much time, or perhaps more, or less? Is the amount of training time required acceptable to you?

_____

What hours do people in this field work? (Remember to include "playing the game" time. These are hours you would put into activities that may not be part of your job description, but are necessary to excel in this work.) Are these hours acceptable to you? _____

Given your current skill level, how long do you estimate it will be before you can begin in this new career? Is this acceptable to you? Why do you think so? Is there any way that you could significantly shorten this time?

_____

Once in this career, how long does it generally take people to hit their stride? Is this time acceptable for you? Is there any way you can significantly reduce this time? If so, how?_____

Personal

What personal activities or interests might you have to sacrifice for a time or altogether in pursuing this career role? Are these trade-offs acceptable to you?

_____

What sacrifices are you likely to have to make in the way you relate to your family, friends, or other loved ones in order to pursue this career? Are these sacrifices acceptable to you?_____

All in all, based on the sacrifices you will have to make, would you give this career role a "no" or "go" at this time? Check one: No___ Go___

Wisdom begins with sacrifice of immediate pleasures for long-range purposes.
Louis Finkelstein

Evaluation #7: Work Environment
Will the work environment match with my personality and preferred work style?

While many factors relating to work environment are specific to particular jobs or work positions, there are some factors that are typical of given careers. Perhaps the most significant of these is the workplace culture. Next to finding a career that allows you to pursue your purpose and express your talents, finding one with a well-suited workplace culture is the most significant noneconomic factor in predicting workplace satisfaction. People end up leaving or being asked to leave positions far more often because they don't mesh with a given workplace culture than because they aren't competent in their work.

Based on your research: Is the general workplace culture associated with this career one that you resonate with? _____

_____

Do people in this career generally share your values and interests? _____

_____

In what physical setting do people in this career generally work? (For example, in a store, home, office, etc.) Is this a physical environment that resonates with you?

_____

How is work typically organized in this career? Do people in this career typically work alone or in a team? Do they tend to be self-employed or do they work for large, medium, or small organizations? Is the way that work is typically organized for people who work in this career a way that you enjoy working? If not, is it possible to work in a different way and still be successful in this career?

_____

_____

Are there any other factors involved with the workplace culture, physical setting, organizational structure, or work habits typically associated with this career that you particularly resonate with? _____

_____

Are there any other factors involved with the workplace culture, physical setting, organizational structure, or work habits typically associated with this career that you particularly dislike? _____

_____

All in all, considering the typical work environment associated with this career, would you give this career move a "no" or a "go" at this time? Check one: No___ Go___

Evaluation #8: Retraining
How much additional education (formal or otherwise) will be required for this new career?

Answer the questions below to help you decide if this career is right for you. Later on, you will have an opportunity to explore retraining options in much greater detail.

_____

_____

What additional education, training, or credentials will you need to begin working in this field? _____

_____

How long (months, years) will it take you to complete these requirements?

_____

_____

Roughly (again, you will have an opportunity to explore this in more detail later) how much will your retraining cost?

_____

_____

What personal sacrifices will you have to make in terms of time and money to acquire the education or training you need?

_____

_____

What will you gain professionally?

_____

_____

What might you gain personally from doing the necessary retraining for this career?

_____

_____

All in all, considering the retraining required to pursue this career, would you give it a "no" or a "go" at this time? Check one: No___ Go___

 Desire creates the power.
Raymond Hollingwell

Evaluation #9: Economic Factors
Will this career work for me financially?

How much do people in this career role earn?_____

At entry level?_____

At top level?_____

Are these earnings acceptable to you?_____

Is there any way that you could significantly increase the money you would make through related products and services? Are you willing to do this?

_____

_____

_____

How much money must you make in order to maintain a lifestyle that is acceptable to you? Can you do it working in this field?

_____

_____

_____

Estimate approximately how much it will cost you to train for this field. Is this amount acceptable to you?_____

_____

_____

Are you likely to lose additional money in the transition? (For example, in addition to the money that you spend on training, there is the amount of income lost while devoting yourself to training. Also, if you are at a high level in your current career, you may be starting at a lower level in your new work.) If these sacrifices apply in your case, how great are they? Are you willing to make them?

_____

_____

_____

All in all, based on financial considerations, would you give this career a "no" or "go" at this time? Check one: No___ Go___

The chief value of money lies in the fact that one lives in a world in which it is overestimated.
H. L. Mencken

Evaluation #10: Demand and Growth
What does the future of this career look like in terms of market demand and opportunities to grow and/or advance professionally?

In choosing your new career, it's wise to assess the current and future market demands for your products or services.

How much in demand are people in your career role? In other words, how hard will you have to work at marketing yourself at this? Is this amount of work acceptable to you?

_____

_____

_____

_____

_____

_____

_____

_____

How strong are your marketing skills? If you plan to work for someone else—job-hunting skills. If you plan to work for yourself—entrepreneurial and, especially, marketing and sales skills. If your career choice is a new field, do you have a good idea of how to market yourself at this and what it's going to take to do it?

_____

_____

_____

_____

_____

_____

_____

Given the demand for the product or service you will be providing, do you feel it is best to proceed with your career choice at this time? Check one: No___ Go___

Every individual has a place to fill in the world and is important in some respect, whether he chooses to be so or not.
Nathaniel Hawthorne

Evaluation Checklist

The following checklist summarizes the process that you have just completed. Answer the questions below with a yes or no for an overview of your work. If you were too lazy to complete the process, this checklist can still give you a good idea of whether the career you have selected is right for you.

Y/N

1. Would this career role allow you to pursue your life's work effectively?   _____

2. Would it make the best use of your talents?   _____

3. Would it provide you with opportunities for continued development and growth?   _____

4. Do you now possess the skills necessary to work in this field?   _____

5. (Answer only if you answered no to question four.) Is the amount of training that would be required to gain the skills necessary to assume this role acceptable to you?   _____

6. Would it give you a work environment that you could excel in?   _____

7. Would it allow for the maximum expression of your creativity?   _____

8. Would you actually be serving the people whom you most want to help?   _____

9. Would you be working with the kind of people who would stimulate, challenge, and support you?   _____

10. Would you earn an acceptable amount of money in this career role?   _____

11. Are the likely trade-offs and sacrifices that you would have to make acceptable to you?   _____

12. Would your self-esteem and self-image allow you to achieve this goal?   _____

13. If your answer to question 12 is no, is there ample time to improve your self-esteem sufficiently, within the required time, to make it work?   _____

14. Is the amount of time it will take you to actually begin doing this work acceptable to you?   _____

15. Given everything you have considered, is this career role right for you?   _____

Nothing is more difficult, and therefore more precious, than to be able to decide.

Napoleon I

Act II Review

Briefly describe your #1 career role. Why did you choose this role?   *(page 278)*

Summarize the key points of what you learned during your interviews with professionals in this field.   *(page 294)*

Of the skills needed to succeed in this career, list those that you are already competent in and those that need work.   *(page 311)*

Describe how this career provides the best way to fulfill your work purpose.   *(page 313)*

Describe how this career provides the opportunity to express your talents.   *(page 314)*

Do you believe you can ultimately do, and excel at, this work?   *(page 315)*

What benefits will you gain from succeeding in this career?   *(page 316)*

List the sacrifices you'll need to make in terms of: *(page 317)*

Time:

Personal Life:

Describe the work environment that best matches your personality and preferred work style.   *(page 318)*

How much additional education (formal or otherwise) will be required for this new career?   *(page 319)*

Describe the financial factors relevant to this field.   *(page 320)*

What does the future of this career look like in terms of market demand and opportunities to grow and/or advance professionally?   *(page 321)*

The Battle for Life's Work

Wherein our hero selects a marketing strategy

Choose always the way that seems the best, however rough it may be. Custom will soon render it easy and agreeable.

Pythagoras

In the play of life's work, the third act is decisive. If you've completed the exercises that accompany Acts I and II, you're on track to create a fulfilling experience of work. You've identified your passion and at least one viable career role through which to express it. That's terrific! Yet without sufficient knowledge of the marketplace, the confidence to act, and/or the will to endure in your marketing efforts, you may abandon your grand intentions to the realm of mere dreams. Whether you choose to work for yourself or to take a job within an existing organization, you'll have to market yourself and your work. "Act III: The Battle for Life's Work" is designed to arm you with what you need to "take it to the street." In addition to providing you with specific information about creating your own business, working as a freelance, starting a nonprofit organization, and landing the right job, Act III ends with a section entitled "Street Smarts" that will explore a number of general marketing skills with applications in virtually any field.

*Note: If additional training is required before you can pursue the career you identified in Act II, you may want to go directly to "Act IV: The School of Life's Work."

Winning in the Marketplace;

Or, How to Kick Butt Without Being a Total Jerk

Everybody lives by selling something.
Robert Louis Stevenson

There is a war going on. Like it or not, you're on the battlefield. Now, as discussed earlier, the really important battles are the ones within yourself, but that does not negate the fact that there is an outer war happening as well. This war is a battle for power and control. It is played out in the economic sphere. In the battlefield of the economy, the large corporations are the superpowers. Superpowers get even bigger by gobbling up the mid-sized companies. So the giant fish eat the large and medium-sized fish. And what do the medium-sized fish eat? Why, the biggest little fish, of course. A fish can only get so big without being noticed by a hungry bigger fish. Giant fish are too large to bother little fish; and medium-sized fish, too large to notice tiny fish.

The tiny fish are, of course, the countless small businesses and freelancers that provide a myriad of services we all use and enjoy every day. These small fry get away only because they aren't really interesting to bigger fish. Tiny-fish companies are what Gerald Michaelson (see highlight on page 329) and others have termed "guerrillas." Their survival depends on their ability to attract the attention of customers, clients, investors, benefactors, etc., without doing this so well that they attract a hungry bigger fish.

Guerrillas, including small business people, nonprofit operators, and freelancers, must have the market savvy to survive in a big-gun environment. Except for occasional strikes, guerrillas don't take on large armies in their strongholds—they hold rugged terrain and rely on the support of the local people. They go under, around, and behind the big armies, but almost never meet them head-on.

Appear where they cannot go, head for where they expect you least.

Sun Tzu

Although most people report that they would like to work for themselves, relatively few actually do. Many who are unhappy working for someone else could make the transition if they had the necessary confidence and marketing skill. If you have long dreamed of working for yourself or have determined that it's the best way to pursue your passion, you owe it to yourself to investigate this option further. Throughout Act III, you will find a good deal of specific information as well as a preliminary planning process for thinking through your new enterprise. I also encourage you to take advantage of the abundant resources available online. (See empoweryou.com for links to a variety of these.)

Instead of working for ourselves, most of us have jobs. No doubt this is partly because we understand that there is a war going on, and a lot of gung-ho guerrillas come back as casualties. We attempt to join forces with large organizations, figuring there is strength in numbers, or because in our field, a job is the best or only vehicle for achieving the results we want. Yet even within the belly of a whale, the market sea can be a dangerous place, with shifting currents and raging winds—and there is always the chance of the whale running aground. Even large companies go bankrupt. Many more face mergers and acquisitions that bring significant layoffs. Still others move huge segments of their operations overseas. Of course, as an employee, your efforts and abilities serve your employer's aims only for as long as that employer deems fit.

Only a life lived for others is a life worthwhile.

Albert Einstein

Bravery never goes out of style.

William M. Thackeray

The vagaries of employment as well as your desire to realize your own best work require that you clarify your own purpose. Your purpose gives you a sense of direction in seeking new employment and something to hold on to when circumstances change. Knowing your own purpose helps you to see how to align your efforts with those of others and to take advantage of opportunities as they arise. It's equally imperative that you understand the purpose of any organization you plan to work for and that you choose one whose purpose is congruent with your own, or at least tolerant of it. You're probably not going to single-handedly reform organizations (especially large ones), so stay with organizations where you can, in good conscience, go with the flow. Landing the jobs you really want (you can easily have a dozen or more in your work life) requires the necessary self-marketing or job-hunting skills. As much as the guerrilla entrepreneur (though in different ways), the job seeker must be a marketing warrior (see the "Landing the Right Job" scenario, beginning on page 415).

The conflict in "The Battle for Life's Work" arises from the tension between the way things are now and the way they could be. This gives your marketing adventure its inherent drama. You want to sell your products or services, spread your message, provide greater community service, or get a job that allows you to express your natural talents and gifts, etc. In other words, you want something and you may or may not get it. Whether or not you do, depends more than anything on you. You will have to fight your own fear and inertia and overcome external barriers. In this sense, our marketing efforts are character building.

Marketing—character building? I can hear it, rolling around not too far in the back of some of your minds, a philosophical debate centered on the question, "Can one be intelligent, moral, *and* successful?" Much of modern literature tells us that we cannot. We've been inundated with images of the anti-hero—the intelligent, moral person as the proverbial outsider. Implied is the notion that all successful, self-confident people must be fools or crooks—"not deep" or "not decent." This is bunk. If by success you mean achieving what you, in your heart, want—not somebody else's idea—then of course, you can and should be successful. If your success or some part of it requires winning in the marketplace—go for it.

Zen will have nothing to do with defeat, self-pity, or retreating to the Ivory Tower of Should Be. It adapts to circumstance. In India and China, Buddhism had a legacy of nonviolence. In Japan, Zen embraced the samurai tradition and transformed it—instilling a higher code of acceptable martial conduct. Zen was not squeamish about the martial arts, and it needn't be squeamish about the marketing arts—today's equivalent. Zen brings its energy, detachment,

The Marketing Battlefield

The following, from Gerald A. Michaelson's *Winning the Marketing War: A Field Manual for Business Leaders*, is a concise description of current battlefield positions and strategies. Reprinted with the permission of the publisher.[1]

The Marketing Battlefield

The big ones own the strongest positions.

Positions on the Battlefield

The marketplace is much like the political geography of the Cold War.

1. The big ones—always in control.
2. The secondary powers—squeezed in the middle.
3. Everyone else—fighting like guerrillas.

The Super Powers

They own the territory.

1. Their best defense is an active offensive.
2. They should allow no one to camp on their battlefield.
3. When the super powers don't protect their armies, they lose their position.

Secondary Powers

They are in the dangerous middle ground.

1. They must get bigger so that they don't get smaller.
2. They don't attack the major powers.
3. They get their territory from the smaller companies.

The Guerrillas

Everyone else with a small market share.

1. Their struggle is for survival.
2. Survivors keep a watchful eye on the super powers.

self-discipline, humor, and grace wherever it goes—even when, like the little piggy, it goes to market.

East and West (around the world, for that matter), there is a tradition of the noble warrior. Martial skill without self-discipline and restraint was recognized as a danger to the community. (Today, the same may be said of marketing skill.) Codes of martial conduct were established to check the potential abuses of this power. Andrea Hopkins, in her wonderful book *Knights*, states that the distinguishing characteristics of the true medieval knight were *bravery*, *skill in combat*, and *integrity*.[2] These can provide a basis for a code of conduct for today's marketing warrior. He or she needs the *bravery* to go into the marketing battle, the *marketing skill* to be masterful, and the *integrity* to remain true to principle throughout. (If today's battleground is the marketplace, then skill in combat means marketing skill.)

Bravery Is a Battle You Can Win or Lose: Overcoming Fear

Within the marketing context, bravery means simply that you believe in what you are doing enough to fight for it, to enter the fray, to risk getting roughed up a bit. If you're looking for a job, go for the one you really want—don't settle for less. If you want to start your own business, get out there and mix it up with the competition. If you want to start a nonprofit organization, drum up support for your ideas, solicit from potential donors, organize events to fund your efforts, hassle with the paperwork, etc. Fight for what you believe in.

A warrior must only take care that his spirit is never broken.

Chozan Shissai

A poet once said, "Only the gentle are brave." Gandhi repeatedly said that the "nonviolence" of the weak is not nonviolence but cowardice, and that only the strong can be nonviolent. The person who stays in a job he hates, and condemns others for being "too ambitious" or "materialistic," is playing the hypocrite. There is no honor in indifference; no virtue in poverty. Self-denial out of cowardice is a waste, not a gift. Your bravery as a marketing warrior springs from your caring, your compassion, your commitment to the vision you hold. The words *valor* and *value* come from the same Latin root, *valere*, meaning "to be strong."[3] Those with the conviction of their values have the strength to initiate, endure, and ultimately triumph.

To be a warrior is to learn to be genuine in every moment of your life.

Chögyam Trungpa

Integrity Is a Battle You Can Win or Lose: Overcoming Laziness and Greed

We lose strength by sacrificing our integrity. Everyone knows that greed can steal integrity; just as often, laziness is the culprit. After all, selling out is the easy way out. Standing up for what you want and believe in takes energy. At every step along the way, you will meet with the temptation to compromise your integrity for the sake of ease, financial reward, recognition, understanding, acceptance, etc. In the employment sector, you may be offered a lucrative position doing work that violates your principles or work that, while not ethically or morally repugnant, isn't what you know in your heart you want.

First see to it that you, yourself, are all right, then think of defeating an opponent.

The Way of the Spear

In business, tests of integrity come into play in the way you conduct yourself with your employees, customers, suppliers, other businesses, and the general public. In the nonprofit sector, you may be asked to abandon controversial programs in order to receive funding from governments and corporations. These are just a few of the integrity issues that may arise. The point is that when we compromise our integrity, we lose more than moral authority; we lose the inner strength and conviction we need to realize the genuine desires of our hearts.

Marketing Skill Is a Battle You Can Win or Lose: Developing Resourcefulness

In the Japanese art of sword fighting (*kendo*), there is a saying: "Zen seven, *ken* three." *Ken* refers to the sword. The meaning of the saying is that success in swordsmanship is seven parts Zen, or inner state of being, and three parts *ken*, or technical ability with the sword. I've already suggested the metaphor of the marketplace as a battlefield. Within this context, the saying "Zen seven, *ken* three" applies equally well with the English meaning of the word *ken*. In English, *ken* means "to know" or "range of knowledge."[4] What you know about the marketplace and the range of knowledge you have about effective market strategies can spell the difference between success and failure. We need this kind of knowledge the way a general needs military intelligence. Yet your awareness, your Zen,

is always the single most important factor. Because preconceived notions of how things are—or should be—block awareness and distort perception, cluttered minds make poor decisions. Emptiness brings the clarity to see and respond naturally.

We can see unmistakeably that there is an inner relationship between Zen and the warrior's life.
D. T. Suzuki

Limiting beliefs weigh us down; but if we are willing, it doesn't take much to turn them around. For example, if you are resisting your "warrior" energy, developing positive images of the creative use of aggressive energy can unleash powerful dormant possibilities. For some, the word *warrior* conjures images of war, brutality, death, and destruction. As I use the term, *warrior* isn't limited to combat veterans, but applies to anyone who uses their aggressive energy in a disciplined, focused way. Aggressive energy is a part of life. There is no getting around it. It can be used creatively or destructively, but it cannot be eliminated. But what about nonviolence?

Nonviolence is the creative use of aggression—not its negation. But don't take my word for it; listen to the world's foremost nonviolence practitioner, Mahatma Gandhi: "I have learned through bitter experience the one supreme lesson to conserve my anger, and as heat conserved is transmuted into energy, even so anger controlled can be transmuted into an energy which can move the world."[5] Gandhi embraced his anger and transformed it into a force that shook the world.

When you reach real ability you will be able to become one with the enemy. Entering his heart you will see that he is not your enemy after all.
Tsuji (Japanese sword master)

How can we learn to "control" our aggressive energy—and in so doing tap the benefits of its power? When you get behind the wheel of an automobile, you respect its power—or pay the price. You know that, depending on how well it is controlled, your car can be a means of locomotion or destruction. Similarly, your aggressive energy can work for or against you. It *will* find expression—either in creativity, initiative, and persistence or in negativity, hostility, and self-sabotage. Determine to respect this energy and make it work for you. In Tibetan Buddhism, the adept is said to "turn around" the energy of anger (sometimes called stubbornness) into tenacity

Joy lies in the fight.

Mahatma Gandhi

or "immovable" determination. Controlled aggression becomes the force of tenacious concentration—the key discipline of the warrior, the source of her power.

In the Western tradition, we find the same understanding in the lore of knights. Today's most prestigious cadre of knights (the Order of the Garter) was originally known as the "Order of St. George." He is still its patron saint. St. George the dragon-slayer (sometimes shown as St. Michael) is one of the great icons of Western art. If you look closely at one these images, you will notice that St. George doesn't actually kill the dragon (symbol of the aggressive energy); he keeps his sword at its throat. He does not destroy his aggressive energy; he keeps it under control. A true knight uses his aggression in a disciplined way. He does not waste this energy in petty, egotistical ways, but concentrates it into an immovable determination to accomplish his objectives.

Some say the warrior metaphor doesn't work well for women. Anyone who makes this claim can take a few lessons from world history, mythology, and current events. Throughout history, scores of women have marched into battle with their menfolk; various cultures produced whole battalions of female warriors, for example, the African Dahomeyan.[6] Mythology abounds with legends of female warriors and warrior goddesses, recognizing the warrior energy within the feminine psychology. History has had its own share of real-life warrior queens, and today women fill the ranks of military units around the world. But all of this is really beside the point. For as I've said before, warrior energy isn't limited to the martial realm. Rosa Parks, Mother Teresa, and Georgia O'Keeffe overcame on their own battlefields, as have countless other famous and not-so-famous women. In today's marketing battlefield, most of the new guerrillas (entrepreneurs) are women.

Smart marketing warriors do a lot better than naive ones. They know that without the right attitudes and the right information, they may get slaughtered in the marketing wars. To be successful in your marketing efforts, you must project confidence. In the long run, confidence can't be faked. You must develop the attitudes and knowledge that breed confidence. Below are a few attitudes that smart marketing warriors adopt.

1. Know there is a way.

2. Find a way.

3. Take action on the basis of the knowledge that you find.

4. Keep at it.

In walking, just walk.
In sitting, just sit.
Above all,
don't wobble.

Yun-men Wen-Yan

They conquer who believe they can.

Emerson

Know There Is a Way

You want people to help you, whether it's by buying your products or services, supporting the mission of your nonprofit, or hiring you for a job that will allow you to pursue your passion. Think of your marketing efforts as nothing more or less than getting people to agree to assist you in doing what you want to do. Marketing warriors never doubt what *they* want. That's why you were asked to take the time to identify exactly what you want from your life's work. When you run up against an obstacle, there is a big difference between saying, "I don't know if I really want this after all" and saying, "This is a damn difficult obstacle." Many people abandon the ship of their dreams as soon as they run into the first strong wind. Marketing warriors don't retreat from their goals. They put the full force of their creative energy into finding a way.

We get out of our marketing efforts what we put into them and since these efforts can spell the difference between doing the work you love or settling for less, why not have fun going after what you really want? Most anything can be fun when we bring our passion to it; nothing is much fun when we don't. If you start with the assumption that people want to help you achieve your goals, you can relax into the process of showing them how they can. You can have fun with it.

Go to the battlefield firmly confident of victory and you come home with no wounds whatsoever.
Kenshin Uesugi (Samurai general)

By now, you have definite goals. Start with the conviction that you are going to achieve them. Affirm that there is a way. In a sense, every marketing problem is simply a lack of knowledge. It could be about how to raise the capital you need to start your business. It might be about the needs and desires of the population you want to serve or it could be about the organizations or individuals that can give you the job you seek. It could also be about how to present yourself and what you have to offer in the best possible light. Whatever you want to achieve, there is a way to win the support you need to make it happen.

Find a Way

These days, one has to be very careful about saying that something can't be done. In fact, 99 percent of the time, someone who has come from equally difficult or more adverse circumstances than you is doing that very thing right now. Marketing warriors take the attitude, "I know there is a way, and I'm going to find it. How am I going to find it? Well, first and foremost, I'm going to keep looking until I do."

You must push yourself beyond your limits, all the time.

Carlos Castaneda, Don Juan

Looking *is* looking, not ruminating on the problem. Many people confuse idle conversation with the action of finding a way. They seem to believe that a little fairy godmother is going to hear their complaints and magically solve their problems. Their approach is: "I want you to listen to me recite my litany of weaknesses, the obstacles I face, and all my reasons why I can't make it work." Of course, we can always do this (and we may do it more than we care to admit), but when we are done complaining, our situation will not have improved. You'd be better off redirecting the energy spent in idle complaint toward figuring out how to advance your dream. One step forward is worth a ton of idle chatter.

If knowledge is power, then ignorance is weakness. Often when we hit a roadblock, we just need more knowledge to gain clarity about what to do next. Determine that you are going to keep looking until you find a way—until the lightbulbs go off. When you don't find a way right away, don't conclude that there *is* no way. Take the approach, "I haven't found a way yet, but I know there is one, and I'm still looking." This is the time to redouble your efforts—get more information. Research. Read. Talk to people who know more than you. Avoid complaining and negative talk of all kinds. Unless your conversation is a matter of seeking information from a more knowledgeable source or bouncing off a sounding board you know you can trust—clam up.

People will tell you that there is no way, before they have done any research to find out. They picture mental "Road Closed" signs where none exist. They allow fear of failure to stop them in their tracks. If you want to be successful, don't worry about failure. All failure is simply a failure to *concentrate*. Fear of failure distracts your attention from the search for a way to make it work. In this way, *the fear of* failure actually helps to create it. There is a way. Keep looking. If you don't see it right away, persist. Go back and affirm that there is a way. Stay with the search like a leopard on the hunt. Know what you want to do, and concentrate on finding a way to make it work.

Whatever is worth doing at all, is worth doing well.

Philip Stanhope

With enough knowledge and self-confidence,
you can do anything.

All the things you want to do will fall into one of two categories. Either it has been done before, but not by you, or it has never been done. In either case, *finding the way is a matter of inner listening (intuition) and outer research*. In proper combination, these are an unbeatable tandem.

It Has Been Done Before, but Not by You: If the thing you want to do has been done before, but not by you, your emphasis will be on outer research. You need to find a good model and follow it. The model will provide the primary guiding force. Of course, you will want to adapt the model to fit your unique situation by listening to your intuition, or gut feelings, and by keeping an awareness of relevant environmental factors. The process, though more complicated in practice, is not unlike that of assembling a bicycle or a piece of furniture that you buy in the box. All of the necessary steps have been laid out for you; if you simply follow the instructions, you'll get results. You don't have to invent something that doesn't exist. Just get good information and follow instructions.

There is a wealth of information available today for improving your marketing skill. If you are seeking employment, developing your job-hunting skills can give you the power to choose the position you really want. You don't have to settle for less—not if you have the power of knowledge working for you. You can select the organizations you want to work for and aggressively go after them. If you're interested in starting your own business, you will need to know about markets and management, accounting and advertising, sales and red tape, capital acquisition and business planning, and more. All of this is in addition to the knowledge specific to operating your particular business. If you want to start a nonprofit organization, you will need to know about the legalities of incorporation and tax-exempt status; legal restrictions on officers, directors, and programs; fundraising; publicity; proposal writing; strategic planning; management; evaluation; record keeping; and more. Again, all of this is in addition to the specific knowledge necessary to providing the services your organization offers.

Action is doing something, reacting is having
it happen.
                                                    Syd Field

Marketing warriors understand that their biggest enemy is their own lack of knowledge. Know your enemy. Identify the specific knowledge areas you need to acquire and attack them relentlessly. Select the areas you will focus on first. (Don't try to learn everything at once.) Next, get general information on the topic. Read a good general survey. This will give you enough of an overview to strategically approach the acquisition of the knowledge you need. Next, select the specific learning options you will use to master this knowledge. For example, you might want to work with a mentor, attend classes or seminars, do additional reading, etc. (see page 530). Likewise, if you need more information about the job market or the market demographic you want to serve, develop a plan for getting the knowledge you need.

If the thing you want to do has been done before, you needn't start from scratch, and you shouldn't. Find good models and follow instructions, adapted, of course, to your particular situation. People often try to invent at the stage where they would be better off copying; that's a mistake. Every artist has to learn how to copy before he can invent. Every warrior has to go into training before she is ready for battle.

He who can copy can do.
Leonardo da Vinci

It Has Never Been Done Before: If the thing you want to do has never been done before, your emphasis will be on intuition, with adaptations based upon your outer research. The primary guiding force will be your own inner promptings and creative ideas. These, of course, must be grounded and adapted to the practical realities of the environments you want to work in. Your research will give you the knowledge necessary to bridge your intuition to the realities of the physical world and the predilections of society. Develop prototypes, mock-ups, and presentation tools that make your new idea come alive. Find or develop metaphors to link your new idea with more familiar things or concepts. The trick is to make people feel comfortable with your new product, innovative program, or organization concept. Don't assume that they will get it. Give them logical reasons to support your new idea *and* an opportunity to buy in emotionally. If you want to see your new idea manifest, you'll need to convince others that you are on to something.

Think first, then do.

Albert Schweitzer

Take Action on the Basis of the Knowledge That You Find

Again, marketing warriors don't waste time trying to reinvent the wheel. They have the self-confidence and humility necessary to follow instructions. *People who can't follow instructions can't direct the course of their own lives.* The self-directed individual selects what she wants (or needs) to learn and do, and sets about following the models necessary for learning and doing it.

It is necessary to any originality to have the courage to be an amateur.

Wallace Stevens

> *In order to arrive at what you do not know*
> *You must go by the way which is the way of*
> *ignorance.*
>
> T. S. Eliot

When an experienced, knowledgeable person says, "This is the way to do it," accept that that is the way to do it, at least until you know enough to find a better way. Act! Don't allow intervening thoughts such as, Oh, but can I do it? or, I don't know if I'm cut out for this, or, Am I doing it wrong? to distract your mind. Concentrate on what you need to do. Do what the model says: Do step one. Begin!

That's the important thing: Did you do step one? Did you actually do it? If you did, you're on your way to achieving your result. Now do step two. This entire discussion seems almost ridiculously obvious, but I am continually struck by how often people tend to focus on tangential issues of self-evaluation (Can I? Can't I? Am I doing it right or wrong?) rather than taking the action that gets the results. Do step three. Do step four. Do what the model tells you. It's not a matter of "Can you do it?" If you do it, you're doing it.

> *Expect nothing; be prepared for anything.*
> *Samurai saying*

Just follow instructions! This gets all the personal angst out of it. If you approach each action with the idea that it's going to make you great (or justify your existence), you'll get so tense that you can't act. It will become such a big deal in your mind that you will be effectively paralyzed from taking action. Instead, concentrate on taking action—step one, step two, step three. Act through from beginning to end. Focus on the model, and you stay objective.

Action is character, right? What a person does is what he is, not what he says.

Syd Field

Now, is this action going to prove that you are a more worthwhile human being or redeem your sins? No, nothing of the kind. It's just going to demonstrate that you can do step one—whatever that is. Does that make you better than anyone else? No, it just means you're getting closer to getting the result you want. Does it mean you're a worse human being if you don't do it? No, it just means you won't get the result associated with that series of steps. Don't take the whole thing personally; just get good information (from intuition and research), and follow through.

Another really obvious but often overlooked point is that a process is a series of steps. For example, if you want to start your own business, there is a series of steps you must take before your idea can become a reality. If you do step one really well and quit, you're not going to get the result. You must do all of the steps, and in appropriate sequence. To take a simple example, let's say the action you are taking involves expressing your feelings in a heartfelt letter. The last step of putting the stamp on the letter and dropping it in a mailbox, though almost inanely simple, is as important to the total process of communicating as the more involved steps of thinking about and actually writing the letter. It doesn't matter how many hours you spent thinking about the letter if you didn't write it. It doesn't matter how much effort you put into crafting a beautiful letter if you didn't send it. Follow step one, step two, step three. Don't skip any step, no matter how difficult or easy.

When you read the book, attend the seminar, or listen to the mentor, and you are told to do A, B, and C, go out and do A, B, and C. Get the result, and see how that feels. Do it again and again, and you may start to think there is nothing you can't learn, digest, and apply in action. If you can follow instructions, this is an incredible time to be alive. Today there is a wealth of organized information on virtually every subject.

If one source says to do it one way, and a second suggests another way, and a third offers still another way, feel your way to which is best. Most likely, a synthesis will be best. For this reason (the superiority of the synthesis), you should almost always (always when dealing with written material alone) seek out more than one source of information. A synthesis of several sources is helpful, but don't let confusion stop you from acting. Any one way is better than none. Act!

Whether you think you can or you can't— you are right.

Henry Ford

Keep At It

Think not so much of what thou hast not, as of what thou hast.

Marcus Aurelius

Don't worry about what you don't have; use what you do. This point is so important that it can't be overstated. Begin where you are. Act into your goals. When you are hiking cross-country, it is often necessary to get to the top of one hill or plateau before you can see the next peak. From the starting point, you couldn't have seen the peak that now stands before you. You had to get on the trail first. Always go as far as you can, and you'll find that you can always go farther. Moreover, the more invested you are in the outcome, the less likely you are to turn back when the going gets rough. Go to the highest peak you can, and see what you can see from there.

A journey of a thousand miles is many thousand steps.

*Don't wait.
The time will never be just right.*

Napoleon Hill

When we are stuck, it's simply because we can't see what to do next. Sometimes we can't see because we aren't looking, that is, we are looking at all that needs to be done instead of what needs to be done next. You can only take one step at a time. You don't look at a pizza and say, "I can't eat it; it's too big to fit into my mouth." You slice it into pieces and eat it one bite at a time. Go back to your model, see where you are in the process, and do the next step. If you start worrying that you will never get there, stop and look at your map (your model), and see how far you have come.

Have you ever asked yourself, What is worry? Isn't worry just the misuse of imagination? When we are exercising our imaginations properly, we are using them to go before us, to mentally see a way to do the things we want to do before we actually do them. When we are worrying, we are allowing our imaginations to picture negative results. Guard your imagination. Be careful of what you mentally associate with your goals.

Let's say that to achieve one of your goals you want to develop skill in public speaking. If, when you think of this goal, your imagination conjures up pictures of embarrassment or ridicule, you'll experience the associated feelings of pain. Out of self-protection, your subconscious mind will move you away from situations where you might experience the painful results you have envisioned. This puts you in a state of struggle; consciously you are trying to move forward (toward the action of public speaking); subconsciously you are moving away. Unite the subconscious imaginative energy with your conscious intention, and you magnify your capacity for constructive action. Our subconscious minds work on a kind of pleasure principle. They naturally move us toward pleasure and away from pain. If you hold only positive (pleasure-producing) pictures in association with your goals, you will move easily toward them.

Approach the moment with the idea that you're in the fight to the finish.

Iso Mataemon

If it seems that you can only associate negative pictures with your goals, it may be because you lack the information necessary to construct positive ones. Think of the children's game of making so many things (e.g., a tree, a house, a man) out of toothpicks. Certainly one can make more arrangements out of fifteen toothpicks than she can out of three, and more out of a hundred than fifteen. Think of each toothpick as a set of knowledge. We can, of course, be more or less creative with any number of toothpicks, but certain arrangements will be impossible with only a few. We might think a teacher cruel who instructed her young students to construct an elaborate barnyard scene complete with buildings and animals, but provided them with only a few toothpicks. Yet, if she gave them several boxes of toothpicks, we know they could do it. The more knowledge you have, the greater the opportunities for creative arrangements. If you are stuck, you may be asking your mind to build a picture without enough toothpicks. Get more information.

Again, you can't force yourself to move into a situation that you envision with negative (pain-producing) pictures. If you find yourself worrying or procrastinating, check your imagination. Make the change directly in your imagination or with the aid of new information. These really go hand in hand. Use both aspects of mind: the rational side to select the behaviors that are going to move you forward, and the imaginative side to associate these behaviors with positive (pleasure-producing) pictures. Hold only positive (pleasure-producing) pictures of the things you want, and you are sure to move into the actions that will bring them to you.

It is the greatest of all mistakes to do nothing because you can only do a little. Do what you can.

Sidney Smith

Value Progress; Or,
Those Beautiful Shades of Gray

Look at a Zen *suiboku* (ink-monochrome) painting. It has no color. Yet all subtlety and suggestion is there in the beautiful shades of gray. Space, depth, infinity itself appear in the beautiful shades of gray. There is a lesson here. We can learn to see and love the many shades of gray in our own lives. There are dangers to living in a world without gray—to viewing things in terms of sharp contrasts between black and white. On the one hand, we may whitewash the world and ourselves and miss important "darker" information that we need to be aware of. On the other hand, we may become submerged in a black pit from which we can see no light.

1. Whitewash: The Avoidance Factor. The black/white construction blocks our openness to feedback: feedback from life, feedback from others, even feedback from ourselves. If you need to have everything be all white, you may block out knowledge about yourself or about the things you're doing that aren't working. The rationale, if you can call it that, goes something like this: "If I allow myself to be aware of this personality fault or this ineffective way of doing things, it will mean that I am bad, inadequate, hopeless, or some such. If there are things about me or what I am doing that are imperfect, then I must be all wrong or all bad." Instead of seizing on important information they require to be more effective, people with the whitewash syndrome tend to avoid anything that they perceive as putting them in a dark light. They also dismiss unfavorable news from the marketing battlefield—information they may need to make shifts in strategy or tactics. If we live in a world where we always look good and never need to learn or grow, it will be a small world indeed.

2. Black Pit: The Baby-with-the-Bath Syndrome. Where the "whitewash" involves the tendency to avoid negative or unpleasant information, the "black pit" is the tendency to get overwhelmed by it. While in the "black pit," all seems black, as though one mistake or failure means one is forever doomed. One tends to fixate one's attention on the failure and block out all intelligent thought of course correction. In the black pit, one rejects and condemns oneself (I'm no good), the objective standard one had been striving to reach (I didn't really want to do it anyway), or the source of the feedback (It's not fair, they're wrong). In the black pit, one misses, not only the shades of white in the black, but also the idea that one might ever be capable of change. After all, black is black, and white is white. Even as falling and stumbling were a part of learning to walk, so, if we want to grow, we must embrace the process of becoming—one step at a time.

Clearly, we can see that we cannot steadily grow until we learn to see the beautiful shades of gray. Discriminate grays *and* appreciate the ground you've already walked on the journey toward your goals. Take an objective standard as your guiding light, and work steadily toward it. You may make mistakes; no doubt you will, but don't exaggerate their importance. Reject neither objective standards of excellence nor yourself in the process of learning. Instead, focus on your successes and the steps you can take toward further improvement. This gives you a sense of momentum, a forward thrust into your full creative expression.

What's Ahead in Act III

In **"Scene I: Taking It to the Street,"** you will have the opportunity to select an organizational form for your new career endeavor. You may choose to create your own business or nonprofit organization, work as a freelance, or land the right job for you.

"Scene II, Scenario I: Sailing the Entrepreneurship" is devoted to starting your own business. The entrepreneurial sector is the fastest growing part of the American economy. Today, an ever-increasing number of individuals are taking a shot at calling their own shots. "Sailing the Entrepreneurship" gives a brief overview of the challenges and opportunities that face today's new entrepreneurs. Detailed worksheets will help you plot out the basic framework of your new business. See empoweryou.com for additional online and book resources.

"Scene II, Scenario II: Wielding the Freelance" is designed for those who are looking for maximum freedom in their work environments and who are comfortable with a minimum of structure. Artists, musicians, craftspeople, consultants, and those with highly specialized technical skills, such as computer programmers, are often good candidates for the freelance option. It offers the greatest control over one's work, with the least bureaucratic and organizational hassle. This section focuses on the three essentials of any freelance business: marketing, negotiation, and administration. Since freelance businesses often require aggressive marketing, you will find a section designed to help you overcome self-marketing barriers. Also included is a section on designing and using promotional pieces and platforms.

In **"Scene II, Scenario III: Crafting the Nonprofit Foundation,"** you will explore some of the major advantages and disadvantages of starting a nonprofit corporation. Though in many ways similar to for-profit businesses, the nonprofit foundation presents some unique management challenges, including defining the purpose of the organization, agreeing upon effective strategies for achieving this purpose, determining objectives, making planning decisions, and measuring the success of your efforts. At the end of this section, you will find a helpful worksheet for clarifying your purpose, strategies, and primary objectives. You will learn how to fund your nonprofit corporation. If you are interested in starting a nonprofit, you'll find extensive links to online and book resources at empoweryou.com.

"Scene II, Scenario IV: Landing the Right Job" is designed to help you locate the organization and the position within the organization where you can best put your talents to work in the pursuit of your purpose. You'll have a chance to map out a job-hunting strategy, zeroing in on the organizations you want to work for and the people within them who have the power to hire you. This "scenario" will explore eight distinct strategies for landing interviews (the single most important key to getting the job you want) and present twenty-five techniques that you can use before, during, and after your interview to make sure it's a success. Again, you'll find extensive links to online and book resources at empoweryou.com.

"Scene III: Street Smarts" covers the essentials of networking, generating publicity for your work, writing grant proposals, and negotiation. With these tools at your command, you'll be ready to take it to the street.

Detour #3: The Availability Trap

The detour of availability comes into play when we look casually over the work landscape and decide that what we want is not available. You may find a little gold on the surface, but the rich veins are deep inside the earth. You have to dig to find them. So it is with putting yourself to work. You may find some opportunities on the surface, but you usually have to dig for the real treasures. The availability trap takes the form of "Can't Find It" or "Can't Make It," depending upon whether you want to work for an existing organization or start your own.

Can't Find It: If you can't find the job you are looking for (and are qualified for), there are only a few possibilities: it doesn't exist, you don't know how to find it, or you have given up too soon. While it's possible that the job you want really does not exist, it generally takes a good deal of research to be sure of that. Some people try a few places, decide it's impossible, and give up. Keep looking! The next thing that could keep you from finding a job is not knowing how to. The job search section should prove helpful. See empoweryou.com for links to a variety of additional online and book resources.

If you don't learn well from books or are confused by what you read, you may want professional assistance. The primary job-hunting skills are learning how to target organizations, land interviews, and succeed in the interview process. While the process is basically simple, there are hundreds of techniques that can help you improve your effectiveness. Keep looking and learning. Don't give up until you get what you want.

Can't Make It: If, after careful consideration, you have decided to create your own organization, don't let the "can't make it bug" get you down. "Can't Make It" takes two forms: "I haven't done it before," or "It hasn't been done before."

If it's been done, but not by you, other people's experience can help see you through. Go after it through books, classes, seminars, workshops, friends, and mentors. Aggressively seek out all you need to know. Assemble a capable team of people committed to the purpose and vision of your organization. Hire outside experts when you are stuck, but never, never give up.

If what you are considering has never been done before, the task ahead of you presents a great challenge. It takes a special kind of person to pull this off. You must be able to see your vision as clear as a bell and communicate it to people who don't see it so well. Even after the prototype's a hit, there will be doubters, but don't quit. All the while, you will be asking people to invest their time, energy, and money into something that doesn't yet exist. It's difficult, but not impossible, if your belief in your vision is unstoppable.

What to Look for in an Existing Organization

Shared Vision/Purpose: Choose an organization whose purpose matches yours, one that you can wholeheartedly and enthusiastically take responsibility for. This is the most important criteria for full involvement and satisfaction in your work.

Purpose-Focused Management: Purpose-focused management means that the leadership of the organization frames and makes important the question: What's right? They don't get bogged down in peripherals or in personality (Who's right?). Where the leadership of an organization is focused on peripherals and personalities, the atmosphere will be one of aimlessness and negativity. Where the leadership is focused on purpose, the entire work force comes to understand that it is their purposeful action that is rewarded and given attention. People's advancement within the organization is based upon their ability to advance the organization's goals, not upon personal favoritism or other considerations.

Encourages Full Participation of Its Employees: Choose an organization that encourages the full participation of its employees, an organization that wants thinking people. Select organizations that won't treat you as a body, or even as a cluster of skills. Choose one that wants your ideas, that gives you the freedom to do your work in the way that works best for you. This relates to the previous point. If an organization is purpose-based, then its interest is in getting quality work done. It doesn't get bogged down with rules and regulations for their own sake. You need to be able to control your work, to have authority that matches your responsibility and the freedom to innovate when you discover a better way.

An Emphasis on Ongoing Learning and Development: Choose an organization that emphasizes ongoing learning and development, both as an organization and for the people within the organization. Times change. Situations change. Successful organizations are able to adapt to changes because they make ongoing learning and development a part of their practice. They are able to capitalize on opportunities, take advantage of emerging trends, and ensure that they do not become obsolete or get left behind. Additionally, these kinds of organizations encourage and facilitate the development of their workforce. They help individuals to discover what they need to learn in order to be more effective, and they encourage them to learn it. They are concerned with the individual as a whole person and help him to understand what he must learn in order to advance.

Why Start Your Own Organization?

You have a vision. Your vision entails a genuine innovation. In other words, you want to do something that is currently going undone, or you see a better way of doing something that is already being done. Innovations come in all shapes and sizes. Your innovation may be a new idea or invention. It may be the application of an existing technology to a new area or purpose. Your innovation could be a combination of existing factors that you organize in a new way. Your innovation should be well thought out and tested. It must be clearly understood by yourself and the members of the team you assemble. An organization without vision and purpose is more likely to drown in runaround than endure in the long run.

You desire greater control than you can find within an existing organization. Entrepreneurial freedom may be something of a myth, but entrepreneurial control is a fact of life. You believe that you could do a better job as captain of your own ship than as first or second mate of someone else's. You want creative or managerial control that you can't get within an existing framework. You enjoy having the rewards for efforts directly tied to your performance and decisions.

You have or are ready to acquire management knowledge and experience. There is not much sense in starting an organization only to watch it fail. You, of course, want to succeed. Success will require effective management. Hit and miss is more often a miss than a hit. If you lack management knowledge and experience, you must be prepared to acquire or hire it.

You enjoy making decisions. As leader of your new organization, the ball will be in your court. You will bear the responsibility for and consequences of your decisions. You must not only enjoy making decisions, but you must make good ones. A combination of intuition and intelligent analysis generally yields the best results.

 It is only when the maker of things is a maker of things by vocation, and not merely holding down a job, that the price of things is approximate to their real value.
Ananda K. Coomaraswamy

The Power of Team Working

*Never doubt that a small group of thoughtful, committed citizens
can change the world. Indeed it is the only thing that ever has.*
Margaret Mead

Together: The Strength of a Common Purpose. Shared vision and purpose collect and focus energy. A team can draw upon the experience, talents, knowledge, skills, and contacts of all its members. They share in a common struggle and adventure that promotes endurance and gives meaning and purpose to their actions. Members of a team combine and share their spiritual and emotional strength. The example of one individual or segment of the team spurs others on to their best. Even peer pressure can have positive influence in enhancing individual and team performance. Committed team members develop strong relationships built on loyalty and trust. The mutual understanding, love, and respect they share provides the emotional support necessary to persevere in the face of great difficulties.

Each: Commitment to Team Motivates Each to Excel and Grow. The sense of shared vision and personal loyalty prompts each individual to go the extra mile—not only to continue beyond where he would normally give up, but to make excellence a consistent value. Within the environment of a supportive team, the individual feels safe to explore new ideas, test new skills, and try out new modes of self-expression. Individuals who have been members of teams involved in extremely difficult undertakings often discover within themselves more strength and ability than they ever knew they had. The group benefits from their efforts and they, as individuals, have tapped into a deep reservoir of strength and confidence that they will carry with them for the rest of their lives. Having been tested in the fire, these individuals are less likely to get rattled by the slings and arrows of outrageous fortune that attend life, generally.

Accomplishes: A Team Is Organized for Action. A well-organized team is an efficient vehicle for advancing an agreed-upon purpose through the achievement of definite objectives. It avoids the wastes of duplication of effort or misappropriation of resources. It organizes and divides labor so as to take full advantage of individual strengths and abilities. The shared goals of the team are measured and assessed by feedback systems that help to keep everyone moving in the same direction. A committed team develops a learning curve of experience. In the process of creating projects and meeting challenges, a team develops effective policies and standard operating procedures that enable it to handle recurring situations with maximum efficiency and ease. A team may even evolve effective ways of dealing with entirely new situations in an optimal manner.

More: The Whole Is Greater Than the Sum of Its Parts. A committed team has, as well as the efficiency of planned action, the indefinable power of synergistic action. As a team develops its own rhythm and harmony, it moves beyond mere rational thought into a realm of intuitive group action. Things happen that never could have been planned or predicted. The dynamic force released when divergent energies become focused around common objectives is truly awesome in its power to generate ideas, attract opportunities, and execute action. Team works!

Taking It to the Street: Choosing Your Marketing Strategy

Take time to deliberate; but when the time for action arrives, stop thinking and go in.

Andrew Jackson

The purpose of this section is to help you select the way (or ways) you intend to market yourself and your work. It begins with a general discussion of marketing. Whether you intend to start your own business, go freelance, get a job, or create a nonprofit organization, you may find it valuable to review this section. Immediately following Scene I, each of these four marketing scenarios will be explored in greater depth. In this section, each of these (along with their advantages and disadvantages) is briefly sketched. You'll also find some questions and checklists to help you decide which of these options is best for you.

Zen and the Art of Marketing

The purpose of the discussion that follows is to consider something like a Zen of marketing. Traditional marketing functions and variables will be considered from this perspective. A good deal of attention will be paid to cultivating the attitudes that will favor success in your marketing efforts. Indicated in the subheadings below are the marketing variables relevant to each section. These are the product, the package, the price, the promotion, and the delivery.

Marketing Is a Fact of Life: The Product

As Robert Louis Stevenson said, "Everybody lives by selling something." Even the Buddhist monk going door to door with his begging bowl is selling a blessing and a chance to accrue karmic benefit by giving alms. The chart below is overly simple, but makes the point—no matter what you choose to do, you are going to be selling something. Of course, you will be selling *yourself* in any case, yet if you choose to work at a job, you (your passion and abilities) are all you will be selling.

For reasons that are rather self-evident, marketing has traditionally been important to entrepreneurs and freelancers. Yet recent trends in the job market and in the nonprofit sector have made marketing increasingly important for folks who work in these areas as well. In the old days, it was not uncommon for an individual to hold a job for twenty or thirty years. Most men—and in those days, most of the workforce was made up of men—looked forward to retiring from the company they began working for while in their twenties or thirties. They might have had two or three jobs in their entire lives. Developing a streetwise marketing sense was not as important for them as it is for today's working women and men.

In today's shifting economy, everyone is self-employed. Today, people have more *careers* in the course of their lives than they had *jobs* thirty years ago. Competition is fierce, and knowledge of effective self-marketing (or job-hunting) techniques can mean the difference between getting what you want and settling for less. Even if you plan on working for large, existing organizations for the rest of your life, you had better know a good deal about self-marketing.

Some years ago, nonprofits were relatively isolated from the demands of the marketplace. Today the situation has changed. Declining private contributions and cutbacks in federal and state grants and programs have forced many nonprofits to come up with new ways of garnering financial support, including cooperative ventures with the corporate sector and profit-making ventures under the nonprofit umbrella. Many nonprofits are selling subscriptions to newsletters or magazines or putting out catalogues of books and merchandise. Some contract out services for profit. Many have become extremely sophisticated in using direct mail and telemarketing techniques. If they want to give their organizations a fighting chance, today's nonprofit managers require an understanding of effective marketing techniques.

The Product: What Are You Selling, Anyway?

Business	Freelance	Nonprofit	Job
a product or service, an organization, and you	creative work or service, and you	a message, an organization, and you	you (your passion and abilities)

The underlying point of this entire discussion is simply this—no matter which way you go, you are going to be marketing something. Accepting this as a fact of life makes it easier to deal with. Be clear on what you are selling.

Marketing Is a Matter of Image and Perception: The Package

Everyone knows that a business, let's say a bank, that is *perceived* as being in trouble (even when it isn't) soon becomes so *in fact*. Wall Street is notorious for its reliance on perception. A company can be "hot," selling at an inflated price one month—and bottom out the next. Global and national economies rise and fall, to a great extent, on the basis of perception. Terms like "consumer confidence" and "investor confidence" reflect the economic power of perception. Perceptions of economic strength or weakness affect practical decisions, which, in turn, affect still more perceptions and practical decisions. Nowhere in the marketplace can we altogether separate perception from fact. Even at the level of the individual seeking a job, the person currently employed typically has an easier time finding the next job than one who is unemployed. This, again, is a matter of the perception of success.

Nothing succeeds like the appearance of success.
Christopher Lasch

Part of the sense of falseness or charade in the world of business comes from the fact that everyone is trying to project success. It isn't just business. Politicians, hospitals, universities, and all kinds of nonprofits are in on the act; and as you know, when you look for a job, you are in on it too.

Many people find the perception game and the need to constantly project success a bit nauseating and dishonest. Yet the truth is, most people don't see you; they see what

you project. They see your image. You really can't judge a book by its cover—but most people do. Studies have shown that people size you up and form a first (and somewhat lasting) impression in the first thirty seconds.[1] The same is true of the product or message you are promoting. People will judge these on the basis of what they (and you) look like before they ever find out what the product can do or what the point of your message is.

Effective marketing requires that we play the image game. Honesty and integrity demand that we have confidence in what we are selling—confidence in its value and confidence that it can deliver what we say it can. Part of the repulsion many have to playing the image (marketing) game is the fact that so much worthless junk is hyped from morning till night over radio and television. Yet if you have confidence in the value of what you are selling—be it a product, a service, a creative work, a message, or your own talent and energy—and you don't make the effort to create and project the appropriate image, you risk doing a disservice to these. You wouldn't present a diamond ring in a smelly old sock. A beautiful package or wrapping is appropriate to a beautiful gift, and a strong image can enhance the perceived and even the real value of what you are selling.

Below are a few image variables. Some appeal to the right brain; some, to the left brain. We can think of a continuum running from, say, aloof to folksy, or from traditional to "hot," and so on. Consider what image works best for you, based on what you are selling, who you are selling it to, and what you feel comfortable with.

Left-Brain	Right-Brain
Respectable	Friendly
Traditional	"Hot"
Stable	Cutting Edge
Established	Growing
Aloof (snobbish)	Folksy

Marketing Is a Matter of Negotiation: The Price

You must determine a fair price for what you are selling. For example, if you are seeking a job, your price is your salary. We'll consider the specifics of negotiation as it relates to the various marketing strategies as we come to them. You'll also find a general discussion of negotiating principles in the "Street Smarts" section. I mention it here to alert you to the fact that it is a critical marketing variable.

Marketing Is a Matter of Personality: The Promotion, Part I

In his autobiography, philosopher and Zen writer Alan Watts wrote that "no one can succeed as an independent author, or as a teacher or minister [let alone a businesswoman or man], without a flair for drama and for coming on strongly as a personality, and by success I mean, not only financial reward, but also effective communication."[2] It's not true that nice guys always finish last—but it's certainly true that weak personalities do.

On the other hand, as Watts points out, "Strength of personality—even though you know very well that it is a big act—is always taken for an 'ego-trip.'"[3] Many of us, certainly most from the middle and lower classes, were taught to downplay ourselves and our strengths. Those of us who do project ourselves in a strong and dynamic way risk being labeled "egomaniacs" or worse. Part of the reaction comes from the violation of the norm itself, a kind of "shame on you." Part of it is jealousy. After all, it is easy to see that those who project themselves well are having fun doing it. Those who feel constrained by the norm from getting in on the fun often resent those who enjoy expressing themselves. The more repressed project an attitude of "Who do you think *you* are?" onto the less inhibited. The implication is that if you were someone else— say, someone rich, famous, or powerful—this behavior would be acceptable.

Everyone on this earth is wearing an ego or persona mask of some kind and, in some way or another, projecting through it. Watts points out that the "enlightened ones" he knew all projected strong personalities. Look at the images of the Zen masters scattered throughout these pages—strong personality comes through every one. Modern-day saints like Gandhi, Schweitzer, and Mother Teresa all had strong personalities. Incidentally, these three were extremely effective promoters (or marketers) of their beliefs. All wrote books and toured the world speaking on behalf of their causes.

Where, then, do we get the idea that projecting a strong personality is "unspiritual"? Much of the popular religion in the West teaches false humility, a sort of psychological self-flagellation. We have been taught that a weak, self-deprecating personality is good (acceptable) and a strong personality is bad (threatening). Putting oneself down or hiding in the crowd is not humility. Humility comes of itself when we have no desire to be better than anyone else. When we let go of this craving, we simultaneously let go of the shame of being worse than anyone. We realize that at the deepest levels, we are no better, no worse, and no different.

The only difference between a wise man and a fool is that the wise man knows he's playing.
Fritz Perls

We all are on an "ego trip," journeying through time and space, projecting to one another through personality masks—egos. The so-called "enlightened ones" realize that this "ego trip" is going nowhere, has of itself no particular point or purpose, but is rather more like theater-in-the-round. They put on their masks, play in the theater, go on the ego trip—remaining all the while at home, perfectly at rest within themselves. The point of the drama *is* the drama, the expression of Infinite Compassion and Bliss in a seemingly endless variety of forms. As Shakespeare said, "The play's the thing."

Projecting a strong personality—essential to marketing success in any arena—is no more or less egotistical than projecting a weak one. Whatever the image portrayed on it, a mask *is* a mask. The kid wearing the Alfred E. Neuman mask on Halloween night is in costume as much as the kid wearing the superhero mask.

Zen would say a strong persona and a weak persona are equally fictitious. Neither is any better or worse than the other. Buddhism, however, does give the notion of *upaya,* or "skillful means." If you want your marketing efforts to succeed, adopting a strong, dynamic personality is the skillful choice. This doesn't mean that you will fail if you don't. It just means that any other choice is likely to bring added frustration and struggle and would therefore be a less skillful choice. One does not use a cross-country ski for waterskiing, or a weak personality for marketing. Whether we are taking a job interview or advocating a particular cause, promoting a business or book, a strong personality helps.

No matter which marketing strategy you choose, you will find a number of ways of marketing yourself within Act III. All require a strong personality to gain maximum benefit from them. If you don't already have a strong personality, you may want to work on developing one—or, more accurately, on letting it out. Everyone has a little ham in him or her. Ham it up, toot your own horn. Just remember that it is all, as Alan Watts says, a "big act."

Marketing Is a Matter of Circulation—The Promotion, Part II

A strong personality is essential because, without it, you'll probably have a hard time getting into circulation. Circulation is the name of the game in marketing—getting into and staying in circulation. Getting out and meeting people is circulating. Targeted networking is circulating. Circulating

brochures, circulating direct-mail pieces, making the talk-show rounds, speaking tours—all types of advertising and publicity expand your circulation. Think of what you are selling and how you can increase its circulation. The means you employ will vary, depending on what you are selling, but the principle of circulation applies across the board. When you come to the marketing party, be ready to circulate.

Our word *circulation* comes from a Latin root meaning "to form a circle."[4] View your marketing strength in terms of the circles you have formed and the circles you intend to form: circles of friends, circles of acquaintances, circles of contacts, circles of sales or job leads, circles of clients or customers, circles of investors, circles of like-minded individuals. Make a graphic representation of these, perhaps on a poster board. Maintaining and expanding these circles opens doors to new opportunities. *Remember, the wealth of the universe comes to you through people. No matter what kind of work you do, you are in the people business.*

To make more sales, inform more people of your cause, or create more or better job opportunities—increase your circulation. There are many ways of doing this. What's best for you will depend on your situation. I've included specific information within each of the four marketing "scenarios" that follow. You'll also find information on networking and generating publicity in the "Street Smarts" section of Act III. I encourage you to think about the best ways for you to increase your circulation.

Marketing Is a Matter of Organization: "The Delivery"

In what kind of organizational structure do you want to perform your work? Below, we'll explore the advantages and disadvantages of four broad organizational settings: starting your own business, working freelance, founding a nonprofit organization, and getting a job working for an existing organization.

Scenario I:
Sailing the Entrepreneurship

If you're a self-reliant, self-motivated person who enjoys taking responsibility and making decisions, starting your own business may be your next step. Do you have an idea for a new product or service that you can't wait to take to market? Have you thought of a genuine innovation on an existing product or service? Ideas like these are often the first steps to creating a successful business. The entrepreneur must be passionately committed to her vision and willing to take risks to make it happen. She must be resourceful and able to motivate others—a take-charge kind of person who enjoys challenge and hard work.

Advantages: Starting your own business offers you the freedom to control and market your product or service as you see fit. You enjoy the responsibilities of being your own boss, creating a crack team, and deciding who gets to play. You are able to use your talents to come up with a new and innovative approach to your product or service, and you reap the financial profits that result from your efforts.

Disadvantages: If your business fails, you may be held liable for some or all of its debts (see page 377). The success or failure of your new endeavor is all in your hands—including all the management and financial hassles. Running your own business usually entails very long hours and lots of hard work, especially in the beginning.

Scenario II:
Wielding the Freelance

If freedom, flexibility, and creative control over your work are strong values for you, you may want to consider working as a freelance. Many writers, craftsmen, musicians, and artists of all kinds find a freelance structure the most conducive to creative work. It takes a self-disciplined, passionate, and committed person to make it as a freelance. You must believe in yourself and your work enough to survive some rejection, especially in the beginning stages. If you do, you will enjoy the freedom to live your life as you see fit, while building a successful career doing what you enjoy most.

Advantages: The freelance option offers the most freedom to create and control your work. You choose your own hours and work environments. This option also tends to minimize the hassles you'll get from others, since a freelance often spends much of her working time alone. You are free to capitalize on your talents and abilities in the way you see fit.

Disadvantages: Your income as a freelance may be unstable, especially in the beginning. You may have to contend with long periods of reduced income or unemployment. You will not have the security of benefits or retirement plans. Also, the freelance option offers less opportunity for teamwork and the feedback of others on a daily basis.

Therefore the considerations of the intelligent always include both benefit and harm. As they consider benefit, their work can expand; as they consider harm, their troubles can be resolved.
                                                           Sun Tzu

Scenario III: Crafting the Nonprofit Foundation

If you are committed to working on a particular social, cultural, or environmental issue, you may want to consider founding a nonprofit organization. Building a successful nonprofit organization can be an exciting challenge. It takes vision, creativity, resourcefulness, and strong "people skills." Since nonprofits are cause-driven organizations, formed to benefit others, they provide excellent opportunities for meaningful and rewarding work.

Advantages: Nonprofits often attract committed people who are dedicated to social or cultural change. Working together with those who share a common altruistic purpose offers unparalleled opportunities to experience genuine teamwork and cooperation in the workplace. Creating a nonprofit allows you to follow your purpose-based agenda and to craft solutions for issues that matter to you. You can solicit contributions and enjoy the tax advantages and increased credibility that accrues to nonprofits. People will know that you're not just "in it for the buck."

Disadvantages: You'll put in a lot of time and effort, without making a lot of money (at least in the beginning). You will probably endure some frustration with the apparent insignificance of your efforts. There are lots of rules and regs in the nonprofit sector—you may have to climb a mountain of paperwork to get anything done. You will need to go through the hassle of getting most of your actions approved by your board of directors.

Scenario IV: Landing the Right Job

If you enjoy working in a structured environment and being a team player, if security and stability are important factors in your work life—you are sure to find some challenging opportunities in the job market, provided you are willing to aggressively look until you do.

Advantages: You will enjoy opportunities for advancement within the organization as you "learn the ropes," and you may get a chance to benefit from the training and skill of fellow employees. You'll get a secure paycheck (which definitely makes it easier to budget), and you may get medical and retirement benefits as well.

Disadvantages: You'll have to subordinate a measure of your freedom to the needs of the organization. You'll have to follow someone else's schedule and, usually, answer to a boss. You may not have much input in the decision-making process involved with your work. You may have to do things that are counter to your purposes or values in order to keep your job.

Note: The pages that follow outline in greater detail the four options of creating your own business, wielding the freelance, creating a nonprofit organization, and getting a job. This will help you get a clearer sense of what avenues are best suited to you at this time.

Success on any major scale requires you to accept responsibility . . . In the final analysis, the one quality that all successful people have . . . is the ability to take on responsibility.
Michael Korda

Getting Organized: Which Way to Go

In considering which of the four options you would like to pursue at this time, the questions that follow may be of assistance to you. Examine the four sets of statements below. If the statement fits you, check "Yes." If it does not, answer "No." Answer as honestly and objectively as possible. See scoring instructions on page 357.

Scenario I—Entrepreneurs

Y/N

1. Having the freedom to create my own work is extremely important to me. _____

2. When I have an idea that I'm excited about, I get everybody around me excited about it too. _____

3. I enjoy aggressively going after what I want. _____

4. When I take on a project, I'm practically married to it until it's done. _____

5. I trust my instincts, and I am able to act decisively. _____

6. I thrive on challenge. _____

7. It's okay with me if people think I'm a little crazy, as long as I believe in what I'm doing. _____

8. I'd say that a natural ability to lead is one of my strongest talents. _____

9. I am prepared to work more than forty hours a week. _____

10. I never let it stop me if I don't know how to do something. I just jump in the middle of it, and pretty soon, I've got it figured out. _____

Scenario II—Freelancers

Y/N

1. The freedom to follow my creative instincts is extremely important to me. _____

2. I do my work because I enjoy it. I'd probably do it whether I was getting paid or not. _____

3. I enjoy working alone—in fact, I thrive on solitude. _____

4. If I'm doing what I love best, I can easily adjust to fluctuations in income. _____

5. It's very important to me to live by my own schedule. _____

6. I have little patience for bureaucracy and red tape. _____

7. I make most of my business decisions intuitively, independent of the feedback of others. _____

8. I don't want to be tied down to any one location. _____

9. I'd say that I possess a good deal of self-discipline. _____

10. I don't want the responsibility or the hassle of managing an organization. _____

The difficulty in life is the choice.
George Moore

Scenario III—Nonprofit Founders

1. Although I am a strong leader, I enjoy teamwork and cooperative decision making.   Y/N _____

2. I am able to work cooperatively with a board of directors, staff, and volunteers in order to accomplish my organization's objectives.   _____

3. Economic profit is not as important to me as working at something I believe in.   _____

4. I have the willingness and the patience to put up with a lot of red tape.   _____

5. I am able to work effectively with a variety of viewpoints and agendas while sticking to my organization's purpose and long-term goals.   _____

6. Making a difference for others is a very strong value for me.   _____

7. I enjoy finding creative ways to fund my organization, and I am willing to do so indefinitely.   _____

8. I am able to delegate responsibility in order to accomplish a variety of tasks.   _____

9. I enjoy getting people motivated around an idea.   _____

10. I am willing to speak out in public for my beliefs and for my organization, and to attract media and community attention when necessary to accomplish my goals.   _____

Scenario IV—Job Seekers

1. The only way I can do my work is as an employee of an existing organization.   Y/N _____

2. I believe there are organizations already in existence where I could pursue my work purpose in alignment with the company's objectives.   _____

3. I like the predictability of a large organization—its policies and opportunities for advancement.   _____

4. I believe I could benefit from the training and experience that I would receive by working at a job in my field.   _____

5. I do not want to enter into any kind of financial venture that might threaten my ability to maintain my present standard of living.   _____

6. I do my best work as a member of a team.   _____

7. One of my strongest talents is an ability to be reliable and consistent.   _____

8. I like work in which my responsibilities are clearly spelled out for me.   _____

9. I want to create a steady, reliable income to support myself while I am training for my chosen field.   _____

10. I like to leave work at work. I try to keep my work life and my personal life separate.   _____

Now check over your answers, and tally up the number of "Yes" responses in each scenario. If most of your "Yes" answers were in the first scenario, you may prefer to create your own business now or later. If you had more "Yes" responses in the second scenario, you may want to try working as a freelance. If most of your "Yes" answers were in the third scenario, you may want to begin your own nonprofit organization. If you had more "Yes" answers in the fourth scenario, you will probably want to work for an organization that fits your goals.

Personality/Organizational Match

Qualities Important for Individuals Who Want to
Start Their Own Business

1. Self-reliant
2. Self-motivated
3. Committed
4. Persuasive
5. Decisive
6. Adventurous
7. Able to motivate others
8. Risk-takers
9. Innovative
10. Quick learners

Qualities Important for Freelancers

1. Creative
2. Intuitive
3. Like to work alone
4. Flexible
5. Independent
6. Self-disciplined
7. Respond well to change
8. Ability to create and market their work
9. Prefer unstructured work environments
10. Acknowledge their own efforts

Qualities Important for Individuals Who Want to
Start Nonprofit Organizations

1. Service-oriented
2. Committed
3. Resourceful
4. Persistent
5. Team players
6. Passionate
7. Patient
8. Good at both long- and short-term planning
9. Focused
10. Tolerant

Qualities Important for Individuals Who Want to
Work within Existing Organizations

1. Reliable
2. Cooperative
3. Cautious
4. Analytical
5. Well organized
6. Objective
7. Other-directed
8. Preference for structure
9. Responsive to feedback
10. Steady

Blessed is he who has found his work. Let him ask no other blessing.

Thomas Carlyle

Your Organization:
To Find It or to Found It

It is a good idea to decide at the outset whether you want to work for yourself or someone else. If you choose to work for someone else, plan on developing your job-hunting skills, not simply as an obligatory nuisance for landing your next job, but as part of a long-term strategy for achieving your life's work. If you plan to work for yourself, start perfecting the entrepreneurial skills you'll need over the course of your work life. It helps in either case to see the development of these skills as part of a long-term process for improving career effectiveness.

The chart on the following page depicts various types of organizational structures and compares them on four key variables: *Independence*, *Structure*, *Benefits*, and *Rewards/Performance Measure*. *Independence* refers to the individual's ability to choose her hours, the kind and quantity of work he will do, the setting that the work is done in, etc. *Structure* refers to the extent to which the organization has formal organizational structure, rules, regulations, policies, etc. *Benefits* refers to those extra-income remunerations, such as sick leave, paid vacations, health care, life insurance, pension plans, vacation, travel, etc. *Rewards/Performance Measure* (R.P.M.), refers to the degree to which the rewards one experiences (be they monetary or others) are related to their efforts.

Note: The relative rankings given each of the organizational categories are general composite ratings. For particular organizations within the categories, different circumstances may apply. Obviously, for this chart to be entirely accurate, it would have to consider these variables for each organization individually. Take these ratings, then, as general guides to broad organizational categories. You will want to research these variables (and others that are important to you) for specific organizations you are considering.

Man finds the meaning of his human existence in his capacity for decision, in his freedom of choice. It is a dreadful freedom, for it also means responsibility, but without it man would be as nothing.

Will Herberg

Organizational Comparison Chart

	Type of Organization	✓	Primary Market Skill Group	Independence	Structure	Benefits	R.P.M.
Create Your Team	Sole Proprietorship		Entrepreneurial Skills	◆◆◆◆◆	◆	◆	◆◆◆◆◆
	Partnership		Entrepreneurial Skills	◆◆◆◆	◆◆	◆	◆◆◆◆
	Corporation		Entrepreneurial Skills	◆◆◆◆	◆◆◆	◆◆	◆◆◆◆
	Nonprofit Corporation		Entrepreneurial Skills	◆◆◆	◆◆◆	◆◆	◆◆◆
	Franchise		Entrepreneurial Skills	◆◆	◆◆◆◆	◆◆◆	◆◆◆◆
Find Your Team	**Commercial Sector**						
	Large		Job-Hunting Skills	◆◆	◆◆◆◆◆	◆◆◆◆	◆◆
	Medium		Job-Hunting Skills	◆◆	◆◆◆◆	◆◆◆	◆◆◆
	Small		Job-Hunting Skills	◆◆◆	◆◆◆	◆◆	◆◆◆
	Public Sector						
	Local		Job-Hunting Skills	◆◆	◆◆◆	◆◆◆	◆◆
	State		Job-Hunting Skills	◆	◆◆◆◆	◆◆◆◆	◆
	National		Job-Hunting Skills	◆	◆◆◆◆◆	◆◆◆◆	◆
	Nonprofit Sector						
	Nonprofit Corporation		Job-Hunting Skills	◆◆◆	◆◆◆	◆◆◆◆	◆◆

Final Selection: _____

Starting Your Own Organization

1. **Sole Proprietorship:** One individual owns and operates the business and has unlimited personal liability for taxes, debts, and legal damages in case of a lawsuit.

2. **Partnership:** Two or more individuals own and operate the business, dividing all profits and dividing the personal responsibility for all taxes, debts, and legal damages in case of a lawsuit. A general partner(s) may take on a limited partner who does not participate in the business operations, but who may invest money in the business and has only limited liability for the business, up to the amount of money he invests.

3. **Corporation:** A corporation is a legal entity that pays taxes and is liable for its own debts and legal damages, apart from the people who own and operate it.

4. **Nonprofit Corporation:** A nonprofit corporation is a legal entity, subject to state and federal laws. Some are tax-exempt.

5. **Franchise:** A franchise is typically a business that is owned by an individual, but operated as a part of a large chain, with standardized products, services, advertising, trademarks, store appearance, etc.

Working for an Existing Organization

Commercial/Private Sector: A business that is privately (as opposed to governmentally) owned and run for a profit.

1. **Large:** A business with over 2,000 employees.
2. **Medium:** A business with 500 to 2,000 employees.
3. **Small:** A business with less than 500 employees.

Public Sector: An organization that is owned and run by the government.

1. **Local:** An organization run by the city or county government.
2. **State:** An organization run by the state government.
3. **National:** An organization run by the federal government.

Nonprofit Corporation: See point 4 above.

Your Life's Work: Step by Step

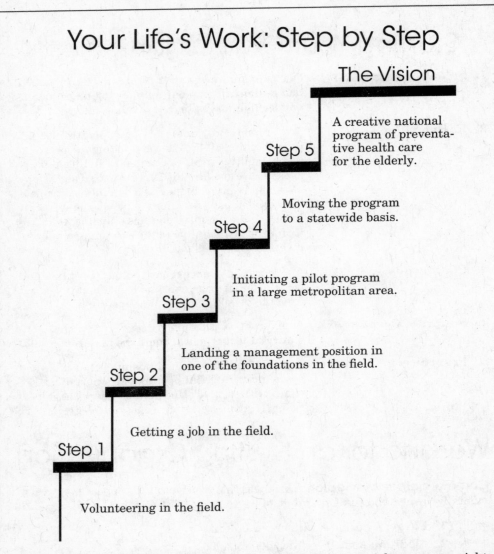

The Vision

A creative national program of preventative health care for the elderly.

Step 5

Moving the program to a statewide basis.

Step 4

Initiating a pilot program in a large metropolitan area.

Step 3

Landing a management position in one of the foundations in the field.

Step 2

Getting a job in the field.

Step 1

Volunteering in the field.

If you decide that your optimal life's work is too much for you right now, you might start with interim steps and work your way up to it. Let's say your vision involves a creative approach to health care for the elderly, which you want to introduce on a nationwide basis. Interim-step 1 might be familiarizing yourself in the field through volunteer work. Interim-step 2 might be getting a job working for what you consider to be a state-of-the-art organization in your field. For interim-step 3, you might take a management position in one of the leading foundations in your field. Interim-step 4 might be starting a pilot program in a large metropolitan city. Interim-step 5 might be expanding your program to encompass an entire state. Not giving up, you work on the intermediate steps, while keeping your eye on your optimal vision.

Social Change and Organizations

Individuals and organizations are both creators and products of the society in which they operate. Even as the already existing house you move into is probably not the house you would design from scratch, so the society you are born into is probably not your idea of utopia. In an already existing society or house, you must acknowledge the structural limitations of the existing framework. You can redecorate, remodel, add on, adapt, or even abandon the structure. Still, you must in some way reckon with things as they are, even while you are creating changes.

If one does not confront the fact that he is a creator of society, he risks alienation, boredom, and emptiness. On the other hand, if one does not confront the fact that he is a product of society, he risks getting clobbered by it. As a practical matter, we have to deal with many aspects of society that may not be to our liking. For example, like it or not, we live in a money economy. This has far-reaching consequences, many of which the individual cannot directly control. As for organizations, those of any size frequently require other people's money to start and maintain themselves. Little money comes without strings attached. The goals and values of the organization will be influenced to a greater or lesser extent by those from whom it receives money.

> *Who gives the bread lays down the law.*
> *Spanish Proverb*

Efforts to effect (social or technological) change always face the tension between the need to enlist the support of the status quo and the danger of being co-opted by it. Here is the dilemma that all who would innovate must face: on the one hand, to remain true to one's ideals and, on the other hand, to be "relatable" enough to the mainstream that one can have an impact on it. One does not want to be so extreme that he has no influence, nor so relatable that he has nothing new to offer. It helps to have either an intuitive or a cultivated understanding of the existing psycho-techno-culture and its likely evolutionary directions.

For those interested in social change, it is important to realize that the more fundamental the social change your organization proposes, the less likely it is to adopt values that will make it effective within the context of the mainstream culture. To be an effective agent of social change, you have to be in the middle of the field; yet to get in the middle of it, you have to adopt many values of the larger society. There are no easy answers to these problems. Every organization must strike its own balance. The question is really: What are the essentials to cling to, and what are more peripheral matters you can yield on?

The larger your organization becomes, the more likely it is to become like what already exists. In our culture, we tend to think bigger is better. Yet when it comes to social change, bigger is not necessarily more effective. Margaret Mead has remarked, "Never doubt that a small group of thoughtful, committed citizens can change the world. Indeed, it's the only thing that ever has." The analysis of historian Michael H. Hart in *The 100: A Ranking of the Most Influential Persons in History*[5] seems to confirm this observation. Five of his top ten most influential persons made their mark as individuals, not as members or leaders of any groups. These were inventors, explorers, and theorists. The other five were spiritual leaders. Only three of the ten, Muhammad, Buddha, and St. Paul, could be said to be leaders of large organizations, and each of these began with a handful of followers.

More important than the size of a group is its dedication, or commitment, to purpose. As Louis Ginzberg has put it, "There is no great thought that has become an impelling power in history which has not been espoused at its origin by men [or women] willing to put all their physical and spiritual powers entirely at its service." This is the kind of commitment that catches fire. We tend to forget that political changes like the American Revolution, technological changes like the personal computer, and social changes like the abolition of slavery or women's suffrage began with a relatively few dedicated individuals.

While an organization is relatively small, it can create its own subculture. The larger it gets, the more heavily it becomes influenced by the broader society, and so the more like that society it becomes. The artist often faces the choice between going commercial, i.e., appealing to a wider audience, or developing in such a way that her work is appreciated only by an esoteric few. Similarly, an organization, in moving to a larger size, may risk the very principles and ideals upon which it was founded. This is simply because, as it grows, it becomes increasingly plugged into what already exists. Dynamic organizations tend over time to become sluggish. They tend to lose their original purpose, not to mention spark, and become self-perpetuating bureaucracies.

Walking the line between the ideals that give birth to an organization and the values of the existing psycho-culture affects decisions at every point in the development of an organization. For example, take a business. When it comes to product development, the creator holds certain values with reference to the quality of the product and the need it is intended to serve. Additionally, there are considerations as to how widely the product will sell. These values are often in conflict. Soul searching and thought must be ongoing.

Sailing the Entrepreneurship

Perfect freedom is reserved for the man who lives by his own work and in that work does what he wants to do.
R. G. Collingwood

There is a perception among some that business—any kind of business—is by definition immoral, materialistic, and otherwise "uncool." This conception is probably a holdover from the sixties, when the term "business" came to be synonymous with "selling out." Of course, this is far too simplistic. Many engage in business without selling out, and many more sell out without becoming entrepreneurs. If we accept that "selling out" means forsaking one's integrity and convictions for some apparent short-term gain, it is easy to see that there are many ways to sell out quite apart from business. This section examines the benefits of the entrepreneurial option, and what it takes to play in this game. Those who decide this is the right option will find a ten-step business builder with which to begin laying out the foundations of their new businesses.

A true definition of an entre-preneur comes closer to: A poet, visionary, or packager of social change.
                    Robert Schwartz

To be sure, the business world *does* provide plenty of opportunities for "character tests." Yet when the character of the businessperson fails, the fault lies, not with business per se, but with the individual's own greed, thirst for power, inhumanity, or any of a number of other personality flaws. Business may exaggerate existing flaws, but it does not create them. If your heart is true and your principles solid, you needn't worry that business will corrupt you. In a sense, you are already "in business."

When we get right down to it, business or "commerce" means "trade." Of course, you can trade fairly, or you can cheat. You can trade quality goods or shoddy goods. You can trade good service or poor service. You just can't get away from trading. The products we need and enjoy come to us by way of trade, from food and clothing to shelter and entertainment. Everyone who works for someone else is in the business of trading his time, effort, and abilities for money. Yet the entrepreneur exercises far greater control than the employee over what his business does, how it treats its staff and customers, and the role that it plays in the community. Many today are seeking the greater opportunities for service, creativity, and control that going into business for themselves offers.

In fact, the small business sector is the most dynamic and fastest growing sector of the American economy. Small business has been responsible for creating more than two-thirds of the new jobs in America over the last three decades. More than seven hundred thousand new businesses are started each year. Two-thirds of the new businesses are owned by women. Clearly,

from the standpoint of economic growth, small business is where the action is. In the words of noted management consultant Peter Drucker, "The old job creators [e.g., Fortune 500 companies] have actually *lost* jobs in these last twenty years." Drucker concludes that most of the "new jobs must have been created by . . . small and medium-sized businesses, and a great many of them, if not the majority, *new* businesses that did not even exist twenty years ago."[1]

What is motivating all of these people to start their own businesses? For many, opening their own business means a chance to escape the conventional nine-to-five job rut. In *Re-inventing the Corporation*, John Naisbitt writes, **"The unspoken factor behind the entrepreneurial boom is that working for most companies is so demeaning to the human spirit that many talented people are forced out the door.** The only way to have a nurturing work environment, they reason, is to create it themselves" [bold type in original].[2]

In *Growing a Business*, Paul Hawken concurs, "This movement toward new enterprise must reflect a certain amount of alienation of the work force from the conditions of their jobs."[3] People who strike out on their own often find working for themselves to be more rewarding and meaningful than the jobs they left behind.

While some few may be motivated by simple greed, most of today's new entrepreneurs have more interesting reasons for setting up shop. Small business owners enjoy the satisfaction of offering products and services they genuinely believe in. They enjoy shaping their business to reflect their social and personal values, setting a tone or atmosphere for their work life that they feel comfortable with. They enjoy making the decisions about the direction of their business and seeing the results of their efforts.

They enjoy the creative opportunities to experiment, to try out new ideas without needing bureaucratic approval. These people are working to be themselves, not to fit into some giant bureaucracy or to gain the approval of a boss. In addition to providing valuable services, an increasing number of today's new entrepreneurs donate some portion of their profits to charities or causes they believe in. Given all these reasons (and others there isn't space to discuss), it is not surprising that job satisfaction surveys consistently find that the self-employed are the most likely of any group to report that they are *very happy* in their work.

In the marketplace, new small businesses often have advantages over the larger, well-established corporate institutions. Think of the difference between a fleet of giant luxury liners and a speedboat. When it comes to making a change, the smaller, more maneuverable speedboat has the edge. Like a speedboat, a small business can easily maneuver around the huge corporate boats. It doesn't require the deep waters of enormous capital investment necessary to launch the giant corporate fleets. It can play in the shallow waters of innovation. Consequently, small businesses often discover and develop ideas that larger corporations won't even touch until there is a "proven market."

While the huge corporations battle it out for the deep water of proven markets, small business is creating new ones close to the shore. From this special vantage point, the entrepreneur can feel the pulse of the people and respond more quickly to their special needs, aspirations, and concerns. Large corporations seldom lead the way to innovation, as a General Electric vice president observed: "I know of no original product invention, not even electric shavers or heating pads, made by any of the giant laboratories or corporations . . . The record of the giants is one of moving in, buying out, and absorbing the small creators."[4]

Time and again, small business has brought innovation and invention. Many a small business has begun as a response to a particular need that was going unmet. The creative entrepreneur recognizes a need in the community or nation that others miss, or she sees a way to serve a well-recognized need in a new or innovative way. Sometimes a small business begins when an individual desires a product or service that no one is providing. She says in effect, "Wouldn't it be great if there was . . . ?" And then she goes on to provide that product or service for others to enjoy.

Today's new entrepreneurs are no stuffed shirts; they are dynamic social innovators living exciting lives on the cutting edge of social and technological transformation. Below you'll find a list of qualities that make a New Entrepreneur. See if they fit you. (Much of the material in the freelance section that follows [page 391] will apply to the start-up entrepreneur.)

What Makes a New Entrepreneur

Sensitivity   To perceive what is needed.

Creativity   To conceive of a way of providing it.

Courage   To try something new, perhaps even something no one has tried before.

Initiative   To act and act and act.

Grit   To stick with it when all the people who don't have the above qualities tell you it can't be done.

Taking It All Home: A Look at Home Business

More and more people are discovering the home-based business as an effective alternative to the traditional nine-to-five job. In fact, not since the days of the cottage industries that helped launch the Industrial Revolution in the late eighteenth and early nineteenth centuries has such a large portion of the population worked from home in nonagrarian activities. According to the U.S. Small Business Administration, one in twelve American households has a home-based business within it. While exact figures are hard to come by, some estimates have put the total number of home businesses at over thirty million. Each day, more than 8,500 new ones are born—about one every ten seconds. Over half of all small businesses (53 percent) are home-based businesses. *Entrepreneur* magazine estimates that home-based businesses generate over $400 billion each year. Home-based businesses are not just an important and growing part of our economy; they also can be quite profitable. According to International Data Corporation, a leading market research firm, income from home-based business averages over $63,000 per year, with twenty thousand home businesses having annual incomes of over a million dollars.

In addition to significant income potential, working at home offers a variety of attractive features that are fueling this boom. First, overhead expenses (and, therefore, capital risks) are low. This undoubtedly helps to account for the much higher success rate that home-based businesses enjoy when compared to other kinds of small business. Fully 85 percent of nonhome small businesses will be out of business within three years of opening up shop. On the other hand, 85 percent of home-based businesses will still be going strong three years after they are born.[5]

When you work at home, you do away with the daily commute. Rush hours and traffic jams and the stress and wasted time that go with them become a thing of the past. The rigidity of the time clock and the absurdity of office politics fade into distant memory. When you work at home, you can structure your work life to harmonize with your own natural energy cycles. You dress in a way that suits you rather than your employer. Most importantly, you can build a life around your most cherished values and take advantage of your real talents and strengths. What's more, many people find that working at home affords them the opportunity to spend more time with the people they love.

When you work at home, you get to be your own boss; but then, of course, you have to be the boss. Without the pressures of a time clock or the physical presence of a supervisor, you are free to work at your own pace in accord with your natural rhythms. You are also free to procrastinate or avoid working altogether. It's easy to spend too much time reading newspapers or magazines, to turn on the television, putter in the garden, yack away on the telephone, surf the Internet, or otherwise avoid getting down to work. On the other hand, if you are a workaholic who can't seem to "call it a day" after eight or ten hours at the office, you might find your life getting even more out of balance when home *is* the office.

In addition to a structured work environment, jobs typically provide opportunities for social interaction. When you leave behind the traditional nine-to-five work setting to work at home, you will probably also be leaving behind a significant part of your social life. Many new to working at home are surprised at the loneliness and isolation they feel after the initial excitement of starting out on their own wears off.

While working at home can add comfort and convenience to your work routine, it can also confound it with interruptions and distractions. The same features that make working at home so appealing—freedom, flexibility, independence, and increased family contact—can limit your effectiveness when not carefully planned for. Below are some tips for making a success of your at-home business:

How to Make Working at Home Work

1. Minimize Your Risk: Every new business venture entails an element of risk. Put the odds in your favor by devoting ample time and attention to planning before you launch your new home business. While you may not need a formal business plan, you should address yourself to each of the elements that comprise one (see page 371). It's usually best to begin in a field you already know. Taking advantage of the expertise and networks you have already developed is less risky than plunging headlong into a brand-new field. If you do want to try your hand at something entirely new, you may want to reduce the financial pressure by holding on to your current job. Work part-time at your new home business. Then, when your home business really starts taking off, you can let go of your regular job. Many people begin planning for a new home business when they suspect their jobs might be in jeopardy or when they feel burned out in their current positions. This allows them to ease into the new venture before it becomes an urgent necessity to do so.

2. Schedule Your Work: Make a daily schedule and stick to it. Determine the number of hours you need to work each week, and schedule your time accordingly. If you are a night owl (and your kind of work allows it), schedule your work for late evenings. If you are an early bird, begin your day at the crack of dawn, and call it quits by mid-afternoon. If your business involves working on long projects, break them up into smaller units and assign intermediate deadlines for each. Trying to cram at the end is no way to run a business, and it isn't worth the added stress. A schedule serves not only as a prod to the would-be procrastinator but also as a balancing tool for the workaholic. Many successful home business owners find it useful to set appointments with themselves for exercise, family outings, community involvement, and so on. Balance work with time for play and fun. Of course, you can and should be flexible with your schedule, altering it with the ups and downs of your workload and adjusting it as your business grows and evolves. It's all right to deviate from your schedule from time to time. Just make sure you have one!

3. Designate a Place for Your Business: If at all possible, designate an entire room (with a door that closes) as the site for your home business. Closing the door will help filter out sounds from pets, children, the garbage disposal, and so on. It also reinforces the feeling that you are now in your "work mode" and should not be interrupted or disturbed. This not only sends a message to members of your family but, just as importantly, helps keep *you* focused. What's more, it closes off your work when it's time to walk away from it. A separate outside entrance is ideal if you will be receiving clients in your home office. Check with the city or county for local zoning ordinances. These may impose limitations on foot traffic, parking, the number of employees you can have working in your home at any given time, and so on.

Make sure you have a comfortable chair and a roomy desk—these items are *not* the place to cut corners. Equip your home office with the technology you need: computers, printers, additional phone lines, fax machines, and so on. Also, be sure to check out the tax laws for home office deductions. You may qualify for some significant tax breaks.

4. Pay Attention to Your Image: Just because you work at home is no reason to have anything less than a professional image. For example, make sure all the written materials representing your business (stationery, business cards, brochures, etc.) are high quality and attractive (see page 396). Similarly, written correspondences with clients should be well written, neat, and free of typos. Have checks printed with your business name and logo.

Where once others in the business community tended to look with suspicion at those working from home, the sheer number of people doing business this way today is rapidly eliminating this prejudice. Nevertheless, you may want to project the illusion of having an outside office or of being a larger organization than you really are. Certainly you will want at least one phone line designated exclusively to your business. Instruct children not to answer this phone. Equip your primary business line with voice mail; its popularity in the corporate world means those calling will have no idea you are at home (or that you are changing diapers) while their call is coming in. You might want to use a mailbox service for your correspondence. This can give your stationery a downtown street address and "suite number." It's also a good idea to create your own Web site (see page 400).

For most home businesses, the telephone is the primary sales tool. Some people find it helpful to get dressed as though they were going to work in a corporate office before they make their calls. It helps put them in a confident and down-to-business mode. If you bring clients to your home office, keep it clean and professional in appearance. If you don't have a separate entrance to your office, make sure your house is neat and presentable and that your clients won't be tripping over children's toys on their way to closing a deal.

5. Build and Strengthen Your Networks: Networking is especially important for the home-based businessperson (see page 457). It gives you an inexpensive way to develop contacts for your business, while helping to alleviate the sense of isolation that can come with spending so much time alone at home. You may want to join leads clubs, service clubs, or trade groups or to volunteer in your community. You might even want to start a networking group of your own.

6. Join Trade Associations: Whatever your specific field, if there is a "National Association for_____"—join it! There are also a number of trade associations that address the needs of home-based business owners in a more generic fashion. These generally publish newsletters and provide seminars and other educational resources of interest to the home-based business person. Some lobby Congress for legislative changes to benefit home-based and small businesses.

Membership in a home-based business trade association can give you the buying clout of a large organization. With a trade association membership (some cost as little as $50 annually), you can get discounts in a number of areas, including business and personal insurance, financial services (tax and legal assistance, investment opportunities, and the ability to accept credit cards from your customers), communications (long-distance rates, Internet service, etc.), and a diverse variety of products and services (travel, car rentals, business products, copying services, etc.).

Working at home provides real opportunities for generating a strong income while creating a balanced and healthy lifestyle. With careful planning, a little ingenuity, and determined effort, the freedom, flexibility, and profitability of a home-based business can be yours.

 There's no substitute for hard work.
Thomas Edison

The Ten-Step Business Builder

What follows on the next several pages is a ten-step formula that will help you begin to sharpen your vision of your new business. While this process should not be confused with a formal business plan (see page 385), completing it will begin to put your new business into focus and give you a good idea of what it will take to get it started. Many have found this to be an extremely valuable exercise.

Step 1. Outline your business: Decide on the products and/or services your new business will offer. What benefits will others derive from these products or services? How will they use them? What are the unique features of your product or service? Who will be your major competitors, and how will you distinguish yourself from them?

Step 2. Know your market: Zero in on exactly who your potential clients or customers are. Define your market by demographics, geography, and lifestyle interests.

Step 3. Determine how to reach your market: Next, determine how you will reach your market. In what ways will you advertise and promote your business? Will you advertise in newspapers or use direct-mail marketing? How will you deliver your products or services? For example, will you establish a retail store or work from a home office?

Step 4. Assemble a team: Will you have employees? If so, at what levels of responsibility? What qualities and skills will you want from them? What outside professionals will you want on your team (for example, lawyers, accountants, advertising agencies, and so on)?

Step 5. Decide on a legal structure: Determine what kind of legal entity your business will be. Will it be a sole proprietorship, partnership, or corporation?

Step 6. Determine the cost of doing business: Next, assess the onetime costs associated with the start-up of your business as well as its regular monthly operating expenses.

Step 7. Raise money: Develop strategies for obtaining the necessary financial resources to launch your business and keep it afloat through the difficult early years. Will you be looking for loans, partners, or equity investors?

Step 8. Establish a system to monitor your dough: Determine how you will keep track of your money. What inventory, accounting, or bookkeeping procedures will you employ?

Step 9. Cut through the red tape jungle: Make sure that your new business will be on solid legal footing with all the appropriate government regulatory and tax agencies.

Step 10. Concentrate your energy and resources: Finally, consider how you see your business growing over the years. What specific objectives would you like to accomplish in the first year? In the first three years? And so on.

Step One: Outline Your Business

1. What products or services do you want to offer?_____
    _____

2. What benefits do your products or services offer?_____
    _____

3. How will your product or service be used?_____
    _____

4. When (from the customer's point of view) will the product or service be used?
    _____
    _____

5. What unique features can you bring to the design, delivery, or marketing of
    this product or service?_____
    _____

6. Who will be your major competition?_____
    _____

7. What are their strengths?_____
    _____

8. What are their weaknesses?_____
    _____

9. How will you distinguish yourself from the competition?
    _____
    _____

10. If a product, will you manufacture it yourself? How? Will you buy ready-made
    products from suppliers? Who? Where?_____
    _____
    _____

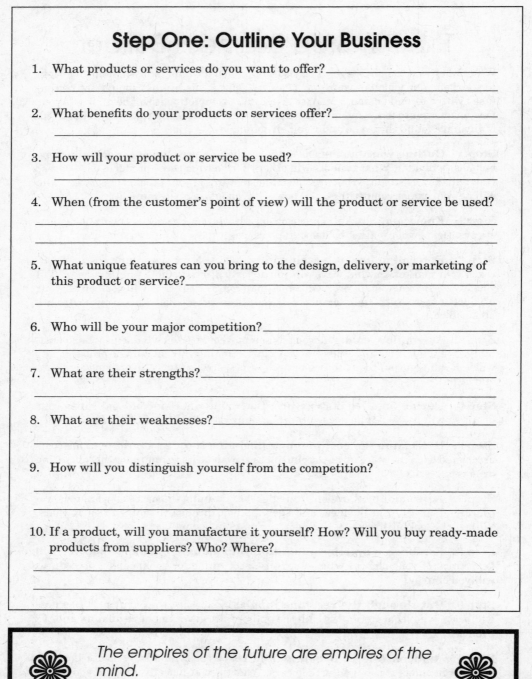

The empires of the future are empires of the mind.

Winston Churchill

Step Two: Know Your Market

Who Is Your Market?

Identify potential buyers of your product or service according to the following criteria:

Demographics

Age	_____	Ethnicity	_____
Sex	_____	Family size	_____
Socioeconomic level	_____	Marital status	_____
Education	_____	Profession	_____
Religion	_____	Income	_____

Geography

Neighborhoods	_____	Regional	_____
Segments of cities	_____	Multistate	_____
Citywide	_____	Nationwide	_____
Countywide	_____	Multinational	_____
Segments of states	_____	Global	_____
Statewide	_____	By climate	_____
Bicoastal	_____	By terrain	_____

Lifestyle

Activities	_____	Interests	_____
Values	_____	Opinions	_____

Using the variables above (or any others pertinent to your ends), identify your market.

_____

_____

_____

_____

_____

_____

_____

 The difference between intelligence and education is this: Intelligence will make you a good living.
Charles Kettering

Step Three:
Determine How to Reach Your Market

Promotion: How will you get the attention of your market? Check the applicable methods:

_____ Word of mouth	_____ Flyers
_____ Newspapers	_____ Brochures
_____ Magazines	_____ Promotional speeches
_____ Television	_____ Demonstrations
_____ Radio	_____ Introductory seminars
_____ Trade publications	_____ Writing books and
_____ Outside advertising	publications
(signs, billboards, etc.)	_____ Direct mail
_____ Trade shows	_____ Telephone directories
_____ Publicity	_____ Internet

Delivery: How will you distribute your product or service to the market? Check the applicable methods:

_____ Retail	_____ Trade shows
_____ Wholesale	_____ Field sales force
_____ Mail order	_____ Manufacturing representatives
_____ Multilevel marketing	_____ Independent agents
_____ Franchising	_____ Sell to manufacturer
_____ Telemarketing	_____ Web site

 A wise man will make more opportunities than he finds.

Francis Bacon

Step Four: Assemble a Team

Put together a team of committed, competent people who agree on the purpose of the organization. Listed below are important qualities to look for in building your team.

Management Team

1. Agreement on purpose
2. Complementary skills
3. Complementary personalities
4. Highly motivated/dedicated
5. Willing to risk getting less in the beginning for more in the end

Professional Support Team

1. Credibility
2. Professional standing
3. Personal rapport
4. Prestige in the community
5. Support for your objectives

Staff Team

1. Able to cooperate
2. Self-reliant
3. Positive
4. Growth-oriented
5. Willing to work long hours

In your view, what is important that members of your team understand to be the purpose of your organization?

_____
_____
_____
_____

What undeveloped skills can you compensate for by having an individual on your team who is strong in that area?

_____
_____
_____
_____

Your associates can be priceless.
Napoleon Hill

What weaknesses in your personality can you compensate for by having an individual on your team who is strong in that area?

_____
_____
_____

What is it about the concept and purpose of your organization that will attract highly dedicated individuals?

_____
_____
_____

What is it that you can offer the people on your team that will entice them to want to give their all (e.g., the opportunity to make a significant contribution, challenge, training and skill development, a financial stake in the organization, the opportunity to work with the very best, camaraderie, etc.)?

_____
_____
_____
_____

What will be the initial size of your team?

_____

How many individuals will you require at each of the following levels?

_____Ownership   _____Supervisory   _____Management   _____Workers

Professional Support Team

Identify the following:

Accountant: _____
Advertising Agent: _____
Attorney: _____
Banker: _____
Business Consultant: _____
Insurance Agent: _____
Other: _____

Step Five: Decide on a Legal Structure

1. Sole Proprietorship

Pros: You have total control over it. Simple and very easy to start. Doesn't need to be registered with the state.

Cons: Personal liability. Limits access to capital.

2. Partnership

Pros: Simple, relatively easy to start. Doesn't need to be registered with the state. (You will probably want a partnership agreement prepared by an attorney.) Greater access to capital than with a sole proprietorship.

Cons: You are personally liable and may be vulnerable to lawsuits. A partnership usually terminates when one of the partners dies. Potential for conflict. (Don't start a partnership unless you really know and trust the individual[s] involved.)

3. Corporation

Pros: Limited liability for debts, taxes, and litigation. Continuous existence.

Cons: More difficult to start. Many corporate actions must be formalized by the board of directors. Legal fees involved. Must be registered with the state.

Investigate further; then determine the type of legal structure you would like to use.

My legal structure: _____

_____

_____

_____

_____

_____

Note: Be advised that tax consequences of the various legal structures are significant and should play a role in your decision. See a certified public accountant for up-to-date details.

 Our greatest glory is not in never falling, but in rising every time we fall.

Confucius

Step Six: Determine the Cost of Doing Business

Onetime Start-up Costs

Equipment	_____
Furnishings	_____
Renovations	_____
Licenses, permits, fees	_____
Professional services	_____
Start-up inventory	_____
Rent prepayments	_____
Insurance prepayments	_____
Special advertising or promotion	_____
Printing stationery, forms, etc.	_____
Utility deposits and installation	_____
Start-up cash	_____
Other_____	_____
Other_____	_____
Other_____	_____
Total	_____

Monthly Operating Costs

Rent	_____	Postage and freight	_____
Utilities	_____	Insurance	_____
Advertising/promotion	_____	Loan payments	_____
Professional fees	_____	Monthly payments	_____
Wage/salaries	_____	Bad debts	_____
Employee benefits	_____	Transportation	_____
Taxes	_____	Printing	_____
Inventory	_____	Other_____	_____
Supplies	_____	Other_____	_____
		Total	_____

Experience is the best of school masters, only the school fees are heavy.

Thomas Carlyle

Step Seven: Raise Money

Where to Get the Money

1. Start on a shoestring and slowly build.
2. Acquire a business on a no-cash basis.
3. Friends and family
4. Banks
5. Savings and loans companies
6. The SBA (Small Business Administration)
7. Venture capitalists
8. Silent partnerships
9. Organize a syndication
10. Small business investment corporations
11. State development commissions
12. Credit unions
13. Investment consultants (can help you find investors)
14. Suppliers (can give you credit)
15. Foundations

Approaching Potential Investors

The first step to approaching potential investors is to decide what kind of investment you want: a security-based investment, an equity-based investment, or a purpose-based investment. Your process will vary according to the avenues you choose.

Security-based Investments: A security-based investment is essentially a loan. The prime consideration for this type of lender is security. Your task is to demonstrate that loaning you money is a safe proposition. Do this by convincing them that:

1. Your venture is based on solid planning, will be well managed, and has a high probability of success; in other words, that it makes economic sense. Be well prepared. Go with your business plan in hand, and make sure that all of the marketing and financial projections are realistic and solid. Bring along other important financial data, for example, recent balance sheets, profit/loss statements, etc.

2. You have sufficient collateral in case the unforeseen occurs. Some common security-based investors include: banks, savings and loans, credit unions, thrifts, small business investment corporations, friends and family. (Be clear and be careful!)

Equity-based Investments: Equity-based investors want a piece of the action. They become part owners of your business, for example, as general or limited partners, or corporate shareholders. The equity investor incurs greater risk than the debt investor, with the prospect of realizing greater profit when the business succeeds. Understand their point of view. First convince them, if you honestly can, that they have little or nothing to lose. Then convince them how much they have to gain. (Again, approach with a realistic and well-prepared business plan.) Your task with the equity investor is to convince him that your idea is viable, marketable, and will realize sizable profits for him. Some examples are: venture capitalists, silent partnerships, syndications, small business investment corporations, friends, and family. (Be clear and be careful!)

Purpose-based Investments: Private foundations, public agencies, and individual philanthropists invest in projects that reflect their purposes, values, and objectives. These investments can take the form of no-strings grants, low-interest loans, free services, or other assistance. Some organizations and individuals will invest directly in a profit-making business without giving prime consideration to either security or equity. Others will only invest in a charitable or nonprofit enterprise. You may still be able to obtain monies from these investors by gaining the sponsorship of a nonprofit organization that receives the money on your behalf. They then pass the money along to you for a nominal service charge. Your primary task is to convince these investors that what you are planning to do furthers their purpose-based investment objectives and that your organization is a credible and responsible one that will reflect well on them. Foundations, individual philanthropists, the SBA (Small Business Administration), state development commissions, and a host of other government agencies are potential sources. Additional sources might include churches, universities, friends, and family.

Now indicate the funding vehicles you plan to employ: _____

_____

_____

_____

_____

_____

_____

_____

_____

_____

Whom will you approach?	By when?
_____	_____
_____	_____
_____	_____
_____	_____
_____	_____
_____	_____
_____	_____

Step Eight:
Establish a System to Monitor Your Dough

You may want to purchase a small-business accounting software program (e.g., Quicken Home and Business or QuickBooks) or subscribe to one online. Similar programs (such as GnuCash) can be downloaded for free. Most of these programs are relatively easy to learn and operate. As your business grows, specialized editions will help you handle virtually any conceivable record-keeping issue. When you're first starting your business, an even simpler system for keeping track of your money will work fine for a time. It is listed below (adapted from *The Small Time Operator* by Bernard Kamoroff).[6]

1. Open a business bank account.

2. Deposit all of your business income. That way you'll know exactly how much money you're taking in.

3. Pay all bills by check. That way you'll have a record of all your expenditures.

4. Never use the business account for anything else. That way you'll be able to keep track of your business income and expenditures.

5. Decide whether you want to use a cash or accrual accounting system. If you use a cash accounting system, you record income when you receive payments and expenditures when you make payments. In an accrual accounting system, you record income and expenses at the time of the transaction, whether or not money has physically changed hands. Though a cash accounting system is simpler, the accrual system gives you a more complete picture of your finances. See an accountant for advice on your accounting system.

Additional Financial Sources

201 Great Ideas for Your Small Business, Revised and Updated. Jane Applegate. Princeton: Bloomberg Press, 2002.

Keeping the Books: Basic Recordkeeping and Accounting for the Successful Small Business. Linda Pinson. New York: Kaplan Business, 2007.

Pratt's Guide to Private Equity and Venture Capital Sources. Boston: Venture Economics. Updated regularly.

Raising Venture Capital for the Serious Entrepreneur. Dermot Berkery. New York: McGraw-Hill, 2007.

The Small Time Operator. Bernard Kamoroff. Laytonville, Calif.: Bell Springs, 2008.

Working for Yourself: Law & Taxes for Independent Contractors, Freelancers & Consultants. Stephen Fishman. Berkeley: Nolo Press, updated regularly.

Step Nine: Cut Through the Red-Tape Jungle

There may be a red-tape jungle separating you from what you want to do. Think of it as an obstacle course, set up to test the intensity of your desire and your willingness to go the extra mile to make your work happen. Here are just a few of the red-tape items you may want to consider.

Business Identity: Almost without exception, you will need to obtain a business license from the city and/or county in which you intend to run your organization. You will need to file for an Employer ID number or Tax ID number from the IRS in order to open a bank account for your organization. Articles of Incorporation will need to be filed for profit and nonprofit corporations. You will need to file a fictitious name statement if you call your business by a name other than your own surname. After completing the necessary research, indicate the red-tape obstacles you need to overcome to establish your business identity. _____

_____

_____

Regulations: You will need to check with your city, county, state, and federal governments to make certain that your organization complies with all of their regulations. Some of these may include: zoning regulations, building codes, health codes, land-use restrictions, and special licenses and permits that are unique to the product or service you are providing. After completing the necessary research, indicate the steps you need to take to ensure that you are in compliance with all pertinent laws and regulations.

_____

_____

Taxes: Consult a tax accountant and make sure that you are aware of and pay all necessary local, state, and federal taxes. These include, but are not limited to: income tax, self-employment tax, sales tax, property tax, payroll tax, federal unemployment tax, state unemployment tax, Social Security, federal excise taxes, etc. After completing the necessary research, indicate the red-tape obstacles you need to overcome to ensure that you are paying all relevant taxes and paying no more than your fair share. _____

_____

_____

   The art of living is more like wrestling than dancing.
Marcus Aurelius

Insurance: Consult an independent professional insurance consultant who will go over with you what insurance coverage is mandatory and what is highly advisable for your particular needs. Armed with this information, you are then ready to approach an insurance agent to purchase the insurance you need. After completing the necessary research, indicate the steps you need to take to ensure that you are properly insured. _____

_____

_____

_____

_____

Employees: As soon as you hire your first employee (or in the case of a corporation, if you are an employee), you geometrically increase the amount of red tape you will need to wade through. Some areas to be aware of include: Social Security Tax and Federal Income Tax Withholding, payroll tax, State and Federal Unemployment Tax, Workman's Compensation Insurance, Federal OSHA (Occupational Safety and Health Act of 1970) record-keeping requirements, as well as pension plans, welfare plans, Federal Wage and Hour Laws, and fair employment practices. Once again, I urge you to seek the help of a qualified professional in determining how best to meet these requirements. After completing the necessary research, indicate the steps you need to take to ensure that you are complying with all existing laws and regulations with regard to employees. _____

_____

_____

_____

_____

Miscellaneous Red Tape: Include any additional action steps necessary to be on top of any red-tape requirements not listed above. _____

_____

_____

_____

_____

The entrepreneur is essentially a visualizer and an actualizer. He can visualize something, and when he visualizes it he sees exactly how to make it happen.

Robert Schwartz

Step Ten:
Concentrate Your Energy and Resources

Grow at a pace you're comfortable with. Seize opportunities while operating from a solid base. Understand that there are advantages to starting small. It allows you to perfect your product or service and your delivery systems before you try to market them on a wide scale. Determine realistic growth projections for the next five years.

Where I want my business to be in one year: _____
_____
_____
_____

Where I want my business to be in two years: _____
_____
_____
_____

Where I want my business to be in three years: _____
_____
_____
_____

Where I want my business to be in four years: _____
_____
_____
_____

Where I want my business to be in five years: _____
_____
_____
_____

Web and Book Resources

Find out more about starting your own business
@ Empoweryou.com.

Create a Business Plan

Why Do You Need a Business Plan?

1. A business plan helps you clarify the exact nature of your business and how you plan to develop it. It is a road map from where you are now to where you want to be—in business. It helps you mark out your objectives and stay on course as you move toward them.
2. A business plan is a tool to attract investors. Your well-thought-out business plan can stimulate potential investors to provide you with the seed money you may need to launch your business.

What Is in a Business Plan?

While business plans vary in format, the four parts below are basic to all.

Summary: The first part of a business plan summarizes the three parts that are to follow, namely the business (operations), the marketing plan, and relevant financial data. It gives the reader "the plan in a capsule."

The Business: This section describes your business operations, including the goods and/or services you will provide, the legal entity (sole proprietorship, partnership, corporation, etc.), the management team, (including resumes of the key players), your staffing plan, your professional support team, the physical facilities of your business, the process and procedures by which your business will run, and an overall scheme of your goals and objectives.

The Market: This section contains your marketing plan, the most essential part of your business plan. Your marketing plan will include a description of the market (what's out there) and your place in it, observable trends in the market, forecasts for the future, and the specific individuals, groups, or organizations that you intend to sell to (your target markets). Additionally, you will describe pricing policies, sales terms, customer service policies, methods of sales and distribution, advertising and promotional strategies, and all other relevant marketing data.

Finances: This section includes a budget for implementing the plans you have made in your business and marketing sections. It details where you expect to get your money from, how much you expect to make, where the proceeds of your business will go, and how much your business would need to make in order to break even. This section will also include a proposal to your investors: what you want from them, what they can expect to gain, and exactly where they would fit into your plans.

Writing Your Business Plan

Read a good book (or two) on writing a business plan (preferably, one with examples of successful plans) before you attempt to write one yourself. You may want to seek the help of professional business consultants, lawyers, tax accountants, and market research firms in the preparation of your plan. If you can't afford professional assistance, contact the Service Corps of Retired Executives (SCORE) via their Web site (www.score.org). While it is helpful to consult experts, I recommend that you do the bulk of the work yourself. That way you will get the full value out of your plan, both as a road map for action and as an investment tool. The effort you put into making your business plan the best it can be will pay off both when you approach potential investors and when you finally get down to business.

 To climb steep hills requires a slow pace at first.
Shakespeare

Self-Employment and the Jeffersonian Ideal

America at its inception—Hamilton and Jefferson debate the future of the new nation. Hamilton wants an urban country with a strong centralized government, a sort of aristocracy of the merchant class. Jefferson wants a land of independent farmers. The farmers would control property and, with it, the means of subsistence. They would be free of the need to sell their labor for wages. Their political strength would come from their economic independence. Of course, our country has evolved along the Hamiltonian model. We are an urban nation with a strong central government. While as late as 1900, 60 percent of the nation's population were living an agrarian lifestyle, today less than 3 percent are independent farmers.

Yesterday's independent farmer has hired himself out to earn his keep and buy his consumer goods. Today his wife is selling her services as well. The landholding farmer is already quaint history in the developed world and is becoming rarer and rarer in the undeveloped world in its rush to modernize. Today's closest facsimile to the Jeffersonian free man is the self-employed individual. Of course, he (or she—today most new businesses are started by women) still has to deal with bureaucratic red tape, but he is free to choose his work and make the decisions that affect it.

When men and women are asked to indicate the career roles they find most attractive, they come up with very different choices—except, that is, for the number one position. Both men and women choose working for themselves as the most attractive career option. Apparently, this is with good reason. In a recent Gallup poll, 58 percent of all people who work for themselves reported that they are "very happy" in their work, while only 35 percent of those who work for others gave a similar response.

Still, it would be wrong to think of self-employment as a panacea or an escape from discipline. To give up the discipline of the time clock is to assume the discipline of capital acquisition, of government red tape, of client needs, of operational expenses, of management. To escape the trials of having a boss is to embrace the trials of being a boss, or of experimenting with cooperative management styles.

It would probably be a mistake to think of self-employment as working for oneself. One is working for clients or customers, for the government, for the bank, for the respect and acceptance of the community. Much of the freedom of self-employment is theoretical. Theoretically, the self-employed person can choose not to show up for work, but in all likelihood he will be working harder and longer than when he was employed by others. Only if his business is very small or very large can he expect greater leisure time. While the self-employed person may not enjoy a great deal more free time, he does have a great deal more control over his destiny. He controls the purpose, objectives, and performance of his company. With control comes the responsibility for making decisions and for enjoying their consequences. In other words, the freedom to live life as you choose.

Over 200 Businesses You Can Start with Little or No Money

Below is a list of ideas for starting businesses or freelance operations with little or no money. Many are ideas for interim ways of making money while you train and prepare for the work you truly want to do. Some have long-term career potential.

1. Abstract or technical writing
2. Ad agency
3. Aerobic instructor
4. Air-conditioning and heating repair services
5. Aquarium service
6. Astrologer
7. Auctioneer
8. Auto detailing
9. Bed-and-breakfast reservation service
10. Bicycle repair and sales
11. Bicycle touring
12. Blind and drapery cleaning
13. Boat maintenance
14. Boat painting
15. Bridal consulting
16. Burglar alarm sales and installation
17. Business consulting
18. Janitorial services
19. Cake delivery
20. Car alarm installer
21. Care of horses and other animals
22. Care of the disabled
23. Care of the elderly
24. Caricaturist
25. Carpet cleaning
26. Cartoon map publishing
27. Catering truck
28. Catering
29. CD, DVD, and cassette duplicating
30. Child care
31. Child-care referral and consulting
32. Children's party planning
33. Chimney sweep
34. Christmas tree lot
35. Clown
36. Coaching services
37. Collection agency
38. College campus tours
39. Commercial freelance writing
40. Companion to the elderly or disabled
41. Computer consultant
42. Computer data retrieval service
43. Computer repair
44. Consignment store
45. Consumer research and protection service
46. Cooking classes
47. Costume sales and rental
48. Corporate coach
49. Courier service
50. Crafts businesses
51. Custom sewing and alterations
52. Dance instructor
53. Dating service
54. Desktop publishing service
55. Dog grooming
56. Dog training
57. Dog-walking service
58. Drafting and blueprint making
59. Drywaller

60. eBay sales or store
61. Editing and proofreading service
62. Errand service
63. Etiquette training
64. Event planning
65. Faux and decorative painting
66. *Feng Shui* consulting
67. Financial planning services
68. Finder's fee service
69. First aid instructor
70. Flea market sales
71. Flower stands
72. Foreign language instruction
73. Fundraising consultant
74. Furniture refinishing
75. Furniture repair
76. Garage sale organizer
77. Gardening and lawn care
78. Gift basket maker
79. Glass tinters
80. Grant-writing consultant
81. Graphic design services
82. Greeting card sending service
83. Gutter cleaning
84. Handyman referral service
85. Handyman
86. Herb farming
87. Holiday decorating, commercial and residential
88. Home inspection service
89. Housecleaning
90. House painting
91. Ice-cream truck
92. Image consultant
93. Import products
94. In-home child care and day care
95. In-home electronics assembly
96. Indexing
97. Information and research services
98. Information brokering
99. Interior decorating
100. Internet consulting services
101. Jewelry design
102. Jewelry repair
103. Juggler
104. Karaoke DJ
105. Knife sharpening
106. Landscaping
107. Limo service
108. Literary agent
109. Loan consultant
110. Local tours (walking, bike, car)
111. Lunch delivery service
112. Mail order
113. Manicurist
114. Marketing consultant
115. Massage therapy
116. Meal delivery
117. Medical claims processing service
118. Meeting planner
119. Message answering service
120. Message delivery (bike)
121. Mime
122. Mobile disc jockey
123. Mobile dog grooming
124. Mobile hair-cutting service
125. Mobile home repair
126. Mobile locksmith service
127. Mobile tune-up service
128. Mobile television and appliance repair
129. Mobile window-screen repair
130. Monogramming service
131. Mover service
132. Multilevel marketing
133. Musical instructor
134. Musical instrument maker
135. Musician

136. Nanny placement service
137. Newsletters
138. Novelty sign rental
139. Novelty telegrams
140. Organizational consultant
141. Outdoor guide
142. Outdoor maintenance
143. Packaging and shipping store
144. Party services
145. Personal cook
146. Personal trainer
147. Pest removal
148. Pet grooming
149. Pet-sitting
150. Pet taxi service
151. Piano tuner
152. Picture framing services
153. Plant maintenance
154. Plasterer
155. Pool service
156. Portrait artist
157. Pottery
158. Prepared foods service
159. Pretzel stands
160. Private investigating
161. Process servers
162. Publicist/agent
163. Puppeteer
164. Radon detection service
165. Real estate investor
166. Real estate staging service
167. Recycling service
168. Relocation service
169. Remodeling planning
170. Rental-finding service
171. Restaurant delivery service
172. Resume writing
173. Retailing by kiosk and cart
174. Reunion planning

175. Roof restoration
176. Sandwich stands
177. Self-publishing
178. Seminar production
179. Seminar promotion
180. Shoe repair
181. Shopping service
182. Small business consultant
183. Specialty advertising brokerage
184. Specialty gardening/sprout growing
185. Stand-up comedian
186. Tax preparation service
187. Teaching crafts classes
188. Teaching English to foreign students
189. Telecommunications consultant
190. Translation service
191. Truck and car washing
192. Tutoring
193. Typing, data-entry service
194. Upholstery cleaning
195. Upholstery repair
196. Used bookstore owner
197. Used car inspections
198. Used car assessment
199. Valet parking service
200. Vehicle moving service
201. Vending machine service
202. Videotaping service
203. Virtual assistant
204. Web site design, management, and maintenance services
205. Wedding planner
206. Wallpaper hanging
207. Window cleaning
208. Windshield repair service
209. Writing service
210. Yoga instructor

Selling Information

Selling information gives you the opportunity to share what you know with others while earning income independent of your job or primary business. It may even become your primary business. Choose subjects about which you have specialized knowledge. Organize and package practical information into easy-to-use formats. "How-to" reports, articles, and books (in traditional or electronic formats), video and audio recordings, teleclasses, and source lists and catalogues, are just a few of the ways you can share what you know with others. Market your items via the Internet or by mail.

Producing Your Product: The digital revolution has made it possible for anyone to inexpensively produce high-quality informational materials. All you need is the right software and equipment. No matter what format you decide upon, make sure your information is well organized. Before you write or produce your materials, break down your subject matter into a series of bullet points. Arrange these in a kind of flow chart that describes how the purchaser of your information moves through the process you are describing. Make your product attractive, but remember, when selling via the Internet or by mail, people are more interested in the information than the package. If you're delivering written materials through the mail, have them printed or photocopied. Written materials made available for online downloads or on computer-readable discs can be published in a PDF format. Audio and video recordings can be produced for delivery via disc or made available for direct download.

Marketing and Delivering Your Product: The most popular ways of marketing information are over the Internet and through direct mail. While you may eventually want to use both options, in the beginning you'll probably want to decide on one and develop it first (see "Ten Steps to Launching Your Web Site" on page 400 and "Direct Mail" on page 398). If you're eager to begin and you don't already have a Web site, you may want to start with selling by mail. With appropriate adaptations, many of the products and marketing pieces developed for your direct-mail campaign can later be used for your Web site. In the long run, a strong Web presence is a good idea whether you choose to deliver your informational products via online download or through the mail. Once you've established a Web site with an online store, the costs of delivering your material via Internet downloads are negligible. If you use the mail, the postal service's Media Mail can significantly reduce your mailing costs. (Media Mail cannot contain advertising, except for incidental announcements of books.) Call the USPS for information on current regulations and costs. Finally, as a beginner, you may want to consider partnering with larger, more established sites to market your materials. For example, Amazon sells e-books, and a number of different sites will sell your audio or video recordings. If you've ever considered selling information, I encourage you to investigate this option further. Some of the resources below may prove helpful:

Selling Information Sources

From Entrepreneur to Infopreneur: Make Money with Books, E-Books and Information Products. Stephanie Chandler. New York: Wiley, 2006.

Start Your Own Mail Order Business. Irvine: Calif.: Entrepreneur Press, 2008.

The Official Get Rich Guide to Information Marketing on the Internet. Bob Regnerus and Robert Skrob. New York: Entrepreneur Press, 2008.

Wielding the Freelance

The people who get on in this world are the people who get up and look for the circumstances they want, and, if they can't find them, make them.
George Bernard Shaw

The term *freelance* has come down to us from medieval times, when knights independent of any lord roamed the countryside in search of fortune and adventure. Because they were unattached, they were known as "free lances." Today, a freelance has come to mean "a person who acts according to his principles and is not influenced by any group; an independent."[1] In the *I Ching*, we find a description that fits both the medieval and modern sense of a freelance: "one who does not serve either a king or a feudal lord, but in a lofty spirit values his own affairs."[2] Modern-day freelances can include artists, writers, musicians, actors, journalists, photographers, inventors, consultants of any kind, commercial artists, editors, and more. This section will outline important issues you may want to consider in setting yourself up as a freelance. (Many of the exercises on pages 372–384 will also prove helpful to would-be freelancers.)

Of course, in a certain sense, a freelance is really operating a small business. The basic difference is this: a freelance is not interested in starting an organization. For our purposes, a restaurant is a small business (even if it only has two employees), but an inventor who sells her ideas to industry is a freelance. As an up-and-coming young country and western singer, Dolly Parton was a freelance; but as an executive of Dollywood, she is running a not-so-small business. Freelancing has nothing to do with how much money you make. A professional sports figure or entertainer may make big bucks as a freelance or may, like Oprah Winfrey, start her own production organization. Successful freelancers don't usually want to run organizations, though many of them could.

Freelancers want the relative freedom and control of managing their own business affairs, without the responsibility of running a company. The freelance has an even greater freedom in how to structure and use time than the small business owner. Most businesses have to keep regular hours (at least if they want to stay in business), but freelancers might start their day at two p.m. and work late into the night, or they may work intensively on a project for six months and take six months off. As a freelance, you can take advantage of your natural life rhythms and work at those times when you feel most creative and have the most energy. You are running your schedule; your schedule is not running you. As with time, so with space; you are free to create. The freelance can work at home in her underwear. I know one who does. Today's technology makes working from home possible in many more fields.

Many personal and informational services that are commonly run as small businesses can easily be adapted to a freelance format. People who enjoy working primarily with ideas or information (e.g., journalists) or those with a great deal of highly specific skills (e.g., pilots) or specialized knowledge (e.g., engineers) are good freelance candidates.

Creative artists often freelance, whether by choice or necessity.

Many former executives find that the knowledge, skill, and experience they acquired in the corporate world can be applied in ways that better reflect their current values by taking advantage of the freelance option. For example, a former management executive for a large defense contractor became an organizational consultant for nonprofits. What he learned about effective management and organization he now shares with nonprofits, helping them to better organize their efforts. He gains satisfaction working for people and causes that more adequately reflect his values. On the other hand, some former executives find they want a minimum of time constraints and organizational hassles. They want to focus on spiritual or psychological growth, which they may have neglected while climbing the ladder of success. These folks often have highly marketable skills that can provide them a comfortable living with a minimum of hassles.

Of course, a freelance may be one by temperament or by necessity. Certain fields require a freelance status, especially in the early stages of a career. You may be a dancer with a dream of starting your own dance troupe, but you will probably have to spend many years as a freelance (and a very exceptional one at that) before you will have the credibility and visibility to gain the necessary financial and audience backing for your organization.

Freelancers are ready to trade security for freedom. There are no pensions, benefit packages, or yearly cost-of-living adjustments waiting for freelancers—unless, of course, they create these for themselves. Some do, but even with these, the freelance life is a bit on the edge. You must like or at least be comfortable with this. Many freelancers spend a good portion of their workdays alone. Ask yourself if this works for you. There are, of course, ways of minimizing one's sense of isolation.

Joining a local club or guild (for example, a writer's or artist's guild, a songwriter's or actor's club, a speaker's or consultant's association, etc.) can provide, especially the beginning freelancer, with much-needed balance, knowledge, and support. Membership is usually a matter of a nominal yearly fee. Joining an organization gives you a chance to get out and meet with other folks in your field. In addition to providing the emotional support of others who share common experiences (and frustrations), these groups offer the individual a chance to exchange ideas and learn from more experienced colleagues. They provide information about opportunities for jobs and late-breaking trends in the field. Besides offering talks and forums by successful individuals in the field, most groups conduct seminars and workshops on subjects including the legal, marketing, and accounting aspects of their profession.

Freelancers often hold jobs, but of short duration. An actor working on a film; a dancer performing in a show; a consultant working for a particular company, nonprofit, or government agency for several months at a stretch; a photographer making a big shoot for a catalogue or magazine—all have jobs, but they know these jobs aren't going to last. Successful freelances have the confidence, connections, and skill to keep creating work. They know how to take care of business, or they hire people who do.

Taking Care of Business

As a freelance, you'll find the business end of your work is likely to be a matter of making contacts, negotiating contracts, and handling paperwork—in other words, marketing, negotiation, and administration. There are, of course, professionals skilled in all of these areas whom you can hire to do most or all of your business work. Should you choose to seek professional help, it is a good idea to stay involved and informed. If you are going to do most of the work yourself, the most essential skills you will need are marketing and negotiation. If you are successful at these, you can hire someone

to do your paperwork, record keeping, and accounting—otherwise, guess who.

Get Yourself Some Hired Guns: Agents, Marketing Consultants, Lawyers, and Accountants

Agents: People who are looking to sell their creative work or talent may be able to profit from the services of an agent. There are agents for authors, artists, musicians, entertainers of all kinds, and professional sportspeople, among others. Agents are professionals who handle the business end of creative work for a percentage fee. Agents are in the business of contacts, making them and keeping them. They endeavor to connect creative artists or their work with opportunities for exposure; they negotiate deals, protect artists' work from infringement, or promote artists' names or reputations. Of course, before an agent will agree to take you on as a client, she must be convinced that her efforts at promoting you will be worthwhile for her. In other words, she has to know that you will be marketable, and that she stands to earn enough on the 10 to 20 percent she gets from the sale of your work, to make it work for her.

Marketing Consultants: There are marketing consultants who specialize in working with small businesses and freelancers. They can create and design a complete marketing program for you. They can help you develop a marketing strategy, target specific markets, design promotional and advertising materials, get publicity, and more. Marketing consultants often work for a flat fee or on a monthly or quarterly retainer. If you can afford it and it is appropriate to your field, hiring a professional in the beginning is usually a good idea. Later, we'll consider how to create effective promotional materials. A marketing consultant can assist you in developing these. For many freelancers, the best way to utilize the services of a marketing consultant is in developing general marketing concepts and materials (e.g., a logo) before the launch of their business. Later on, you can come to them with specific requests—for example, to help design specific promotions.

Lawyers: Even if you decide you don't need or can't get an agent or marketing consultant, you should have a good attorney. This is for the simple reason that contracts can be a boon or bane for the freelance, and a good lawyer can make the difference. From authors to artists, from songwriters to consultants, from inventors to speakers, contracts are basic to doing business in a freelance way. In some fields, you may be able to have an attorney draw up a standard contract (or several) that you can use over and over with slight alterations (like varying the numbers). Lawyers can also help you deal with issues like copyrights, trademarks, patents, and their protection. They can tell you what to do if someone is infringing on you and/or your work.

Accountants: You should avail yourself of the advice of a good accountant, preferably one who specializes in working with people in your field. Special tax considerations can apply to independent contractors, artists, authors, actors, and others. These frequently change. It is your accountant's job to stay on top of these and help you get the best breaks.

Do It Yourself: Give Yourself a Promotion

In many fields, hiring an agent doesn't apply. Even in those where it does, there are circumstances where you may not want (or be able to get) an agent. Similarly, you may not be able to afford or you may not want to work with a marketing consultant. In that case, you are on your own. Fortunately, there are many good books on the subject. On the road to freelance freedom, there are several barriers, which the beginner must overcome. The way you deal with these barriers can mean the difference between making it as a freelance and returning to the job market.

Break Through Self-Marketing Barriers

Antimarketing Bias: If you have a job, you try to do good work and hope that someone will notice and promote you. If you work for yourself, you have the opportunity or the obligation to promote yourself. Whether you view it as an opportunity or an obligation could spell the difference between success or failure in your marketing attempts. If you resent having to market yourself—the time that it takes away from other activities, the sometimes silly horn-blowing, the ingratiating inanities—you will probably be ineffective. If Zen can be Zen chopping wood and carrying water, then Zen can be Zen through the marketing drama—a modern-day equivalent. Understand that this whole business of ego is a show, and you can drop any hang-ups about being a showman or show-woman.

Embarrassment: If you feel too shy or embarrassed to promote yourself, this could stop you in your tracks. Get a friend to help you, one who can see you objectively and help you to accent your strengths and minimize your weaknesses. The real marketing geniuses turn weaknesses into strengths. Even if you are able to get others to assist you in your efforts, you will need to think through your strategy and be able to look at your image with a degree of objectivity. Believe in you and in what you do, and have fun promoting yourself.

Perfectionism: The perfect has been called "the enemy of the good." The good you can enjoy today is often better than the perfection you might have someday. Somedays have a way of never coming. Eventually, you just have to do it.

Lack of Persistence: To be successful, you generally must accept self-marketing as an essential, ongoing part of your business. If you land one big account, you have to maintain it and get the next one. If you complete one project, no matter how well you did it, there's always the next. If you write one book, paint one painting, or compose one piece of music, there's always the next, no matter how good the last one was. It's easy to rest on your laurels and coast on your last success, but if you're going to make it as a freelance, you have to keep at it. The promotion you do today will pay off later on.

Lack of Knowledge: I'll assume you already have the specialized knowledge necessary to do your work. (If not, see Act IV, Scene II.) Beyond this, you will need marketing knowledge, including how to create effective marketing strategies, how to locate and cultivate specific markets in your field, how to assemble relevant marketing pieces, how to network and negotiate effectively, and more.

Take Action

Research Your Markets: Artists need to make connections with dealers and galleries, actors with producers or studios, writers with publishers, songwriters with music publishers or recording companies. There are publications such as *Writer's Market, Artist's and Graphic Designer's Market, Songwriter's Market,* and *Photographer's Market* (all published by Writer's Digest), which will help you make your connections on a kind of do-it-yourself basis. You may want to work as a professional speaker; there are speakers' bureaus you should know about. You may have inventions to market; you should know how to submit these products to industry. For all of these options and more, there is a wealth of information available on the Internet. It's always a good idea to

contact several people in the field you are considering and ask them what they have found to be their most effective marketing approaches. The point is: Thoroughly investigate how you will market your work before jumping in. Develop a plan that is grounded in reality.

Shake the Grant Tree: There are many grants available for the freelance. Special grants exist for writers, artists, dancers, theater directors, musicians, researchers, analysts, and many others. You can apply directly, through organizations such as the National Endowment for the Arts, 1100 Pennsylvania Avenue, NW, Washington, D.C., 20506. They have grants available in areas including opera, theater, music, visual arts, film, radio, television, dance, literature, design arts, folk arts, museums, etc. It helps if you know how to write a good proposal. For a brief sketch of the process and a list of books that you may want to consult, see pages 411–412. Many grants can only be given to tax-deductible nonprofit organizations. You may be able to receive a grant that "flows through" one of these organizations. They receive the money from a donor you have selected and pass it on to you. The organization will usually charge you a fee for this service (around 10 percent).

Develop a Self-promotional Orientation and Network: Get aggressive about promoting what you do. Use the promotional pieces and tips on publicity that appear below. If appropriate, carry samples of your work with you. Pass your business cards out to people you meet. Develop networking skills. See the networking and association sections on pages 457–466.

Sharpen Your Image: Like it or not, people judge you by the way you look. It's their first impression of you and often the strongest. Choose your image with care, because it is following you everywhere. Most freelancers do not have to conform to the standard business dress code. Whatever look you choose, make sure that it is well put together. Be aware that people are attracted to success. Of course, the way that an author or an artist looks successful may be different from the way a business consultant does; still, no matter your profession, look like you're making it. Finally, recognize that if your appearance runs to the unconventional, you could be getting yourself into a box. If you always dress like a Guatemalan peasant or a cowboy, people will think that's what you are.

Negotiate

There are dozens of books on the subject of negotiating. Links to several of the better ones can be found at empoweryou.com. On pages 471–473, you'll find some general tips on negotiation. Beyond this, I will simply restate that it's a good idea to have a lawyer examine any contracts before you sign. Beginners in fields such as songwriting and screenwriting have often been taken to the cleaners, so beware. Several hundred dollars in attorney's fees up front could save many thousands later on.

By All Accounts: The Paperwork

If you don't already have one, buy a personal computer to help you get a handle on the paper end of your business. With the right software and your own effort, you can save thousands of dollars a year on the services of a bookkeeper, appointment secretary, graphic designer, typographer, file clerk, or research assistant.

No matter how much you rely on a computer, you will probably never completely eliminate the need for paper. One key to keeping your paperwork under control is to make certain you have plenty of ways to "receive" your paper; these include file folders, filing cabinets, notebooks, index cards, index files, paper trays, paper clips, labels, etc. Where you see a workspace piled with disorderly papers, you will almost always find a lack of these important supplies (or their effective use).

Put It in Writing and Get the Word Out

One vital thing to understand about our society is that it runs on paper. Many people think that if it isn't on paper, it can't be real. On the other hand, the written word carries a kind of mystique. Perhaps this goes back to ancient times when priests or magicians were the only ones who could read and write. Whatever the origin of our fascination with the written word, it is definitely something of which to be aware and take advantage. Additionally, studies have shown that most people process information visually: show beats tell every time. Keep these points in mind when creating and designing your promotional materials.

Many beginning freelancers don't like to deal with creating promotion pieces, but sooner or later, most professionals come around to seeing their importance. You save time, hassle, and lost business by doing it right from the start. Begin by thinking through the image you want to present to the public (see page 526). You will most likely want to take advantage of the promotional pieces below:

Logo: It may be worth your while to hire a professional graphic designer to create a logo for your business. For some freelance businesses, a logo is practically mandatory; for others, it's not important. A logo is especially useful if you use a business name other than your own name. Once you have the logo, you can use it on all of your promotional pieces, e.g., business cards, stationery, brochures, flyers, advertisements, etc. If you are going to use a logo, take the time to create one you will be comfortable with for years to come. In marketing, it is important to be consistent—it helps you build name recognition over time.

Business Cards: A business card allows you to promote your business wherever you go. Take the time, thought, and care to create the right card for you. Look at other people's cards to get ideas for what will work best for yours. Be appropriate to your field. In most cases, a business consultant's card should be rather conventional, sending the message, "I'm competent and reliable." The same card design for a photographer, artist, or jewelry designer would be a mistake; it should say, "I create." For the freelance, using your own name for your business name is often best. Even if you decide to incorporate, you can still be Susan Smith, Ltd. Include on your card a graphic logo and/or tagline motto for your business if you have these. (If you don't, you may want to create them.)

Many freelancers put additional information on the back of their cards. You can use yours to list services and benefits or to indicate how your work is different from your competitors. There are Web sites (e.g., businesscards.com, VistaPrint.com) that allow you to create a card (and letterhead and stationery) online and have the finished products shipped to your door. Whether you use an online service or your local printer, make sure your card looks professional. Choose high-quality cardstock. It's also a good idea to purchase a card organizer and collect other people's business cards. A well-organized card file provides a ready reference for contacts, leads, and clients and can serve as a Rolodex. Periodically, transfer the card data of your most important new contacts into your computer or mobile device.

Stationery and Envelopes: Everything that applies to business cards goes for your stationery. It should be professional, appropriate, high quality, and "you." Again, if you have a logo, use it.

Portfolio: Every freelance should have a portfolio. One of the most common mistakes that beginning freelances make is failing to document in words and pictures exactly what they do. A portfolio is good for your self-confidence. It helps you to see where you have come from and stimulates you to grow. Most importantly, it shows people what you can do by showing what you have done. Obviously, the ingredients in the portfolio of a fine artist and computer consultant are going to vary greatly, but every freelance needs a portfolio. Select a high-quality binder or portfolio. As to the contents of your portfolio, choose from the list below. Create a showcase that fits your particular field and image, one that highlights your best work.

> *Resume*
> *Examples of work*
> *Photos*
> *Letters of recommendation*
> *Testimonials*

Brochures: If you can afford to hire someone to write, photograph, design, and print a glossy four-color brochure, that's great. If not, it doesn't mean you can't create an effective, inexpensive brochure that will get people excited about what you are doing. The simplest brochure is an 8 $\frac{1}{2}$ x 11 sheet of paper folded in three to produce six panels. (An 8 $\frac{1}{2}$ x 14 sheet is often folded in four to produce eight panels.) You likely already have software templates for making brochures on your computer and more sophisticated programs are readily available online. Some Web sites allow you to create (or upload) your design online and have the printed brochures shipped to you.

What goes on your brochure will, of course, depend on the line of work you are in. Whatever you do, take time to distill your thoughts before you begin creating your brochure. A few clear ideas, well communicated in words and pictures, make a much stronger impression than trying to say too much. Look at successful brochures in your field to get ideas. An eye-catching headline on your brochure cover is essential. Keep the text of your brochure precise and brief. Be positive and use simple, jargon-free language. Define your service and spell out its features and benefits in terms that appeal to your clients or buyers. Let your readers know how you are different from your competitors (e.g., quality, price, specialized or comprehensive service, etc.). You may want to include testimonials from satisfied clients. Balance your text with eye-catching graphics and "white space." Include photographs of your work or of people engaged in the service you are selling. Since most freelancers are offering personal services or their own creative work, it's also a good idea to include a photograph of yourself. Finally, don't neglect the aesthetics of your brochure—make it visually attractive. Once you are satisfied with your brochure, take (or upload) it to a professional printer. Don't print it from your computer unless you have a *very* high-quality printer. Like all of your marketing materials, your brochure should have a professional look and feel. Better a small, high-quality two-color brochure than a large, cheap-looking four-color job.

Flyers: Flyers are one of the most inexpensive ways of getting the word out about your offerings. Make a simple but attractive flyer describing what you do. Again, you likely have software templates for making flyers on your computer. Print or photocopy your flyers and post them around town. Many communities have kiosks in areas with a high volume of pedestrian traffic. Retail store windows and bulletin boards in local libraries, colleges and universities, laundromats, and employee lounges are good places to post your flyers. Some people hand them out on busy street corners or go door-to-door with them. Some even put them on car windshields, as you have probably noticed.

Advertising: Get the biggest bang for your advertising buck. Internet ads, newspaper and magazine space ads, as well as classified ads, telephone directories, and radio and television spots are just a few of the ways you can advertise. You don't need to spend a great deal of money to effectively advertise your work. Some freelancers do very well by simply running classified ads in magazines

that alert the public to what they have to offer, then using the responses to develop contacts for direct-mail campaigns. Others run Internet ads and promotions that drive traffic to their Web sites.

Direct Mail: For some freelancers, direct mail can be an excellent marketing technique. All you need is a well-targeted and up-to-date mailing list, a marketing package, and postage. While your marketing pieces must be simple, clear, well written, and pitched to your potential clients, marketing professionals will tell you that nothing is more important to your success than the quality of your mailing list. Check the Internet or your local yellow pages for professional services that sell mailing lists. Develop your own list of clients or buyers who might like to know about future offerings. There are fine books available on how to write effective copy that will draw responses. Also read your own junk mail and get ideas. The standard direct-mail package includes:

> *A brochure or flyer*
> *A letter*
> *A return card (a postcard with your*
> *   name and address printed on it)*

Experiment and find what works best for you and your budget. Your package may be as simple as a letter with an enclosed business card. Don't write off direct mail until you are absolutely sure it can't work for you. If you find that the postage is too expensive, you may be able to do a cooperative mailing with others—share the costs, and everyone benefits.

Promotional Video: A promotional video helps performers such as speakers, musicians, comedians, actors, dancers, etc., demonstrate what they can do. Many agencies and would-be employers require you to submit a video prior to meeting with and/ or even considering you. Again, make it a professional presentation—hire or make friends with a pro.

Viral Advertising: Viral marketing and advertising take advantage of preexisting social networks to sell products or services, create "buzz," or enhance brand awareness. All new forms of viral advertising take advantage of the oldest of all—word of mouth. Today, that word can spread through cyberspace (or other forms of telecommunications) without the spreader and the "spreadee" ever meeting, much less knowing one another. Many viral marketers have used blogs and social networking sites (e.g., Facebook, MySpace) to great effect. YouTube videos have launched a number of careers. All of the sites mentioned above are themselves highly successful examples of viral marketing. By understanding people's desires, by giving away a service that could easily be transferred to others, and by taking advantage of subscribers' existing communication networks, these sites catapulted to success. Using similar principles, you can create your viral success on the Internet or on the street.

Contracting Your Services

You may choose to operate as an independent professional who contracts services to existing organizations. As an independent contractor, you maintain the independence of being your own boss and choosing your clients. Yet since your relationship with these types of clients is generally sustained over a long period of time, you may have greater security than you would in other freelance endeavors.

General Steps to Contracting Your Services

1. Identify organizations that are fulfilling purposes you support or that might be persuaded to pursue purposes that you support.

2. Prioritize these, based upon your desire to work with them.

3. Research these organizations. Understand their relative strengths and weaknesses. What problems do they have that you can help solve? What areas are they neglecting that you could help put into focus? Find out.

4. Identify the individual or individuals who have the authority to hire you.

5. Develop a proposal that demonstrates your credibility and how you can benefit their organization.

6. Approach these organizations with your proposal.

Note: Be advised that there are legal questions about exactly what constitutes an independent contractor versus what constitutes an employee. The IRS says if you act like an employee, you are an employee as far as they are concerned. Check with a competent tax attorney or the IRS for updated details.

Web and Book Resources

Find out more about starting a freelance business
@ Empoweryou.com.

Ten Steps to Launching Your Web Site

If you're thinking that your freelance work or new business should have a Web presence, you're probably right. Below is a list of steps to consider as you begin to design and market your Web site.

Step 1: Define the purpose and goals of your Web site. What do you want to accomplish with your site? Do you want to build a major online store or do you want what amounts to an online brochure? Are you trying to reach a local, national, or international market?

Step 2: Decide on strategies to meet your goals. For example, if you plan to use your site to market your offline local business, a simple static site may be adequate. If your goal is to make money online, you will need an e-commerce site. If you want to create a community-based site where people can interact, you'll want to include chat rooms, blogs, forums, and/or other interactive content.

Step 3: Select a domain name. In selecting a domain name make sure it is easy to remember, easy to spell, relevant to your product or service, and that it is not too long or too short. Additionally, make sure you select the appropriate domain-name extension for the type of site you are creating (i.e., .com, .net, .biz, .org.)

Step 4: Register your domain name and select a Web site hosting company. Currently, some of the better-known companies offering registration services include Networksolutions.com, Godaddy.com, Register.com, and Mydomain.com. These sites also allow you to search through existing domain names to find out if the one you want is available. While it's a good idea to register your domain name as soon as possible, shop around for the best combination of price and features before settling on a Web-hosting company. All of the companies listed above offer Web-hosting services. You may also want to investigate the costs and benefits of using your existing ISP (Internet service provider) or other ISPs.

Step 5: Research other sites to get ideas for yours. Though you've been using the Internet for years, you may not have given much thought to Web site design. Review successful Web sites that do similar things to what you would like yours to do. Pay attention to how these sites are constructed. How do you navigate around these sites? How much content do they have per page? Do they break the content into columns or do they use the full width of the page? What about photos and graphics? What kind of color scheme seems to work best? If the sites have an e-commerce facility, is it easy to use? These are just some of the issues you are likely to encounter as you put together your own site. Reviewing other sites with these kinds of questions in mind will help you decide on how best to build your own.

Step 6: Map out the structure of your site. Determine how people will navigate your site. Some familiar navigation elements include: Home, Products/Services, Testimonials, Portfolio/Samples, Fees, About us, FAQs, Contact info, Site map, etc. If your site is under thirty pages, you needn't bother putting a site map on your Web site. Still, it's worth the trouble to sketch one out for your own sake. Identify and list as many pages as you think you will need and then group these under several major headings. Once you have determined what your principal links and sublinks will be, the next step is to determine how people will move around your site. Decide which links will appear on all pages, which will appear on major heading pages, and which will be embedded into the text of certain pages.

Step 7: Write a rough draft of the contents of your site. Begin to flesh out the content of each of the pages you identified in the step above. At this point, don't worry about getting it right, just get something down for each page. Also create a title for each page.

Step 8: Develop your site's SEO parameters. Google and other search engines find and (in large part) rank your site based on its keywords and key phrases. Selecting the right keywords and key phrases can spell the difference between visibility and invisibility on the Net. Keywords appear in both the viewable areas and in the underlying source code of each page. Understanding how SEO (Search Engine Optimization) works and selecting the right keywords and key phrases for your site can be somewhat difficult for the beginner. Research this topic thoroughly on the Internet and/or hire an SEO specialist to assist you with this step.

Step 9: Finalize the content for your site. Once you have a rough draft for each page and have identified the keywords you want to highlight, it's time to bring it all together. Rewrite and finalize your text, incorporating your top keywords and phrases throughout. Make sure your text includes a clear message to your market with a call to action (sign up for our newsletter, join a forum, take a free test, buy our product or service, etc.). Also finalize the page descriptions (the text viewable on the search engine under the link to each page) and your page titles.

Step 10: Design your site. Whether you do it yourself or hire a pro, keep in mind these Web-design elements: Design it with your market in mind. Select a look that is clean, not too busy, and that matches well with your offline business. Throughout your site, the fonts, colors, graphics, and other design elements should be consistent or at least complementary. Make sure the site works well on all major browsers, and design it so it loads relatively quickly.

Do it yourself: If you want to design your site, you'll likely want to acquire a Web-design program. Adobe Dreamweaver is a favorite of many professional Web designers. It will allow you to create state-of-the-art Web pages with all the bells and whistles. The drawbacks are that this program is somewhat complicated and difficult for the beginner and it is expensive. If your needs are more basic, Coffeecup is an inexpensive program that is relatively easy to use. Nvu is a free program that allows anyone to create Web pages and manage a Web site with no technical expertise or knowledge of HTML. Do some research before purchasing a Web-design program, as new ones are constantly being developed. Hosting companies typically offer a free (but rather basic) site-building program to customers. These site-building programs include predesigned templates with limited font and color selection. While it is relatively easy to create a site this way, these programs do not offer the flexibility of design and interactivity that end-user programs can. Review the features your hosting company offers before deciding to go this route.

Hire a pro: Even if you decide to hire a pro, it will still be helpful for you to do, or at least be actively involved in, most of the steps listed above. After all, it is your site, and no one knows better what you want than you. You are likely to get a much better result if you stay actively involved throughout the process. When looking for a pro, try to find a Web developer who has the skills necessary to: write and/or edit your page text, design your site, and create a Web-marketing plan for your site. Get referrals from other business owners. Ask prospective Web developers for references, samples of their work, and a proposal (with price quotes). Once you decide whom you want to hire, make sure to draw up a contract that (among other things) ensures you maintain the copyright to all your materials. In addition to assisting you in designing and launching your Web site, a Web developer can help you maintain and market it. You will usually pay a monthly fee for these services.

Where Do Artists Sell Their Work?

Do you have a body of work you would like to show? Are you ready to get feedback on it? Are you willing to spend the time, energy, and money to get your work out there? If you answered yes to the above questions, you may be ready to begin marketing your work. Check out the following:

Galleries: Research the galleries that you are most interested in. Check them out with the Better Business Bureau, and ask for feedback from other artists who have used them. When you've finished your research, make a list of the galleries that you are most interested in. Call them and set up as many appointments as possible.

Studio Viewings: Studio viewings provide a good opportunity for a curator or collector to see all of your work, and you don't have to schlep it.

Studio Shows: Studio shows provide you with an opportunity to show your work to many in an atmosphere of fun and play. Hold a reception with drink and food, and get them in a cheery mood—to buy.

Cooperative Galleries: Because cooperative galleries are run by artists, they may allow you to show works commercial galleries would not touch. Also, you can network with and learn from other artists.

Commissions: A commissioned work is one you are paid to make from scratch. Commissions might come from record or publishing companies, city airports, corporations, or city government—even friends and acquaintances.

Sidewalk Shows: Sidewalk shows represent artists of all levels who show and sell their work. You don't have to be a pro to show your art here. Contact your local artists' association to find out about shows in your area.

Art Fairs: Art fairs are similar to sidewalk shows, except that they are juried events. In many cases, prizes are awarded. Entering these exhibitions can open up doors to other opportunities. Often dealers and collectors go to shows seeking out new talent. You can contact your city's parks and recreation department for a schedule of such shows.

Artists' Sources

Artist's and Graphic Designer's Market. Writer's Digest. Cincinnati: Writer's Digest. Published annually.

The Artist's Marketing and Action Plan Workbook, 5th ed. Jonathan Talbot and Geoffrey Howard. Warwick, N.Y.: Jonathan Talbot, 2005.

Business and Legal Forms for Fine Artists, 3rd ed. Tad Crawford. New York: Allworth Press, 2005.

Crafting the Nonprofit Foundation

Such gardens are not made
By singing:—"Oh, how beautiful" and
sitting in the shade.

Rudyard Kipling

Let's say you have a vision in mind of a particular good you'd like to accomplish, one requiring the efforts of several people, at least. Let's further say the nature of this effort rules out forming a profit-based company and that there is no existing nonprofit already doing what you would like to do, or doing it in the way you would like to do it. You may want to consider starting a nonprofit corporation of your own. This section will help you to determine if this option is right for you.

A nonprofit corporation is a legally chartered state corporation. Establishing such a corporation is not a particularly difficult procedure, though you generally must follow specific guidelines about how your organization is formed and how its business is to be conducted. These procedures vary from state to state. More complicated and often more difficult to meet are the requirements for tax-exempt status, which, of course, most potential nonprofit organizations would like to get.

The variance from state to state of incorporation and other regulations and the possibility of continued changes in federal tax law make it difficult to say much in detail about the legal aspects of nonprofit corporations. If you are really serious about forming a tax-exempt nonprofit corporation, you should consult a qualified attorney who works in this field.

If the nonprofit form of organization is best for you, don't be intimidated by the procedures or paperwork. Remember, thousands of others have started nonprofits, which today are actively providing many valuable services to their communities and the world that never would have happened had they been unwilling to deal with the red tape.

Apart from legal considerations, nonprofit corporations have their own unique set of problems and opportunities. The discussion below considers some of the major advantages and disadvantages of starting a nonprofit corporation, as well as some of the major challenges faced by those interested in running this kind of organization.

Advantages

Credibility: People are more likely to trust you when they know that your organization has met certain legal requirements for operation and that you are not "just in it for the buck." In this world, where it often seems that everyone is trying to sell you something, the fact that your organization was set up for altruistic purposes carries considerable weight with the general public. People will be more likely to listen to your message and publicize or participate in your activities if you carry nonprofit status. Of course, your organization's continued credibility depends on the quality of its performance.

Access: In order for your organization to do certain kinds of work, you simply must have nonprofit tax-exempt status. It's the law, and again, it varies from state to state. If you're interested in working in or with certain types of organizations (for example, elementary or secondary schools, colleges and universities, hospitals, prisons, the armed forces, state or national legislatures, churches, etc.) or with certain types of individuals (for example, veterans, runaways, the handicapped, the mentally retarded, the elderly, etc.), your opportunities for access are greatly enhanced when you make your approach as a representative of a nonprofit organization.

Publicity: People love to hear about good things that are happening in their community and the world at large. Consequently, your nonprofit organization may enjoy enhanced opportunities for free media attention. Newspapers and magazines are often very receptive to doing stories on nonprofit activities, as are local television and radio stations. Local and national radio and television talk shows are constantly looking for credible and interesting guests and often invite controversial and issue-oriented speakers. Additionally, radio and television stations are obliged to grant free air time for public service announcements. You can take advantage of these to get your message out, enlist volunteer support, or announce your upcoming fundraising events and opportunities.

Funding: Obtaining tax-exempt status —otherwise known as qualifying with the IRS as a 501(c)(3) organization—greatly expands your ability to obtain the funding necessary to accomplish your organization's goals. Most of the large philanthropic foundations will only give grants to organizations that have obtained tax-exempt status. Nonprofit tax-exempt status can likewise help you obtain grants from federal and state governments and donations from corporations and individuals. Nonprofit tax-exempt status may also increase the possibility of obtaining gifts, low-interest loans, or donated products and services. You can cut costs with volunteers, interns, nonprofit mail privileges, and by buying products and services at a discount. Members and subscribers can provide continuing support. You can solicit funds through direct-mail campaigns or get local or national celebrities to put on benefits on your organization's behalf. These are just a few of the many funding possibilities available to nonprofit organizations, many of which simply don't apply to other types of organizations.

Volunteers: As a nonprofit corporation, you can attract an army of committed individuals to further your organization's mission. Each year, thousands of Americans and people around the world donate their time and effort to working for causes they believe in. A certain percentage of these become extremely dedicated to particular organizations. As your organization grows, you may want to select from these individuals when filling permanent positions. You know their commitment, and they know your organization—its goals and needs, its opportunities and challenges. In addition to free help from volunteers, many organizations take advantage of the efforts of interns who, in exchange for learning and training, work for nominal wages.

Disadvantages

Cost: Launching a nonprofit corporation can be a considerable expense. Legal and consulting fees and research-and-development costs add up. Your start-up team may be able to do some or all of the nonlegal work itself or with the help of other volunteers. You might even find a lawyer willing to donate his services. Even if you can't find an oblig-

ing, qualified lawyer, you may—depending on the type of organization you want to start and the availability of good self-help materials in your state—be able to do much or all of the legal work yourself. Nolo Press (http://www.nolo.com) provides excellent legal materials for the self-starter.

Complexity: Nonprofits are somewhat complicated to begin and maintain. Starting your nonprofit corporation includes writing articles of incorporation and bylaws (spelling out the purpose of your organization and the way its business is to be conducted) and filing a number of forms with various agencies, including the Internal Revenue Service. Following the proper start-up procedure is only the beginning of many requirements set by state and federal government agencies with which you must comply.

Again, the rules and regulations vary from state to state and tend to be somewhat involved. Failure to comply can result in the loss of your nonprofit standing or in even more severe penalties. Be sure that your board of directors and all officers and employees know exactly what the law requires of them. Again, if you are serious about starting a nonprofit organization, qualified legal and accounting professional help is a must—and be sure you understand the information or advice they give.

Paper Jungle: You can expect to file a steady stream of paper, not only with various governmental agencies, but with members and donors, as well as with philanthropic organizations, contractors, and others, all of which someone must write. With minutes, reports, proposals, neverending government forms and filings, balance sheets, mailings, newsletters, public service announcements—nonprofits can seem awash in a sea of paper. The larger your organization gets, the more administrative mumbo jumbo it will have to deal with. Of course, this can and does take time and energy away from fulfilling the purpose for which your organization was founded. It's not a perfect world we live in and, like it or not, red tape is a fact of life.

Limited Financial Compensation: While you can eventually earn a comfortable living, recognize that no one ever got rich in the nonprofit sector. Especially in the beginning, you can expect to work long, hard hours for a modest salary. Still, if you have gotten this far into the process of discovering and realizing your life's work, it is safe to assume that you are committed to values and a vision that mean more to you than a profit motive, and that the experience of giving your gifts to mankind means more to you than getting rich.

Management Challenges

In many respects, managing a nonprofit organization is similar to managing a business or any other type of organization. You start with your vision and state your purpose for existence. Next, you shape broad strategies for the fulfillment of that purpose. Then you step those strategies down into specific objectives and plan exactly how you will achieve these goals. Finally, you evaluate the results of your efforts in light of your original vision and purpose.

Though in many ways similar to other types of organizational management, the nonprofit organization presents managers with unique opportunities and challenges. Here's an advance look at a few of the special management challenges you can expect to face should you decide to build your own nonprofit organization.

1. The challenge of defining the purpose or mission of the organization

2. The challenge of determining and agreeing upon effective strategies for achieving the organization's mission

3. The challenge of determining objectives for achieving agreed-upon strategies

4. The challenge of making planning decisions and allocating resources to achieve agreed-upon objectives

5. The challenge of measuring the effectiveness of efforts to achieve objectives

Defining Mission: Nonprofits differ from for-profit organizations in that their missions are usually more difficult to define and their performance in fulfilling these missions, more difficult to measure.

The for-profit corporation's main purpose is to make money. A nonprofit organization's purpose may be as open-ended as promoting world peace or protecting the environment, advancing education or promoting volunteerism. These kinds of purposes are less clear-cut than the simple "make profit." The first step, then, for your start-up team will be to define as clearly as possible the purpose of your nonprofit organization.

Selecting Strategies: Let's say you all agree that the purpose of your organization will be to promote world peace. How will you do it? What will be your strategies? Will you focus on education? If so, will you try to educate the young (the future generation) or world leaders? Will you attempt to limit nuclear proliferation or promote international understanding; or will you try to work on root causes of greed and violence—or some combination? These are just a few of the possibilities you might come up with.

One difficulty that nonprofit planners face is the dilemma between long-term and short-term strategies for action. Will your foundation focus most of its energy on long-term change or short-term solutions? Short-term solutions often seem more attractive because:

a) *Your staff will receive more recognition and feedback and receive it more quickly for short-term solutions.* Efforts at short-term solutions have dramatic and immediate impacts, both on their recipients and on those providing the service. It feels good to see your efforts result in immediate improvements in the quality of the lives of those you work with. Tackling long-term objectives may be more frustrating. (Examples: Distributing food and blankets to the homeless vs. working to alleviate the underlying causes of homelessness. Providing famine relief to hungry children vs. building irrigation systems or promoting farming practices that may prevent future famines from occurring.)

b) *It is often easier to raise funds and enlist support for dramatic short-term solutions.* For example, in recent years, extensive droughts in sub-Saharan Africa brought massive emergency relief from around the world. Yet though there were effective strategies for establishing long-term self-sufficiency, the influx of support began to dry up as soon as the immediate crisis was alleviated—leaving the seeds of another crisis. When a problem has reached crisis proportions, it seems more "real" to people. The image of famine communicated the need in a dramatic and powerful way. When the need you want to serve is less immediately dramatic, it may require more creativity and effort to communicate it effectively to your would-be supporters.

Long-term strategies often involve fundamental changes, including changes in basic values, long-ingrained customs or procedures, and calcified thinking. The more fundamental the changes you are proposing, the greater resistance you are likely to encounter.

In addition to consideration of long- vs. short-term efforts, you must determine the scope your organization will work at. Will it work primarily on a local, state, national, or global scale—or some mix? Who in particular will your organization focus on serving?

Whatever mix your organization comes up with in selecting strategies for action, it is important that it reach a consensus. Coming to consensus can be a time-consuming and even divisive process. Yet it is vital that members of your organization agree on its strategies if they are to work effectively and harmoniously toward achieving them. Whatever strategies you choose, keep moving forward, step by step, holding to your purpose while remaining flexible in your response to changing times and circumstances.

Determining Goals: Picking up on the earlier example, let's say that your organization has chosen to fulfill its purpose of promoting world peace through the strategy of education. Even though all of the key members of your organization have agreed upon the organization's purpose and strategies, there may be as many ideas on how to actually implement these strategies as there are participants in your organization.

For example, Tom wants to teach elementary school children about sharing and the value of caring for others. Judy has just come back from a seminar on conflict mediation and believes that teaching these skills is, without a doubt, the quickest and surest road to world peace. Roger is convinced that international exchange-student programs at the college level should be the organization's primary focus. Carlotta wants to produce a peace play, featuring an international cast of children, and take it on a global tour. And the list goes on.

All of these objectives and others could further the organization's mission of furthering world peace through education. The point is simply that choices must be made.

Allocating Resources: What weight will various objectives be given within the organization? How do projects and programs stack up against administrative and fundraising efforts in terms of the share of available time and money resources? These are difficult questions that provide the possibility of ongoing friction and tension within the organization.

Various members of your organization may have their own pet projects. Each wants the greatest possible allocation of financial and personnel resources for his or her favorite. In addition to potential conflict over which programs will get what piece of the allocation pie, there are questions about the balance between the activities that further an organization's mission and those that pay for them.

How much emphasis should be placed on raising funds, and how much on the pure pursuit of the organization's mission? When does the organization risk compromising its principles in furthering its pocketbook? Do environmental groups, for example, accept large contributions from oil companies or industrial polluters? Many will say no. Others will say the good the organization can do with the money outweighs the potential harm to credibility and morale.

Every organization has to find its own balance and ethics. If an organization concerns itself too much with fundraising, it may become distracted from its mission. If, on the other hand, the foundation devalues the fundraising process, it may soon find its power to serve greatly reduced or eliminated entirely. This is a tightrope that every nonprofit foundation must walk: to generate enough income to keep itself viable, without becoming consumed by fundraising and administrative functions.

Whenever possible, try to combine fundraising activities with direct action on your mission objectives. (For example, organizing a benefit concert or event performs the dual functions of publicizing your cause and generating income.)

Assessing Feedback: Another striking difference between profit and nonprofit companies comes in evaluating performance. Management consultants have long known that clear feedback on performance is one of the strongest motivations for sustained action. Yet for many nonprofit enterprises, it is often difficult to measure exactly how effective the organization's efforts are.

For profit-based companies, measures set up to evaluate the company's performance are rather clear-cut—cost per unit, market share, quarterly sales figures, balance sheets, etc. The profit-based corporation is, after all, dealing with quantities—numbers related to money. Measuring nonprofit performance often does not lend itself to reduction to numbers. Issues of quality—the kind of things you just can't put a number on—are often more important than issues of quantity. For example, efforts in public education, or "consciousness raising," while important, are difficult to measure.

Another difficulty with a nonprofit corporation is deciding when it has accomplished its purpose. Let's say you begin an organization to stop commercial development on a local mountain. You found a nonprofit organization called "The Coalition to Save Mt. X." After many years of struggle, and much to your delight, Congress passes a provision protecting this mountain from future development. The purpose of the organization has now been achieved. But by this time you have a well-trained staff, a long list of donors and volunteers, and an extensive mailing list. The question now becomes: Do you disband or become "The Coalition to Save Mt. Y"? Or do you perhaps expand the purpose of your organization to include more far-reaching objectives, such as slowing global deforestation?

After thinking through the factors discussed above, you can begin to get a sense of whether or not creating a nonprofit foundation is the best way for you to accomplish your mission objectives. If you feel that it might be, by all means, do more research.

 If the only prayer you say in your whole life is "thank you," that would suffice.
Meister Eckhart

Starting Your Nonprofit Organization

State Your Purpose

The mission of the _____ organization is:

_____

_____

Determine Effective Strategies

The most effective strategies for achieving the mission of the organization include:

_____

_____

_____

State Prime Objectives

The primary objectives of strategy number one, for the period from_____
to _____ include: _____

_____

The primary objectives of strategy number one, for the period from_____
to _____ include: _____

_____

The primary objectives of strategy number one, for the period from_____
to _____ include: _____

_____

The primary objectives of strategy number one, for the period from_____
to _____ include: _____

_____

The primary objectives of strategy number one, for the period from_____
to _____ include: _____

_____

The great use of life is to spend it for something that will outlast it.

William James

Funding Your Nonprofit Corporation

Clarify Your Vision: Clarify on paper the goals and objectives of your program or organization. What do you want to accomplish? Whom do you want to serve? How do you plan to accomplish these objectives? How much money do you need? How will you document your results? Think it through; getting absolutely clear on what you want and why you want it is the first and most vital step to obtaining the results you desire.

Research: The purpose of the research process is to target those funding sources that most appropriately fit your specific needs. This may be the most time-consuming (and often the most tedious) part of the funding process. Hang in there. Time spent in careful research is time that will pay off in a greater percentage of successfully funded proposals. There are six factors involved in choosing your potential funding sources:

1. Field of interest: Many funding sources only give grants in specific fields. Target those awarding grants in your field.

2. Geographic limitations: Many foundations only fund projects within a given locale or region.

3. Type of support needed: Determine exactly what kind of assistance your project needs (seed money, equipment, building funds, etc.).

4. Type of recipient: Find out who your potential funding source gives to (nonprofit organizations, individuals, schools, hospitals, youth groups, etc.).

5. Amount to request: Make sure the amount you request in your proposal is consistent with the amounts this funder has granted before.

6. Application process: Find out how this funder prefers to receive proposals, and whether their funding cycle is consistent with your needs.

Write Your Proposal: Stress the benefits your project will provide. Tailor your proposal to the goals and objectives of your funding source. Keep it short and to the point. Include any information that enhances your credibility. Convince potential funders you have the credentials and the experience necessary to successfully complete your project. Make sure to include a carefully thought out, itemized budget. Mention any other sources or donations you've received, and include financial projections for the future of your project or program.

Follow Through: Find out the name of and get background information on the person(s) who make(s) final funding decisions. Call to set up an appointment to discuss your proposal. Come well prepared. First impressions are essential. If your proposal is rejected, find out why and keep in contact. You may want to send another proposal in the next funding cycle. Persist until you succeed. Consider these potential sources of funding: local foundations, statewide and national foundations, government grants, grants to individuals, corporate philanthropic programs.

> *I feel the capacity to care is the thing which gives life its deepest significance and meaning.*
> Pablo Casals

Proposal Writing at a Glance

Every year, billions of dollars in grants are awarded by private, public, and federal institutions to individuals, nonprofit organizations, and businesses. It has been estimated that there are roughly seventy-two thousand privately endowed grant-giving foundations in the United States (in 2007, grants from these organizations totaled $42.9 billion). In addition, there are thousands of grant-giving programs administered by the federal government.

Grants are awarded in a variety of areas, including education, research, training, health, performing arts, acquisition of equipment, conferences, travel, or to supplement operating costs. In virtually any area you may be working in, there is the possibility of gaining funding assistance through some type of grant.

Here are just a few examples of grant awards: Three chemical engineering researchers from Mississippi State were awarded $200,000 from the Environmental Protection Agency for a project designed to convert wastewater sludge into biodiesel fuel; the John Templeton Foundation awarded $500,000 to Enterprise Africa!, an organization devoted to finding local solutions to the problems of poverty in Africa. Soprano Dawn Upshaw was named a MacArthur Fellow and awarded $500,000 by the MacArthur Foundation; the Old Globe Theatre was awarded $750,000 from the James Irvine Foundation to develop arts-related programs in southeastern San Diego; the Pew Memorial Trust awarded $100,000 to the Big Brothers/Big Sisters of America in Philadelphia in support of their District Field Service System; the Kellogg Foundation awarded $206,093 to Youth for Understanding in Washington, D.C., to help them develop and deliver a national intercultural volunteer leadership development program.

Start by developing the general concept of your project; consider the issues you want to address, along with the methods you will use in your approach to them. Once you have clarified your project objectives, the keys to receiving a grant to fund your project are three: comprehensive research of appropriate and available grants, the writing of effective proposals, and persistence.

The last point is critical. I know of one case where a man seeking a grant for a unique educational program he had developed received over three hundred rejections before his proposal was finally funded. The private foundation that eventually funded his program liked his idea so much, they gave him more money than he had originally requested. The last I heard, his program was being taught in hundreds of schools throughout the nation. If you are serious about proposal writing, it's a good idea to develop a thick skin about rejection. At the same time, you will want to develop the skills that will increase your chances of success—selecting the right organizations to approach and writing effective proposals.

Your local library will probably have many of the sources you need to research grant options. When you are seeking a grant, check sources such as *Grant Seekers Guide, The Taft Foundation Reporter: Comprehensive Profiles and Analyses of America's Private Foundations, The Foundation Grants Index,* and *Foundation Grants to Individuals.* (You can also check "Grant-writing Resources" at empoweryou.com for links to up-to-date resources.) These sources will give you a general idea of who is giving grants and for what purposes, along with information on how to contact the grant-giving organizations.

Like any other, proposal writing is a skill that improves with practice. The information that can be provided in this space is necessarily limited. I include it to give you a general idea of the process and to stimulate those who are interested to check out additional resources. I suggest you visit http://foundationcenter.org, or contact the Foundation Center, 79 5th Ave., New York, NY 10003, (212) 620-4230, for more information. Besides providing a wealth of information and sources, the Grantsmanship Center offers seminars and workshops (around the country) that give you a chance to learn directly from those who have had experience and success in grant writing. Similar courses are provided by the Foundation Center and the Fund Raising School. In addition, there are a number of excellent how-to books on proposal writing (see the list on this page). There are also private grant-writing consultants who specialize in areas such as writing proposals for government agencies. You may want to investigate these.

Government and many of the large private foundations have application check lists or specific guidelines dictating the way a proposal must be submitted. Contact your target organizations, and ask them to send you their guidelines. While you are waiting for these (and many organizations don't have them), write a preliminary or rough draft proposal. This will assist you in clarifying your own thinking. As Francis Bacon said, "writing [maketh] an exact man [or woman]."[1] Besides clarifying your thinking, writing your rough draft will show you what you know and what you need to find out.

Grant-Writing Sources

Complete Book of Grant Writing. Nancy Burke Smith. Naperville, Ill.: Sourcebooks, 2006.

Demystifying Grant Seeking: What You REALLY Need to Do to Get Grants. Larissa Golden Brown and Martin Brown. New York: Wiley, 2008.

The Everything Grant Writing Book: Create the Perfect Proposal to Raise the Funds You Need. Nancy Burke Smith and Judy Tremore. Holbrook, Mass.: Adams Media Corp., 2008.

Getting Funded: A Complete Guide to Proposal Writing. Mary S. Hall. Portland, Ore.: Continuing Education Press, 2003.

Grant Writing for Dummies, 2nd ed. Beverly A. Browning. New York: For Dummies, 2005.

Grassroots Grants: An Activist's Guide to Proposal Writing. Andy Robinson and Kim Klein. San Francisco: Jossey-Bass, 2004.

The Only Grant Writing Book You'll Ever Need: Top Grant Writers and Grant Givers Share Their Secrets!, 2nd ed. Ellen Karsh and Arlen Sue Fox. New York: Carroll & Graf, 2006.

Proposal Planning and Writing, 3rd ed. Lynn E. Miner and Jeremy T. Miner. Westport, Conn.: Greenwood Press, 2008.

Web and Book Resources

Find Web and book resources about creating a nonprofit foundation @ Empoweryou.com.

Nonprofit Incorporation Checklist

The list below is incomplete but can serve as a general guide to track your progress as you define and launch your nonprofit organization.

1. Select a legal name for your organization.   _____

2. Form your board of directors.   _____

3. File fictitious business name statement.   _____

4. Obtain business licenses and permits.   _____

5. Draft bylaws.   _____

6. Prepare and file articles of incorporation.   _____

7. Prepare and file state tax exemption application.   _____

8. Prepare and file federal tax exemption application.   _____

9. Create a strategic plan.   _____

10. Develop and submit fundraising proposals.   _____

11. Develop a budget and financial plan.   _____

12. Develop accounting and record-keeping systems.   _____

13. Apply for a nonprofit mailing permit.   _____

14. Obtain an EIN (Federal Employer ID number) from the Internal
    Revenue Service.   _____

15. Open a separate bank account for your nonprofit.   _____

16. File the necessary documentation to comply with state, county, and
    municipal charitable solicitation laws.   _____

17. Obtain liability insurance.   _____

Twelve Principles That Motivate
the Creation of Nonprofit Organizations

VISION
*Inspired action
based on a vision of the Good.*
Self-motivating

HARMONY
*Balanced feelings; accord; shared
responsibilities; cooperation.*
Cooperating

POWER
*Providing resources
the authority to act.*
Establishing

PURIFICATION
*Seeking out hidden problems to
effect transformation.*
Transforming

TRUTH
*Knowledge of
the incontrovertible.*
Educating

LAW
*Principles on which
shared ethics are based.*
Leading

LOVE
*Fidelity to the
principle of benevolence.*
Sharing

FOUNDATION
*Forms which support
the function of institutions.*
Structuring

WISDOM
Expressing intelligence in life.
Creating

VIRTUE
*Evolving life through practical
adherence to ideals.*
Refining

COMPASSION
*Serving others; providing
for basic life needs.*
Serving

SUSTAINMENT
*Preservation of the
social, conceptual, and artistic
institutions of society.*
Protecting

Landing the Right Job

*God gives every bird its food,
but He doesn't throw it in the nest.*
                    J. G. Holland

This section begins with a brief overview of the job landscape, then focuses specifically on the corporate, government, non-profit, and small-business sectors. It goes on to outline a complete program for conducting an aggressive job search. From identifying your goals and targeting potential employers, through landing and taking job interviews, all the way through salary negotiation—the material that follows will guide you every step of the way. The efforts you put into researching the jobs you really want, into aggressively seeking out potential employers, and into making sure that you really stand out at interview time will all pay off in the long run. In fact, they could spell the difference between starting each day excited about the work in front of you or dreading that alarm clock because it signals the start of another dreary day of meaningless or monotonous routine.

Why Do I Need an Aggressive Job Search?

In little over a hundred years, we have gone from an agrarian to an urban society. It is hard to believe that as late as the 1890s, most Americans grew their own food, made their own clothes, built their own homes; many even made their own soap. Today, few of us do any of these things for ourselves. Beyond this, the number of "necessary" consumer products has exploded. In the modern economy, we need money to survive and more money to enjoy life. Yet relatively few of us make the money we need and want by working for ourselves. Consequently, most of us are, or believe we are, in need of jobs to survive and have the things we want for our loved ones and ourselves. It is little wonder then that many ask for nothing more than economic rewards from the work they spend their lives doing. Since you are reading this book, it's likely that you are asking for more—and you should.

You deserve to spend your life doing something that brings you happiness and joy, something you can take pride in and be really passionate about. While you might be lucky, chances are that you will have to work to find a job like that. The effort you put into your search will be well rewarded. No matter your education, experience, or skill level, you can find a better job through an aggressive, targeted job search than you can through the more typical happenstance approach to job hunting.

Why Aren't There More Good Jobs?

Have you ever asked yourself: Why aren't there more good jobs? By "good jobs" I mean jobs that challenge, jobs that inspire, jobs that encourage maximum self-development and allow people to make meaningful contributions. This is not to say that these jobs do not exist. (Indeed, they do and the tools and strategies in this section will help you find one of these jobs to call your own.) It is simply to ask: Why aren't there more good jobs? Implicit in this question is another: Why do I need to develop an aggressive approach to my job search? After all, if there were an abundance of good jobs, anyone could easily obtain one. While finding *a* job can be more or less difficult, depending on the economy, finding a job that allows you to be and express yourself always presents a challenge. Below I will briefly consider how work is organized today and see if we can't, perhaps, discover an answer to the question: Why aren't there more good jobs?

The Organization of Work

In the United States, roughly twenty million people are self-employed. The rest of the U.S. workforce works for somebody else. In order, the major employers are for-profit corporations, nonprofit corporations, and government. The corporate sector—large, mid-sized, and small corporations—employs the largest number of people by far. Roughly one in eight of all working Americans work for a Fortune 500 company. Of course, there are a great many large corporations that are not in the exclusive Fortune 500 club. In fact, small businesses employ more than half of all private-sector employees. Government (local, state, and federal) directly employs over twenty-three million people—and millions more indirectly through contracts. Most government jobs are at the state and local level. While the U.S. federal government is the nation's single largest employer, its three million employees represent a small fraction of the total U.S. workforce. The nonprofit sector is one of the fastest-growing employment sectors, employing roughly thirteen million people. While there has been a steady trend in recent years toward smaller organizations, the fact remains that most people who work for someone else work for large organizations.

Large organizations are a fact of modern life. In the words of famed management consultant Peter Drucker, "Our society has become, within an incredibly short fifty years, a society of institutions. It has become a pluralist society in which every major social task has been entrusted to large organizations—from producing economic goods and services to healthcare, from social security and welfare to education, from the search for new knowledge to the protection of the natural environment."[1] Today, for-profit corporations are the dominant organizational form. In our highly institutionalized and organized society, massive amounts of capital are required to establish and maintain large organizations. Most large nongovernmental organizations are corporations, for the simple reason that this is how they are financed (through the sale of shares of corporate stock), and further, because the existing legal and tax structures favor incorporation.

As the dominant type of large organization, the modern corporation has great influence over our lives. Many feel that this influence is too great. In a recent survey of Americans, 80 percent said they believed that corporations have too much power. Ultimately, the most important power that the corporations wield is the power to employ people—to employ not simply their labor, but their knowledge and intelligence toward ends that the corporations deem worthy. Remember, every existing job reflects visions and values that someone deems worthy of support. Modern corporations determine, to a great extent, the visions and values that society reflects through the work they set for millions to do.

Clearly, if we are to understand how work is organized, we must understand something of the role that the large corporations play. Large corporations have certain characteristics that shape their social role: Corporations are profit-driven

organizations that limit personal responsibility and tend to consolidate wealth and power.

Profit-driven: Profits are the essential discipline of the modern corporation, its elemental decision-making criterion. "[Profits are] the immediate, unique, unifying, quantitative aim of corporate success."[2] This is somewhat ironic because corporations exist at the behest of the states (which charter them), and states once demanded far more for the privilege. In early American history, states only granted corporate charters, and the extraordinary powers they confer, to organizations that agreed to undertake projects that the states deemed of benefit to the public good (e.g., building roads or canals). These corporations were allowed to make a profit, but only for a limited time and only for a purpose that the state recognized as serving the public good. By contrast, the modern corporation can exist in perpetuity for no other purpose than to make money. The modern corporation's exclusive emphasis on profit does not reflect some mystical law of market economics but rather public policy, which is to say, political decisions. Since the state holds the power to grant corporate charters, the state could theoretically set any qualifying criteria it wanted, including demonstrated service to the greater good. Although the state (and thus, through the political process, the public) maintains some control over corporations through regulation, it no longer requires that corporations serve the public interest.

The modern corporation's primary responsibility is to serve the private economic interests of their debt and equity holders—not the public. Because of the way they are organized, corporations are only interested in working in areas with profit potential. For example, while there may be profit in providing nursing-home care (and therefore, corporate involvement), there is not the same interest in providing care for the homeless. Additionally, the quality of care that corporate nursing homes provide will be dictated by profit considerations at every turn. This doesn't necessarily mean the service provided will be shoddy. Nursing homes for the well-to-do are likely to provide excellent service because there is greater profit potential in doing so. The point is simply that the basic question asked is not, "How do we provide the best care?" but, "How do we make the most profit?"

Today, in making corporate decisions, the short-term economic interests of the company's debt and equity holders take precedence over the interests of its workforce and customers, the general public, and the environment. While, as an individual, a corporate manager may be a kind and caring person, a corporation, as an institution, is only interested in the well-being of its employees to the extent that "a happy worker is a productive worker," one who is likely to produce more profit for the corporation. The worker (white collar or blue) is viewed, first and foremost, as a business expense made for the realization of profit. Corporations are interested in the quality of the environment or the public welfare to the degree that there is profit potential in addressing them. This service may generate profit directly, through the sale of goods and services, or indirectly, through an enhanced public image. Of course, an emphasis on profit applies to all business, from the medieval town fair to the mom-and-pop grocery. Yet the profit orientation of the modern corporation is especially severe in its application for a couple of reasons.

First, corporations have great influence over the other sectors of society (government, nonprofit, small business). Through their control of capital and their employment of labor, corporations set the agenda for most of the work that gets done in our society. This has effects that are felt throughout national and global communities. For example, it is clearly essential for life on this planet that we develop clean, safe, renewable energy. Yet we've long been told the profit incentive just isn't there. No one doubts, however, that there is plenty of profit in the dirty,

dangerous, and nonrenewable energy we currently rely on. Government is reticent to do anything that might interfere with the profits of the large corporations. After all, politicians depend on corporations for campaign contributions. In Washington D.C., and most state capitals, corporate lobbyists far outnumber legislators. These lobbyists often draft bills that friendly legislators then introduce to the full legislative body for ratification. The large corporations likewise exercise a good deal of control over the nonprofit sector through the awarding of grants, sponsorships, and the sharing of board members. Further, the large corporations exercise influence over small business through ownership of banks and other lending institutions. Small business needs money to grow, and since the large corporations control the lion's share of available capital, they can greatly influence the visions and values that small businesses are likely to actualize.

Second, the larger the corporation, the more removed the decision makers are likely to be from the human implications of their decisions. Small businesses are more likely to include other value considerations when

Make It Count

"My employer uses twenty-six years of my life for every year I get to keep. And what do I get in return for the enormous thing I am giving? What do I get in return for my life?"

Michael Ventura,
L.A. Weekly

making decisions because they are more likely to meet and know the people whom their decisions affect. Because they typically have more human interaction with their employees, customers, clients, and communities, small-business decision makers are more likely to view these folks as people like themselves. On the other hand, corporate managers frequently set company policy in isolation. They never see, feel, or in any way directly experience the effects their decisions have on employees, customers, the general public, or the environment. Physical distance breeds emotional and psychological distance. As a general rule, the greater the physical proximity of key decision makers to those affected by their decisions, the more human factors become variables in the decision-making process. In the case of a major corporation, those working at the corporate headquarters, even at the lower staff levels, are likely to receive greater consideration (human and monetary) than those working in the field offices (excepting those regional directors, etc., who have regular physical contact with key decision makers). It's not surprising then that corporate decision makers often insulate and isolate themselves high atop great glass towers, where they are free to make decisions with a cool eye to the bottom line. The exclusive emphasis on profit performance gives them a kind of tunnel vision. Indeed, survival in management positions often depends upon acquiring and maintaining this vision. Corporate managers are likely to have "their feet held to the fire" for their financial performance, not for their service to humanity.

Limited Responsibility: Legally, a modern corporation is a fictional person with limited personal responsibility. A corporation is granted the rights of an individual person (e.g., the right to enter into contracts, equal protection under law, freedom of speech, etc.) yet is exempted from many of the responsibilities that an individual faces. For example, every major corporation keeps two sets of books. With one set, they are allowed to say to shareholders and creditors (and would-be shareholders and creditors), "Look, these are the profits we made." Yet, at tax time, they are allowed to present a second set of books to the government in which, remarkably, they've made significantly less profit or even showed a loss. An individual who tried to do the same could well be looking at jail time. In a variety of ways, the financial and legal liability of corporate shareholders is limited. States were once reticent to grant corporate charters because they recognized that they were bestowing extraordinary powers on those who comprise this "person."

For corporate managers, personal responsibility is limited by making the economic interests of the debt and equity holders primary to all other considerations. Again, corporate managers are not expected to be interested in anything that will not enhance shareholder value and preserve creditors' interests. A corporate manager who bases his decisions on other criteria is likely to be replaced by one who "knows the value of the bottom line." Today, even managers who base their decisions on profit considerations but are perceived as taking a too-long view are likely to be replaced. No person, be he CEO or chairman of the board, is exempt from short-term profit pressure. In this sense, there are no people running corporations. They are run, instead, by the drive to maximize short-term profits.

Monopolistic: In practice, this tends to make the large corporations rather like hungry ghosts, which roam the earth devouring natural resources, human labor, knowledge, and culture, and other corporations, in an attempt to satisfy an insatiable appetite for growth. The corporate logic of "eat or be eaten" demands sustained growth. "Grow or die" is the corporate battle cry. This growth tends to be malignant to life. Large corporations feed on the real wealth of life, labor, and knowledge to produce an abstraction called "economic profit."

This drive for growth tends to consolidate wealth in monopolies controlled by a relative few. Since corporate interests tend to dominate governments, they are able to construct favorable legal metaphysics that ensure ever-greater consolidation of wealth. In fact, this is the case. Relatively few individuals control a large percentage of the abstract wealth called "capital assets," and through it, the real wealth of knowledge, labor, and resources. Today, fewer than five hundred families control more wealth than the poorest half of the planet's population—more than three billion people!

The Bottom Line

As we have seen, a corporation is required to serve the economic interests of its debt and equity holders. While it may be engaged in an enterprise that benefits the greater good, there is no requirement that it must be. What this means for you is that if you want your job to be about more than economic rewards, if you want to feel that your daily efforts are contributing to the greater good, you will need to be selective when choosing a company to work for. It is the individual's responsibility to choose work that expresses values he or she considers worthy of his or her time and energy. Those who offer money for work and those who offer their talents, skills, and energy for hire share responsibility for the world they create. The argument that the corporation must be socially irresponsible to make a profit is no more or less spurious than the argument that the individual must join an organization whose goals he does not believe in, simply to survive.

Organizations can (and some do) profit quite nicely by doing socially useful things. Many organizations profiting from less noble pursuits could redirect their efforts toward more socially valuable efforts if they had the will to do so. Similarly, many individuals work within organizations whose purposes they genuinely agree with and deem valuable and useful to the greater good. Many individuals who do not could do so if they had the will to continue their search until they found such organizations. The large organizations that control huge capital funds have a responsibility for the use of the natural resources, human knowledge, and labor that it represents. (Again, enormous capital assets do not fall from the sky; they represent an accumulation of the labor, knowledge, skill, and intelligence of thousands of individuals, not to mention the beneficence of the planet, and its living and mineral resources.) Each of us is, likewise, responsible for how we use our talent, knowledge, skill, intelligence, labor, time, and energy.

> *Many times a day I realize how much my own outer and inner life is built upon the labors of my fellow men, both living and dead, and how earnestly I must exert myself in order to give in return as much as I have received.*
>
> *Albert Einstein*

Take, for example, the knowledge you possess. As Francis Bacon said, "Knowledge is power." Today, that power is truly enormous. Consider the power that practitioners of physics, chemistry, genetics, and engineering wield today. Yet all one has to do to gain initiation into these powerful "knowledges" is to go to any university in the land. No attempt will be made to measure one's wisdom or character before he is initiated into these fantastic powers. He will not even be admonished that the power he controls (through his knowledge) is extraordinary and should be used with great care. He need only be clever and have money for school.

Knowledge, which is an accumulation of centuries of human endeavor, is taken by him to be his personal property. Since he believes that he owns this knowledge, he deems it his right to sell it to the highest bidder, regardless of the purpose the bidder has in mind. Then he takes the cloak of scientific respectability as his defense and says, "Well, I'm just 'doing science.' (Or, I just work here.) It is not my responsibility how my work will be used." Of course, there are exceptions, but this kind of attitude is rampant, not only in science, but in many professions.

When you go to a university and learn physics or genetics, chemistry or computer science, engineering or architecture, or any science, or art for that matter, what you learn represents thousands of years of intellectual accumulation and millions of years of human evolution. The notion that each of us ought to do with this planetary accumulation whatever he or she pleases, without a sense of social responsibility or obligation, is a prescription for global disaster. A society of hired guns, selling off planetary accumulation for personal profit, without consideration of the use to which that accumulation is put, can only turn our beautiful blue planet into a nightmare world.

I understood . . . that those who desired salvation should act like the trustee who, though having control over great possessions, regards not an iota of them as his own.

Gandhi

Of course, everything I've said with respect to responsibility for how you use your knowledge applies equally to your talents, skill, time, and energy. When you join your efforts to any organization, consider how this organization is likely to use *your* assets. Your sense of obligation to the past and responsibility for the future will naturally move you toward an organization whose purpose is valuable and humane.

The Secrets to Finding the Right Organization

Famed management consultant and author Peter Drucker has discussed motivation in work, noting changes in today's workers from previous generations. He has concluded that the stick (fear) no longer motivates, except in rare instances. Neither does the carrot (material rewards)—not, at least, with any degree of consistency. This, Drucker explains, is for the simple reason that the more we get, the more we want. He suggests that embracing responsibility for the organization and its contribution to the larger society is the best long-term motivator.[3]

Choose an Organization You Can Take Responsibility For: Here, then, is a key to continued motivation in the workplace, but also, and more importantly, a key to selecting the organizations you choose to work for. It is imperative that you select an organization for which you can actively and wholeheartedly take responsibility. Any other choice will, eventually, lead to motivational problems and their attendant side effects: apathy, depression, poor performance, and the like. *Remember, only if you can take full responsibility for the organization you are working for and its contribution can you do your best work.* You must agree with and support the organization's purpose.

Look for Agreement and Commitment: In addition to choosing an organization for which you can take responsibility, look for an organization that has strong agreement among its members as to purpose. This will help ensure that the work environment will be productive and harmonious. Remember the axiom: *Peripherals move in to fill the void left by lack of purpose.* Peripherals in the work environment can take the shape of pointless bickering, useless rivalries, distracting preoccupations, routine redundancies, or endless delays. They drain you emotionally and leave little energy for

the important work. People who have only
worked in this type of work environment
come to believe that all work is draining
and exhausting. In fact, purposeful work
replenishes and renews; it gives as much
energy as it takes. It is working on peripherals that is exhausting, and all the more so
because one recognizes that they are such
a waste. Choose, then, an organization you
can take responsibility for and one with an
energetic esprit de corps.

Working the Corporate Scene

Nothing said above should be taken as a
wholesale indictment of corporations or
of corporate employment. It is, rather, my
intent to indicate some of the structural
dynamics that tend to limit corporations'
capacities to provide fulfilling work. Still,
there are thousands of worthwhile jobs
within the corporate sector. Those interested
in jobs in this sector are encouraged to take
advantage of the resource links available at
empoweryou.com. You should be able to find
many of the books listed there in your public
library or college career center.

Working for Small Business

The small-business sector is the fastest-
growing segment of the American economy.
For research purposes, the U.S. Office of
Small Business Administration (SBA) defines small businesses as companies that
employ fewer than five hundred employees.
According to the SBA, small businesses
employ more than half of all private-sector
employees and generate 60 to 80 percent of
new jobs annually. This booming sector offers
many exciting job opportunities, especially
for aggressive, self-motivated individuals.
Many of these jobs are relatively high-paying
professional positions. For example, small
business employs nearly 40 percent of high-
tech workers (such as scientists, engineers,
and computer workers.)

The work environment in small businesses is usually less structured and formal
than in larger companies. Smaller firms
generally offer greater opportunities to learn
new skills and take on new responsibilities. They also are more apt to encourage
creativity and initiative on the part of their
employees. Start-up businesses account for
many of the new jobs created each year.
These companies are often run by individuals with a kind of missionary zeal for their
enterprises. When hiring, these employers
look for dedicated people who are willing to
go above and beyond the call of duty. While
they often expect more of their employees
(e.g., greater loyalty, longer hours, fewer
benefits and vacations), entrepreneurs offer
greater opportunities to become involved in
the equity side of the business—to own a
piece of the action. Additionally, if you become
involved in a rapidly growing business and
show real leadership ability, you may have
unique opportunities for rapid advancement.
Finally, small businesses often provide opportunities for deeper personal relationships
than larger firms—a chance to feel like you
are part of a team or even a family.

For a list of small businesses in your
area, look for a local business directory on the
Internet. For current openings, check local
and national online job boards, craigslist,
and newspaper classifieds.

Energy and persistence conquer all things.
Benjamin Franklin

Working for the Federal, State, or Local Government

When you think of government jobs, you may think of postal clerks or bureaucratic office workers. Fortunately, these are not the only jobs available within the government sector. Government jobs vary as much as those in the private sector—ranging from baker to typist, nurse to zoologist, accountant to physical therapist, radio operator to community planner, lawyer to economist. There are more than nine hundred job classifications within the federal government, and many more at state, county, and city levels.

Whatever your field of interest, opportunities exist to serve the public good by working within the government. Those interested in public action may want to explore programs within the Departments of: Housing and Urban Development, Labor, Education, or Health and Human Services. If you are interested in environmental issues, you may want to consider programs within the Department of the Interior or the Environmental Protection Agency. Those interested in civil rights might consider the Justice Department; in international relations, the State Department. State and local governments often develop innovative programs designed to address specific needs. For example, the state of California developed a statewide program to enhance the self-esteem of schoolchildren. Washington State developed an innovative program to assist welfare recipients in starting their own small businesses. According to the U.S. Census Bureau, roughly twenty-three million Americans work in government at the federal, state, and local level. Each year, the federal government alone hires over three hundred thousand new employees. Behind these statistics lie a lot of dull, and some really great, jobs. You will probably have to sift through a lot of chaff to find the wheat. There are a number of excellent resources that can assist you in finding out about good government jobs. In addition to all the regular places you look for a job (job Web sites, newspapers, etc.), there are a number of sites especially targeted to government jobs.

Applying for Federal Jobs: You can obtain complete information about federal job openings by visiting USAJOBS at: www.usajobs .opm.gov. Applicants for federal jobs are no longer required to fill out Standard Form 171. Instead you can create your own resume or use the Optional Application for Federal Employment (OF 612). If you choose to use the OF 612, be sure to fill it out carefully, and tailor each application to the particular job you are applying for. If you choose to create your own job-specific resume, be sure to provide complete information. Keep in mind that the standard job resume is seldom adequate for a federal job. In the private sector, the purpose of a resume is to grab the attention of a potential employer so you will be called in for an initial interview. In the government sector, virtually all screening is done on paper, while in the private sector, candidates are screened lightly on the basis of their resumes and more thoroughly on the basis of their interviews. Because government agencies typically conduct fewer job interviews when filling a position, your application or resume for a federal job must be much more thorough. If your application or resume doesn't adequately portray you, your qualifications, and work experience, you won't get an interview.

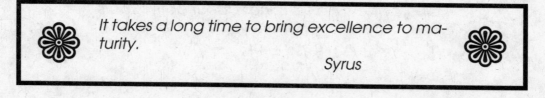

It takes a long time to bring excellence to maturity.

Syrus

The Federal Vacancy Announcement: Review the Federal Vacancy Announcement (available at www.usajobs.opm.gov) carefully prior to filling out your OF 612 or writing your position-specific resume. It provides you with a thorough description of the vacancy: its title, job requirements, salary, growth potential, geographic location, description of duties, and posting and closing dates. It will also tell you if you are required to take a written Civil Service exam. (For most positions, this is not required.) Take note of the "Quality Ranking Factors" section. It describes the specific skills, knowledge, and abilities you will need for the position, stating the criteria that will be used in scoring your application. Federal Vacancy Announcements list the name and phone number of a designated staffing specialist who usually is the only person authorized to give you specific information about the position. Call this person if you have any questions about the job prior to submitting your OF 612 or resume.

Additional Sources of Federal Job Listings: An additional source for job information is the *Federal Jobs Digest,* available online at www.jobsfed.com (or look for a hard copy in your local library). The Federal Research Service (www.fedjobs.com) also offers listings of available federal jobs, in addition to a variety of products and services for federal job seekers. It publishes *Federal Career Opportunities*, a magazine available in many libraries. Ask your reference librarian for assistance in finding this and other nongovernmental newsletters and Web sites that list federal job vacancies. Additionally, many better-paying and/or professional jobs in the government are listed in the classified section of your local newspaper (especially the Sunday edition) and are posted on the major job sites (Careerbuilder, etc).

State Jobs: Every state has a central Web site that lists all the state government jobs currently available in that state. Most are searchable by a range of criteria. Empoweryou.com has links to all fifty of the state government job sites.

City Jobs: Like the states, most large urban centers have central Web sites that list all city government jobs. Links to the city job Web sites of about fifty major U.S. cities can be found at empoweryou.com. If you are looking for a job in a smaller city, much of what of is discussed below in reference to counties applies for smaller cities as well.

County Jobs: Visit your county Web site. Many, but by no means all, counties list county job openings on their sites. If yours doesn't, you should at least find the phone number of your local county personnel office. Call and ask how you can find county jobs in your area. Also, if you are looking for a government job in a specific area, for example, teaching (www.teachers-teachers.com) or law enforcement (www.lawenforcementjobs.com), be aware that there are job Web sites targeted to many specific vocational areas.

 One of the simplest things about all the facts of life is that to get where you want to go, you must keep on keeping on.
Norman Vincent Peale

Working in the Nonprofit Sector

If teamwork, challenge, and a service motivation interest you, the nonprofit sector is likely to offer excellent employment opportunities. If you are interested in starting your own nonprofit organization, you will find working for a nonprofit already established in your field to be an invaluable source of experience.

Commitment to Service: Generally, work in the nonprofit sector provides an opportunity for service to others. People enjoy the opportunity to work with colleagues who share a similar commitment and vision. Motive counts in the nonprofit sector. Most employees enjoy the sense of purpose, commitment, and integrity that comes from believing in what they're doing. Many people who work in the nonprofit sector start out as volunteers and end up filling paid positions.

Comraderie: Nonprofits generally offer a less competitive and more harmonious work environment than corporations. Many nonprofits operate on a consensus basis and value each individual's input in decision making. While building consensus takes considerably more time, people tend to be more committed to successfully implementing resulting decisions.

Freedom to Initiate: Individuals who succeed in the nonprofit sector are generally self-motivated and desire the freedom and flexibility to design programs and solutions to problems as they see fit. They often enjoy greater autonomy and challenge than in similar business or government jobs.

Organizational Structure: Nonprofits tend to be somewhat looser in structure than business or government organizations. The average nonprofit is a smaller organization with a more varied workload. For this reason, many nonprofits can be flexible in responding quickly to changes and developments in their field. Nonprofits can often be quickly and effectively organized to deal with local or short-term issues.

Stress Level in Work: Nonprofit workers experience a different type of stress than their counterparts in business or government. There is less high-pressure stress than in the corporate world, but there may be more immediate contact with human suffering. This can take an emotional toll. Further, many nonprofits, for example, in the arts, continually face funding crises and the associated stress.

Earnings and Benefits: Although pay in the nonprofit sector is usually lower than in business, the gap has been steadily closing. A good nonprofit manager can expect to earn almost as much as his corporate counterpart. In addition, nonprofit workers usually enjoy greater flexibility in hours. Medical coverage, working conditions, and fringe benefits vary greatly from organization to organization.

Note: Do careful research on each organization you are considering. If possible, talk to the people who work there.

Web and Book Resources
Find targeted Web resources for finding private sector, government, and nonprofit jobs @ Empoweryou.com.

Aggressive Job-Search Strategies

The competitive demands of the marketplace and the desire to realize your own best work require that you take an aggressive approach to the job-hunting process. Whether you choose to work for a large or small business, in government, or in the nonprofit sector, the dynamics of an aggressive job search are essentially the same. The first step is to specify exactly what you want from a potential employer. Next, thoroughly research organizations in your field and determine the ones you most want to work for. Make contact with these organizations and set up interviews. (This section will cover a number of ways to do this.) Then prepare for and take the interviews and, when all goes well, negotiate salary and other considerations. Before considering these steps in more detail, let's step back and briefly contrast aggressive job-search strategies with some more traditional approaches.

The Hit-and-Miss Approach: The hit-and-miss approach is the most common job-search strategy. It involves responding to newspaper ads, posting resumes online, and going to private employment agencies and state employment offices (see page 443).

Attitude: Passive selection. "I'll leave it to employers to tell me what positions they have available and hope they offer one that matches what I want to do."

Weakness: Limited selection (only 30 percent of all jobs are advertised) and lack of control in the selection (many of the best jobs are never advertised).

The Broadcast Approach: This approach involves posting, e-mailing, or mailing a barrage of resumes to as many job boards or potential employers as possible in the hope of eliciting requests for interviews.

Attitude: Fire and wait. "I will put my resume everywhere I can and hope that among the employers who might see it, a few can give me a match with what I want to do."

Weakness: You are depending on a resume—a cold piece of paper, or set of characters on a screen—to find you a job. This is a mistake for two reasons: (1) First, there is no guarantee that the person who has the power to hire you will ever see it. Your resume may be screened out by computer software or by a bureaucrat in the human resources department. Large organizations are inundated with resumes and yours simply becomes one more in the stack. In a small organization without a personnel department, the individual you're soliciting is most likely swamped with routine paperwork. Expecting him or her to even read your resume (let alone respond to it) may be asking too much, especially if the position you are seeking has not been advertised. (2) No resume can possibly represent you as well as you can. Employers hire people, not qualifications listed on a resume.

The Laser-Focused Approach: This approach involves determining in advance the organizations you would like to work for and arranging to set up interviews.

Attitude: Take charge of the process from beginning to end. "I will select the organizations I want to work for and will creatively and consistently go after them until I get the position I want."

Weakness: Only the limits of your creativity, effort, and persistence.

The Laser-Focused Job Search

The discussion below concentrates on the laser-focused approach. You're probably familiar with how the others work and see the advantages of a more aggressive approach. Aggressiveness is critical in two key areas: in researching organizations and in approaching them. It will take planning, research, and effort. It will take courage, determination, and persistence. A positive, winning attitude is a must. P. T. Barnum said that a sucker is born every minute. Suckers get beat in the job hunt because they focus on their weaknesses. They are missing a few years in their work history or changed jobs too many times; the college or university they attended was not prestigious enough or they don't have a graduate degree. Whatever it may be, they concentrate on what they are lacking rather than focusing on the value of what they have to give.

You're no sucker if you know you have the power in your job search. And power *is* a matter of perception. Ultimately, your power comes from your confidence and belief in yourself. Recognize that the process of landing a job is a negotiation and that the first person you're negotiating with is yourself. If you lose this negotiation and settle for less than what you really want, you're beaten before you've even started. Raise your aspirations, up your expectations, and you'll get more of what you want. You'll never get more by settling for less. Be in your own corner.

Job-Search Strategies in a Nutshell

Step 1: Decide: Identify what you want from an organization.

Step 2: Research: Know your market. Research organizations.

Step 3: Select: Target the organizations you want to work for. Identify the exact position you want and the person with the power to hire you.

Step 4: Write: Create or update your resume.

Step 5: Solicit: Get the interview.

Step 6: Prepare: Prepare for interviews.

Step 7: Communicate: Conduct successful interviews.

Step 8: Celebrate: Get the job you want.

10 Keys to Making Your Job Search Successful

1. Believe in yourself and the value of what you have to give.

2. Know your strengths: the tangibles (knowledge, experience, skills, and abilities) as well as intangibles (creativity, intuition, determination, etc.)

3. Know how to present yourself and your strengths. Develop stories that highlight your strengths in action.

4. Know exactly what you want. Develop criteria for your employer.

5. Throughout all your efforts, take the attitude that you are self-employed. You are hiring yourself an employer.

6. Be selective. Target. Target. Target. There is nothing more frustrating or demeaning than working your tail off to get a job you don't really want.

7. Master self-marketing and job-hunting skills to give yourself more freedom. Many people report staying in jobs they can't stand, simply because they dread the "hunting" process so much.

8. Networking is key. The more people you know, the more ways you have to go, the more room you have to grow. This applies after you get your next position, as well as before.

9. You are seeking membership in an organization—of people. Play with paper as required (resumes, cover letters, applications, etc.), but remember, people ask *people* to join their organizations.

10. Remember—in all forms of marketing, nothing succeeds like the appearance of success. Project a strong personality. Confidence counts.

The Mechanics

Before examining aggressive job-search strategies, let's consider a few mechanics that will facilitate getting the most from your efforts.

1. **Set a schedule.** If you're out of a job and looking for work full-time, then do it full time. That doesn't mean post or send your resume hundreds of times every month. It means try to schedule at least one interview a day, four days a week, perhaps, Tuesday through Friday. Take Mondays (and evenings if necessary) for research and preparation.

    If you are currently employed, set a regular schedule and follow it. Perhaps you can take one day a month off for interviews, or arrange to take a number of interviews during your vacation. If you have a flexible job schedule, you may be able to get away for a couple of hours; if not, try to arrange interviews for early mornings or after regular office hours. Whatever type of arrangement works best for you, create a schedule and stick to it until you get what you want.

2. **Establish a base of operation, a regular workplace.** Set yourself up with a desk or table with computer and a telephone. Have all relevant reading material handy, as well as your appointment book, calendar, and perhaps a copy of this book. Make sure this is a place where you can work uninterrupted and undistracted. From here, you can also write thank-you notes to people who give you leads and help, and thank-you letters to those with whom you have had interviews.

3. **Enlist the support of your family.** Unemployed people frequently spend a lot of their time answering phones, running errands, babysitting, and the like. Tell your family that you are looking for a job on a full-time basis and that you will need their cooperation in allowing you to work uninterrupted during this time. Get someone to answer the phone for you and take messages when you are not in. You might get a family member to type resumes, letters, and proposals for you.

4. **Assemble letters of recommendation, personal and professional references.** Develop and have on hand copies of letters of recommendation and personal and professional references.

 It's the constant and determined effort that breaks down all resistance, sweeps away all obstacles.
                    Claude M. Bristol

Step One—Decide: Identify What You Want from an Organization

Take creative control of the job-hunting process. Begin by establishing criteria for potential employers. First, they have to pass your test; later, you will have to pass theirs.

What type of organization do you want (e.g., government agency, nonprofit, small-business, etc.)? _____

The Big Picture

What kind of values or philosophy must this organization reflect? _____
_____

What goals or objectives must this organization have? _____
_____

What kind of people do you want to work with? _____
_____

What level of responsibility do you seek within this organization?
_____
_____

How much do you want to earn working for this organization?
_____
_____

The Details

Assuming that two or more organizations offer similar opportunities to satisfy your big-picture work goals, which of these additional factors are most important to you?

1. Schedule flexibility _____
2. Creative environment _____
3. Attractive work setting _____
4. Job security _____
5. Convenience from your home _____
6. Health and dental _____
7. Pensions _____
8. Opportunities for advancement _____
9. Prestige _____
10. Day-care facilities _____
11. Opportunities for additional training _____
12. Other: _____

Establish Criteria for Your Employer

In the space below, prioritize your employment needs, using the following three criteria. An example appears at the bottom of the page.

1. **Bottom-line needs:** These conditions must be met by an employer before you give the employer any consideration. They are nonnegotiable.

2. **Priority needs:** These are important (more important at the top of the list, less important as you descend), but not absolutely essential.

3. **Extras:** These are benefits that exceed your bottom-line and priority needs.

Bottom-line Needs	Priority Needs	Extras
1._____	1._____	1._____
2._____	2._____	2._____
3._____	3._____	3._____
4._____	4._____	4._____
5._____	5._____	5._____
6._____	6._____	6._____
7._____	7._____	7._____
8._____	8._____	8._____
9._____	9._____	9._____
10._____	10._____	10._____
11._____	11._____	11._____
12._____	12._____	12._____

Bottom-line Needs	Priority Needs	Extras
1. Common purpose	1. Health and dental insurance	1. Convenient location
2. Harmonious relationships	2. Pension plan	2. Attractive environment
3. Advancement opportunities	3. Profit-sharing	3. Travel opportunities
4. Career development opps.	4. Flexible hours	4. Bonuses
5. Income $55,000–$60,000	5. Day care	5. Company car

Step Two—Research Organizations: Know Your Market

Once you have identified what you're looking for in an organization, the next step is to research existing organizations and find those best suited to you. In many ways, this is the most important part of the job-hunting process. The more information you have, the more options you have and the better the choices you can make. You wouldn't think of opening a business without conducting market research, and you ought not think of taking a job without conducting a thorough search for the right organization. Also refer to the resources below. Take notes as you go and keep track of what you learn. You may want to organize the information related to the companies you are most interested in on three-by-five cards. This will make the information you've collected easy to quickly review when it comes time to take the interview.

Researching Organizations Sources

Glassdoor.com: At glassdoor.com, employees rate companies. It's a great place to find "inside" information on salary ranges and corporate culture, including prevailing management style and ethics, level of teamwork within the company, and expectations with respect to hours.

Corporate Annual Reports. Most corporations publish their annual reports online.

Ward's Business Directory of U.S. Private and Public Companies. Farmington Hills, Mich.: Thomson/Gale. Published annually.

Standard and Poor's Register of Corporations, Directories and Executives. New York: Standard and Poor's. Published annually.

Individuals and Organizations

1. Current employees (best source, take these folks to lunch)
2. Former employees
3. Competitors
4. Clients
5. Community leaders
6. Suppliers
7. Chamber of Commerce
8. Better Business Bureau
9. Professional associations in the field
10. University professors in the field

Web and Book Resources

Find out more about researching companies and organizations @ Empoweryou.com.

Step Three—Select the Organizations You Want to Work for and the Position(s) You Want

Based upon your initial research, list the organizations you are most interested in working for.

1. Organization: _____
    Position: _____

2. Organization: _____
    Position: _____

3. Organization: _____
    Position: _____

4. Organization: _____
    Position: _____

5. Organization: _____
    Position: _____

6. Organization: _____
    Position: _____

7. Organization: _____
    Position: _____

8. Organization: _____
    Position: _____

9. Organization: _____
    Position: _____

10. Organization: _____
    Position: _____

 There is nothing which persevering effort and unceasing and diligent care can not accomplish.   *Seneca*

Create a Job Where There Is None

When looking for a job, you are not limited to existing positions. You can help an employer create a position for you. The following are a few of the common situations that provide opportunities for creating jobs:

1. **They are aware of the need, but haven't filled it.** They know that they need help, but they haven't gotten around to advertising a position. You remind them of the obvious need and demonstrate how you are the person best qualified to fill it.

2. **They're not aware of the need.** You make them aware. They're having chronic problems in a specific area where you have expertise. They don't understand the problem, either because they lack the expertise or because they are too busy focusing on other things. You identify the problem, point out how much it's costing them, and indicate how you can help solve it. On the other hand, you might show them how they are missing opportunities to grow or expand into new areas or markets. You demonstrate how hiring you will help them take advantage of these opportunities.

3. **Consolidate and streamline what they have.** They may be currently paying several people to do the work that you, because of your special talents and abilities, could do more efficiently on your own (or with a smaller team). You demonstrate how, by reorganizing and hiring you, they will be more effective in achieving their goals.

4. **Start at another position and gradually assume the responsibilities of the position you want.** You create the new position after you make it into the organization. This takes patience and a clear idea of your ultimate goal.

Below, indicate organizations for which one of these job-creating strategies might be appropriate and how you can convince the employer to give you a job.

Organization	Position to Create	Strategy of Approach
_____	_____	_____
_____	_____	_____
_____	_____	_____
_____	_____	_____

 It isn't that they can't see the solution. It is that they can't see the problem.

G. K. Chesterton

Step Four—Write: Create or Update Your Resume

Resumes are not all they're cracked up to be. They're certainly not worth getting anxious over. There are about as many different approaches to this subject as there are experts on it. Some say, "Forget about resumes." Others would call that blasphemy. Your purpose in sending out resumes is to get interviews. This seldom happens without a follow-up call. While it's true that nobody gets hired because of a terrific resume, a good resume can help you get an interview, and interviews get you hired.

While there are many variations, as a practical matter, most resumes fall into one of two categories. The first and more traditional is the *chronological resume;* the second, the *functional resume*. A chronological resume usually works best when you want to continue working in the same field. A functional resume is often the best choice for the career changer, the first-time job seeker, and those who have been long absent from the workplace. The difference comes into play in the way you demonstrate how your experience qualifies you for the position you are seeking (see point 3 below). Whether you write a chronological or a functional resume, it should include the following, and usually in this order:

A "Formula" for a Two-Page Resume

1. Personal information: Be sure to include name, address, and phone number. Beyond this, everything is optional. Health information and military record are examples of things you might include.

2. Education: Start with your most advanced degrees. If you have postgraduate degrees, list those and then your undergraduate college work. If you graduated from a university, you don't need to put down your high school. Include nondegree educational training pertinent to the position you are seeking.

3. Work experience or accomplishments: This will vary according to whether you are using a chronological or a functional resume.

Chronological: Put your most recent work experience at the bottom of the first page. Go into what you did quite extensively— your position, responsibilities, salary, and accomplishments. Be sure to include the name and address of your employer and the name and number of your immediate supervisor. Continue on the next page (in most cases, your resume should not be more than two pages) to list additional work experience. A good rule of thumb is to allow each entry of previous work experience one-half the space of the one that preceded it. In other words, if the first entry of work experience requires ten lines, give the second five, and the third, two and a half. The employer is more interested in what you have done recently, less interested in your distant past.

Functional: The functional resume is organized around your skills and abilities rather than your work history. This gives you the opportunity to anticipate what your potential employer is looking for and to convince him that you are the best qualified for the job. Identify the skills and abilities required for the position you are seeking. Then look over your experience and describe the things you have achieved or accomplished that best demonstrate that you possess the requisite skill.

Note: Your personal information, education, accomplishments, and/or work experience represent the meat of your resume. Include the information that follows only as space permits.

4. Community involvement: Includes any community service involvement or leadership that indicates how you are an asset to your community and, by extension, how hiring you will reflect well on the company that you are asking to hire you.

5. Special interests: If there is space remaining, you might include hobbies, special interests, etc. This is less important than other entries.

6. Personal references: If you have remaining space (this will probably only apply to people new in the world of work), include personal references. Otherwise simply state: "References available upon request."

Additional Points about Resumes

If you're applying for employment with a large organization, private or public, be aware that your resume may only get ten to fifteen seconds' attention. You can increase the odds that your resume will be noticed by:

1. The paper that you select. (High-quality linen is best. Stay away from colored paper or from cheap typing paper.)

2. Paying special attention to your use of language. Make every word count.

3. Keeping your resume under two pages.

4. Using a good-quality typewriter or computer printer or paying someone to type for you. Photocopied resumes are usually fine. Cover letters should be freshly typed.

5. Of course, spelling and punctuation are important. Additionally, the layout of the material on the page ought to give an attractive, neat appearance that is well balanced and proportioned.

When to Use a Cover Letter

A cover letter briefly describes who you are, the position you're seeking, and the contribution you feel you can make. Use a cover letter when: (1) you know the exact position you are applying for, and (2) you know the name of the person doing the hiring. (If you don't know, do more research.)

Key Points for an Effective Cover Letter

1. Address it to the specific individual who has the capacity to hire you.

2. State the position that you are seeking.

3. Highlight important features of your qualifications and how you will help their organization achieve their goals.

4. Ask for an interview. Indicate that you will call to set up a time.

5. Keep your letter short (two or three short paragraphs).

6. Make it interesting, clear, and well-written. Try to distinguish your letter from the others on his or her desk.

7. Type each one fresh, no photocopies.

 Whatever we conceive well we express clearly.
Nicolas Boileau-Despréaux

Step Five—Solicit: Get the Interview

While all of the fundamentals laid out in the first four steps are a necessary part of finding a job you love, nothing really significant happens until you "get your foot in the door," that is, until you get an interview. This section considers several different strategies for securing interviews with the people who can help make your dreams come true.

Strategies for Soliciting Employers

Choose the strategies best suited to your personality and career objectives. Each method is considered in greater depth in the pages that follow.

Strategy 1: Mine the Internet. Today, responding to online job listings is the most popular job-search strategy and not without good reason. One recent study reporting on the hiring practices of forty-nine large companies (over five thousand employees) found that 25 percent of all new hires came as a result of online job listings (including the companies' own Web sites).[4] This is probably the best single strategy if you need a job right away. If you want a job you really love, be creative in your approach to the Net. Don't limit yourself to responding to the job listings you find posted. Use the Web as a research, networking, and promotional tool to reach the organizations you have targeted.

Strategy 2: Work Your Networks. Depending on the size and relevance of your networks, this can be one of the best strategies—not just for finding a job, but for finding one you really love. The study cited above found that about 28 percent of new hires came from referrals. While referrals can come from a wide variety of sources, the study found that the ones that were most likely to lead to a job came from current employees. In addition to working your existing networks, develop strategies for developing new contacts who will begin to give you access to the specific organizations you have targeted.

Strategy 3: Approach Targeted Organizations Directly. If you have identified a specific way that you can help a particular organization, write a personalized letter targeted to a specific individual within that organization. Follow up with a phone call or e-mail and attempt to arrange a meeting with that person. This is not a formal interview—could be a

The only thing that keeps a man going is energy. And what is energy but liking life?
Louis Auchincloss

lunch or coffee—just a chance to share your ideas and begin to develop a relationship. Alternatively, you can send a targeted cover letter and resume soliciting an interview and then follow up with a phone call to set up the interview. In either case, don't expect a response to your mailings. Everything will depend on your follow-up. You could try cold-calling (calling without first sending a resume or gaining a referral), but this is tough—not recommended unless you have strong sales skills.

Strategy 4: Seek Professional Help. There are times when a professional's help can be useful. If you are seeking a high-paying executive or professional position, recruiters can be helpful, especially if you want to change positions within the same or a similar field. Personnel agencies tend to place people in more midlevel positions. While a recruiter's services are free to qualified job candidates, personnel agencies typically charge the job seeker a significant portion of the first year's salary. For this and other reasons, personnel agencies are only recommended as a last resort.

Strategy 5: Parlay Your Way. This is an excellent strategy for those new to the workforce as well as those reentering after a long absence. It also presents opportunities for those who are currently employed and can afford to work for a time for little or no pay or who are able to take on additional responsibilities for a period of time. Internships, and in some cases volunteer opportunities, can not only be a great way to get on-the-job training for a new career but also help you develop contacts that will prove invaluable. Others have used temp agencies to get their foot in the door of an organization they want to work for. Some have even parlayed informational interviews directly into great jobs.

Strategy 6: Consider Unconventional Approaches. These strategies involve putting yourself right in the middle of the action and making it pay off for you. Not for the faint of heart, these kinds of bold moves have enabled some to take giant leaps in their careers

Strategy 7: Try the Old Stand-bys. Don't neglect responding to hard-copy newspaper ads or taking advantage of state employment offices and other more traditional job-search options.

Fortune favors the audacious.
Desiderius Erasmus

Strategy 1: Mine the Internet

Many things about the job-hunting experience have changed in the digital age. Yet the key remains getting in front of the person who has the power to hire you and making a good impression when you do. In other words, it is still all about the interview. You're succeeding in your job-hunting efforts to the extent that you're getting interviews with people who have the power to hire you into the companies that you want to work for. While the goal of the job-hunting process remains the same, the way we go about achieving it has changed dramatically in recent years. Today, as many as five million new jobs are posted online each month. Visit empoweryou.com for an up-to-date list of Web sites that will help you find the job you are looking for. Below are a few general factors to keep in mind as you conduct your search.

1. Don't Get Lost in Cyberspace: No doubt you have noticed that the Internet has a way of making time disappear. When you're sitting in front of your computer for hours at a time, searching for jobs and posting resumes, it can seem as you though you are accomplishing a lot more than you really are. For many, it is also easier and less threatening than dealing with real people in the real world. If you are engaged in a full-time job search, try to limit your online efforts to the evening hours. Use the daytime hours for interviews, making calls, and networking.

2. Relevance is the Resume Keyword: At many larger companies, no one will ever look at all of the resumes that are posted for an open position. Instead, they run software searches based on relevant keyword matches that sort through hundreds, or even thousands, of resumes to produce a much more limited pool that an actual human will later review. The best way of surmising what these keywords might be is simply to look at words and phrases used in the online job description. Mimic as many of these in your resume as you honestly can.

3. Go Beyond the Monstrously Large Job-Hunting Sites: For most people looking for a job, the big job-hunting sites (e.g., Monster.com) are *the* online destinations. Don't neglect smaller and more targeted niche sites. For example, journalists might want to visit JournalismJobs.com; doctors, PracticeMatch.com; those seeking jobs in the nonprofit sector, Idealist.com; and so on. Many jobs are also posted on craigslist.com. Today, some employers skip the big boards and rely on social networking sites such as LinkedIn to fill positions.

4. Be Aware that Potential Employers are Aware of the Cyber You: Employers can find virtually anything and everything that has ever been posted online by or about you. Today, potential employees are screened not only via criminal background and credit checks but also through the content of their social networking pages. One recent survey by the Society for Human Resource Management found that would-be employers are influenced much more by what they perceive as the negative parts of the "cyber you" than by the positive points. While it may cramp your style a bit, try to view all photos, videos, and written text that you upload from the standpoint of future potential employers. If you wouldn't want them to see it, you might want to think twice about posting it.

Making the Most of Your Online Job Search

Posting or Uploading Your Resume: Posting or uploading your resume in the public areas of large job-search Web sites is not to be confused with undertaking an aggressive job search. Moreover, despite the claims of some of these sites, employers seldom search through existing resume databases, let alone contact those who keep their resumes "private." When they hire from online listings (and today nearly 30 percent of all new hires come in this way), they typically examine resumes sent in response to specific job openings. Today, many employers and job boards allow you to upload your standard-format (Word or WordPerfect) resume. Nevertheless, as many still do not, you'll need an e-resume to make the most of your online job search efforts.

The e-Resume: E-resumes differ in form and character from the traditional hard-copy variety, relying on keywords and phrases rather than on writing style, organization, or presentation. When responding to a specific job opening, review the job description carefully and include as many of its keywords and phrases in your resume as you honestly can. While you will want to adapt your postings to accommodate specific keywords, it will save you time and energy to create and save a master "plain text" version of your resume. You'll be able to quickly adapt it and then copy and paste into online forms, post into online resume databases, or send in the body of an e-mail (see below). When you post your resume online, the subject line you choose is critical. It's the first thing a potential employer sees (in large font) and will determine whether or not that employer chooses to read the rest.

While you'll want to customize the keywords, the place to start your e-resume is with your traditional hard-copy version. Open the print version of your resume in Microsoft Word, and save it as a "plain text" file. Close the file but NOT Word. Now open the text file again. You will notice that it has been stripped of all font variations (bold or italic, large/small, etc). Next, make any needed formatting adjustments. (For example, replace bullets with asterisks, remove header content, etc.) Save this file and use as needed. Creating an HTML version of your resume allows you to make a much more attractive presentation than you can get with plain text alone. Some of the large job boards (e.g., CareerBuilder) and

many smaller ones (that don't accept Word docs) will allow you to upload an HTML resume.

E-mailing Your Resume: When responding to online e-mail forms, the format you choose will be dictated by what the Web site accepts. For online job listings that give e-mail addresses for reply, avoid the temptation to send your beautifully formatted print version, unless you have been specifically asked to send your resume as an attachment. Instead, put your text-only version into the body of an e-mail. Many employers (or their software) will simply delete e-mails with file attachments from unknown sources. Paste your plain-text version into the body of an e-mail (see above) and correct for the line-length distortions. Send an e-mail copy to yourself to see how it appears when sent, and adjust the formatting accordingly. Once you get it right, save a copy for future e-mails. As with online posts and uploads, the subject lines of your e-mails are critical.

Privacy Issues: Ostensibly, access to resume databases is only made available to potential employers. Nevertheless, there is no guarantee your information will not eventually find its way into the hands of marketers. Those to whom you would never have directly consented to give your street and e-mail address, phone numbers, work history, and other information may end up with it. Once out there, your data may persist long after you have found a new job. Also, be aware that your employer could well be among those with access to the very resume databases that you are posting on. Of course, employers will generally not be happy to discover that you are looking for another job. While they may not go as far as firing you, in most cases there is little stopping your employer from doing so. (Contractual agreements or specific state or federal laws may protect you in some cases.) Carefully read the job board's privacy policy, and review its confidentiality and security options before posting on any site.

Strategy 2:
Work Your Networks

When professionals in the career field talk about the so-called "hidden job market," they are referring to the 65 to 70 percent of all jobs that are never publicly advertised. These jobs are filled internally or through referrals. Obviously, if you want a job with a new organization, referrals are your key to the hidden job market. In turning this key, the old saying "It's not what you know, it's who you know" is truer than ever.

If you need a job right away, contacting the people you know to let them know that you are looking and what you are looking for is a must. (You just never know who knows whom or what they know about opportunities that you have never heard of.) Yet whether or not this approach will prove effective in landing a job you really love will depend in large part upon the size and relevance of your existing networks. A long-term strategy starts with identifying organizations you want to work for and then developing networking strategies for getting to know people within these organizations. (Think in terms of degrees of separation and move ever closer to the source.) Alumni associations, vendors, and colleagues who work outside of the organizations you are targeting can all be great sources of referrals. Nevertheless, the vast majority of referrals that result in job hires come from current employees. They represent your best chance to tap into the hidden job market.

Of course, the best time to network, especially for a job you really want, is when you don't need to make a change right away. Even the thought of networking for a job can bring up considerable anxiety.

Fears of rejection and/or failure can keep us from reaching out. Beyond this, many feel uncomfortable needing—to say nothing of asking for—help from others. You certainly don't want to come across as desperate. On the other hand, there is no reason to feel embarrassed about asking for what you really want. On the contrary, the whole point of an aggressive job search is to create the opportunity to do what you truly love. People will appreciate and respect your passion and will want to help you if you, in turn, are considerate and respectful of their time and efforts. Developing effective networking skills and strategies are essential keys to maximizing your opportunities to pursue your dreams. (For more on networking, see "Turning on Your Networks," page 457.)

Put your network to work by:

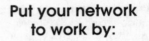

1. Having them set up an interview (not always appropriate).

2. Getting them to speak to the person you want to contact and obtain that person's agreement to meet with you. You call and confirm.

3. Getting them to write letters of introduction or recommendation that you can send along with your resume.

4. Getting their permission to use their name when you call to set up an interview.

The man who makes no mistakes does not usually make anything.
Edward Phelps

Strategy 3:
Approach Targeted Organizations Directly

This can be approached in a several different ways. If you've identified a specific way you can help a particular organization, write a personalized letter targeted to a specific individual within that organization. (Of course, prior to undertaking this option, you'll need to have done enough research to understand the goals, needs, and challenges of the organization in question and to have identified the individual[s] with the power to hire you.) In your letter, briefly describe some of your ideas for helping this organization better achieve its goals, and indicate the unique strengths you bring to the table. Make the letter dynamic, brief, and to the point. Include a brief statement of your past accomplishments, your skills, and the kind of results you are likely to produce for the organization. Don't oversell or make exaggerated promises. Close by indicating that you would like to arrange an informal meeting and that you will be calling for that purpose in the near future. Another approach is to send a carefully crafted cover letter, along with your resume, to a specific individual in an organization you have targeted.

In either case, don't expect the potential employer to contact you. When you call, be cheerful and persistent. Be patient if you don't get a call back. Try varying your contact vehicle—phone call, then e-mail, etc. Don't ever be rude or indicate that you are in any way annoyed that the employer hasn't gotten back to you. If you are always pleasant and upbeat and allow sufficient time between inquiries, you may eventually get the interview. If, on the other hand, you are specifically told not to contact this party again, then by all means respect his or her wishes. For some ideas on how to handle your follow-up calls see pages 444–445.

Strategy 4:
Seek Professional Help

There are times when you may want to seek out the aid of a job-placement professional in a recruiting firm or personnel agency. The difference between recruiters (headhunters) and personnel agencies is in the level of the positions sought and in who pays. Recruiters attempt to fill higher-paying executive and professional positions, and the employer typically pays. Personnel agencies work to fill more mid-level positions, and the employee usually pays a portion of the first year's salary. While headhunters continue to be utilized by companies seeking to fill executive and professional positions, there has been a marked decline in the use of private employment agencies to fill mid-level positions in recent years. Avoid personnel agencies that make you pay up-front fees. If you choose either option, make sure you are dealing with a reputable firm, as there are dubious operators in both fields.

Recruiters: Recruiters (aka executive search firms) specialize in locating executives and professionals (e.g., lawyers) for their client companies. Most prefer to work for executives and professionals who are currently employed. Some firms will interview people not currently working. If at all possible, don't just send a resume. Recruiters are essentially salespeople. They are busy trying to close existing positions and are likely to put an unsolicited resume in a stack. Call and schedule an interview related to a position they are currently trying to fill—even if it's not your ideal. (Once they have met you and seen your work-related documents, they are more likely to suggest you for other positions.) Consider this a screening interview for your new job—wear what you would wear—and conduct yourself as you would at a job interview. Once you are in their pool, it's fine for you to call from time to time to see how it is going. Generally, these services are free to the potential employee (the employer pays). There are three primary advantages of working with a recruiter: (1) He knows where the jobs are (many of which are unadvertised). (2) He has contacts within the companies that can get you the job you want. Instead of approaching these companies as a stranger, you are approaching them via an inside connection. (3) If he thinks you are a qualified candidate, he will aggressively "sell" you to employers.

Personnel Agencies: Personnel agencies attempt to match job seekers with employment opportunities within their communities. It is important that you know exactly what you want going in. Since you will likely be paying the agency a hefty chunk of your first year's salary, make sure it is really a job you want before accepting an offer. Be sure you understand what you are getting yourself into before you sign a contract. Generally, it's best to exhaust all of your other options first—treat this one as a last resort.

Strategy 5: Parlay Your Way

Below are a few of the ways that you can parlay off-the-job-site experience into a networking opportunity or even a job offer.

1. **Internships:** Internships can be a great way to gain hands-on experience in a new field while making connections that could lead to a job you love. College students, recent graduates, and those returning to the workforce after a long absence will find internships especially attractive. Internships give these folks a chance to gain some (or some recent) work experience in their fields to include on their resumes. Moreover, interns make real-world connections and often have the inside track for permanent full-time positions when

they become available. Those in midcareer who are looking to make a significant change shouldn't rule out this option without further investigation. At any age, internships present challenges. Issues related to money and time, as well as to the quality of the work experience and relevance of the connections made, top the list. While some Fortune 500 companies and large law firms offer relatively generous compensation, internships typically come with little or no pay. (Some companies offer grants to those who qualify under diversity guidelines.) Unless you have significant savings or someone else's financial support, your internship will likely be in addition to a job that pays the bills. Some internships are structured to offer real on-the-job training. Others will keep you occupied with relatively menial tasks. Similarly, internships vary in terms of the access they provide to the key decision makers who can offer you a job. With well over one hundred thousand internships offered each year, it's worthwhile to do some research before deciding on one (links to internship resources available at empoweryou.com). Finally, you might consider creating an internship where none exists. Approach organizations you are interested in working for and ask if they would allow you to work (unpaid) for them in exchange for some hands-on experience. Your proven desire and initiative could well lead to a job.

2. **Volunteer Work:** Volunteer work is not only an excellent way to make contacts that could lead to jobs; it is also an excellent way to gain knowledge and experience, build up a track record, and test your dream career in the laboratory of reality. Many employers in overcrowded fields have unwritten hiring policies that favor volunteers and interns.

Web and Book Resources

Find recruiter firms, internships, volunteer opportunities and networking resources @ Empoweryou.com.

3. Informational Interviews: The contacts that you make during informational interviews can assist you in realizing your career objectives. For a review of how this process works, see pages 291–294 in the "Reality Testing" section.

Strategy 6: Consider Unconventional Approaches

Be on the lookout for unconventional ways of getting to the people who can give you what you want. For example, Aristotle Onassis broke into the big time in the shipping business by waiting for thirty-seven days outside of the office of the man he wanted to talk to. He was prepared, he knew what he wanted, and he was persistent. When the man he was trying to see finally relented, the deal was done in a matter of hours, and Onassis was on his way to a huge fortune. People have landed jobs, negotiated deals, and funded projects because they "just happened" to be staying in the right hotel, drinking in the right lounge, or even riding in the right elevator.

Note: Try to avoid job interviews over lunch. Do this only as a last resort if you're really interested in the company. There are too many distractions at lunch, and you may be judged on factors that have nothing to do with the job (for example, the food you order, or the noise you make when you chew).

Strategy 7: Try the Old Standbys

For those who would like to take a shot at the more traditional job-hunting sources, consider the following:

Answering Newspaper Ads: Perhaps the most popular method of finding a job, answering newspaper ads, is by no means the best. If you are going to use this method, keep in mind some of the other techniques described above. Also, remember that qualifications are not written in stone. Individuals seeking employment often take themselves out of the running for jobs they would enjoy because they take written statements outlining qualifications as decrees from on high.

If the want ad says, "Must have X degree and five years' experience" and you only have two years' experience, and you want the job, apply anyway. If they ask you why you applied, even though you didn't meet the criteria, tell them, "While I may not meet the exact criteria you've listed, I do feel that I'm qualified for this position, and here's why . . ." Proceed to tell them why you are the best person for the job. You have nothing to lose, and if you present yourself well, you may have just won yourself a job. Remember, employers hire people, not qualifications. Everything said here applies to positions listed on in-house bulletin boards as well as to those advertised in newspapers, magazines, trade journals, and newsletters.

State Employment Offices: If you like drab offices, long lines, and are looking for a low-paying entry-level job, then a state employment office may be a good bet for you. Most employers tend to fill their middle- and upper-level positions through other sources. Even at the entry level, your odds of landing a job through an employment office are not good, as the number of applicants is typically far greater than the number of available openings.

College Placement Offices: College students, go to the career placement office at your school (preferably well before graduation). Get to know the staff and what they have to offer. College placement offices are especially good when you go in knowing what you want instead of expecting them to tell you. Some schools provide training in job-hunting skills. Ask staff members to keep you informed of recruiters from the various companies who visit your school and of other positions they know of through various sources.

The Follow-up Call

You've already sent a resume and a cover letter, which gives you a reason (or an excuse) to follow up with a call. Call in the mornings. (People are generally sharper and more responsive in the morning.) You'll either be talking to a secretary/receptionist or with the individual who will be conducting the interview. If you are talking to the secretary, understand that it is her job to get rid of you. It is your job to see that she doesn't (politely). Once you have the person you want the interview with on the line, your conversation might go something like this:

Caller: Hello, Mr._____, this is Ms. _____calling.

Potential Employer: Yes, how can I help you?

Caller: Last week I sent you my resume and a letter outlining ways that I feel I could contribute to your organization. Have you had a chance to look at it?

Potential Employer: No. [Chances are good that he hasn't.]

Caller: I know, Mr._____, that you're a busy man and that your time is valuable. That's why I'd like to come in and discuss with you how I can be an asset to your company.

Potential Employer: We really don't have a position available right now.

Caller: I understand that within the context of the usual way of looking at things, you don't have any openings available right now. Still, I've been studying your organization, and I have some exciting ideas that I'd like to discuss with you about how we can work together.

Potential Employer: You'll probably be wasting your time, Ms._____.

Caller: I can understand how you might feel that way, especially since you haven't had a chance to look over my proposal. I value my time and yours. I wouldn't ask for an appointment unless I felt it was going to be a valuable use of time for both of us.

Potential Employer: Well, Ms._____, you are persistent; I must say that.

Caller: Thank you. I'd like to get together with you next week and discuss this with you in person. How about Tuesday at nine a.m.?

Potential Employer: Well, ten would be better for me.

Caller: Very well, ten it is.

In the space below, list the important points you'd like to get across in your phone conversation.

1._____

2._____

3._____

4._____

5._____

6._____

7._____

Now list possible objections that the potential employer may have to meeting with you, and ways that you might overcome them.

1. Objection:_____

Solution: _____

_____

_____

_____

_____

2. Objection:_____

Solution: _____

_____

_____

_____

3. Objection:_____

Solution: _____

_____

_____

_____

_____

Either do not attempt at all or go through with it.

Ovid

Your Plan for Landing the Interview

Name of Organization: _____

Position You Are Seeking: _____

Name of Person Who Can Hire You: _____

Position: _____

How You Will Get to Them: _____

_____

_____

Plan B: _____

_____

Plan C: _____

_____

Name of Organization: _____

Position You Are Seeking: _____

Name of Person Who Can Hire You: _____

Position: _____

How You Will Get to Them: _____

_____

_____

Plan B: _____

_____

Plan C: _____

_____

Name of Organization: _____

Position You Are Seeking: _____

Name of Person Who Can Hire You: _____

Position: _____

How You Will Get to Them: _____

_____

_____

Plan B: _____

_____

Plan C: _____

_____

Step Six— Prepare for Interviews

Put Yourself in the Interviewer's Shoes

Imagine that you are in charge of hiring employees for a large organization. The future of your organization depends upon your judgment. After all, the quality of its employees, more than any other factor, will affect this organization's ability to achieve its goals. Additionally, at even a modest salary, the organization will be spending hundreds of thousands of dollars over the course of a few years on each employee. Hiring, then, is one of the most important business transactions any organization undertakes. Given all of this, you might be in a state of mild anxiety as you are faced with deciding the fate of your organization—selecting its employees.

One way that employers attempt to reduce this anxiety is through familiarity, that is, by hiring people they know or hiring people recommended by those they know and trust. From the interviewer's point of view, he's taking a chance in hiring a stranger, a chance that may affect his own standing in the company. He would rather deal with a known commodity than take a risk with an unknown. It is not surprising, then, that 67 percent of all positions filled result from personal and professional contacts. The list opposite suggests some ways you can become familiar to the interviewer and thus reduce his anxiety about hiring you.

Employers want to interview you because they want to see a real person, not a piece of paper. They don't simply want someone who looks good on paper. They want someone who functions well in the work environment. The interviewer is interested in how you look, how you respond to difficult questions, how developed your verbal skills are, how well you are likely to get along with other people, how passive or assertive you are, how apathetic or dynamic. In short, he wants to get to know you. The tips on the next few pages can help you ensure that he meets you at your best.

How to Become "Familiar" with the Interviewer

1. Get to know the person doing the hiring, through an informational interview or through social or professional contacts.

2. Come recommended by someone within the organization whom that person knows and trusts.

3. Come recommended by someone outside the organization whom that person knows and trusts.

4. Come recommended by someone who has a position of credibility and respect within the field.

5. Come recommended by someone who has a position of high standing and respect within the community.

6. Be persistent in approaching them. Without becoming a nuisance, make sure that the interviewer remembers you.

Knowledge is power if you know about the right person.

Ethel Mumford

Do Your Homework

Research and Read: Thanks to the Internet, it's pretty easy to find out loads of information on any organization with more than a dozen employees. Get on your favorite search engine and start looking around. For companies listed on the stock exchanges, visit the company's page on financial sites (e.g., Yahoo or Google finance). There you'll find links to a variety of articles by the business press that will help you understand current trends, challenges, and opportunities relevant to the company. Also don't neglect sites like Glassdoor, for information on companies, and LinkedIn, to find more about the individual(s) with the power to hire you. Generally speaking, the higher you go up the economic and professional scale, the more information you will find on the people with the power to hire you, but it's worth a thorough search in any case. The more you know going in, the better you are likely to do when you get there. (Find additional resources for preparing and conducting job interviews at empoweryou.com.)

Talk to People: If at all possible, try to talk to people who know the person who will interview you. You might want to speak to former employees or *discreetly* with current employees. Speak with others in the community who may know this person personally or who interact with him or her on a professional basis.

Practice: Be sure to do a number of practice interviews. (Get a friend to play the interviewer and ask you tough questions.) In your practice interviews (at least for some of them), dress as you would for the real thing. Ask your partner to critique you, not only on what you say, but on your appearance and nonverbals as well. If at all possible, make a video recording of a dress rehearsal interview. Viewing yourself as you appear to others is the best way to get a sense of how you are coming across. You may discover a few quirks that are relatively easy to correct and will dramatically improve your presentation. On the other hand, you may discover that you are coming over much better than you thought—a definite boost to your confidence. Sample interview questions can be found on the following page.

Interview Questions

Here's a brief list of questions that you may encounter in the interview process. Practice answering these and/or other questions you believe are likely to arise. For a more complete list of potential interview questions, see *Sweaty Palms: The Neglected Art of Being Interviewed*, by Anthony Medley.

1. Tell me about yourself.

When interviewers ask this question, they're not interested in your great rock collection or favorite rock 'n' roll band. Remember, they're sizing you up for the position they have in mind. Don't answer the way you would if asked by a blind date.

2. Why should I hire you?

Now, don't get defensive, intimidated, or hostile. Be cool and state how your skills, attitude, enthusiasm, and experience will contribute to their organization.

3. What are your career goals? Where do you want to be in five to ten years?

This is a good test question. They want you to sign up for life. You want to move on in a year and a half. Handle this one with deftness and sincerity, but don't make unrealistic promises. Speak in terms of positions you'd like to achieve or things you'd like to accomplish.

4. Why did you leave your last position?

Don't tell them you hated the job, were bored out of your mind, or were ready to shoot your boss. Tell them that you'd gone as far as you could go in your previous or current job, and you're looking for the opportunity to work for a growth-oriented and challenging company like theirs. If you have done your research properly, you ought to be able to indicate what attracts you to their organization, and mean it.

5. Why are you interested in this position?

This question is an exciting, wide-open door. It's your chance to demonstrate all that you know about their company, its history, philosophy, products, and services.

6. Why did you choose this field of work?

You have a tremendous advantage when answering this question. Assuming you have followed the formula given in this book, you have discovered the work you really love to do. Let that love show through as you clearly articulate your reasons for entering the field.

7. How much do you expect to earn?

You should know approximately what they're offering and find it acceptable or not waste your time on the interview. Your answer to this question, then, should be within their range, only a tad higher. For example, if their range is $75,000–$82,000 you could suggest $80,000–$85,000. This way, you're letting them know that you believe that you are worth at least the high end of what they offer.

When asked tough questions, for example, "What are your weaknesses?" avoid being "honest" to a fault: state the weakness so that it sounds like a strength. For example, "If anything, I probably work too hard..." Or else state the weakness as something that was operative in the past, under specific circumstances that no longer apply. For example, "In the past, in a few instances, I would get irritated by customers who were overbearing and rude. I've matured since then and learned to deal with the situation in a way that works well for everyone."

Take a Pre-interview Inventory

The process of landing a job is a negotiation. In any negotiation, it is important to know what your needs and strengths are. Likewise, it is important that you know the other party's needs and strengths. The key is to match your strengths to their needs, and their strengths to your needs. The purpose of the exercise below is to help you identify what you have to offer employers and what they have to offer you. (All potential employers should meet the criteria you established on page 430.)

Name of Organization: _____

Position Sought: _____

Your Employment Strengths: In the space below, list the things that make you desirable to a potential employer.

How do your skills make you a valuable asset to this organization?

_____

_____

_____

_____

In what ways do your experience and knowledge of the field make you an asset to this organization?

_____

_____

_____

_____

How does your knowledge of this organization make you an asset?

_____

_____

_____

_____

Why would you make a good addition to their team? (What makes you a good team player?)

_____

_____

_____

_____

Potential Employer's Needs: In the space below, make a prioritized list of your potential employer's needs or goals and how you can help satisfy or achieve them.

**Current Needs and Goals
and How You Can Help**

1. _____
   _____
2. _____
   _____
3. _____
   _____
4. _____
   _____

**Future Needs and Goals
and How You Can Help**

1. _____
   _____
2. _____
   _____
3. _____
   _____
4. _____
   _____

Potential Employer's Strengths: In the space below, list what you perceive to be your potential employer's current and future strengths. Why is this a good organization to work for now? In the future?

**Current Strengths:
What They Can Offer You Now**

1. _____
   _____
2. _____
   _____
3. _____
   _____
4. _____
   _____

**Future Strengths
What They Can Offer Later**

1. _____
   _____
2. _____
   _____
3. _____
   _____
4. _____
   _____

*Great works are performed not by strength,
but by perseverance.*

Samuel Johnson

Step Seven— Communicate: Conduct Successful Interviews

Setting the Scene

The Prelims: These are screening interviews, designed to sift the wheat from the chaff. They are the most formal and structured of employment interviews. Everything that applies to the "main event" applies to the "prelims," with the following addition: be a bit more cautious in these interviews— less aggressive, and careful not to offend. Your objective in the screening interview is simply to pass the first cut.

The Main Event: Now, don't fret, lament, or stick your head in cement. You're ready to stay in control through preparation. You've already done a good deal of research and planning. Now it's time to make sure that you are mentally prepared.

An interview is a high-stress situation. But then, so is a great deal of work in the real world. If you choke under the pressure of the interview, you can't blame the interviewer for generalizing that you will choke under the pressure of the work situation. Similarly, if you handle the interview well, you use it to showcase (though not in a flashy way) your capacity to excel under pressure.

In today's job market, interviewers often have a host of (or at least several) qualified candidates. They're going to pick the ones they like best, the ones that make the best overall impression. There's nothing terribly objective about this, and it varies from interviewer to interviewer. While there's no magic formula, two attitudes, used in proper balance, will always work to your advantage. These are *confidence* and *caring*, and they are both linked to preparation. Preparation increases your confidence in yourself and exhibits your caring for your new organization.

Confidence: Confidence increases as you focus on your strengths and diminishes as you focus on your weaknesses. If you go in for an interview focused on your weaknesses, you'll make a poor impression. People typically focus on their weaknesses only because they haven't taken the time to identify and practice projecting their strengths. If your confidence is lacking, put more time and effort into preparation.

Confident people tend to be well prepared, and preparation increases confidence. People sometimes assume that lack of preparation comes from overconfidence. Actually, it demonstrates a lack of confidence—a chronic tendency to avoid their weaknesses (low self-esteem). Low self-esteem can keep you from doing the homework you need to do before the interview, and from making your best presentation during the interview. It can also keep you from doing your best once you get the job, and interviewers know that. When you make the effort to identify and focus on your strengths, you may be doing more than preparing for a job interview. You may be giving yourself a permanent self-esteem boost.

Caring: There is an old saying that *people don't care what you know until they know that you care.* This certainly applies to job interviews. When you show potential employers that you understand their needs and objectives, you demonstrate that you care about their organization. Come well prepared, and they'll be glad that you were the one they snared.

 The successful man will profit from his mistakes and try again in a different way.
Dale Carnegie

The Interview

Interviewers are trained to observe you from beginning to end. They are rating you at least as much on how well you project yourself as on what you say. Indeed, one of the best reasons to be well prepared in your answers is so you can concentrate on projecting confidence while answering them.

1. **Groom:** Dress the way that you would dress if you were working for this organization. Make sure your clothes are neatly pressed, your shoes carefully polished, and your hair neatly combed. Don't overdo it with makeup, perfume, cologne, or aftershave.

2. **Right from the Start:** Realize that the interview begins the moment you come into the interviewer's view. Don't wait for the first serious question to begin making a good impression; start immediately. Greet the interviewer warmly, with a sincere smile and a handshake. If you can give the interviewer a sincere compliment, do so. Many interviewers begin with a little chitchat. Be graciously engaged, not impatient, antsy, or nervous. Don't worry, you'll get to the serious questions soon enough.

3. **Project Confidence:** Your voice, well used, is one of the surest ways of projecting confidence. Watch the pitch, the tone, the volume, and the speed of your communication. Project self-command, enthusiasm, and dynamic energy. Recognize that your body language is speaking for you. Make sure that it is saying what you want it to say.

4. **Listen:** In most interviews, the interviewer is talking nearly as much as the interviewee. Yet the interviewee is often preoccupied with what he himself is saying and paying too little attention to what the interviewer is saying. This is a big and common mistake. Remember, the interviewer is a person (not a rating machine). Like all people, interviewers want to feel important. One of the best ways of making anyone feel important is by listening to them. Demonstrate alert interest through eye contact, facial gestures, and body language. Answer the questions they are asking. (It is surprising how many people don't.) Active listening is one of the best ways of ensuring that interviewers like you (and whether they admit it or not, interviewers hire people they like).

5. **Tell Stories:** Be sure to include stories that demonstrate the qualities you want to highlight. Telling a story captures the interest of the interviewer. It enhances your credibility by demonstrating not only that you possess a certain skill, attitude, or talent, but that you also know how to use it in real-life situations that may be similar to those you will encounter in your new position. Most important, people remember stories better than dry facts.

6. **Respond:** Keep it short, but not too short. According to Richard Bolles (*What Color Is Your Parachute?*), research has found the ideal response time to interviewer questions to be between twenty seconds and two minutes.

7. **Ask:** Take advantage of your opportunity to ask questions. Be prepared with questions in advance. For example: Whom will I be reporting to? Can you tell me a little something about this person? Develop your own list of questions, and practice asking them. Ask questions when given the opportunity. It shows interest and confidence.

8. **Like:** Make a sincere effort to genuinely like the person who is interviewing you. If you genuinely like that person, the chances greatly increase that he or she will like you, and, again, interviewers hire people they like.

Step Eight— Celebrate and Analyze

1. **Celebrate:** Preparing for and taking interviews is hard work. When the work is done, it's time to have some fun. Taking time to play afterward will help to keep you fresh and ensure that you maintain your enthusiasm for the search.

2. **Analyze:** Reflect on the interview you have just completed. Where were you strong? How could you improve? You might want to develop a checklist and give yourself points based upon your performance. Interviewing is a game as much as a skill. Unless you are very experienced and/or extremely well prepared, you may not want to start with the organization you most want to work for. If at all possible, get a few interviews under your belt before you take them on. Practicing with a partner is an invaluable part of your preparation, but there's nothing like getting real experience when the pressure's on.

3. **Express appreciation:** Let the interviewer know that you are glad he considered you for the position. Write the interviewer a formal letter thanking him for the opportunity to discuss the position with him. Restate what you consider to be the high points of the interview, for example, your qualifications, personal attributes, or expertise in the field. Indicate that you are looking forward to further association with him, and close formally. Try to send this letter out in the next day's mail. It's an added reminder, not only of your qualifications, but of your conscientiousness, and it comes at the most critical time— while the interviewer is still making up his mind.

4. **Follow through:** It is appropriate to call back and find out if you got the position. If you didn't get it, ask the interviewer to tell you why. If she mentions factors you know can be improved, thank her for her feedback, and tell her that you intend to work on these. Ask the employer to keep you in mind for any future positions. If it is clear that there is no possibility of working with this organization, you might ask her if she knows of opportunities with other organizations.

Evaluate Your Interviews

For each interview, answer the following:

Name of Organization: _____

Position Sought: _____

Interviewer: _____

What went well during the interview?

_____

_____

_____

What could you have improved?

_____

_____

_____

What steps will you take to follow up?

_____

_____

_____

Web and Book Resources

Find a complete list of resources for all aspects of the job search process @ Empoweryou.com.

Street Smarts

Zen is not some kind of excitement, but concentration on our usual everyday routine.
                    Shunryu Suzuki

If you don't have street smarts, you could be losing battles you might otherwise win. The "Street Smarts" section introduces you to the fundamentals of networking, publicity, and negotiation. Networking expands your options, often in ways you never could have imagined. Publicity gets the word out about you and/or your organization. Good negotiation skills can move you forward and cover your rear. Think of these as skills to develop over the long run to improve your street savvy. Many if not all these skills can be used regardless of whether you choose to work as an entrepreneur, a freelancer, a nonprofit administrator, or an employee in business or government.

It often takes considerable effort to create opportunities to do the work we really love. Say, for instance, that you are a naturally gifted speaker. Speaking comes easily and effortlessly to you. On those occasions when you have had the opportunity to speak, you have felt, not a tingle, but a tornado run up your spine. You know from the comments of others that you have reached them. So you love to speak, and you have natural talent. You may even be clear on what you want to communicate. Yet you experience difficulty in creating a context that allows you to express this talent as fully or as often as you would like. You may lack the persona, the role, the expertise, the image of authority, or other connecting bridges that would draw people to you. A speaker must be able to create an audience.

In creating an audience or market, you may have to do many things that are not as fun or exciting (for you) as the direct expression of your talent. Still, making the effort can often make the difference between fulfillment and might-have-beens. Even when it seems like opportunities fall in your lap, it takes street savvy to recognize and make the most of them.

Opportunities come to all, but only the well prepared take full advantage of them. In the words of Winston Churchill, "To every man there comes in his lifetime that special moment when he is figuratively tapped on the shoulder and offered the chance to do a very special thing, unique to him and fitted to his talents. What a tragedy if that moment finds him unprepared or unqualified for the work which could be his finest hour." Being "street smart" can make all the difference. The section that follows will consider these street-smart skills.

Networking: On one level, you are the star of your life, with others cast in supporting roles. On another level, we are all participants in a grand play—the scope of which we can hardly imagine. Creative engagement requires seeing and making opportunities for synergistic connections with other players, even those in seemingly unrelated fields. We can't simply hope that all of our connections will fall into place; we need to seek out and maintain a strong network of support. This section will consider how to develop and maintain a strong reputation, how to sharpen your networking skills, and how to select and work with associations and organizations that will further your work.

Publicity: Being street smart means you know how to get the word out about the exciting products, services, or events that you or your organization have to offer. You need to know how to work with the various media and take advantage of the assistance they can offer in promoting your work and that of your organization. This section includes information on writing news releases and obtaining feature stories, reviews, and interviews. Additionally, it considers how to promote your work by writing your own magazine or newspaper column, as well as a variety of miscellaneous publicity tips. For those who seek more in-depth information, some additional sources are provided.

Negotiation: It has been said that every human interaction is a negotiation. The more skilled you are as a negotiator, the more likely it is that you will be able to achieve your objectives in every area of life. This section will briefly outline negotiation strategies and encourage you to think of negotiation as a win-win proposition. For those who want more information, additional sources are included on page 473.

No man is an island, entire of itself; every man is a piece of the continent, a part of the main.
John Donne

Turning on Your Networks

The New York Stock Exchange is a formal, organized trading exchange, where stocks are bought and sold. A personal or professional network is an informal trading exchange that trades in trust. Individuals, through their care, effort, and integrity, build up a certain store of trust and goodwill with people. They then trade portions of this trust in exchange for access to the trust store that others have garnered.

Even as trust is the "commodity" traded in a network, reputation is the currency of exchange. With a great reputation, you can obtain a good deal of trust and thereby gain access to the networks of others. As long as you act in a manner that maintains your reputation, your access continues to grow. If you have a poor reputation, you will not be able to garner much trust. Your network will be small and unattractive, and you will have little to trade with others whose networks you may want to penetrate. Developing effective networks, then, is not simply a matter of meeting a lot of people. Meeting people is important, but your reputation is even more important.

How to Develop and Maintain Your Reputation

1. Be Sharp: Look your best. It shows that you care about yourself and others. After all, they are the ones who are looking at you. Be alert. Give people your attention, and you will get their respect.

2. Be Prompt: Be on time. If you're too early, you will rush people; if you're too late, they will resent your making them wait.

3. Be Trustworthy: Follow-through separates the men from the boys, the women from the girls. It is easy to break promises and to fail to recognize the importance of the value of agreements you have made. *Though a promise is easy to break, the damage is often difficult to repair*. Failing to keep your promises is a sure way to ruin your reputation and to inflict deep wounds, even fatal blows, to your relationships with others. Keep your promises, and you demonstrate to people that they can count on you. You also demonstrate your trustworthiness by keeping confidences and by refraining from speaking negatively about others. After all, if you speak negatively about others to me, I have every reason to assume that you are speaking negatively about me when I am not around.

4. Be Honest: Honesty is not simply a matter of not telling lies. It includes the capacity to be precise in your statements and measured in your judgments. If you develop a reputation of being prone to wild exaggeration or distortion, people may not believe you even when you are being careful to state things clearly and precisely. Don't be a know-it-all. Avoid trying to be an "expert" on everything. Be willing to say, "I don't know. That's not my area of expertise." Value the experience of others.

5. Be Responsible: Accept total responsibility for your actions. When you make mistakes, admit them without blame, excuse, or defense. Whenever you enlist the aid of

More business decisions occur over lunch and dinner than at any other time, yet no MBA courses are given on the subject.
Peter Drucker

others, maintain responsibility for decision making and for the consequences. Don't attempt to dump your problems onto others. Wear your responsibilities well, with competence, confidence, and good cheer.

6. Be Courteous: Show consideration. Politeness and courtesy are always well received. One of the best ways of showing people that you respect them is by respecting the value of their time. Don't impose. Don't overstay your welcome. Don't embarrass people or put them in awkward situations. *Show thoughtfulness.* Remember birthdays, children's names, favorite things, places, and events.

7. Be Prepared: Demonstrate that you value the relationship by giving your best. Show that you care enough to prepare. *Prepare for your time together.* Whether it be a business transaction, a social event, or a day at the beach, preparation can spell the difference between a successful encounter and a disappointing one. Prepare for your outings with others by clearing the decks of possible distractions or interruptions and by anticipating how best to accomplish your common goals. Organize the things you need to bring along as well as notes on subjects you want to discuss.

Prepare when you ask for help. Don't impose on people by asking them to solve problems that you could have solved yourself with a little thought, research, or legwork. If you ask people to help you before you have done your homework, you risk their irritation and displeasure. When you do ask for assistance, be clear on exactly how people can help you *before* you approach them. *Prepare what you have to give.* Don't spill the beans. It is often better to keep an idea to yourself than to bring it up before you are prepared to discuss it fully. Bite your tongue until you are ready to make your best case.

8. Be Appropriate: A sense of appropriateness is critical to successful human relations. Appropriateness is a matter of knowledge, sensitivity, and timing.

Knowledge: There are ways in which certain things are done. These involve issues of protocol and custom: whom to invite to various functions, what gifts to buy for whom, how to address and conduct oneself with various individuals, and so on. Happily, this can all be learned. Mentors help. Books on social and professional etiquette and foreign customs are widely available.

Sensitivity: A good deal of appropriateness is simply a matter of empathy and common sense. It's sensing when it's appropriate to broach a subject, or to give a word of encouragement or a gentle chide. If we are alert and really listening with all of our senses, we will know what is appropriate and what is not.

Timing: Recognize that what might be appropriate in one situation could be entirely inappropriate in another. For example, if you have established a friendship with a superior, it may be appropriate for you to call him by his first name and relate to him in an informal manner in his home. However, when you are in the company of subordinates or clients, a more formal interaction is appropriate.

9. Be Discriminating: People with discriminating tastes are held in high regard. It is especially important that you *choose your associates carefully.* Far more than you may realize, you are judged by the company you keep.

10. Be Valuable: Add value to the lives of those you touch. Make their lives better for every encounter they have with you. Increase your value by making a lifelong commitment to learning and growing. The bottom line of a good reputation is that people have good things to say about you. Work on your behavior and demeanor so that's all they have to say. *Your reputation precedes you. It is either paving your way or getting in the way.*

Strengthening Your Reputation

Using the list on pages 457–458, and any other factors that are important to you, indicate below how you can improve your reputation by developing in each of the following:

Appearance: _____

_____

Promptness: _____

_____

Trustworthiness: _____

_____

Honesty: _____

_____

Responsibility: _____

_____

Courtesy: _____

_____

Preparedness: _____

_____

Appropriateness: _____

_____

Discrimination: _____

_____

Service: _____

_____

Other: _____

_____

Undertake not what you can not perform, but be careful to keep your promises.
George Washington

Developing Contacts and Relationships

1. Don't miss opportunities to develop contacts. We are virtually surrounded by people who are ready and willing to help us. If we have our eyes and ears open, we will be able to take advantage of many opportunities we might otherwise miss. Be on the lookout for individuals who can help you. Sometimes opportunity comes in ways you might not expect. Be alert. Don't dismiss opportunities because you don't see exactly how certain people can further your career objectives.

2. Ask for help. Regardless of whether you need information, leads, or referrals, ask for what you need. Express appreciation for the help you receive. Let people know that they are important to you and that you value their help.

3. Follow up on information, advice, or leads given you and communicate back. If it turns out that certain leads are not appropriate for you, you will be able to communicate that back to the party who has helped you get together. If you take some action on the advice that people give you and let them know about it, they will be much more likely to help you further. If you do nothing, they may not want to spend their valuable time trying to help you.

4. Develop well-rounded relationships that are not "all business." Obviously, you do not have the time to do this with everyone; however, for the really key members of your networks, it is essential.

5. Give more than you get. Share what you have to give with the members of your network. It may be your knowledge and experience; it may be your encouragement and support; it may be access to important people. You can share current information, perhaps a book or magazine article that members of your network might enjoy or benefit from.

6. Live up to the trust that others place in you. Recognize that when people share important contacts with you, they are giving you a vote of confidence and placing their trust in you. Do not violate that trust or fail to appreciate it. When you meet with someone who has been referred or introduced to you by a member of your network, the way that you conduct yourself is going to reflect upon that individual as well as on you. If you present yourself well, the esteem that you garner accrues to the one who sent you. If you present yourself poorly, you reflect badly, not only on yourself, but on the one who helped you establish the contact.

7. Protect the members of your network. In the same way, those whom you refer go out as your ambassadors as well as their own. Don't refer people who will reflect badly on you and themselves by failing to appreciate the opportunity. Remember, it takes time and energy to cultivate trust, and while trust often takes a long time to develop, it can easily be weakened or destroyed.

8. Identify your social strengths and weaknesses, and develop strategies for improving your effectiveness. In developing a networking strategy, you will want to look at your style of relating to people in various settings. Identify your social strengths and weaknesses (e.g., formal, informal, one-on-one, small groups, large groups, etc.). You might say, "I'm fine one-on-one, but feel awkward in small groups," or "I do well in informal settings, but feel uncomfortable in a formal environment," or "I feel comfortable with people my own age, but have difficulty with those who are much older." Know what your strengths are and, as much as possible, take advantage of them.

Anticipate potential problem areas, and endeavor to strengthen or mitigate weaknesses in advance. Play it out in your mind beforehand. Visualize the scene in advance, and identify exactly what it is that makes you feel uncomfortable. It may be a lack of knowledge. It may be that you are judging yourself or others harshly. It may be that you are recalling some past failure. The important thing in this process is to identify exactly what the problem is and then make the correction. As always, understanding gives you power over fear.

9. Get to know the right people. Recognize that people judge you by who you know as much as by who you are or what you have accomplished. In virtually any endeavor, there are people whom you should know, key people who can help you gain access to others. They may be within your field, or simply so influential within your community that their names open doors. Get to know them.

Your Networking Strategy

In the space below, indicate your strategy for developing and maintaining effective relationships with each of the following that are applicable to you:

Mentors:_____

_____

Colleagues/coworkers: _____

_____

Superiors: _____

_____

Subordinates:_____

_____

Miscellaneous

1. Benefactors: _____

2. Investors: _____

3. Clients and customers:_____

4. Suppliers:_____

5. Distributors: _____

Trust men, and they will be true to you. Treat them greatly, and they will show themselves great.
Emerson

Associations: The American Way

Americans of all ages, all conditions and all dispositions constantly form associations. They have not only commercial and manufacturing companies in which all take part but associations of a thousand other kinds: religious, moral, serious, futile, restricted, enormous, or diminutive.
Alexis de Tocqueville,
Democracy in America

Associations play as important a role in American society today as they did when Tocqueville wrote this in the early nineteenth century. In many professions, membership is an absolute must. In most any profession, they're a definite plus. Associations serve as places of fellowship and clearinghouses of information. They provide a sense of a common identity to people with common interests. Associations, through the vehicle of peer pressure, attempt to direct the behavior of their membership toward the attainment of certain values, goals, or principles. Joining associations can enhance your prestige and credibility and expand your networks. Identify and join the associations that will enhance your effectiveness in fulfilling your life's work.

Key Points for Association Membership

1. Select organizations you want to develop long-term relationships with. In making your selections, take a long-range view. Select quality organizations with quality people who have a lot to offer.

Be as interested in what you have to give to the organization as you are in what you have to get out of it.

2. Show appreciation for the organization and its leadership. It is important that you show appreciation for the privilege of membership in the organization and respect for its current leadership. (After all, they have usually been elected by the membership and are held in esteem by them.) Validating the group and its leadership is honoring a basic principle of sociology: *Groups give acceptance to those who support the group's social structure.* Some have suggested links between this phenomenon in human behavior and the hierarchical social orders among certain animals, for example, baboons. Whatever its origin, its existence cannot be denied.

Individuals who try to ignore this fact and operate as though their organization were a meritocracy are usually disappointed. They assume that they are being judged on the basis of their work alone. This often leads to frustration as individuals attempt to gain greater recognition and responsibility within the group by working harder. They dismiss other considerations as merely "politics." Often they are disappointed before they come to realize that if you want to "play the game," you have to play politics. *Validate the group and its leadership.*

3. Look for responsibility vacuums and fill them as appropriate. Show your interest in the group by assuming responsibility for areas that are currently being neglected. Look for ways you can help. Be sure, when you do this, that you are operating "within channels." Sometimes "go-getter" types try to assume too much responsibil-

Life is to be fortified by many friendships. To love and to be loved is the greatest happiness.
Sydney Smith

ity too early, in the hope of ingratiating themselves with the membership. They are just as likely to be viewed as pushy and overbearing as they are to be appreciated for the work they do. This is especially true if they appear arrogant and do not express sincere appreciation for the organization and for the privilege of being a member of it. *Without being pushy, assume as much responsibility as you can.*

4. Develop long-term win-win relationships with members of the organization.
Give at every available opportunity to individuals as individuals. Recognize that every individual in the association is a representative of a particular network, which he or she has developed. *If people are thanking you or expressing gratitude when they leave you, you are probably on the right track.*

5. Consider organizations in the following categories:

Professional: e.g., ABA, AMA.

_____

_____

_____

_____

Community Service: Habitat for Humanity, Rotary, Optimists, PTA, etc.

_____

_____

_____

_____

Recreational/Social: Health clubs, sports teams, sailing clubs, community theater, etc.

_____

_____

_____

International/Current Affairs: World Affairs Council, Commonwealth Club.

_____

_____

_____

Special Interest Associations: Sierra Club, League of Women Voters, Audubon Society.

_____

_____

_____

Religious Associations:

_____

_____

_____

Political Parties and Associations:

_____

_____

_____

Associations Source

Encyclopedia of Associations. Thomson/Gale. Farmington Hills, Mich.: Thomson/Gale. Published annually.

Back of every noble life there are principles that have fashioned it.
George Horace Lorimer

Your Mission Team Mastermind

Find the key individuals in your life who share your dreams, and assemble them in a team. Give yourself the added benefits of a mastermind team, people who will support your goals and work in a spirit of cooperation. Meet with these individuals for breakfast, or have them over for coffee once a week.

Assemble your mastermind team:

Team member #1:_____

Motivation for helping you: _____

Strengths:_____

_____

Team member #2:_____

Motivation for helping you: _____

Strengths:_____

_____

Team member #3:_____

Motivation for helping you: _____

Strengths:_____

_____

Team member #4:_____

Motivation for helping you: _____

Strengths:_____

_____

Team member #5:_____

Motivation for helping you: _____

Strengths:_____

The sole meaning of life is to serve humanity.
Leo Tolstoy

Creating Your Mental Mastermind

Libraries are full of great conversations. You can pick up a book and have a conversation with Homer, Plato, or Einstein. In his book *Think and Grow Rich,* Napoleon Hill describes how he had mental meetings with the greats of history who represented particular virtues he wanted to develop. (*Emerson*—an understanding nature; *Burbank*—a harmonizing nature; *Napoleon*—inspiration, faith; *Paine*—freedom of thought; *Darwin*—patience; *Lincoln*—justice, patience, humor, and tolerance; *Carnegie*—principles of organized effort; *Ford*—persistence, determination, poise, self-confidence; *Edison*—faith.) Take some time to develop your mental mastermind.

Individual	Quality
1._____	_____
2._____	_____
3._____	_____
4._____	_____
5._____	_____
6._____	_____
7._____	_____
8._____	_____
9._____	_____
10._____	_____

Go into daily (or regular) meditation, and ask these individuals to assist you, to give you ideas, to help you solve problems. Conduct a mental board meeting.

Mastermind Sources

Current Biography Yearbook. Clifford Thompson, ed. Bronx, N.Y.: H. W. Wilson Company. Published annually.

Encyclopedia of World Biography. Thomson/Gale. Farmington Hills, Mich.: Thomson/Gale. Published annually.

Think and Grow Rich, rev. ed. Napoleon Hill. New York: Tarcher, 2005.

Man's brain may be compared to an electric battery . . . a group of electric batteries will provide more energy than a single battery.
Napoleon Hill

Networking Objectives

Write your networking goals in the space below. Make them as specific as possible. You may want to include goals about the number and kinds of contacts you want to make, the organizations or associations you want to join, positions you might want to hold within various organizations, the assemblage of your mastermind team, or any other networking goals of importance to you. Be sure to include the date by which you expect to have each goal completed.

Networking Goal 1: _____

_____

_____

_____

Networking Goal 2: _____

_____

_____

_____

Networking Goal 3: _____

_____

_____

_____

Networking Goal 4: _____

_____

_____

_____

Networking Goal 5: _____

_____

_____

_____

Web and Book Resources

Find links to associations and a variety of other networking resources @ Empoweryou.com.

Publicity: Working the Media

The purpose of publicity is to enhance public awareness of yourself and your offerings. Think of publicity as free advertising. When planning your publicity strategy, keep in mind the goals of the various media, as well as your own goal (exposure). Generally, the media want to inform, educate, and entertain. If you can help them to do any of these things (and you can), you are helping them to achieve their objectives while meeting yours. Remember, every day throughout the land, the media write thousands of articles and broadcast hundreds of hours of radio and television programming. They need help in finding new stories. That's where you come in.

Look at publicity as a long-term activity. It helps to build from the ground up. For example, even if your goal is to be on *The Oprah Winfrey Show,* you probably will want to start with your local cable access channel and work your way up through local television and radio interviews. Research local media options, and determine which will work best for you.

Start with the easy-access media, and move up to the big time as you gain skill, experience, and a publicity track record. Use easy-access media as a springboard to gaining access to major market newspapers, radio, and television stations. A man I know, who lives in the San Diego area, promoted his self-published books by starting with articles and reviews in local suburban newspapers. He was able to parlay these into reviews from the *San Diego Union* and then the *L.A. Times.* Below are a few tips on how to let people know about you and your offering.

> *The worst fear is the fear of living.*
> *Theodore Roosevelt*

Write a News Release

The centerpiece of any publicity campaign is a well-written news release. If you want people to know what you are doing, write a press release, and send it to all the local newspapers, magazines, radio shows, and television stations. Take some time with your news release. The style of a press release is that of a journalistic report. Many beginners make the mistake of writing a press release as though it were advertising copy.

Remember, your press release is the first impression that an editor or interviewer has of you, and it will determine whether or not he or she is going to be interested in doing a story on or an interview with you. Also, many small newspapers, newsletters, and magazines print press releases as news stories in their publications with little or no editing. Spend some time honing your message. Make sure it communicates accurately the essence of your work.

Use your letterhead stationery. Include the release date, for example, "For Release May 1, 2012," or the words, "For Immediate Release." Also include the name of a contact person and that person's (day and evening) phone number. Type the words "PRESS RELEASE" across the top. Headline your press release with an attention-getting line that encapsulates your message.

There are three parts to a standard news release—the lead, the body, and the conclusion. The *lead* is the first three or four sentences. It gives the essence of what you have to say—in capsule form. Start with an attention-grabber. You may want to use a question, quotation, or a bit of humor here to catch the reader's attention. The *body* is three or four paragraphs in length and contains, in descending order of importance, everything you think the reader should know about what you are doing. The *close,* or final paragraph, summarizes your message. Close with something that will stick in the editor's or producer's mind. Follow up your news release with a phone call. Media people are often inundated with paper. Persistence pays.

Ways of Publicity

Here is a list of publicity options that gives you an idea of different access levels.

Easy-Access Media

Calendars and Bulletins:

Calendar and event sections of local
    newspapers
Radio and television bulletin boards
Church bulletins
Newsletters

Features and Interviews:

Low-wattage college radio programs
Cable television public access programs
Small-town newspapers
Weekly newspapers
Local magazines

Guerrilla Internet Publicity:

Blogs/Web sites
YouTube
Social networking sites, e.g., MySpace, Facebook, etc.

Intermediate-Access Media

Level A

Features and Interviews:

Public affairs programs
Radio and television talk shows
Features in local radio and television
    news programs
Mid-sized city newspapers
National trade publications
Association magazines
Professional trade journals

Level B

The same types of avenues, only in major
city and regional markets.

"The Big Time"

Major National Newspapers:

New York Times	*Washington Post*	*Wall Street Journal*
USA Today	*Los Angeles Times*	*Chicago Tribune*
Boston Globe	*Philadelphia Inquirer*	

National Magazines of All Varieties, Such As:

Time	*Newsweek*	*People*
O, The Oprah Magazine	*Rolling Stone*	*The Atlantic*
Esquire	*Vanity Fair*	*The New Yorker*

Television Programs:

ABC News Nightline	*The Oprah Winfrey Show*	*The Charlie Rose Show*
Good Morning America	*Late Night with*	*Morning Joe*
60 Minutes	* David Letterman*	*The Ellen DeGeneres Show*
20/20	*Larry King Live*	*Primetime*
The Today Show	*The Tonight Show*	*The Daily Show*
Dateline	*The View*	*The Colbert Report*

Make a Press Kit

On many occasions, a press release alone won't do—you'll need a press kit. A press kit is a packet of information that offers editors, producers, and interviewers the information they need to know about you. The most important item in your press kit is a carefully written news release. Your kit should also include a one- or two-page "bio," or summary of your educational background, marital and family status, current and prior occupations, professional credentials, local awards, and community service participation.

Write a short cover letter, typed on a single page and directed toward the specific individual who will be making the interviewing decisions. Tell him why you would make a great guest and why his readers, listeners, or viewers will want to hear what you have to say. Include a black-and-white photograph of yourself, either 5 x 7 or 8 x 10. If you have color slides, don't send them, but simply write "Color Slides Available on Request" on your cover letter. Also send along a list of ten to twenty sample interview questions that you would like to be asked. Arrange all of these items in a sturdy, attractive, and fairly conservative-looking folder, and you're off to let the public know about you and your gig!

Include in your press kit:

1. *A one- or two-page news release, offset or typeset*
2. *A cover letter*
3. *A one- or two-page biography*
4. *One or two photographs*
5. *A list of "suggested interview questions"*
6. *Sample clippings or quotes from previous interviews or features*
7. *A preprinted Rolodex card with your contact information*
8. *Your business card*
9. *A folder with your name or your company or organization's name, either preprinted or stuck on the cover with a mailing label*

Be the Feature Attraction: Get Them to Do a Feature Article or Story on You

A feature article on you in a local newspaper or a feature story by a radio or television show can get the word out about what you are doing faster and more effectively than paid advertising, and it's free besides. Articles about you and/or about what you do are perhaps the single most effective piece of written publicity. It's more believable than an advertisement because the credibility of the newspaper or magazine accrues to you. Of course, the same applies to television and radio feature stories. A two- to four-minute feature on you is worth a great deal of paid advertising. Again, it's more credible and suggests that you are "hot." Television has the advantage of showing you in action.

Be the Talk of the Town: Get Interviews

Newspapers, radio, and television stations also do interviews. Cable or public access television, local newspapers, and morning radio talk shows are good places for the beginner to start. Approach your interviews with confidence. Focus on the valuable information you have to share and watch nervousness vanish into thin air. Have in mind three or four points you would like your audience to remember, and keep coming back to these. (If people remember this much of what you say, you can consider yourself fortunate.) You may want to rehearse your answers, especially to tough questions. This will help you to stay relaxed. Don't get defensive, even if the interviewer is hostile. Be gracious in manner, measured and precise in speech. Speak with authority and command; after all, you are being interviewed because you're the expert. Television interviews present added dimensions. Make sure your look (dress, posture, gesture, facial expression) effectively conveys the image you want to project. Keep in mind that over 90 percent of all communication is nonverbal.

The "U-Revue": Get Them to Review Your Work

Writers have books reviewed. Artists have gallery showings reviewed. Musicians and entertainers of all kinds have performances reviewed. Even caterers get reviewed. Be sure that people who write the local reviews are aware of you and your work. Send them a press release and a copy of your work (if appropriate).

The Write Way to Publicity: Write Your Own Article or Column

If you've got something to say that could be of ongoing interest to readers, try writing your own newspaper article or perhaps a column. You can spread your message, showcase your expertise, and offer a service to your audience at the same time. Write some sample columns, and then approach the editor of your local newspaper. The "Lifestyle" section of your newspaper has regular columns on health, entertainment, food and nutrition, astrology, consumer affairs, education, parenting, and many other subjects of general interest. When writing your article, choose your words carefully, and consider how the reader will perceive what you are saying. Anticipate questions, and think your answers through in advance.

Most professions, trades, and special interest groups publish newsletters that offer readers the most current information in their field. Use *Newsletters in Print* at your local library to target newsletters most likely to be read by the people you want to reach, and submit an article. (Or ask them to interview you.) This is an easy way to get publicity that's targeted to a specific audience.

Public Service Announcements

Radio and television stations are required to allot a certain portion of their airtime for public service announcements. If you're promoting a free or charity event, or any-thing that could be defined as a community service, take advantage of these. Call your local radio and television stations, and find out how to get your PSA on the air.

Other Publicity Ideas

1. Create a blog.
2. Write letters to the editor.
3. Give a speech.
4. Sponsor an event.
5. Produce your own cable-access show or regular program.
6. List in community calendars
7. Get yourself listed in: *Yearbook of Experts, Authorities, & Spokespersons*. Their Web site is www.yearbook.com

Publicity Sources

Full Frontal PR: Building Buzz About Your Business, Your Product, or You. Richard Laermer. New York: Bloomberg Press, 2004.

High Visibility: Transforming Your Personal and Professional Brand. Irving J. Rein, Philip Kotler, Michael Hamlin, and Martin R. Stoller. New York: McGraw-Hill, 2005.

The New Rules of Marketing and PR: How to Use News Releases, Blogs, Podcasting, Viral Marketing and Online Media to Reach Buyers Directly. David Meerman Scott. New York: Wiley, 2007.

Your Public Best: The Complete Guide to Making Successful Public Appearances, 2nd ed. Lillian Brown. New York: Norton, 2003.

Negotiation

Whether you're discussing an important contract with a new client, talking to your boss about a raise, or finding the financial support to begin a new business, good negotiating skills are critical to your success. There are two basic styles of negotiation: hardball and win-win. Use a win-win approach whenever possible.

Hardball Negotiations

In the business world, most people are playing the hardball game. It helps to be aware of this game when you're dealing with someone who insists on being your opponent, or is trying to take advantage of you. The object of the hardball game is to make sure one gets what one wants, no matter what happens to the other guy. If you're aware of these tactics, you're more likely to overcome them. There will also be times when you may need to use them yourself.

The Hardball Game

1. **Whenever possible, take the initiative in the negotiation.** This gives you added power. You increase the likelihood that you will get what you want when you are calling the shots. If you make an outrageous offer, the other party might just take it. (They might not know about point number four below.)

2. **Be prepared to walk away.** The one who needs the deal the most is at the biggest disadvantage. Everything is negotiable, but you don't *have* to negotiate. Still, *don't make threats unless you're prepared to back them up*. Don't threaten to walk away unless you really mean it, or you will lose credibility fast.

3. **Understand their objectives as well as their weaknesses and vulnerabil-**ities. Do your homework. Smoke out their real bottom line. Get them talking and keep them talking—discover where their soft underbelly is. Many hardballers have a sort of "underbelly" sixth sense. They know how to find it and how to tear into it.

4. **You don't ever have to take the first offer.** You can always try to get a better deal. Sometimes silence helps—if you say nothing, they may start scrambling to offer you something better. In any case, *don't agree to anything right away*. If you're not sure about your decision, give yourself plenty of time to think it over. You can always postpone and set up a later meeting.

5. **Always ask for more than what you really want.** In this way, you can seem to be giving up more than you really are. While you are negotiating away small points, the other side is making real concessions. Get something for everything you give up, even the smallest points. Minimize what they are giving up while maximizing what you are.

6. **Create demand by starting a bidding war.** People want what they think other people want. Create an image of yourself as hot and in demand. Let them know that if they don't take your offer, somebody else will. Remember, there are plenty of fish in the sea.

7. **Always have a backup plan in mind in case something doesn't work out.** Have a "Plan B." In fact, make "Plan C" and "Plan D" while you're at it. This will help you to keep your cool, no matter what happens. You won't have to cave in out of desperation.

8. **Get your adversary saying "Yes" to you as often as possible.** This will get him or her into the habit of saying yes when it comes to the final decision.

9. **Get everything in writing.** Whenever possible, have *your* lawyer write the contract. Carefully check out your adversary's credentials. Some people will try to screw you, so protect yourself. Make them put it in writing, and by all means, don't sign anything until you are clear about what it says.

10. **Remember, you don't have to settle for less than what you want.** If you're willing to persist, you can usually get a good deal.

Win-Win Negotiations

Win-win negotiations start with the premise that when the people involved combine creative energies, they most often come up with a better solution than either party originally had in mind. When dealing with people with whom you have a continuing relationship, for instance your spouse or your boss, it is obviously in your best interest to emphasize win-win negotiating strategies. Yet in all you do, you sincerely want people to be happy with the results of the negotiations you enter into. Win-win works best; after all, what goes around comes around.

The Win-Win Game

1. **Think in terms of a long-term relationship.** In hardball negotiations, you might win the battle and lose the war. You might take the guy to the cleaners once, but now you've made an enemy, and he's going to be looking to get you at the first available opportunity. At the very least, he's not going to be very cooperative the next time you need his agreement. Also, you may get a reputation for being a real jerk, in which case people whom you have never dealt with before may be gunning for you and take satisfaction in nailing "that S.O.B." Trust that if you do right by people, it will come around again and again.

2. **Approach your win-win negotiations with certainty.** Start with the assurance that there is a way for both parties to win. Come in knowing that you will continue to explore ideas and generate options until you find a mutually beneficial solution.

3. **Come prepared.** Before you meet, find out as much as you can about the other party, including his lifestyle, personality, and interests, as well as his likely attitudes on the issues you will be considering together. Explore all factors relevant to your negotiation. For example, consider how third parties might play a role or how the situation is likely to change or evolve over time. Begin generating mutually beneficial solutions even before you meet for discussion. Be creative.

4. **Be agreeable—view the other party as a partner.** In the hardball game, the other guy is your adversary. It's easier to work with a partner than an adversary. Be friendly. Stay focused on agreement; don't get into hard positions. Remember, agreement is the goal. Genuinely want to help the other party.

5. **Listen.** Although it helps to find out as much as you can in advance, don't come in with set solutions. Take the time to understand the other party's needs, concerns, and desires. Ask questions and really listen. Active listening can help you hear what is not being said, as well as what is. In some situations, it may be necessary to draw the other party out—to help her clarify her needs and desires. To make sure you understand her clearly, feed back what she has shared with you, until she indicates that you have got it right.

6. **Be honest about what you want and ask for it.** That means you have to know what you want. State it clearly and be specific. Then show the other party how he or she can help you get it.

Especially in personal relationships, it is important to state exactly what you want. Otherwise, you may frustrate the other party by making yourself impossible to please. Others can help you get what you want, but they can't save you from your own moods.

7. **Don't view compromise as loss.** We have been trained to think that we have to win every point or be thought a fool. Pride and self-righteousness can keep us from making compromises that will be better for everyone in the long run. Alexander Hamilton wanted a form of government more closely akin to a monarchy than the representative democracy that the Constitutional Convention decided upon. Still, once the decision had been taken, he supported the Constitution and lobbied hard for it. He saw the country had more to win by his supporting this decision than by taking his marbles and going home. *Win-win players keep a greater good in mind.*

8. **See conflict as opportunity.** An apparent conflict or dispute offers an opportunity for creative solutions. Often conflict comes in when we get into rigid or limited thinking. All that may be needed is to look at the situation from a fresh perspective. Stay detached and objective. Don't take conflict personally or as an affront. Keep the emotional tone from getting overheated—if you need to, take a break.

9. **Remember you are entering into a dynamic creative process.** The spirit of win-win negotiation is creative and playful, fluid and fun. Like a jazz improvisation, it starts to jive when the players are harmonizing and staying loose. The music that you make in these negotiations will surprise and delight. Harmonious playfulness triggers the right-brain wholistic and inspirational solutions that you can never get from scheming or from a defensive adversarial posture. You tap into something beyond the range of critical thought.

10. **Don't settle for less than the right solution for both parties.** If you've tried in every way to come up with a mutually beneficial solution and you find that there really isn't one in this instance—let it go. Don't jeopardize the relationship by trying to make sparks fly from wet sticks. After a time, you'll know if it is not going to click. Part company as friends, and leave the door open to work together again.

Be on the lookout for new opportunities to use a win-win approach. As you develop and practice your win-win negotiation skills, you'll find hundreds of opportunities to apply them, not simply in work, but in every aspect of your life. It gives you an ongoing experience of a world that works for everyone.

Negotiation Sources

The Art of Closing Any Deal: How to Be a Master Closer in Everything You Do. James W. Pickens. New York: Warner Books, 2003.

Beyond Reason: Using Emotions as You Negotiate. Roger Fisher and Daniel Shapiro. New York: Viking, 2005.

Essentials of Negotiation, 3rd ed. Roy J. Lewicki, Bruce Barry, David M. Saunders, and John W. Minton. New York: McGraw-Hill, 2006.

Getting to Yes: Negotiating Agreement without Giving In. Roger Fisher, William Ury, and Bruce M. Patton. New York: Random House, 2003.

Harvard Business Essentials Guide to Negotiation. Watertown, Mass.: Harvard Business School Press, 2003.

Ten Keys to Effective Selling

1. **Believe in what you are selling.** When you're totally convinced that your product or service is of genuine benefit to your clients and you sincerely want to provide them with the best, your enthusiasm is irresistible, and your sales will soar!

2. **Project the right image.** Be neat, organized, and professional in your sales presentation. Remember—the first impression you make on a prospective buyer is the most important factor in whether or not you will close the sale. Nonverbals are at least as important as verbals.

3. **Become an expert.** Learn as much as you can about your product or service. Your knowledge and confidence will put your customers at ease and make it easy for them to trust you.

4. **Qualify your prospects.** Make sure you're talking to a qualified buyer who has both the authority and the means to make the final decision. Be aware that qualifying goes both ways. Make sure that what you are selling is really appropriate to your client.

5. **Assess your clients' needs.** If possible, do homework on clients before you meet. Learn as much as you can. If you know what they want, it'll be easy to show them how owning and enjoying your product or service will help them get it. Conduct interviews with your clients to help you identify their needs. Let them tell you what they want, then match it to what you have to offer.

6. **Stress the benefits when making your presentation.** Talk about the benefits that your new clients will receive from owning your product or service. Do they want more challenge and excitement in their lives? A greater sense of self-esteem? Do they want to save money or time?

People buy for emotional reasons. They buy benefits, not products and services. If you can demonstrate that owning your product or service will help them get what they want, you've made the sale.

7. **Handle their objections.** If they say no, find out why. Get clear on their objections. Once you know what their problems are, you'll be able to solve them and close the sale. Because you believe in the value of what you are selling and know your client is qualified and will benefit from your product or service, you'll be able to handle any objections with ease and confidence.

8. **Close the sale naturally.** This is the most crucial and most challenging aspect of the sales process. More sales are lost because the salesperson was afraid to ask for the sale than for any other reason. Go ahead—close the sale. Make sure that your buyer gets to enjoy the benefits of your product or service.

9. **Follow through.** Give your clients follow-up calls to make sure they're satisfied. If they are, this is a great opportunity to ask for referrals. If not, find out why, and handle the problem right away. Focus on developing long-term business relationships with satisfied customers. Consistent follow-through is the most important key to keeping track of satisfied clients and building your business.

10. **Stay positive.** Every sales presentation is a valuable learning experience. Think about what you did well and what you could improve upon. Find out how many "No's" it takes you to close one sale. Then remind yourself that each "No" brings you one step closer to your next "Yes"! Don't get discouraged. An unrelentingly positive attitude is the greatest asset of an effective salesperson. If you persist, you will succeed.

Information, Please

For many years, economists and workforce experts of every hue and stripe have been telling us about the rise of the "information economy." Of course, it isn't just talk. Today, "knowledge workers" make up more than 20 percent of the workforce, with nearly five million directly involved in supplying information services, according to the Bureau of Labor Statistics. But it goes far beyond this. In fact, if you were to view all business as the sale of organized information, you wouldn't be too far off the mark. What is a doctor, lawyer, accountant, engineer, or any professional selling—if not knowledge? Even in commodity-based industries like manufacturing and mining, nothing happens without the knowledge to convert raw materials into finished products and the knowledge to market these products. Today's information economy affords tremendous opportunities for those with the skills and abilities to take advantage of them. These skills include:

1. The ability to research and collect data
2. The ability to organize information
3. The ability to target specific markets
4. The ability to package information
5. The ability to sell information

The more you can develop these skills, the more valuable you'll make yourself in this economy. If you don't already have them, it pays to develop your informational skills. If you are already involved in knowledge work, you might want to think about how you can convert your knowledge into intellectual property. For example, consultants, project managers, and sales and leadership development trainers (among others) often create systems, presentations, manuals, or seminars in the course of their work that have applications that extend far beyond the immediate purpose for which they were developed. If applicable, you may want to examine work that you have done or will do in the future with an eye toward creating information products and/or services that you can market directly to the consumers of this information. (Of course, first be sure that you haven't signed or even verbally agreed to anything that would restrict your ownership of the intellectual property you create.)

Others may have learned a great deal about subjects that are only peripherally or not at all related to their current jobs. If you find yourself in either position, you might develop seminars, professional speaking opportunities, teleclasses, books, audio or video recordings, or other vehicles through which to share your knowledge and experience. In time, you may develop opportunities to significantly augment or even replace the income you get from your existing job.

Act III Review

If you've decided to create your own organization, answer the following questions. If you want to work in an already existing organization, turn to page 478.

Sailing the Entrepreneurship

Describe the products and/or services you will provide.   *(page 372)*

Identify the chief markets for your product or service.   *(page 373)*

Briefly, how will you get their attention?   *(page 374)*

How will you distribute your product or service?   *(page 374)*

List the key players on your management team.   *(page 375)*

List the key players on your professional support team.   *(page 376)*

What legal structure will you use (partnership, sole proprietorship, corporation, etc.)?
(page 377)

Indicate the funding vehicles you plan to employ.
(page 380)

Summarize your strategy for dealing with the "red tape" involved in creating your business.
(page 382)

Write a goal for the completion of your business plan here.
(page 385)

Wielding the Freelance

The advantages of my freelance option are:
(page 391)

The top markets for my project are:
(page 395)

Crafting the Nonprofit Foundation

State the mission of your organization. *(page 409)*

List your top three strategies for fulfilling this mission. *(page 409)*

List three potential sources of funding. *(page 410)*

My ideas for further exploring proposal writing are: *(page 411)*

Landing the Right Job

Identify what you want from an organization. *(page 429)*

List your top employment needs. *(page 430)*

Identify the top three organizations you would most like to work for, and the position you want. *(page 432)*

Describe your strategy for landing the interview with employer #1. *(page 446)*

List your employment strengths. *(page 450)*

List your #1 potential employer's needs, and how you can help. *(page 451)*

List your #1 potential employer's strengths, including current and future opportunities. *(page 451)*

Street Smarts

My networking strategy will be: *(page 461)*

The media options I will use to promote myself are: *(page 468)*

The negotiation strategy I will emphasize in regard to my current negotiation is: *(page 472)*

The School of Life's Work

Wherein our hero learns to change and grow

One is always seeking the touchstone that will dissolve one's deficiencies as a person and as a craftsman. And one is always bumping up against the fact that there is none except hard work, concentration, and continued application.

Paul Gallico

So far, we've considered your life's work as an Art, a Quest, a Game, and a Battle. Act IV looks at your life's work as a School—an ongoing learning process. This book began with a discussion about recognizing and honoring the timeless in life. It closes by honoring the role that time plays in creating and developing a life's work. The nature of *time* is *change*; the two words are virtually synonymous. "Act IV: The School of Life's Work" is about making the changes that will enable you to pursue your life's work. It will consider training and skill development, developing an effective transition strategy, improving your self-image, enlisting support, and getting the most out of what you're doing now. Before getting into these specifics, we'll explore lifelong learning in creating—and responding to—change.

Learning to Change:
The Old Boy and the Student-Sage

The only person who is educated is the one who has learned how to learn . . . and change.
Carl Rogers

The following remarks from *Megatrends* author John Naisbitt help us understand how vital it is that we learn to *create* change and learn to effectively *deal with* the changes we are not directly creating. "In the new information society, where the only constant is change, we can no longer expect to get an education and be done with it. There is no one education, no one skill that lasts a lifetime now. Like it or not, the information society has turned us all into lifelong learners."[1] I would suggest that it makes a difference whether we "like it or not," that our attitudes toward change and learning are critical to our effectiveness.

Change. Does the word conjure up anticipation or fear? With anticipation, we look forward to change, demonstrating an inherent trust in our ability to learn and grow, and in the basic goodness of life. Fear reflects a lack of trust in ourselves and in life. We can distinguish between the fear of *changing* and the fear of *change*. The fear of changing, of actively initiating change, comes from a lack of confidence in our ability to learn. The fear of change, the fear of the effects of any portion of a generalized "other" (for example, people, circumstances, the weather, God, etc.), comes from the belief that life is basically hostile, that what's coming is likely to be bad. We can say in the vernacular that the fear of changing is the fear of screwing up; the fear of change, the fear of getting screwed.

Do not cherish the unworthy desire that the changeable might become the unchanging.
Teachings of the Buddha

Learning plays a part, both in creating change (for example, in retraining and skill development) and in responding or adapting to change (for example, changes in the economy or in specific markets). The Latin origins of two English words long associated with learning suggest approaches for effectively creating and responding to change. Our word *student* comes from *studere,* "to be eager about, to study"; the word *sage,* from *sapere,* "to know, to taste."[2]

The student is eager to learn, to acquire knowledge; the sage has the patience to taste wisdom. As students of life, we are eager to learn the new. As would-be sages, we develop the patience and insight to taste, experience, and penetrate into the very essence of change itself. The true student of life has mastered the fear of changing; the true sage, the fear of change.

If ever there was a book designed to illuminate the essence of change, it is the ancient Chinese classic the *I Ching,* or *Book of Changes.* Of course, I can only touch on the profound wisdom in this book, which some claim as the oldest of earth. A lifetime of devoted study will not exhaust its treasures. The *I Ching* reflects the distilled wisdom of the "ancients" and their profound understanding of change. The *I Ching* instructs that "the Creative and the Receptive are the real secret of the Changes."[3]

From the standpoint of the *I Ching,* what I've called "the fear of changing" (or indecisiveness) can be viewed as a deficiency or blockage of the Creative energy. What I've called "the fear of change" can be conceived of as a deficiency or blockage of the Receptive energy.

There is no security in life, only opportunity.

Mark Twain

*Learning is
movement
from moment
to moment.*

J. Krishnamurti

The following lines from the "Ta Chun" ("The Great Treatise") of the *I Ching* give the sense of what is meant by the "Creative" and the "Receptive":

> *The Creative knows the great beginnings.*
> *The Receptive completes the finished things.*
> *The Creative is decided and therefore shows to men the easy.*
> *The Receptive is yielding and therefore shows to men the simple.*[4]

The Creative brings the end of difficulties through the strength of decisive action. In developing a life's work, our creative power is enhanced by learning how to learn. The way of creative change is easy for those who know how to learn. True students of life bring an eagerness, a joyous ease into every circumstance. "Knowing the great beginnings," they easily decide upon a way and set about learning what is required. They create a course of study, practice, and action that brings the desired result.

Thomas Jefferson said, "Nothing is troublesome that we do willingly." We are willing when we are decided. Where we lack ease in our lives, we lack the strength of decisive action. Our word *crisis* comes from the Greek *krinein,* "to decide."[5] *Crisis is what happens when we don't decide.* For example, you know it's time for a career change, but you lack the skills or knowledge necessary to move into the career you desire. If you don't take decisive action and aggressively seek the skills and knowledge you need, you could end up feeling trapped in a dead-end job.

The Receptive brings the end of complications through simplicity of motive. Where there is complexity in our lives, we have too many motives crashing into each other. For example, retraining for a new career might mean the temporary loss of income and status. Unless you are clear about your motive, you may quit before you have achieved your goals. The desire for the approval of others can all at once or bit by bit pull you away from your stated objectives. When we are devoted to our objectives, we can let go of our concern about how we appear to others. We let go the vain attempt to control things that we can't (like the opinions of others) and concentrate on what we can control (our own thoughts, feelings, and actions).

The Receptive aspect of change in developing a life's work demonstrates itself in the flexibility and sensitivity to follow the line of least resistance. Those with the wisdom of the sage know that the plans and intentions of our conscious minds are but a small part of life, so they remain flexible. They realize that success is often a matter of moving with events that are larger than themselves, so they remain sensitive to the flow of events. Receptivity doesn't mean abandoning our goals, but moving toward them in a way that is as simple and harmonious as possible. A surfer has an aim (toward shore), yet to realize it, he must put himself in accord with the rhythm of the ocean and ride the waves. To be Receptive, we must, like the surfer, expand our attention and trust that the great ocean of life will carry us forward if we are patient enough to catch the right wave and let it do most of the work.

We can think of the Creative as the *will* and the Receptive as the *willingness* of change—the will to transform, the willingness to let go, to receive. As we develop confidence in our ability to learn, we become students of Creative change, confidently creating the transformations (inner and outer) we desire. As we simplify our motives, we become willing to embrace and harmonize with the larger-than-self changes, all the while moving patiently and steadily toward our goals. To be good students of life, we need to retain (or reclaim) the childlike eagerness to learn. Yet too much eagerness leads to frustration and disappointment, and so, like a wise old sage, we must be able to detach—to stand back, look at where we are going, and consider the best way.

The only way to make sense out of change is to plunge into it, move with it, and join the dance.
Alan Watts

The name of the Taoist sage Lao Tzu has been translated "Old Boy." We can all learn to be old boys or old girls—eager, playful, and decisive, and yet wise, patient, and enduring. When we are confident in our ability to learn, we can plunge into the life we have imagined, like a child at play. When we are clear in our motives, we can let go any need to justify or defend ourselves or our actions, or to desperately seek approval. Like the wise old sage, we keep our own counsel. Long after others have given up or burned out, we endure—flowing with circumstances while remaining devoted to our ideals. We pace ourselves, like the venerable turtle of Aesop, and win the race through steady application.

Again and again, the *I Ching* instructs on the merits of perseverance, and encourages us to take a long view: "The secret of action lies in duration. Good fortune and misfortune are slow in the making."[6] If we are to persevere, we must exercise both the Creative and the Receptive potentials, possessing both the eagerness of the student and the wisdom of the sage. Next, we will consider how we can improve our capacity to learn and, in so doing, enhance our ability for creative, decisive action. Later, we'll explore the wisdom of patient, persistent action.

In the world of the future, the new illiterate will be the person who has not learned how to learn.

Alvin Toffler

Learning: The Difference Between Here and There

In a world that is constantly changing, there is no one subject or set of subjects that will serve you for the foreseeable future, let alone for the rest of your life. The most important skill to acquire now is learning how to learn.

John Naisbitt

Through the ages, man has searched for the secret of youth. In the Middle Ages, witches and magicians invoked spirits with spells, potions, and amulets to confer the vigor of youth. Western and Chinese (Taoist) alchemists mixed strange herbal brews and concocted elaborate mineral combinations in the hope of prolonging life. In the eighteenth century, Ponce de León traversed vast expanses of the American continent in search of the Fountain of Youth. In the nineteenth century, elixirs were sold from the backs of medicine wagons and at carnival shows. Today health food, nutritional supplements, and regular exercise are touted as the answers. While the efficacy of these methods can be debated, in the end the secret of youth may be found in learning—keeping the fresh perspective that new knowledge and experience bring— keeping an open mind!

Anyone who stops learning is old, whether twenty or eighty. Anyone who keeps learning today is young. The greatest thing in life is to keep your mind young.

Henry Ford

A well-educated man once went to a Zen master to acquire understanding of Zen. After greeting him, the master instructed the visitor to be seated and proceeded to pour him a cup of tea. The cup was filled, and still he poured. Tea spilled over the sides of the table onto the floor, and still the Zen master poured. Finally, the visitor could contain himself no longer. "The cup is already full! It can hold no more!" The Zen master replied, "So it is. Just as you come to me so full of what you know that you can receive nothing new."

Learning requires an empty cup, what some Zen practitioners refer to as "the beginner's mind." The wide-open zest and spontaneity of the child reveal the beginner's mind. Young children learn at a fantastic rate. Pushing this pace is an incessant driving beat of the simple question: Why? Why? Why? Often their questioning outlasts our patience. At times, it threatens our deeply held assumptions and pat answers.

As Mark Twain put it, "The trouble with most of us is that we know too much that ain't so." We've lost the questioning of youth. We settle for answers we don't understand, but oh, well, they sound okay, and who wants to make the effort to look anew? We become mentally old and rigid as we attach ourselves to ignorance. We reclaim the beginner's mind when answering the question *Why?* once more becomes more important to us than protecting any particular point of view.

But what does this have to do with achieving your career goals? Simply this: every goal requires learning. Were it not so, it would not be a goal but an accomplished fact. Given ample desire (and that's a big "given"), all that stands between you and your new career is ignorance: what you don't know (knowledge and skills) and who you don't know (contacts). The remedy for both is learning.

All human beings, by nature, desire to know.

Aristotle

Self-education is, I firmly believe, the only kind of education there is.

Isaac Asimov

While your understanding is incomplete, you are sure to be frustrated in your efforts to reach your goals. As long as your skill is undeveloped, you'll feel overwhelmed and out of your league. While unable to enlist the help of others, the ship of your dreams is dead in the water. Learning how to learn can help in all these areas.

Learning is also the primary means of improving self-esteem. In his book *Awareness Through Movement*, Moshé Feldenkrais points out that self-image is determined by "[1] physical and genetic heritage, [2] education, and [3] self-education."[7] Over the first, our genetic endowment, we have no control. The second too is largely out of our hands; as Feldenkrais puts it, "Education makes each of us a member of some definite human society and seeks to make us as like every other member of that society as possible." Then, as Feldenkrais writes, "Of the three active areas in the establishment of our self-image, self-education alone is somewhat in our hands."[8] Active engagement in lifelong learning improves your self-image and, in so doing, enhances not only your ability to achieve but also your sense of well-being. The steps that follow will help you reclaim the beginner's mind and improve your learning capacity.

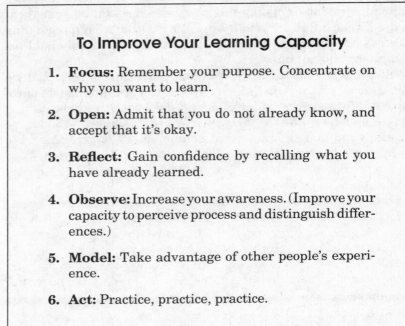

To Improve Your Learning Capacity

1. **Focus:** Remember your purpose. Concentrate on why you want to learn.

2. **Open:** Admit that you do not already know, and accept that it's okay.

3. **Reflect:** Gain confidence by recalling what you have already learned.

4. **Observe:** Increase your awareness. (Improve your capacity to perceive process and distinguish differences.)

5. **Model:** Take advantage of other people's experience.

6. **Act:** Practice, practice, practice.

Remember Your Purpose: Concentrate on Why You Want to Learn

Learning can be defined as the process of remembering what you are interested in.
        Richard Saul Wurman

Attention is the key to learning. Anything you can do to increase your attention will increase your capacity to learn. I knew a woman who was an understudy in a play with a city repertory company. She had learned her lines well enough, but paid little attention to the subtleties of delivery. Then one night, just before the curtain came up, the lead learned that her mother, who lived on the other side of the country, was seriously ill. She had to return immediately after that night's performance. Suddenly it dawned on the understudy that the next evening she would be playing the part for real. That night she watched and learned as never before.

The story illustrates a simple point: *whenever we increase our intention, we increase our attention and, with it, our ability to learn.* The understudy's intention increased when she had a practical purpose for learning. Think of how many times a child has seen his parents starting and driving the family car. Yet most kids don't really pay attention until they are sixteen or so. Suddenly what they had taken for granted becomes fascinating. This mundane activity now means freedom, dates, social acceptance—and that makes it interesting. Again, a clear purpose brings increased intention and, with it, increased attention, and thereby accelerates the learning process.

> *The readiness is all.*
> *William Shakespeare*

Learning the mundane aspects of your subject matter (and every subject has them) becomes more interesting when you keep in mind why you want to learn them. What does it mean to you to gain this new knowledge or skill? How will it affect your life? In addition to sharpening your attention, keeping your purpose in mind helps you to prioritize the various elements of your subject matter. Looking at all you need to learn can seem overwhelming or threatening. Focusing on purpose helps you sort out the principal from the peripheral, the essential from the extraneous. You'll be able to plot your course and pursue it without distraction. At every point, you will know why you are doing what you are doing.

George Washington Carver said, "There is nothing that will not reveal its secrets if you love it enough." This statement holds another great key for increasing your attention and, with it, your learning capacity. Learn to pursue knowledge like a lover wooing a would-be sweetheart, and you find great joy in the learning process itself. A lover loves the courting process. Knowledge will flirt with you, tease you, smile on you, run from you, disappoint you; and yet, if you are true to your love, she will at last be won. I trust that if you are taking the trouble to train for a new career, it's because you have a real love for this field. Keep loving it until you are on intimate terms with it, until it whispers all its secrets.

Your desire to achieve your goals and your love for your subject give a natural impetus to your learning efforts. Focusing on these will propel you to act, to get out and learn all you require to be successful. Desire always leads to action, unless it is somehow inhibited. What often inhibits our natural desire to learn is judging ourselves for not already knowing.

> *To know that you do not know is the best. To pretend to know when you do not know is a disease.*
>
> *Lao Tzu*

Admit Your Ignorance, and Accept That It's Okay

Who has no faults?
To err and yet be
able to correct it is
best of all.

Yuanwu

Let's face it; it's difficult to learn anything while we are trying to prove that we already know it all. None of us likes to admit our ignorance. Yet most of us will admit we don't know everything, which means we are ignorant of something. Once we admit ignorance, we can do something about it. We can take responsibility to learn. Admitting ignorance can come after a long and difficult process or as simply and as innocently as a child asks why.

Everyone is ignorant, only in different subjects.
Will Rogers

What is it that makes us think we should have learned something before we have studied it or even thought of studying it? Let's say you go to a party and you meet someone there who is, or appears to be, a genuine expert in their field. You find yourself feeling uncomfortable around this person and intimidated by what they know. What's happening internally is that you're judging yourself for not knowing what they know. This is a little silly because you've made no effort to learn this subject, while they've devoted years to it. When you judge yourself for not knowing, you miss the opportunity to learn more by asking questions that further your understanding. This illustrates a principle that operates whenever we are engaged in the process of learning: *when we judge ourselves for not already knowing, we miss the opportunity to learn now.*

What keeps us from admitting our ignorance is a compulsive need to be right, expecting ourselves to know before we have learned. Accepting yourself for not already knowing allows you to keep your attention on what you want to learn. Until we admit our ignorance, part of the attention that we need in order to learn becomes tied up with defending ignorance. These defenses take three forms: denying, blaming, and playing sour grapes.

In the context in which it's used here, *denying* means refusing to admit that what you don't know can hurt you. Joan's career objective requires going into business for herself. Yet she knows very little about administering a business. She says, "I can make the sales; administration isn't important." She's denying that a vital aspect of her business is important, simply because she doesn't know much about it. She feels anxious and uneasy about her goal because she's avoiding an area that is vital to her success. Deep down she knows this, but insecurity prevents her from admitting it. She is blocked from learning until she admits that something she doesn't know is important. As long as she refuses to admit her ignorance, she blocks the perception of potential solutions (for example, taking night classes in business administration, hiring full- or part-time help, reading, etc.). *Remedy: Stop denying and take action!*

In the context in which it is used here, *blaming* means channeling your attention into building a fortress of excuse instead of directing it into learning what you must to be successful. The moment we start rehearsing our excuses or pointing the finger of blame, in that moment we are defeated. Jack is blaming his wife and kids for holding him back from getting the retraining he needs to achieve his career objectives. Because his responsibilities and his wife's earning capacity prevent him from pursuing his career objective by going back to school full-time, he is looking at giving up altogether. If he does, he may blame and resent his wife and his children for the rest of his life. As soon as he stops blaming, he can begin to take a realistic look at what he can do to further his training right now. *Remedy: Stop blaming and take action!*

Learning is the very essence of humility.
J. Krishnamurti

As used here, *playing sour grapes* means pretending you don't really want what you want because you're not ready to risk what it would take to get it. Eileen had a natural gift for working with people. People often told her she would make a great therapist. She was constantly doing informal therapy with her friends and family, helping them to clarify and express their feelings. With only two years of college training, she felt that the master's degree she would need to become a marriage and family counselor would take too long and was beyond her reach. While a bright woman, Eileen was never strong academically. She feared that she would not be able to complete the necessary academic work to get her credential. Eileen was pretending that she could be satisfied with using this, her strongest talent, in a peripheral way. She was ready to give up on her strongest talent without giving it a fair chance. Once she admitted what she really wanted, she was ready to give it her best shot. *Remedy: Stop pretending you don't want it and take action!*

In every case, the remedy is to take action.
Get clear about exactly what you need to learn
and exactly what you need to do to learn it.
BEING CLEAR KILLS FEAR.

Admit your ignorance, and learning is possible. Deny, blame, pretend, and you are sure to hit a dead end. As we detach ourselves from our shortcomings and begin to look at them objectively, we find new ways of approaching our goals. Accepting ourselves for not knowing allows us to grow and expand. Judgment brings anxiety, tension, and a sense of struggle that inhibits learning. It creates interference. Simply put, judging yourself hurts and keeps you from learning. Self-acceptance fosters learning, and it feels good. Despite what some of us may have been taught at school, learning is fun. The moment of learning is always a moment of exhilaration. It is not necessary to struggle in order to learn. The first step to easy learning is to recall what you have already learned. This gives you the confidence to learn even more.

Recall What You Have Already Learned

Lest you feel overwhelmed as you ponder all you must learn in order to pursue your new career, consider the following: when you were born, you could not walk, talk, write, drive an automobile, comb your hair, go to the bathroom, brush your teeth, or add figures, yet you probably do all of these things every day. But these are simple things, right? Try telling that to a child learning to walk or talk. Few things you will ever learn are as complex as these. Valuing what you have already learned gives you the confidence to learn still more. You may be ignorant of many things, as we all are, but you certainly are not stupid (unable to learn). As a practical matter, *intelligence is simply confidence in your ability to learn.*

Make it thy business to know thyself, which is the most difficult lesson in the world.
                                            Miguel de Cervantes

---

Review all you have learned. You may be surprised. If you think you have difficulty learning, take a look at the evidence (see the exercise on page 509). Simply to function in our highly complex society, you have had to learn a great deal already. Say to yourself: If I can learn _____, I can certainly learn _____, and you leverage your learning. Now let's look a little deeper into what learning is.

Increase Your Awareness:
Perceive Process and Distinguish Differences

I found that I was fitted for nothing so well as for the study of truth: as having a mind nimble and versatile enough to catch the resemblances of things (which is the chief point) and at the same time steady enough to fix and distinguish the subtle differences.

Francis Bacon

Your capacity to learn is your capacity to perceive process and distinguish differences. Let's consider each in turn. The ability to recognize process—to understand what gives a complex operation or function its fundamental unity, to notice the similarities within and between operations—is a powerful tool for organizing and comprehending vast amounts of information.

The great Confucian scholars referred to this as *ko wu,* "apprehending the principle in things."[9] Jacob Bronowski, in *Science and Human Values*, describes it as the essence of science and art. "All science is the search for unity in hidden likenesses . . . Science is nothing else than the search to discover unity in a wide variety of nature—or, more exactly, in the variety of our experience. Poetry, painting, the arts are the same search."[10]

In the work of Joseph Campbell, one recognizes a profound understanding of process, the "apprehension of the principle in things." Campbell's greatest contribution was his well-documented presentation of the essential unity of world mythology. By identifying a fundamental and universal symbolic language, Campbell was able to make sense of the various supernatural beings, animals, totems, and archetypal heroes that populate the myths of the world. Through a symbolic understanding, he could see how what was portrayed in one culture's mythology by, say, a buffalo, and in another culture's by a tree, were representations of the same archetypal energy.

If one looked at the material forms, one only saw differences. However, Campbell could see the process and, therefore, recognized the similarity of the function of various forms. His ability to perceive process gave him a tool for organizing vast amounts of information from diverse sources. He could move into an unfamiliar culture, with a totally foreign set of symbols, and make sense of them quickly and accurately because he understood process.

Incidentally, Joseph Campbell said, "Everything I know I've gotten from reading."[11] Neo-Confucians such as Chu Hsi viewed reading as a means of enlightenment. They taught that one could most clearly and easily recognize "the one principle that resides in all things" by reading the Confucian classics. Having realized it thus, one then could proceed to recognize the one principle within all things. Of course, what Chu Hsi had in mind was not a casual or even a merely intellectual reading. The reading he advocated was a rigorous discipline that required the right subject matter, a reverential and yet critical approach, and a calmness of mind enhanced by meditation, tenacious application, and endless patience.[12]

There is then creative reading as well as creative writing.

Emerson

Individuals who are especially adept in a given area communicate about it in a simple language laypeople can understand. An understanding of process makes this possible. People who do not understand process get lost in complexity or simply bore us. As Thoreau put it, "I am put off with a parcel of dry technical language. Anything living is easily and naturally expressed in popular language."

Penetrate to process. Fix in your mind the essence of the particular career you want to pursue. Break it down into process. What are the four or five essential elements of this career? As you move into the complexity of the details, keep in mind the simplicity of process. Concentrating on the essence of your career will not only make you more effective in practicing its essential elements but will also help you organize what you need to learn. There may be a host of skills and knowledge that you will need to learn. A focus on process helps you stay on track and move confidently into new areas. An understanding of process brings simplicity, clarity, and breadth to your work, but you also want depth. You want to become a genuine expert in the field of your choice. This brings in the other aspect of learning, i.e., distinguishing differences.

Distinguish Differences

To the uninitiated, computer-programming language looks like a mass of incomprehensibility. We lump it all together and say, "It's Greek to me." Yet the trained expert easily perceives the various languages and their applications. Any area of knowledge in which

The chief object of education is not to learn things but to unlearn things.

G. K. Chesterton

you have a high degree of mastery is an area in which you are able to distinguish a high degree of difference. This is true regardless of your field of expertise. It could be gardening, designing aircraft, baking cookies, managing corporations, installing telephone equipment, or administering city governments.

One is an expert because she knows the subtleties of her craft. The uninitiated can enjoy the end products, but not all the details that go into creating them. For example, the uninitiated may say, "That was a delicious cookie," or "This new software is amazing," but how the cookie was made or exactly how the software does what it does, the uninitiated do not know. *The greater knowledge we have in any field, the subtler the degree of difference we can perceive.*

Because the "differences" vary so much from subject to subject, there is little that can be said about them generally. One thing that can be said: Start with the general and move to the specific; understand the "differences" at each stage along the way. Build on a foundation of understanding. Thoroughly chew each bite of knowledge you take, and minimize the indigestion of confusion. Make sure you understand the vocabulary of your subject area. Don't proceed past words you don't understand.

Take Advantage of Other People's Experience

There is an easy way and a hard way to learn most anything. The hard way is by trial and error; the easy way is by using other people's experience (O.P.E.). Take the attitude, "If I don't know, someone does. It's my responsibility to find out who knows and either hire their experience or learn from them." Where can you find O.P.E.? We live in the midst of an information explosion. Other people's experience is readily available in whatever form suits you best.

We can be knowledgeable with another man's knowledge, but we cannot be wise with another man's wisdom.

Michel de Montaigne

Here are just a few of the ways you can access it: live interviews, conversations, classes, seminars, the Internet, books, audio and video recordings, films, trade journals, newsletters, magazines, and newspaper articles. All of these methods and more provide you with that most valuable of treasures, other people's experience. I encourage you to seek it out.

By tapping other people's experience, you can internalize a great deal of knowledge in a relatively brief time. For example, it may have taken an individual fifteen years to learn the ins and outs of her business, yet you can learn many of the essential aspects in an eight-hour seminar or by reading a two-hundred-page book. Because she is sharing her hard-won experience, you can spare yourself many of the costly and time-consuming mistakes she has made. Learn as much as you can from everyone. The following are some of the ways you can take full advantage of other people's experience:

Imaginative projection allows you to take advantage of other people's experience, even when they're not physically present. Through the creative use of imagination, you can gain maximum benefit from learning materials such as "how-to" books, audio and video recordings, and so on. As you read (or listen or watch), pause periodically to mentally project yourself into the situations you are learning about. Read, digest, and then build mental images of yourself doing the thing described. This is an extremely effective way of learning from "how-to" books and audio and video recordings. All you learn in this fashion is "prewired" into your subconscious—making a new task seem easier and more familiar when it comes time to execute it.

Accumulate learning by study, understand what you learn by questioning.

Mingjiao

Once you have pre-experienced the content through imaginative projection, you can deal more confidently and effectively with it when you meet it in actual experience. The remaining ways of taking advantage of other people's experience require the physical presence of the person you want to learn from, though in some cases you could use video recordings.

Osmosis involves simply being in the presence of individuals you want to learn from. Getting yourself in their presence and having the intention to learn from them starts things happening. Without effort, you pick up their vibes and attitudes. Your subconscious mind is constantly learning and incorporating ways of being and acting, of carrying and presenting yourself, simply by being in that person's presence.

Observation requires that you deliberately and consciously pay attention to what the individual you want to learn from is doing. Additionally, you're bringing in a critical analysis. Remember, even the best role models can teach what not to do as well as what to do. You want to pick up what they do well, without collecting their bad

Earthly things must be known to be loved: divine things must be loved to be known.

Blaise Pascal

habits. Determine what they are doing that works well, and zero in on the step-by-step process of doing it. Likewise, as you encounter practices and procedures (or the lack of them) that aren't working quite so well, make note of these. You may want to observe a better role model for that particular aspect or else devise your own method.

Modeling is similar to observation, except instead of making notes about what you will apply later, you are going one step further to actually imitate, or copy, what the individual is doing as he or she is doing it. This is a natural process in learning. It's sometimes referred to as "monkey see, monkey do." It brings the learning all the way into your body. It's the way the great masters of art taught their students. Children do this all the time, quite spontaneously. They see someone making cookies and want to jump in the batter. The monkey business of modeling plays a big part in the speed with which children learn.

As adults, we don't imitate because we want to be original, "different," and unique. We miss out on tremendous opportunities to accelerate learning when we refuse to copy, or model, behavior. Of course, once you gain mastery, you can bring in your own touch, but you can usually learn the basics much more quickly if you're willing to imitate.

Skiing was one of the first behaviors to be systematically modeled. Observers carefully analyzed films of expert skiers and broke down the process into small components that could be easily duplicated. Then they had simply to teach the various components in succession, and the complex set of skills necessary for skiing could be learned easily and rapidly by virtually anyone. Study how people who are expert in your field approach their work. How do they prepare themselves? How do they execute? Break it down into steps you can apply. Make their skill your own.

Is there anyone so wise as to learn by the experience of others?

Voltaire

Seek Out Mentors

One of the most effective ways of tapping other people's experience is working with a mentor. If you were to travel cross-country through a strange and distant land, it would certainly help to have a guide. Similarly, when it comes to understanding (and excelling in) a new work environment, a mentor can be an indispensable guide. Mentors know the way and can show you around. Take advantage of their experience. A good mentor provides you with a total learning experience. The mentor shows you what he is doing; he tells you about what he is doing, and you get a feel for it. After a short time with a mentor, you will know whether or not the mentor's work is something you want to pursue.

Often what blocks us from learning is being too proud or too shy to ask people who know. This comes from failing to perceive the difference between ignorance and stupidity. I have never met a man or woman who isn't ignorant (about something) nor yet met anyone who is inherently stupid (unable to learn). If you find yourself failing to avail yourself of the help you might receive by asking others, ask yourself if it is because:

- You won't admit your ignorance.
- You have a compulsive need to be right.
- You lack confidence in your ability to learn.
- You are too emotionally attached to "getting it."
- You fear the other party may reject you.
- You are afraid they may ask you to work too hard.

Practice

The final step to learning is to practice, practice, practice. Actors in Broadway plays average about three months of rehearsal before a new production. Olympic athletes train for years. Great speakers practice their speeches. Comedians practice their jokes. You will want to practice the skills that you require to achieve your objectives. Be willing to make mistakes. Refrain from making the ridiculous demand of yourself that you must be able to do something perfectly before you'll do it at all. Anything worth doing is worth doing poorly at first. Practice makes perfect.

> *Tell me, I'll forget. Show me, I may remember. But involve me and I'll understand.*
> *Chinese Proverb*

Let Go: Detach and Learn

Detachment can be seen as the essence of Zen. From the Buddhist perspective, attachment is the source of suffering. Attachment to "having it my way" binds us to ignorance and the suffering it fosters. Before we can overcome ignorance, we must detach from automatic emotional reactions to events. Only then are we free to embrace all of our experience and learn from it.

Trying too hard can actually keep us from learning. One reason young children learn so rapidly is that they've yet to develop any emotional hang-ups about learning. They can stay relaxed and present. As adults, we often burden ourselves with performance anxiety and negative memories. We are not interested in learning for its own sake, but as a means of justifying or proving ourselves. If you are having difficulty learning anything, take your emotional temperature before you decide that it's too hard or you are "too stupid." You may just be too emotionally involved. Let go of the emotional charge, and you may discover you were pretty bright all along.

In antiquity men studied for their own sake; nowadays men study for the sake of (impressing) others.

Confucius

Before the transmission of your car can go from reverse to forward, it must pass through neutral. When you are learning, your life is going forward. When you are emotionally reacting, you are going in reverse. To get things moving forward again, shift into the neutral gear of detachment. Humor helps. When you laugh at your emotional attachment and drama, you release your hold on ignorance and pass into neutral. Now you are ready to go full speed ahead toward your objectives. Don't take yourself too seriously. The joke may be on you.

On average, an infant laughs nearly two hundred times a day; an adult, only twelve. Maybe they are laughing so much because they are looking at us.

Learning Summary

In review, the attitudes best suited for creative learning can be verbalized as follows: "I have a strong desire to learn. I know what I want to learn and why. Instead of wasting my energy by judging myself for not already knowing, I will keep my attention fixed on my objectives. I can detach emotionally and penetrate to process and distinguish differences. I will seek out knowledge and those who know. I will practice and practice and keep a sense of humor."

I love laughing.

William Blake

Dancing Through the Changes

I once knew a Zen teacher whose favorite saying was, "One by one. Day by day." He often repeated this expression to his too-eager students. Impatient with daily application, they demanded instant results and wondered out loud if they would *ever* "get it." The wisdom he shared reflected the patience that comes with age and experience. Youth is eager and enthusiastic, yet tends to be impetuous and easily frustrated. The wisdom of age brings a long-view perspective, one that knows that nothing of lasting value was ever accomplished without long and patient effort. So far, this discussion has focused on how we can improve our capacity to learn to effectively and deliberately create change. Now let's look at how we can foster the staying power to go the distance by learning how to respond well to changes we are not directly intending.

> *To be able to preserve joyousness of heart and yet to be concerned in thought: in this way we can determine good fortune and misfortune on earth, and bring to perfection everything on earth.*
>
> I Ching

In *creating* change, we are acting intentionally. In *responding to* change, we act best when we act receptively. Many of the changes we must respond to are beyond our direct control, changes that result from the actions of others or from "acts of God." Sometimes, however, the changes we are responding to are, in fact, our own creations, though not fully intended. If we think of our lives as whole systems, we can easily understand that significant change in any one part of the system will bring considerable change to other aspects of the system. Some of these changes may be anticipated, some even intended, but many will be neither intended nor anticipated. (Of course, it is best to anticipate as much as possible. The exercises that follow are designed to assist you in doing just that.) How well we respond to these unintended, peripheral changes is as much a part of our success as our ability to initiate and effect intentional change.

The process of creation is, after all, a rather messy business. Look at a painter or sculptor at work. While creating order on the canvas or the stone, he is making a mess of his clothes and studio. Writers, scholars, and research scientists, who may be extremely precise, neat, and orderly in their work, are notorious for having chaotic offices piled high with books, files, and scraps of paper, particularly while in the white heat of a creative flow. Some peripheral disorder always attends the process of creating a new order.

> *The work of art is above all a process of creation, it is never experienced as a mere product.*
> *Paul Klee*

The movement to create a truer manifestation of your life's work is an attempt to bring a greater order into your life. By integrating more fully your visions, values, and talents into daily expression, you are creating a more ordered (harmonious) life. In the process, you can expect to generate a good deal of peripheral disorder. The first step to dealing effectively with the increased disorder is accepting it as a sign that you are making progress.

Before you can better order your closet, you first make a bigger mess of the room it's in. If you focus on the mess, it seems that you are getting nowhere and that things are actually getting worse. Of course, with the simple task of cleaning a closet (which may take a few hours), you understand and accept the temporary chaos as part of the process of creating a new order. However, when you are dealing with the much larger task of creating a fulfilling life's work (a process that may take years), the resulting temporary disorder can seem overwhelming.

This is especially true if moving toward your new career requires major lifestyle changes. Changes such as going back to college, letting go of a financially secure and steady job, or moving to another city, can be very disruptive. The additional demands on your time can put a strain on your relationships and other aspects of your life. If you lose sight of purpose, these additional demands may seem like more than you can bear.

> *Simplify!*
> *Henry David Thoreau*

A strong sense of purpose enables you to respond positively to the inevitable difficulties, annoyances, and inconveniences of life in general and change in particular. Your sense of purpose brings both meaning and direction to the problems associated with change. This is yet another reason why the importance of purpose has been emphasized throughout this book. It will provide you with the motivation, not only to move ahead, but also to deal with some of the waves that forward movement creates.

Dealing with Disorder

There are three things we can do with disorder. First, we can learn to live with it and do nothing about it. Second, we can decide to leave it alone for now. Third, we can deal with it immediately. While disorder doesn't always need to be dealt with or dealt with right away, it does need to be confronted. What we are not aware of can, and usually does, hurt us. Being aware of something and deciding to leave it alone is not the same as avoiding it.

Some disorder can be dealt with on a systematic basis. You may want to establish a regular time to review your disorder. In household or support team meetings, assign priority ratings to various areas. Determine whether to learn to live with it, leave it alone for now, or deal with it immediately. Of course, your decisions may change as your decision-making criteria or the circumstances of your life change.

Everything is in flux.
Heraclitus

While some kinds of disorder can be dealt with systematically, other kinds of disorder come more immediately into our experience. Here again, the key is to be aware of it and consciously decide to accept it as it is, leave it alone for now, or deal with it.

While on a backpacking trip, I was awakened in the middle of the night by my friend. He informed me with some alarm that there was a "bunch of bears" nosing around near our campsite (a disorderly situation). I told him that was nice and began to go back to sleep. (I was deciding to accept the bears.) He was not interested in rest right then and asked me what we should do. I told him, "Nothing," which he wasn't quite ready to accept. So I told him to stay awake and keep an eye on them, and if they got any closer or started pawing on his sleeping bag, to wake me. (In other words, I told him to leave it alone for now.) This he could accept, though it didn't help him get much sleep. Despite the fact that the bears had soon left (as I found out in the morning), his all-night vigil had left him exhausted. Much of our disorder is simply bears in the night. We can accept them or leave them alone for now. Had these bears been known for feasting on human flesh, I would have, no doubt, made a different decision. The bears that are ready to eat us must be dealt with now.

Learn to Live with It: You can't do everything. If you start going back to school and your house gets a little messier (and you can't enlist someone to help you), learn to live with it. Don't judge yourself. The important thing is that you do the important things.

Leave It Alone for Now: Many of our problems will resolve themselves simply by leaving them alone (as any good doctor or psychologist will tell you). The American sage Mark Twain remarked on how he had dealt with a lot of trouble in his life, most of which never happened. In addition to the fears that never manifest, there are the situations that we eventually will want to deal with, but for whatever reason, now is not the time.

Deal with It Now: Things that are critical to your purpose and well-being must be dealt with right away. To delay here is dangerous. It might cost you a missed opportunity or put you in needless jeopardy. There is an old Czech folk saying: "Trouble comes in a door left open." The door is a hole in your awareness. Fortunately, most opportunities and potential pitfalls come with advance notice. If you're alert, you can usually see them coming. The sooner you respond, the more likely you are to have a successful outcome.

Everything flows on and on like this river, without pause, day and night.

Confucius

It may not be necessary to totally handle a situation that must be dealt with now. Some circumstances lend themselves to a partial disposement. A partial disposement could take the form of putting a fence around a problem or achieving limited objectives that leave a need for later mopping up. Remember, containing the potentially dangerous aspects of a situation or achieving only limited objectives generally requires that you get back to the issue. Only take this option if you are certain that it is not better to totally handle the situation now. Much time is lost in getting back to problems or opportunities we have taken our attention off of.

The Simple Power of Purpose

When we are clear on our purpose, we simply act. We put an end to the complexity of the better/worse game of comparisons and competitiveness, of looking over our shoulders to see what others are doing. We accept that we cannot be all things to all people and concentrate on doing our best to achieve our purpose. Purpose provides an organizing principle to our lives, bringing greater order and a higher degree of integration and synergy. As we have seen, acting on purpose can bring with it a certain degree of temporary disorder, yet purpose provides us with an indispensable guidepost for effective decision making.

This is true regardless of the level of decision under consideration. Of course, when making major decisions, we want to keep in mind our purpose in life. But purpose can also help us as we approach specific, even routine, tasks. Ask yourself, "What is the purpose of this task?" Your answer will tell you, not only how much energy a particular task deserves, i.e., its relative importance, but also where to concentrate your energy to effect the best result. In other words, purpose helps you establish priorities among competing tasks, as well as within a task or set of tasks.

State Your Purpose and Stay with It

Many people become a bit compulsive about what they are doing and lose sight of their original purpose. One way that you can help yourself to stay on purpose is to write down your objective and how long you think it will take you to complete it. This will help you to stay on track and make sure that the activities you undertake are the result of a conscious decision. Energy has momentum. It can take on a force of its own, and you can quickly become involved in peripheral pursuits.

> *It is not enough to be busy, so are the ants. The question is, what are we busy about?*
> Henry David Thoreau

For example, one day you decide to clean out a shelf in your garage so that you can save time in finding certain tools. Your purpose was to organize the shelf, and you imagined it would take you about an hour to complete the task. Once you get involved, you find yourself cleaning out the entire garage. The afternoon has passed, and things are still in disorder. Your one-hour task has already taken four, and it's going to take another hour to put all this stuff away. Of course, there is nothing wrong with cleaning out the entire garage, but that was not your purpose. What is true for simple tasks like this goes double for more complex operations. Clearly stating your purpose in advance helps you stay on track.

We can get confused with ideas and with people as easily as we can with things. Let's say you have a report to write. Clearly stating your purpose in advance with a time estimate will help you

Make your work to be in keeping with your purpose.

Leonardo da Vinci

stay on track. Periodically check yourself to make sure that what you're doing is pertinent to your original purpose. This will keep you from getting lost in tangents and will stimulate additional thoughts relevant to the report.

We've all had the professor or teacher who enjoys telling his stories so much that he forgets what his original point was. He starts out dutifully with his lecture notes in hand, but soon he is rambling on and on. He becomes so fascinated with the sound of his own voice that, before you know it, the bell has rung and, "We'll talk about that next time." State your purpose and stay on track.

Establish Completion Criteria

Of course, nothing we do is perfect, so completion is, in a sense, arbitrary. It's up to each of us to determine what completion means by establishing criteria for the task. For example, in making a transition into a new career, when do you know enough to jump into a new field? Of course, if you don't jump in, you'll never get wet. Knowing when you are ready can make the difference between a belly flop and a triple somersault. Establish criteria in advance so you will know when the time has come. Some of these criteria are external (completing degree requirements, passing the bar, or obtaining a license), but many are internal, subjective perceptions of readiness.

Completion and the Energy of Success

There is great satisfaction in the completion of a task well done. It is an exhilarating and energizing experience. This energy provides the force and momentum to make the large change that a transition into a new career represents. Making your transition in discreet, quantifiable steps keeps you from getting overwhelmed in the process and energizes you along the way. Spell out the major action steps to your transition as well as the subpoints that comprise them. Value each step you take.

The Receptive completes the finished things.
I Ching

The satisfaction and energy that you feel from the completion of any task is proportional to the amount of energy and concentration you have put into it. For example, it's energizing and satisfying to wash and clean your car. It's more satisfying to graduate from college. The students who have been most purposeful and have put the most energy into their work will feel the greatest sense of satisfaction and energy from their completion (graduation).

This is true so long as the individual actually experiences completion. If, for example, the student is ruminating after the fact about how he should have earned a higher GPA, his mental energy is still involved in pregraduation activity. In his mind, he has not completed. In order to be able to tap into the wellspring of energy that completion brings, we must know when something is complete—when it is time to let it go.

A Final Word

Persistence: Your persistence level is a function of your emotional investment in your purpose and your belief in your ability to accomplish that purpose. Persistent application toward the realization of a given purpose is the result of a burning desire to see it manifest. Don't give up. Believe in yourself and your purpose. Everyone who takes a risk, tries new things, or does things in new ways will fail from time to time. Success is not about going through life without making mistakes. It rather has to do with a determined effort to see it through. Learn from your mistakes, and stay on track. Remember, as the *I Ching* says, "Perseverance furthers."

'Tis a lesson you should heed: Try, try again. If at first you don't succeed, try, try again.
William Hickson

What's Ahead in Act IV

Think of the transition between where you are now and where you want to be as a journey to a new life. Act IV is about planning the journey to make sure that it is as smooth, pleasurable, and exciting as possible. You have the opportunity to express the eager movement into change of the student and the sagelike patience to endure.

"Scene I: Getting There: Transition Strategies." When you plan a trip, you start by identifying your destination; this you have already done in your previous work in this book. You have determined where you want to go and what you have to do to get there. Now you need to determine how fast you will travel. Will you travel by plane, bullet train, or compact car? These decisions involve considerations of time, money, and other responsibilities.

"Scene II: Training Thrills: Knowledge and Skills." In this section, you will have a chance to formulate a strategy for the acquisition of the additional skills and knowledge you will require to move into your new career. You will differentiate between the training you require to improve your ability, your credibility, and your marketability. This will help you to keep your purpose in mind throughout your training. You will examine the most effective ways to go about learning what you need to learn. Then you will research the best places to go to learn it.

"Scene III: Creating the Self-Image You Need to Succeed." This section provides you with specific methods for improving your subconscious image of yourself. You will learn to apply techniques of visualization, affirmation, and behavior modification to reshape your old self-image into a new one that allows you to express your best.

"Scene IV: Help!: Enlisting Support." We are so tied to our families and immediate friends that a major change for us is a significant change for them. Simply because they are so closely related to us, they're going on the journey with us, whether they know it or not, whether they like it or not. How well we manage to enlist the support of our friends and family may well determine how successful we will be in making the change to a new life, as well as how enjoyable the process will be.

"Scene V: Loving What You Do (Till You Are Doing What You Love)." No matter how great your destination or how beautiful the scenery along the way, if you have a bad attitude, you're probably not going to enjoy the trip. In the same way, you need a constructive attitude while making the journey to your new life's work. That's what this section is about.

Detour #4: The Lack of Self-Confidence Trap

Lack of self-confidence is, more often than not, simple laziness. We feel confused and uncertain because we do not know. But instead of making the effort to investigate, we procrastinate and worry. We tell ourselves we can't instead of learning how we can. If we used the mental energy we expend in worry and fear to get out and find out about what we do not know, we would see our self-confidence grow. Lack of self-confidence is not overcome by faith but by action. It is a lack, not of certainty, but of effort. Too often we are certain that we can't before we give ourselves a fair chance.

Act on the impulse that says, "I want to know. I want to find out." If you "know" you don't have time to take a certain class or are "sure" you couldn't pass it, find out about it anyway. Start taking action. Move in the direction of your desire, and watch your confidence increase. Let your sense of duty to purpose and to the potential that lives within you propel you to act. Remember, taking it personally causes delay. Focusing on purpose smooths the way. The first thing to learn is what you need to learn. Next, how and where you can best learn it. Beware these hang-ups: "Don't Investigate" and "Don't Act."

Don't Investigate: Assuming you've gotten past laziness and you're ready to act, it helps if you know how to organize information so that it doesn't overwhelm you. Learn to approach a new subject by first understanding its general principles and practices. Outline them. Next, go to more specialized information within the general headings. Of course, we were all taught to do this at school, but it is surprising how many people do not seem to know how to research or investigate new subject matter. Even if you approach the subject in a systematic and organized fashion, you still may become confused, especially if you don't understand the "language of the field." Learn the requisite terms, and persevere until the light goes on in your head.

Don't Act: Some of us have no difficulty investigating all the ways to learn about a new subject. We buy books we never read, audio recordings we never listen to. We collect brochures on every training, seminar, and workshop from here to China and back, but we never act. Others of us will take the class, read the book, but as soon as the bell rings or the cover is closed, we forget all we "learned." When it comes to skill, it takes application; you learn by doing. You have learned, not what you can remember, but what you can apply. Take action! Read the book, attend the meeting, approach a mentor, watch a video, practice what you know, learn about it now—it's not too late. Every piece of knowledge leads to the next. Move aggressively and persistently toward the knowledge you desire.

Recall What You Have Learned

Make a list of at least thirty things you have learned to do. Be sure to include things that may be obvious, things you may discount as insignificant but that, in fact, are important, e.g., learning to walk, learning to talk, learning to drive a car, learning to read, etc.

1. Write everything you have learned in the last five years.

_____

_____

_____

_____

_____

_____

_____

_____

2. Write everything you have learned in the previous ten years (five to fifteen years ago).

_____

_____

_____

_____

_____

_____

_____

_____

3. Write everything you have learned prior to this (from birth to fifteen years ago).

_____

_____

_____

_____

_____

_____

_____

_____

The School of Life's Work Affirmations

1. I am confident in my ability to learn all I need to excel in my new career.

2. I now see the easiest, best, and most credible ways of learning all I need to realize my life's work.

3. I am now developing a definite strategy for acquiring the skills and knowledge I need to succeed in my new career.

4. My desire to achieve my life's work and my belief in myself attract all those who can help me to realize my dreams for myself and humanity.

5. I am now attracting people who are helping me to achieve success in all areas of my life.

6. Because I want to help others, I know that others want to help me. I easily accept their help and support.

7. I never feel ashamed or embarrassed for not knowing the skills, knowledge, or people that I need to know in order to succeed. I accept myself and take the action that moves me ever closer to my life's work.

8. I love and accept myself; therefore, I easily admit what I do not know and take the necessary steps to acquire additional understanding and skill.

9. Since my desire is to serve others, I know that the money I require for training in my new career is available and is coming quickly to me now.

10. There is more than enough love, support, time, energy, and money for me to acquire all I need to fulfill my destiny.

Getting There:
Transition Strategies

We must ask where we are and whither we are tending.
Abraham Lincoln

The purpose of this brief section is to help you design a program for moving into your new career as quickly as possible. You'll determine whether you are ready to leave your current position or if you will need to continue in your current work while developing yourself for your new career. If you require retraining, you'll have a chance to evaluate how much time and energy you can devote to it. "Scene II, Training Thrills: Knowledge and Skills" will consider training in depth.

The purpose of pointing out a number of transition strategies is to suggest that there is more than one way to make it work. Perhaps you can't devote yourself to full-time retraining, and you're not prepared to begin your new career right away. This doesn't mean you have to abandon your dreams. You can still find a way to make it work. In the discussion that follows, you'll find six transition strategies that have been divided into two broad categories: transitions that involve immediately quitting your current position and transitions predicated on maintaining your current position for a time.

Quit Your Current Position

1. Quick Shift: The quick shift is for individuals who are ready to quit their current work and move immediately into new careers. If, after careful research, you have determined that: (1) you currently have the necessary skill and knowledge for your new career and (2) you have a realistic strategy for marketing yourself in this field, you're ready for a quick shift. Quick-shift candidates would include individuals ready to begin practice as independent consultants in fields they've worked in for some time or individuals who have worked in a given field for some time and are ready to go into business for themselves.

2. Full-time Training: Full-time training is for those with the financial wherewithal to devote themselves full-time to learning what they need to pursue their new careers. This strategy is also appropriate for those who are willing to sacrifice their current lifestyle for the sake of training for a new career. (You may have to rely on student financial aid.)

3. Interim Job and Part-time Training: This strategy is for those who want an immediate change, but are not yet prepared to begin working in the career role they have envisioned. Perhaps you feel as though you have gone as far as you can go in the job you now hold. You know you need a change—

and quick. The challenge and excitement have gone out of what you're doing. Still, you're not ready to begin work in the new field, at least not at the level that you ultimately desire. You might be able to take an interim job that allows you to pick up additional training, experience, contacts, and self-confidence. This will enable you to move toward your new career at a deliberate pace, even if you haven't the time or money for full-time retraining. There are several ways you can approach this:

• *You could work in your new field at a lower level of responsibility.* For example, let's say you're interested in starting a nonprofit organization. You might work for an existing one in your field. In this way, you gain on-the-job training that will come in handy when you start your own organization. You could augment this with additional training through classes, seminars, and independent reading.

If you want to start your own business, you might work for someone else in the same business and learn as much as you can from that person. You would endeavor to assume as much responsibility as possible, keeping in mind that one day very soon, you will be doing all of this for yourself. Practical training of this kind is far more useful than anything you can get from educational institutions. You learn how things actually work, not how they're supposed to work. After a time of doing this kind of work for someone else, it will become clear to you whether or not you want to make a career of it. Meanwhile, you will be making contacts that can help you later.

• *You could work in a different field at a position that would give you an opportunity to develop needed skill.* Again, let's say you want to start a nonprofit foundation. You recognize that you currently lack the necessary management skills to be effective at this. You could gain valuable management experience working in business or in government. Meanwhile, you might take some of the evening classes in nonprofit administration offered by many universities in major metropolitan areas.

Maintain Your Current Position

1. Part-time Training: You've decided that you want to stay where you are while training for your new career. Evenings and weekends are devoted to training. Perhaps you can negotiate more flexible hours in your current position that will allow you to get some daytime training. You may even be able to arrange for your current employer to pay for additional training.

2. Part-time New Work: This strategy is similar to part-time retraining, except that instead of spending your spare time in retraining, you spend it in working at your new career. You are ready to begin, even if you can't make a full-time living from your new business. You might, for example, start a business working part-time out of your home. This strategy especially applies to those who are interested in working freelance or creating their own organizations.

3. Part-time Training and Part-time New Work: This strategy is for those who want to move quickly into their new career, but don't have the financial resources for full-time training, or sufficient skills to make the quick shift. People using this strategy might start businesses from their homes and begin taking business classes at night school, all the while maintaining their current employment. This path requires a lot of forethought and planning and is generally best for people who do not have a lot of additional responsibilities (for example, raising a family).

"Making the Transition" Sources

Getting Organized: Learning How to Focus, Organize and Prioritize. Chris Crouch. Memphis, Tenn.: Dawson Publishing, 2004.

How to Get Control of Your Time and Your Life. Alan Lakein. New York: Signet, 1997.

Managing Change and Transition. Boston: Harvard Business School Press, 2003.

The Now Habit: A Strategic Program for Overcoming Procrastination and Enjoying Guilt-Free Play. Neil Fiore. New York: Tarcher, 2007.

Self-Discipline in 10 Days: How to Go from Thinking to Doing. Theodore Bryant. Seattle: HUB, 2004.

Smart Choices: A Practical Guide to Making Better Decisions. John S. Hammond, Ralph L. Keeney, and Howard Raiffa. New York: Broadway, 2002.

Taming Your Gremlin: A Surprisingly Simple Method for Getting Out of Your Own Way. Rick Carson. San Francisco: Collins, 2003.

The Time Trap: The Classic Book on Time Management, 3rd. ed. Alec MacKenzie. New York: MJF Books, 2002.

Transitions: Making Sense of Life's Changes, rev. 25th anniv. ed. William Bridges. New York: Da Capo Press, 2004.

 The present is great with the future.
Gottfried Leibniz

Transition Strategy

1. What transition strategy have you chosen? Check one.

    Quit Current Position   **Maintain Current Position**

    ❐ 1. Quick shift   ❐ 1. Part-time training
    ❐ 2. Full-time training   ❐ 2. Part-time new work
    ❐ 3. Interim job and   ❐ 3. Part-time training and
           part-time training   part-time new work

2. Why do you feel this is the best choice for you?_____
    _____
    _____
    _____

    What are the benefits of this approach?_____
    _____
    _____
    _____

    What are the potential risks, costs, and sacrifices to this approach?_____
    _____
    _____
    _____

    Are they acceptable to you?_____

3. What steps do you need to take to implement this strategy?   **Date**

    Step One: _____   _____
    Step Two: _____   _____
    Step Three: _____   _____
    Step Four: _____   _____
    Step Five:_____   _____

4. When do you plan to be fully engaged in your new career? (Give specific dates.)
    _____
    _____
    _____
    _____

Living the Dream

Remember when you were a child? Do you remember how your parents talked about what they did? Was there anything they ever talked about doing that they never did? And I don't mean failed at. I mean never really worked at. Do you remember what that did for your belief in yourself, for your understanding about life, and for your expectations of it? Do you want to do that to your children? Or do you want to show by example what they can do when they trust themselves and make the commitment to follow their hearts? Do you want to give your children a world where people are divorced from themselves, alienated from their own desires, or a world where people dare to express themselves fully in making this world the best it can be?

Nothing has a stronger influence psychologically on their environment, and especially on their children, than the unlived life of their parents.
Carl Jung

Isn't alienation at the root of so many of our problems? Alienated individuals make an alienated society. And we are that—alienated from nature, from the Great Spirit of life, from our own souls and their gifts, and from each other. Isn't there at the base of apathy, at the root of every mean and violent act, an alienated individual who feels powerless and adrift? Isn't so much of the hostility we see reflected in our youth today simply a cry, a scream that says, "I can't do it. I can't express. I can't make a constructive difference"? Perhaps as a society we are better to encourage and develop the good within young people than to concentrate on answering their cries with greater punishment. People are good and will do good if they think they can. Youth look to their elders for the way, but they will not be deceived. There is no substitute for authentic examples.

Life is not simply a process of disillusionment, where childhood fantasies are crushed and ground to dust by the heavy "you can't do it" wheel. Life is a growth of competency, an expansion in love, in which one's desire to give propels one into new universes, new interests, new skills. When you doubt whether or not you can live your dreams, remember, someone is counting on you.

It's Never Too Late to Change Your Career

Many people believe that because they have trained in one field, they are stuck with it for the rest of their lives. If the people below had stuck with their original work, none of us ever would have heard of them. Sometimes formal retraining is required, as in the case of Dr. Albert Schweitzer. However, all of the others on our list made the transition to new or auxiliary careers without formal retraining.

Mohandas K. Gandhi was trained as a lawyer and became a spiritual leader who developed effective principles of nonviolent resistance and was instrumental in liberating his country.

Michael Faraday trained as a bookbinder and made important contributions to physics.

Vincent van Gogh studied for the ministry and became a great artist.

Mother Teresa was a nun who worked as a schoolteacher and principal before she began her missionary work with the Sisters of Charity.

Nicolaus Copernicus studied law and medicine and was a part-time astronomer.

Dr. Martin Luther King, Jr., was a Baptist minister who left his mark as a civil rights leader.

Medical missionary **Dr. Albert Schweitzer** originally trained as a musician and theologian.

Benjamin Franklin was trained as a printer and left his mark in science and technology, government and diplomacy.

Thomas Jefferson was a gentleman farmer who trained as a lawyer. He made significant contributions as a political theorist and writer, an architect, a botanist, an educator, a diplomat, and a president.

Playwright and poet **William Shakespeare** was trained as an actor.

Gregor Mendel (Mendel's laws of heredity) was an Austrian monk and an amateur scientist.

Poet **Wallace Stevens** was a practicing lawyer.

Philosopher and art critic **Ananda K. Coomaraswamy** originally trained as a geologist.

Zen art historian **Yasuichi Awakawa** was trained as an economist.

Of course, many not-so-famous people have made equally dramatic career changes, often well into midlife. It's never too late to follow your dreams. Even if you can't or don't want to take formal retraining, recognize that avocations often turn into vocations.

Training Thrills: Knowledge and Skills

I'm a great believer in luck, and I find that the harder I work, the more I have of it.

Thomas Jefferson

Now that you've determined how much time you have to devote to your training efforts, it's time to think about how you can acquire the skill and knowledge you need to succeed—as quickly and painlessly as possible. That's what this section is about—developing an effective strategy for skill development and knowledge acquisition. To begin with, it helps to identify your primary purpose in seeking training. You'll be asked to differentiate between training designed to enhance your ability, credibility, and marketability. Unless a particular degree or credential is mandated by state (or, in some cases, federal) law in your field, it often pays to look for alternatives to traditional academic coursework. Alternative methods can often help you learn exactly what you need in less time and at less expense.

For the most part, universities and colleges don't do a very good job of teaching new skills (some specific vocational training programs excepted). As a career changer, you've been around for a while. You've probably learned most of the *skills* that college work has to teach you—for example, writing, research, study, listening, note taking, etc. What you *can* learn in college is specialized knowledge, but even this can often be learned more quickly and effectively through self-directed study.

Assuming you have the initiative and discipline, self-directed study has a lot to offer. First, it puts you in control. You learn what you want to learn, when you want to learn it, *because* you want to learn it. It sparks creative synthesis and enhances retention because you learn with an eye toward applying what you learn.

Self-directed study, especially when combined with some form of apprenticeship, is often superior to the formal lecture/exam mode of training. Where you need new skills, try to get into a program where you can actually practice what you learn.

Skills are best learned through practice. Even when you are seeking specialized knowledge, stay away from relying entirely upon books. As much as possible, learn from people who are doing what you want to do. On page 528, you'll find a number of learning resources. Select those that are right for you in constructing your self-directed program.

When degrees are mandated by law or where they are de facto requirements, look for alternative university and college programs. These programs may allow you to take advantage of previous work experience, participate in selecting your curriculum, develop flexible hours that fit your schedule, and save money. See *Bears Guide To Earning Degrees By Distance Learning,* Mariah P. Bear and Thomas Nixon (Berkeley: Ten Speed Press, 2006.)

Why Go Back to College?

1. You have to. It's the law in your field.

2. It will significantly improve your credibility.

3. The school you are considering has an outstanding program in your field, with individuals who have real experience in it.

4. You lack the discipline necessary for self-directed study, and you like the learning environment.

5. You've never been before, and you want to check out the experience.

6. You're looking to date people half your age.

Why Not Go to College?

1. A degree is no guarantee of a job; you'd still have to market yourself after you got it.

2. You may be bored with work not specifically related to your interest.

3. It will take your precious time.

4. It costs a lot of money and keeps you from making any.

5. You may have more life experience than your professors.

6. You'll be the oldest kid in the class.

"Training Thrills" in a Nutshell

Step 1: Identify what you need to learn and your purpose for learning it. From the research you did in "Act II: The Game of Life's Work," indicate what you need to learn in each of three categories: ability, credibility, and marketability. See pages 519–527.

Step 2: Select the ways you want to learn. See page 528.

Step 3: Conduct research and identify specific learning options. See page 529.

Step 4: Research Cost and Availability of Financial Aid. See page 529.

Step 5: Analyze learning options. Compare the benefits of various learning options in terms of the cost, the time it's going to take, and the relative payoff from each of these training options. See page 530.

Step 6: Develop a training strategy and schedule. See page 531.

Step One: Identify What You Need to Learn and Your Purpose for Learning It

Now it's time to develop your training strategy. The first step is to determine your purpose for learning. Do you need training in terms of your ability to actually do the job? Do you need training so that you can be more credible in this work? Do you need training in marketability, in your ability to market yourself in this career role? Perhaps you require training in all three or some combination? Below you'll find a few examples of what I mean by *ability, credibility,* and *marketability.*

Ability

Jennie, who was trained as a geologist, has worked in other fields for many years. She now wants to pursue a career in a specific branch of geology related to environmental concerns. Though she has a Ph.D. in geology, she hasn't worked in this field in nearly fifteen years. Her *ability* is lacking.

She's had little practical experience and has forgotten much of what she learned in school. Going back to school for another Ph.D. would not be an effective training strategy for her. She is better off concentrating on raising her ability by brushing up on general material on her own, taking classes in her specialization, and working with people in her new field.

Jennie's Strategy: *Focus on ability by working as an apprentice, studying on her own, and taking targeted classes.*

If there is anything education does not lack today it is critics.

Nathan M. Pusey

Credibility

Tom worked as an accountant in a large metropolitan area. His dream was to open his own accounting firm, specializing in service to nonprofit corporations. He felt that he could make a meaningful contribution by offering his services to organizations that he recognized as special assets to the community and nation. He had worked for a CPA for many years, and though he essentially did the CPA's work, he himself was not a CPA He did the work, and his boss signed the papers and enjoyed the status, income, and independence of a CPA.

Tom had the ability (he could, in fact, do the work); still, he was not allowed to start his own practice because the law stipulates that only a CPA can do certain kinds of work. He lacked a college degree, and his state required such a degree before he could take the Uniform CPA Examination. In his training, the essential point was to focus on getting the credential, which would enable him to do this kind of work more effectively and at a higher level of contribution, satisfaction, income, and status.

Tom's Strategy: *Focus on credibility by going to the local university (evenings as much as possible), acquiring his degree, and passing the Uniform CPA Exam.*

Marketability

Monica deeply values physical health and well-being. She wants to work as a massage therapist. She has the ability—plenty of training and hands-on experience. Additionally, she has the necessary credentials, having completed the training and licensing requirements established by her state. But she lacks the marketing skill necessary to practice her trade on a full-time basis as an entrepreneur. She has worked in hotels, resorts, and health spas, but has found this unsatisfactory and would prefer to work on her own. In looking at the training necessary to pursue her career the way she wants to, she recognizes she needs to concentrate on developing marketing skills.

Monica's Strategy: *Monica focuses on marketability by taking seminars on marketing techniques for small businesses and by arranging to exchange professional advertising, graphic design, and marketing services for massage therapy.*

Of course, you may need to develop yourself in all three areas. The purpose of the exercises that follow is to help you ascertain exactly what you need to learn, and develop a strategy for learning it. The definitions below may help to clarify the differences between ability, credibility, and marketability.

Ability: that combination of skill and knowledge necessary to execute the particular work you are pursuing. This includes: formal training, previous work experience, apprenticeships, internships, and independent training or scholarship.

Credibility: that which is legally required or that which makes you appear to be especially qualified or outstanding in your field. This includes: previous work experience, degrees, titles, awards, the quality or prestige of the companies or clients you have worked for, endorsements, testimonials, associations, certifications, affiliations, publications, and media attention.

Marketability: that group of self-presentation skills (be they in the area of job-hunting and career development or entrepreneurial skills) that enhance your standing in the marketplace. These include: job-hunting skills, sales skills, entrepreneurial skills, grantsmanship skills, promotion and advertising skills, negotiating skills, and human relations skills.

Variables to Consider in Training

It is important to specify the exact nature of the training you need because training (or retraining, as the case may be) can be an expensive and time-consuming proposition. You want to make your investment of time, money, and energy pay off. Toward this end, it's helpful to rate your **ability**, **credibility**, and **marketability** relative to your would-be new career. Give yourself a percentage score between one and one hundred. For example, if you have 80 percent of the skills necessary to do the job, give yourself eighty percent in the area of ability, and so on. If you don't feel confident filling in the chart below at this time, complete the chart *after* you have completed the exercises that follow.

Ability	Credibility	Marketability
_____%	_____%	_____%
Skill: What additional skills will you need to learn and practice? _____ _____ _____ _____ _____ _____	**Requisite Credentials:** Requisite credentials are those needed to legally operate in your career role. (For example, a lawyer must pass a state bar in order to practice law; a realtor must pass a licensing exam, etc.) What requisite credentials will you need? _____ _____ _____	**Image:** How can you improve or clarify your image? _____ _____ _____ _____ _____
Specialized Knowledge: What information will make you more effective in the performance of your new career role? _____ _____ _____ _____ _____ _____	**Additional:** Additional credentials refer to anything that improves your credibility that is not mandated by law. What additional credentials do you need? _____ _____ _____ _____	**Projection:** How can you better project your image in the marketplace? _____ _____ _____ _____ _____

Ability Training

While every career requires different skills and abilities, there are certain general abilities that apply to many fields. Two lists of these skills are included below. You may want to take them into consideration when developing your training strategy. The first list contains factors that were rated most important by employers when selecting college candidates for positions in their organizations. The study was conducted by Michigan University Placement Services. This data was compiled from a survey of five hundred employers throughout the United States.

Skills Most Sought After by Employers

1. Ability to get things done
2. Common sense
3. Honesty/integrity
4. Dependability
5. Initiative
6. Well-developed work habits
7. Reliability
8. Interpersonal skills
9. Enthusiasm
10. Judgment skills
11. Motivation to achieve
12. Adaptability
13. Intelligence
14. Decision-making skills
15. Oral communication skills
16. Energy level
17. Problem-solving abilities
18. Attitude toward work ethic
19. Mental alertness
20. Emotional control

Here is a list of the ten hottest transferable skills compiled by Harold Figler, and found in *The Complete Job Search Handbook*,[1] an excellent primer on the skills necessary to the job seeker.

Ten Hottest Transferable Skills

1. Budget management
2. Supervising
3. Public relations
4. Coping with deadline pressure
5. Negotiating/arbitrating
6. Speaking
7. Writing
8. Organizing/managing/coordinating
9. Interviewing
10. Teaching/instructing

Skills Transfer More Readily Than Specialized Knowledge

It is not unusual for individuals in top-level management to move from field to seemingly unrelated field. For example, John W. Gardner served as Secretary of Health, Education, and Welfare. He then became chairman of the National Urban Coalition. Later he founded the public interest group Common Cause. Then he founded a new organization called "Independent Sector" to increase the strength and effectiveness of America's volunteer sector. In addition, he was a distinguished editor and author. Although these positions spanned a great variety of fields and endeavors, he used many of the same skills in each position. (Note how many of the skills listed above Gardner used in all four positions.)

 Every man takes the limits of his field of vision for the limits of the world.
Arthur Schopenhauer

Ability Training Worksheet

This process summarizes for easy reference the work you did in Act II on identifying skills and specialized knowledge.

Doing-the-Work Skills: What skills do you most need to acquire to do this work effectively? Refer to "My Skills Map" on page 311.

1._____
2._____
3._____
4._____
5._____
6._____
7._____
8._____
9._____
10._____

Playing-the-Game Skills: These are the auxiliary skills necessary to maintain and enhance your acceptance in this profession. Refer to "Playing-the-Game Skills: Some Examples" on pages 299–300.

1._____
2._____
3._____
4._____
5._____
6._____
7._____
8._____
9._____
10._____

 Try to know everything of something and something of everything.
Lord Brougham

Credibility Training: Requisite Credentials

Check with the proper agencies in your state, and determine which of the following (if any) you will need to operate legally in your state. Next, indicate what you need to do to acquire the credentials in question.

Entrance Requirements	✓	What Do I Need to Do?
Boards (State)		
Degrees		
Certification (State)		
Licenses (Federal and State)		
Bonding and Insurance		
Fees		
Mandatory Monitoring	✓	What Do I Need to Do?
Inspection		
Continuing Education		
Standards		
Ongoing Review		
Renewals		
Others		

Issuing and Oversight Agencies: List the relevant agencies you will be dealing with:

_____

_____

 One learns through the heart, not the eyes or the intellect.

Mark Twain

Additional Ways to Enhance Your Credibility

Ways to Enhance Credibility	✓	What?	Where?	How?
Degrees				
Titles				
Certifications				
Endorsements				
Registers				
Testimonials				
Letters of Recommendation				
Join Associations				
Participate in Affiliations				
Join Service and Social Clubs				
Get Media Attention (Articles, Interviews, etc.)				
Write Books				
Produce Audio and Video Recordings				
Conduct Seminars				
Write Articles				
Do Public Speaking				
Other:				

Marketability Training

Whether you're thinking of creating your own organization or working for an existing one, the way you present yourself can spell the difference between success and failure, recognition and anonymity. Employers report that the single most important factor to the success of an employment interview is the first impression the interviewee makes. Making the right impression can be even more important for people who own their own business. We have included an image and projection section under "Marketability" because these factors apply to both the job seeker and the entrepreneur. For more specific information on the mechanics of marketing yourself, refer to "Act III: The Battle for Life's Work."

Image

The following are examples of certain qualities that make up the images of various companies and individuals.

Apple: Innovative, smart, unconventional

Nike: Hip, energetic, showy

BMW: Performance, engineering, quality

Oprah Winfrey: Integrity, spirituality, compassion

David Letterman: Cynical, witty, middle-of-the-road

Now write no more than five key qualities that you want to project as part of your image.

1._____

2._____

3._____

4._____

5._____

If you are planning to create your own organization, write the key points of the image you want it to project:

1._____

2._____

3._____

4._____

5._____

 In matters of principle, stand like a rock; in matters of taste, swim with the current.
Thomas Jefferson

Projecting Your Image

Now that you have determined the image you want to project, consider how you can systematically and consistently build and project this image. Some vehicles for accomplishing this are dress, language, voice, posture, body language, stories of past experience, resumes, brochures, business cards, stationery, etc. Indicate below how you will project each of the main points of your image.

Quality #1: _____

How you will project it: _____

_____

_____

_____

Quality #2: _____

How you will project it: _____

_____

_____

_____

Quality #3: _____

How you will project it: _____

_____

_____

_____

Quality #4: _____

How you will project it: _____

_____

_____

_____

Quality #5: _____

How you will project it: _____

_____

_____

_____

Step Two: Select the Ways You Want to Learn

Learning Resources: Skill Blocks. After reviewing your answers on the previous pages, list the skills you want to learn. Next, check the ways that you will go about learning these. See the example below for *Public Speaking*.

Example: *Public Speaking*

Skill #1:_____

Skill #2:_____

Skill #3:_____

Skill #4:_____

Skill #5:_____

Skill #6:_____

Skill #7:_____

Skill #8:_____

Skill #9:_____

Ways to Learn	Example	Skill #1	Skill #2	Skill #3	Skill #4	Skill #5	Skill #6	Skill #7	Skill #8	Skill #9
Formal Academic Training	✓									
Nondegree Classes	✓									
Seminars										
Home Study Courses	✓									
Direct Observation	✓									
Mentors										
Internships										
Volunteer Work	✓									
Books	✓									
Videos, CDs DVDs										
Informational Interviews	✓									
Films										
Trade Journals	✓									
Newsletters										
Magazines										
Newspapers										
Other:										

Step Three: Conduct Research and Identify Specific Learning Options

The next step is to conduct research and specify exactly where and from whom you will acquire the knowledge and training you need for your new career. Some of the places where you might do research include the Internet, career centers, libraries, adult education centers, community colleges, university extension offices, and bookstores.

Develop a List of Potential Learning Options: Make a list of potential learning options based on your goals. For example, let's say your long-term goal is to launch your own nonprofit organization and you've determined that you need to acquire a good deal of knowledge and specialized training to achieve it. You may determine that your learning options are a matter of choosing between taking a master's degree program in nonprofit administration from University X, Y, or Z. Alternatively, you may determine that the best approach for you is a self-directed course of study including academic coursework in nonprofit management, human resources, and strategic planning; seminar training in grant writing, fundraising, and nonprofit marketing: as well as an internship at a local nonprofit. In this case, you will want to determine where you will acquire each of the various elements of your training. Indicate where you will learn what you need below, and/or on a separate sheet of paper.

Specific places where I could acquire the knowledge and training I need:

1._____
2._____
3._____
4._____
5._____

Step Four: Research Cost and Availability of Financial Aid

For each of your potential learning options, determine the financial cost and the availability of financial aid. At this writing, over $55 billion in financial aid is available annually in the United States.[2] If you're female, have a low income, are a member of a racial or ethnic minority, are handicapped or disabled, are a veteran, or if you have a parent belonging to any of the above groups, you may qualify for special financial assistance programs. Organizations centered around specific vocations (e.g., health care, agriculture, or teaching) often provide financial assistance to students pursuing careers in these fields. The best way to find out is to visit a financial aid counselor, either at the school you plan to attend or at your local community college or career center. Religious or community service organizations are also potential sources of financial aid. Additionally, many employers offer financial assistance to employees who wish to attend college. Research all of the above in your search for funding. You may also wish to explore the sources listed on empoweryou.com.

> *Thousands of people have talent. I might as well congratulate you for having eyes in your head. The one and only thing that counts is: Do you have staying power?*
>
> *Noël Coward*

Step Five: Analyze Learning Options

Now that you have clearly identified the skills necessary to your success, and have researched how you might go about acquiring these, it's time to assess the relative merits of the various kinds of training. Evaluate each of the training options you are considering according to the criteria below. Remember, employers and clients are concerned with what you can do and what you know. How you came to the ability is of less importance than the fact that you possess it.

Skill or Specialized Knowledge #1	Quality of Instruction	Cost	Time Required
Learning Option #1_____			
Learning Option #2_____			
Learning Option #3_____			
Learning Option #4_____			
Skill or Specialized Knowledge #2	Quality of Instruction	Cost	Time Required
Learning Option #1_____			
Learning Option #2_____			
Learning Option #3_____			
Learning Option #4_____			
Skill or Specialized Knowledge #3	Quality of Instruction	Cost	Time Required
Learning Option #1_____			
Learning Option #2_____			
Learning Option #3_____			
Learning Option #4_____			

Step Six:
Develop a Training Strategy and Schedule
Training Strategy 1: Ability

Skills to Acquire	How?	By When?

Specialized Knowledge to Acquire	How?	By When?

 A little learning is a dangerous thing; drink deep or taste not the Pierian spring.
Alexander Pope

Training Strategy 2: Credibility

Requisite Credentials to Acquire	How?	By When?
Additional Credentials to Acquire	**How?**	**By When?**

 For every credibility gap there is a gullibility fill.
Richard Clopton

Training Strategy 3: Marketability

Marketing Skill to Acquire	How?	By When?

Marketing Knowledge to Acquire	How?	By When?

 The superior man understands what is right; the inferior understands what will sell.
Confucius

Training Summary

Review your answers on the three previous pages and indicate your training strategy below.

One Year	Three Years	Five Years
Over the next year, my training objectives in priority order are:	Over the next three years, my training objectives in priority order are:	Over the next five years, my training objectives in priority order are:
1.	1.	1.
2.	2.	2.
3.	3.	3.
4.	4.	4.
5.	5.	5.
6.	6.	6.
7.	7.	7.
8.	8.	8.
9.	9.	9.
10.	10.	10.

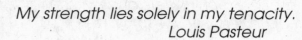

My strength lies solely in my tenacity.
Louis Pasteur

Creating the Self-Image You Need to Succeed

Every man has three characters: That which he exhibits, that which he has, and that which he thinks he has.
Alphonse Karr

The most important factor to your total success in life is your self-image. It's more important than your IQ, family background, place of birth, education, or training. Your self-image determines your ability to motivate yourself to get going on your new career objectives. It determines the respect you receive from others, which in turn largely affects your ability to accomplish your goals. In the words of Moshé Feldenkrais, "Each of us speaks, moves, thinks, and feels in a different way, each according to the image of himself that he has built up over the years. In order to change our mode of action, we must change the image of ourselves that we carry within us."[1]

Your self-image is constructed of mental pictures of yourself in the past. These mental pictures may not reflect you at your best. Fortunately, you can change your self-image for the better. When you expose the negative pictures that linger in the dark corners of your subconscious past to the present light of conscious awareness, you strike a mortal blow to the bondage these negative pictures have held you in. In this section, you will find powerful tools for changing your self-image for the better. The first step in this process is to take a self-image inventory, identifying the problem areas of your self-image and the changes you would like to make (see next page).

"Creating the Self-Image You Need to Succeed" in a Nutshell

Once you know the specific self-image changes that you would like to make, the next step is to begin creating these changes. Try the following:

Step 1: Take a self-image inventory.

Step 2: Visualize your success.

Step 3: Affirm your success.

Step 4: Reinforce: stroke your way to success.

 All of the significant battles are waged within the self.

Sheldon Kopp

Take a Self-Image Inventory

In the column marked "Old Negative Image," list all of the aspects of your self-image that might limit success in your new career role. Next, under the heading "My New Image," write the opposite of the negative traits you listed. For example, the opposite of "sloppy" might be "organized," the opposite of "awkward" might be "at ease," and so on.

Old Negative Image	My New Image
1.	1.
2.	2.
3.	3.
4.	4.
5.	5.
6.	6.
7.	7.
8.	8.
9.	9.
10.	10.
11.	11.
12.	12.
13.	13.
14.	14.
15.	15.
16.	16.
17.	17.
18.	18.
19.	19.
20.	20.
21.	21.
22.	22.
23.	23.
24.	24.
25.	25.

Now use the traits you listed under "My New Image" to help you in the visualization and affirmation processes that follow.

Visualization:
What You See Is What You Get

Visualization is a powerful technique, both for achieving specific goals and for improving your self-image. We are all constantly visualizing. However, most of our visualizations are subconscious, and many times they are actually destructive to our success. For many years, athletes, entertainers, and successful people from all walks of life have understood and used the power of consciously directed visualization. Below is a simple, easy-to-use formula for effective visualization.

Visualization in Seven Steps

1. **Deserve:** Know that you can have what you repeatedly see. Be willing to create the picture exactly as you want it.

2. **Intend:** Direct the picture; concentrate your mind. See the picture and hold it. Don't let your mind wander.

3. **Ease:** Relax, don't tense or strain. You may want to do muscle relaxation exercises first.

4. **Intensity:** Pour your feelings into the image. Let yourself feel an intense longing, or desire, for what you see.

5. **Detail:** Step into your picture and see the detail. See the grain in the wood, the dew in the grass.

6. **Include:** If you want the object of your visualization, be sure to include yourself in the picture.

7. **Enjoy:** Feel good about what you see. Express gratitude for receiving it. Let it go. Know that it *is* done.

Visualization Sources

Creative Visualization. Shakti Gawain. Novato, Calif.: New World Library, 2002.

Mental Training for Peak Performance: Top Athletes Reveal the Mind Exercises They Use to Excel. Steven Ungerleider. Emmaus, Pa.: Rodale Press, 2005.

Psycho-Pictography: The New Way to Use the Miracle Power of Your Mind. Vernon Howard. Pine, Ariz.: New Life Foundation, 2001.

When the task is done beforehand, then it is easy.

Yuantong

Seeing Success Scenarios

Visualize yourself in various scenarios related to your new career. Describe these in the space below. What are you doing? What are the surroundings? What are you feeling? Note: It is important that you go into as much detail as possible. If there is not sufficient space below, write your scenarios on a separate piece of paper.

Scenario 1: _____
_____
_____
_____
_____
_____
_____

Scenario 2: _____
_____
_____
_____
_____
_____
_____

Scenario 3: _____
_____
_____
_____
_____
_____
_____

You may want to make an audio recording. It can assist you in maintaining a regular routine of visualization and thus maximize the creative benefits of this process. Begin the recording by giving yourself instructions to relax, to feel deeply calm and at peace. Next, instruct yourself to visualize one of the scenarios you have written above. Allow a thirty-second to one-minute pause on the recording to visualize the scenario. Repeat this process for as many scenarios as you like. It's best to do your visualizations every night just before you retire. If this is not practical for you, do them as often as possible.

Building a Vision

You can translate your goals into positive images of success. Make a scrapbook. Fill it with vivid images of you successfully doing your life's work. Draw them. Cut pictures out of a magazine. Take photographs and paste them in. Be creative and have fun. Get out your scissors, drawing pencils, glue, tape, and paints. Work in whatever medium most appeals to you. Write captions beneath your illustrations, referring to them as if they have already occurred.

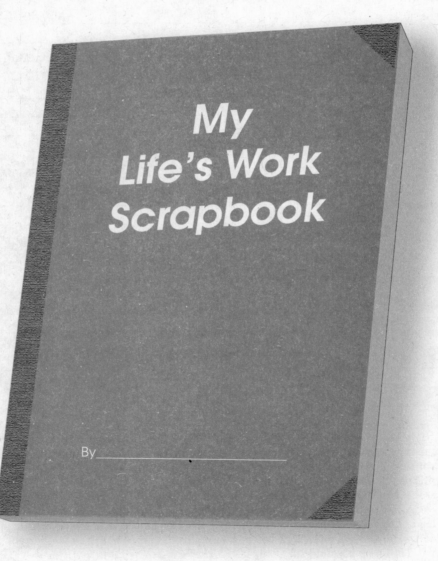

Affirmation: The Power of Positive Belief

Changing careers can be a difficult process. There are plenty of opportunities for doubts to arise. You may doubt your ability. You may doubt whether there is sufficient demand in the marketplace for what you want to give. You may doubt your ultimate success. In addition to your own doubts, you are surrounded by the doubts of others. You must believe in yourself and in the course you have chosen. Recognize that *you believe what you hear repeated* and, most of all, what you repeat to yourself. Repetition opens the doors to your subconscious mind. Think of how a song sticks in your mind after repeated hearings.

The subconscious mind works like a computer. If you try to execute a function on your computer that the program you are running is not designed to handle (e.g., sophisticated graphics on a word-processing program), you have no luck. Yet if you take out that program and put in the proper one, you can do it easily. It works the same way with your mind. If you put in programming that says you can, you'll be able to do things you could never do with the old program.

One way to enter a new program is through a process called "affirmation." The most powerful way to use affirmation is to say *"I am"* before that which you want to be, do, or have. The words *I am* form the primary link to your self-image. Therefore, they should be used with the greatest of care. Remember, *I am* makes a strong impression. Be careful not to link negative thoughts with the words *I am, I, me,* or *mine,* or these negative thoughts will attach to your self-image. Always affirm something positive and beneficial.

Now write positive statements that will reflect the kind of progress you want to make. Here are a few examples:

I love my work. It energizes me and challenges me to give my very best. Excellence is my goal and my reality.

I am a positive, productive, and happy person. I'm glad to be alive, and I'm glad to be who I am.

I always do what I know is right, easily and without delay.

I am confident of my ability to get the job done and done right.

_____

_____

_____

 Speak the affirmative; emphasize your choice by utterly ignoring all that you reject.
                        Emerson

Behavior Modification: Stroke Your Way to Success

It may be some time before you are actually doing your life's work. You will need to maintain your interest, concentration, and enthusiasm along the way if you are to make steady progress toward your goals. Reinforce your progress by giving yourself positive strokes along the way. Your heart has its desires to give, to share, to make a constructive contribution. Your ego also has desires. The ego wants stimulation and attention. Get the ego on board. The ego's desire for attention is not necessarily in conflict with the heart's desire to express its love. However, you may want to look at how you can get them working together right from the start.

Indicate your career goals below. Then write down when you plan to complete them and what positive strokes you may want to give yourself along the way. These goals might include acquiring necessary training, landing your first position, or achieving a particular objective in your career.

Career Goal #1: _____

_____

Estimated Arrival Time: _____

Positive Strokes Along the Way: _____

_____

Career Goal #2: _____

_____

Estimated Arrival Time: _____

Positive Strokes Along the Way: _____

_____

Career Goal #3: _____

_____

Estimated Arrival Time: _____

Positive Strokes Along the Way: _____

_____

Behavior Modification Sources

The Power of Your Subconscious Mind. Joseph Murphy. Englewood Cliffs, N.J.: Prentice Hall, 2008.

New Psycho-Cybernetics. Maxwell Maltz. Englewood Cliffs, N.J.: Prentice-Hall, 2002.

Get An Act-As-If Degree

Act as if. Beware the voice that says you can't, the one that says you have to get permission or that you must have a title, a degree, or certification before you can begin. In some fields, you may be legally prohibited from beginning without a given degree or certification, but, more often than not, your desire and willingness to act the part are all you need to start. The fact that Ezra Cornell never graduated from any school didn't stop him from founding Cornell University. The fact that Thomas Edison had three weeks of formal education didn't keep him from making scores of historic inventions. The fact that George Bernard Shaw had but five years of schooling didn't keep him from acting like a great intellectual. The fact that Anna (Grandma) Moses never had a painting lesson and didn't start painting until she was in her seventies didn't keep her from receiving critical acclaim for her work. He had a year and a half or formal education, yet most historians rate Abraham Lincoln first or second in their reviews of America's greatest presidents. Michael Faraday was a bookbinder by training—not a chemist or physicist. All the folks mentioned above were essentially self-taught individuals who excelled in their fields despite a lack of formal education.

There is education by degrees. You are no doubt familiar with these: B.A., B.S., M.A., M.S., Ph.D., L.L.D., etc. Then there are degrees of education by experience. You gain experience by acting the part. Go ahead and start. Don't let the lack of formal education stop you from doing what you want. If you want additional formal training or really think you need it, go for it, but don't let it stop you from acting as if in the meantime. After all, by the time you get your degree, you may have four (or more) years of practical experience under your belt. Start doing what you want to do in your spare time. Try it on for size.

For those of you who feel bad about not having a degree or diploma, you will find one on page 544 (suitable for framing). While it is true that this degree is not accredited by any university, you must remember that neither was the scarecrow's (in *The Wizard of Oz*), and that didn't keep him from using his brain. Anyone outrageous enough to post this degree publicly has already earned it.

Self-Educated Greats

All the greats below were entirely, or in respects important to their contributions, self-educated.

> *Abraham Lincoln*
>
> *Eric Hoffer*
>
> *Thomas Edison*
>
> *Charles Dickens*
>
> *Alan Watts*
>
> *Walt Whitman*
>
> *William Blake*
>
> *Vincent van Gogh*
>
> *William Shakespeare*
>
> *George Bernard Shaw*

The true perfection of man lies not in what man has, but in what man is.
Oscar Wilde

Doctor of Audacity

This certifies that on this date _____,

the bearer _____ has been conferred a

Doctor of Audacity Degree (Au.D.) for

_____

Count Von Suksiss
PRESIDENT EMERITUS AND MOST EXALTED EXCELLENCY

Keith D. Fayth
SECRETARY AND HIGH COUNSELOR

Royal Order of the Bold and Audacious

Help!:
Enlisting Support

*If you want to get the best out of a man, you must
look for the best that is in him.*

Bernard Haldane

This section explores how you can garner the support you
need to achieve your goals. It begins by looking at how to
make sure you have your own support. Next, it examines
how you can gain the support of your family. Finally, it
looks at the particular issues of relationships and how
these affect life's work.

Enlisting Your Own Support:
Getting Past Guilt and the Need to Blame

Before you go looking for support from others, make sure you have your own. Remember, no matter what you are doing, *the desire to make it work is the most important factor to your success.* Begin by making sure that you are not burdened by guilt. It could rob you of the energy you need to succeed. Many people were told as children that they were the reason why their parents were unable to pursue their dreams. The implication is that if the child had not been born, the parent would have gone on to do great things. Children who accept this often become adults who are burdened with guilt. Guilt, in turn, saps them of the strength they need to tackle their life's work.

Implicit in guilt is a perceived need for punishment. In order to relieve the sense of guilt that the individual feels, she may create circumstances that allow her to feel that what she "did to her parents" is being "done to her." That is, just as she held her parents back, someone (her children, her mate, etc.) is now holding her back. The release from all of this comes in the realization that each individual is responsible for his or her own life and the choices that he or she makes. Recognizing that you are not now, and never were, responsible for your parents' achievements reclaims the energy tied up in guilt and allows you to put it to good use.

It's easy to support someone who knows what she wants and where she is going. Instead of needing others to make you feel okay in spite of your guilt (a hopeless task), you can suggest specific things they can do to see you through. Below are a few pointers for enlisting the support of your family once you are sure you have your own.

Enlisting Support from Your Family

1. Let them know that you are committed to your objectives, and ask for their support.

2. Give them your support in the things they care about.

3. Give them specific ways of helping you.

4. Set clear, definite boundaries that enable you to carry on your work.

5. Delegate areas of responsibility to each family member, and instill a sense of pride in each person for his or her area.

6. Schedule a meeting time to organize, plan, and coordinate efforts.

7. Express gratitude and appreciation for their help.

8. Share your achievements with them. Give them generous credit for their part in your accomplishments.

9. Keep the lines of communication open.

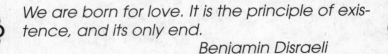

We are born for love. It is the principle of existence, and its only end.

Benjamin Disraeli

Relationships That Work

Below I explore three kinds of partner relationships and how they impact on the pursuit of a life's work.

The Growth-based Relationship

Growth-based relationships are mutually supporting. They are entered into by mature, self-reliant individuals who take responsibility for their lives, as individuals and as partners in a relationship. Each is dedicated to the growth of the other as well as to his or her own. Growth-based relationships don't just happen. They are created by people who know themselves and what they want. Being in touch with their own desire to express their best, each partner recognizes and supports that desire in their mate. Because they themselves are risk-takers, they are supportive of the risks their partners take and understand the vulnerability of the creative life. These individuals are working on themselves as whole people, not halves of a relationship. They know that $1/2 \times 1/2 = 1/4$, not one.

The Need-based Relationship

Often relationships are based, not on growth, but on need. The premise is that each individual is too weak to make it on his or her own, so they need to be together. This we might call a distractive-destructive relationship. It distracts the individuals, through diversion or mutual resignation, from devoting themselves to being the best they can be. It destroys the opportunity for both of the individuals to achieve their best, so long as they are tied to this kind of relationship. Individuals in these types of relationships for many years tend to blur their identities. John and Mary become "we this" and "we that."

In order to achieve your life's work, you must grow. As you grow, you are moving away from where you have been. If your partner is not willing to move with you to a new level of strength and ability, he will tend to perceive you as moving away from him. He will tend to resist your forward progress, because he perceives you, not as growing toward your best, but as moving away from him. His need has blinded him. He cannot see you as an individual, but only as an object who either satisfies or frustrates his need. Occasionally, need-based relationships masquerade as growth-based ones. If you have any doubt about whether you are in a growth-based or need-based relationship, it will certainly show when you take a major step to grow.

When one person in a need-based relationship starts to grow, they need the other less. They have less need for excuses, less need to reinforce their weakness, less need to attack those who try and those who succeed. Consequently, the one "less needed" feels the relationship threatened. This is a real threat. The old need relationship is in jeopardy. Since it was mutual need that formed the relationship and mutual need that sustained it, when need diminishes on one end, the balance of power in the relationship, and ultimately the relationship itself, is in jeopardy.

Individuals in need-based relationships are very aware of each other's faults. They are often taken aback when one party no longer believes in a limitation he has been holding on to for years. *As long as the relationship remains based upon need, the party who is not growing must subconsciously thwart the progress of the other*. If you recognize that you are in a need-based relationship, you needn't feel guilty, hopeless, or bitter. First realize that your awareness is your best friend and will help you through the tests that lie ahead. Next, recognize that there are three basic options.

1. You continue to grow and your partner grows along with you. (This option is discussed below under "The Transforming Relationship.")

2. You continue to grow, and you sever your destructive relationship. This is a painful and difficult decision, to be sure, but sometimes it is the only viable option. Surely, every effort should be made to move into a new growth-based relationship. However, if your partner refuses to grow, and by extension refuses to support your growth, you may, at last, be faced with this choice. Recognize that if you make a break, you may feel a bit vulnerable and shaky for a time. Stand strong in your intention to give and be your best, and you will go on to better days.

3. You give up your efforts to grow, and maintain your relationship (with added bitterness and/or depression). This is the least desirable and most painful of the alternatives. You may end up hating yourself and your partner.

The Transforming Relationship

The transforming relationship is one in the process of moving from a need-based relationship into a growth-based one. A pivotal turning point is reached when both individuals recognize that, while they no longer need each other, they love and respect one another and want to grow together as individuals. A "want to" that is free of need is an exhilarating feeling. Though one party in the relationship may initiate the process of transforming the relationship, it will ultimately take the desire of both parties to make it work. Often the best thing for the relationship is to focus, not on the relationship, but on the individuals in it.

How does one transform a need-based relationship into a growth-based one? You must discover this for yourself. Here are a few suggestions that might prove helpful.

1. Admit the need of the past. Communicate openly and freely. Admit the pain that the need-based relationship has fostered. Ask the other party to share his or her hurts as well. While sharing, avoid blaming each other. Recognize that it was the premise of the relationship that was wrong, not the individuals in it.

2. Discuss what a growth-based relationship means to you. Discuss your goals and dreams. List ways in which each of you could be more supportive of the other. Compare notes.

3. Communicate clearly and emphatically that you are dedicated to being your best and that you are going to do it with or without him. You love him and want his support. You admit that in the past you let fear rule you and hold you back. But no more! You will not be stopped. To try to stop you is futile!

4. Let your partner know you support his best, and encourage him to grow into it. Tell him that you realize you could have been more supportive in the past and that now you are ready to be so.

5. If your partner is willing to take a risk that will test his belief in himself, encourage him to do so and be supportive of the process.

6. The more you can get your partner focused on his own life and working to make it the best it can be, the more supportive and less resistant he will be to your growth.

May you live all the days of your life.
Jonathan Swift

Loving What You Do (Till You Are Doing What You Love)

The power of man's virtue should not be measured by his special efforts, but by his ordinary doings.
        Blaise Pascal

I've talked a great deal about the value of planning for the future and about developing a strategy for achieving your goals. Still, many of us are not in a position to quit our current jobs immediately and begin pursuing our new career objectives. The question then becomes: How do we do our work in the meantime? What kind of attitudes do we take to work with us every day? If we view our current jobs negatively, we will rob ourselves of the energy we need to go beyond them. Throughout this book, I've emphasized the importance of identifying clear objectives and working toward them. You will have far more success if you view your new work as something you are moving toward, than if you view your old work as something to get away from.

Frustration with your current work has served you well. It helped motivate you to discover and develop a plan for achieving your life's work. Now it's time to put frustration aside. Redirect the energy that once went into frustration toward developing yourself for your new career. Put it into working at your current job in such a way as to glean from it all you can. Put it into making the greatest contribution you can through your current work. Don't let negative emotions get the best of you. Stop and objectively consider what works and what doesn't.

What Doesn't Work

1. Being discouraged, reactive, and depressed

2. Hating your job and doing it poorly

3. Hoping it will get better and fearing it won't

4. Complaining, blaming, or procrastinating and staying where you are

5. Feeling inferior because you lack training, experience, or connections—and doing nothing

What Works

1. Staying positive, objective, and motivated

2. Loving what you're doing and putting your best into it

3. Having a plan and making it work

4. Accepting responsibility for where you are now and for putting yourself where you want to be

5. Believing in yourself and doing what it takes

Basically, what it comes down to is this: Work as though you are working for yourself, even though you're not. Work as though you're doing your ultimate life's work, even while you aren't. Work with the same commitment to excellence, the same intensity that you will put into your ultimate work. This gives you the confidence to conceive of yourself doing more. If you think, "Well, this is just a dumb job, it's not important," you won't totally put yourself in. If you don't totally put yourself in, you will lose self-respect. Any kind of work can be done with dignity, pride, and self-respect. Every day you are developing habits. You're either developing good habits that will serve you later on or poor ones that will frustrate your future plans.

While writing this book, I was working one evening at a local coffee shop. The waitress asked me what I was doing, and I told her that I was writing a book on career planning and fulfilling life's work. She said, "Oh, I really need that." She then went on to discount her work as a waitress, to lament what a meaningless and nothing job it was. Not suprisingly, she was not a very competent waitress. While she professed to want something better, she was acting in a way that locked her into work far below her potential. Hating your current job, complaining, and hoping that it will get better without taking constructive action are all prescriptions for failure. In Communist Poland, the workers had a saying: "We pretend to work and they pretend to pay us." That kind of attitude is a prescription for failure and low self-esteem.

If you give your all to a position that is below your capacity, you will outgrow it. If, on the other hand, you do poor-quality work or work that you know is less than your best, you will begin to lose confidence in yourself. You start out thinking, "I could do better, but I won't." But after a while, you end up wondering, "Could I do better, even if I wanted to?" Value what you're doing. Treat it with respect. Learn everything it has to teach you. You might learn practical skills that you can transfer to later work. Even if you don't learn any skills or knowledge that you can directly apply later (and this is highly unlikely), you can still develop attitudes and work habits that will stand you in good stead for the rest of your life. Recognize that there is something to learn from everything, and determine to learn it.

Loving what you do will give you the confidence you need to do what you love, if you understand that expressing your best in your current work is your ticket out of it, not a sign of resignation to it. The person who is resigned to less than her best holds back. The person who is determined to fulfill her life's work gives her all to everyone she works for. It's a matter of honor, integrity, and decency. Should you become an employer, you will, in turn, expect the best of others. You'll know what it takes to do quality work, and you'll know that it's good for people to do it—good for their self-respect. You cheat people far more by expecting too little out of them than by expecting them to give their best. This goes double for yourself. Focus on the value of what you have to give, and do your best work. Channel frustration with your current circumstance into constructive action.

Love It and Leave It

1. Staying positive, objective, and motivated.
   How am I doing?_____
   How can I improve?_____

2. Loving what you're doing and putting your best into it.
   How am I doing?_____
   How can I improve?_____

3. Having a plan and making it work.
   How am I doing?_____
   How can I improve?_____

4. Accepting responsibility for where you are now and for putting yourself where you want to be.
   How am I doing?_____
   How can I improve?_____

5. Believing in yourself and doing what it takes.
   How am I doing?_____
   How can I improve?_____

The best preparation for good work tomorrow is to do good work today.
Elbert Hubbard

Act IV Review

In the space below, write the transition strategy you've chosen. Why is this the most effective strategy for you? *(page 514)*

Summarize your plan for developing yourself in your career in terms of:

    a. Ability   *(pages 519–526)*

    b. Credibility

    c. Marketability

List the top three qualities you want to project as part of your new image, and how you plan to do this. *(page 527)*

Briefly describe your positive visions of your new career in the space below. *(page 538)*

Write three affirmations that reflect the growth you want to see in your new career. *(page 541)*

How will you give your ego some positive strokes along the way? *(page 542)*

List several ways you could improve on loving what you are doing until you are doing what you love. *(page 551)*

A Final Note

Milder Gradients to Life's Work

Throughout this book, you've been encouraged to approach your life's work from the standpoint of your creative passion and your desire to maximize your contribution to the world. I recognize that this can be a difficult and demanding task. Fortunately, it does not have to be all or nothing, and it doesn't have to be all right now. If this seems like too steep a gradient for you right now, you might want to consider the alternatives suggested below. In any case, I encourage you to act.

Alternatives

1. **Become involved.** "Act I: The Quest for Life's Work" discussed discovering your purpose in life. Even if you don't know exactly what your purpose is, get involved in something you can believe in.

2. **Part-time work.** "Act II: The Game of Life's Work" discussed shaping your work purpose into career roles. If you cannot (for whatever reason) or are not ready to dedicate yourself to make a career of it, take some action part-time in an area of interest to you.

3. **Support or volunteer or recruit for an existing organization.** "Act III: The Battle for Life's Work" discussed finding a job or creating your own organization. It also addressed the importance of organized effort and teamwork in making a difference. If you're not ready to either take a job in the field or create your own organization, you can still take advantage of organized effort by becoming a member of groups or organizations that are interested in your area of focus. (See empoweryou.com for links to Web sites that promote volunteerism.)

4. **Do the best you can with what you already have and continue to develop yourself.** "Act IV: The School of Life's Work" discussed creating a strategy for developing your knowledge, skill, and contacts. If you are not ready to go after these in a concerted fashion, make the most of the skills and resources you already possess. If you're not ready to make the transition from your current work at this time, you may want to periodically review your situation and determine if, perhaps, you might be ready to do so in the future. In any case, if you commit yourself to continued learning and personal growth, you'll have a more interesting life—and you may just discover your passion in the bargain.

 Never give in, never give in, never, never, never, never.

Winston Churchill

CHAPTER NOTES

Preface

1. Kakuzo Okakura, *The Book of Tea* (Tokyo: Kodansha International, 1989), 70.
2. D. T. Suzuki, *Zen and Japanese Culture* (Princeton: Princeton University Press, 1959), 63.

Introduction: The Grail Quest or the Bourgeois Nest?

1. For example, historians speculate that our day is divided into two twelve-hour units because the Egyptians, whose sundials were the forerunners to our clocks, preferred counting in twelves. They took the three joints of four fingers instead of the five digits on two hands (as we do) as the basis for their counting system. The point is that there is no commonsense reason for twelve-hour clocks or sixty-minute hours. These are arbitrary abstractions.
2. *Webster's New Twentieth Century Dictionary, 2d ed.*, s.v. "leisure."
3. Erich Fromm, *The Art of Loving: An Enquiry into the Nature of Love* (New York: Harper & Row, 1956), 72.
4. Quoted by Dudley Lynch and Paul L. Kordis, *Strategy of the Dolphin* (New York: Ballantine, 1988), 131.
5. Joseph Campbell, *The Power of Myth* (New York: Doubleday, 1988), 41.
6. Colin Wilson, *The Craft of the Novel* (Bath, Great Britain: Ashgrove Press Limited, 1990), 233.
7. For a general introduction to Jung, see: Carl G. Jung, *Man and His Symbols* (New York: Dell, 1964); Carl G. Jung, *The Portable Jung,* ed. Joseph Campbell, trans. R.F.C. Mull (New York: Penguin, 1976); Harry A. Wilmen, M.D., *Practical Jung: Nuts and Bolts of Jungian Psychotherapy* (Wilmette, Ill.: Chiron Publications, 1987).
8. Joseph Campbell, *The Hero with a Thousand Faces* (Princeton: Princeton University Press, 1949), 229.
9. Anne M. Lindbergh, *Gift from the Sea* (New York: Vintage, 1955), 57.
10. A. B. Keith, Aitareya Aranyaka, 1909, 42. cited in Ananda K. Coomaraswamy, *Christian & Oriental Philosophy of Art* (New York: Dover, 1956), 33.
11. Quoted by Jack Meadows, *The Great Scientists* (New York: Oxford University Press, 1987).
12. Freud referred to love and work as "the parents of civilization." See Sigmund Freud, *Civilization and Its Discontents*, ed. and trans. James Strachey (New York: Norton, 1961).
13. This discussion draws on the work of Ananda K. Coomaraswamy, an exceptionally gifted philosopher and art historian of the twentieth century. See especially *Christian and Oriental Philosophy of Art* and *The Transformation of Nature in Art*, both published by Dover. Cited passage from Ananda K. Coomaraswamy, "Art and Craftmanship," in *Reflections on Art*, ed. Susanne Langer (New York: Oxford University Press, 1961).
14. Ananda K. Coomaraswamy, *Christian & Oriental Philosophy of Art,* 18.
15. Quoted in D. T. Suzuki, *Zen and Japanese Culture* (Princeton: Princeton University Press, 1959), 16.
16. William Blake, *The Portable Blake*, ed. Alfred Kazin (New York: Viking, 1946), 499.
17. Coomaraswamy, *Christian & Oriental Philosophy of Art,* 72.
18. Coomaraswamy, "Art and Craftmanship," in *Reflections on Art,* 242.
19. Ellen Dooling Draper, "Focus," *Parabola* 17 (1992): 2.
20. *Webster's New Twentieth Century Dictionary, 2d ed.*, s.v. "culture."
21. Coomaraswamy, "Art and Craftmanship," in *Reflections on Art,* 240.
22. Joseph Campbell, *The Way of Art* (New York: Mystic Fire Audio, 1990). Audiocassette.
23. For a discussion of the limits of logic to prove or disprove God, see: Immanuel Kant, *Critique of Pure Reason,* trans. Norman Kemp Smith (New York: St. Martin's, 1929).

24. Aldous Huxley, Introduction to *The Song of God: Bhagavad-Gita,* trans. Swami Prabhavananda and Christopher Isherwood (New York: Mentor Books, 1951), 13.

25. Campbell, *The Power of Myth*, 117.

26. See *The Perennial Philosophy*, by Aldous Huxley (New York: Perennial Library, 1944) and *The Transcendent Unity of Religions*, by Frithjof Schoun (Quest, 1984).

27. Arthur Schopenhauer, *Foundations of Morality*, quoted by Joseph Campbell in *Transformations of Myth Through Time* (New York: Harper & Row, 1990).

28. Quoted by Joseph Campbell, *The Flight of the Wild Gander* (New York: HarperCollins 1990), 45.

29. *Webster's New Twentieth Century Dictionary, 2d ed.,* s.v. "conscience."

30. Miguel Serrano, *Carl G. Jung and Herman Hesse: A Record of Two Friendships*, trans. Frank Mac-Shane (New York: Schocken Books, 1968), 42.

31. R. Buckminster Fuller and E. J. Applewhite, *Synergetics* (New York: Macmillan, 1982), XXVII.

32. Campbell, *The Power of Myth*, 99.

33. T. S. Eliot, *The Waste Land,* 1922.

34. E. F. Schumacher, *A Guide for the Perplexed* (New York: Harper & Row, 1977), 138.

35. Coomaraswamy, *Christian & Oriental Philosophy of Art.*

Prologue: The Art of Life's Work

Chapter One

1. For an introduction to Taoist thought, see Lao Tzu, *The Way of Life*, trans. R. B. Blakney (New York: Mentor Books, 1955); Alan Watts, *Tao: The Watercourse Way* (New York: Pantheon Books, 1975); Herrlee G. Creel, *What Is Taoism?* (Chicago: University of Chicago Press, 1970); Chang Chung-yuan, *Creativity and Taoism* (New York: Harper & Row, 1963).

2. For a simple introduction to the uncertainty principle, see Gary Zukav, *The Dancing Wu Li Masters* (New York: Bantam, 1979), 111–114.

3. Rollo May, *The Courage to Create* (New York: Bantam, 1975), 44–45.

4. *Webster's New Twentieth Century Dictionary, 2d ed.,* s.v. "job."

5. Even in primitive societies, most work involves something other than the effort to obtain the water and food calories necessary to sustain life. See Smil, Vaclav, *Energy in World History* (Boulder, Colo.: Westview, 1994.)

6. Thomas Mann as quoted by Joseph Campbell in: Stephen and Robin Larsen, *Fire in the Mind* (New York: Doubleday, 1991), 250.

7. Leonardo da Vinci, *The Notebooks of Leonardo da Vinci,* ed. Irma A. Richter (New York: Oxford University Press, 1982).

8. Ralph Waldo Emerson, *Ralph Waldo Emerson: Selected Prose and Poetry*, ed. Reginald L. Cook (New York: Holt, Rinehart & Winston, 1963).

Chapter Two

1. The Zen master Tosu reportedly gave just this answer:
   Monk: "What is Zen?"
   Tosu: "Zen."
   Quoted by D. T. Suzuki, *Zen and Japanese Culture,* (Princeton: Princeton University Press, 1959), 34.

2. David Ben-Gurion, *The Jews in Their Land*, trans. Madechai Nurock, and Misha Louvish (New York: Doubleday, 1974), 79.

3. Paul Williams, *Mahayana Buddhism: The Doctrinal Foundations* (Routeledge: Chapman Hall, 1989).

4. Aldous Huxley, Introduction to *The Song of God: Bhagavad-Gita,* trans. Swami Prabhavananda and Christopher Isherwood (New York: Mentor Books, 1951), 12.

5. Troy Wilson Organ, *Hinduism: Its Historical Development* (Woodbury, N.Y.: Barron's Educational Series, 1974), 57.

6. *Webster's New Twentieth Century Dictionary*, 2d ed., s.v. "poet."

7. Quoted by Whitall N. Perry, *A Treasury of Traditional Wisdom* (San Francisco: Harper & Row, 1971), 336.

8. Lao Tzu quoted in Alan Watts, *The Way of Zen* (New York: Vintage, 1957), xii.

9. *Karuna* (Sanskrit), literally "compassion." *Karuna* is one of the two principle virtues of Mahayana Buddhism, the other being *prajna* (Sanskrit), literally, "consciousness," or "wisdom." *Ananda* is a Sanskrit word meaning literally "bliss," or "absolute joy." *Ananda* is one of the three properties of the *Atman—sat* (being, or existence), *chit* (consciousness), and *ananda* (bliss).

10. George Bernard Shaw, *Man and Superman* (New York: Airmont, 1965), 27.

11. Phil Cousineau, *The Hero's Journey: The World of Joseph Campbell* (New York: Harper & Row, 1990), 65.

12. D. T. Suzuki, *Essays in Zen Buddhism* (New York: Grove, 1994), 126.

13. *Webster's New Twentieth Century Dictionary*, 2d ed., s.v. "art."

14. From the Greek, *theoritica*, literally "a look at." *Webster's New Twentieth Century Dictionary*, 2d ed., s.v. "theory."

15. James Joyce, *The Portable James Joyce*, ed. Harry Levin (New York: Penguin, 1976).

16. Herbert Read, *The Meaning of Art* (London: Faber & Faber, 1931), 18.

17. While it is clear that the word *Zen* comes from the Indian *dhyana* by way of the Chinese *ch'an* (or *ch'an-na*), there is some dispute as to whether *Zen* is a shortening of *Zazen* (i.e., sitting meditation), or simply of *Zenna* (meditation). This may seem a small point, but the difference in emphasis which each gives reflects a long-standing dispute within the Zen community as to the exigency of sitting meditation to ultimate Zen realization.

18. See D. T. Suzuki, *The Zen Doctrine of No Mind* (York Beach, Minn.: Samuel Weiser, 1972).

19. Sōetsu Yanagi, *The Unknown Craftsman*.

20. Arthur Schopenhauer, "On Aesthetics" in *Essays and Aphorisms* (New York: Penguin Classics, 1986), 159.

21. Lao Tzu, quoted in *The Secret of the Golden Flower*, trans. Richard Wilhelm (New York: Harcourt, Brace & World, 1962), 21.

22. Quoted by Ananda K. Coomaraswamy, *Christian & Oriental Philosophy of Art* (New York: Dover, 1956).

23. Joseph Campbell, *The Way of Art* (New York: Mystic Fire Audio, 1990). Audiocassette.

24. Quoted by Ananda K. Coomaraswamy, *The Dance of Shiva* (New York: Noonday Press, 1957), 179.

25. Quoted in Cousineau, *The Hero's Journey: The World of Joseph Campbell*, 32.

26. Quoted by Coomaraswamy, *Christian & Oriental Philosophy of Art*.

27. Quoted by Coomaraswamy, *The Dance of Shiva*, 179.

28. Gottfried von Strassburg, *Tristan* (New York: Penguin, 1960), 41.

29. *Webster's New Twentieth Century Dictionary*, 2d ed., s.v. "design."

30. Joseph Campbell, *The Power of Myth* (New York: Doubleday, 1988), 150–151.

31. William Blake, *The Portable Blake*, ed. Alfred Kazin (New York: Viking, 1946), 253.

32. Roy Harris, *The Bases of Artistic Creation* (New Brunswick, N.J.: Rutgers University Press, 1942).

33. Suzuki, *Zen and Japanese Culture*, 84.

34. Coomaraswamy, *Christian & Oriental Philosophy of Art*, 65.

35. Jacob Bronowski (condensed from a speech to the American Academy of Arts and Letters).

Chapter Three

1. Phil Cousineau, *The Hero's Journey: The World of Joseph Campbell* (New York: Harper & Row, 1990), 40. Campbell says he got the term "transparent to transcendence" from Karlfreid Graf Dürkheim.

2. Joseph Campbell, *The Hero with a Thousand Faces* (Princeton: Princeton University Press, l949), 3.

3. Carl G. Jung, *On the Nature of the Psyche*, Bollingen Ser., vol. 20 (Princeton: Princeton University Press, 1969).

4. Carl G. Jung, *Symbols of Transformation*, Bollingen Ser., vol. 5 (Collected Works) (Princeton: Princeton University Press, 1956).

5. Carl G. Jung, *Man and His Symbols* (New York: Dell, 1964).

6. Isshu Miura and Ruth Fuller Sasaki, *The Zen Koan* (New York: Harcourt, Brace & World, 1965), 66.

7. Jung, *Man and His Symbols*.

8. **Hero/Heroine:** Rather than using the awkward hero/heroine construction throughout, I will use the term *hero* to apply to both genders, not unlike the way the term *actor* today is commonly used to refer to thespians of both genders. This gender-neutral usage of *hero* is already in common use.

9. The word *Maya*, as well as *illusion*, means "magic, art, and that with which we create."

10. *Webster's New Twentieth Century Dictionary, 2d ed.*, s.v. "illusion."

11. The reference here is to a passage quoted on page 226 of this work, taken from Alan Watts, *The Way of Zen* (New York: Vintage, 1957), 125.

12. See Steven Ungerleider, *Mental Training for Peak Performance: Top Athletes Reveal the Mind Exercises They Use to Excel* (Emmaus, Pa.: Rodale Press, 1996) and Bernie Siegal, *Love, Medicine and Miracles* (New York: Harper, 1990).

13. *Bushido* has been translated "the way of the Warrior" and is a developed code of conduct for the Japanese Samurai warrior. The "Luke" referred to here is Luke Skywalker, a Jedi knight or warrior, from the fictional film trilogy *Star Wars, The Empire Strikes Back*, and *Return of the Jedi.*

14. Lao Tzu, *The Way of Life*, trans. R. B. Blakney (New York: Mentor Books, 1964), 62.

15. Joseph Caster, *Putnam's Concise Mythological Dictionary* (New York: G. P. Putnam's Sons, 1980), 89.

16. Michael Harner, *The Way of the Shaman* (New York: Mentor Books, 1964).

17. Quoted in *The Spirit of Shamanism* (Los Angeles: Jeremy P. Tarcher, 1990), 141.

18. Quoted by Whitall N. Perry, *A Treasury of Traditional Wisdom* (San Francisco: Harper & Row, 1971), 206.

19. Frances Gies, *The Knight in History* (New York: Harper & Row, 1984).

20. I saw this on American television (PBS), but have been unable to track the title.

21. Chu Hsi, *Learning to Be a Sage*, trans. Daniel K. Gardner (Berkeley & Los Angeles: University of California Press, 1990).

22. Lu Chi, *The Art of Writing*, trans. Sam Hamill (Minneapolis: Milkweed Editions, 1991), 29–30.

23. Quoted by Ananda K. Coomaraswamy, *Christian & Oriental Philosophy of Art* (New York: Dover, 1956).

24. Jung, *Man and His Symbols*, 87.

25. Joseph Campbell, *The Power of Myth* (New York: Doubleday, 1988), 4.

26. Jung, *Man and His Symbols*.

Chapter Four

1. Albert Camus, *The Myth of Sisyphus*, trans. Justin O'Brien (New York: Vintage, 1955), 3.

2. George Bernard Shaw, *Man and Superman* (New York: Airmont, 1965), 27.

3. *Mother Teresa* (Petrie Productions, Inc., Home Today Entertainment, 1986). Videocassette.

4. Albert Einstein, *The World as I See It* (Secaucus, N.J.: Citadel Press, 1979), 21.

5. From the Greek, *katharsis*, purification. *Webster's New Twentieth Century Dictionary, 2d ed.*, s.v. "catharsis."

Act I: The Quest for Life's Work

The Quest for Your Best

1. Joseph Campbell, *Transformations of Myth Through Time* (New York: Harper & Row, 1990), 211.

2. *Webster's New Twentieth Century Dictionary, 2d ed.*, s.v. "heretic."

3. Joseph Campbell, *The Hero with a Thousand Faces* (Princeton: Princeton University Press, 1949), 78.

4. John Matthews, *The Elements of the Grail Tradition* (Longmead, Shaftesbury, Dorset, Great Britain: Element Books, 1990).

5. Colin Wilson, *The Craft of the Novel* (Bath, Great Britain: Ashgrove Press Limited, 1990), 20.

6. Leonardo da Vinci, *The Notebooks of Leonardo da Vinci*, ed. Irma A. Richter (New York: Oxford University Press, 1982).

7. Wilson, *The Craft of the Novel*, 151–152.

8. Ibid., 87.

9. Quoted by Ibid., 28.

10. Wilson, *The Craft of the Novel*.

11. Ralph Waldo Emerson, *Ralph Waldo Emerson: Selected Prose and Poetry*, ed. Reginald L. Cook (New York: Holt, Rinehart & Winston, 1963), 168.

12. Heinrich Dumoulin, *Zen Enlightenment* (New York: Weatherhill, 1979, 1983), 73.

13. Isshu Miura and Ruth Fuller Sasaki, *The Zen Koan* (New York: Harcourt, Brace & World, 1965), 42–43.

14. Wolfram von Eschenbach, *Parzival* (New York: Penguin,1980).

15. Ibid., 75.

16. Dag Hammarskjöld, *Markings*, trans. Leif Sjoberg and W. H. Auden from the Swedish (New York: Alfred A. Knopf, 1970).

17. Eschenbach, *Parzival*, 15.

18. Ibid., 131.

19. Ibid., 135.

20. Ibid., 396.

21. Chrétien de Troyes, *Perceval: The Story of the Grail*, (including "The Three Continuations") trans. N. Briant (D. S. Brewer, 1982).

22. Eknath Easwaran, *Gandhi the Man* (Petaluma, Calif.: Nilgiri Press, 1973), 29.

23. Edmund Burke, *On the Sublime and Beautiful* (New York: P. F. Collier & Son, 1937, 1969), 35.

24. Leo Tolstoy, *War and Peace* (New York: The Modern Library, 1931), 1039.

25. Ibid., 1060.

26. Mary Harrington Hall, "A Conversation with Peter Drucker," *Psychology Today*, (March 1968): 21 ff.

27. Campbell, *The Hero with a Thousand Faces*, 59.

28. Dumoulin, *Zen Enlightenment*, 72.

29. George Herbert, *The Complete Works in Verse and Prose of George Herbert*, 3 vols. (New York: AMS, Reprint of 1874 ed.).

30. Harold C. Schonberg, *The Lives of Great Composers* (New York: W. W. Norton & Company, 1981, 1970), 99.

31. This painting was thirty years in the planning. Theodore Rousseau, Jr., *Cézanne* (New York: Pocket Books, 1953), plate 25.

32. Oxford University Press has recently put out an excellent biography: *Goethe: The Poet and the Age* in two volumes. Nicholas Bayle, *Goethe: The Poet and the Age*, 2 vols. (New York: Oxford University Press, 1991).

Scene I: Vision Questing

1. A. R. Lacey, *Dictionary of Philosophy* (New York: Macmillan, 1977), 319.

2. *Webster's New Twentieth Century Dictionary*, 2d ed., s.v. "sacred."

3. Fritjof Capra, *The Tao of Physics* (New York: Bantam, 1977).

4. Erica Anderson, additional text by Albert Schweitzer, *The Schweitzer Album* (New York: Harper & Row, 1965), 47.

5. Albert Einstein, *The World as I See It* (Secaucus, N.J.: Citadel Press, 1979), 29.

6. Ibid.

7. E. F. Schumacher, *Small Is Beautiful: Economics As If People Mattered* (New York: Harper & Row, 1975). Schumacher may have got this from Ananda K. Coomaraswamy. He says something remarkably similar in *Christian & Oriental Philosophy of Art* (New York: Dover, 1956), 62.

8. Eknath Easwaran, *Gandhi the Man* (Petaluma, Calif.: Nilgiri Press, 1973), 75.

9. Peter Tompkins and Christopher Bird, *Secret Life of Plants: A Fascinating Account of the Physical, Emotional, & Spiritual Relations between Plants and Man* (New York: Harper & Row, 1984).

10. Diane Sukiennik, Lisa Raufman, and William Bendat, *The Career Fitness Program: Exercising Your Career Options* (Scottsdale, Ariz.: Gorsuch Scarisbrick, 1986), 13.

11. See L. Reti, *The Unknown Leonardo* (New York: McGraw-Hill, 1974).

12. R. Buckminster Fuller, *Critical Path* (New York: St. Martin's, 1981), 125.

13. Leonardo da Vinci, *The Notebooks of Leonardo da Vinci*, ed. Irma A. Richter (New York: Oxford University Press, 1982).

14. Fuller, *Critical Path*, 217.

15. Gautama Buddha, *Dhammapada*, trans. Irving Babbitt (New York: New Directions, 1965).

16. *Webster's New Twentieth Century Dictionary, 2d ed.*, s.v. "imagination."

17. Quoted in Miyamoto Mushaski, *Book of Five Rings*, trans. Victor Harris (Woodstock, N.Y.: Overlook Press, 1982), 39.

18. Confucius, *Wisdom of Confucius*, ed. Lin Yutang (New York: Random House, 1938).

19. Voltaire, *The Portable Voltaire*, ed. Ben R. Redman (New York: Penguin, 1977).

20. Ken Keyes, *The Hundredth Monkey* (Coos Bay, Ore.: Living Love, 1984).

21. Henry David Thoreau, *The Portable Thoreau*, ed. Carl Bode (New York: Penguin, 1977).

Scene II: Clarifying Values

1. Thomas Jefferson, *Complete Jefferson*, facs. ed., ed. Saul K. Pandover (Salem, N.H.: Ayer, 1943).

2. D. T. Suzuki, *Zen and Japanese Culture* (Princeton: Princeton University Press, 1959), 41–57.

3. Confucius, *Wisdom of Confucius*, ed. Lin Yutang (New York: Random House, 1938).

4. See Idries Shah, *The Sufis* (London: Octagon Press, 1964).

5. Oswald Spengler, *The Decline of the West* (New York: Modern Library, 1965).

6. Quoted by Joseph Campbell in *The Inner Reaches of Outer Space: Metaphor as Myth and as Religion* (New York: Harper & Row, 1988), 53.

Scene III: Pointing to Purpose

1. Maxwell Anderson et al., *The Bases of Artistic Creation* (New Brunswick, N.J.: Rutgers University Press, 1942).

2. Joseph Campbell, *The Power of Myth* (New York: Doubleday, 1988), 123.

3. Ibid., 126.

Scene IV: Targeting Talents

1. John Addington Symonds, *The Life of Michelangelo* (New York: Carlton House, n.d.), 46–47.

2. Matthew 25:14–30.

3. Quoted by Ananda K. Coomaraswamy in *The Dance of Shiva* (New York: Noonday Press, 1957), 144.

Act II: The Game of Life's Work

Playing the Game: Winners, Losers, and Choosers

1. For popular books on this subject, see: Patricia Garfield, *Creative Dreaming* (New York: Ballantine, 1976), and Stephen LaBerge, *Lucid Dreaming* (New York: Ballantine, 1986).

2. William James, *Varieties of Religious Experience*, ed. Martin Marty (New York: Penguin, 1982).

3. Henry Grady Weaver, *The Mainspring of Human Progress* (Irvington-on-Hudson, N.Y.: Talbot Books, 1947), 105–106.

4. Francis Bacon, *Essays*, ed. John Pitcher (New York: Penguin, 1986), 196.

5. Erich Fromm, *The Art of Loving: An Enquiry into the Nature of Love* (New York: Harper & Row, 1956), 72.

Act III: The Battle for Life's Work

Winning in the Marketplace

1. Gerald A. Michaelson, *Winning the Marketing War: A Field Manual for Business Leaders* (Lanham, M.D.: Abt Books, 1987).
2. Andrea Hopkins, *Knights* (New York: Quarto, 1990).
3. *Webster's New Twentieth Century Dictionary, 2d ed.,* s.v. "valor," "value."
4. Ibid, s.v. "ken."
5. Eknath Easwaran, *Gandhi the Man* (Petaluma, Calif.: Nilgiri Press, 1973).
6. Tim Newark, *Women Warlords: An Illustrated Military History of Female Warriors* (London: Blandford, 1989), 40–52.

Scene I, Taking It to the Street: Choosing Your Marketing Strategy

1. Leonard Zunin with Natalie Zunin, *Contact: The First Four Minutes* (New York: Ballantine, 1972).
2. Alan Watts, *In My Own Way: An Autobiography* (New York: Pantheon Books, 1972), 278.
3. Ibid.
4. *Webster's New Twentieth Century Dictionary, 2d ed.,* s.v. "circulation."
5. Michael H. Hart, *The 100: A Ranking of the Most Influential Persons in History* (New York: Beaufort Books, 1985).

Scene II, Scenario I: Sailing the Entrepreneurship

1. Peter F. Drucker, *Innovation and Entrepreneurship: Practice and Principles* (New York: Harper & Row, 1986), 2–3.
2. John Naisbitt and Patricia Aburdene, *Re-inventing the Corporation* (New York: Warner Books, 1985), 95.
3. Paul Hawken, *Growing a Business* (New York: Fireside, 1987), 13.
4. John Molloy, *Molloy's Live for Success* (New York: Bantam, 1983).
5. Barbara Weltman, *The Complete Idiot's Guide to Starting a Home-Based Business, 2nd Edition* (New York: Alpha Books, 2007), 7.
6. Bernard Kamoroff, *The Small Time Operator* (Laytonville, Calif.: Bell Springs, 1988).

Scene II, Scenario II: Wielding the Freelance

1. *Webster's New Twentieth Century Dictionary, 2d ed.,* s.v. "freelance."
2. Richard Wilhelm and Cary F. Baynes, trans., *The I Ching* (Princeton: Princeton University Press, 1967).

Scene II, Scenario III: Crafting the Nonprofit Foundation

1. Francis Bacon, *The Essays or Councils, Civil and Moral, of Francis Ld. Verulan* (Mt. Vernon, N.Y.: Peter Pauper Press, n.d.).

Scene II, Scenario IV: Landing the Right Job

1. Peter F. Drucker, *Management: Tasks, Practices, Responsibilities* (New York: HarperCollins, 1974).
2. Paul Baran and Paul Sweezy, *Monopoly Capital* (New York: Monthly Review Press, 1968).
3. See *Management: Tasks, Responsibilities, Practices*, by Peter Drucker (New York: HarperBusiness, 1993).
4. Gerry Crispin and Mark Mehler, "Sources of Hire," 2008, http://www.careerxroads.com/

Act IV: The School of Life's Work

Learning to Change: The Old Boy and the Student-Sage

1. John Naisbitt, *Megatrends: Ten New Directions Transforming Our Lives* (New York: Warner Books, 1983).

2. *Webster's New Twentieth Century Dictionary, 2d ed.*, s.v. "student," "sage."

3. Richard Wilhelm and Cary F. Baynes, trans., *The I Ching* (Princeton: Princeton University Press, 1967), 322.

4. Ibid, 227.

5. *Webster's New Twentieth Century Dictionary, 2d ed.*, s.v., "crisis."

6. Wilhelm and Baynes, trans., *The I Ching*, 326.

7. Moshe Feldenkrais, *Awareness Through Movement* (San Francisco: HarperCollins, 1972, 1977), 3.

8. Ibid., 4.

9. Chu Hsi, *Learning to Be a Sage*, trans. Daniel K. Gardner (Berkeley & Los Angeles: University of California Press, 1990).

10. Jacob Bronowski, *Science and Human Values* (New York: Harper & Row, 1972).

11. Joseph Campbell, *The World of Joseph Campbell: In Search of the Holy Grail: The Parzival Legend* (NP: Mythology Limited, 1989). Audiocassette.

12. Chu Hsi, *Learning to Be a Sage*.

Scene II: Training Thrills: Knowledge and Skills

1. Harold Figler, *The Complete Job Search Handbook* (New York: H. Holt, 1980).

2. See: http://www.nextstudent.com/financial-aid-news/articles/strategies.asp

Scene III: Creating the Self-Image You Need to Succeed

1. Moshé Feldenkrais, *Awareness Through Movement* (San Francisco: HarperCollins, 1972, 1977), 10.

INDEX

—THE END—

Everything must end;
meanwhile we must
amuse ourselves.
Voltaire

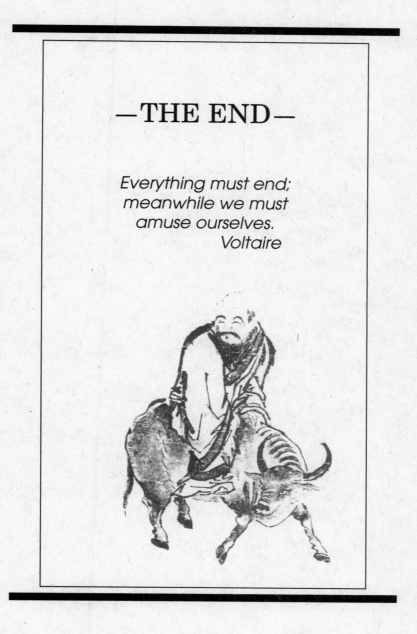

Visit the Center for Creative Empowerment at

www.empoweryou.com

for a variety of career resources and online links as well
as information on career coaching, licensing, and more.